Privacy, Data Protection and Data-driven Technologies

AF849358

This book brings together contributions from leading scholars in law and technology, analysing the privacy issues raised by new data-driven technologies.

Highlighting the challenges that technology poses to existing European Union (EU) data protection laws, the book assesses whether current legal frameworks are fit for purpose, while maintaining a balance between supporting innovation and the protection of individuals' privacy. Data privacy issues range from targeted advertising and facial recognition, systems based on artificial intelligence (AI) and blockchain, and machine-to-machine (M2M) communication, to technologies that enable the detection of emotions and personal care robots.

The book will be of interest to scholars, policymakers and practitioners working in the fields of law and technology, EU law and data protection.

Martin Ebers is President of the Robotics & AI Law Society (RAILS) and Associate Professor of IT Law at the University of Tartu (Estonia). He taught and presented at more than 100 international conferences, is a member of several national and international research networks and published 16 books and over 120 articles in the field of law and technology, especially artificial intelligence, as well as in commercial, private, European, comparative and international law. His latest books include *Algorithms and Law* (2020), *Algorithmic Governance and Governance of Algorithms* (2021), *Contracting and Contract Law in the Age of Artificial Intelligence* (2022) and the *Stichwortkommentar Legal Tech* (2023).

Karin Sein is a Professor of Civil Law in the Faculty of Law of the University of Tartu, Estonia. Her main research interests cover domestic and European contract law, consumer law, private international law and international civil procedure and also law and digitalisation. In recent years, she has provided expertise for the Estonian Ministry of Justice on implementing European consumer protection directives into Estonian contract law. During the Estonian EU Presidency in July–December 2017, she was acting as Chair for the Council Working Group for the Proposals of the Directive on Digital Content and of the Directive on Sale of Consumer Goods.

Routledge Research in the Law of Emerging Technologies

Regulating Artificial Intelligence
Binary Ethics and the Law
Dominika Ewa Harasimiuk and Tomasz Braun

Cryptocurrencies and Regulatory Challenge
Allan C. Hutchinson

Regulating Artificial Intelligence in Industry
Edited by Damian M. Bielicki

The Law of Global Digitality
Edited by Matthias C. Kettemann, Alexander Peukert and Indra Spiecker gen. Döhmann

Internet of Things and the Law
Legal Strategies for Consumer-Centric Smart Technologies
Guido Noto La Diega

Regulating the Metaverse
A Critical Assessment
Ignas Kalpokas and Julija Kalpokienė

The Regulation of Digital Technologies in the EU
Act-ification, GDPR Mimesis and EU Law Brutality at Play
Vagelis Papakonstantinou and Paul de Hert

Privacy, Data Protection and Data-driven Technologies
Edited by Martin Ebers and Karin Sein

For more information about this series, please visit: www.routledge.com/Routledge-Research-in-the-Law-of-Emerging-Technologies/book-series/LAWTECHNOLOGY

Privacy, Data Protection and Data-driven Technologies

Edited by Martin Ebers and Karin Sein

Routledge
Taylor & Francis Group
LONDON AND NEW YORK

First published 2025
by Routledge
4 Park Square, Milton Park, Abingdon, Oxon OX14 4RN

and by Routledge
605 Third Avenue, New York, NY 10158

Routledge is an imprint of the Taylor & Francis Group, an informa business

© 2025 selection and editorial matter, Martin Ebers and Karin Sein; individual chapters, the contributors

The right of Martin Ebers and Karin Sein to be identified as the authors of the editorial material, and of the authors for their individual chapters, has been asserted in accordance with sections 77 and 78 of the Copyright, Designs and Patents Act 1988.

All rights reserved. No part of this book may be reprinted or reproduced or utilised in any form or by any electronic, mechanical, or other means, now known or hereafter invented, including photocopying and recording, or in any information storage or retrieval system, without permission in writing from the publishers.

Trademark notice: Product or corporate names may be trademarks or registered trademarks, and are used only for identification and explanation without intent to infringe.

British Library Cataloguing-in-Publication Data
A catalogue record for this book is available from the British Library

Library of Congress Cataloging-in-Publication Data
Names: Ebers, Martin, 1970- editor. | Sein, Karin, 1974- editor.
Title: Privacy, data protection, and data-driven technologies / edited by Martin Ebers and Karin Sein.
Description: Abingdon, Oxon [UK] ; New York, NY : Routledge, 2024. | Series: Routledge research in law of emerging technologies | Includes bibliographical references and index.
Identifiers: LCCN 2024016100 (print) | LCCN 2024016101 (ebook) | ISBN 9781032614472 (hardback) | ISBN 9781032820682 (paperback) | ISBN 9781003502791 (ebook)
Subjects: LCSH: Privacy, Right of—European Union countries. | Data protection—Law and legislation—European Union countries. | European Parliament. General Data Protection Regulation. | Technological innovations—Law and legislation—European Union countries. | Blockchains (Databases)—Law and legislation—European Union countries.
Classification: LCC KJE6071 .P755 2024 (print) | LCC KJE6071 (ebook) | DDC 342.2408/58—dc23/eng/20240412
LC record available at https://lccn.loc.gov/2024016100
LC ebook record available at https://lccn.loc.gov/2024016101

ISBN: 978-1-032-61447-2 (hbk)
ISBN: 978-1-032-82068-2 (pbk)
ISBN: 978-1-003-50279-1 (ebk)

DOI: 10.4324/9781003502791

Typeset in Times New Roman
by Apex CoVantage, LLC

Contents

Contributors

Tommaso Corno is an Italian journalist and recent graduate of the Dickson Poon School of Law at King's College London. Having completed an LLB in Politics, Philosophy and Law in 2023, his interest in European jurisdictions will soon bring him to pursue Masters of Laws in Université Paris II Panthéon-Assas and La Sapienza in Rome as part of the *Juriste Européen* programme. His focus is on technological regulation, in particular within the field of artificial intelligence.

Mateja Durovic is a professor in contract and commercial law, and Co-Director of the Centre for Technology, Ethics, Law and Society (TELOS) at King's College London. Previous to this, he was an assistant professor (2015–2017) at the School of Law, City University of Hong Kong. The work of Dr. Durovic was published in leading law journals (*European Review of Private Law*, *European Review of Contract Law*, *Journal of Consumer Policy*) and by most prominent publishers (Oxford University Press, Hart Publishing). He is a member of the European Law Institute, Society of Legal Scholars and Society for European Contract Law.

Martin Ebers is President of the Robotics & AI Law Society (RAILS) and Associate Professor of IT Law at the University of Tartu (Estonia). He taught and presented at more than 100 international conferences, is a member of several national and international research networks and published 16 books and over 120 articles in the field of law and technology, especially artificial intelligence, as well as in commercial, private, European, comparative and international law. His latest books include *Algorithms and Law* (2020), *Algorithmic Governance and Governance of Algorithms* (2021), *Contracting and Contract Law in the Age of Artificial Intelligence* (2022) and the *Stichwortkommentar Legal Tech* (2023).

Federico Galli is a junior assistant professor at the Department of Legal Studies, University of Bologna. In 2021, he obtained a PhD in law, science and technology from the University of Bologna and in computer science from University of Luxembourg. During this period, he has gained research experiences in the field of computer law (in particular, privacy, data protection law, contract, and consumer law of AI) and in law and ethics of AI. He has published on Italian and international journals. He is currently involved in several projects in legal and ethical issues of computation and in legal informatics.

Giorgia Guerra is assistant professor in comparative private law at the School of Law of the University of Verona (Italy). She teaches comparative legal systems (law school program), and transnational and comparative law and technology (data science program). She has held the national qualification (habilitation) as second-level professor (associate) since August 2021. She has an extensive track record of publications with leading international publishers, particularly on disruptive technologies. Her latest book is *Redesigning Protection for Consumer Autonomy: The Case-study of Dark Patterns in European Private Law* (FrancoAngeli, 2023).

Mykyta Petik holds an LL.B degree from Taras Shevchenko Kyiv National University (2016), an LL.M degree from Ghent University (2017, cum laude), and an MA in IT law degree from Tartu University (2018, MFA scholarship). He is currently pursuing a PhD degree as an MSCA scholar at KU Leuven CiTiP focusing on privacy and cybersecurity in 5G networks. His professional experience includes consulting Estonian, U.S., and Ukrainian companies in matters of information technology and intellectual property law and working as a Senior Privacy Specialist for a major international company.

Kärt Pormeister is a legal scholar and practitioner whose work focuses on data protection and health law. Kärt obtained a LLM in health law as a Fulbright scholar from the University of Houston (Texas, USA). Her PhD thesis focused on transparency in genetic research, and after completing her PhD, Kärt served as the legal counsel of the Estonian Biobank. Prior to this, Kärt taught law at the University of Tartu and Tallinn University, and has practiced law both in the private sector as an attorney and in the public sector as a lawyer for the State Agency of Medicines.

Vera Lúcia Raposo is currently an assistant professor of law and technology at Nova School of Law in Lisbon, Portugal, where she is the leading researcher at FutureHealth, focused on the use of new technologies in healthcare. She was also a supervisor at the Centre for Medical Ethics and Law, University of Hong Kong and a collaborator of the National Yang Ming Chiao Tung University School of Law in Taiwan. She is the author of more than 100 studies, particularly in digital law (AI, data protection, metaverse) and biomedical law, many of which were published in indexed journals.

Peter Rott is a professor of civil law, commercial law and information law at the University of Oldenburg. Prior to this, he held positions as lecturer at the University of Sheffield, junior professor at the University of Bremen, associate professor at the University of Copenhagen, professor at the University of Kassel and visiting professor at the University of Ghent. Peter specialises in European private law and in German and European consumer law. Currently, he focuses on the effects of digitalisation on private law, on sustainable consumer law and on the enforcement of consumer law.

Galileo Sartor is a PhD student at Swansea University, Wales, Department of Computer Science. He obtained a bachelor's degree in computer engineering from the University of Bologna in 2019. His current research includes the analysis of risk-based approaches in socio-technical systems and AI- and logic-based knowledge representation in the legal context. He has published in Italian and international journals and is currently involved in projects in legal informatics and AI and law.

Karin Sein is a Professor of Civil Law in the Faculty of Law of the University of Tartu, Estonia. Her main research interests cover domestic and European contract law, consumer law, private international law and international civil procedure and also law and digitalisation. In recent years, she has provided expertise for the Estonian Ministry of Justice on implementing European consumer protection directives into Estonian contract law. During the Estonian EU Presidency in July–December 2017, she was acting as Chair for the Council Working Group for the Proposals of the Directive on Digital Content and of the Directive on Sale of Consumer Goods.

Gerald Spindler was a fully tenured professor of civil law, commercial and economic law, comparative law, and multimedia and telecommunication law at the University of Göttingen, mainly occupied with legal issues regarding e-commerce, i.e., Internet and telecommunication law. He was elected as a fully tenured member of the German Academy of Sciences, Göttingen, in 2004. He has published more than 20 books, commentaries and more than 400 papers in law reviews, as well as expert legal opinions. He was elected as general rapporteur for the bi-annual German Law Conference regarding privacy and personality rights on the Internet (2012).

Paul Vogel studied law at the University of Würzburg. Between 2017 and 2022, he was a graduate assistant at the Chair of Prof. Hilgendorf. As of 2018, he completed postgraduate studies in European Law at the University of Würzburg for which he attained a Master of Laws in European Law (LL.M. Eur.). He completed his legal clerkship from 2020–2022, graduating as a fully qualified lawyer in 2022. In his dissertation, he dealt with the compatibility of artificial intelligence with applicable data protection law. Since 2022, he is working as an attorney at the German law firm Noerr.

Wojciech Wiewiórowski is the European Data Protection Supervisor, the EU's independent data protection authority.

Monika Zalnieriute is a Senior Fellow at the Lithuanian Centre for Social Sciences. Monika's research on law and technology has been published widely and has been drawn upon by international organizations such as the Council of Europe, World Bank, the European Parliament and the World Health Organization. Monika's work has been translated into Mandarin, Russian and German, and has also appeared in international media outlets *such as BBC and the Guardian.* She is the co-editor of *Money Power and AI* (Cambridge University Press, 2023) and *Cambridge Handbook of Facial Recognition in the Modern State* (Cambridge University Press, 2024).

Preface

Privacy and data protection are cornerstones in any democratic society based on the rule of law and fundamental rights. Data protection is one of the last lines of defence for persons. The EU Charter is for everybody, not just EU citizens, and so Arts. 7 and 8 of the Charter on the rights to privacy and to data protection are there for all.

Neither privacy nor data protection are absolute rights, however; therefore, important objectives of general interest, such as internal security or public health, may justify limitations on its exercise. However, such limitations should be necessary and proportionate, and in any event must respect the essence of the fundamental rights and freedoms. The EU Court of Justice has provided us with a clear guidance in this regard – in a nutshell – the more serious interference with fundamental rights requires the more serious justification and stronger safeguards, and vice versa. Against this background, the actual policy challenge is to translate the legal requirements into practical steps and measures.

The authors of this book have been observing carefully how data protection and its application grows, develops and changes – not only in itself, but predominantly due to ever-changing context in which it is applied. This context, or rather contexts, are influenced in particular in recent years by a rapid technological advancement. In these observations we all make in the data protection community, there are two types of temptations: (1) to maintain the unwavering faith in effectiveness of data protection concepts irrespectively of the matter which they are facing, or (2) to approach each new technological development with an undocumented conviction that new regulatory approaches are immediately necessary.

The book does not fall into the trap of both fallacies. Instead, it engages with both, attempting to find evidence-based answers (be they normative or empirical); not shying away from questioning general views when evidence supports, and, equally, not afraid of reinforcing them when the analysis confirm.

An assessment of the realisation of the fundamental rights to privacy and to data protection in various sectors, or in different applications of technology, is key to understand whether the data protection laws in fact protect well the "data protection right." Data protection being conceived as a framework law poses that its functioning in different aspects is key to determine whether a specific regulation or a specific intervention is needed or not. These are never instead of data protection laws, but on top of it, and the book is a welcome and much needed contribution in this regard, given how new technologies, or even certain "hype" around them, require careful attention and diligent analysis.

The book identifies such contexts both on the level of technologies and areas, e.g., biobanking or health data, where the EU lawmaker – especially in recent years – has focused its regulatory initiatives. And not coincidentally. The approaches taken by the EU lawmaker are par excellence a very good exemplification of data protection not precluding as such the creation of instruments aimed at achieving specific policy objectives through a use of data, as long as a tailor-made structure in place respects and ensures the fundamental rights to privacy and data protection.

The authors also reflect on and recognise the national contexts. These indeed cannot be overestimated. The EU nature of data protection laws (or new regulations such as AI Act) should not diminish our attention to the national contexts, be it in designing the letters of law on EU level, and not less importantly in terms of the governance structures and practical implementation and enforcement aspects – especially when a country has a pioneer experience in subject matter, as is the case with Estonia.

The constraints of the procedural nature of data protection law, and a critical take presented in the book on the limitations this procedural nature brings, remain an interesting and valuable angle, sometimes forgotten in the public debate that expects from data protection solving somehow all the problems of the digital world. Such limitations, however, remain for me "a feature, not a bug" – an opportunity to approach the variety of challenges stemming from different areas, different applications of technology, in a largely coherent (even if not perfect) way, a methodology, a mind-set, that does not preclude further regulatory interventions.

I would like to thank warmly all the contributors to this book, with special appreciation to Prof. Martin Ebers and Prof. Karin Sein.

Wojciech Wiewiórowski
European Data Protection Supervisor

Acknowledgements

This book is part of the "Geriatronics" project, a lighthouse initiative of the Munich Institute of Robotics and Machine Intelligence (MIRMI) at the Technical University Munich (TUM). The contributions in this book are mainly based on the presentations given at a two-day conference on "Privacy, Data Protection and New Technologies" held in Tallinn, Estonia, on 16–17 June, 2022, and funded by the ENLIGHT network. We would like to express our gratitude to Ms Tiina Jaksman, the coordinator of ENLIGHT in Tartu University, for her great help. We would also like to thank those who helped us to edit this book, especially Ms. Valeria Argento, Mr. Gabriel Udoh and Mr. Daniel Hauck.

During the production process of this book, a number of developments have taken place at the European level. In particular, the AI Act has been under negotiation since April 2021 and was not formally adopted until early 2024. While Chapter 1 was able to take this legislative development into account, the other chapters were already completed in mid-2023. Readers should therefore be aware of the changes made in the political agreement as enacted into law. Nevertheless, most of the legal observations are still relevant, as the AI Act is a horizontal instrument that applies in addition to existing EU data protection law.

Martin Ebers
Karin Sein

Part I

Introduction

1 Data-driven Technologies

Challenges for Privacy and EU Data Protection Law*

Martin Ebers and Karin Sein

1.1 Introduction

The General Data Protection Regulation (GDPR),[1] which came into force in 2018, has become a landmark in the field of privacy and data protection, setting legally binding standards for the European Union (EU) and beyond.[2] Although the GDPR attempts to keep pace with technological and socio-economic changes – notably, by following the principle of technology neutrality[3] and providing for flexible, openly worded principles and articles – concerns have been growing in recent years as to whether the regulation is being outpaced by new technological developments and their use of data.[4]

Indeed, data-driven technologies introduce new privacy risks that are currently not (explicitly) addressed by European data protection law. The specific characteristics of data-driven technologies pose significant challenges to current data protection law, in particular due to: (i) their functional dependence on large amounts of (personal) data and on the quality of the data; (ii) their lack of transparency, which makes it difficult to understand how data-driven systems operate, including how data are processed and for what purpose; (iii) the complexity of data processing activities and the multiplicity of actors involved, which raises the question of how to identify and control data controllers and processors; (iv) the ability of some data-driven systems to continuously "learn" and "adapt" their behavior leading to new unpredictable risks; and (v) their (partially) autonomous behavior, which may affect privacy without direct human intervention.

Against this backdrop, this book – consisting of chapters by leading scholars in law and technology – analyzes the manifold privacy issues raised by data-driven

* This work is part of the "Geriatronics" project, a lighthouse initiative of the Munich Institute of Robotics and Machine Intelligence (MIRMI) at the Technical University Munich (TUM).

1 Regulation (EU) 2016/679 of the European Parliament and of the Council of 27 April 2016 on the protection of natural persons with regard to the processing of personal data and on the free movement of such data and repealing Directive 95/46/EC [2016] OJ L119/1.

2 On the so-called Brussels effect of the GDPR, cf., A Bradford, *The Brussels Effect: How the European Union Rules the World* (Oxford University Press 2020).

3 Cf., Recital 15 GDPR.

4 eg A Voss, 'Position Paper on Fixing the GDPR: Towards Version 2.0' (2021) <www.axel-voss-europa.de/wp-content/uploads/2021/05/GDPR-2.0-ENG.pdf> accessed 5 January 2024.

DOI: 10.4324/9781003502791-2

technologies, ranging from systems based on artificial intelligence (AI) and blockchain, machine-to-machine (M2M) communication and social robots, to behavioral advertising, biometrics and technologies that enable the detection of emotions.

This introduction builds on the findings of the book by first discussing the general conceptual shortcomings and limits of the GDPR (Section 1.2), followed by an overview of the various issues that arise when applying EU data protection law to data-driven technologies (Section 1.3) and an analysis of the (often unclear and incoherent) relationship between the GDPR and EU digital law (Section 1.4). The final section (Section 1.5) draws conclusions and provides recommendations on how the EU data protection legal framework could be improved to take sufficient account of data-driven technologies.

1.2 Conceptual Flaws and Limits of the GDPR

1.2.1 The "One-Size-Fits-All" Approach

One of the most imminent conceptual shortcomings of the GDPR is its "one-size-fits-all" approach. As is well known, the regulation does not distinguish between different use-cases or sectors (e.g., retail, health or finance) or technologies (e.g., AI or blockchain). Rather, it strives to protect everything at the same time.

Unlike much other recent EU legislation in the field of digital law,[5] the GDPR lacks a risk-based approach that tailors the choice and design of regulatory instruments based on the level of risk, following the rule: "the higher the risk, the stricter the rules." Instead, it treats most data processing activities uniformly, regardless of their level of risk. Admittedly, the GDPR also contains few elements of a risk-based approach. For example, the regulation distinguishes between "normal" and "sensitive" personal data, with the latter category of data receiving a higher level of protection under Art. 9 GDPR. In addition, when imposing administrative fines, the supervisory authorities must take into account the circumstances of each case; in particular, the nature, gravity and duration of the infringement, having regard to the nature, scope or purpose of the processing concerned, the number of data subjects affected and the level of the damage suffered by them (Art. 83[2] GDPR). Other than that, the articles of the GDPR do not take into account the severity of the breach. To the extent that *personal data* is processed, the entire body of the GDPR is applicable, with all its obligations and rights, regardless of the nature, gravity or duration of the infringement.

5 Cf., G De Gregorio and P Dunn, 'The European Risk-Based Approaches: Connecting Constitutional Dots in the Digital Age' (2022) 59(2) *Common Market Law Review* 473. See also R Gellert, 'The Role of the Risk-Based Approach in the General Data Protection Regulation and in the European Commission's Proposed Artificial Intelligence Act: Business as Usual?' (2021) 3(2) *Journal of Ethics and Legal Technologies* 15; M Tzanou, 'Addressing Big Data and AI Challenges: A Taxonomy and Why the GDPR Cannot Provide a One-Size-Fits-All Solution' in M Tzanou (ed), *Health Data Privacy under the GDPR: Big Data Challenges and Regulatory Responses* (Routledge 2021) <https://papers.ssrn.com/sol3/papers.cfm?abstract_id=3654119> accessed 5 January 2024.

However, the GDPR leaves the assessment of risk and choice of mitigation measures to the data controller and processor.[6] This is evident with regard to the responsibilities of data controllers. According to Art. 24 GDPR, data controllers are required to implement "appropriate" technical and organizational measures "[t]aking into account the nature, scope, context and purposes of processing as well as the risks of varying likelihood and severity for the rights and freedoms of natural persons." However, there is no specification as to definite or mandatory risk thresholds. Accordingly, to comply with the GDPR, data controllers must conduct a thorough assessment of the risks to the fundamental rights of data subjects when processing personal data and implement appropriate mitigation strategies.[7] In addition, data controllers are primarily responsible for conducting a Data Protection Impact Assessment (DPIA) prior to processing if it is likely to result in a high risk to the rights and freedoms of natural persons (Art. 35[1] GDPR). Also, by Art. 35(4)(5) GDPR, supervisory authorities may require a DPIA if they consider that a particular processing operation poses a high risk and the processor has not yet carried out a DPIA, either by publishing a public list of processing operations for which a DPIA is required or of processing operations for which a DPIA is not required. For many data-driven technologies, however, such a list does not exist,[8] making it difficult for processors to assess the need for a DPIA. In such cases, controllers should proactively assess the risks and, if uncertain, seek guidance from privacy experts or consult the relevant supervisory authority.

The rise of data-driven technologies raises the question as to whether this approach is still appropriate. The European Court of Justice (ECJ) has recently taken a strict stance on claims for damages under Art. 82 GDPR by increasing the liability risk for companies handling personal data.[9] To manage this increased liability risk, adopting a risk-based approach can serve as a mitigating factor. After all, different data processing activities carried out by different actors in different sectors for different purposes pose very different risks to the right to privacy and other fundamental rights. A one-size-fits-all approach that treats all types of data processing activities with similar rigor often leads to higher costs and burdens without effectively targeting particularly high-risk activities. In contrast, a codified risk-based regime – taking into account the specific risks and providing for appropriately tiered obligations and rights[10] – would be much better suited to address the specific risks of different technologies in different sectors.

6 De Gregorio and Dunn (n 5) 476.

7 Ibid., 478.

8 The ongoing debate concerns the question whether or not the legislator should include a specific list of technologies in Art. 35(5) GDPR and continuously update it as new technologies emerge.

9 Case C-300/21 *UI v Österreichische Post* ECLI:EU:C:2023:370; Case C-340/21 *VB v Natsionalna agentsia za prihodite* ECLI:EU:C:2023:986. According to the latter judgment, the mere fear of a possible misuse of personal data is capable, in itself, of constituting non-material damage.

10 Strongly opposed to such a graduated approach, cf., Art. 29 Data Protection Working Party, 'Statement on the Role of a Risk-Based Approach in Data Protection Legal Frameworks' adopted on 30 May 2014, 2 <https://ec.europa.eu/justice/article-29/documentation/opinion-recommendation/

This approach involves organizations assessing and prioritizing potential risks to data subjects' rights and freedoms. Entities can demonstrate a proactive commitment to data protection by identifying and addressing high-risk processing activities. Such measures may be considered favorably in the event of legal challenges. This approach aligns with the GDPR's objective of promoting accountability and ensuring that organizations take appropriate measures to protect the privacy of individuals.

Implementing robust risk assessments and adopting measures to mitigate identified risks can help organizations demonstrate compliance and a commitment to protecting personal data. Incorporating privacy impact assessments when necessary not only enhances legal defensibility, but also aligns with the GDPR's principles of accountability and proportionality.

1.2.2 The Individual Rights Approach

Another problematic feature is the GDPR's exclusive focus on individual rights, which shapes both its scope and remedies. The regulation only applies to personal data of known and identifiable individuals, not to anonymous or anonymized data.[11] Moreover, the remedies for GDPR violations are primarily designed as individual rights,[12] granting data subjects exclusive rights, particularly with respect to access and deletion of their personal data.

This approach dates back to the origins of privacy and data protection law. Historically, privacy has focused on giving individuals control over their personal information. However, in today's digital age when data is continuously and automatically collected and stored, establishing individual control is challenging. Moreover, the combination of individual data with other datasets in the realm of Big Data raises concerns about harm to groups, particularly in vulnerable contexts.[13]

Machine learning (ML) models used for profiling make the limits of data protection law based on individual rights even more apparent. As most of the data

---

files/2014/wp218_en.pdf> accessed 5 January 2024: "It is important to note that – even with the adoption of a risk-based approach – there is no question of the rights of individuals being weakened in respect of their personal data. Those rights must be just as strong even if the processing in question is relatively 'low risk'."

11 Cf., Recital 26 GDPR.

12 This becomes evident in the light of Art. 80(1) GDPR. Even the representation of data subjects requires that the mandated body is active in the field of the protection of data subjects' rights and freedoms with regard to the protection of their personal data. Furthermore, a successfully lodged complaint requires infringement of the data subjects' rights. This becomes even clearer with regard to Art. 80(2) GDPR, according to which non-profit organizations can litigate data protection rights without being mandated, only if they consider that the rights of a data subject have been infringed as a result of the processing. According to the ECJ, this requires that the rights of *identified* or *identifiable* natural persons have been infringed; Case C-319/20 *Meta Platforms Ireland Limited, Formerly Facebook Ireland Limited v Bundesverband der Verbraucherzentralen und Verbraucherverbände – Verbraucherzentrale Bundesverband e.V.* ECLI:EU:C:2022:322.

13 L Kammourieh and others, 'Group Privacy in the Age of Big Data' in L Taylor, L Floridi and B van der Sloot (eds), *Group Privacy: New Challenges of Data Technologies* (Springer 2017) 37.

that drives AI systems is either directly linked to a person, or (if pseudonymized) is at least identifiable by an algorithm, the GDPR applies regularly both when AI is under development (since it governs the collection and use of data in generating ML models) and under certain limited conditions when it is used to analyze or reach decisions about individuals. However, there are no data protection rights or obligations concerning the ML models themselves in the period after they have been built but before any decisions have been made about using them. As a rule, ML models do not contain any personal data, but only information about groups and classes of persons. Although algorithmically designed group profiles may have a big impact on a person, (ad hoc) groups are not recognized as holders of privacy rights. Hence, automated data processing by which individuals are clustered into groups or classes (based on their behavior, preferences, and other characteristics) creates a loophole in data protection law.[14]

To illustrate, an algorithm that filters content can discriminate against someone based on their race, gender, or sexual orientation without identifying the person.[15] The algorithm only needs access to these characteristics or their proxy data. The individual can remain anonymous and still be discriminated against. In addition, statistical data about human behavior can be used in general ways, such as redesigning the interface of some services or adjusting the timing of notifications. However, this generic use may intentionally or unintentionally increase the addictive nature of such services, which may be harmful to the mental health of users.[16]

These examples show that the GDPR – with its concept of individual rights and remedies – is reaching its limits in the age of Big Data. Thus, many scholars have proposed ways to fill these gaps, such as recognizing some form of "group privacy,"[17] a new right "to reasonable inferences"[18] or a right to "predictive privacy."[19] Arguably, in order to protect citizens and groups from unfair Big Data (group) profiles and inferences, it is not necessary to provide such protections in the GDPR itself. After all, data protection law is primarily concerned with the unjustified *disclosure* of data and not so much with the harmful *use* of data. As a result, other regulations such as the recently adopted AI Act, in combination with other laws (competition law, civil law, non-discrimination law, or criminal law) could and should primarily address the harmful use of data, thus creating a comprehensive legal framework.

14 M Ebers, 'Regulating AI and Robotics: Ethical and Legal Challenges' in M Ebers and S Navas (eds), *Algorithms and Law* (Cambridge University Press 2020) 63.

15 P Pałka, 'Harmed While Anonymous' (2023) *Technology and Regulation* 22 <https://techreg.org/article/view/13829> accessed 5 January 2024.

16 Ibid.

17 L Floridi, 'Group Privacy: A Defence and an Interpretation' in L Taylor, L Floridi and B van der Sloot (eds), *Group Privacy: New Challenges of Data Technologies* (Springer 2017) 83 <https://papers.ssrn.com/sol3/papers.cfm?abstract_id=3854483> accessed 5 January 2024.

18 S Wachter and B Mittelstadt, 'A Right to Reasonable Inferences: Re-Thinking Data Protection Law in the Age of Big Data and AI' (2019) 2 *Columbia Business Law Review* 1.

19 R Mühlhoff, 'Predictive Privacy: Towards an Applied Ethics of Data Analytics, Ethics and Information Technology' (2021) 23 *Ethics and Information Technology* 675 <https://link.springer.com/article/10.1007/s10676-021-09606-x> accessed 5 January 2024.

1.2.3 The "Prohibition Principle" in Private Law Relationships

Some authors have argued that the so-called prohibition principle[20] can be seen as an inherent flaw of the GDPR insofar as it applies to private law relationships. The GDPR treats any processing of personal data as a potential risk. According to Art. 6 GDPR and also Art. 8(2)(1) CFR (Charter of Fundamental Rights),[21] processing of personal data is prohibited unless there is a specific legal ground (such as consent or statutory permission) justifying it. Whereas most scholars agree that the "prohibition principle" is legitimate as far as vertical relationships between citizens and administrative institutions are concerned, such a restrictive legal concept of data protection has been criticized as being ill-equipped to regulate horizontal data transactions.[22]

Indeed, the "prohibition principle" is in tension with the general objective of Art. 1(3) GDPR regarding the promotion of the free movement of data. One could argue that it also conflicts with the very foundations of private law, which is based on the principle of party autonomy, thus stressing the freedom to act according to one's own will. Yet, private law has a lot of restrictions on party autonomy, especially where fundamental rights and vulnerable parties are concerned, such as, e.g., in consumer, labor and even insurance law. Data protection law follows this regulatory model and reverses this rule/exception relationship. Since the processing of personal data is generally prohibited, private parties who contract for the commercial use of personal data always run the risk of violating data protection law. Some lawyers have therefore described the "prohibition principle" as a straightforward "interventionist paternalism"[23] that creates an "informational heteronomy" ("informationelle Fremdbestimmung"),[24] leading to a hypertrophic protection of fundamental rights accompanied by a loss of freedom for data controllers and data subjects.[25] Others, however, argue that the "prohibition principle" is not only mandatory due to Art. 8(2)(1) CFR, but that it can also be combined with the proposed risk-based approach.[26]

20 A Roßnagel, 'Kein "Verbotsprinzip" und kein "Verbot mit Erlaubnisvorbehalt" im Datenschutzrecht' (2019) *Neue Juristische Wochenschrift* 1 argues that the legal terms "prohibition principle" and "prohibition subject to authorization" are not suitable for data protection law because they do not acknowledge the fundamental rights basis of data protection law.

21 Charter of Fundamental Rights of the European Union [2016] OJ C202/389.

22 Cf., K von Lewinski, *Die Matrix des Datenschutzrechts* (Mohr Siebeck 2014) 46; H P Bull, *Sinn und Unsinn des Datenschutzrechts* (Mohr Siebeck 2015) 1; A Sattler, 'Personenbezogene Daten als Leistungsgegenstand' (2017) 72(21) *Juristen Zeitung* 1036; J Reinhardt, 'Realizing the Fundamental Right to Data Protection in a Digitized Society' in M Albers and I Sarlet (eds), *Personality and Data Protection Rights on the Internet* (Springer 2022) 55.

23 C Krönke, 'Datenpaternalismus' (2016) 55 *Der Staat* 319; Bull (n 22); von Lewinski (n 22) 46.

24 Von Lewinski (n 22) 46 ("informationelle Fremdbestimmung"). See also Bull (n 22).

25 C Herresthal, 'Grundrechtecharta und Privatrecht' (2014) *Zeitschrift für Europäisches Privatrecht* 238.

26 B Buchner and T Petri, 'Art. 6 Rechtmäßigkeit der Verarbeitung' in J Kühling and B Buchner (eds), *DS-GVO-BDFG* (4th edn, C.H. Beck 2024) para 14; cf., also B Buchner, *Informationelle Selbstbestimmung im Privatrecht* (Mohr Siebeck 2006) 175ff (individual rights to personal data as a necessary requirement for an efficient distribution of data as an economic good). Prohibition principle is also welcomed by Hornung, see G Hornung, 'Eine Datenschutz-Grundverordnung für Europa? – Licht und Schatten im Kommissionsentwurf vom 25.1.2012' (2012) *Zeitschrift für Datenschutz* 101.

The apparent conflict between data protection law on the one hand, and the needs of the modern data economy for data exchange contracts on the other hand, cannot be resolved by the Member States. National legislators are not allowed to create national divergent provisions on consent requirements in contract law (cf., Art. 6[2] GDPR) and hence national rules on mistake, duress etc., usually employed in order to guarantee the free will of the person, are not applicable. However, in cases of certain categories of sensitive data, national legislators are permitted to foresee more stringent rules for consent (Art. 9[4] GDPR). The adoption of a common European data obligation law (beyond the Data Act)[27] is also very unlikely in the near future, as the years of negotiations on the GDPR have resulted in little interest in revising the European requirements for the protection of personal data.[28] Additionally, both the ECJ and the European Data Protection Board (EDPB) tend to interpret the key concepts of "informed consent,"[29] "performance of contract"[30] and "legitimate interest"[31] restrictively in practice. However, an alternative way forward would be expanding and reformulating certain statutory legal bases and hence relying less on consent as the expression of personal autonomy.

1.2.4 The Primacy of Consent

Although the GDPR provides for six equally adequate legal bases, the most important provision for the processing of personal data in practice is "informed consent" (Art. 6[1][a] GDPR). This concept is also subject to strong criticism, mainly because, often, users do not have a clear understanding of what they are agreeing to. Also, they often have no choice but to consent, as refusal would exclude them from the use of certain services. Therefore, critics argue that the notion of individual control over personal data is an illusion, as data controllers exploit this concept by shifting their responsibilities to users through complex and extensive privacy statements. Some legal scholars even view consent as fiction that gives companies a blank check to process data,[32] because they often confront and overwhelm users

27 Cf., thereto Section 1.4.3.

28 Sattler (n 22) 1036.

29 Case C-61/19 *Orange România SA v. Autoritatea Națională de Supraveghere a Prelucrării Datelor cu Caracter Persona* ECLI:EU:C:2020:901; Case C-673/17 *Bundesverband der Verbraucherzentralen und Verbraucherverbände – Verbraucherzentrale Bundesverband e.V. v Planet49 GmbH* ECLI:EU:C:2019:801; EDPB Guidelines 05/2020 on consent under Regulation 2016/679 15.

30 Case C-252/21 *Meta vs Bundeskartellamt* ECLI:EU:C:2023:537; EDPB, Guidelines 2/2019 on the processing of personal data under Art. 6(1)(b) GDPR in the context of the provision of online services to data subjects, 9.

31 Case C-252/21 *Meta vs Bundeskartellamt* ECLI:EU:C:2023:537; Case C-13/16 *Valsts policijas Rīgas reģiona pārvaldes Kārtības policijas pārvalde v Rīgas pašvaldības SIA "Rīgas satiksme* ECLI:EU:C:2017:336, cf., EDPB, Guidelines 06/2020 on the interplay of the Second Payment Services Directive and the GDPR, 16.

32 D J Solove, 'Murky Consent: An Approach to the Fictions of Consent in Privacy Law' (2024) 104 *Boston University Law Review* 593; N Richards and W Hartzog, 'The Pathologies of Digital Consent' (2019) 96 *Washington University Law Review* 1461, 1476–1491; G Hornung and S

with privacy banners (e.g., cookie banners), leading them to agree to an overload of consents as a condition for accessing certain services. This not only undermines the original idea of informed consent but also gives a few large companies a competitive advantage over small to medium-sized enterprises (SMEs) and start-ups. Such companies can obtain consent (often automatically)[33] for all their services in a centralized manner (e.g., through terms and conditions) and use the collected data for innovation and product development.

Against this backdrop, several solutions are being discussed. Some have called for a strict interpretation of Art. 6(1)(a) GDPR.[34] In addition, the notion of "informed consent" could be further strengthened by applying EU (and national) consumer law, in particular by reviewing pre-formulated data processing clauses in light of the Unfair Contract Terms Directive (UCTD) 93/13/EEC.[35] According to Recital 42 GDPR, a pre-formulated declaration of consent "should be provided in an intelligible and easily accessible form, using clear and plain language and it should not contain unfair terms." This implies that a pre-formulated data processing consent clause must comply not only with the GDPR, but also with the requirements of the UCTD – i.e., both the fairness requirement under Art. 3 UCTD and the transparency requirement under Art. 5 UCTD.[36]

Others argue that a strict interpretation of the concept of "informed consent" may stifle technological innovation.[37] As some chapters in this book make clear,[38] it is almost impossible to require consent for every data processing operation, especially in the case of automated networked services. Against this backdrop, some scholars argue that the concept of "informed consent" should be replaced by "technological consent," i.e., agreement technologies[39] that automate the consent procedure based on privacy preferences. In addition, many advocate giving data subjects the right to actively choose whether to pay for a service indirectly through their data or directly through monetary payments.[40]

Schomberg, 'Datensouveränität im Spannungsfeld zwischen Datenschutz und Datennutzung: das Beispiel des Data Governance Acts' (2022) *Computer und Recht* 508–516 with further references.

33 Cf., G Guerra, Chapter 2 in this book.

34 EDPB, Guidelines 05/2020 on consent under Regulation 2016/679,15.

35 Council Directive 93/13/EEC of 5 April 1993 on unfair terms in consumer contracts [1993] OJ L95/29.

36 Accordingly, national courts review pre-formulated consent clauses also against the provisions transposing the UCTD. For Germany, see OLG Köln, judgment of 03.11.2023–6 U 58/23 Rn 37; S Ernst, 'Die Einwilligung nach der Datenschutzgrundverordnung' (2017) 3 *Zeitschrift für Datenschutz* 110.

37 Voss (n 4).

38 Cf., G Guerra, Chapter 2; M Petik, Chapter 5; M Ebers, Chapter 9.

39 Cf., C Santos and others, *Artificial Intelligence and Law* 2019 1(2ff); H Billhardt and others, 'Agreement Technologies for Coordination in Smart Cities' (2018) 8(5) *Applied Sciences Article* 816 1 (2ff with overview on applications at 6ff); M Luck and P McBurney, 'Computing as Interaction: Agent and Agreement Technologies' (2008) *IEEE SMC Conference on Distributed Human-Machine Systems* 1; see also S Ossowski (ed), *Agreement Technologies. Second International Conference, AT 2013, Beijing, China, August 1–2, 2013. Proceedings* (Springer 2013).

40 P Hacker, *Datenprivatrecht: Neue Technologien im Spannungsfeld von Datenschutzrecht und BGB* (Mohr Siebeck 2020) 621 footnote 442.

Alternatively, there have also been calls to replace consent as the primary means of justifying data processing with the "legitimate interest" test.[41] According to these opinions, such a test would provide a more robust data protection framework and enhance legitimacy in contrast to the current legal regime, which primarily emphasizes the intended purposes of data collection and use. Nevertheless, it remains unclear how this test will be carried out and what criteria will determine whether an interest is legitimate. Art. 6(1)(f) GDPR gives supervisory authorities and the courts considerable leeway for a flexible ex-post assessment in individual cases. Hence, private data controllers who base their business model on legitimate interest face a great deal of legal uncertainty, as they cannot say ex ante whether the courts will give higher priority to the interests of data controllers (general freedom of action, freedom of contract, freedom of profession) or to the right to the protection of personal data in their ex-post assessment of individual cases.

An alternative strategy to overcome the current reliance on consent as the primary legal basis for data processing in private law is to rely more on statutory legal bases – by creating specific legal grounds for data processing or by expanding existing ones.

1.2.5 Unclear Responsibilities

A further problem with the GDPR, as interpreted by the ECJ, is the unclear responsibilities of data processors and controllers in the context of data-driven technologies. Since these technologies typically collect and store personal data in a decentralized manner, they involve multiple actors. Additionally, according to the judicial interpretation of "control", joint controllers only require a low threshold of influence over the means. The decisive criterion is that the individual concerned enables the collection and transfer of personal data, possibly linked to some input that such a joint controller has as to the parameters.[42] This confirms earlier warnings that as more individuals become data creators, they also become controllers, and raises questions about the controllers' liability.[43]

However, these broad interpretations of control not only fail to achieve the goal of providing comprehensive and efficient protection for data subjects, but also prove problematic from a political economy perspective. Furthermore, such far-reaching definitions hinder the effectiveness of the law itself, as the intricate

41 L Moerel and C Prins, 'Privacy for the Homo Digitalis: Proposal for a New Regulatory Framework for Data Protection in the Light of Big Data and the Internet of Things' (2016) <https://papers.ssrn.com/sol3/papers.cfm?abstract_id=2784123> accessed 5 January 2024. See moreover D J Solove and W Hartzog, 'Kafka in the Age of AI and the Futility of Privacy as Control' (2024) 104 *Boston University Law Review* (forthcoming), with the proposal to replace the "individual control model" based on consent with the "societal structure model" which seeks to protect privacy by regulating the behavior of organizations that collect, use and disclose personal data, rather than relying solely on individual empowerment.

42 Case C-210/16 *Wirtschaftsakademie Schleswig-Holstein* ECLI:EU:C:2018:388.

43 M Finck, 'Cobwebs of Control: The Two Imaginations of the Data Controller in EU Law' (2021) 11(4) *International Data Privacy Law* 333; G Spindler, Chapter 8, in this book, under 3.3.1.

network of responsibilities lacks clarity and precision, thereby making enforcement challenging and leaving gaps in the protection of individuals' data rights.[44]

A possible solution could be a new control test: instead of asking if a controller controls the data and software used, one could devise a de minimis threshold of influence over the means of the processing. According to this, only entities that influence both the objectives and methods beyond the simple selection of a platform or service and facilitating another party's processing should be considered controllers,[45] so a company or state authority that chooses to keep personal data in a certain cloud should not be considered a controller and hence liable. Such an approach would, however, create false incentives whereby controllers could outsource certain high-risk activities to other entities and thereby escape liability for data breaches. This can be illustrated by the recent case decided by the ECJ in which the Lithuanian National Public Health Centre commissioned a private company with the development of a COVID-19 app and provided instructions regarding its development but later tried to evade liability on the ground that it did not process personal data itself.[46] Moreover, a new control test is not necessary to avoid an unreasonably high risk of liability. If a controller has no real influence over the data processing, they could often prove that he or she is not 'in any way responsible' for the breach and hence not financially liable for the damages under Art. 82(3) GDPR. The same applies to administrative fines: as confirmed by the recent judgments of the ECJ, the imposition of a fine under Art. 83 GDPR requires wrongful conduct on the part of the data controller.[47] Controllers with no or minimal influence can rarely be accused of intentional or negligent conduct.

1.2.6 Regulatory Burdens

An additional issue that is often pointed out is the regulatory burden of GDPR compliance, which can be particularly hard on SMEs. Some studies have shown that the GDPR has had noteworthy implications for the European common market. Notably, businesses subject to the GDPR have reportedly experienced an 8% decline in profits, with small companies bearing a nearly double average reduction.[48] Another study examining data from 4.1 million apps on the Google Play Store between 2016 and 2019 came to the conclusion that the GDPR triggered the exit of approximately one-third of available apps.[49] Moreover, in the quarters following

44 Finck (n 43) 333; F N Wittner, *Verantwortlichkeit in komplexen Ökosystemen. Attempt to Further Develop Data Protection in the Context of Distributed Processing Reality* (Mohr Siebeck 2022).

45 Finck (n 43) 347.

46 Case C-683/21 *Nacionalinis visuomenės sveikatos centras prie Sveikatos apsaugos ministerijos v Valstybinė duomenų apsaugos inspekcija* ECLI:EU:C:2023:949.

47 Ibid.; Case C-807/21 *Deutsche Wohnen SE v Staatsanwaltschaft Berlin* ECLI:EU:C:2023:950.

48 C Chen, C B Frey and G Presidente, 'Disrupting Science' (2022) *Oxford Martin School Working Paper* <www.oxfordmartin.ox.ac.uk/downloads/academic/Disrupting-Science-Upload-2022-4.pdf> accessed 5 January 2024.

49 R Janßen, R Keßler, M E Kummer and J Waldfogel, 'GDPR and the Lost Generation of Innovative Apps' (2022) *NBER Working Paper 30028* <www.nber.org/system/files/working_papers/w30028/w30028.pdf> accessed 5 January 2024.

its implementation, the entry of new apps significantly decreased by half. While the GDPR aims to enhance consumer protection and safety, it also brings to light potential constraints on product choice in the market, particularly as consumer and safety laws may limit the availability of certain products. Furthermore, concerns have been raised about how the GDPR has contributed to an increase in digital market concentration, suggesting a complex interplay between regulatory efforts and market dynamics in the European digital landscape.[50]

A solution to mitigate this economic impact could be the risk-based approach discussed previously or the inclusion of more exemptions.

1.2.7 Enforcement Gaps

Finally, policymakers and academics alike assert that there is a significant mismatch between the GDPR's legal framework and its actual enforcement, despite the fact that the regulation allows for both public and private enforcement.[51] Due to this gap between the law in the books and the law in action, some of the GDPR's strongest supporters have even warned that it risks becoming a "fantasy law."[52]

Indeed, the GDPR has been enforced differently across the EU in the past. While some Member States (such as Spain, Italy, France and Germany) have been very proactive in issuing fines,[53] public enforcement in other countries, notably Ireland, has been so weak that the European Parliament in 2021 voted in favor of a resolution calling on the European Commission to open infringement proceedings against Ireland for failing to enforce the GDPR.[54] The main reason for this disparity is the

50 G A Johnson, S K Shriver and S G Goldberg, 'Privacy & Market Concentration: Intended & Unintended Consequences of the GDPR' (2020) <https://papers.ssrn.com/sol3/papers.cfm?abstract_id=3477686> accessed 5 January 2024.

51 European Parliament, *Press Release*, 25.3.21, Parliament Calls for Improved Implementation and Enforcement of the GDPR <www.europarl.europa.eu/news/en/press-room/20210322IPR00527/parliament-calls-for-improved-implementation-and-enforcement-of-the-gdpr> accessed 5 January 2024; F Lancieri, 'Narrowing Data Protection's Enforcement Gaps' (2022) 74 *Maine Law Review* 16 <https://digitalcommons.mainelaw.maine.edu/cgi/viewcontent.cgi?article=1753&context=mlr> accessed 5 January 2024.

52 Lancieri (n 51).

53 Spain has issued the highest number of fines, with 277 (212 of which were issued in 2021), followed by Italy (88), Romania (62), Hungary (44), and Germany (32). In terms of the total fine amount, Italy leads with €84 million, followed by France (€57 million), Germany (€49 million), the UK (€44 million), and Spain (€32 million). Recently, Luxembourg joined these ranks by issuing the largest fine to date on Amazon, amounting to €746 million. Cf., I Heine, '3 Years Later: An Analysis of GDPR Enforcement' (*Center for Strategic and International Studies*, 13 September 2021) <www.csis.org/blogs/strategic-technologies-blog/3-years-later-analysis-gdpr-enforcement> accessed 5 January 2024; cf., J Ruohonen and K Hjerppe, 'The GDPR Enforcement Fines at Glance' (2022) 106 *Information Systems* 101876. See also EDPB, Study on the enforcement of GDPR obligations against entities established outside the EEA but falling under Art. 3(2) GDPR.

54 L Bertuzzi, 'MEPs Call for Infringement Procedure Against Ireland' (20 May 2021) *Euractiv* <www.euractiv.com/section/data-protection/news/european-parliament-calls-for-infringement-procedure-against-ireland/> accessed 5 January 2024.

one-stop-shop (OSS) mechanism introduced by the GDPR,[55] under which multinational companies are only subject to the regulator in the jurisdiction where the organization has its main or only branch. Countries such as Ireland, where many big tech companies are headquartered, have therefore long been able to refrain from strict GDPR enforcement in order to protect their domestic economy. Estonia, in turn, has been very modest in issuing fines or administrative orders due to the lack of resources of the national enforcement authority, as well as to the unclear legislation on the requirements of applying administrative fines.[56]

However, this has recently changed. On 13 April 2023, the EDPB issued a binding dispute resolution decision[57] against the Irish data protection authority, directing it to impose fines on Meta Platforms Ireland Limited for Meta's transfers of personal data to the United States since 16 July 2020. As a result, Ireland imposed the largest ever GDPR fine on Meta, amounting to €1.2 billion.[58]

At the same time, the ECJ strengthened the mechanisms of private enforcement of the GDPR in a couple of cases. In *Natsionalna agentsia za prihodite*[59] the Court ruled that the mere fear of a possible misuse of personal data may, in itself, constitute non-material damage. This broad interpretation of Art. 82 GDPR will most likely have a deterrent effect, encouraging companies to step up their efforts to comply with EU data protection law. Furthermore, in *Meta Platforms Ireland*,[60] the ECJ emphasized that the GDPR does not preclude the bringing of additional representative actions in the field of consumer protection, and that consumer protection associations are entitled to bring actions against infringements of the GDPR on the basis of the Unfair Commercial Practices Directive (UCPD) 2005/29[61] and the Injunctions Directive 2009/22.[62] The latter Directive has now been replaced by the Representative Action Directive (RAD) 2020/1828,[63] which explicitly states in

55 Cf., Art. 56(1) GDPR.

56 K Sein, 'The Growing Interplay of Consumer and Data Protection Law' in H-W Micklitz and C Twigg-Flesner (eds), *The Transformation of Consumer Law and Policy in Europe* (Bloomsbury 2023) 154. See also K Sein, Chapter 3, in this book, on the innovative data-sharing platform created by the state in order to allow citizens to share their personal data held in public databases.

57 EDPB, Binding Decision 1/2023 on the dispute submitted by the Irish SA on data transfers by Meta Platforms Ireland Limited for its Facebook service (Art. 65 GDPR), adopted on 13 April 2023.

58 <https://edpb.europa.eu/news/news/2023/12-billion-euro-fine-facebook-result-edpb-binding-decision_en> accessed 5 January 2024.

59 Case C-340/21 *VB v Natsionalna agentsia za prihodite* ECLI:EU:C:2023:986.

60 Case C-319/20, *Meta Platforms Ireland Limited, Formerly Facebook Ireland Limited v Bundesverband der Verbraucherzentralen und Verbraucherverbände – Verbraucherzentrale Bundesverband e.V.* ECLI:EU:C:2022:322, para 79.

61 European Parliament and Council Directive 2005/29/EC of 11 May 2005 concerning unfair business-to-consumer commercial practices in the internal market and amending Council Directive 84/450/EEC, Directives 97/7/EC, 98/27/EC and 2002/65/EC of the European Parliament and of the Council and Regulation (EC) No 2006/2004 of the European Parliament and of the Council [2005] OJ L149/22 (Unfair Commercial Practices Directive).

62 Directive 2009/22/EC of the European Parliament and of the Council of 23 April 2009 on injunctions for the protection of consumers' interests (Codified version) [2009] OJ L110/30.

63 Directive (EU) 2020/1828 of the European Parliament and of the Council of 25 November 2020 on representative actions for the protection of the collective interests of consumers and repealing Directive 2009/22/EC [2020] OJ L409/1.

Art. 2(1), Annex I No. 56, that the Directive also applies to representative actions brought against infringements of the GDPR that harm or may harm the collective interests of consumers. Last but not least, competition law can also contribute to a more efficient enforcement of data protection law. According to the ECJ's judgment in *Meta Platforms and Others*,[64] national competition authorities may find an abuse of a dominant position (Art. 102 TFEU) when the company's general terms and conditions for the processing of personal data infringe the GDPR.

In the meantime, the European Commission has also reacted to the enforcement deficits that have become apparent in the past. In July 2023, the Commission published a proposal for a GDPR Procedural Regulation[65] to set up concrete procedural rules for the authorities when applying the GDPR in cases which affect individuals located in more than one Member State. In particular, the proposal introduces an obligation for the lead data protection authority to send a "summary of key issues" to their counterparts concerned, identifying the main elements of the investigation and its views on the case, thereby allowing them to provide their views early on. By this, the proposal aims to reduce disagreements and facilitate consensus among authorities from the initial stages of the process.

1.3 GDPR and Data-driven Technologies

In addition to the conceptual shortcomings and limits of the GDPR discussed previously, there is the question of how new, data-driven technologies can comply with EU data protection law. Critics from politics point out that the GDPR is incompatible with many emerging technologies and rather prevents them from reaching their full potential.[66] This is probably not generally true. Yet, as various chapters of our book show, data-driven technologies – such as AI systems, blockchain technology, social robots, M2M communication in Internet of Things (IoT) environments and smart cities, behavioral advertising and biometrics – do indeed raise a number of data protection issues.

1.3.1 AI Systems

AI systems process a significant amount of data, which is likely to include personal data, triggering the application of the GDPR. Therefore, when applied to certain AI applications, including large language models, their training may conflict with EU data protection law. This became particularly clear at the end of March 2023, when the Italian data protection authority decided to impose a temporary restriction on OpenAI's

64 Case C-252/21 *Meta v Bundeskartellamt* ECLI:EU:C:2023:537, para 62. At the same time, the ECJ developed criteria to assure a coherent GDPR application on interactions between competition and data protection authorities, paras 53ff.

65 European Commission, Proposal for a Regulation laying down additional procedural rules relating to the enforcement of GDPR, COM(2023) 348 final. Cf., thereto EDPB-EDPS, Joint Opinion 01/2023 on the Proposal for a Regulation of the European Parliament and of the Council laying down additional procedural rules relating to the enforcement of Regulation (EU) 2016/679.

66 Voss (n 4) 9.

processing of Italian users' data due to alleged GDPR violations.[67] While this ban has since been lifted, the EDPB set up a task force in April 2023 to cooperate and exchange information on the enforcement of EU laws against ChatGPT maker OpenAI.[68]

Indeed, the training of AI models may violate the general principles of the GDPR, above all the principles of transparency (Art. 5[1][a] GDPR), purpose limitation (Art. 5[1][b] GDPR) and data minimization (Art. 5[1][c] GDPR). Of these, purpose limitation is especially problematic. According to this principle, data must be collected for specified, explicit and legitimate purposes and not further processed in a way that is incompatible with those purposes. The purpose must be stated at the time of data collection. Importantly, the purpose limitation principle is at odds with the way Big Data is collected and used, which is characterized by the collection of large amounts of data, while the methods of analysis and the specific purpose of the data processing are only determined during or after collection. Furthermore, the purpose limitation principle requires the purpose to be clearly stated. A purpose statement such as "to improve the service" is not considered specific enough.[69] In practice, however, neither the data controller nor the data subject will often know at the time of data collection what precise purposes the processing may serve in the future.

Finding a legal ground for processing data to train AI systems[70] and complying with the GDPR's information duties[71] are other key challenges for AI system developers. Moreover, it is currently unclear whether and how data subjects can exercise their rights of access, rectification and erasure in relation to training datasets.[72]

67 <www.garanteprivacy.it/web/guest/home/docweb/-/docweb-display/docweb/9870847#english> accessed 5 January 2024.

68 <https://edpb.europa.eu/news/news/2023/edpb-resolves-dispute-transfers-meta-and-creates-task-force-chat-gpt_en> accessed 5 January 2024.

69 Recital 39 GDPR; M Finch and A Biega, 'Reviving Purpose Limitation and Data Minimisation in Personalisation, Profiling and Decision-Making Systems' (2021) *Max Planck Institute for Innovation and Competition (research paper series)* 1 <www.utupub.fi/bitstream/handle/10024/174974/Aho_Sami_progradu.pdf;jsessionid=0753DB2A519AD776DDBF1503DE5DDE70?sequence=1> accessed 5 January 2024. See also Art. 29 Data Protection Working Party, 'Opinion 03/2013 on Purpose Limitation' (2013) 00569/13/EN 16.

70 Cf., P T Kramcsák, 'Can Legitimate Interest Be an Appropriate Lawful Basis for Processing Artificial Intelligence Training Datasets?' (2022) *Computer Law & Security Review* 1 <www.sciencedirect.com/science/article/abs/pii/S026736492200108X> accessed 5 January 2024.

71 Cf., L Mitrou, 'Data Protection, Artificial Intelligence and Cognitive Services: Is the General Data Protection Regulation (GDPR) "Artificial Intelligence-Proof"?' (2018) 53 <https://papers.ssrn.com/sol3/papers.cfm?abstract_id=3386914> accessed 5 January 2024.

72 B Custers and A S Heijne, 'The Right of Access in Automated Decision-Making: The Scope of Article 15(1)(h) GDPR in Theory and Practice' (2022) 46 *Computer Law & Security Review* 1; S Cabral, 'Forgetful AI: AI and the Right to Erasure under the GDPR' (2020) 6 *The European Data Protection Law Review* 378; T Li, E Fosch Villaronga and P Kieseberg, 'Humans Forget, Machines Remember: Artificial Intelligence and the Right to Be Forgotten' (2018) 34 *Computer Law & Security Review* 12; T Li, 'Algorithmic Destruction' (2022) 75(3) *SMU Law Review* <https://ssrn.com/abstract=4066845> accessed 5 January 2024; L Floridi, 'Machine Unlearning: Its Nature, Scope, and Importance for a "Delete Culture"' (2023) *Philosophy & Technology* <https://ssrn.com/abstract=4455976> accessed 5 January 2024.

Another key provision of the GDPR that is highly relevant for AI systems is Art. 22 GDPR, according to which the adoption of a "decision based solely on automated processing" (Art. 22[1] GDPR) is only permitted if: (i) the decision is necessary for the conclusion or performance of a contract; (ii) it is authorized by EU or Member State law; or (iii) it is based on the data subject's explicit consent (Art. 22[2] GDPR). In the recent *Schufa* judgment,[73] the ECJ interpreted the term "decision based solely on automated processing" very broadly. According to the Court, the provision does not only cover those transactions that have direct legal effects vis-à-vis the data subject without any human intervention. Rather, Art. 22(1) GDPR also covers prior automated predictions (such as credit scoring) made by a particular company (Schufa), provided that a third company (bank) subsequently "draws strongly on that probability value to establish, implement or terminate a contractual relationship with that person."[74]

The *Schufa* ruling is likely to have far-reaching consequences for companies that use AI systems to generate scores that "strongly" influence legally relevant decisions, regardless of whether these decisions are made by those companies themselves or by third parties. Since such predictions fulfill the criteria of Art. 22(1) according to the ECJ, they will henceforth require a justification under Art. 22(2) GDPR and trigger the data subject's rights under Arts. 15(1)(h) and 22(3) GDPR.

All these considerations show how difficult it is for providers and users of AI systems to comply with the GDPR. Arguably, the recently adopted AI Act has not brought clarity, but rather created more problems, as the AI Act applies additionally to the GDPR.[75] Against this backdrop, some critical voices perceive European data protection law as an "obstacle" to the development and use of AI systems,[76] while others highlight that despite these problems, it is quite possible for developers and users to navigate and comply with the requirements of the GDPR.[77]

1.3.2 Blockchain Technology

Significant data protection issues also arise with blockchain technology – a distributed ledger technology based upon a peer-to-peer network which forms the basis for cryptocurrencies and smart contracts.

73 Case C-634/21 *OQ v Land Hessen* ECLI:EU:C:2023:957.

74 Ibid., para 73.

75 Cf., Art. 2(7) AI Act; additionally, Recital 10 AI Act clarifies "that data subjects continue to enjoy all the rights and guarantees awarded to them by such Union law, including the rights related to solely automated individual decision-making, including profiling." On the relationship between the AI Act and data protection law see more generally Section 1.4.4.

76 Cf., C Lawson-Hetchley, 'The Potential Impact of the Future AI Act on the GDPR' (Master's thesis, University of Oslo 2022) <www.duo.uio.no/bitstream/handle/10852/101369/1/The-potential-impact-of-the-future-AI-Act-on-the-GDPR.pdf> accessed 5 January 2024; <www.euractiv.com/section/5g/interview/gdpr-could-obstruct-ai-development-mep-says/> accessed 5 January 2024.

77 A Vogel, Chapter 6, in this book; G Sartor, 'The Impact of the General Data Protection Regulation (GDPR) on Artificial Intelligence' (2020) *European Parliamentary Research Service* <www.europarl.europa.eu/RegData/etudes/STUD/2020/641530/EPRS_STU(2020)641530_EN.pdf> accessed 5 January 2024.

In most cases, blockchains process personal data within the meaning of Art. 4(1) GDPR.[78] Although blockchain generally only assigns a pseudonym to data whose concrete assignment leads to persons outside blockchain, pseudonymized data is personal data because such data relates at least to an identifiable natural person.[79]

One key feature of blockchain technology is that the data stored on blockchain is secured against modification and deletion. Once data is stored in a decentralized block, it is impossible to delete or alter. Another characteristic is that blockchains are often decentralized as peer-to-peer networks without their own administrators or servers, with which in principle anyone can therefore participate.

Both features are in conflict with the GDPR. First, the fact that data on blockchain cannot be deleted or modified is hardly compatible with the requirements of Art. 16 GDPR (right to rectification) and Art. 17 GDPR (right to erasure). Second, decentralized blockchains make it difficult to assign responsibility and accountability, whereas the GDPR is based on the assumption that for each personal data point, there is at least one person – the data controller – to whom data subjects can turn to enforce their rights under EU data protection law.

Other questions arise in relation to the data minimization principle. Data is replicated on many different computers, and distributed ledgers are constantly growing, so how the purpose limitation principle can be complied with when data is not only processed once for a specific purpose but continues to be processed after it has been placed on the chain, remains in contention.

Accordingly, Chapter 8 of this book concludes that the provisions of the GDPR and blockchain technology can hardly be reconciled.

1.3.3 Social Robots, Especially Medical and Care Robots

Another technology that raises many open questions under the GDPR is social robotics – i.e., physically embodied, (partially) autonomous agents that communicate and interact with humans on an emotional level. Chapter 7 and Chapter 9 focus, in particular, on medical and care robots, which are designed to assist users, family members or professional caregivers, in providing physical, cognitive or emotional support.

Social robots may have impacts on privacy, especially, in three ways: facilitating direct surveillance, introducing new access points to traditionally protected spaces and leading to new varieties of highly sensitive personal information.[80] The inherent vulnerability of some users (patients, care recipients) raises specific questions concerning the relationship between data processors and data subject,

78 M Finck, *Blockchain and the General Data Protection Regulation* (European Parliament 2019) 14ff; J Schrey and T Thalhofer, 'Rechtliche Aspekte der Blockchain' (2017) *Neue Juristische Wochenschrift* 1431.

79 G Spindler, Chapter 8, in this book.

80 M Ebers, Chapter 9, in this book.

especially with regard to information duties and transparency requirements, informed consent and legal capacity.[81] In addition, human users often develop an emotional and empathic bond with personal (care) robots, considering them as friends or even partners.[82] This well-known "anthropomorphization effect" might lead to significant misconceptions about data processing and challenge the very concept of informed consent. On the other hand, the cooperative nature of human–robot interaction offers a number of opportunities to protect privacy in new ways. Against this backdrop, Chapter 9 discusses novel solutions on how personal (care) robots can comply with the GDPR, especially design options, data anonymization methods and the cutting-edge ideas of dynamic consent and conversational privacy.

Additional issues arise in relation with the reuse of personal data, in particular health data. As Chapter 7 shows, the GDPR imposes many restrictions on the processing of health data, and especially on the repurposing of such data. On the other hand, the envisaged regulation on a European Health Data Space (EHDS)[83] aims to facilitate the use, reuse, and repurposing of health data for AI systems in healthcare. Accordingly, the question arises as to how this new piece of legislation will relate to the GDPR. A number of issues remain to be clarified in this regard, not least the legal basis for data processing.[84]

1.3.4 M2M Communication, Especially in IoT Environments and Smart Cities

With the proliferation of IoT devices and 5G networks, data generation activities are increasing, particularly in M2M communications, which poses legal challenges under the GDPR (and also the ePrivacy Directive[85] and the proposed ePrivacy Regulation[86]), particularly with regard to the principles of transparency and data minimization, as well as the concept of informed consent. The shift to real-time data processing in M2M, especially in IoT and smart city applications, requires

81 Ibid.; C Ho, 'Privacy and Transparency in Human-Robot Interaction' in W Barfield, Y Weng and U Pagallo (eds), *Cambridge Handbook on Law, Policy, and Regulations for Human-Robot Interaction* (Cambridge University Press, 2024) 589.

82 M Scheutz, 'The Inherent Dangers of Unidirectional Emotional Bonds between Humans and Social Robots' in P Lin, K Abney and G A Bekey (eds), *Robot Ethics: The Ethical and Social Implications of Robotics* (The MIT Press 2012) 205; K Ishii, 'Comparative Legal Study on Privacy and Personal Data Protection for Robots Equipped with Artificial Intelligence: Looking at Functional and Technological Aspects' (2019) 34 *AI and Society* 509 with further references, 515.

83 European Commission, Proposal for a regulation of the European Parliament and of the Council establishing the Union Health Data Space, COM(2022) 197 final.

84 V L Raposo, Chapter 7, in this book.

85 Directive 2002/58/EC of the European Parliament and of the Council of 12 July 2002 concerning the processing of personal data and the protection of privacy in the electronic communications sector (Directive on privacy and electronic communications) [2002] OJ L201/37.

86 European Commission, Proposal for a Regulation of the European Parliament and of the Council concerning the respect for private life and the protection of personal data in electronic communications and repealing Directive 2002/58/EC (Regulation on Privacy and Electronic Communications), COM(2017) 10 final.

robust data protection measures. The integration of 5G and edge computing further emphasizes the need for GDPR compliance. Although 5G has promising aspects, there is a need for a comprehensive examination of privacy (and also security) vulnerabilities in M2M communications, including technical, societal, ethical and regulatory dimensions. At the same time, it is important that legal frameworks are dynamic and adaptable to the evolving 5G technology.

The cornerstone of data protection – consent – faces challenges in balancing operational efficiency with the stringent requirements of the GDPR, creating the need for a nuanced approach. A broader application of GDPR principles and industry-wide standards for managing consent in M2M environments could be a solution.[87] Advanced and dynamic consent procedures and notifications are critical to upholding individual rights within M2M-generated data in 5G.[88] This may require regulatory adjustments. Overall, the interplay between M2M communications and 5G networks within EU data protection standards remains a dynamic area of focus as both technologies continue to evolve.

1.3.5 Behavioral Advertising

Online Behavioral Advertising (OBA) practices have several market and societal implications. They process large amounts of data to personalize advertisements by predicting the potential customers' behavior and to make online marketing more effective. Data protection law therefore applies in many cases, but numerous questions remain. Generally speaking, OBA raises issues regarding compliance with data protection principles, challenges in distinguishing between data controllers and processors, the complex issue of obtaining valid consent, lack of enforcement on profiling and automated decision-making prohibitions, and insufficient accountability among data controllers in cases of cross-border transfers.[89] These shortcomings are the result of a lack of coherence between EU data protection law with regard to the use of consent in online advertising.

To address this regulatory impasse, there are essentially two regulatory options. The first option focuses on techno-legal reforms to reinstate data protection in OBA and ensure that users can more effectively have consent and control of their personal data.[90] These options include privacy-friendly interfaces, user-accessible options, and

87 M Petik, Chapter 5, in this book.

88 Ibid.; E Del Re, 'Which Future Strategy and Policies for Privacy in 5G and Beyond?' (2020) *IEEE 3rd 5G World Forum (5GWF)* 236 <https://doi.org/10.1109/5gwf49715.2020.9221371> accessed 5 January 2024.

89 F Galli and G Sartor, Chapter 11, in this book.

90 See, eg, E Hsiao, 'Ethical Design: Obligations of a UX Designer That Are Never Talked about Enough' (*BoorCamp UX Design*, 8 December 2022) <https://bootcamp.uxdesign.cc/ethical-design-obligations-of-a-ux-designer-thats-never-talked-about-enough-452692529a2b> accessed 5 January 2024; N Lawrence, 'UI/UX Design: 5 Major Ethics' (*UX Planet*, 24 January 2022) <https://uxplanet.org/ui-ux-design-5-major-ethics-116a7fc14df7> accessed 5 January 2024. Studies and courses are also emerging to teach ethical design to UX students, see G N Vilaza and P Bækgaard, 'Teaching User Experience Design Ethics to Engineering Students: Lessons Learned' (2022) 4 *Frontiers in Computer Science* 793879.

controlled browser gatekeeping mechanisms. The second option – preferred by the authors of Chapter 11 – proposes a new approach to data regulation,[91] namely, to regulate data use in OBA, dissecting different options – substantive prohibitions, the disclosure of ad selection criteria and the regulatory attitudes necessary for effective oversight.

1.3.6 Biometrics: Facial Recognition and Emotional AI

The processing of biometric data also raises questions under the GDPR. A typical example is that of facial recognition technologies (FRT), which are used for various purposes, including policing and law enforcement, welfare and banking. While a biometric identification system (BIS) identifies natural persons on the basis of biometric data, a biometric categorization system (BCS) is able to assign a natural person to specific categories, such as sex, age, ethnic origin or sexual or political orientation.[92] An emotion recognition system (ERS), on the other hand, tries to detect different emotions through the integration of information from facial expressions, body movement, gestures and speech.[93]

The use of biometrics has sparked concerns around the world.[94] While many organizations and lawmakers advocate for strict(er) regulation or bans,[95] the GDPR has been criticized for its non-specific and general approach towards the use of biometrics[96] and for its heavy reliance on procedural safeguards, which may not be sufficient to counteract the expansion of state and corporate power enabled by this technology.[97]

Against this backdrop, the regulation of biometrics was one of the most contentious issues during the negotiations on the AI Act. In its proposal, the European Commission advocated prohibiting (with notable exceptions) real-time remote biometric systems used in publicly accessible spaces for law enforcement purposes,[98] while other forms of BIS were (partially) recognized as high-risk AI

91 F Galli and G Sartor, Chapter 11, in this book.

92 Cf., Art. 3(40) AI Act; C Wendehorst and Y Duller, 'Biometric Recognition and Behavioural Detection' *Study Requested by the JURI and PETI Committees of the European Parliament, PE 696.968*, August 2021 56ff, available 28 July 2022 at: <www.europarl.europa.eu/RegData/etudes/STUD/2021/696968/IPOL_STU(2021)696968_EN.pdf> accessed 5 January 2024.

93 Cf., Art. 3(39) AI Act.

94 T Madiega and H Mildebrath, *Regulating Facial Recognition in the EU* (European Parliament 2021) 32–34.

95 V L Raposo, '(Do Not) Remember My Face: Uses of Facial Recognition Technology in Light of the General Data Protection Regulation' (2023) 32 *Information & Communications Technology Law* 45; J Vincent, 'Automatic Gender Recognition Tech Is Dangerous, Say Campaigners: It's Time to Ban It' (*The Verge*, 14 April 2021) <www.theverge.com/2021/4/14/22381370/automatic-gender-recognition-sexual-orientation-facial-ai-analysis-ban-campaign> accessed 5 January 2024; cf., M Zahn, 'Controversy Illuminates Rise of Facial Recognition in Private Sector' (*ABC News*, 8 January 2023) <https://abcnews.go.com/Business/controversy-illuminates-rise-facial-recognition-private-sector/story?id=96116545> accessed 5 January 2024.

96 M Zalnieriute, Chapter 12 in this book.

97 Ibid., Section 12.6.

98 European Commission, 'Proposal for a Regulation Laying Down Harmonised Rules on Artificial Intelligence (Artificial Intelligence Act)' COM(2021) 206 final, Art. 5(1)(d).

systems.[99] BCS and ERS, on the other hand, were only subject to transparency obligations[100] and were not necessarily considered high-risk under the Commission's proposal,[101] even though these systems have a history of bias.

In contrast, the European Parliament insisted in its negotiating position[102] for a full ban of: (i) real-time remote BIS in publicly accessible spaces; (ii) "post" remote BIS, with the only exception of law enforcement for the prosecution of serious crimes and only after judicial authorization; (iii) BCS using sensitive characteristics; and (iv) ERS in law enforcement, border management, workplaces and educational institutions.

The compromise agreement reached on 8 December 2023 took a middle course, according to the press releases of the Council[103] and the European Parliament.[104] Recognizing the potential threat to citizens' rights, the co-legislators agreed to prohibit in Art. 5(1) AI Act the following: (i) untargeted scraping of facial images from the Internet or CCTV footage to create or expand facial recognition databases; (ii) ERS in workplaces and educational institutions; (iii) BCS that use sensitive characteristics; and (iv) real-time remote BIS in publicly accessible spaces for the purpose of law enforcement, unless and in so far as such use is strictly necessary under certain conditions.

1.4 The GDPR and Its Relationship to EU Digital Law

Since 2018, the European legislature has adopted and proposed new legal acts regulating issues related to digitalization and data economy that will interact with the GDPR in cases when personal data is being processed, the most recent of these being the proposed Financial Data Access Regulation.[105] The texts of these legal acts are characterized by the difficulty of the EU legislature to reconcile the aims of data protection and data economy/innovation, as these aims are partially contradictory. There are structural controversies such as the principle of data minimization versus the interest in large data pools.[106] In a recently published position paper on the GDPR, the Council of the European Union stressed that any new EU legislation containing provisions on the processing of personal data should be consistent with the GDPR and with ECJ case law.[107]

99 Annex III.1.a. AI Act Proposal of the European Commission.

100 Art. 52 AI Act Proposal of the European Commission.

101 Critically discussed in M Ebers and others, 'The European Commission's Proposal for an Artificial Intelligence Act – A Critical Assessment by Members of the Robotics and AI Law Society (RAILS)' <www.mdpi.com/2571-8800/4/4/43> accessed 5 January 2024; N A Smuha and others, 'How the EU Can Achieve Legally Trustworthy AI: A Response to the European Commission's Proposal for an Artificial Intelligence Act' (2021) <https://papers.ssrn.com/sol3/papers.cfm?abstract_id=3899991> accessed 5 January 2024.

102 European Parliament, Amendments adopted by the European Parliament on 14 June 2023 on the proposal for a regulation of the European Parliament and of the Council on laying down harmonised rules on artificial intelligence (AI Act) and amending certain Union legislative acts, P9_TA(2023)0236.

103 Council of the EU, Press Release 986/23 of 9 December 2023.

104 European Parliament, Press Release 20231206IPR15699, of 9 December 2023.

105 European Commission, Proposal for a Regulation of the European Parliament and of the Council on a Framework for Financial Data Access and Amending Regulations (EU) No 1093/2010, (EU) No 1094/2010, (EU) No 1095/2010 and (EU) 2022/2554, COM(2023) 360 final.

106 D Tolks, 'Die finale Fassung des Data Governance Act' (2022) *Multimedia und Recht* 444.

107 Council of the European Union, Council position and findings on the application of the General Data Protection Regulation (GDPR), 15507/23, 17 November 2023, para 40.

As Specht-Riemenschneider observes, "regulatory addressees will regularly find themselves in the situation of acting contrary to data protection law or of acting contrary to the obligations under the data law."[108] Although the GDPR has been called an elephant in the room for data economy, it is also argued that it should not be considered an antagonist to data exchange but rather an expression of the standards to which the exchange of personal data in the EU must adhere.[109]

Subsequent sections describe the complicated interplay of the GDPR with the most important EU digital law legislative initiatives: Data Governance Act,[110] Digital Services Act,[111] Data Act[112] and the very recently adopted AI Act,[113] as well as the EHDS proposal[114] that is still in the negotiation phase. It highlights certain inconsistencies as well as issues that have been solved during the legislative process.

1.4.1 GDPR and Data Governance Act

The Data Governance Act (DGA) – applicable since September 2023 – regulates conditions, structures and procedures of data use for individuals, public bodies and traders. Its relationship with the GDPR is set forth in Art. 1(3) DGA, stating that the Act is without prejudice to data protection law. It further clarifies that in case of a conflict between the DGA and European or national data protection law, the latter has priority. It is, however, quite tricky to determine when there is a conflict between these regimes, as the GDPR has many open clauses that entitle the EU legislature to adopt further regulation and, in some cases, the provisions of the DGA could be considered such further regulation and thus a filler of the GDPR's opening clauses.[115]

108 L Specht-Riemenschneider, 'Datennutz und Datenschutz: Zum Verhältnis zwischen Datenwirtschaftsrecht und DSGVO' (2023) *Zeitschrift für Europäisches Privatrecht* 638.

109 C Wendehorst, 'Of Elephants in the Room and Paper Tigers: How to Reconcile Data Protection and the Data Economy' in S Lohsse, R Schulze and D Staudenmayer (eds), *Trading Data in the Digital Economy: Legal Concepts and Tools* (Nomos/Hart Publishing 2017); B P Paal and M Fenik, 'Access to Data in the Data Act Proposal' (2023) *Zeitschrift für Digitalisierung und Recht* 249.

110 Regulation (EU) 2022/868 of the European Parliament and of the Council of 30 May 2022 on European Data Governance and Amending Regulation (EU) 2018/1724 (Data Governance Act) [2022] OJ L152/1.

111 Regulation (EU) 2022/2065 of the European Parliament and of the Council of 19 October 2022 on a Single Market for Digital Services and Amending Directive 2000/31/EC (Digital Services Act) [2022] OJ L277/1.

112 Regulation (EU) 2023/2854 of the European Parliament and of the Council of 13 December 2023 on Harmonised Rules on Fair Access to and Use of Data and Amending Regulation (EU) 2017/2394 and Directive (EU) 2020/1828 (Data Act) [2023] OJ L1.

113 While the AI Act had not yet been published in the Official Journal of the EU, at the time of writing this chapter, the authors have taken into account the final version which was approved by the European Parliament (March 13, 2024), by the Council (May 21, 2024) and finally signed into law (June 13, 2024), PE-CONS 24/1/24 REV 1, available at: https://data.consilium.europa.eu/doc/document/PE-24-2024-REV-1/en/pdf.

114 European Commission, Proposal for a Regulation of the European Parliament and of the Council on the European Health Data Space, COM(2022)197 final.

115 L Specht-Riemenschneider (n 108). It is further unclear whether the GDPR and the DGA are parallelly applicable to mixed datasets. R Gellert and I Graef, 'The European Commission's Proposed

For example, it has been argued that Art. 12(a) and (e) DGA that regulate the provision of data intermediation services should be understood as a Union law within the meaning of Art. 6(4) GDPR setting forth the compatibility test for the further use of personal data.[116] This interpretation would mean that the original legal basis for data processing is enough, and a new legal basis is not needed for data processing under Art. 12(a) and (e) DGA. Article 1(3) DGA states that the DGA does not create a legal basis for personal data processing, nor does it affect any of the rights and obligations set out in the EU data protection law. Therefore, the aforementioned Art. 12(d) and (e) DGA are not to be seen as independent legal bases but only as additional requirements for certain data processing activities that must be met in addition to the legal basis of the GDPR.[117]

As the DGA aims to strengthen the trust of market actors in data intermediaries,[118] one of the crucial issues is how data intermediaries – including the Personal Information Management Systems (PIMS) – can foster the exchange of personal data to manage the consent and support data subjects in exercising their data-related rights. On this, several authors have argued that the answer to these questions should be found in the data protection law and not the DGA. However, it is still unclear whether (for instance) the possibility of the data holder to mandate data trustees can be contractually excluded.[119] The DGA does not provide any rules on that issue and simply sets further requirements in addition to the requirements of the GDPR.[120]

The interplay of the DGA and GDPR is also reflected in the important issue of liability of data intermediaries. Under the DGA, data intermediaries have a fiduciary duty toward individuals to ensure that they act in the best interest of the data subjects. Before the adoption of the DGA, it was discussed whether it should set out rules on the liability of data trustees for data breaches that the trustee should have foreseen.[121] In the final version, this important issue – that also arises in the case of the Estonian consent service[122] – is left to the national liability regimes.[123] Hence, the validity of contractual liability restrictions also depends on national contract law. However, if the data intermediary breaches this fiduciary duty, such intermediary may be qualified as a joint controller within the meaning of Art. 26 GDPR and, hence, be liable for the material and immaterial damages inflicted to the data subject under Art. 82 GDPR.[124]

Data Governance Act: Some Initial Reflections on the Increasingly Complex EU Regulatory Puzzle of Stimulating Data Sharing' *TILEC Discussion Paper No DP2021–006* (2021) 16.

116 L Specht-Riemenschneider (n 108).

117 Ibid., 638, 658.

118 See recitals 4 and 5 DGA.

119 H Richter, 'Looking at the Data Governance Act and Beyond: How to Better Integrate Data Intermediaries in the Market Order for Data Sharing' (2023) 72 *GRUR International* 458; Tolks (n 106) 444.

120 L Specht-Riemenschneider (n 108) 656.

121 H Richter (n 119) 467.

122 K Sein, Chapter 3 in this book.

123 Recital 33 DGA.

124 J Kühling, 'Der datenschutzrechtliche Rahmen für Datentreuhänder' (2021) *Zeitschrift für Digitalisierung und Recht* 26.

1.4.2 GDPR and Digital Services Act

The Digital Services Act (DSA) aims to foster a safe, predictable and trusted online environment by laying down harmonized rules on the provision of intermediary services. As providing digital intermediary services is inextricably linked to processing personal data, the regimes of DSA and GDPR become intertwined. Similar to other EU digital law acts, its interplay with the data protection law is characterized by the "without prejudice" rule in Art. 2(4)(g) DSA. Again, it is prone to create uncertainties as to its consequences. First, it is unclear whether provisions of the DSA can create a legal obligation and hence a legal basis for data processing within the meaning of Art. 6(1)(c) GDPR. Presumably, this is the case – provided that the requirements in Art. 6(3) GDPR are met.[125] Furthermore, certain provisions of the DSA stress that the compliance with its obligations places no obligation on online platform providers to process more personal data than they already have.[126]

Second, the DSA will interact with data protection law (as well as EU consumer law) in cases of dark patterns. According to Art. 25(2) DSA, the prohibition of dark patterns in Art. 25(1) DSA does not apply to practices covered by the UCPD or the GDPR. Consequently, it will only be applicable to such dark patterns that do not rely upon processing of personal data. This provision, leading to the mutual exclusivity of the DSA and GDPR (and UCPD) will be counterproductive to the aim of fighting dark patterns as its unclear content will render enforcement overly complicated and hence ineffective.[127]

Finally, Arts. 26, 28 and 38 DSA complement the rules of the GDPR on profiling, forbidding presenting advertisements based on profiling using special categories of personal data or the personal data of minors and obliging the very large online platforms and very large online search engines to provide at least one recommender system not based on profiling. Hence, the protection of privacy in the EU is not restricted to the GDPR but is also fostered by certain digital law acts. At the same time, it should be noted that this additional layer of protection only applies to these players that are not micro and small-sized enterprises, whereas the rules of the GDPR continue to apply to all data controllers, notwithstanding their size.

Last but not least, the complicated relationship between the GDPR and the DSA becomes obvious in case of liability of intermediary services providers. According to Art. 2(4) GDPR, these rules remain untouched by the GDPR. Yet, in turn, under Art. 2(4)(g) DSA, its provisions are without prejudice to the GDPR. Consequently, both regimes are applicable in parallel and hence the online platform providers cannot rely upon the safe harbor privileges of the DSA in case of data protection breaches.

125 S Schwamberger, 'Zusammenspiel und Friktionen mit anderen Rechtsakten' in B Steinrötter (ed), *Europäische Platformregulierung* (Nomos 2023) 273.

126 See Art. 28(3) and recitals (71) and (77) DSA.

127 See, in detail, the European Law Institute, Response to the European Commission's Public Consultation on Digital Fairness – Fitness Check on EU Consumer Law (2023) 9–10. It rightly suggests deleting Art. 25(2) DSA.

1.4.3 GDPR and Data Act

The recently adopted Data Act (DA) regulates, inter alia, the access rights of users as well as the contractual relationships between different actors of the data economy. Both the new DA as well as the GDPR break up the de facto monopoly of data holders by requiring a legal basis (GDPR) or user's permission (DA) for the use of data.[128] The Commission's DA proposal was criticized as to its unclear relationship with EU data protection rules – most importantly with the GDPR. While many of these critical points have been addressed and solved during the legislative procedure, some are still left open. For example, originally, even the question of whether the DA applies at all to personal data was disputed in the legal literature.[129] Yet, the final text of Art. 1(2) DA clearly states that the Act applies both to personal and non-personal data. Indeed, in the case of IoT,[130] data is usually connected with a person and hence qualifies as personal data within the meaning of the GDPR. It should also be kept in mind that the protection of personal data under the GDPR goes way beyond the protection of the product and related services data under the DA.[131]

The criticism about the unclear meaning of Art. 1(2) (third sentence) of the Commission's proposal declaring that the DA does not affect the applicability of the GDPR[132] is taken into account and reflected in Art. 1(3) of the final text – which states that in case of contradictions the data protection rules should take precedence. In addition, Art. 1(5) DA clarifies the relationship of the data access and data portability rules of DA and GDPR, stating that these regimes are complementary.

In the case of the data access rights under the DA, it has been questioned whether (for instance) Art. 3(1) DA constitutes an independent legal basis for data processing or should at least be qualified as a legal obligation within the meaning of Art. 6(1)(c) GDPR.[133] Although plausible at the first sight, the EDPS and EDPB have correctly pointed out the privacy risks associated with such interpretation. For example, in case of employer-owned smart products, this could lead to a violation of data subjects' rights when the employer provides its employees with a virtual voice assistant and uses its right of direct access under Art. 3(1) DA to monitor their search history.[134] Moreover, in case of sensitive personal data, such interpretation would be contrary to Art. 9 GDPR. The final texts of Art. 4(12) and Art. 5(7) DA rightly provide that, if the user is not the data subject whose personal data is requested, any personal data generated by the use

128 B J Hartmann, R McGuire and H Schulte-Nölke, 'Datenzugang bei smarten Produkten nach dem Entwurf für ein Datengesetz (Data Act)' (2023) *Recht Digital* 49.

129 B Steinrötter, 'Verhältnis von Data Act und DS-GVO' (2023) *GRUR International* 216.

130 See Recital 14 DA listing IoT objects (connected products) such as household and medical appliances or cars: data created by these smart objects will in most cases qualify as personal data and hence lead to the parallel applicability of the GDPR.

131 S Assion and L Willecke, 'Der EU Data Act. Die neuen Regelungen zu vernetzten Produkten und Diensten' (2023) *Multimedia und Recht* 805.

132 European Commission, 'Proposal for a Regulation of the European Parliament and of the Council on Harmonised Rules on Fair Access to and Use of Data (Data Act)' COM (2022) 68 final, 4.

133 B Steinrötter, 'Verhältnis von Data Act und DS-GVO' (n 129) 220.

134 EDPB and EDPS, Joint Opinion 2/2022 on the Proposal of the Data Act, 10.

of a product or related service may only be made available by the data holder if there is a valid legal basis.[135] Consequently, Arts. 4 and 5 DA can constitute a legal basis for personal data processing only in cases when the data subject is the user. In other cases, i.e., when the user is not the data subject but an employer, the user must prove that he/she has a legal basis for the data transfer – like the consent of the data subject.

Finally, it has been rightly pointed out that after the enactment of the Data Act, distinguishing between personal and non-personal data will become vitally important, as an incorrect classification will lead to a violation of either the DA or the GDPR.[136] This will become extremely complicated in case of mixed datasets and mean considerable legal uncertainty for data holders.

1.4.4 GDPR and AI Act

The recently adopted AI Act is a horizontal instrument[137] that applies in addition to existing EU legislation. Article 2(7) AI Act clarifies that the regulation does not affect EU data protection law,[138] in particular the GDPR, the LED[139] or the EUDPR.[140] Accordingly, AI systems the use personal data must comply with both the AI Act and EU data protection law. This is only logical, as the GDPR, the LED and the EUDPR establish a detailed and comprehensive system for the protection of personal data in the EU. The AI Act, on the other hand, does not contain explicit preconditions for AI systems to comply with the GDPR requirements in order to

135 Recital 7 DA further explains that:

> Where the user is not the data subject, this Regulation does not create a legal basis to provide access to personal data or make it available to a third party and should not be understood as conferring any new right on the data holder to use personal data generated by the use of a product or related service. In these cases, it could be in the interest of the user to facilitate meeting the requirements of Article 6 of Regulation (EU) 2016/679. As this Regulation should not adversely affect the data protection rights of others, including the data subject, the data holder can comply with requests inter alia by anonymizing personal data or transferring only personal data relating to the user.

136 D Bomhard and M Merkle, 'Der Entwurf eines EU Data Acts' (2022) *Recht Digital* 168.

137 Cf., M Ebers, 'Standardizing AI – The Case of the European Commission's Proposal for an Artificial Intelligence Act' in L A DeMatteo, C Poncibò and M Cannarsa (eds), *The Cambridge Handbook of Artificial Intelligence: Global Perspectives on Law and Ethics* (Cambridge University Press 2022) 13.

138 Explicitly excluded are, according to Art. 2(7)(2) AI Act, data processing for the purpose of ensuring bias detection in high-risk AI systems (Art. 10[5] AI Act) and data processing in AI regulatory sandboxes (Art. 59 AI Act).

139 Directive (EU) 2016/680 of the European Parliament and of the Council of 27 April 2016 on the protection of natural persons with regard to the processing of personal data by competent authorities for the purposes of the prevention, investigation, detection or prosecution of criminal offences or the execution of criminal penalties, and on the free movement of such data, and repealing Council Framework Decision 2008/977/JHA [2016] OJ L119/89.

140 Regulation (EU) 2018/1725 of the European Parliament and of the Council of 23 October 2018 on the protection of natural persons with regard to the processing of personal data by the Union institutions, bodies, offices and agencies and on the free movement of such data and repealing Regulation (EC) No 45/2001 and Decision No 1247/2002/EC [2018] OJ L295/39.

enter the European market – although both the EDPS and the EDPB asked the co-legislators to include such a requirement in the AI Act. In particular, both bodies recommended that the certification of high-risk AI systems should expressly include a verification of compliance with the GDPR.[141] In contrast, Recital 63 AI Act points out that the fact that an AI system is classified as a high-risk AI system

> should not be interpreted as indicating that the use of the system is lawful under other acts of Union law or under national law compatible with Union law, such as on the protection of personal data, on the use of polygraphs and similar tools or other systems to detect the emotional state of natural persons.

Additionally, Recital 63 clarifies that the AI Act "should not be understood as providing for the legal ground for processing of personal data, including special categories of personal data, where relevant" unless it is specifically provided for otherwise in the AI Act.

As the AI Act and EU data protection law apply in parallel, both the EDPB and the EDPS pointed out that it is important for the AI Act to clearly avoid any inconsistencies and possible conflicts with the GDPR, the LED and the EUDPR.[142] Indeed, several concepts and provisions of the AI Act overlap with EU data protection law, potentially leading to legal uncertainties, diverse interpretations and contradictions. For example, both the GDPR and the AI Act impose transparency obligations, but the scope and the requirements are regulated differently under the two acts.[143] Another example is the requirement for human intervention and/or human oversight. While the GDPR requires human intervention for decisions based solely on automated processing, including profiling (Art. 22[3] GDPR), the AI Act requires human oversight for high-risk AI systems (Art. 14 AI Act).

In addition, the AI Act carries the risk of creating parallel enforcement structures with data protection authorities, which could also lead to legal uncertainty.[144] While the EDPB and the EDPS stressed that the national data protection authorities should be entrusted with the enforcement of the AI Act,[145] Art. 70 AI Act leaves

141 EDPB-EDPS, Joint Opinion 5/2021 on the proposal for a Regulation of the European Parliament and of the Council laying down harmonised rules on artificial intelligence (AI Act), 18 June 2021, para 23; EDPS, Opinion 44/2023 on the Proposal for AI Act in the light of legislative, 23 October 2023, para 27.

142 EDPB-EDPS, Joint Opinion 5/2021, para 57.

143 The GDPR establishes the principle of transparency to facilitate the exercise of data subjects' rights under Art. 15–22, including the right to erasure, to rectification and to data portability. In contrast, the AI Act contains transparency obligations only for high-risk AI systems (Art. 13 AI Act) and for other certain AI systems (Art. 50 AI Act). Moreover, Art. 13 AI Act focuses on the interests of the deployer of an AI system rather than on the final user and/or data subject.

144 P Hajduk, 'AI Act and GDPR: On the Path Towards Overlap of the Enforcement Structures' (*RAILS-Blogpost*, 1 October 2023) <https://blog.ai-laws.org/ai-act-and-gdpr-on-the-path-towards-overlap-of-the-enforcement-structures/> accessed 5 January 2024.

145 EDPB-EDPS, Joint Opinion 5/2021, para 48.

the designation of competent authorities to the Member States.[146] This will most likely lead to the authorization of different entities with overlapping competences, as shown by the example of the recently created Spanish Agency for the Supervision of AI.[147]

1.4.5 The GDPR and the European Health Data Space Act

While the previously discussed legal acts were cross-sectoral, the new EHDS Act proposal would only cover a narrow sector of medical data, aiming at encouraging innovation and research and thereby facilitating better healthcare. Yet, as is also the case with the previously discussed legislation, the EHDS is characterized by the complicated interplay with data protection law. In their joint opinion on the proposal, the EDPB and the EDPS note that the EHDS will add yet another layer to the already extremely complex set of provisions under the EU and national law on health data processing and call for further clarification.[148]

Most importantly, there is considerable legal uncertainty as to the EHDS Act's linkage with the legal bases for personal data processing under the GDPR. In several instances, the EHDS does not seem to be in line with the requirement of the GDPR that every data processing must have a legal basis. For example, the EDPB and the EDPS note that Art. 4(1) EHDS Proposal, which grants every health professional access to the electronic health data of natural persons under their treatment, is not in line with the data minimization and purpose limitation principles, since access is not granted independently of whether it is necessary and only on a need-to-know basis.[149]

Similarly, there is a problem with the legal basis requirement under Art. 34(1)(f) EHDS Proposal which obliges health data access bodies to grant access to electronic health data whereby the intended purpose of processing is "development and innovation activities for products or services contributing to public health or social security or ensuring high levels of quality and safety of healthcare, of medicinal products or of medical devices." According to the Commission's proposal, the EHDS is meant to complement it and function as "the Union law" within the meaning of Art. 9(2) GDPR. Recital 37 EHDS Proposal states that "[t]his Regulation also meets the conditions for such processing pursuant to Arts. 9(2)(h),(i),(j) of the Regulation (EU) 2016/679," indicating that by meeting the purpose of development and innovation activity, the data user automatically satisfies the legal basis requirement under Art. 9(2)(h), (i) or (j) GDPR as well. Hence the proposal

146 See also Recital 157 AI Act: "This Regulation is without prejudice to the competences, tasks, powers and independence of relevant national public authorities or bodies which supervise the application of Union law protecting fundamental rights, including equality bodies and data protection authorities."

147 <https://decrypt.co/153482/spain-just-created-the-first-european-ai-supervision-agency> accessed 5 January 2024.

148 EDPB-EDPS, Joint Opinion 03/2022 on the Proposal for a Regulation on the European Health Data Space 3.

149 Ibid., 17.

proceeds from the assumption that the user does not need to prove compliance with Art. 9 GDPR separately.[150] Yet, it has been demonstrated that while in many cases, Art. 9(2)(j) GDPR is an appropriate legal basis for development and innovation activities with health data, and in exceptional cases, reliance on Art. 9(2)(h) and Art. 9(2)(i) is also possible, this is not necessarily so in all cases where health data is used for development and innovation activities.[151] Therefore, it is plausible to conclude that the EHDS Proposal, as it currently stands, does not fully comply with the legal basis requirement of Art. 9 GDPR.

The EDPB and the EDPS have also expressed the view that to guarantee the protection of personal data, the EHDS should be further circumscribed when there is a sufficient connection with public health and/or social security within the meaning of Art. 34(1) EHDS, and that the criteria of the GDPR should additionally be taken into account when deciding upon issuance of the data access permit.[152] Moreover, the EDPB and the EDPS recommend excluding wellness applications and other digital applications, as well as wellness and behavior-related health data from Art. 33(1)(f) EHDS, or at least subjecting them to the requirement of consent. Should these applications remain within the scope of the EHDS, they further recommend including a reference to the ePrivacy Directive.[153] Finally, there is a need for legal clarity on the interplay between the data subject's rights under the EDHS and under the GDPR.[154]

1.5 Conclusions and Outlook

Data protection is and remains a vital component of responsible and ethical innovation. We should only allow technology that complies with our core values and ethical principles, and we should not modify these principles just because there is new technology available on the market. As Gerald Spindler stresses in his Chapter 8 of this book on blockchain and data protection, when discussing the right to be forgotten in case of blockchain technology: "Thus, the argument with regard to Art. 17 GDPR that deletion is fundamentally unreasonable cannot be accepted either, because the technology is deliberately used here."[155] His reference to Steinrötter that otherwise the legal system would always have to capitulate when persons deliberately maneuver themselves into a situation that makes it impossible to enforce

150 Artt 33(1), 45(1, 2), 45(4), 46(1) EHDS; M Shabani and S Yilmaz, 'Lawfulness in Secondary Use of Health Data: Interplay between Three Regulatory Frameworks of GDPR, DGA & EHDS' (2022) *Technology and Regulation* 128; S Slokenberga, 'Scientific Research Regime 2.0? Transformations of the Research Regime and the Protection of the Data Subject That the Proposed EHDS Regulation Promises to Bring Along' (2022) *Technology and Regulation* 135.

151 M Kruus, 'Development and Innovation Activities with Health Data: On What Legal Basis? Examples of Estonia, Finland, and the EHDS Proposal' (2023) *European Journal of Health Law* 97.

152 EDPB-EDPS, Joint Opinion 03/2022 on the Proposal for a Regulation on the European Health Data Space 3.

153 Ibid., 4, 9.

154 Ibid., 4.

155 G Spindler, Chapter 8, in this book.

the law[156] (e.g., by using certain technology) is of utmost importance. Instead of constantly changing the law, we should try to develop and deploy technology that complies with existing law.

Nevertheless, new technologies are leading us to rethink certain central issues of privacy law. First, a risk-based approach may be better suited to the era of Big Data and data-intensive technologies than the current "one-size-fits-all" approach. Estonia's recent example of a major data leak – which potentially affected more than 10,000 individuals when a genetic testing laboratory fell victim to a cyber-attack – is a good illustration of the high risks to privacy posed by evolving technologies. The leaked data arguably included paternity tests, fertility tests and tests related to genetic conditions.[157] At the same time, it also shows that technology could be of cure and prevention. The head of the Estonian Data Protection Inspectorate argued that the consequences of the leak could have been mitigated if the health data had been encrypted or pseudonymized.[158] Therefore, investing more in privacy-enhancing technology and raising awareness about the importance of its use, especially for high-risk data, would be an important step forward.

Second, technological developments have highlighted, more clearly, the problem of the primacy of consent over other legal bases for data processing. Although this problem existed before the era of Big Data and AI, it is now impossible to ignore. As a result, we should rely more on statutory legal bases (and possibly modify them in certain cases) in order to take into account the public interest in innovation. Similarly, the Estonian biobanking example shows that the "one-size-fits-all" approach to consent for data processing under the GDPR is not feasible when it comes to biobanks and genetic research.[159] Additionally, when consent is used as a legal basis, there is an increasing need to use dynamic consent models.[160]

Another problem related to the data-driven technologies and the protection of personal data is the growing intertwining of data protection and data law. The new EU legal initiatives concerning digitalization and data create new legal challenges and uncertainties regarding the coherence of the instruments and their interrelationship with the data protection framework. These inconsistencies are rooted in the difficulty to reconcile the aims of data protection and data economy/innovation. On a positive note, some of them have already been corrected during the legislative process. However, some still remain and can only be fully resolved through case law. In addition, the Council of the EU has recently encouraged the EDPB to adopt specific opinions and guidelines to clarify how the provisions of the GDPR should be applied together

156 B Steinrötter, 'Datenschutzrechtliche Probleme beim Einsatz der Blockchain' (2021) *Zeitschrift für Bankrecht und Bankwirtschaft* 373.

157 ERR, 'Paternity and Fertility Tests Among Data Stolen in Asper Biogene Cyberattack' (15 December 2023) <https://news.err.ee/1609195705/paternity-and-fertility-tests-among-data-stolen-in-asper-biogene-cyberattack> accessed 5 January 2024.

158 Ibid.

159 See K Pormeister, Chapter 4 in this book.

160 Cf., thereto M Ebers, Chapter 9 in this book.

with, inter alia, the DMA, the DSA, the DGA, the DA, the AI Act, etc.[161] Such guidelines would be essential for legal certainty, especially if they take into account – as the Council suggests – the development of the digital economy in the Union and the need to support innovation and the development of new technologies.[162] Otherwise, it would often be extremely complicated for data controllers to ensure compliance with all these legal frameworks at the same time. This would be even more complex in the case of mixed datasets.

Finally, we should also recognize the limits of data protection law in protecting individuals and groups from the unfair use of Big Data. It is not the task of data protection law to address all possibilities of misuse of personal data. Specific technology-oriented regulations, such as the recently adopted AI Act, and other areas of law – such as competition law, civil law, anti-discrimination law and criminal law – should primarily address the harmful use of personal data and ensure that we as citizens can benefit from the development of technology while preserving our privacy.

Bibliography

Article 29 Data Protection Working Party, 'Opinion 03/2013 on Purpose Limitation' (2013) 00569/13/EN 16

Article 29 Data Protection Working Party, 'Statement on the Role of a Risk-Based Approach in Data Protection Legal Frameworks' (30 May 2014) <https://ec.europa.eu/justice/article-29/documentation/opinion-recommendation/files/2014/wp218_en.pdf> accessed 5 January 2024

Assion S and Willecke L, 'Der EU Data Act. Die neuen Regelungen zu vernetzten Produkten und Diensten' (2023) *Multimedia und Recht* 805

Bertuzzi L, 'MEPs Call for Infringement Procedure against Ireland' (*Euractiv*, 20 May 2021) <www.euractiv.com/section/data-protection/news/european-parliament-calls-for-infringement-procedure-against-ireland/> accessed 5 January 2024

Billhardt H and others, 'Agreement Technologies for Coordination in Smart Cities' (2018) 8(5) *Applied Sciences* Article 816

Bomhard D and Merkle M, 'Der Entwurf eines EU Data Acts' (2022) *Recht Digital* 168

Bradford A, *The Brussels Effect: How the European Union Rules the World* (Oxford University Press 2020)

Buchner B, *Informationelle Selbstbestimmung im Privatrecht* (Mohr Siebeck 2006)

Buchner B and Petri T, 'Art. 6 Rechtmäßigkeit der Verarbeitung' in Kühling J and Buchner B (eds), *DS-GVO-BDFG* (4th edn, C.H. Beck 2024)

Bull HP, *Sinn und Unsinn des Datenschutzrechts* (Mohr Siebeck 2015)

Cabral S, 'Forgetful AI: AI and the Right to Erasure under the GDPR' (2020) 6 *The European Data Protection Law Review* 378

Chen C, Frey CB and Presidente G, 'Disrupting Science' (Oxford Martin School Working Paper 2022) <www.oxfordmartin.ox.ac.uk/downloads/academic/Disrupting-Science-Upload-2022-4.pdf> accessed 5 January 2024

161 Council of the European Union, Council position and findings on the application of the General Data Protection Regulation (GDPR), 15507/23, 17 November 2023, para 41.

162 Council of the European Union, Council position and findings on the application of the General Data Protection Regulation (GDPR), 15507/23, 17 November 2023, para 20.

Custers B and Heijne AS, 'The Right of Access in Automated Decision-Making: The Scope of Article 15(1)(h) GDPR in Theory and Practice' (2022) 46 *Computer Law & Security Review* 1

De Gregorio G and Dunn P, 'The European Risk-Based Approaches: Connecting Constitutional Dots in the Digital Age' (2022) 59(2) *Common Market Law Review* 473

Del Re E, 'Which Future Strategy and Policies for Privacy in 5G and Beyond?' (2020) *IEEE 3rd 5G World Forum (5GWF)* 236 <https://doi.org/10.1109/5gwf49715.2020.9221371> accessed 5 January 2024

Ebers M, 'Regulating AI and Robotics: Ethical and Legal Challenges' in Ebers M and Navas S (eds), *Algorithms and Law* (Cambridge University Press 2020) 37

Ebers M, 'Standardizing AI – The Case of the European Commission's Proposal for an Artificial Intelligence Act' in DeMatteo LA, Poncibò C and Cannarsa M (eds), *The Cambridge Handbook of Artificial Intelligence: Global Perspectives on Law and Ethics* (Cambridge University Press 2022) 321

Ebers M and others, 'The European Commission's Proposal for an Artificial Intelligence Act – A Critical Assessment by Members of the Robotics and AI Law Society (RAILS)' <www.mdpi.com/2571-8800/4/4/43> accessed 5 January 2024

EDPB, Binding Decision 01/2023 on the Dispute Submitted by the Irish SA on Data Transfers by Meta Platforms Ireland Limited for Its Facebook Service (Art. 65 GDPR), adopted on 13 April 2023

EDPB, Guidelines 02/2019 on the Processing of Personal Data under Article 6(1)(b) GDPR in the Context of the Provision of Online Services to Data Subjects

EDPB, Guidelines 05/2020 on Consent under Regulation 2016/679

EDPB, Guidelines 06/2020 on the Interplay of the Second Payment Services Directive and the GDPR

EDPB, Study on the Enforcement of GDPR Obligations against Entities Established Outside the EEA But Falling under Article 3(2) GDPR

EDPB and EDPS, Joint Opinion 02/2022 on the Proposal of the Data Act

EDPB and EDPS, Joint Opinion 03/2022 on the Proposal for a Regulation on the European Health Data Space

EDPB-EDPS, Joint Opinion 05/2021 on the Proposal for a Regulation of the European Parliament and of the Council Laying down Harmonised Rules on Artificial Intelligence (Artificial Intelligence Act), 18 June 2021

EDPB-EDPS, Joint Opinion 01/2023 on the Proposal for a Regulation of the European Parliament and of the Council Laying down Additional Procedural Rules Relating to the Enforcement of Regulation (EU) 2016/679

EDPS, Opinion 44/2023 on the Proposal for Artificial Intelligence Act in the Light of Legislative, 23 October 2023

Ernst S, 'Die Einwilligung nach der Datenschutzgrundverordnung' (2017) 3 *Zeitschrift für Datenschutz* 110

ERR, 'Paternity and Fertility Tests among Data Stolen in Asper Biogene Cyberattack' (15 December 2023) <https://news.err.ee/1609195705/paternity-and-fertility-tests-among-data-stolen-in-asper-biogene-cyberattack> accessed 5 January 2024

European Law Institute, 'Response to the European Commission's Public Consultation on Digital Fairness – Fitness Check on EU Consumer Law' (2023)

Finch M and Biega A, 'Reviving Purpose Limitation and Data Minimisation in Personalisation, Profiling and Decision-Making Systems' (2021) *Max Planck Institute for Innovation and Competition* (Research Paper Series) 1 <www.utupub.fi/bitstream/handle/10024/174974/Aho_Sami_progradu.pdf;jsessionid=0753DB2A519AD776DDBF1503DE5DDE70?sequence=1> accessed 5 January 2024

Finck M, 'Blockchain and the General Data Protection Regulation' (Study for the European Parliament, Panel for the Future of Science and Technology, PE 634.445, European Parliament 2019)

Finck M, 'Cobwebs of Control: The Two Imaginations of the Data Controller in EU Law' (2021) 11(4) *International Data Privacy Law* 333

Floridi L, 'Group Privacy: A Defence and an Interpretation' in Taylor L, Floridi L and van der Sloot B (eds), *Group Privacy: New Challenges of Data Technologies* (Springer 2017) <https://papers.ssrn.com/sol3/papers.cfm?abstract_id=3854483> accessed 5 January 2024

Floridi L, 'Machine Unlearning: Its Nature, Scope, and Importance for a "Delete Culture"' *Philosophy & Technology* (2023) <https://ssrn.com/abstract=4455976> accessed 5 January 2024

Gellert R, 'The Role of the Risk-Based Approach in the General Data Protection Regulation and in the European Commission's Proposed Artificial Intelligence Act: Business as Usual?' (2021) 3(2) *Journal of Ethics and Legal Technologies* 15

Gellert R and Graef I, 'The European Commission's Proposed Data Governance Act: Some Initial Reflections on the Increasingly Complex EU Regulatory Puzzle of Stimulating Data Sharing' (TILEC Discussion Paper No DP2021-006 2021) 16

Hacker P, *Datenprivatrecht: Neue Technologien im Spannungsfeld von Datenschutzrecht und BGB* (Mohr Siebeck 2020)

Hajduk P, 'AI Act and GDPR: On the Path towards Overlap of the Enforcement Structures' (*RAILS-Blogpost*, 1 October 2023) <https://blog.ai-laws.org/ai-act-and-gdpr-on-the-path-towards-overlap-of-the-enforcement-structures/> accessed 5 January 2024

Hartmann BJ, McGuire R and Schulte-Nölke H, 'Datenzugang bei smarten Produkten nach dem Entwurf für ein Datengesetz (Data Act)' (2023) *Recht Digital* 49

Heine I, '3 Years Later: An Analysis of GDPR Enforcement' (*Center for Strategic and International Studies*, 13 September 2021) <www.csis.org/blogs/strategic-technologies-blog/3-years-later-analysis-gdpr-enforcement> accessed 5 January 2024

Herresthal C, 'Grundrechtecharta und Privatrecht' (2014) *Zeitschrift für Europäisches Privatrecht* 238

Ho C, 'Privacy and Transparency in Human-Robot Interaction' in Barfield W, Weng Y and Pagallo U (eds), *Cambridge Handbook on Law, Policy, and Regulations for Human-Robot Interaction* (Cambridge University Press, 2024) 589

Hornung G, 'Eine Datenschutz-Grundverordnung für Europa? – Licht und Schatten im Kommissionsentwurf vom 25.1.2012' (2012) *Zeitschrift für Datenschutz* 101

Hornung G and Schomberg S, 'Datensouveränität im Spannungsfeld zwischen Datenschutz und Datennutzung: das Beispiel des Data Governance Acts' (2022) *Computer und Recht* 508

Hsiao E, 'Ethical Design: Obligations of a UX Designer That Are Never Talked about Enough' (*BoorCamp UX Design*, 8 December 2022) <https://bootcamp.uxdesign.cc/ethical-design-obligations-of-a-ux-designer-thats-never-talked-about-enough-452692529a2b> accessed 5 January 2024

Ishii K, 'Comparative Legal Study on Privacy and Personal Data Protection for Robots Equipped with Artificial Intelligence: Looking at Functional and Technological Aspects' (2019) 34 *AI and Society* 509

Janßen R, Keßler R, Kummer ME and Waldfogel J, 'GDPR and the Lost Generation of Innovative Apps' (NBER Working Paper 30028 2022) <www.nber.org/system/files/working_papers/w30028/w30028.pdf> accessed 5 January 2024

Johnson GA, Shriver SK and Goldberg SG, 'Privacy & Market Concentration: Intended & Unintended Consequences of the GDPR' (2020) <https://papers.ssrn.com/sol3/papers.cfm?abstract_id=3477686> accessed 5 January 2024

Kammourieh L and others, 'Group Privacy in the Age of Big Data' in Taylor L, Floridi L and van der Sloot B (eds), *Group Privacy: New Challenges of Data Technologies* (Springer 2017) 37

Kramcsák PT, 'Can Legitimate Interest Be an Appropriate Lawful Basis for Processing Artificial Intelligence Training Datasets?' (2022) *Computer Law & Security Review* 1 <www.sciencedirect.com/science/article/abs/pii/S026736492200108X> accessed 5 January 2024

Krönke C, 'Datenpaternalismus' (2016) 55 *Der Staat* 319
Kruus M, 'Development and Innovation Activities with Health Data: On What Legal Basis? Examples of Estonia, Finland, and the EHDS Proposal' (2023) *European Journal of Health Law* 97
Kühling J, 'Der datenschutzrechtliche Rahmen für Datentreuhänder' (2021) *Zeitschrift für Digitalisierung und Recht* 26
Lancieri F, 'Narrowing Data Protection's Enforcement Gaps' (2022) 74 *Maine Law Review* 16 <https://digitalcommons.mainelaw.maine.edu/cgi/viewcontent.cgi?article=1753&context=mlr> accessed 5 January 2024
Lawrence N, 'UI/UX Design: 5 Major Ethics' (*UX Planet*, 24 January 2022) <https://uxplanet.org/ui-ux-design-5-major-ethics-116a7fc14df7> accessed 5 January 2024
Lawson-Hetchley C, 'The Potential Impact of the Future AI Act on the GDPR' (Master's Thesis, University of Oslo 2022) <www.duo.uio.no/bitstream/handle/10852/101369/1/The-potential-impact-of-the-future-AI-Act-on-the-GDPR.pdf> accessed 5 January 2024; <www.euractiv.com/section/5g/interview/gdpr-could-obstruct-ai-development-mep-says/> accessed 5 January 2024
Li T, 'Algorithmic Destruction' (2022) 75(3) *SMU Law Review* <https://ssrn.com/abstract=4066845> accessed 5 January 2024
Li T, Fosch Villaronga E and Kieseberg P, 'Humans Forget, Machines Remember: Artificial Intelligence and the Right to Be Forgotten' (2018) 34 *Computer Law & Security Review* 12 <www.sciencedirect.com/science/article/abs/pii/S0267364917302091> accessed 5 January 2024
Luck M and McBurney P, 'Computing as Interaction: Agent and Agreement Technologies' (IEEE SMC Conference on Distributed Human-Machine Systems 2008)
Madiega T and Mildebrath H, *Regulating Facial Recognition in the EU* (European Parliament 2021)
Mitrou L, 'Data Protection, Artificial Intelligence and Cognitive Services: Is the General Data Protection Regulation (GDPR) "Artificial Intelligence-Proof"? (2018) 53 <https://papers.ssrn.com/sol3/papers.cfm?abstract_id=3386914> accessed 5 January 2024
Moerel L and Prins C, 'Privacy for the Homo Digitalis: Proposal for a New Regulatory Framework for Data Protection in the Light of Big Data and the Internet of Things' (2016) <https://papers.ssrn.com/sol3/papers.cfm?abstract_id=2784123> accessed 5 January 2024
Mühlhoff R, 'Predictive Privacy: Towards an Applied Ethics of Data Analytics, Ethics and Information Technology' (2021) 23 *Ethics and Information Technology* 675 <https://link.springer.com/article/10.1007/s10676-021-09606-x> accessed 5 January 2024
Ossowski S (ed), *Agreement Technologies: Second International: Conference, AT 2013, Beijing, China, August 1–2, 2013: Proceedings* (Springer 2013)
Paal BP and Fenik M, 'Access to Data in the Data Act Proposal' (2023) *Zeitschrift für Digitalisierung und Recht* 249
Pałka P, 'Harmed While Anonymous' (2023) *Technology and Regulation* <https://techreg.org/article/view/13829> accessed 5 January 2024
Raposo VL, '(Do Not) Remember My Face: Uses of Facial Recognition Technology in Light of the General Data Protection Regulation' (2023) 32 *Information & Communications Technology Law* 45
Reinhardt J, 'Realizing the Fundamental Right to Data Protection in a Digitized Society' in Albers M and Sarlet I (eds), *Personality and Data Protection Rights on the Internet* (Springer 2022) <www.springerprofessional.de/realizing-the-fundamental-right-to-data-protection-in-a-digitize/20213844> accessed 5 January 2024
Richards N and Hartzog W, 'The Pathologies of Digital Consent' (2019) 96 *Washington University Law Review* 1461
Richter H, 'Looking at the Data Governance Act and Beyond: How to Better Integrate Data Intermediaries in the Market Order for Data Sharing' (2023) 72 *GRUR International* 458

Roßnagel A, 'Kein "Verbotsprinzip" und kein "Verbot mit Erlaubnisvorbehalt" im Datenschutzrecht' (2019) *Neue Juristische Wochenschrift* 1

Ruohonen J and Hjerppe K, 'The GDPR Enforcement Fines at Glance' (2022) 106 *Information Systems* 101876

Santos C and others, *Artificial Intelligence and Law* (2019) 1(2) <https://doi.org/10.1007/s10506-019-09259-8> accessed 5 January 2024

Sartor G, 'The Impact of the General Data Protection Regulation (GDPR) on Artificial Intelligence' *European Parliamentary Research Service* (2020) <www.europarl.europa.eu/RegData/etudes/STUD/2020/641530/EPRS_STU(2020)641530_EN.pdf> accessed 5 January 2024

Sattler A, 'Personenbezogene Daten als Leistungsgegenstand' (2017) 72(21) *Juristen Zeitung* 1036

Scheutz M, 'The Inherent Dangers of Unidirectional Emotional Bonds between Humans and Social Robots' in Lin P, Abney K and Bekey GA (eds), *Robot Ethics: The Ethical and Social Implications of Robotics* (The MIT Press 2012)

Schrey J and Thalhofer T, 'Rechtliche Aspekte der Blockchain' (2017) *Neue Juristische Wochenschrift* 1431

Schwamberger S, 'Zusammenspiel und Friktionen mit anderen Rechtsakten' in Steinrötter B (ed), *Europäische Platformregulierung* (Nomos 2023) 255–288

Sein K, 'The Growing Interplay of Consumer and Data Protection Law' in Micklitz H-W and Twigg-Flesner C (eds), *The Transformation of Consumer Law and Policy in Europe* (Bloomsbury 2023) 139

Shabani M and Yilmaz S, 'Lawfulness in Secondary Use of Health Data: Interplay between Three Regulatory Frameworks of GDPR, DGA & EHDS' (2022) *Technology and Regulation* 128

Slokenberga S, 'Scientific Research Regime 2.0? Transformations of the Research Regime and the Protection of the Data Subject That the Proposed EHDS Regulation Promises to Bring Along' (2022) *Technology and Regulation* 135

Smuha NA and others, 'How the EU Can Achieve Legally Trustworthy AI: A Response to the European Commission's Proposal for an Artificial Intelligence Act' (2021) <https://papers.ssrn.com/sol3/papers.cfm?abstract_id=3899991> accessed 5 January 2024

Solove DJ, 'Murky Consent: An Approach to the Fictions of Consent in Privacy Law' (2024) 104 *Boston University Law Review* 593

Solove DJ and Hartzog W, 'Kafka in the Age of AI and the Futility of Privacy as Control' (2024) 104 *Boston University Law Review* forthcoming

Specht-Riemenschneider L, 'Datennutz und Datenschutz: Zum Verhältnis zwischen Datenwirtschaftsrecht und DSGVO' (2023) *Zeitschrift für Europäisches Privatrecht* 638

Steinrötter B, 'Datenschutzrechtliche Probleme beim Einsatz der Blockchain' (2021) *Zeitschrift für Bankrecht und Bankwirtschaft* 373

Steinrötter B, 'Verhältnis von Data Act und DS-GVO' (2023) *GRUR International* 216

Tolks D, 'Die finale Fassung des Data Governance Act' (2022) *Multimedia und Recht* 444

Tzanou M, 'Addressing Big Data and AI Challenges: A Taxonomy and Why the GDPR Cannot Provide a One-Size-Fits-All Solution' in M Tzanou (ed), *Health Data Privacy under the GDPR: Big Data Challenges and Regulatory Responses* (Routledge 2021) <https://papers.ssrn.com/sol3/papers.cfm?abstract_id=3654119> accessed 5 January 2024

Vilaza GN and Bækgaard P, 'Teaching User Experience Design Ethics to Engineering Students: Lessons Learned' (2022) 4 *Frontiers in Computer Science* 793879

Vincent J, 'Automatic Gender Recognition Tech Is Dangerous, Say Campaigners: It's Time to Ban It' (*The Verge*, 14 April 2021) <www.theverge.com/2021/4/14/22381370/automatic-gender-recognition-sexual-orientation-facial-ai-analysis-ban-campaign> accessed 5 January 2024

Von Lewinski K, *Die Matrix des Datenschutzrechts* (Mohr Siebeck 2014) <www.mohrsiebeck.com/buch/die-matrix-des-datenschutzes-9783161533730?no_cache=1> accessed 5 January 2024

Voss A, 'Position Paper on Fixing the GDPR: Towards Version 2.0' (2021) <www.axel-voss-europa.de/wp-content/uploads/2021/05/GDPR-2.0-ENG.pdf> accessed 5 January 2024

Wachter S and Mittelstadt B, 'A Right to Reasonable Inferences: Re-Thinking Data Protection Law in the Age of Big Data and AI' (2019) 2 *Columbia Business Law Review* 1

Wendehorst C, 'Of Elephants in the Room and Paper Tigers: How to Reconcile Data Protection and the Data Economy' in Lohsse S, Schulze R and Staudenmayer D (eds), *Trading Data in the Digital Economy: Legal Concepts and Tools* (Nomos/Hart Publishing 2017) 327

Wendehorst C and Duller Y, 'Biometric Recognition and Behavioural Detection' (Study Requested by the JURI and PETI Committees of the European Parliament, PE 696.968, August 2021) <www.europarl.europa.eu/RegData/etudes/STUD/2021/696968/IPOL_STU(2021)696968_EN.pdf> accessed 5 January 2024

Wittner FN, *Verantwortlichkeit in Komplexen Ökosystemen: Attempt to Further Develop Data Protection in the Context of Distributed Processing Reality* (Mohr Siebeck 2022)

Zahn M, 'Controversy Illuminates Rise of Facial Recognition in Private Sector' (*ABC News*, 8 January 2023) <https://abcnews.go.com/Business/controversy-illuminates-rise-facial-recognition-private-sector/story?id=96116545> accessed 5 January 2024

Part II

Consent, Data Protection and New Technologies

2 Dark Patterns and the Scraping Consumer Consent

Comparative Remarks on More Effective Legal Compliance

Giorgia Guerra

2.1 Introduction

The choice of a digital architecture affects the presentation of information to the user and, consequently, the user's decisions. Consent must reflect the data subject's genuine and informed choice – a clear indication that data protection law must be perceived as an important pillar of consumer protection law.[1]

Nevertheless, the issue of user consent remains one of the most sensitive and controversial in the European context, as well as in other legal contexts, because digital architectures are complex to such an extent that what is considered sufficient notice, and what counts as legally acceptable consent, significantly differs depending on the geographical and regulatory scope that an actor falls in.[2]

Although the protection of free consent has already been provided by the Directive 95/46/EC on the protection of individuals with regard to the processing of personal data and on the free movement of such data, changes introduced by the General Data Protection Regulation (GDPR) emanate from the awareness that standard privacy policies are ineffective because they are a 'take it or leave it' condition.[3] Generally, the main provisions about the protection of data subject's consent are included in GDPR and the Electronic Privacy Directive (ePD) also known as the ePrivacy Directive, or simply the EU cookie law.[4] However, this chapter will focus mainly on the GDPR.

1 See Jan Trzaskowski, 'Persuasion, Manipulation, Choice Architecture, and "Dark Patterns"' in Andrej Savin and Jan Trzaskowski (eds), *Research Handbook on EU Internet Law* (chapter 15, 2nd edn, Edward Elgar 2023).

2 Midas Nouwens, Iaria Liccardi, Michael Veale and David Karger, 'Dark Patterns after the GDPR: Scraping Consent Pop-ups and Demonstrating their Influence' (2020) *CHI 2020 Paper*.

3 Parliament, Council, Regulation 2016/679 of 27 April 2016 on the protection of natural persons with regard to the processing of personal data and on the free movement of such data and repealing Directive 95/46/EC (General Data Protection Regulation) [2016] OJ L 119.

4 Parliament, Council, Directive 2002/58/EC of 12 July 2002 concerning the processing of personal data and the protection of privacy in the electronic communications sector (Directive on privacy and electronic communications) [2002] OJ L 201, 37 On February 10, 2021, a finalized text was agreed upon by the EU Council that pushes the ePrivacy Regulation into a whole new phase of

DOI: 10.4324/9781003502791-4

Data protection authorities in Europe have questioned whether compliance with data protection law provisions is sufficient, or whether a more in-depth substantive compliance is needed when considering the emerging new, mostly cognitive, vulnerabilities. To differentiate this peculiar nature of vulnerability from the traditional one, stakeholders have started to identify it as digital vulnerability.[5] Data-driven technologies are techniques used to exploit emotional and cognitive consumer resources eroding consumer attention. Some scholars have called this the phenomenon of 'attentional theft'.[6]

In line with the most recent debate on dark patterns, the chapter aims to analyze the effectiveness of the existing current legal rules in providing protection to the data subject/consumer consent scraping by digital deceptive architectures. Suitable trajectories to respond to the new challenges will be traced, as well.

This chapter is structured into three parts. The first part describes digital designs and dark patterns, underlining their still unexplored effects on the data subject consent (Section 2.2). The next part analyzes the problem – framing the discrepancy between formal and effective consent protection into the current articulated framework composed of data protection law and consumer law (Section 2.3, Section 2.4, and Section 2.5). The last part will review the emerged crucial concerns for consent protection into the ongoing regulatory/political European debate toward dark patterns (Section 2.6). Conclusive remarks will be sketched out towards strengthening the preventive legal approach, such as the one based on the pivotal role of legal design (Section 2.7).

2.2 The Variety of Consent-related Challenges Under a Unique Label: 'Dark Patterns'

Computer language and new digital designs introduce a wide range of critical issues for the *human-centered interaction* (HCI) setting between the user and the digital world. Today, HCI goes much further than the sole communication purpose, also covering the process of designing and prototyping legal artifacts, services, organizations, and systems.

Originally, design patterns were useful techniques especially employed in computer science and other fields.[7] Subsequently, they were employed for digital

---

trialogue negotiations, from which a new data privacy law might emerge and take effect across the European Union.

5 Among others, preliminary readings on the new concept are: Klaus Wertenbroch, Rom Y Schrift, Joseph W Alba and others, 'Autonomy in Consumer Choice' (2020) 31 *Mark Letter* 429–439; Natalie Helberger, Marijn Sax, Joanne Strycharz and others, 'Choice Architectures in the Digital Economy: Towards a New Understanding of Digital Vulnerability' (2022) 45(2) *Journal of Consumer Policy* 178; BEUC, EU Consumer Protection 2.0. Structural Asymmetries in Digital Consumer Markets. A Joint Report from Research Conducted Under the EUCP2.0 Project (2021) <www.beuc.eu/publications/beucx-2021> accessed 10 June 2023.

6 Tim Wu, 'Blind Spot: The Attention Economy and the Law' (2017) 82 *Antitrust Law Journal* 771, 778.

7 Erich Gamma and others, *Design Patterns: Elements of Reusable Object-Oriented Software* (Addison-Wesley 1995).

architectures, gaining a crucial role in legal design. This became identified as a discipline that combines law, technology, and design to create user-friendly legal documents and, more generally, make the legal system more accessible to people.[8] Legal design patterns are essential problem-solving tools that can prevent disputes and be reused for handling recurring problems,[9] triggering more transparent and understandable communication, based on recognized good practices and efficient standards.[10]

Simply said, legal design often works by nudging users toward a predetermined choice, as behavioral economics and cognitive sciences have extensively explored.

A slightly different application of the phenomenon nowadays worries legislators in Europe and in many other countries. These include the exploitation of nudges to exclusively pursue the operator's interest to the detriment of user interests or public interests. Very often, in fact, what seems to contribute to the design of a poorly designed web interface is the result of choices made specifically to misuse user cognitive bias and increase the profits of providers.[11] This malicious aim does not fit in a fair legal digital design that should give priority to the protection of human rights, including the right of self-determination – assured by substantial transparency and compliance with ethical and normative principles.

Such persuasive designs induce users to unconsciously perform certain actions.[12] These tactics are known as 'dark patterns', a term originally coined by Harry Brignull. In 2010, Brignull identified 12 types of dark patterns. By 2021, the number of dark patterns variants had increased to about 27.[13]

Given the increased number and variety of dark patterns, this research notes that every specific form of dark patterns, and consequently their legal assessment, depend on how they are used and the purposes for which they are used ('preformulated declarations of consent', or 'click-wrap' contracts; 'cookie walls' specifically aim at scraping consent).[14]

Recently, efforts of researchers and European authorities have been focused on identifying and classifying these polyhydric practices. Looking first at the academic contributions dedicated to the topic,[15] there seems to be a common idea that

8 Chiara Rauccio, 'How Legal Design Can Improve Data Protection Communication and Make Privacy Policy More Attractive' (2021) 1 *European Journal of Privacy Law & Technologies* 224.

9 Cristopher Alexander and others, *A Pattern Language – Towns, Buildings, Construction* (Oxford University Press 1977).

10 Arianna Rossi, Rossana Ducato, Helena Haapio and Stefania Passera, 'When Design Met Law: Design Patterns for Information Transparency' (2019) (I)122 *Droit de la consommation* 7.1.

11 Amos Tversky and Daniel Kahneman, 'Judgment under Uncertainty. Heuristics and Biases' (1974) 185(4157) *«Science» New Series* 1124.

12 Karen Yeung, 'Hypernudge: Big Data as a Mode of Regulation by Design' (2017) 20 *Information, Communication & Society* 118.

13 All the information could be found in Harry Brignull, *Deceptive Patterns. Exposing the Tricks Tech Companies Use to Control You* (Testimonium Ltd 2023).

14 Midas Nouwens, Iaria Liccardi, Michael Veale and David Karger, 'Dark Patterns after the GDPR: Scraping Consent Pop-ups and Demonstrating their Influence' (2020) *CHI 2020 Paper*.

15 Mark R Leiser and Wen-Ting Yang, 'Illuminating Manipulative Design: From "Dark Patterns" to Information Asymmetry and the Repression of Free Choice Under the Unfair Commercial Practices

dark patterns can be identified as "user interface design choices that benefit an online service by coercing, steering, or deceiving users into making unintended and potentially harmful decisions".[16] Behavioral economists prefer to consider dark patterns as species of sludge,[17] while other academic researchers consider them to be a type of market manipulation.[18]

The idea is not new. It is reminiscent of unfair commercial practices, even though, because e-commerce has a global reach, the dark patterns in digital environments are more complex, dangerous, and prevalent than those well-known practices. Dark patterns do not only appear in cookie banners. They are also prevalent, with variations, in social media settings, e-commerce, and fitness apps that users install on their mobile devices. This also includes the proliferation of chatbots and virtual assistants – whose mission is not only to learn about their users and generate knowledge to persuade, but also to proactively engage in triggering – or even originating new vulnerabilities.

These practices affect consumers in a variety of ways – by misleading them, distorting their choice or behavior, or making certain decisions more prominent, more difficult, or easier. Dark patterns can create a false feeling of urgency or a 'missing out' fear (e.g., the use of a 'high-demand' message), or a feeling of guilt via social influence or peer pressure, or they can obstruct or confuse consumers, also by sneaking items into the shopping basket.

Within such a diverse scenario, Luguri and Strahilevitz observed that a first wave of scholarship seeks to create a useful taxonomy of dark patterns, while a second wave of research established the growing prevalence of these techniques.[19] The overall goal of numerous taxonomies is to better understand the legal challenges behind dark patterns, especially how designers affect the data

Directive' (2022) note No. 8 SocArXiv Examples of taxonomy (in part overlapping with the Brignull's original classification are: Gregory Conti and Edward Sobiesk, 'Malicious Interface Design: Exploiting the User' (*Proceedings of the 19th International Conference on World Wide Web 271*, 2010), 272 <https://doi.org/10.1145/1772690.1772719> accessed 27 September 2021; Colin Gray, Yubo Kou, Bryan Battles, Joseph Hoggatt and Austin Toombs, 'The Dark (Patterns) Side of UX Design' (*Proceedings of the 2018 CHI Conference on Human Factors in Computing Systems*, Article no. 534, 2018); Arunesh Mathur, Gunes Acar, Michael Friedman, Elena Lucherini, Jonathan Mayer, Marshini Chetty and Arvind Narayanan, 'Dark Patterns at Scale: Findings from a Crawl of 11 K Shopping Websites' (2019) 3 *Proceedings of the ACM on Human Computer Interaction* 81, 82; Şebnem Özdemir, 'Digital Nudges and Dark Patterns: The Angels and the Archfiends of Digital Communication' (2020) 35 *Digital Scholarship in the Humanities* 417.

16 Shruthi Sai, Chris Watkins, Lucca McKay and Colin M Gray, 'Nothing Comes Before Profit': Asshole Design in the Wild' (2019) *CHI Conference on Human Factors in Computing Systems* 1 <https://doi.org/10.1145/3290607.3312863> accessed 10 February 2023.

17 Richard H Thaler, 'Nudge, Not Sludge' (2018) 361(6401) *Science* 431; Cass R Sunstein (2020) 6 *Sludge audits Behav Publ Policy* 654.

18 Ryan Calo, 'Digital Market Manipulation' (2014) 82 *The George Washington Law Review* 995–1051; Jon D Hanson and Douglas A Kysar, 'Taking Behavioralism Seriously: The Problem of Market Manipulation' (1999) 74(3) *New York University Law Review* 632.

19 Jamie Luguri and Lior Strahilevitz, 'Shining a Light on Dark Patterns' (2021) 13 *Journal of Legal Analysis* 43.

subject decision-making process.[20] For the scope of this chapter, it is not necessary to present the full extent of categorization proposed by academics. This chapter is limited to the description of the sole official policy and legal documents that describe the phenomenon.

A commonly accepted taxonomy of dark patterns has recently been published by the European authorities. Specifically, the reference model is based on content and type of interface. The research was carried out by the European Data Protection Board (EDPB), based on Art. 60 of the GDPR. The Board published the Guidelines 3/2022 dedicated to *Dark Patterns in Social Media Platform Interfaces: How to Recognise and Avoid Them*.[21] They instruct designers to avoid the insertion of dark patterns within sites, social platforms, and consent management platforms (CMPs) in websites to manage user privacy consent.[22]

The following short description of the main characteristics of every category proposed by the EDPB will be helpful to the current analysis.

The *overloading* requests confront users with a large amount of information or options to prompt them to share more data or unintentionally allow personal data processing against the expectations of the data subject.

Within this first category, three specific types are included: *continuous prompting*, *privacy maze*, and *too many options*. Continuous prompting is the practice of re-proposing at each access the same request for information that the user refused to grant at first. As a result, the user will be inclined to give the requested information in order not to see the request reappearing again.

The so-called content-based privacy maze occurs when data protection information, instead of being placed in the same place, is in different tabs, resulting in inconvenience to the user. Such a situation can occur when the privacy notice is structured to make it more difficult for the user to read and understand the information contained within it. A Norwegian study, for example, showed how, in the default settings of some websites, dark patterns are used to 'push' users toward more privacy intrusive options.[23] The study was conducted by Forbrukerrädet, an organization that protects consumer interests and was founded by the Norwegian government. Part of its work is to promote consumer rights such as the right to privacy and the right to secure and balanced contracts when purchasing digital

20 Luiza Jarovsky, 'Dark Patterns in Personal Data Collection: Definition, Taxonomy and Lawfulness' (1 March 2022) <https://papers.ssrn.com/sol3/papers.cfm?abstract_id=4048582> accessed 10 June 2022.

21 European Data Protection Board (EDPB), *Guidelines 3/2022 on Dark pattern*, version 1.0, adopted on March 14, 2022.

22 Cristine Utz, Martin Degeling, Sascha Fahl, Florian Schaub and Thorsten Holz, '(Un)Informed Consent: Studying GDPR Consent Notices in the Field' (2019) *Proceedings (ACM SIGSAC Conference on Computer and Communications Security)* <http://doi.org/10.1145/3319535.3354212> accessed 15 May 2023.

23 Norway Forbrukerr˚adet, *Deceived by Design: How Tech Companies Use Dark Patterns to Discourage Us from Exercising Our Rights to Privacy*. Forbrukerr˚adet, Norway, 2018 <https://fil.forbrukerradet.no/wp-content/uploads/2018/06/2018-06-27-deceived-by-design-final.pdf> accessed 20 March 2022.

products or services. The study includes among the elements that manipulate users into giving up their data under the illusion of control the use of default settings, misleading words, and the choice of 'architectures' of websites that require the user to put more effort into taking measures to protect their personal data, thus discouraging them from taking such actions.[24]

With the *too many options pattern*, the number of choices leaves users unable to make any choice, or makes them overlook some settings, especially if information is not available. It can lead them to finally give up or miss the settings of their data protection preferences.

The *skipping* pattern class induces the user to forget or to not think about all or some of the data protection aspects. *Deceptive snugness* and *"look over there"* are subcategories. The former is exclusively related to the interface. An example is intrusive data features and options enabled by default – which constitutes a dark pattern because usually the user keeps the preselected options without evaluating others.

The second (the *"look over there"*) is an interface used to distract the user attention toward elements that are unrelated to data protection. Here, the controller reports through text that contains a lot of non-relevant information and omits the relevant details.

The category of *stirring* patterns affects the choice users would make by appealing to their emotions or using visual nudges. Subcategories of this are *emotional steering* and *hidden in plain sight* patterns. In the former, wordings or visuals are used in a way that conveys information to users in either a highly positive outlook, making users feel good or safe, or a highly negative one, making users feel anxious or guilty. The latter uses a visual style for information or data controls that nudge users away from advantageous data protection options toward less restrictive – and thus, more invasive – options.

Hindering patterns hamper users in various ways, such as obstructing or blocking users in their process of becoming informed or managing their data by making the action difficult or impossible to achieve. Subcategories of this include *dead ends*, *longer than necessary*, and *misleading information*. In the case of *dead ends*, some links that would allow users to exercise their rights are missing, or the interfaces appear to be unresponsive to commands. *Longer than necessary* cases involve the unnecessary prolongation of the choice process or the proliferation of opt-out versus opt-in steps characterized the interface. *Misleading information* is used to make the user believe that the information to be provided is indispensable. In this specific case, the dark pattern also violates the principle of minimization, which requires that only data strictly necessary to achieve the purposes can be collected and processed.

Fickle patterns generate an unclear design. Here, the interface is inconsistent and makes it difficult for the user to navigate through the data protection control tools and understand the purpose of processing.

Lacking hierarchy and *decontextualizing* are subcategories. The first case occurs when the information given to the user is not divided into sections or paragraphs,

24 Ibid.

making it difficult to read or (in cases when the social platform differs a little from the usual design model) the settings are displayed with a different symbol in different device versions of a social platform. *Decontextualizing* occurs when an information or data protection control option is located on a page out of context and becomes difficult for the user to find because it has a non-intuitive location.

Uncertainty prevails with the *left in the dark pattern*, as the interface is designed to hide information or data protection control tools, or to leave users unsure about how their data is processed and what kind of control they might have over it regarding the exercise of their rights. Language discontinuity, conflicting information, or ambiguous wording are subcategories of this. *Language discontinuity* occurs when information about data protection is not provided in the official languages of the country where users live, as opposed to the service. *Conflicting information* leaves the user uncertain about what they should do and the consequences of their actions; for example, where the social network informs the user of control over their sharing preferences but at the same time specifies that it is impossible to change them on content posted.

Finally, the use of *ambiguous words* or information is a problematic practice. This could involve using conditional or vague wording that leaves the user uncertain about the use of the data and the purpose of collection or, using specific or technical language that is difficult for the average user to understand.

Clearly, from this brief overview, the variety and diversity of circumstances place problems primarily at the crossroad between both data protection and consumer law.[25]

From an ethical point of view, user concerns also increase as data collectors have the tools to manipulate individual information.[26] Knowing or inferring a person's preferences allows one to exert considerable influence over that person. Also, it creates the possibility of finding out their goals, their weaknesses and vulnerabilities, and when and how they are influenced.

2.3 Data Subject/Consumer Consent in Between Data Protection Law and Consumer Law

As noted by the European Commission,[27] dark patterns are manipulative means to distort privacy and control the processing of personal data. What the dark patterns 'materialize' is very often a design lacking due transparency. Transparency, in turn,

25 European Consumer Organization (BEUC), 'Report on Eu Consumer Protection 2.0 Structural Asymmetries in Digital Consumer Markets', written by Natali Helberger, Orla Lynskey, Hans W Micklitz, Peter Rott, Marijan Sax, Joanna Strycharz, Brussels, 2021. See also European Consumer Organization: 'Dark Patterns' and The Eu Consumer Law Acquis. Recommendations for better enforcement and reform, 2022 <www.beuc.eu/publications/beuc-x-2022-013_dark_patters_paper.pdf> accessed 23 June 2023.

26 Daniel Susser, Beate Roessler and Helen Nissenbaum, 'Technology, Autonomy, and Manipulation' (2019) 8(2) *Internet Policy Review* <https://doi.org/10.14763/2019.2.1410> accessed 14 December 2022.

27 Commission, 'Communication from the Commission to the European Parliament, the Council and the European Economic and Social Committee A New Deal for Consumers' COM (2018) 0183 final.

is a prerequisite for empowerment, and information requirements permeate both consumer protection law and data protection.[28]

Thus, transparency is closely linked to the consumer's right to self-determination. Consumers are supposed to take informed decisions in accordance with their individual goals, values, and preferences.

The analysis of the criticalities affecting consumer consent scraped by dark digital architectures requires, first, the ability to individualize the European regulatory framework concurring to discipline consent and digital design. An interplay of different policies emerges, composed mainly of consumer protection and data protection.[29]

It is worth to briefly introduce the main trajectories of this patchwork before going into details of the specific topic here examined. The analysis of this interplay between areas of EU private law started in 2014 when the European Data Protection Supervisor made the proposal as a topic of debate. A very proactive role was played by different authorities, even through soft law instruments. From this perspective, the European Consumer Organization (BEUC) and the European Data Protection Board (EDPB) played important roles.

Notably, with the growth of the digital market, consumer protection and data protection have begun to overlap, becoming more and more complementary to one another.

Regarding the scope of the two policies, a quite remarkable difference consists of the fact that consumer law aims at providing consumers an adequate level of protection (as a minimum standard); indeed, data protection law strike an appropriate balance between the protection of personal data and the free movement of data.[30] While consumer protection law can be seen to merely set a floor in its pursuit of a high level of consumer protection, data protection law sets both a floor and a ceiling, due to its clearly articulated dual purposes: (i) protecting individuals with regard to the processing of personal data; and (ii) providing for the free movement of such data.[31]

The constitutional foundations of each policy are different: data protection is a fundamental right, based on Arts. 7 and 8 of the Charter of Fundamental Rights of the European Union[32]; while the protection of consumer interests is the object of Art. 169 of the Treaty on the Functioning of the European Union (TFUE), and consumer

28 Savin and Trzaskowski, chapter 9 (n. 1).

29 Some references on the analysis of the intersectoral area are: Mark R Leiser, 'Chapter 10: Dark Patterns: The Case for Regulatory Pluralism between the European Union Consumer and Data Protection Regimes' in Eleni Kosta, Ronald Leenes and Irene Kamara (eds), *Research Handbook on EU Data Protection Law* (Edward Elgar Publishing 2022); Philipp Hacker, 'Manipulation by Algorithms. Exploring the Triangle of Unfair Commercial Practice, Data Protection, and Privacy Law' (2021) *European Law Journal* 1; Mark R Leiser and Mirelle M Caruana, 'Dark Patterns: Light to be Found in Europe's Consumer Protection Regime' (2021) 10 *European Consumer and Market Journal* 237.

30 Dan Jerker B Svantesson, 'Enter the Quagmire – The Complicated Relationship Between Data Protection Law and Consumer Protection Law' (2018) 34 *Computer Law & Security Review* 25.

31 Ibid.

32 Plixavra Vogiatzoglou and Peggy Valcke, 'Chapter 1: Two Decades of Article 8 CFR: A Critical Exploration of the Fundamental Right to Personal Data Protection in EU Law' in Eleni Kosta, Ronald Leenes and Irene Kamara (eds), *Research Handbook on EU Data Protection Law* (Edward Elgar Publishing 2022).

protection regulation is still an internal market competence (Art. 114 TFUE). Data protection law in the processing of personal data grants rights to data subjects and imposes obligations on data controllers. On the other hand, the rationale of consumer law is less clear, because it does not immediately appear to protect a specific fundamental right. Generally, the object of a "high level of consumer protection" stated in Art. 38 of the EU Charter of Fundamental Rights largely responds to two different rationales: (i) to protect consumer rights and information to act; and (ii) to protect consumers in situations where they act as a weaker party.

Data protection law and consumer law also share common goals (e.g., to spread innovation and the promotion of economic growth), and both utilize many legal tools to pursue these goals.

An exemplary common tool is informed consent; a crucial part of empowerment and a functional means to addressing power asymmetry.[33] Informed consent is the basis for the lawful processing of personal data. Further, consumer law adds some more requirements to inform consumers – for instance, when the personalization of services, products, and information is at stake. Data protection aims to address power differentials based, inter alia, on information asymmetries and/or bargaining power. Like data protection law, consumer law is aimed at strengthening consumer rights, with specific attention to their ability to make informed decisions.

The Consumer Rights Directive (CRD),[34] focusing on the digital content, for example, requires companies to inform consumers about the tracking of consumer behavior (Recital 19, Art. 5 and 6 of the CRD). Theoretical analysis about the relationship between consent on data processing and its potential functionality to conclude a contract represents a key issue about the interconnection between data protection law and consumer law.[35] When the GDPR came into force, the debate changed its perspective, as the regulation introduced an autonomous provision for the consent on data, rooted in the sole European regulation, as completely autonomous from the national disciplines on consent in all the other specific fields of private law.[36]

Currently, concerns about the effectiveness of the informed consent in all the circumstances where digital manipulation need to be faced.[37] For this reason, the following analysis of the data protection regulation will focus on the principles

33 Michiel Rhoen, 'Beyond Consent: Improving Data Protection Through Consumer Protection Law' (2016) 5(1) *Internet Policy Review* 1.

34 Consolidated version (after the amendments introduced by the Directive (EU) 2019/2161 of 27 November 2019 on better enforcement and modernisation of Union consumer protection rules): Parliament, Council, Directive 2011/83/EU of 25 October 2011 on consumer rights, amending Council Directive 93/13/EEC and Directive 1999/44/EC of the European Parliament and of the Council and repealing Council Directive 85/577/EEC and Directive 97/7/EC of the European Parliament and of the Council [2011] OJ L 304.

35 Claudia Irti, *Consenso "negoziato" e circolazione dei dati personali* (Giappichelli 2021); Giuseppe Versaci, *La contrattualizzazione dei dati personali dei consumatori* (ESI Quaderni di «Studi Senesi» vol. 5 2020); Alberto De Franceschi, *La circolazione dei dati personali tra privacy e contratto* (ESI 2017).

36 Elise Poillot, 'La protection des données personnelles par le droit européen de la consommation' in Mathieu Combet (ed), *Le droit européen de la consommation au XXIe siècle. État des lieux et perspectives* (Bruylant 2022).

37 Geraint Howells, 'The Potential and Limits of Consumer Empowerment by Information' (2005) 32 *Journal of Law and Society* 349.

regulating consent, before shifting toward the important role that design rules could play in promoting user-friendly information.[38] Similar concerns have shaped the structure of the analysis of the consumer law (Section 2.5).

Ultimately, many consumer transactions for free online services enable companies to collect consumer data. Against this backdrop, an instance of a data protection liability claim for dark patterns could be potentially pursued against a non-controller third party under consumer law. It can happen that a breach of information requirements could also be interpreted as an unfair commercial practice because, depending on national law, the failure to provide information or the provision of misleading information could make the contract void. In such circumstances, it is consumer law that provides contractual remedies for the breach of transparency requirements.

Consumer and data protection EU policies seem not to be functional when it comes to forbidding anti-privacy designs embedded in websites – every time consumers enter into a contractual agreement that would not have happened without the influence of dark patterns. Insights will indirectly emerge about the need for a tighter (and clear) synergy between the two policies and their enforcement tools.

Looking at the freedom of self-determination, doctrinal and policy contributions flourish.[39] Approximately all of the critical issues are described by the recent report of the European Consumer Organization (BEUC) titled *EU Consumer Protection 2.0: Structural Asymmetries in Digital Consumer Markets*.[40] In sum, open questions relate to: (i) how consumers can be meaningfully informed about technically complex issues such as data collection online; (ii) how realistic an informed consent approach is in times of information overload and constantly divided attention; and (iii) what role the GDPR and consumer law play in helping consumers to manage their data once consent has been given (post-consent management).

2.4 Focus on Consent Under Data Protection Law

A recurring question in data protection law is the effectiveness of the most empowerment mechanism currently employed in practice – the 'notice and choice mechanism'. Another inquiry investigates to what extent effectiveness of informed consent, primarily guaranteed by Arts. 4–7 and 9 of the GDPR, will still assure the fundamental requirements of a lawful consent, given the fact that current EU private law was not set up for 'digital vulnerability'.

Users are asked to give consent in ways that comply with the requirements of the GDPR, assuming that this prerequisite will be sufficient to ensure full protection of

38 Ryan Calo, 'Digital Market Manipulation' (2014) 82 *The George Washington Law Review* 995.

39 Plixavra Vogiatzoglou and Peggy Valcke 'Chapter 1: Two Decades of Article 8 CFR: A Critical Exploration of the Fundamental Right to Personal Data Protection in EU Law' in Eleni Kosta, Ronald Leenes and Irene Kamara (eds), *Research Handbook on EU Data Protection Law* (Edward Elgar Publishing 2022).

40 European Consumer Organization (BEUC), Report on Eu Consumer Protection 2.0 (n. 21).

freedom of choice. This is, however, an optimistic view that does not correspond to reality.

GDPR provisions were written when dark digital architectures were not yet widespread.[41] Nonetheless, the interpretative function of the European Court of Justice in recent cases concretely determined to what extent the meeting of GDPR requirements for a freely given consent is still sufficient and suitable to cope with the challenges of dark patterns.

It is interesting to note that influencing decisions by providing biased information to individuals can generally be considered as an unfair practice, contrary to the principle of fairness of processing set in Art. 5(1)(a) GDPR. It can occur throughout the entire user experience within a social media platform. However, at the sign-up process stage, the stirring effect can be especially strong, considering the overload of information that users might have to deal with in addition to the steps needed to complete the registration.[42]

Some GDPR provisions protect the freedom of consent. For example, by Art. 7(4), consent is presumed not to be freely given if it does not allow separate consent to be given to different personal data processing operations, despite it being appropriate in the individual case. This also applies to cases when the performance of a contract, including the provision of a service, is dependent on the consent, despite such consent not being necessary for such performance.

Several other provisions in the GDPR seek to promote a high degree of transparency in the processing of personal data. In general, these provisions require data controllers to provide data subjects with information about the processing of their personal data and to do so in a concise, transparent, intelligible, and easily accessible form, using clear and plain language.

The crucial problem in managing dark patterns' violation of consumer rights under the GDPR is that GDPR focuses on transparency protection, while the protection of digital vulnerability requires architecture control, which, ultimately, means to assess fairness. The control of architecture can be conducted by the shape of standardization and through a specific individual phase, which refers to concrete circumstances. For this reason, the Unfair Commercial Practices Directive (UCPD) cannot be neglected when assessing the fairness of data exploitation strategies under the GDPR.

For example, when personal data is obtained from the data subject, Art. 13(2)(f) requires data controllers to provide data subjects with information about "the existence of automated decision-making, including profiling . . . and meaningful

41 At that time, behavioral studies were not yet employed to analyze consent clauses. Lucilla Gatt, Roberta Montanari and Ilaria Amelia Caggiano, 'Consenso al trattamento dei dati personali e analisi giuridico-comportamentale. Spunti di riflessione sull'effettività della tutela dei dati personali' (2017) 2 *Politica del diritto* 363.

42 European Data Protection Board (Edpb), 'Guidelines 03/2022 on Deceptive Design Patterns in Social Media Platform Interfaces: How to Recognise and Avoid Them' (Version 2.0), 14 February 2023, 17 <https://edpb.europa.eu/our-work-tools/our-documents/guidelines/guidelines-032022-deceptive-design-patterns-social-media_en> accessed 11 August 2023.

information about the logic involved, as well as the significance and the envisaged consequences of such processing for the data subject". The purpose of such information provision is said "to ensure fair and transparent processing". The GDPR requires that the mandated disclosures listed under Art. 13 GDPR has to be provided at the moment of the collection of personal data. Clear and plain communication with data subject regarding the processed data is an essential condition together with other interconnected European principles like fairness and lawfulness.

Transparency is, despite many weaknesses, a core concept of the GDPR (Arts. 5, 12–14, 26, 40, 41–43, 53 and 88 and in Recitals 13, 39, 58, 60, 71, 78, 100 and 121 GDPR). However, data exploitation regards the fairness of the design architecture. Consequently, according to legal scholars, potential application of the transparency-by-design principle could better contribute to struggle with dark patterns.[43]

More precisely, transparency is, on the one hand, connected to the accountability of controllers in areas of mandatory information (Arts. 12–14 of the GDPR); and, on the other hand, to the accessibility of information, the meaningfulness of choices, and the reduction of information vulnerabilities.

The twofold structure of the principle of transparency (temporal and formal requirements), like the way it is described in the consumer field, can be found in data protection law, as well. Where data is derived from third party sources (which is the case enshrined at Art. 14 GDPR), information requirements have to be fulfilled within a reasonable time period, depending on the specific circumstances of the processing (which cannot exceed one month in any case). If the personal data is intended for communicating with the data subject, then the information must be given, at the latest, at the occurrence of the first communication, or (when the data controller plans to disclose the personal data) at the time of the first disclosure (Art. 14.3 GDPR).

Regarding formal requirements, the GDPR echoes consumer protection rules – the data controllers shall take appropriate measures to provide the information required by law (Arts. 13–14 GDPR) and any communication regarding the right of access, the use of automated individual decision-making, and personal data breach – in a concise, transparent, intelligible, and easily accessible form; using clear and plain language; provided in writing or by other means, including, when appropriate, by electronic means; or provided orally, if requested so by the data subject. Furthermore, where the processing is based on the data subject's consent, the request for it has to be presented in a manner which is clearly distinguishable from other matters.

For the GDPR, visualization and iconography (Art. 12[8] GDPR) are surely means of guaranteeing transparency, in similar format with food labeling regulations. In essence, the literal and formal importance given to these aspects were not accompanied by more concrete guidelines, as against the case of the transparency principle with WP29.

43 Luiza Jarovsky, 'Dark Patterns in Personal Data Collection: Definition, Taxonomy and Lawfulness' (1 March 2022) <https://papers.ssrn.com/sol3/papers.cfm?abstract_id=4048582> accessed 10 June 2022.

Given the nature of the technological designs examined, another crucial contribution of data protection law is the integration of individual rights into the data systems' operation based of the concept of 'data protection by design' enshrined in the GDPR. It constitutes the most direct way to structure the design, avoiding the use of circumvention techniques that avoid the effectiveness of techno-regulatory measures.

The idea is to build in legal policies right from the design of the technology, mainly through the functions of algorithms concerning several specific profiles as the already mentioned transparency by design, safety by design, competition by design,[44] and 'data protection by design' – explicitly recognized in Art. 25(1) of GDPR; which requires system designers to consider the privacy risks of their digital architectures as early as possible, and throughout the entire process.[45]

Based on the data protection by design requirement, controllers implement data protection principles like accountability and fairness into the design of data processing systems. Practically speaking, through this mechanism, data protection becomes part of data processing. In comparison to the more traditional data protection approach based on post-production remedies, the design approach shifts to a proactive and preventive perspective.

The EDPB adopted the Guidelines 4/2019 on Art. 25 Data Protection by Design and by Default (version 2.0) underlay the necessity for data controllers to implement GDPR obligations when designing processing operations.[46] Moreover, the EDPB gives guidance on appropriate measures to provide effective implementation of Art. 25 obligations. Thus, the controller must understand data protection principles and the data subject rights and freedoms to properly implement the legal requirements.

Data controllers need to consider the effectiveness of legal principles' protection in practice as early as possible. Key verifiable elements are clarity, semantics, accessibility, relevance, comprehensibility, and the universal design multi-channel. These last ones are relevant for the facilitation of rights protection, as well as the avoidance of discrimination (EDPB, Guidelines 4/2019). Often, in fact, companies such as Tinder or Facebook recognize the rights of the user under the GDPR, but they do not do enough in practice to facilitate the application of such rights within the user's exercise.

Academic opinions concerning the guidelines underlined deceptive practices are contrary to both the data protection by design and by default obligations.[47] By adopting a design pattern that unduly impedes the free choice of data subjects, the

44 Margrethe Vestager, 'Algorithms and Competition', *Speech at the Bundeskartellamt 18th Conference on Competition* (Berlin 16 March 2017).

45 Ann Cavoukian, 'Privacy by Design – The 7 Foundational Principles, Information and Privacy Commissioner of Ontario' (2009) 3 <www.ipc.on.ca/wp-content/uploads/resources/7foundationalprinciples.pdf> accessed 11 November 2022.

46 EDPB, 'Opinion 1/2021 on the Proposal for a Digital Services Act' 10 February 2021 <https://edps.europa.eu/system/files/2021-02/21-02-10-opinion_on_digital_services_act_en.pdf> accessed 10 June 2023.

47 Derek McAuley, Ansgar Koene and Jiahong Chen, 'Comments on the European Data Protection Board's Guidelines 4/2019 on Article 25 Data Protection by Design and by Default' (2020) <https://edpb.europa.eu/sites/edpb/files/webform/public_consultation_reply/comments_on_edpb_guidelines_on_a_25_dpbdd_-_horizon.pdf> accessed 20 May 2023.

data controller would fail to fulfill their duty to implement appropriate technical and organizational measures in an effective manner. In certain cases, this may even constitute a violation of the transparency principle, as well as the lawfulness principle, because the consent given via a manipulative pattern cannot be considered 'freely given' and thus cannot serve as a valid legal basis for consent on data processing.

It must be noted that, in recent times, private forms of regulation – such as private voluntary standards and soft law – have greatly contributed to shape the principle of transparency. Article 29 Working Party, for example, issues guidelines on transparency under Regulation 2016/679 in April 2018, which influence the interpretation and applicability of the GDPR in a remarkable way. Concretely, WP29 delineates general principles, clauses, and practical indications as the succinct and efficient way to present information and to implement transparency as a "user-centric [concept] rather than legalistic".[48]

WP29 guarantees that the consumer has the suitable tools to foresee the scope, the potential risks, and the consequences of the data processing, also in line with consumer law case law decisions. Overall, the guidelines also benefit from empirical behavioral insights.

The interdisciplinary insights into understanding mandated disclosures and transparency become central, so empirical findings from linguistics, information design, human–computer interaction, and behavioral sciences can efficiently contribute to shape the content of the principle of transparency, providing not only ex ante guidance to traders and data controllers, but also a toolkit to enforcement authorities and courts to assess legal obligations.[49]

Based on these keen academic observations, the design way of proactively thinking reveals itself as an effective tool for the coherent application of these new directions in complying with transparency. Consequently, patterns operatively translate the legal principle of transparency into practice through behavioral and design lenses.

2.4.1 European Case Law on Data Subjects' Consent

European cases are determinant to tracing the current trajectories of transparency and informed choices protection in a data-driven technological context. Recent jurisprudential interpretations address the most innovative profiles of user's self-determination protection against data exploitation mechanisms (e.g., *web scraping*).

In *Planet49*,[50] the Grand Chamber ruled on the active and unequivocal nature of consent, establishing that it is not valid when expressed using a pre-ticked check-box that the user must deselect to refuse his or her consent (para 65).

48 Point 4 of the document (Guidelines on transparency under Regulation 2016/679).

49 Rossi and others, *When Design Met Law* (n. 7).

50 Case C-673/17, *Planet49 GmbH v Bundesverband der Verbraucherzentralen und Verbraucherverbände – Verbraucherzentrale Bundesverband e. V.*, ECLI:EU:C:2019:246.

Furthermore, the Court of Justice of the European Union (CJEU) stated that unchecking the consent box does not require any consumer action. The ruling is on the same wavelength with Recital 32 GDPR, which stipulates that 'silence, pre-ticked boxes or inactivity should not, therefore, constitute consent'.

In the case at hand, a German company had used a pre-ticketed checkbox by which regular users, who aspired to participate in sweepstakes, expressed consent to the installation of cookies aimed at collecting information for advertising purposes. The Court held that consent to the installation and consultation of cookies on the terminal equipment was not validly manifested through a preselected checkbox, which the user had to uncheck to deny consent to the processing of his or her data. The CJEU helped identifying the specific conditions under which consent is effectively free and informed to constitute a suitable legal basis for data processing. Consent must be expressed in a positive action, distinct from the activity that the user wishes to pursue.

In cookie consent management, dark patterns can also prevent effective consent in the sense of Art. 5(3) of the ePrivacy Directive. Statements on this can be found in the opinions of the German data protection supervisory authorities described as inadmissible 'nudging'.[51]

In sum, implied consent which occurs when one continues to use a website without actively objecting to a *notice* (or *cookie*), will not establish a valid legal basis for data processing and collection, because it does not involve user action.

Withdrawing consent should be as simple as providing it.[52] After consent is given, the same consent withdrawal form should be available at each access. Unfortunately, this is not always the case.

The need for affirmative action that proves that the user understands the disclosure has already been emphasized by the terminology used. Consent mechanisms employed with different visual techniques or colors for terms such as 'agree' or 'allow', and for terms such as 'reject' or 'block', are not legally compliant, as the system influences users to opt for the acceptance.

Information should be truly comprehensible; otherwise, consent (be it even contractual consent) would be deprived of its authentic nature as a manifestation of free will as it is conscious, discouraging instead the so-called consent (and reading)-fatigue.[53]

In *Orange Romania*,[54] the CJEU goes further than what it did in *Planet49*. Regarding the active nature of consent, the CJEU states that consent is not valid if the

51 See DSK, 'Orientierungshilfe der Aufsichtsbehörden für Anbieter: innen von Telemedien' (*OH Telemedien* 2021) 1 December 2021, as of December 2022 <efaidnbmnnnibpcajpcglclefindmkaj/www.datenschutzkonferenz-online.de/media/oh/20221130_OH_Telemedien_Version_1.1.pdf> accessed 11 February 2023; LfD Niedersachsen, 'Handreichung: Datenschutzkonforme Einwilligungen auf Webseiten – Anforderungen an Consent-Layer', September 2022.

52 Giorgio Resta, 'Revoca del consenso ed interesse al trattamento nella legge sulla protezione dei dati personali' (2000) *Riv Crit Dir Priv* 299.

53 BEUC, Report on EU Consumer Protection 2.0 (n. 21).

54 Judgment in Case C-61/19 Orange România SA v Autoritatea Naţională de Supraveghere a Prelucrării Datelorcu Caracter Personal (ANSPDCP).

pre-ticked box attached has been checked by the data controller prior to the signing of that contract.

As regards to the freely given and informed nature of consent, the Court stated that the consent is not valid when the terms of the contract are capable of misleading the data subject as to the possibility of concluding the contract in question.[55] Consequently, forcing customers to complete another form to specify their refusal may confuse data subjects, affecting their right to information.

Reading the decision from the perspective of business, it could be challenging for them to meet the CJEU's requirements regarding the active, freely given, and informed nature of consent.

Although Art. 29 Working Party had stated that consent on data processing should not be a mandatory condition for the conclusion of a contract, the Court of Luxemburg goes further: it shows how the inclusion of additional conditions, for example the completion of an additional form invalid consent to data processing. In conclusion, in *Orange Romania*, the Court proposed a restricted vision, attributing an absolute value to consent when used as a legal basis for data processing. It significantly raises the standards of consent, and will undoubtedly have a significant influence in practice. It invites national courts to interpret consent to the highest standards.[56]

Finally, a quick reference to the interpretation of data protection law and competition is also needed to complete the frame of cases.

Notably, a relevant European interpretative proceeding on issues about consent has been expected for long on the well-known German Facebook (now Meta Platforms) case,[57] whereby the *Bundeskartellamt* imposed far-reaching restrictions on Facebook in the processing of user data.[58] Finally, this European Court of Justice (ECJ) decision was delivered on 4 July 2023 (C-252–21),[59] when the Court of Justice resolved the problem around the potential interaction between data protection regulation and competition law following the legal opera that started in 2019 with the German competition authorities on the Meta case. The decision also imposes important requirements in relation to the interpretation of the GDPR, in particular with regards to the personalized use of consumers' personal data for targeted advertising by social media platforms.

The decision will have far-reaching implications for those organizations that are in a dominant marketing position and accumulating large amounts of personal data from various sources.

55 Para. 52.

56 Italian Cass. Civ., Order 14381/2021, the Italian Court of Cassation has gone so far as to assess the content of the information in cases of automated decisions (ex Art. 22 GDPR). A comment of the decision is available at <www.medialaws.eu/consenso-intelligenza-artificiale-e-privacy-commento-a-corte-di-cassazione-sez-i-civ-25–05–2021-n-14381/> accessed 21 August 2023.

57 Facebook changed its name to Meta Platforms on 28 October 2021.

58 Bundeskartellamt, 6 February 2019, B6–22/16 – Facebook. For a critical analysis, see Giuseppe Colangelo, Mariastella Maggiolino, 'Antitrust über alles. Whither competition law after Facebook?' (2019) 42 *World Competition* 355.

59 Case C-252–21 *Meta Platform and Others* (General terms of use of a social network) [2023] EU:C:2023:537.

The CJEU ruled that competition authorities of a Member State have the authority to investigate and sanction an infringement of the GDPR, if companies exploit their dominant market position. In case of data protection violations, the competition authorities must consult with the competent data protection supervisory authority.

In addition, the case deals with requirements for the combined personalized processing of Facebook users' personal data collected by Meta within Facebook, and of off-Facebook data collected by websites and applications outside of the social media platform. In this regard, the CJEU imposes strict limitations on the interpretation of the 'necessity for the performance of a contract' legal basis. According to the decision, the interpretation must be objectively indispensable for a purpose that is integral to the contractual obligation intended for the data subject. The Luxemburg Court also limits Facebook's legitimate interests to process users' personalized social network data and imposes strict requirements for obtaining lawful consent for a company dominant in the market.

2.5 Focus on Consent Protection Under Consumer Law in a Nutshell

With the Consumers New Deal, the Commission intends to modernize and complete the consumer acquis – through the strengthening of enforcement, the adaptation of the regulatory framework to the characteristics of online markets, and the supply of digital content and services. Notwithstanding this, the New Deal fails to liberate itself from the old paradigms of consumer protection rooted in pre-Big Data era. It is still far from reaching its scope toward addressing the inequality of bargaining power in consumer transactions.[60] In 2018, the European Commission mentioned that the purpose of the New Deal was to fill the gaps of the regulatory discontinuity in consumer law.[61] Early signs of a necessary shift emerged in legal discussion currently carried on by legal institutions toward a holistic regulatory response, reformulating the consumer law field. Consequently, the relationship with data protection law becomes more synergic, demonstrating how complicated it is in arranging a regulatory response into the current framework for protection.

Dark patterns are transforming consumers "from service recipients to servants of the data industry companies".[62] This is a problem that emerges in public and political discussions. During the roundtable on digital dark commercial patterns held in 2021, the OECD analyzed the growing range of dark commercial patterns and highlighted the difficulties to distinguish them from other marketing techniques. In that occasion, the OECD already hypothesized a way to distinguish them. They

60 Mateja Durovic and Franciszek Lech, 'A Consumer Law Perspective on the Commercialization of Data, European Review of Private Law' (2021) 5 *European Review of Private Law* 701, 703.

61 Please consider pages 3–4 of the document.

62 Speech by Giovanni Buttarelli, 'Dark Patterns in Data Protection: Law, Nudging, Design and the Role of Technology', at *Legal Design Roundtable*, 29 April 2019, Brussels, Belgium.

could modify choice architecture to hamper consumer decision-making through changes to the decision space, or manipulation of information flow.

Many of those practices that exploit cognitive vulnerabilities can be characterized as such unfair commercial practices regulated by the Directive 2005/29/EC (UCPD) as amended by the Directive 2019/2161.[63] As such, it is important to investigate if, and to what extent, the UCPD contributes to safeguard individual transactional decisions in the case of technology-driven manipulation.[64] Unfair commercial practices legislation has an important role in assessing the fairness of the business-to-consumer commercial practices, in addition to other instruments in the European framework, such as the ePrivacy Directive, the GDPR, or sector-specific legislation applicable to online platforms. Pragmatically, this is due to the functional origins of digital vulnerability.

Indeed, the European Consumer Organization (BEUC), in the same year of 2021, published a report titled *Consumer Protection 2.0: Structural Asymmetries in Digital Consumer Markets*. This report emphasized major issues in the digital market including digital vulnerability and digital asymmetry.[65] In a digital society, vulnerability is architectural because the digital choice architectures we navigate daily are designed to imply or even create vulnerabilities. The vulnerabilities that consumers can experience are the product of digital consumer markets. If consumers keep using the same services, apps, or platforms over time, the commercial entities offering those services, apps, or platforms will be able to collect and analyze more user data and, as a result, be better able to identify exploitable vulnerabilities, increasing the asymmetrical nature of ongoing commercial relationships.

The modality of expressing information is also crucial. Transparency means to inform in a clear and intelligible manner so that the 'average consumer' can understand information without a legal advice. Such requirement is difficult to grasp as consumer law (UTD and CRD) usually provides very broad statements, underling the need for 'plain and intelligible language', where intelligibility stands also for the legibility of that information. Plain and intelligible language has been broadly interpreted by the European Court of Justice.[66]

Consumers must be able to evaluate the legal and economic consequences of choice by considering all the elements of the transaction to give consent: marketing process and the reasonable expectation of attention from the average consumer.

Disruptive features of dark patterns re-emphasized the need to review the traditional legal concepts strictly connected with consent rules. European Law Institute

63 Parliament, Council, Directive (EU) 2019/2161 amending Council Directive 93/13/EEC and Directives 98/6/EC, 2005/29/EC and 2011/83/EU of the European Parliament and of the Council as regards the better enforcement and modernisation of Union consumer protection rules [2019] OJ L 328, 7–28.

64 Mateja Durovic, *European Law on Unfair Commercial Practices and Contract Law* (Hart Publishing 2016).

65 BEUC, 'Report on EU Consumer Protection 2.0 (n. 21).

66 E.g., Case C-472/10 *Nemzeti Fogyasztdvidelmi Hatdsdg v Invitel Tvkozlesi Zrt* [2012] ECLI:EU:C:2012:242, para. 27.

(ELI) stakeholders, for example, answered to the question No. 19 of the *Fitness Check of EU Consumer Law on Digital Fairness* launched by the Commission in 2022,[67] regarding "Adapting the Concept of the 'Average Consumer' or 'Vulnerable Consumer'". The stakeholders agreed to emphasize that 'average consumer' or 'vulnerable consumer' could be adapted or complemented by additional benchmarks or factors,[68] since the factual circumstances are complex.

As shown by empirical studies, in fact, companies use different tactics to prevent customers from quitting the subscribed service. These techniques are considered forms of dark patterns, based on cognitive bias.[69] This empirical data must be viewed from the perspective of the digital market to which the European Institutions dedicate the legislation package composed by the Digital Services Act (DSA) and the Digital Markets Act (DMA). On 20 January 2022, the European Commission passed the final amendments, and the Acts constitute some of the most significant reforms to Internet platform legislation in recent times.[70] Due to the particular importance of DSA for dark patterns regulation, the following subsection is entirely dedicated to it.

2.5.1 DSA, Data Processing Activities, and Dark Patterns

The DSA primarily states the requirements for innovative digital services in the internal market. Also, it contributes to the guarantees on online safety and protect fundamental rights, setting a robust and durable governance structure for the effective supervision of intermediary service providers.

Although the DSA is not expressly structured with a view to protect consumers,[71] several provisions indirectly achieve this objective (e.g., the handling of harmful online content, the protection of online users' fundamental rights, and restrictions on the collection of personal data for advertising purposes and limitations on online behavioral advertising).[72] Based on the universal obligation to fairness, online

67 Commission, 'Fitness Check of EU Consumer Law on Digital Fairness' 2022 <https://ec.europa.eu/info/law/better-regulation/have-your-say/initiatives/13413-Digital-fairness-fitness-check-on-EU-consumer-law_en> accessed 20 June 2023.

68 ELI (drafters: Marie Jull Sørensen, Peter Rott and Karin Sein), Webinar on ELI Response to European Commission's Public Consultation on Digital Fairness – Fitness Check on EU Consumer Law, 2023.

69 Empirical findings are proposed by Julian Runge, Daniel Wentzel, Ji Young Huh and others, 'Dark Patterns' in Online Services in Online Services: A Motivating Study and Agenda for Future Research' (2023) 34 *Mark Letter* 155.

70 <https://digital-strategy.ec.europa.eu/en/policies/digital-services-act-package> accessed 20 July 2023.

71 Users can be consumers and firms. DSA aims at harmonizing conditions for innovative cross-border services to develop in the EU, addressing and preventing the emergence of obstacles to these activities, as well as providing for adequate supervision to the provided services. It ensures that digital service providers are not misused for illegal activities and that operators act responsibly. See Jorge M Carvalho, Francisco Arga Lima and Martim Farinha, 'Introduction to the Digital Services Act, Content Moderation and Consumer Protection' (2021) 3 *Revista de Direito e Tecnologia* 71.

72 Aina Turillazzi, Federico Casolari, Mariarosaria Taddeo and Luciano Floridi, 'The Digital Services Act: An Analysis of Its Ethical, Legal, and Social Implications' (2023) 15 *Law, Innovation and Technology* 83.

platforms must design the organization and operation of their interfaces in a way that minimizes or completely avoids the material distortion or impairment of their users' ability to make free and informed decisions.

The DSA is qualified as a lex specialis that complements sector-specific instruments.[73] The complementary nature to the GDPR is evident when it comes to the right of information – precisely, when Art. 12–1DSA integrates Arts. 12 to 14 GDPR. This is also evident in the additional transparency and accountability to targeted advertisement provided by Arts. 24 and 30 of the Act, without prejudice to the rights and remedies available to data subjects.

While the specific rules on consumer-facing practices remain applicable (e.g., the UCPD), the DSA effectively legislates provisions against misrepresentation and aggressive practices, in all horizontal relationships that are not covered in any sector-specific legislation (e.g., Art. 25). The only requirement is that the practices must be conducted via apps, websites, or other surfaces, operated by online platforms that are not small or micro.[74]

Given its broader applicability to all online 'intermediaries' (from Internet service providers and hosting services, to messaging apps, email providers, and Amazon-style marketplaces), the DSA has drawn more attention to dark patterns. According to Recital 67, dark patterns are practices that aim to prevent users from making autonomous and informed choices or decisions. This is less about the content of (e.g., advertising) statements, but more about the 'structure, design or functionalities' of online interfaces (i.e., primarily websites or apps): for instance, when the choices are not presented in a neutral way, and certain choices are given more prominence through 'visual, auditory or other components' – a topic, that was recently discussed above all by data protection supervisory authorities in connection with cookie banners. Also mentioned is the practice of repeatedly asking a user to resubmit a choice they have already made or making it more difficult to cancel compared to logging in, making default settings difficult to change, and misleading users by enticing them to make certain transactions.

The DSA has banned providers of intermediary services from using deceiving or nudging techniques on recipients of their services and from using dark patterns to distort or impair user autonomy. It appears to break new legal ground with the prohibition of dark patterns in Arts. 25 and 31 DSA, declaring as a decisive criterion that the user's freedom of choice is distorted or impaired. According to Art. 25(1) DSA, the "providers of online platforms shall not design, organize or operate their online interfaces in a way that deceives, manipulates or otherwise materially distorts or impairs the ability of recipients of their service to make free and

73 EDPB, 'Opinion 1/2021 on the Proposal for a Digital Services Act' (10 February) 2021 <https://edps.europa.eu/system/files/2021-02/21-02-10-opinion_on_digital_services_act_en.pdf> accessed 10 April 2023.

74 The online platforms are also subject to an obligation to ensure a high level of privacy, safety, and security of minors on their services. July Martin Husovec and Irene Roche Laguna, *Principles of the Digital Services Act* (Oxford University Press 2023) <https://ssrn.com/abstract=4153796> accessed 20 April 2023.

informed decisions". Read in conjunction with the GDPR, Art. 25 offers relevant protection for complying with provisions detailing lawful grounds for processing, requiring data minimization, setting out how valid consent can be obtained and withdrawn, or how controllers must apply data protection by design and by default when building their systems and processes.

At a general overview, both the GDPR and the new DSA strike on dark patterns. However, a bit different from the GDPR, the DSA is set to put a ban on websites' use of dark patterns. Consequently, one of the main expected effects could be on cookie banners, often used without users being able to reject consent.

Considering that the ban of dark patterns and the request for easier withdrawal of consent will affect the design of cookie banners, with the synergy of the GDPR and the new DSA, providers will pay more attention to designing cookie banner in a way that users know exactly what they give consent to. For example, cookie banner buttons for accepting or rejecting cookies will also change. Buttons must be equally weighted in terms of color, size, and placement. This means that the 'Accept' button may no longer be more prominent or of a different color than the 'Reject' button.

By specifying that the prohibition of such deceptive design tactics applies only to online platforms, the drafters of the DSA opted to scope down the legal potential impact on the use of dark patterns. Consequently, the ban has no effect on a wide range of intermediary services, including businesses foundational to online commerce, such as web-hosting services and domain name registrars. Other concerns of the ban are on what practices are affected.

The aforementioned Art. 25 DSA has a great impact on dark patterns regulation, because it stipulates that the prohibition of dark patterns does not apply to practices covered by the UCPD and the GDPR: DSA is a merely subsidiary prohibition alongside a broad definition of dark patterns. Also, it fails to establish clear criteria for distinguishing illegal practices from legitimate ones and makes the concrete regulation of dark patterns dependent on EC guidelines.

Essentially, neither the GDPR nor the UCPD have succeeded to conclusively hinder dark patterns. Even though these two laws make room for regulating dark patterns, their enforcement has been relatively weak and constrained to narrow contexts, such as cookie consents. Depending on how regulators choose to interpret the DSA, this framing could have profound implications on how gatekeepers' future architectures are presented to consumers. A design that asymmetrically emphasizes one choice over another – for example, by highlighting a decisional button through size, color, or both and leaving the other deemphasized or grayed out – will likely be deemed 'non-neutral', especially if it emphasizes a choice with economic or data disclosure impacts for the user.

2.6 Current Concerns on Consent Protection Within the Ongoing European Debate

Summarizing the main findings of the previous pages, some positive and some critical remarks could be sketched out about the current way to cope with the problem of dark patterns for consent.

On a positive note, the jurisprudential interpretation of GDPR along the years has first contributed to protect the consumer's effective will and substantial consent.

Second, an overview of the horizontal EU consumer law *acquis* shows that misleading and unfair design impacting on effective consent can be addressed by many legal acts. This is because the main problem with lawful consent emerged not only with regard to the lack of information or misleading information, but also with regard to the exploitation of consumer data – a problem structured by the architectural design.

Third, the DSA has already introduced specific provisions to forbid dark patterns, surely increasing the level of digital consumer protection.

On the other hand, it is evident that GDPR – as many other legal acts – does not fully consider the empirical findings of behavioral studies in order to evaluate the efficacy of consent.[75] This could be a crucial limit as digital designs exploit cognitive and emotional human resources. Data-driven marketing is mostly focused on behavior at the expense of higher-order psychological processes such as preferences, emotions, and moral judgments. A machine that reveals consumer preferences from Google searches or browsing history on Amazon may ignore mental processes that lead to individual behavior.

Ignoring meta-preferences (which are inaccessible to the algorithm) and rather focusing on the preferences suggested by past choices, data-driven marketing might deprive consumers of the ability to improve their own character and encourage them to repeat choices that they would wish not to make again. In such a situation, even the 'regular' nudging of digital architectures could persuade consumer toward the 'wrong' choices that are not necessarily in line with the authentic and timely will. Indeed, the potential deviation that dark patterns can provoke between the consumer choice and the authentic preference is a circumstance that hardly can be demonstrated, both for the data subject and the consumer entering a transaction. In other words, the strong focus on informed consent as a legal basis for data processing in consumer transactions may not always provide optimal protection of digital consumer interests.

As already mentioned, European Parliament and Council intervene into the regulatory framework with specific provisions for dark patterns (e.g., DSA). More decisive action is needed to foster the adaptation of the new protection exigencies where two elements clearly exist – the multitude and 'dynamic' tactics that fall under the unique umbrella concept of dark patterns, but truly make impacts in different ways and cause several types of harm to the data subject/consumer consent, and the fact that there is currently a multitude of provisions to protect consent but they belong to a multiplicity of regulation which require a higher level of coordination. Moreover, there is a need to rethink traditional concepts such as trader, average

75 Lucilla Gatt, Roberto Montanari and Ilaria Amelia Caggiano, 'Consenso al trattamento dei dati personali e analisi giuridico-comportamentale. Spunti di riflessione sull'effettività della tutela dei dati personali' (2017) 2 *Politica del diritto* 363.

consumer, and vulnerability, which are currently debated both at regulatory and jurisprudential levels.

It is worth remembering that in spring 2022, the Commission launched a *Fitness Check of EU Consumer Law on Digital Fairness* to determine whether the existing key horizontal consumer law instruments remained adequate for ensuring a high level of consumer protection in the digital environment. The 'check' is general, as the provided program covers five main evaluation criteria: effectiveness (fulfilling expectations and meeting its objectives), efficiency (cost-effectiveness and proportionality of actual costs to benefits), relevance (to current and emerging needs), coherence (internal and external with other EU interventions or international agreements), and EU added value (producing results beyond what would have been achieved by Member States acting alone). Depending on the results, the follow-up outcome of the Fitness Check could take the form of a new legislative proposal, an improved implementation through better enforcement and guidance, or further monitoring.[76] During the second annual digital consumer event held by the European Commission on 21 November 2022[77] and dedicated to *Ensuring Fairness and Safety for Consumers in the Digital World*, stakeholders underlined the necessity to reflect on whether the existing EU legal framework is still fit for the purpose. Several panelists answered negatively, considering consumer law not to be sufficiently fit, especially in tackling 'digital asymmetry' – a structural state of power imbalance between consumers and traders (that, notably, have access to consumer data). One panelist called for putting forward a 'Digital Fairness Act' that would tackle the issues not yet addressed in recent legislation in a satisfactory and more holistic manner. Several panelists further emphasized the importance of taking a holistic approach, both when assessing the legislative framework (notably consumer law's interplay with data protection, competition law, the Digital Services Act, DMA, AI Act) and in the context of enforcement.[78]

2.7 Investing in Digital Architectural Design for More Effective Consent: Concluding Remarks

Considering the limits of having a 'one-size-fits-all' legal model – like the GDPR – for regulating the variety of dark patterns, this research suggests that choice architecture could itself become an innovative solution to strengthen consent protection. Consumer law can, in this perspective, complement the GDPR, for example, by adding the right to check the fairness of choice architectural design used in pre-formulated consent clauses, according to the UCPD, and the precondition that 'external vulnerabilities' are qualified as aggressive practices.

76 Commission, 'Fitness Check of EU Consumer Law on Digital Fairness' (n. 65).

77 Commission, Second Annual Digital Consumer, webinar on 21st November 2022, Brussels.

78 <https://commission.europa.eu/system/files/2023-03/Report%20ADCE22%20final.pdf> accessed 20 September 2023.

Thus, it appears useful to turn the point of view from an ex post perspective (remedies) to an ex ante one. Thinking from the preventive perspective of legal design means to focus on regulation, adopting what the Nordic School identifies as a proactive law approach.[79]

Legal design as a discipline combines law, technology, and design studies to create user-friendly legal documents. Generally, it contributes toward the transformation of the legal system to a more accessible service and structure for the people. Through legal design, the opportunity to integrate legal principles and rules regarding consent with the behavioral economics and empirical cognitive studies arise. These are at the basis of 'bright' patterns that persuade consumer, obtaining a valid consent.

A fair architectural design is indispensable in complying with transparency obligations, as it embeds values and empowers data subjects throughout their interaction with the controller.

Hypothesizing to implement transparency by design architecture, it would mean to embrace the idea of privacy by design (Art. 25 GDPR), as well as to share the same principles. It must be noted that transparency spans beyond privacy. It is not only a matter of data protection but also an issue of consumer law. To meet the obligation of fairness, online platforms must design, organize, and operate their interfaces in a way that avoids manipulation and other material impairments of the user's ability to make free and informed decisions. Indeed, transparency by design implies a focus on accountability and fairness.[80] To promote fairness, the controller must be aware of the key design elements that compose a privacy choice, choosing mechanisms that can mitigate user (cognitive) vulnerabilities.

Data subjects should be served with information that is meaningful and actionable, instead of a standard block of text that acts as a liability document for the controller mission. They need specific protective measures against exploitation. For this reason, transparency by design could establish that: (i) controllers have to transmit a set of information to data subjects and to facilitate the exercise of data protection rights ('accountability'); and (ii) that this must be done in a timely, adequate, and accessible way, through the promotion of meaningful privacy choices, to reduce the informational vulnerabilities that enable dark patterns and unfair privacy policies ('fairness'). Consequently, the UCPD cannot be set aside when assessing data exploitation strategies under the GDPR. Thus, legal coordination permits a concrete integration between regulations and interdisciplinary components.

For fast-evolving data-driven developments, it seems not to be sufficient to think like a traditional lawyer.[81] Instead, designing choice architectures, considering the described coordinated framework, will contribute to shape legal change

79 Helena Haapio, 'Introduction to Proactive Law: A Business Lawyer's View' (2006) 49 *Stockholm Institute for Scandinavian Law, Stockholm* 21.

80 Gianclaudio Malgieri, 'The Concept of Fairness in the GDPR: A Linguistic and Contextual Interpretation' (2020) *Proceedings of Fat* 27.

81 David Sless, 'Designing Documents for People to Use (2018) 4(2) *The Journal of Design, Economics, and Innovation* 125–142, 131.

into a suitable direction toward a more effective protection of consent. This is also in line with the aim of numerous present-day technologies – for example, privacy-enhancing technologies – which are already in action.

Bibliography

Alexander C and others, *A Pattern Language – Towns, Buildings, Construction* (Oxford University Press 1977)

Brignull H, 'Types of Dark Patterns' (2020) <https://darkpatterns.org/types-of-dark-pattern.html> accessed 10 October 2022

Calo R, 'Digital Market Manipulation' (2014) 82 *The George Washington Law Review* 995–1051

Cavoukian A, 'Privacy by Design – The 7 Foundational Principles, Information and Privacy Commissioner of Ontario' (2009) <www.ipc.on.ca/wp-content/uploads/resources/7foundationalprinciples.pdf>

Conti G and Sobiesk E, 'Malicious Interface Design: Exploiting the User' (Proceedings of the 19th International Conference on World Wide Web 271 2010) 272 <https://doi.org/10.1145/1772690.1772719> accessed 27 September 2021

De Franceschi A, *La circolazione dei dati personali tra privacy e contratto* (ESI 2017)

Durovic M, *European Law on Unfair Commercial Practices and Contract Law* (Hart Publishing 2016)

Durovic M and Lech F, 'A Consumer Law Perspective on the Commercialization of Data' (2021) 5 *European Review of Private Law* 701, 703

Gamma E and others, *Design Patterns: Elements of Reusable Object-Oriented Software* (Addison-Wesley 1995)

Gatt L, Montanari R and Caggiano IA, 'Consenso al trattamento dei dati personali e analisi giuridico-comportamentale. Spunti di riflessione sull'effettività della tutela dei dati personali' (2017) 2 *Politica del diritto* 363

Gray C, Kou Y, Battles B, Hoggatt J and Toombs A, 'The Dark (Patterns) Side of UX Design' (Proceedings of the 2018 CHI Conference on Human Factors in Computing Systems 2018) Article no. 534

Haapio H, 'Introduction to Proactive Law: A Business Lawyer's View' in Wahlgren P (ed), *A Proactive Approach, Scandinavian Studies in Law* (vol. 49, Stockholm Institute for Scandinavian Law 2006) 21

Hanson JD and Kysar DA, 'Taking Behavioralism Seriously: The Problem of Market Manipulation' (1999) 74 *New York University Law Review* 632

Helberger N, Sax M, Strycharz J and others, 'Choice Architectures in the Digital Economy: Towards a New Understanding of Digital Vulnerability' (2022) 45(2) *Journal of Consumer Policy* 178

Howells G, 'The Potential and Limits of Consumer Empowerment by Information' (2005) 32 *Journal of Law and Society* 349

Irti C, *Consenso "negoziato" e circolazione dei dati personali* (Giappichelli 2021)

Jarovsky L, 'Dark Patterns in Personal Data Collection: Definition, Taxonomy and Lawfulness' (1 March 2022) <https://papers.ssrn.com/sol3/papers.cfm?abstract_id=4048582> accessed 10 June 2022

Jarovsky L, 'Transparency by Design: Reducing Informational Vulnerabilities through UX Design' (May 25, 2022)

Leiser MR, 'Chapter 10: Dark Patterns: The Case for Regulatory Pluralism between the European Unions Consumer and Data Protection Regimes', in Kosta E, Leenes R and Kamara I (eds), *Research Handbook on EU Data Protection Law* (Edward Elgar Publishing 2022)

Leiser MR and Yang W-T, 'Illuminating Manipulative Design: From "Dark Patterns" to Information Asymmetry and the Repression of Free Choice under the Unfair Commercial Practices Directive' (2022) note No. 8 SocArXiv

Luguri J and Strahilevitz L, 'Shining a Light on Dark Patterns' (2021) 13(1) *Journal of Legal Analysis* 43

Malgieri G, 'The Concept of Fairness in the GDPR: A Linguistic and Contextual Interpretation' (2020) *Proceedings of Fat* 27

Mathur A, Acar G, Friedman M, Lucherini E, Mayer J, Chetty M and Narayanan A, 'Dark Patterns at Scale: Findings from a Crawl of 11K Shopping Websites' (2019) 3 *Proceedings of the ACM on Human Computer Interaction* 81

McAuley D, Koene A and Chen J, 'Comments on the European Data Protection Board's Guidelines 4/2019 on Article 25 Data Protection by Design and by Default' (2020) <https://edpb.europa.eu/sites/edpb/files/webform/public_consultation_reply/comments_on_edpb_guidelines_on_a_25_dpbdd_-_horizon.pdf> accessed 20 May 2023

Nouwens M, Liccardi I, Veale M and Karger D, 'Dark Patterns after the GDPR: Scraping Consent Pop-Ups and Demonstrating Their Influence' (2020) CHI 2020 Paper

Özdemir Ş, 'Digital Nudges and Dark Patterns: The Angels and the Archfiends of Digital Communication' (2020) 35 *Digital Scholarship in the Humanities* 417

Pasa B and Sinni G, 'New Frontiers of Legal Knowledge: How Design Provotypes Can Contribute to Legal Change', in Ducato R and Strowel A (eds), *Design(s) for Law* (Ledizioni 2023 forecoming)

Poillot E, 'La protection des données personnelles par le droit européen de la consommation' in Combet M (ed), *Le droit européen de la consommation au XXIe siècle. État des lieux et perspectives* (Bruylant 2022)

Rauccio C, 'How Legal Design Can Improve Data Protection Communication and Make Privacy Policy More Attractive' (2021) 1 *European Journal of Privacy Law & Technologies*

Resta G, 'Revoca del consenso ed interesse al trattamento nella legge sulla protezione dei dati personali' (2000) *Rivista Critica di Diritto Privato* 299

Rhoen M, 'Beyond Consent: Improving Data Protection through Consumer Protection Law' (2016) 5 *Internet Policy Review* 1

Rossi A, Ducato R, Haapio H and Passera S, 'When Design Met Law: Design Patterns for Information Transparency' (2019) (1)122 *Droit de la consommation* 7.1

Sai S, Watkins C, McKay L and Gray CM, 'Nothing Comes before Profit: Asshole Design in the Wild' (CHI Conference on Human Factors in Computing Systems 2019) 1 <https://doi.org/10.1145/3290607.3312863>

Sless D, 'Designing Documents for People to Use', in Ji S (ed), (2018) 4(2) *The Journal of Design, Economics, and Innovation* 125, 131

Susser D, Roessler B and Nissenbaum H, 'Technology, Autonomy, and Manipulation' (2019) 8 *Internet Policy Review* <https://doi.org/10.14763/2019.2.1410>

Sustain C, 'Sludge and Ordeals' (2019) 68 *Duke Law Journal* 1843

Svantesson DJB, 'Enter the Quagmire – The Complicated Relationship between Data Protection Law and Consumer Protection Law' (2018) 34 *Computer Law & Security Review* 25

Thaler RH, 'Nudge, Not Sludge' (2018) 361 *Science* 431

Trzaskowski J, 'Persuasion, Manipulation, Choice Architecture, and "Dark Patterns"' in Savin A and Trzaskowski J (eds), *Research Handbook on EU Internet Law* (chapter 15, 2nd edn, Edward Elgar 2023)

Tversky A and Kahneman D, 'Judgment under Uncertainty: Heuristics and Biases' (1974) 185(New Series) *Science* 1124

Utz C, Degeling M, Fahl S, Schaub F and Holz T, '(Un)Informed Consent: Studying GDPR Consent Notices in the Field' (2019) (Proceedings ACM SIGSAC Conference on Computer and Communications Security) <http://dx.doi.org/10.1145/3319535.3354212>

Versaci G, *La contrattualizzazione dei dati personali dei consumatori* (vol. 5, ESI Quaderni di "Studi Senesi" 2020)

Vestager M, 'Algorithms and Competition' (Speech at the Bundeskartellamt 18th Conference on Competition, 16 March 2017)

Vogiatzoglou P and Valcke P, 'Chapter 1: Two Decades of Article 8 CFR: A Critical Exploration of the Fundamental Right to Personal Data Protection in EU Law', in Kosta E, Leenes R and Kamara I (eds), *Research Handbook on EU Data Protection Law* (Edward Elgar Publishing 2022)

Wu T, 'Blind Spot: The Attention Economy and the Law' (2017) 82 *Antitrust Law Journal* 771, 778

Yeung K, 'Hypernudge: Big Data as a Mode of Regulation by Design' (2017) 20 *Information, Communication & Society* 118

3 The Consent Service in Estonia

Enhancement of State-held Data Sharing vs. Privacy Risks

Karin Sein

3.1 Introduction

Innovation needs data, including personal data. In the 2020 European Strategy for Data, the European Commission expressed the ambition to change the European Union into 'the most dynamic data-agile economy in the world.'[1] The Commission warns that if the EU 'is to acquire a leading role in the data economy, it has to act now and . . . increase its pools of quality data available for use and reuse,' as there is currently not enough data available for innovative reuse, including for the development of artificial intelligence (AI).[2] Since then, the European legislator has moved swiftly: the Data Governance Act (DGA),[3] aimed at fostering the availability of data for use by increasing trust in data intermediaries and by strengthening data-sharing mechanisms, was adopted on 30 May 2022 and is applicable from 24 September 2023. The plans for creating a European Health Data Space[4] are being discussed intensively by national governments, stakeholders, and privacy scholars.[5] The Data Act was presented by the European Commission on 25 February 2022[6] and adopted in late 2023. It is, however, important to stress that these acts are not supposed to create new legal bases for data processing: on the contrary, the rules of the General Data Protection Regulation (GDPR)[7] will remain applicable and, in case of a conflict, will have priority.[8]

1 Commission, 'A European Strategy for Data' (Communication) COM (2020) 66 final 25.
2 Ibid., 1, 6.
3 Regulation (EU) 2022/868 of the European Parliament and of the Council on European Data Governance and Amending Regulation (EU) 2018/1724 (Data Governance Act) [2022] OJ L152/1.
4 European Commission, 'Proposal for a Regulation of the European Parliament and of the Council on the European Health Data Space' COM (2022) 197 final.
5 M Shabani and S Yilmaz, 'Lawfulness in Secondary Use of Health Data. Interplay between Three Regulatory Frameworks of GDPR, DGA & EHDS' (2022) *Technology and Regulation* 128, 133; P Terzis, 'Compromises and Asymmetries in the European Health Data Space' (2022) *European Journal of Health Law* 1, 12.
6 European Commission, 'Proposal for a Regulation of the European Parliament and of the Council on Harmonised Rules on Fair Access to and Use of Data (Data Act)' COM (2022) 68 final.
7 Regulation (EU) 2016/679 of the European Parliament and of the Council on the protection of natural persons with regard to the processing of personal data and on the free movement of such data, and repealing Directive 95/46/EC (General Data Protection Regulation) [2016] OJ L119/1.
8 See Art. 1(3) DGA; Art. 1(5) of the Data Act.

DOI: 10.4324/9781003502791-5

While fostering data sharing has been declared a common European goal, Estonia as a digitally advanced Member State offers an interesting example with its new and unique concept of a so-called consent service, i.e., a digital solution enabling data subjects to consent to the sharing of their personal data (including health data) held in state registries. Estonia has a history of early, rapid and successful digitalisation starting from the 1990s,[9] and as a result thereof, also advanced digital public registries, e.g., a population registry, a complete and interconnected registry for health data, etc. Moreover, Estonians are also known for a rather relaxed attitude to privacy and for valuing the idea of an open information society,[10] probably a heritage of Soviet history, combined with the 'nothing to hide' fallacy used as a coping strategy.[11] On top of it comes the political ambition to be the frontrunner in digitalisation and innovation and a resulting start-up attitude at the governmental level.

Creating a state-held personal data-sharing service raises questions about possible privacy risks, especially as the reuse of sensitive personal data (health data) is concerned. This contribution will take a critical look at the Estonian consent service aiming at fostering innovative digital services and asks what kind of privacy risks such a data-sharing mechanism is likely to create, whether it is compatible with the requirements of the GDPR and whether the Estonian state would be liable for the possible privacy breaches. On a more general level, it allows assessing whether fostering data-sharing as encouraged in the Data Governance Act via digital solutions currently envisaged in Estonia might serve as a blueprint for the whole European Union (EU), or whether the associated privacy risks outweigh the potential innovation gains.

The chapter starts with introducing the concept and technical solution of the consent service (Section 3.2), followed by the legal analysis of its GDPR compliance (Section 3.3). After discussing the privacy risks that this kind of data-sharing mechanism potentially creates for the data subjects (Section 3.4), it turns to the applicability of the Data Governance Act and whether and how its mechanisms could mitigate these risks (Section 3.5). It then asks whether the Estonian

9 Including widely used public digital services, including digital signatures. Estonia is one of the rare countries to use electronic voting and became the first state where more than 50% of its citizens voted electronically at the parliamentary elections. ERR, 'Estonia Sets New e-Voting Record at Riigikogu 2023 Elections' (4 March 2023) <https://news.err.ee/1608904730/estonia-sets-new-e-voting-record-at-riigikogu-2023-elections> accessed 25 May 2023. On the Estonian e-voting see P Vinkel and R Krimmer, 'The How and Why to Internet Voting. An Attempt to Explain E-Stonia' in R Krimmer et al. (eds), *Proceedings of the First International Joint Conference on Electronic Voting* (Springer 2016) 178–191.

10 For a critical overview, see P K Tupay, 'Estonia, the Digital Nation: Reflections on a Digital Citizen's Rights in the European Union' (2020) 6 *European Data Protection Law Review* 294–300. On the Estonian understanding of open society see also P K Tupay and M Mikiver, 'Der estnische E-Staat – Zukunftsweisendes Vorbild oder befremdlicher Einzelgänger?' (2015) *Osteuropa Recht* 6–9.

11 M Murumaa-Mengel, K Laas-Mikko and P Pruulmann-Vengerfeldt, 'I Have Nothing to Hide'. A Coping Strategy in a Risk Society' in L Kramp et al. (eds), *Journalism, Representation and the Public Sphere* (Bremen: edition lumière 2015), 195–207.

state can be considered a joint controller together with the service provider in such constellations (Section 3.6), as well as about the potential state liability (Section 3.7). The chapter ends with some conclusions (Section 3.8).

3.2 Description of the Concept of the Consent Service and the Technical Solution

Creating a digital data-sharing system such as the Estonian consent service presupposes that the personal data are held in the state registries in digital form. Developing digital public registries has always been a priority in Estonia. The process started already in the early 1990s when the Estonian Ministry of Justice started to create a digital commercial register, as well as a digital land register,[12] and Estonia since then has become one of the frontrunners in digitalising public services, including digital tax declarations and everyday use of digital signatures, as well as a central health data registry for compulsory use by all doctors and other medical services providers.[13] As a consequence, the Estonian state holds a vast amount of personal data of its citizens in different – and interconnected – digital registries. The idea of opening these registries for commercialisation arose already in the late 2010s, and the development of the consent service was declared to be one of the government's aims in the Estonian Information Society Development Plan 2020.[14] The service has two interlinked purposes: first, to allow individuals to disclose their personal data held in national databases to data users (personal autonomy), and second, to enable companies to use this data to develop and provide innovative services.[15]

The Estonian consent service allows data subject to tick a box in the state portal eesti.ee[16] and thereby consent to give access to their personal data held in public registries to a private enterprise (e.g., insurance company or credit provider, or to a private sector medical services provider).[17] The government explains that the service enables citizens to allow the transfer of their personal data to companies that offer innovative and personalised services, and that

12 K Sein and M Ristikivi, *Õigusriigi taastamine. Eesti seaduste ja institutsioonide reformid 1992–2002* (Tartu Ülikooli Kirjastus 2022) 216–233.

13 On the Estonian health data portal, see K Pormeister, 'Patsiendiseire ehk ennetamise eesmärgil andmete töötlemine ilma patsiendi nõusolekuta' (2021) 2 *Juridica* 125–126.

14 Eesti Infoühiskonna Arengukava 2020, 1.

15 Ernst & Young, *Nõusolekuteenuse analüüs. Analüüsi aruanne* (5 February 2021) 4.

16 This is a digital governmental environment where you can find information on many relevant topics related to administrative procedures concerning eg the health and social care system, other public services as well as to log in to the self-service environment to view your data and perform certain operations. One can identify oneself and log in to the eesti.ee environment via mobile-ID, ID-card, digital-ID and Smart-ID. The digital state portal eesti.ee enables the cross-usage of data between different registers and databases based on the identity code of the person. See <www.id.ee/en/article/state-portal-eesti-ee> accessed 25 May 2023.

17 Riigi Infosüsteemi Amet, *Aastaraamat 2020* (Riigi Infosüsteemi Amet 2020) 26ff.

consent can only be given for the transfer of the dataset required for a specific service.[18] It is highlighted as the possibility to make use of your personal autonomy: the consent service allows the data subject to decide whether and with whom he or she wants to share personal data, and it is also possible for the data subject to charge a fee for the data.[19]

Granting the data subject's consent begins in the service provider's digital environment, as it is the service provider (e.g., the credit provider) who requires the user's personal data for certain purposes (e.g., the data subject's tax data for performing an assessment of creditworthiness). From the service provider's digital environment, the data subject will be redirected to the eesti.ee state portal to grant consent. Before granting consent, the data subject will be informed about the dataset that will be transferred based on such consent, as well as the purpose of the data processing. After granting consent, the process continues in the service provider's digital environment.[20]

At the time of writing this chapter, the digital environment for consent service is ready, the first pilot project enabling the transfer of the tax authority data to a credit institution for the purposes of the consumer's creditworthiness assessment[21] has been completed and the consent service has now started in practice. The government official in charge of the consent service project at the Estonian State Information System Authority, the Estonian state authority responsible for the coordination of cybersecurity actions and the development of public digital services, indicated via email that as of April 2023, the consent service is used mostly by different credit providers (altogether 19 financial services providers were listed) but more recently medical services providers[22] are joining, as well.[23] Indeed, sharing state-held health data to develop and use more comprehensive, data-driven and personalised medical services has been one of the aims of the consent service from the outset.[24]

18 State Information System Authority, 'Consent Service' <www.ria.ee/en/state-information-system/people-centred-data-exchange/consent-service> accessed 25 May 2023.

19 Ministry of Economic Affairs and Communication, 'Nõusolekuteenus võimaldab ettevõttel riigilt sinu andmeid küsida' (30 December 2021) <www.mkm.ee/uudised/nousolekuteenus-voimaldab-ettevottel-riigilt-sinu-andmeid-kusida> accessed 25 May 2023.

20 State Information System Authority (n 18).

21 Äripäev, 'UUS: nõusolekuteenusega saavad ettevõtted riigilt sinu andmeid küsida, osustad sina' (5 January 2022) <www.raamatupidaja.ee/uudised/2022/01/05/uus-nousolekuteenusega-saavad-ettevotted-riigilt-sinu-andmeid-kusida-osustad-sina> accessed 25 May 2023.

22 Such as Medidoc OÜ, which acts as an intermediary offering a platform for doctors giving medical consultations in virtual meetings. Indeed, fostering the development of innovative digital services in the area of personal medicine has been pointed out in the explanatory memorandum of the proposed legislation. Explanatory memorandum to the Draft Law for changing the public information act, the environmental surveillance act and spatial data (17 November 2021) 4.

23 Email from P Pärna on behalf of the State Information System Authority to author (11 April 2023).

24 Explanatory memorandum (n 22) 4. One example is a start-up that aims to collect data on a person's prescriptions to inform him or her about the health risks arising due to the interaction of the prescribed medicines.

When the data subject enters the Estonian official digital state portal eesti.ee to inquire about the consent service or to give his or her consent, he or she is confronted with the following text.

> By using the Consent Service, you can grant companies access to your personal data in the national databases.
>
> The Consent Service enables you to allow the transfer of your personal data to those companies which provide novel and customised services based on personal data. Consents can only be given for the transfer of a specific dataset which is required for the provision of a specific service. Once you have given your consent, the data held by the state will be transferred to the selected company.
>
> By using the Consent Service, you can exercise your legal right to make decisions on the processing of your personal data by selecting the third parties which will be able to access your data. The Consent Service is always used and consents are granted on a voluntary basis. Any consents granted can be withdrawn at any time.[25]

In addition to granting consents, the digital environment also allows the data subjects to view all consents that they have granted, including their content, the dates of expiry and the history of use of the consents. The state portal can also be used for withdrawing the consent at any time. However, there is currently no official data available on how many consents have been given since the launch of the service, or how many private enterprises have joined the digital environment. Using the consent service requires valid strong authentication methods within the meaning of eIDAS Regulation:[26] i.e., the Estonian ID-card, Mobile-ID or Smart-ID.[27] Consequently, only persons who are either residents of Estonia or are using the Estonian e-residency programme[28] giving them access to the Estonian public e-services can use the consent service and transfer their data. The consent service is being developed and administered by the State Information System Authority and advertised in the official state portal as ensuring the following benefits for the users.

- convenience – consents are always given in one trusted environment, regardless of the service provider;

25 The state portal is operated both in Estonian and English. This is the official English text used in the state portal for the consent service.

26 Regulation (EU) No 910/2014 of the European Parliament and of the Council of 23 July 2014 on electronic identification and trust services for electronic transactions in the internal market and repealing Directive 1999/93/EC [2014] OJ L257/73.

27 On the Estonian digital signature types, see I Kull and L Kask, 'Electronic Signature Under the eIDAS Regulation in Domestic and Cross-Border Communication: Estonian Example' 12 (2019) *Juridiskā zinātne* 33–34.

28 On the Estonian e-residency program, see <www.e-resident.gov.ee/> accessed 25 May 2023.

- transparency – consents and their usage history are available and managed in one place;
- safety – consents are stored in a national database with a high level of security.[29]

However, several important aspects remain unclarified. For example, explained nowhere is the time frame during which the consent will stay valid and whether it may be used to access the data subject's data several times or even constantly on an updating basis. When giving consent to the state to transfer the tax data to the credit institution, it is not regulated in a statutory law whether the consent given for the purpose of checking the person's financial situation may last as long as the credit agreement is in force, whether it is one-time access or if multiple updates can be requested.

3.3 Legal Background

3.3.1 Compliance With the GDPR

It is remarkable that the consent service has been launched without any national legislative framework in place. Yet, the preparatory work for such a framework started already back in 2020 when the Estonian government published a call for tender for creating the legal and technical concept for the consent service. The tender was won by the auditing and consulting company Ernst & Young and its final report was published at the beginning of 2021.[30] It is interesting that the analysis did not contain any noteworthy discussion on its compliance with the GDPR; yet, based on this analysis, the draft law regulating the legal aspects of the service was submitted by the government in November 2021.[31] After the parliamentary elections in March 2023, the draft law has not yet been adopted and the future of it is unclear. It is even more striking that the Estonian government decided to proceed with the project and start data-sharing without the relevant regulatory framework in place. Currently, only the relevant European rules – most importantly the GDPR – apply to the consent service, and several important legal issues such as the requirements for private enterprises for getting access to the service remain unregulated. Consequently, a lot of issues are left within the discretion of the executives of the State Information System Authority.

It seems that the Estonian government bases the whole system on the idea of private autonomy: if the data subject consents to the sharing of his or her data under Arts. 6(1)(a), 7 and 9(2)(a) GDPR, then there is no need to foresee additional rules on the national level.[32] Indeed, this is in line with the public communication

29 This is the official English text used in the state portal for the consent service.

30 Ernst & Young (n 15).

31 Avaliku teabe seaduse, keskkonnaseire seaduse ja ruumiandmete seaduse muutmise seaduse eelnõu (17 November 2021).

32 It should be clarified that creating a state-held data-sharing system cannot be based on the data subject's data portability right. The right to data portability under Art. 20(1) GDPR only exists

accompanying the launch of the consent service. At the end of 2021 when the pilot project was started, Ott Velsberg, Head of Digital State Data at the Estonian Ministry of Economic Affairs and Communications, noted that:

> As part of the 2030 development plan for the digital society, we want to move towards a more people-centred digital state. . . . The consent service is the next step, giving people more control over what happens to their personal information. On the one hand, the state's role is to enable the sharing of personal data with the private sector and other interested parties, and on the other hand, to ensure transparent data processing. This creates a unique opportunity to boost the data economy and create new and innovative services. Among other things, people will have the opportunity to charge for the use of their data if they so wish.[33]

This resembles the argument of the European Commission in the European Strategy for Data that if tools and means are given to individuals to decide what is done with their data, it can lead to 'significant benefits to individuals, including to their health and wellness, better personal finances, reduced environmental footprint, hassle-free access to public and private services and greater oversight and transparency over their personal data.'[34]

Although there is currently no holistic legal framework for the consent service, two national-level provisions with limited scope should be mentioned: first, § 593(7) of the Health Services Organisation Act[35] entitles the data subject to consent to issue his or her health data and, second, § 20(1) of the Statutes of the Health Information System[36] allows the data subject to give access to his or her data in the state-held digital health data information system to the third parties on the basis of informed consent. The latter provision explicitly rules that such consent must meet the requirements of the GDPR. Although such a provision can only have clarifying legal effect, one must ask whether the consent given by the data subject to share his/her state-held personal data with a third party via the so-called consent service is compatible with the requirements of the GDPR and hence valid.

According to Art. 4(11) GDPR, consent of the data subject means any freely given, specific, informed and unambiguous indication of the data subject's wishes by which he or she signifies, by a statement or by a clear affirmative action,

---

in cases when the data subject provided the personal data on the basis of his or her consent or the processing is necessary for the performance of a contract. However, health data in the patient portal nor tax or other data held in different state registries were not provided on either of these grounds. Furthermore, Recital 68 of the GDPR stresses that the right to data portability should not apply where the processing of personal data is necessary for the performance of a task carried out in the public interest or in the exercise of an official authority vested in the controller.

33 Ministry of Economy and Communications (n 19).

34 Commission (n 1) 10.

35 Tervishoiuteenuste korraldamise seadus, RT I, 11.03.2023, 9.

36 Tervise infosüsteemi põhimäärus, RT I, 05.04.2023, 19.

agreement to the processing of personal data relating to him or her. First of all, consent must be voluntary – i.e., freely given – to enable real choice and control for data subjects.[37] Although consent should not provide a valid legal ground for the processing of personal data in cases when there is a clear imbalance between the data subject and the controller, in particular when the controller is a public authority and it is therefore unlikely that consent was freely given,[38] it does not necessarily mean that the consent given via consent service is not free. Using the consent service is not mandatory for the citizens, but only optional[39] – and hence, in these situations, the data subject is not in a clearly subordinate situation vis-à-vis the state that would rule out his or her free will.

The story might be different vis-à-vis the service provider requiring that the data subject 'releases' his or her personal data from the state-held registry to offer the innovative service. The bundling prohibition principle laid down in Art. 7(4) GDPR stipulates that when assessing whether consent is freely given, utmost account shall be taken of whether, inter alia, the performance of a contract, including the provision of a service, is conditional on consent to the processing of personal data that is not necessary for the performance of that contract. A coupling exists if the conclusion of a contract or the provision of a service is made dependent on the consent of the data subject to a further collection or processing of its personal data that is not necessary for the performance of that contract.[40] The bundling prohibition is intended to protect the free and independent expression of the individual's will and to prevent de facto compulsion to consent to the use of personal data.[41] The EDPB guidelines for consent explain that consent will not be considered to be free if the data subject is unable to refuse or withdraw his or her consent without detriment, including when he or she runs the risk of being denied services.[42] It can very well happen that the employer asks the future employee to disclose all his or her health data via the consent service as a prerequisite for getting the job, that the credit institution requests more tax data history than is actually necessary for the creditworthiness assessment or that a medical services start-up obtains consent for considerably more health data than necessary for the digital service. Whereas all these consents might be invalid under Art. 7(4) GDPR, it does not lead to the invalidity of the consent for transferring the personal data from the state registry to the private enterprise, as we must distinguish between two legal relationships: one between the state and the data subject and the other between the data subject and

37 European Data Protection Board, Guidelines 05/2020 on consent under Regulation 2016/679 13.

38 Recital 43 GDPR.

39 The EDPB Guidelines for consent also bring several examples where consent can be used as a legal basis by a public authority. European Data Protection Board (n 37) 18–20.

40 Ibid., paras 14ff; J Kühling and B Buchner in J Kühling, B Buchner (eds), *Datenschutz-Grundverordnung*, 3rd edn (C.H. Beck 2022) DSGVO Art. 7 paras 46–47.

41 European Data Protection Board (n 37) paras 26 ff; D Clifford, I Graef and P Valcke, 'Pre-Formulated Declarations of Data Subject Consent – Citizen-Consumer Empowerment and the Alignment of Data, Consumer and Competition Law Protections' (2019) 20 *German Law Journal* 713ff.

42 European Data Protection Board (n 37) paras 13, 28.

the service provider. The invalidity of the consent (or the absence of some other legal ground), as such, does not invalidate the consent in the relationship between the state and the data subject. Consequently, the consent given via consent service may be valid even if the consent given to the service provider is not.

In addition to being voluntary, under Art. 4(11) and Art. 9(2)(a) GDPR, consent must always be given for a specific case. Article 9(2)(a) GDPR requires that the specific purposes of processing are laid out in the consent when it comes to the use of special categories of personal data like health data. This includes, for example, specific data processing acts, as well as a concrete purpose.[43] The purpose must be as precise as possible in order to protect the data subject from a gradual expansion or blurring of the purposes;[44] there should be no processing for purposes which the data subject did not expect and/or could not have been expected at the time of granting consent.[45] As the consent given to the state only relates to the transfer of specific personal data from the state registry to the private enterprise, the specific purpose requirement does not pose any problems. It must be stressed that this consent is not directly related to the processing of that data later by the private enterprise: this purpose should be specified in the consent given by the data subject to the enterprise.

The GDPR also foresees that consent must be informed. Article 7(2) GDPR requires the request for consent to be presented in a manner that is clearly distinguishable from the other matters, in an intelligible and easily accessible form, using clear and plain language. As shown in Section 3.3.1, the transparency requirement is met in the case of the Estonian consent service and hence no legal problems arise in this respect. Recital 42 GDPR – clarifying that for consent to be informed, the data subject should be aware at least of the identity of the controller and the purposes of the processing for which the personal data are intended – does not pose any problems, either. The consent is also actively given[46] in the state portal with a mouse click so that requirement of clear affirmative action is met, as well. The requirement of 'explicit consent' under Art. 9(2)(a) GDPR for sensitive personal data only excludes implied consent; otherwise, there are hardly any deviations from the general consent requirements. It must be stressed that there are also no formal requirements: according to Recital 32 GDPR, consent can be given in any form – meaning that written form is not required.[47]

Article 7(3) GDPR stipulates that consent must be freely revocable: the controller must inform the data subject about this possibility and has to ensure that the data subject can withdraw consent at any time. According to Art. 7(3) GDPR, the

43 Ibid., paras 51 ff.; Buchner and Kühling (n 40) DS-GVO Art. 7 para 61.

44 European Data Protection Board (n 37) para 16; S Ernst in B Paal and D A Pauly (eds), *Datenschutz-Grundverordnung* (3rd edn, C.H. Beck 2021) DS-GVO Art. 4 para 78.

45 Buchner and Kühling (n 40) DS-GVO Art. 7 para 61.

46 Cf., Recital 32 sentence 3 and CJEU Case C-673/17, *Verbraucherzentrale Bundesverband e.V.* v. *Planet49 GmbH* EU:C:2019:801 para 63.

47 S Schulz in P Gola and D Heckmann (eds), *Datenschutz-Grundverordnung* (3rd edn, C.H. Beck 2022) DS-GVO Art. 9 para 24.

withdrawal of consent can be carried out in the same way as consent was given. The consent service clearly complies with this requirement, as the data subject has an easy possibility to withdraw his or her consent given to the state as the data controller in the state portal[48] and the data subject is also notified of this possibility when he or she is originally giving the consent to transfer his or her data from the state registry to the private enterprise.

All in all, it must be concluded that consents given by the data subjects to transfer their personal data from the state registries to third parties are valid under the GDPR, as a rule. Neither the requirements of voluntariness nor specificity nor transparency pose any considerable legal obstacles in this respect.

It is more questionable whether the Estonian consent service that allows sharing of health data with third parties would be compatible with the underlying values of the planned EHDS regulation. This regulation – if adopted in the proposed form – requires Member States to set up one or more health data access bodies that can provide access to electronic health data to third parties, either as a new organisation or part of an existing organisation.[49] According to Art. 34(1) of the proposal, such access bodies shall only provide access to electronic health data when the intended purpose of processing pursued by the applicant meets certain requirements such as, e.g., providing personalised healthcare. Moreover, under Art. 50 of the proposal, the access bodies should put those data at the disposal of data users in a secure processing environment and ensure regular audits of the secure processing environments. The current Estonian consent service does not comply with these requirements: first, there are no restricting requirements for processing purposes, and second, the state does not provide for a secure health data processing environment. Hence, there are good reasons not to support unlimited state-held (health) data sharing, as it would most probably not contradict the values and principles of the upcoming EU legislation in respect of health data.

3.3.2 Requirements for the Service Provider to Get Access to the State Database

To start using the state-held personal data, the service provider must get access to the consent service interface.[50] As the draft law has not yet been adopted, there is currently no legal framework regulating the conditions for getting access to the consent service interface in place. Although the explanatory memorandum of the draft law noted that the constitutional principle of legality – and the fact that the consent service enables to process personal data – requires that this service is regulated by law and its use be based on a transparent legal basis,[51] this has not yet

48 Consents can be withdrawn at any time, and the withdrawn consent will stop further data transfer to a third party.

49 Article 36 of the proposed Regulation on European Health Data Space.

50 The Application Programming Interface of the consent service is available at <x-tee.ee/catalogue-data/EE/EE/GOV/70006317/consent/consent_13.json> accessed 25 May 2023.

51 Explanatory memorandum (n 22) 2.

materialised. The web page of the State Information Systems Authority contains just a very basic application template, as well as a description of the technical requirements, descriptions and procedures.[52]

The situation is not going to change much even if the proposed draft law is adopted, as the criteria listed there are not very restrictive. The draft lists only a couple of conditions with which the service provider must comply to get access to the consent service. When a service provider applies for acquiring access to the consent service interface, the State Information Systems Authority will carry out only a limited check on the service providers and control: (1) whether the service provider or its board members have been penalised lately or have been found guilty of data protection breaches during the preceding two years; (2) what kind of personal data the service provider requires for its planned service; and (3) whether the service provider has given confirmation that it has created a Data Protection Impact Assessment (DPIA) or that it is not subject to such obligation.[53]

The first requirement – that the service provider has not been subject to recent criminal convictions or sanctions for breaching data protection rules – aims to guarantee that the consent service can only be used by law-abiding and trustworthy service providers and to mitigate the risk of potential data breaches.[54] However, as we see from the third requirement, even the existence of the DPIA – let alone its completeness – is not assessed by the state before giving access to the interface. The explanatory memorandum explains this by the lack of public resources and notes that should doubts arise as to the potential privacy problems, the state retains the right to require the DPIA.[55] At the same time, the explanatory memorandum stresses that checking compliance with the conditions of the law is necessary in order to assess whether the service provider is reliable and whether the personal data would be adequately protected if transferred to him.[56] It is interesting to note that the whole administrative procedure should be carried out within only ten working days with the possibility to extend this deadline once for another ten working days.[57] An additional ten days are available to assess whether the personal data required by the service provider for its planned service is actually necessary for that service and whether the data minimisation principle is complied with.[58]

Whereas the State Information Systems Authority will – and currently does – play a vital role in deciding upon the access to the consent system, it is less clear

52 See <//github.com/e-gov/NT/blob/master/RIA%20n%C3%B5usolekuteenuse%20kasutamine%20ja%20liidestamine%20ver%201.0%20-%2015.09.2021/RIA%20n%C3%B5usolekuteenuse%20kasutamine%20ja%20liidestamine%20ver%201.0%20-%2015.09.2021.md#n%C3%B5usolekute-haldus> (only in Estonian) accessed 25 May 2023.

53 Draft Law (n 31) § 1 p 7 suggesting adding 43^{12} to the Public Data Act.

54 Explanatory memorandum (n 22) 9.

55 Ibid.

56 Ibid.

57 Draft Law (n 31) § 1 p 7 suggesting adding 43^{13} to the Public Data Act; explanatory memorandum (n 22) 10.

58 Explanatory memorandum (n 22) 9.

whether the Estonian Data Protection Authority will have any say on the access to the consent service based on privacy concerns. According to the draft law, the Estonian Data Protection Authority will be notified when a new service provider has applied to be connected to the consent service to guarantee the protection of personal data and to verify that the exercise of discretion is guaranteed.[59] However, under the draft law, it is unclear whether the Data Protection Authority's negative position will have any legal consequences whatsoever. At least currently, with no national legal framework in place, there is no legislative basis for the Data Protection Authority to restrict access of a certain service provider to the consent service based on privacy risks.

3.4 Privacy Risks Created by the Consent Service

Creating a digital consent service for sharing state-held personal data raises questions about possible privacy and discrimination risks, especially as the reuse of sensitive personal data (health data) is concerned. Should the state incentivise people to sell their personal data, including health data, for money, and should indebted people use it as an option to cover their debts? Would it be desirable for a society that people start transferring their complete health data records, e.g., to a private company promising to perform a holistic medical assessment based on this data? What if these data are then sold to insurance companies and a later deterioration in health leads to the loss of your insurance coverage? Mällo has pointed out that while different regulations introduced in recent years, most importantly the GDPR, have given individuals greater control over their personal data, in line with the European understanding of the right to self-determination, these regulations have until now not been accompanied by awareness-raising measures to support the individual's ability to take responsibility for and demand greater control over their personal data. He stresses that personal data management capabilities of data subjects develop slowly – and until it happens, any data-related solutions should also include measures to mitigate privacy risks.[60]

In the call for a tender on the conceptual basis of the consent service, the Estonian Ministry of Economic Affairs and Communications identified five severe privacy risks associated with the consent service and asked to propose measures to mitigate them. First, there is a risk that the consent service will create a higher need for data and that requiring more data from the clients becomes a 'new normal.' The data users such as financial institutions, insurers and employers will justify their need for more data with a necessity for a thorough assessment of the client's solvency or the candidate's background, and hence, initially innovative digital solutions become ubiquitous and the new normal after a while.[61]

59 Ibid., 5. See Draft Law (n 31) § 1 p 7 suggesting adding 43^{14} to the Public Data Act.
60 T Mällo, 'Nutikas veepudel III' *Sirp* (5 November 2021).
61 Ministry of Economic Affairs and Communications, Annex 3 of the tender call documents 1.

Second, the government identified the risk of excessive data processing, pointing out that it is already very common for mobile apps to ask for access to all sorts of non–service-related data. Moreover, insurers ask medical institutions for the patient's entire medical history, even though they only need health data relevant to the insurance case. So far, it is up to the medical institutions and doctors to decide what data is relevant and what can be released, but with the new consent service, this intermediary step will be abolished – and it can be expected that insurers will start to process health data on a much larger scale.[62]

Indeed, the problem with insurance companies' access to patients' health data is not a new one. As early as 2007, the WP29 expressed the opinion that special measures should be taken to prevent that patients are illegally induced to disclose their electronic health registry data, e.g., upon request of a possible future employer or a private insurance company. Private insurance companies might be entitled to 'receive some (limited) information concerning health records, when necessary in the context of fulfilling their contractual obligations towards insured patients,' but technical means might have to be applied to special requirements for full print-outs from an electronic health registry.[63] One should also recall that under Art. 35(a) and (b) of the Proposed Regulation on EHDS, seeking access to and processing electronic health data obtained via a data permit shall be prohibited, inter alia, for the purposes of making decisions detrimental to a natural person based on their electronic health data, as well as of taking decisions in relation to a natural person or groups of natural persons to exclude them from the benefit of an insurance contract or to modify their contributions and insurance premiums. In other words, the planned European regulation aimed at fostering the secondary use of health data foresees certain restrictions as to the purposes of such use of data. These restrictions concern especially the sharing of health data with the insurance sector. The Estonian consent service, unfortunately, does not employ such mitigation measures.

Third, when publishing the call for a public tender for the consent service concept, the Estonian government also expressed concerns in one of the tender documents that the increasing data sharing may lead to less autonomy of the data subject as the consent becomes a de facto condition for access to services. Although the data transfer is arguably a decision of the data subject, in reality, it easily becomes a condition for the service. For example, in the terms and conditions for obtaining credit from a financial institution, there will be a requirement for the data to be transmitted either to the financial institution or to the data processing company which it uses. Moreover, in exchange for the transfer of data, a reduced price or similar economic benefit may be offered.[64]

62 Ibid.

63 WP29, 'Working Document on the Processing of Personal Data Relating to Health in Electronic Health Records (EHR)' (15 February 2007) 18.

64 Ministry of Economic Affairs and Communications (n 61) 1.

The fourth risk related to the consent service is the creation of super-databases about data subjects, leading to higher risks (more data in one place, and hence, a more attractive target for cyber-attacks against the large profile of a person in the super-database). Moreover, it is not excluded that the data is obtained at the behest of a hostile foreign state, and hence, the consent service may even become a political security threat.[65]

Finally, the risk for rising socio-economic stratification was stressed, as gathering more data about individuals enables creation of their profiles and scores, leading to the increasing prices for those who are at high risk and hence are rated with 'bad scores.'[66] This in turn will likely increase the social costs for the state, as the experiences with the usurious and irresponsible lending practices have already shown in Estonia.[67] Indeed, personal autonomy has been used also in other contexts to justify activities such as the unrestricted selling of cigarettes or alcohol that eventually have led to considerable societal problems and, accordingly, to legal restrictions. Therefore, we should learn from these experiences and be cautious not to over-stress the personal autonomy argument.

It is remarkable that the study conducted by Ernst & Young commissioned by the Estonian government admitted the existence of these risks – but still the most important mitigating measures proposed in the study were raising the awareness of the data subjects, as well as fostering the best practices of data processing for the enterprises.[68] It should be stressed that the study did not propose any legal restrictions for the type, amount or time of the personal data that may be transferred based on consent; in other words, it relied mostly on the ability of the data subject to make informed and responsible choices regarding his or her personal data. The study mostly concentrated on the positive aspects of developing innovative data-driven services and promoting Estonia as a digitally advanced Member State[69] and the vision for 2032 is described as:

> sharing of data with tens and hundreds of services at any given moment is governed by a personal AI solution that gives or denies consent to data processing based on conditions defined at a general human level, against which, in each individual case, conditions are compared. In cases different from the standard conditions, the AI solution sends the person the request for informed consent.[70]

65 Ibid., 2.
66 Ibid., 2.
67 On the Estonian practices of usurious instant credit and the resulting socio-economic problems, see K Sein and U Volens, 'Legal Problems and Regulations Related to Easy-access Non-secured Consumer Loans in Estonia' (2014) 22 *Juridica International* 120, 120–137.
68 Ernst & Young (n 15) 28–29, 35–36, 43, 81ff.
69 Ibid., 10–13.
70 Ibid., 92.

The Estonian Digital Agenda 2030, apart from forecasting the positive impact of current plans,[71] also lacks a risk assessment.[72] Despite these shortcomings, the Estonian government decided to proceed with the development of the consent service and prepare the legal framework for it – and even launched it before the legislation was adopted.

3.5 Implications of the Data Governance Act

Whereas the consent service does not raise fundamental questions as to the compatibility with the GDPR, we will now turn to the newly adopted Data Governance Act and ask whether this act foresees any checks and balances capable of mitigating the described risks related to state-held data sharing. First, we should recall that Recital 15 DGA explicitly encourages public sector bodies to:

> facilitate the re-use of data on the basis of the consent of data subjects . . . on the re-use of data pertaining to them through adequate technical means. In that respect, the public sector body should make best efforts to provide assistance to potential re-users in seeking such consent or permission by establishing technical mechanisms that permit transmitting requests for consent or permission from re-users, where practically feasible.

Of course, the recital does not mention state-held personal data and may therefore be read in the context of the discussions on private data intermediaries.[73] Yet, as the Estonian state has launched a service that enables sharing of state-held personal data with third parties, the question arises whether the state itself is becoming a data intermediation services provider within the meaning of Art. 10(b) DGA. Should the state be qualified as a data intermediation services provider, it will be subject to a notification procedure under Art. 11 DGA, as well as to certain advising and other obligations under Art. 12 DGA.

According to Art. 10(b) DGA, these provisions apply to intermediation services between data subjects that seek to make their personal data available, and potential data users, including making available the technical or other means to enable such services, and in particular enabling the exercise of the data subjects' rights provided in the GDPR. It should be stressed that according to Recital 27 DGA, data intermediation services providers may include public sector bodies. At first glance, the consent service offered by the Estonian state corresponds to the intermediation

71 Ministry of Economic Affairs and Communications, Estonian Digital Agenda 2030, 17–18. <www.mkm.ee/media/6970/download> accessed 25 May 2023. The document explicitly mentions the possibility to sell personal data as it declares one aim to be that 'Private persons and entrepreneurs can use digital solutions to decide who can use the data shared by them and determine the purposes and conditions of use (*for a fee if they wish*)'. Emphasis by the author.

72 T Mällo, 'Nutikas Veepudel II' *Sirp* (22 October 2021).

73 On that, see H Richter, 'Looking at the Data Governance Act and Beyond: How to Better Integrate Data Intermediaries in the Market Order for Data Sharing' (72) 5 *GRUR International* 458–470.

services described in Art. 10(b) DGA: it is making available the technical means to enable the intermediation services between the data subjects wishing to make use of their private autonomy, and the potential data users.[74] It seems that it also fulfils the requirements of the data intermediation service of Art. 2(11) DGA defining 'data intermediation service' as a service that aims to establish commercial relationships for the purposes of data sharing between an undetermined number of data subjects and data holders, on the one hand, and data users, on the other hand, through technical, legal or other means, including for the purpose of exercising the rights of data subjects in relation to personal data. According to this definition, any suitable means of assistance in the initiation of commercial transactions, i.e., mere match-making between data owners and users without further legal or technical assistance, is sufficient.[75] This requirement is clearly fulfilled as the consent service provides technical assistance in match-making. Data intermediation services could include bilateral or multilateral sharing of data or the creation of platforms or databases enabling the sharing or joint use of data, as well as the establishment of specific infrastructure for the interconnection of data subjects and data holders with data users.

It is more complicated to answer whether the Estonian consent service might fall under the exclusion for 'data sharing services offered by public sector bodies that do not aim to establish commercial relationships'[76] as it is unclear whether the commercial relationship within the meaning of this exclusion must exist between the data holders and data users or between the data users and data subjects. According to Hennemann and Ditfurth, a commercial relationship must exist between data owners and data users.[77] If this is the case, then the Estonian consent service does not need to comply with the requirements of Arts. 10–15 DGA. Should we instead ask whether a commercial relationship must exist between the data subjects and data users, then the exclusion in Art. 2(11) DGA can hardly apply to the Estonian consent service, as its purpose is exactly to facilitate commercial relationships such as obtaining credit or using a digital medical service. According to the first sentence of Recital 28 DGA, commercial relationships for the purposes of data sharing must exist between an undetermined number of data subjects and data holders on the one hand and data users on the other. This seems to indicate that the consent service does not fall under the exception of Art. 2(11) DGA as the public sector

74 Cf., also the last sentence of Recital 27 DGA.

75 M Hennemann and L V Ditfurth, 'Datenintermediäre und Data Governance Act' (2022) *Neue Juristische Wochenschrift* 1905. Their position seems to be backed by the wording of the third sentence of Recital 28 DGA.

76 Art. 2(11)(d) DGA. The definition of data intermediation service in the DGA has been criticised for its vagueness by J Baloup et al., 'White Paper on Data Governance Act' (2021) *CiTiP Working Paper* 27 <www.researchgate.net/publication/352690055_White_Paper_on_the_Data_Governance_Act> accessed 25 May 2023.

77 Hennemann and Ditfurth (n 75) 1905. Cf., Richter (n 73) 462: 'the DGA includes commercial and non-commercial entities as DISs only if they aim to establish commercial relationships with regard to data sharing.'

body, i.e., the Estonian state indeed does aim to establish commercial relationships via the consent service.

Should the Estonian consent service underlie the provisions of data intermediation services of the DGA, we have to ask whether its mandatory compliance regime[78] – most importantly, the notification obligation of Art. 11 DGA and certain obligations under Art. 12 DGA – can effectively mitigate the privacy risks previously identified. The answer, unfortunately, will be to the negative. The notification obligation of the Estonian state to the competent authority, and subsequently to the European Commission,[79] clearly cannot prevent the excessive data gathering, the rise of super-databases or the socio-economic risks related to the social scoring of data subjects.[80] The same applies to the rather vaguely worded fiduciary obligation, i.e., the obligation to act in the data subject's best interests by informing and advising him or her about intended data uses by data users and standard terms and conditions attached to such uses before data subjects give consent,[81] to the information obligation regarding the jurisdiction in which the data use is intended to take place,[82] as well as to the logging obligations under Art. 12(o) DGA. The obligation to have procedures in place to prevent fraudulent or abusive practices in relation to parties seeking access through its data intermediation services under Art. 12(g) DGA[83] is a step ahead but lacks specificity as to what these procedures might look like, and hence, leaves a considerable amount of discretion to the Member States. It must be noted, though, that the Estonian consent service does not currently meet the requirements set forth by Art. 12 DGA, nor does it provide for penalties for law infringements as required by Art. 34(1) DGA. Continuing the consent service without adopting the necessary legislative framework required by the DGA, the Estonian state could be violating its provisions as of 24 September 2025 when the provisions of the DGA are to be applied. Moreover, in the legal literature, the question has been raised whether liability might apply in cases in which the data trustee transfers data to a user who breaches data protection law, and the data trustee could have foreseen such breaches.[84]

78 Baloup et al. (n 76) 26.

79 See Art. 11(10) DGA.

80 Note that under Art. 5(1)(c) of the proposed AI Act, social scoring is only prohibited for the state but not for private enterprises or other entities. Commission, 'Proposal for a Regulation of the European Parliament and of the Council laying down harmonised rules on artificial intelligence (Artificial Intelligence Act) and amending certain union legislative acts' COM (2021) 206 final.

81 Article 12(m) DGA. The aim of this provision is to prevent individuals from using such services to make more data relating to them available than what is in their own interest. Richter (n 73) 464. See Recital 30 DGA stating that:

> it is important that the business model of such providers ensures that there are no misaligned incentives that encourage individuals to use such services to make more data relating to them available for processing than would be in their interest.

82 Article 12 (n) DGA.

83 Cf., also Recital 36 DGA.

84 Richter (n 73) 467.

Should the consent service qualify as a data intermediary service within the meaning of DGA, then the Estonian state will not only be violating the provisions of Art. 12 DGA aimed at the protection of data subjects but also the obligation under Art. 12(f) DGA to create an access procedure to its service on a fair, transparent and non-discriminatory basis. As described previously, there are no rules in place regulating the requirements for obtaining access to the consent service. Hence, the fair, transparent and non-discriminatory access procedure is currently not guaranteed. Moreover, important questions arise such as whether the state can refuse access to the consent service for state security reasons,[85] or if it assesses privacy risks to be too high for a particular service provider (e.g., an Estonian subsidiary of a Big Tech corporation).

3.6 Breach of Data Protection Rules by the Service Provider: Would the Estonian State Be Liable Under the GDPR?

Whereas the Estonian state clearly is liable for any security issues of the consent service and the resulting data loss or other privacy breaches, it is more complicated to answer whether this liability also extends to breaches of data protection rules by the service providers to whom the state-held personal data is transferred. Would the Estonian state be liable if the service provider misuses the personal data, selling it for example to a Russian enterprise without the data subject's consent, or if the data is leaked from the service provider's digital environment due to inefficient cybersecurity measures? Is the state transferring personal data from its state databases to private service providers liable for what happens to this data afterwards?

According to the Terms of Use of the Consent Service displayed in the state portal, the State Information Systems Authority is not liable for damages or lost income caused by the use or non-use of the consent service and by the further processing of data transmitted to a third party via the consent service.[86] Apart from point 2.5 of the Terms of Use being incompatible with the Unfair Contract Terms Directive,[87] the Estonian State would be liable for damages under Art. 82 GDPR if it could be considered a joint controller within the meaning of GDPR. Article 26 GDPR defines joint controllers as two or more controllers jointly determining the purposes and means of processing. The question, therefore, is whether or not the state determines jointly with the service provider the purposes of data processing, as well as the means for it.

To answer this question, one should first recall the relationships between the data subject, the state as the data holder and the service provider as the data user. There is a triangular relationship whereby the data subject gives his consent

85 For example, granting access to Russian state-related taxi service Yandex which operated in Estonia before April 2022 and gathered a vast amount of personal data, including the home addresses of its clients.

86 Terms of Use of the Consent Service, points 2.5 and 2.6.

87 Council Directive 93/13/EEC on unfair terms in consumer contracts [1993] OJ L95/29.

under Art. 6(1)(a), and, in the case of sensitive data, under Art. 9(2)(a) GDPR to the state to transfer his or her personal data to the service provider. In addition to that, the data subject also has a relationship – usually contractual or pre-contractual –with the service provider under which the service provider provides, e.g., credit, insurance coverage or innovative medical services such as a vaccination or medication reminder system to the data subject. For these purposes, the service provider either processes the personal data of the data subject on the basis of Art. 6(1)(b), or of Art. 6(1)(a) or 9(2)(a) GDPR, i.e., consent. Hence, the state is processing the data when transferring the data from the state database to the service provider, and the service provider is processing it afterward for the purposes agreed with the data subject. The state and the service provider pursue different interests when processing the data: the service provider pursues its commercial interests, while the state is interested in fostering data sharing and thereby indirectly promoting Estonia as a digital-forward and innovative country.[88] Would that be enough to exclude the state from being a joint controller together with the service provider?

Whereas joint controllership is not ruled out in cases where both controllers pursue different interests,[89] both parties are still required to participate in the determination of the purposes and means of the data processing.[90] The pivotal issue is whether the state determines jointly with the service provider the means and purposes for the data processing performed by the latter. The EDPB guidelines on joint controllership offer the following guidance in this respect:

> Decisions can be considered as converging on purposes and means if they complement each other and are necessary for the processing to take place in such manner that they have a tangible impact on the determination of the purposes and means of the processing. As such, an important criterion to identify converging decisions in this context is whether the processing would not be possible without both parties' participation in the sense that the processing by each party is inseparable, i.e. inextricably linked.[91]

The fact that data processing by the service provider would not be possible without the initial transfer of the data by the state seems to point to the inextricable link between the data processing by each party. Yet, as we see from the *Fashion ID* case

88 According to the explanatory memorandum of the Draft Act, the state has an interest in supporting entrepreneurship, the development of new digital public services and an innovative, functional and user-friendly digital state experience. Explanatory memorandum (n 22) 5. It is evident that the state cannot be viewed as the data processor offering services to the service provider and following its guidance.

89 C-210/16 *Unabhängiges Landeszentrum für Datenschutz Schleswig-Holstein v Wirtschaftsakademie Schleswig-Holstein GmbH* ECLI:EU:C:2018:388, 34, 39.

90 European Data Protection Board, Guidelines 07/2020 on the concepts of controller and processor in the GDPR (2 September 2020) 59, 61.

91 Ibid., 53.

decided by the Court of Justice of the European Union (CJEU), joint controllership does not occur in cases when there is a chain of data processing, and a person participating in this chain does not determine either the purposes or the means for subsequent data processing operations.[92] The Court stated:

> a natural or legal person may be a controller, within the meaning of Article 2(d) of Directive 95/46, jointly with others only in respect of operations involving the processing of personal data for which it determines jointly the purposes and means. By contrast, and without prejudice to any civil liability provided for in national law in this respect, that natural or legal person cannot be considered to be a controller, within the meaning of that provision, in the context of operations that precede or are subsequent in the overall chain of processing for which that person does not determine either the purposes or the means.[93]

The Court stressed that the liability of a data controller is limited to the operation or set of operations involving the processing of personal data in respect of which it determines the purposes and means.[94] Hence, the liability of the state is limited to the data processing consisting of the transfer of personal data to the service provider, as the state only determines the purposes and means for this processing operation.

One may wonder, though, whether supervision of the state over the purposes for which the service provider processes the data would amount to the joint determination of the purposes of data processing. It is important to stress that at the time of writing this chapter, it is not possible to determine from the publicly available sources whether the state performs any checks on whether the services provider meets the requirements for legal personal data processing vis-à-vis the data subject before transferring the data to it. This might be different after the adoption of the regulatory framework. According to the explanatory memorandum of the Draft Act, in order to join the consent service and get access to the respective application programming interface, the service provider must provide the state with the set of data needed to provide the service and a description of the service. Arguably, this should enable the state to assess the consistency between the description of the service provided and the dataset required for this purpose, including whether the data minimisation and purpose limitation principles have been complied with.[95] Although it has been questioned earlier in this chapter how, by whom and to what extent such control could take place, it could be a reason for considering joint controllership. Yet, even if the control does take place, it is doubtful whether this is indeed enough to create joint controllership. The fact that the state exercises certain

92 C-40/17 *Fashion ID GmbH & Co.KG v Verbraucherzentrale NRW eV* ECLI:EU:C:2019:629, 74.
93 Ibid., 74.
94 Ibid., 85.
95 Explanatory Memorandum (n 22) 5.

supervision about the purposes described by the service provider does not amount to joint determination of the purposes within the meaning of Art. 26 GDPR as the service provider still decides alone the purposes and means for its data processing (e.g., providing an innovative digital health service). The state provides only the technical solution for obtaining consent from the data subject as well as the following transfer of the personal data but does not determine or provide the means (e.g., digital environment or platform) for the subsequent data processing by the service provider.

Even if that were the case, the EDPB guidelines stress that the use of a common data processing system will not always qualify the parties as joint controllers, in particular, if their processing is separable and could be performed by one party without intervention from the other.[96] Furthermore, joint controllership may also be excluded in a situation whereby several entities use a shared database or a common infrastructure if each entity independently determines its own purposes.[97] Hence, even if the state would allow the service providers access to the state database, the state would not necessarily qualify as a joint controller within the meaning of Art. 26 GDPR for data processing operations which purposes it does not co-determine. Consequently, the state is not liable for the service provider's data protection breaches under Art. 82 GDPR.

3.7 Potential State Liability?

The fundamental question to be asked is whether a state should create a digital service that indirectly sets incentives to share (sensitive) personal data without almost any risk-mitigating measures and that encourages businesses to require more personal data without a real necessity. Can the state leave everything to the personal autonomy of the data subjects, or might the state have positive obligations to foresee restrictions or other measures to balance the privacy risks? It is worrying that there is almost no public discussion in Estonia about privacy and discrimination risks related to the consent service, especially as the reuse of sensitive personal data (health data) is concerned. The only critical voice in the media has been a psychologist and personal data researcher Tanel Mällo, whose series of articles on the risks of a data-based society have argued that when collecting personal data, the state has also taken an obligation to protect them. He points out that with the current privacy understanding and skills of the general public, the introduction of a consent service that allows people to share their personal data with third parties without balancing the risks means abdicating responsibility – or more precisely, putting it on the shoulders of the incompetent citizen. He compares it to distributing an experimental drug to all population groups instead of sending it to clinical trials: let's see what happens![98]

96 European Data Protection Board (n 90) 66.
97 Ibid., 69.
98 T Mällo (n 60).

Indeed, as discussed previously in this chapter, there are considerable privacy risks connected to borderless personal data sharing, and raising awareness of the data subjects cannot be the only risk mitigation measure. Estonian society has already experienced that leaving everything to the private autonomy of individuals can lead to major socio-economic problems. One of the worst experiences was the wide use of usurious instant loans that brought about massive over-indebtedness and personal bankruptcy of consumers and eventually ended in the change of consumer credit legislation in 2015.[99] The problems with excessive alcohol and tobacco consumption and the legislative restrictions to combat these problems constitute another well-known example. The question to be asked is whether the state has an obligation to intervene on the legislative level to avoid such socio-economic problems. As shown in Section 3.6, the Estonian state would not be liable under Art. 82 GDPR for data breaches of the service providers obtaining personal data via consent service. One may wonder, though, whether the state might be liable under the Estonian State Liability Act[100] or even under the European Convention of Human Rights (EHCR).[101]

Estonian law allows claims for compensation from the state for damages caused by legislative acts. More precisely, § 14(1) of the State Liability Act stipulates that a person may claim compensation for damage caused by the legislation of general application or by failure to issue legislation of general application only if the damage was caused by a significant violation of the obligations of a public authority, the legal provision forming the basis for the violated obligation is directly applicable and the person belongs to a group of persons who have been specially injured due to the legislation or by failure to issue legislation. As we see, under this provision the state can be also liable for inactivity, i.e., in case of failure to issue legislation. However, both the explanatory memorandum to the State Liability Act,[102] as well as the Estonian Supreme Court (Riigikohus), have stressed that the state liability for legislative (in)action may occur only in very limited cases[103] when the failure of the legislature has been severe and resulted in a clearly unjust situation for the individual. This can be the case in severe breaches of a fundamental right.[104]

The preconditions for state liability under the State Liability Act have been subject to several rulings of the Supreme Court.[105] Looking at these decisions, we find

99 Inter alia, APRC caps were introduced for consumer loans. K Sein, 'Regulation of Abusive Debt Collection Practices in Estonia' in C G Stanescu (ed), *The Regulation of Abusive Debt Collection Practices in the European Union and the United Kingdom – Lessons from National Experiences* (Routledge 2022) 101, 106.

100 RT I, 11.03.2023, 86.

101 Convention for the Protection of Human Rights and Fundamental Freedoms, Rome, 4 November 1950.

102 Explanatory memorandum to the Act amending the State Liability Act and the Constitutional Review Court Procedure Act.

103 Decision of the Estonian Supreme Court no 3–3–1–53–13, 40.

104 Explanatory memorandum (n 102).

105 See, for example, the decision of the Estonian Supreme Court 3–3–1–84–12 para 13 listing and elaborating these preconditions.

several obstacles to filing a successful damage claim against the state for legislative inactivity. First, one needs to determine a legislative provision from which the obligation to adopt a legislative act derives and what the content of such obligation is. Moreover, the Court must determine a breach of a corresponding subjective right of the victim.[106]

The Supreme Court has admitted that such an obligation and the subjective right may derive from §§ 13–14 of the Estonian Constitution.[107] The first sentence of Art. 13(1) of the Estonian Constitution[108] states that everyone has the right to the protection of the state and the law. This provision is related to § 14 of the Constitution, stating that the guarantee of rights and freedoms is the duty of the legislative, executive and judicial powers, and of local authorities. The Supreme Court has noted that these provisions impose an obligation on the state to protect fundamental rights[109] and under § 26 of the Estonian Constitution, privacy – including the collection, storage, use and disclosure of personal data – is protected as a fundamental right.[110] The state must ensure protection both against direct attacks of a fundamental right and to help to balance relationships whereby the interests of different persons may be in conflict.[111] When establishing the breach of a fundamental right, it is necessary to assess whether the existing legal regulation ensures the required level of protection or whether certain vital circumstances have been unconstitutionally left unregulated. The Supreme Court has stressed that the legislature has wide discretion in deciding how to reach the constitutionally required level,[112] and it should be also noted that the Supreme Court has only in nine cases determined unconstitutionality due to inaction by the legislature.[113] Hence, the wide margin of discretion left to the legislature may constitute a considerable hurdle for a successful damage claim against the state.

Second, under § 14(1) of the State Liability Act, the legal provision forming the basis for the violated obligation must be directly applicable. The Supreme Court has explained that provisions giving a wide margin of discretion are not directly applicable within the meaning of § 14(1) of the State Liability Act, as they are not sufficiently clear and precise to be relied upon in court proceedings.[114] The Court made a caveat that in case of an extraordinary restriction of fundamental rights, it is not excluded that also a breach of a not directly applicable provision may entitle

106 Decision of the Estonian Supreme Court 5–17–42, 39.

107 Decision of the Estonian Supreme Court 3–3–1–53–13, 34, 39.

108 RT I, 15.05.2015, 2.

109 Decision of the Estonian Supreme Court 3–4–1–15–12, 30.

110 Decision of the Estonian Supreme Court 3–3–1–3–12, 19.

111 Ü Madise et al. (eds), *Eesti Vabariigi Põhiseadus. Kommenteeritud väljaanne* (Juura 2020) § 13 paras 8–9.

112 Decision of the Estonian Supreme Court 5–17–42/9, 36.

113 P K Tupay, 'Seadusandja otsus või kohtu sõna – kelle käes on võim õiguskorra üle?' 3 (2023) *Juridica* 201.

114 Decision of the Estonian Supreme Court 3–3–1–84–12, 48.

the individual to a fair compensation;[115] however, it is highly disputable whether enabling personal data sharing without risk mitigation measures could amount to an 'extraordinary breach of fundamental right' by the state.

Finally, the state's liability may be precluded by the requirement that the victim must belong to a group of particularly affected persons. The explanatory memorandum of the State Liability Act describes that the purpose of this requirement is to prevent mass claims,[116] and the Supreme Court has explained that mass claims may impose an excessive burden on taxpayers and the state budget, thus making it more difficult for the state to fulfil its other functions, including, for example, the guarantee of fundamental social rights.[117] Therefore, the requirement of belonging to a group of particularly affected persons should limit the right to compensation in a situation when failure to act infringes the rights of a very large number of persons. Only when the damage caused by the legislative act or failure to enact is more or less evenly distributed among persons throughout the country must the claimant justify why his or her suffering is more special than that of others.[118] In case of privacy breaches induced by the creation of consent service, the state's failure to provide safeguards for data subjects' rights, the situation is exactly one where the rights of a very large number of persons are potentially infringed. Belonging to a group of particularly affected persons has been acknowledged by the Supreme Court in the case of sellers of pharmaceuticals,[119] as well as authors in case of copyright infringements;[120] however, these groups are clearly distinguishable and rather small compared to the whole population of Estonia. Hence, the requirement of belonging to the particularly affected persons effectively rules out the potential damages claim.

Consequently, it is more than doubtful whether a data subject who has suffered damage due to a lack of risk mitigation measures for the consent service is entitled to claim damages from the state under the State Liability Act: the wide margin of discretion of the legislature, the requirement of extraordinary breach of a fundamental right and the requirement that the victim must belong to a group of particularly affected persons prevent such claims. It is generally accepted that the State Liability Act has not enabled extensive damages awards or mass compensations to a wide circle of persons in Estonia,[121] and it is therefore very likely that there is no effective remedy for the data subject under Estonian law.

This leads to the question of whether the data subject could invoke the European Convention on Human Rights: is it possible that the Estonian state has breached Art.

115 Ibid., 49.
116 Explanatory memorandum (n 102).
117 Decision of the Estonian Supreme Court 3-3-1-53-13.
118 Decision of the Estonian Supreme Court 3-3-1-84-12, 23.
119 Ibid., 24.
120 Decision of the Estonian Supreme Court 3-3-1-9-16.
121 K Lind, 'Riik vastutab: kas päriselt ja piisavalt? 20 aastat arengut: sooviti üht ja saadi . . .' 3 (2023) *Juridica* 176.

8 EHCR[122] when it has not set any restrictions, e.g., to the amount and types of personal data that the data subject can share with third parties via the consent service? In other words, can a state breach the EHCR through failure to protect the individual against himself or herself? Knowingly, Art. 8 EHCR also comprises positive obligations which may 'involve the adoption of measures designed to secure respect for private life even in the sphere of the relations of individuals between themselves.'[123] For example, in the case *Söderman v Sweden*, the European Court of Human Rights found that Sweden had breached its obligations under Art. 8 ECHR for failing to have enacted laws that would protect the applicant from being covertly filmed naked by her stepfather in their bathroom for a sexual purpose. The Court stressed that in case of less serious acts between individuals, Art. 8 EHCR does not necessarily require an efficient criminal sanction: a civil law remedy may also be able to afford sufficient protection.[124] The Court further noted that the correct test involved considering whether Sweden's legal framework is in compliance with its positive obligations under Art. 8 ECHR and provides adequate protection to Ms Söderman against the acts of her stepfather.[125] Although in a different context than data sharing, the Court has ruled that the domestic law must afford appropriate safeguards to prevent any such disclosure of personal health data as may be inconsistent with the guarantees in Art. 8 of the Convention.[126] However, the Court has never had to decide a case in which the central question is the obligation of the state to protect someone from himself or herself. This would involve a complicated balancing between the right to self-realisation, on the one hand, and on the other hand, to the right to privacy.

3.8 Conclusions

Fostering data sharing has been declared a common European goal, as more data is needed for innovation. Estonia – with its interconnected public registries and a rather relaxed attitude – offers an interesting example with its new and unique concept of a so-called consent service, i.e., a digital solution enabling data subjects to consent to the sharing of their personal data (including health data) held in state registries to private sector players. This digital solution has already been launched, although the relevant legislation is yet to be adopted. The draft legislation, however, fails to adequately address privacy threats that a liberal approach totally relying on the data subject's private autonomy is likely to bring about. Although the model of personal data sharing does not directly contradict the rules of GDPR, as consents given by the data subjects to transfer their personal data from the state registries to third parties are valid, as a rule, the solution raises more fundamental issues and systematic risks for the privacy of the citizens. These risks are not mitigated by the

122 Article 8 of the Convention has a broad scope and covers also the right to the protection of personal data. See eg the decision of the European Court of Human Rights Z v Finland (1997) 95.

123 ECHR *Söderman v Sweden* [GC] (2013) 78.

124 Ibid., 85 and the case law cited there.

125 Söderman (n 123) 91.

126 Z v Finland (n 122) 95.

Data Governance Act's provisions on data intermediation services, nor does the state setting up an incentive to sell (sensitive) personal data face liability for the potential data protection breaches of the private sector data users under the GDPR or state liability rules. Therefore, although surely fostering innovative digital services and thereby contributing to the ideals of European data strategy, the Estonian consent service model – i.e., public data intermediation service – cannot be recommended as a pan-European model in its current format without a thorough discussion about how to balance the demand for data, on the one side, with the need to protect data subjects, on the other side. One must agree with Tanel Mällo that by empowering individuals to freely share all their personal data in a situation when most of them are unaware of the consequences, the state assumes that individuals do not share data with unethical data users. In reality, however, people lack the cognitive capacity and information to make such decisions.[127]

Bibliography

Baloup J, et al, 'White Paper on Data Governance Act' (CiTiP Working Paper 27 2021) <www.researchgate.net/publication/352690055_White_Paper_on_the_Data_Governance_Act> accessed 25 May 2023

Clifford D, Graef I and Valcke P, 'Pre-Formulated Declarations of Data Subject Consent – Citizen-Consumer Empowerment and the Alignment of Data, Consumer and Competition Law Protections' (2019) 20 *German Law Journal* 713

Commission, 'A European Dtrategy for Data' (Communication) COM (2020) 66 final

Commission, 'Proposal for a Regulation of the European Parliament and of the Council Laying Down Harmonised Rules on Artificial Intelligence (Artificial Intelligence Act) and Amending Certain Union Legislative Acts' COM (2021) 206 final

Convention for the Protection of Human Rights and Fundamental Freedoms, Rome, 4 November 1950

Eesti Infoühiskonna Arengukava 2020

Email from P Pärna on behalf of the State Information System Authority to author (11 April 2023)

Ernst S, 'Art. 4' in Paal B and Pauly DA (eds), *Datenschutz-Grundverordnung* (3rd edn, C.H. Beck 2021)

Ernst & Young, *Nõusolekuteenuse analüüs. Analüüsi aruanne* (5 February 2021) <www.sm.ee/sites/default/files/content-editors/Ministeerium_kontaktid/Uuringu_ja_analuusid/nt_aruanne_final_3.pdf> accessed 25 May 2023

ERR, 'Estonia Sets New e-Voting Record at Riigikogu 2023 Elections' (4 March 2023) <https://news.err.ee/1608904730/estonia-sets-new-e-voting-record-at-riigikogu-2023-elections> accessed 25 May 2023 accessed 25 May 2023

Estonian e-Residency Program <www.e-resident.gov.ee/> accessed 25 May 2023

Estonian State Portal eesti.ee <www.id.ee/en/article/state-portal-eesti-ee> accessed 25 May 2023; <//github.com/e-gov/NT/blob/master/RIA%20n%C3%B5usolekuteenuse%20kasutamine%20ja%20liidestamine%20ver%201.0%20-%2015.09.2021/RIA%20n%C3%B5usolekuteenuse%20kasutamine%20ja%20liidestamine%20ver%201.0%20-%2015.09.2021.md#n%C3%B5usolekute-haldus> accessed 25 May 2023

Explanatory Memorandum to the Act Amending the State Liability Act and the Constitutional Review Court Procedure Act

127 T Mällo (n 60).

Explanatory Memorandum to the Draft Law for Changing the Public Information Act, the Environmental Surveillance Act and Spatial Data (17 November 2021)

European Commission, 'Proposal for a Regulation of the European Parliament and of the Council on the European Health Data Space' COM (2022) 197 final

European Commission, 'Proposal for a Regulation of the European Parliament and of the Council on Harmonised Rules on Fair Access to and Use of Data (Data Act)' COM (2022) 68 final

European Data Protection Board, Guidelines 05/2020 on Consent under Regulation 2016/679

European Data Protection Board, Guidelines 07/2020 on the Concepts of Controller and Processor in the GDPR (2 September 2020)

Hennemann M and Von Ditfurth L, 'Datenintermediäre und Data Governance Act' (2022) *Neue Juristiche Wochenschrift* 1905

Kull I and Kask L, 'Electronic Signature Under the eIDAS Regulation in Domestic and Cross-Border Communication: Estonian Example' 12 (2019) *Juridiskā zinātne* 33

Kühling J and Buchner B, 'Art. 7' in Kühling J and Buchner B (eds), *Datenschutz-Grundverordnung* (3rd edn, C.H. Beck 2022)

Lind K, 'Riik vastutab: kas päriselt ja piisavalt? 20 aastat arengut: sooviti üht ja saadi . . .' (2023) 3 *Juridica* 176

Madise Ü, et al (eds), *Eesti Vabariigi Põhiseadus. Kommenteeritud väljaanne* (Juura 2020)

Ministry of Economic Affairs and Communications, Annex 3 of the tender call documents

Ministry of Economic Affairs and Communications, Estonian Digital Agenda 2030 <www.mkm.ee/media/6970/download> accessed 25 May 2023

Ministry of Economic Affairs and Communication, 'Nõusolekuteenus võimaldab ettevõttel riigilt sinu andmeid küsida' (30 December 2021) <www.mkm.ee/uudised/nousolekuteenus-voimaldab-ettevottel-riigilt-sinu-andmeid-kusida> accessed 25 May 2023

Murumaa-Mengel M, Laas-Mikko K and Pruulmann-Vengerfeldt P, 'I Have Nothing to Hide: A Coping Strategy in a Risk Society' in Kramp L, et al (eds), *Journalism, Representation and the Public Sphere* (edition lumière 2015) 195–207

Mällo T, 'Nutikas veepudel II' *Sirp* (22 October 2021)

Mällo T, 'Nutikas veepudel III' *Sirp* (5 November 2021)

Pormeister K, 'Patsiendiseire ehk ennetamise eesmärgil andmete töötlemine ilma patsiendi nõusolekuta' (2021) 2 *Juridica*

Richter H, 'Looking at the Data Governance Act and Beyond: How to Better Integrate Data Intermediaries in the Market Order for Data Sharing' (72) 5 *GRUR International* 458

Riigi Infosüsteemi Amet, *Aastaraamat 2020* (Riigi Infosüsteemi Amet 2020) <https://dea.digar.ee/cgi-bin/dea?a=d&d=JVriaarmt202005> accessed 25 May 2023

Schulz S, 'Art. 9' in Gola P and Heckmann D (eds), *Datenschutz-Grundverordnung* (3rd edn, C.H. Beck 2022)

Sein K, 'Regulation of Abusive Debt Collection Practices in Estonia' in Stanescu CG (ed), *The Regulation of Abusive Debt Collection Practices in the European Union and the United Kingdom – Lessons from National Experiences* (Routledge 2022) 101

Sein K and Volens U, 'Legal Problems and Regulations Related to Easy-Access Non-Secured Consumer Loans in Estonia' (2014) 22 *Juridica International* 120

Sein K and Ristikivi M, *Õigusriigi taastamine. Eesti seaduste ja institutsioonide reformid 1992–2002* (Tartu Ülikooli Kirjastus 2022)

Shabani M, Yilmaz S, 'Lawfulness in Secondary Use of Health Data: Interplay between Three Regulatory Frameworks of GDPR, DGA & EHDS' (2022) *Technology and Regulation* 128

State Information System Authority, 'Consent Service' <www.ria.ee/en/state-information-system/people-centred-data-exchange/consent-service> accessed 25 May 2023

Terzis P, 'Compromises and Asymmetries in the European Health Data Space' (2022) *European Journal of Health Law* 1

Tupay PK, 'Estonia, the Digital Nation: Reflections on a Digital Citizen's Rights in the European Union' (2020) 6 *European Data Protection Law Review* 294

Tupay PK, 'Seadusandja otsus või kohtu sõna – kelle käes on võim õiguskorra üle?' 3 (2023) *Juridica* 201

Tupay PK and Mikiver M, 'Der estnische E-Staat – Zukunftsweisendes Vorbild oder befremdlicher Einzelgänger?' (2015) *Osteuropa Recht* 6

Vinkel P and Krimmer R, 'The How and Why to Internet Voting: An Attempt to Explain E-Stonia' in Krimmer R, et al (eds), *Proceedings of the First International Joint Conference on Electronic Voting* (Springer 2016) 178

WP29, 'Working Document on the Processing of Personal Data Relating to Health in Electronic Health Records (EHR)' (15 February 2007)

Äripäev, 'UUS: nõusolekuteenusega saavad ettevõtted riigilt sinu andmeid küsida, otsustad sina' (5 January 2022) <www.raamatupidaja.ee/uudised/2022/01/05/uus-nousolekuteenusega-saavad-ettevotted-riigilt-sinu-andmeid-kusida-osustad-sina> accessed 25 May 2023

4 Consent to Data Processing in Biobanking

Regulatory Challenges of Data Processing in Biobanking, Using the Estonian Example

Kärt Pormeister

4.1 Introduction

Estonia is in a unique position, whereby almost 20% of its population has opted to be part of the Estonian Biobank (EBB).[1] This makes the EBB a great example to explore legal and regulatory challenges related to data processing in biobanks, the use of which is not limited to specific areas of research (unless one were to deem 'genetic research' a specific area of research).

The EBB was initially established in 2001 in the legal form of a foundation by the Estonian government.[2] In 2007, however, the foundation was dissolved, and the EBB became part of the University of Tartu, operating under its Institute of Genomics. The legal framework, most notably the Estonian Human Genes Research Act (HGRA),[3] under which the EBB operates, has remained much the same since 2001. What has significantly changed in recent decades, however, is the understanding and interpretation of data protection law. These changes have immense practical impact on the operation of biobanks, most notably population-based biobanks such as the EBB. This chapter will explore the issue of consent as a legal basis for data processing in biobank research on the example of the EBB.

Generally, consent to data processing can only be given for one or more specific purpose(s) as established under the General Data Protection Regulation (GDPR)[4] (Arts. 4[11], 6[1][a], 9[2][a] GDPR). This general rule can be referred to as the 'requirement of specificity'. The GDPR seems to facilitate (the possibility of) one single exception to this general rule. The exception is expressed in Recital 33

1 See the website of the Institute of Genomics, University of Tartu at <https://genomics.ut.ee/en/content/estonian-biobank> accessed 19 December 2022.

2 The order of the Government of the Republic of Estonia establishing the EBB is available only in Estonian at <www.riigiteataja.ee/akt/84864> accessed 19 December 2022.

3 Human Genes Research Act (HGRA), RT I 2000, 104, 685, available in English online at <www.riigiteataja.ee/en/eli/508042019001/consolide> accessed 19 December 2022.

4 Regulation (EU) 2016/679 of the European Parliament and of the Council of 27 April 2016 on the protection of natural persons with regard to the processing of personal data and on the free movement of such data, and repealing Directive 95/46/EC (General Data Protection Regulation) [2016] OJ L119/1.

DOI: 10.4324/9781003502791-6

GDPR, which establishes that individuals should be 'allowed to give their consent to *certain areas* of scientific research' (emphasis added). The underlying reasoning for this exception, according to Recital 33 GDPR, is that, 'It is often not possible to fully identify the purpose of personal data processing for scientific research purposes at the time of data collection'. The practical meaning and effect of this exception in Recital 33 GDPR will be explored in the first part of this chapter.

The first part of the chapter will analyse the evolution of the approach to consent to data processing for research purposes in EU data protection law, culminating with the ultimate stance of the European Data Protection Board (EDPB) published in 2021, stating that open consent is not compatible with the GDPR. The position of the EDPB regarding its understanding of 'GDPR-compliant consent to data processing in research' will be subject to critical review. It seems that the EDPB's approach effectively nullifies the efforts of the drafters of the GDPR expressed in Recital 33 GDPR in regard to a broader concept of consent to data processing when it pertains to scientific research. Furthermore, the EDPB's efforts to limit the feasibility of consent as a legal basis for data processing in research run counter to efforts of EU legislators expressed in other (upcoming) EU laws that aim to enable and facilitate the (secondary) research use of already obtained personal data.

In terms of structure, the first part of this chapter explores the evolution of consent to data processing in research in a chronological order, starting from consent to data processing for research purposes prior to the GDPR (Section 4.2.1), thereafter exploring the 'could have been' scenario that emerged during the drafting of the GDPR (Section 4.2.2). The next subsection will delves into the status quo of consent to data processing in research (Section 4.2.3), which will be analysed through a legal-technical lens (Section 4.2.3.1) and through the interpretations given to it by various competent bodies such as the Art. 29 Working Party (Section 4.2.3.2), the European Data Protection Supervisor (Section 4.2.3.3), and the EDPB (Section 4.2.3.4). The following subsection (Section 4.2.4) offers comparative remarks on the somewhat contradictory approaches in EU data protection law, on the one hand, and other (upcoming) EU law, on the other hand, as it pertains to the (secondary) use of personal data for research purposes. Finally, the section concludes with critical remarks on the EDPB's stance on the GDPR-compliant breadth of consent to data processing in research (Section 4.2.5).

The second part of the chapter presents the evolution of the legal framework of the EBB to illustrate how the inability of the EDPB to properly address consent to data processing in research and its denial of the possibility of open consent under the GDPR might bring about a need for regulatory changes regarding biobanking. In the first subsection, the author lays out the concept of the open consent used by the EBB for, inter alia, data processing (Section 4.3.1). Thereafter, the dilemma of the appropriate legal basis for data processing by the EBB is explored (Section 4.3.2). Subsequently, possible upcoming regulatory changes regarding data processing by the EBB are discussed (Section 4.3.3). Finally, the author will outline regulatory gaps for biobanking in Estonia as it pertains to data protection law (Section 4.3.4).

4.2 Consent to Data Processing for Research Purposes in EU Data Protection Law

4.2.1 Consent to Data Processing for Research Purposes Prior to the GDPR

The EU 1995 Data Protection Directive[5] (1995 Directive) barely made any specific mention of the research use of personal data. In fact, the 1995 Directive refers to '(scientific) research' on just a handful of occasions. As laid out in what follows, most of the references to the scientific use of personal data in the 1995 Directive resemble those in the current GDR (which is equally as scarce regarding such references).

First, Recital 34 of the 1995 Directive recognised the need for Member States to allow for derogations from the general 'prohibition on processing sensitive categories of data where important reasons of public interest so justify in areas such as . . . scientific research'. The 1995 Directive also set out that further processing of such data for, inter alia, 'scientific purposes' would not be deemed incompatible with the initial purposes for which the data were collected (Recital 29 and Art. 6[1][b] of the 1995 Directive). Like the GDPR, the 1995 Directive allowed for storage of personal data for longer periods of time if necessary for research needs, subject to 'appropriate safeguards' laid down by each Member State (Art. 6[1][e] of the 1995 Directive).

Furthermore – again, like the GDPR – while the 1995 Directive established an obligation for data controllers to provide information to data subjects, where data had been obtained from sources other than the data subject, an exception was granted for when processing was undertaken for purposes of scientific research (Recital 40 and Art. 11[2] of the 1995 Directive). The 1995 Directive also gave Member States discretion on certain conditions to create derogations from the data subjects' right to access when data were processed solely for purposes of scientific research (Art. 12[2] of the 1995 Directive).

Thus, the 1995 Directive did not specifically address the issue of consent to data processing for purposes of scientific research. Instead, that was a matter left at the sole discretion of Member States. Consent to data processing in general, of course, was subject to the requirement of being specific (Art. 2[h] of the 1995 Directive).

However, the question as to whether Member States ought to have been bound by the general requirement of specificity of consent in the realm of scientific research, as well, remains unanswered. As will be shown on the Estonian example, in the second part of this chapter, some countries might have exercised their perceived discretion in regulating consent to data processing in research to allow in their national law for open consent to data processing for purposes of scientific research.

5 Directive 95/46/EC of the European Parliament and of the Council of 24 October 1995 on the protection of individuals with regard to the processing of personal data and on the free movement of such data [1995] OJ L281/31 (the 1995 Directive).

4.2.2 Consent to Data Processing for Research Purposes During the Drafting of the GDPR

An examination of the drafting process of the GDPR reveals that the issue of consent to data processing in research could have found its way to the legally binding parts of the GDPR, as opposed to the recitals, where it eventually ended up (i.e., Recital 33 GDPR).[6] Had the relevant amendment proposal been adopted, the regulation of consent to data processing in research would have arguably been stricter than it is now under the GDPR (though the EDPB's interpretation of Recital 33 GDPR effectively renders the status quo just as strict, as will be argued later in this subsection).[7]

Namely, during the drafting process of the GDPR, an amendment was proposed by the European Parliament's Committee on Civil Liberties, Justice and Home Affairs, that would have resulted in the following legal rule governing consent to data processing in research (emphasis added):

> Where the data subject's consent is required for the processing of medical data exclusively for public health purposes of scientific research, the *consent may be given for one or more specific and similar researches*. However, the data subject may withdraw the consent at any time.[8]

However, this proposal was ultimately unsuccessful and rules on consent to personal data processing specifically in research were not adopted as part of the legally binding parts of the final text of the GDPR. Instead, the GDPR only mentions this specific question in one single recital: Recital 33 GDPR. One can assume that the proposed rule failed to be incorporated into the final version of the GDPR due to opposition from the medical and research sector for the simple reason that it would have created a clear hindrance to data processing in research.[9]

4.2.3 Consent to Data Processing for Research Purposes Under the GDPR

4.2.3.1 The Legal Effect of Recital 33 GDPR

The general rule under the GDPR is that consent to data processing can only be given for one or more specific purpose(s), a.k.a. the 'requirement of specificity' (as

6 Kärt Pormeister, 'Transparency in Relation to the Data Subject in Genetic Research – An Analysis on the Example of Estonia' (PhD thesis, Dissertationes Iuridicae Universitatis Tartuensis 76 (University of Tartu Press 2019), 37–42.

7 Ibid 41.

8 Amendment 191, Proposal for a regulation, Art. 81. Report on the proposal for a regulation of the European Parliament and of the Council on the protection of individuals with regard to the processing of personal data and on the free movement of such data (General Data Protection Regulation) (COM(2012)0011 – C7–0025/2012–2012/0011(COD)). 22 November 2013, Committee on Civil Liberties, Justice and Home Affairs.

9 Pormeister (n 6) 41. See, e.g., Paolo G Casali on behalf of the European Society for Medical Oncology (ESMO) Switzerland, 'Risks of the new EU Data Protection Regulation: An ESMO Position Paper Endorsed by the European Oncology Community' (2014) 25(8) *Annals of Oncology* 1458.

expressed in Arts. 4[11], 6[1][a], 9[2][a] GDPR). However, Recital 33 GDPR recognises that a strict requirement of specificity may not be appropriate where data are being processed for research purposes (emphasis added).

> It is often not possible to fully identify the purpose of personal data processing for scientific research purposes at the time of data collection. *Therefore, data subjects should be allowed to give their consent to certain areas of scientific research when in keeping with recognised ethical standards for scientific research.* Data subjects should have the opportunity to give their consent only to certain areas of research or parts of research projects to the extent allowed by the intended purpose.

It is clear that the aim of Recital 33 GDPR is to allow for some sort of deviation from the general requirement of specificity of consent. However, the practical meaning of Recital 33 GDPR remains debatable.[10] On the one hand, from the case law of the Court of Justice of the European Union (CJEU), it is clear that recitals of EU legal acts are not legally binding.[11] As the CJEU has noted, 'the preamble to a Community act has no binding legal force and cannot be relied on as a ground for derogating from the actual provisions of the act in question'.[12] Recitals have been seen as interpretive tools, sometimes performing 'a supplementary normative role'.[13]

On the other hand, the GDPR specifically grants Member States discretion to regulate the research use of special categories of data in their national laws (Art. 9[2][j] GDPR). This means that by applying the method of systematic interpretation of law one would have to reach the following two conclusions:

1 Recital 33 GDPR as part of the preamble of the GDPR cannot disapply the rules for consent established within the legally binding parts of the GDPR (including the requirement of specificity as established in Arts. 4[11], 6[1][a], 9[2][a] GDPR).
2 Recital 33 GDPR can be applied in the course of the exercise of discretion afforded to Member States and EU lawmakers under Article 9(2)(j) GDPR when regulating the research use of special categories of data in either national laws or other EU law.

As of yet, there unfortunately is no clear guidance concerning the meaning of Recital 33 GDPR and the question of consent to data processing in scientific

10 Pormeister (n 6), 37–42.
11 Case C-162/97 *Nilsson and Others* [1998] ECR I-07477, para 54.
12 Ibid.
13 Roberto Baratta. Complexity of EU law in the domestic implementing process. 19th Quality of Legislation Seminar 'EU Legislative Drafting: Views from Those Applying EU Law in the Member States' 3 July 2014 <https://ec.europa.eu/dgs/legal_service/seminars/20140703_baratta_speech.pdf> accessed 3 April 2023.

research under the GDPR. Instead of providing clarifications, the relevant authoritative bodies within the EU have muddied the waters even further by giving vague and unsystematic interpretations, ultimately rendering Recital 33 GDPR meaningless.

4.2.3.2 Article 29 Working Party on Consent to Data Processing for Research Purposes

After the adoption of the GDPR in 2016, but before its date of application in May 2018, the Working Party established under Art. 29 of the 1995 Directive (WP29) issued an opinion in 2017 on consent to data processing under the GDPR.[14] This opinion was revised in 2018.[15] In the initial version of the opinion in 2017, the WP29 set out that (emphasis added):

> First, it should be noted that Recital 33 does not disapply the obligations with regard to the requirement of specific consent. This means that, in principle, scientific research projects can only include personal data on the basis of consent if they have a well-described purpose. *Where purposes are unclear at the start of a scientific research programme, controllers will have difficulty to pursue the programme in compliance with the GDPR.*[16]

However, in the final version of this opinion in 2018, the WP29 apparently had changed its mind regarding the possibility of broader consent under the GDPR and had altered the preceding sentence highlighted in italics to read instead as (emphasis added):

> For the cases where purposes for data processing within a scientific research project cannot be specified at the outset, *Recital 33 allows as an exception that the purpose may be described at a more general level.*[17]

Thus, it seems that the WP29 went from negating the possibility of using consent as a legal basis in research when the purposes of said research cannot be clearly defined at the outset to recognising that Recital 33 GDPR does indeed allow for processing purposes to be described 'at a more general level'. The WP29 noted that, 'Recital 33 seems to bring some flexibility to the degree of specification and granularity of consent in the context of scientific research'.[18]

14 Article 29 Working Party, 'Guidelines on Consent Under Regulation 2016/679', adopted 28 November 2017, 17/EN WP 259.

15 Article 29 Working Party, 'Guidelines on Consent Under Regulation 2016/679', adopted on 28 November 2017, as last revised and adopted 10 April 2018, 17/EN WP 259 rev.01.

16 Article 29 Working Party, 'Guidelines on Consent Under Regulation 2016/679', (n 14), 27; Pormeister (n 6), 39.

17 Article 29 Working Party, 'Guidelines on Consent Under Regulation 2016/679' rev.01 (n 15), 28.

18 Ibid.

As previously noted, the legally binding parts of the GDPR include the requirement of specificity of consent to data processing, i.e., for the specific purpose(s) of processing to be made clear to the data subject prior to obtaining consent. This rule in the legally binding parts of the GDPR seems to be quite clear, thus not requiring reliance on recitals for its interpretation. Hence, considering the legal meaning of preambles and recitals, as previously explained, Recital 33 GDPR could not allow for deviations from legally binding rules within the GDPR by means of direct application of the GDPR. Thereby, the position of the WP29 – which lacks any reference to possible implementations of the principle expressed in Recital 33 GDPR in national laws or other EU law – remains in this regard questionable as it seems to purport the idea that Recital 33 GDPR could be directly applicable.

Though the WP29 made a reference to Art. 9(2)(j) GDPR, this reference was contained to the context of legal bases for data processing in research that are alternative to consent. Curiously, the WP29 made no reference to the discretion afforded to Member States in Art. 9(2)(j) GDPR in connection with Recital 33 GDPR, and how this discretion could be used to adopt a broader concept of consent to data processing in research specifically.[19]

To make an already confusing matter worse, the WP29 then added that regarding special categories of personal data within the meaning of Art. 9 GDPR, 'applying the flexible approach of Recital 33 will be subject to a stricter interpretation and requires a high degree of scrutiny'.[20] In this light, one is compelled to question what meaning then, if any, is left to Recital 33 GDPR as it pertains to research involving health data?

4.2.3.3 *European Data Protection Supervisor on Consent to Data Processing for Research Purposes*

In 2020, the European Data Protection Supervisor (EDPS) issued a preliminary opinion on data protection and scientific research.[21] The EDPS emphasised that Recital 33 GDPR does not 'take precedence over the conditions for consent set out in Arts. 4(11), 6(1)(a), 7 and 9(2)(a) of the GDPR'.[22] However, like the WP29, the EDPS maintained that Recital 33 GDPR could be relied on directly by controllers, i.e., without mentioning possible applicable national laws or Member States' discretion in regulating the research use of special categories of data. In this regard, the EDPS referred to the controller's responsibility in adopting appropriate additional safeguards, including providing as much transparency as possible.

19 Ibid.

20 Ibid., 28.

21 European Data Protection Supervisor, 'Preliminary Opinion on Data Protection and Scientific Research' 6 January 2020 <https://edps.europa.eu/sites/edp/files/publication/20-01-06_opinion_research_en.pdf> accessed 3 April 2023.

22 Ibid., 19.

The opinion of the EDPS, however, leaves unanswered the question whether open consent –in biobanking, for example – could be GDPR-compliant when additional safeguards are adopted (e.g., providing for full transparency, i.e., a complete overview of all research projects which are undertaken that include the participant's data, etc.).

4.2.3.4 European Data Protection Board on Consent to Data Processing for Research Purposes

4.2.3.4.1 THE 'PRESUMPTION OF COMPATIBILITY' AND ITS EFFECT ON THE QUESTION OF SPECIFICITY OF CONSENT

In 2019, the EDPB addressed questions raised by the European Commission regarding the interplay between the GDPR and the clinical trials regulation (CTR).[23] The positions taken by the EDPB regarding consent to data processing in clinical trials are very much debatable.[24] As objectionable as the overall stance of the EDPB regarding consent to data processing in clinical trials might be in that document, the EDPB did make references to an interesting point that is of immense practical relevance when it comes to the debate about the requirement of specificity of consent to data processing in scientific research: namely, in that opinion the EDPB referred to Recital 50 GDPR, which explains the exceptions to the 'purpose limitation' set out in Art. 5(1)(b) GDPR. The latter states that although generally personal data should only be processed for the purpose(s) for which the data was collected,

> and not further processed in a manner that is incompatible with those purposes; further processing for archiving purposes in the public interest, scientific or historical research purposes or statistical purposes shall, in accordance with Article 89(1), not be considered to be incompatible with the initial purposes.

Recital 50 GDPR explicitly states that in such cases, regarding further processing of data for, inter alia, research purpose(s), 'no legal basis separate from that which allowed the collection of the personal data is required'.

To put this in very simple terms, according to Art. 5(1)(b) GDPR as explained in Recital 50 GDPR, any personal data already collected for whichever purpose

23 European Data Protection Board, 'Opinion of the Board Art. 70.1.b. Opinion 3/2019 Concerning the Questions and Answers on the Interplay between the Clinical Trials Regulation (CTR) and the General Data Protection Regulation (GDPR) (Art. 70.1.b))', adopted on 23 January 2019 <https://edpb.europa.eu/our-work-tools/our-documents/opinion-art-70/opinion-32019-concerning-questions-and-answers_en> accessed 3 April 2023.

24 Kärt Pormeister, 'The Logical Fallacies of the Legal Bases for Data Processing in and Beyond Clinical Trials' (2022) 12 IDPL 2 <https://doi.org/10.1093/idpl/ipac003> accessed 3 April 2023, 132–142; David Peloquin and others, 'Disruptive and Avoidable: GDPR Challenges to Secondary Research Uses of Data' (2020) 28 *European Journal of Human Genetics* 697, 700.

can be further used for scientific research without the need for a new or separate legal basis. This would mean that, e.g., data obtained and processed in the course of research project A based on consent specifying as the processing purpose 'project A' can be further used in projects B–Z with no new or separate legal basis needed. This, of course, seems absurd from a common sense standpoint. This could make sense where the data was initially collected for purposes other than scientific research. However, if the data was initially collected for a specific research purpose(s) as specified in the consent forms, allowing for the reuse of the data for other research without renewed or separate consent would render the initial specific consent morally moot. If no legal basis is needed for the reuse of personal data in scientific research, then why would consent for the primary research use of data need to be specific and limited to only pre-determined specific research projects?

It is notable, then, that it was the EDPB which pointed to Recital 50 GDPR and explained in its opinion on the interplay between the GDPR and the CTR that if a sponsor of a clinical trial wishes to use the data obtained for the purposes of a specific trial outside of that protocol, the sponsor might not need a new legal basis. At the same time, the EDPB approached this with caution stating in reference to Recital 50 GDPR that,

> These conditions, due to their horizontal and complex nature, will require specific attention and guidance from the EDPB in the future. For the time being, the presumption of compatibility, subject to the conditions set forth in Article 89, should not be excluded, in all circumstances, for the secondary use of clinical trial data outside the clinical trial protocol for other scientific purposes.[25]

No such specific attention or guidance has been issued by the EDPB on this matter as of May 2023.

Thus, the question remains unanswered: if the GDPR seems to facilitate the reuse or secondary use of personal data for purposes of scientific research without the need for a new or separate legal basis, then what sense does it make to require the consent obtained for the primary research use of the data to be (project-) specific? If the data can be reused for another research purpose without a new legal basis – or when there is another legal basis alternative to renewed consent that would enable the secondary use of the data in research – would allowing for a broader initial consent not provide more transparency towards the data subject as opposed to specific consent, which creates the illusion that the use of the data will be limited to the specific research purpose(s) as set out prior to obtaining consent? The EDPB do not seem to concern itself or even acknowledge the existence of this dilemma, as it proceed in 2021 to comment on broad consent under the GDPR.

25 Opinion 3/2019 (n 23), 8.

4.2.3.4.2 GDPR-COMPLIANT CONSENT TO DATA PROCESSING FOR RESEARCH PURPOSES

Regarding GDPR-compliant consent to data processing for research purposes, the EDPB continued the path of its predecessor WP29 in viewing Recital 33 GDPR mostly through the lens of direct applicability of the GDPR. In its 2020 guidelines on consent, the EDPB reiterated word by word what the WP29 had stated in their 2018 guidelines regarding consent to data processing in scientific research.[26]

However, when the world faced the COVID-19 pandemic, the EDPB had to face direct and concrete questions from the European Commission about data protection requirements in health research, as the matter became acute and inescapably relevant in the context of the global pandemic. Unfortunately, the EDPB failed to deliver clear and adequate responses.

In its 2021 answers to questions raised by the Commission regarding the application of the GDPR in health research,[27] the EDPB commented on the notion of 'broad consent' to data processing, noting that this concept is foreign to the GDPR, though it could be used in reference to the flexibility referred to in Recital 33 GDPR.[28] Without using the term explicitly, the EDPB ruled out the compatibility of 'open consent' with the GDPR. The EDPB explained that GDPR-compliant consent cannot be given to 'any kind of – unspecified – future research purposes',[29] thereby excluding the possibility of what is often referred to as 'open consent' (as will be illustrated based on the Estonian example in the second part of this chapter).

Concerning the limits to the breadth of GDPR-compliant consent, the EDPB explained that 'the concept of broad consent could be relied on for different research projects that fall within the scope of that broad consent and that meet certain additional safeguards'.[30] One could label this approach as an 'umbrella consent' – i.e., a broader consent that covers a multitude of pre-defined different research projects, but is not open-ended.

The EDPB thereby made it clear that open consent is not compatible with the GDPR, but broad consent could be. The necessity of this differentiation comes into question when one thinks back at the EDPB's references to Recital 50 GDPR and the 'presumption of compatibility' that seem to allow for the secondary research use of personal data without the need for a further or separate legal basis. Furthermore, the explanations offered by the EDPB regarding broad consent under the GDPR evoke at least two follow-up questions, which the EDPB failed to adequately answer. First, the perfectly clear question raised by the Commission about

26 European Data Protection Board, 'Guidelines 05/2020 on Consent under Regulation 2016/679', version 1.1, adopted 4 May 2020, 30–32.
27 European Data Protection Board, 'EDPB Documents. EDPB Document on response to the request from the European Commission for clarifications on the consistent application of the GDPR, focusing on health research', adopted on 2 February 2021.
28 Ibid., 7, para 25.
29 Ibid., 9, para 31.
30 Ibid.

what then is or is not GDPR-compliant specific consent in the context of scientific research. The Commission asked the following.

> Q12. Recital 33 GDPR provides that consent may be given to 'certain areas' of scientific research. What should the formulation of these 'certain areas' look like in the course of obtaining a participants/data subjects consent, in particular as concerns future research projects which cannot be determined at the point of collection of the data (e.g., consent for 'cancer research' or consent for 'breast cancer research').[31]

The question raised by the Commission is exactly one which researchers operating under the GDPR must ask themselves daily – data collection is a costly process and secondary use of data, a question so very crucial for any research institution and the research community at large. Unfortunately, the EDPB failed to provide an answer to this question, and instead referred to the general principles of data processing under Art. 5 GDPR (lawfulness, fairness, transparency). By doing so, the EDPB emphasised that, 'It is therefore imperative that the research areas are narrowed down, there is an obvious link to the context in which the personal data are collected and reasonable expectations of the data subjects are taken into account'.[32]

It is very regrettable that the EDPB purposefully neglected to address the examples brought by the Commission at the end of the question, i.e., whether 'cancer research' or 'breast cancer research' could be specific enough as purposes to obtain GDPR-compliant consent to data processing for research purposes.

Concerning this specific question raised by the Commission, the EDPB went on to refer to potential national legislation. On a positive note, the EDPB this time around at least acknowledged the discretion that Member States have under the GDPR in regulating the research use of special categories of personal data. This also presents the second follow-up question stemming from the EDPB negating the possibility of open consent under the GDPR: could Member States allow for open consent for the research use of personal data under national law? Unfortunately, instead of providing clear guidance on this, the EDPB made a very peculiar reference to Art. 9(4) instead of Art. 9(2)(j) GDPR. Namely, the EDPB stated:

> It will also be necessary to take into account any provisions in MS law as allowed for in Article 9(4) GDPR containing further conditions pertaining to processing of health data, since those provisions in MS law could also impact (enable, facilitate or impede) the usability of 'broad consent' in that MS.[33]

The reference is peculiar, because Art. 9(4) GDPR was originally not meant for 'enabling' or 'facilitating' the use of genetic data, biometric data or data concerning health. In fact, Art. 9(4) GDPR literally states that under this clause 'Member

31 Ibid., 8.
32 Ibid., 8–9.
33 Ibid., 9, para 30.

States may maintain or introduce *further conditions, including limitations*' (emphasis added). There is absolutely no mention of 'facilitating' or 'enabling' the use of these three categories of data. Art. 9(4) GDPR was clearly meant to allow Member States to maintain stricter rules in comparison to the GDPR, as opposed to allow for more lenient ways for the processing of these three special categories of data.[34] This conclusion is further validated by the explanatory warning in Recital 53 GDPR, which emphasises that the discretion afforded to Member States in Art. 9(4) GDPR 'should not hamper the free flow of personal data within the Union when those conditions apply to cross-border processing of such data'.

Thus, the EDPB's reference to Art. 9(4) GDPR is truly nonsensical when it comes to facilitating a broader or possibly even open consent in the context of research use of special categories of personal data. The EDPB should have instead referenced Art. 9(2)(j) GDPR, which gives Member States discretion to regulate the research use of special categories of personal data in national laws, keeping in line with the principles set out in Art. 89(1) GDPR.

Notwithstanding the EDPB's erroneous reference to Art. 9(4) GDPR, the core point of the provided quotation illustrates that according to the EDPB, it seems possible that Member States may have the right to 'facilitate' or 'enable' the use of 'broad consent' to data processing for research purposes in their national laws. However, this raises the question: how broad? Did the EDPB mean an even broader consent than that referred to in Recital 33 GDPR and as interpreted by the EDPB (i.e., an umbrella consent)? Or did the EDPB mean that Member States could adopt national regulations allowing for the same type of broad consent as Recital 33 GDPR? In the latter case, why would that even be necessary if the EDPB seems to allow for Recital 33 GDPR to be used as an interpretive tool in the direct application of the GDPR? To remind the reader here, within its question, the Commission brought the examples of 'cancer research' and 'breast cancer research', asking whether such purpose statements would be GDPR-compliant. These clearly would be 'open-ended' consents if the processing purposes were stated as broadly, and the

34 For example, although Fruzsina Molnár-Gábor and others refer to Art. 9(4) GDPR as providing Member States with 'full flexibility to deviate from the GDPR standard and create own rules', they also note that this flexibility is meant for 'imposing additional or stricter requirements' to 'strengthen the protection provided by the GDPR'. Fruzsina Molnár-Gábor and others, 'Harmonization after the GDPR? Divergences in the Rules for Genetic and Health Data Sharing in Four Member States and Ways to Overcome Them by EU Measures: Insights from Germany, Greece, Latvia and Sweden' (2022) 84 *Seminars in Cancer Biology* <https://doi.org/10.1016/j.semcancer.2021.12.001> accessed 17 August 2023. See also Gerald Spindler and Lukas Dalby, 'DS-GVO Art. 9' in Gerald Spindler and Fabian Schuster (eds), *Recht der Elektronischen Medien* (C.H. Beck oHG 2019) Art. 9(4), para 27.

One German commentary on the GDPR refers to a source that allegedly affirms the possibility of Art. 9(4) including the discretion for Member States to further broaden possibilities for the processing of health, genetic and biometric data; however, the author of this chapter was unable to access the referred source. The reference can be found in 'DS-GVO Art. 9 Verarbeitung besonderer Kategorien personenbezogener Daten' in Heinrich Amadeus Wolff, Stefan Brink and Antje v. Ungern-Sternberg (eds), *BeckOK Datenschutzrecht, DS-GVO, BDSG, Grundlagen, Bereichsspezifischer Datenschutz* (C.H. Beck München 2023) Art. 9(4), para 110.

EDPB's answer to this specific question leaves room for an assumption that open consent could be GDPR-compliant if national legislation were to facilitate it, since the EDPB did not outright negate the possibility of such purpose statements (i.e., 'cancer research' or 'breast cancer research').

Unfortunately, the EDPB utterly failed to provide a systematic approach to consent to data processing in research under the GDPR. In general, the EDPB averted giving clear answers to many specific questions raised by the Commission, instead making references to its planned future guidelines on processing personal data for scientific research purposes that were under preparation at the time and were supposed to be due in 2021.[35] As of April 2023, no such guidelines had been published by the EDPB. One can hope that these guidelines will create more clarity and provide a more systematic and comprehensive approach than the EDPB's publications so far.

4.2.4 Data Protection vs. Other EU Law

The breadth of consent in the research context is first and foremost a question of the possibilities for the secondary use of data obtained for specific research projects. The narrower the consent, the narrower the possibilities for the primary research use of the data, and thus the more prevalent the question of possible legal bases for secondary uses – that is, if one were to ignore Recital 50 and Art. 5(1)(b) GDPR, establishing 'the presumption of compatibility', and the notion that secondary uses of data for research purposes do not seem to require a new legal basis under the GDPR. Based on the EDPB's comments cited previously in this chapter on this subject, the 'presumption of compatibility' regarding the secondary use of personal data for research purposes remains an unknown dimension for now.

However, as it pertains to the secondary use of personal data for research purposes, in addition to the GDPR, there are at least three other EU legal acts that (might) affect the (re)use of personal data for research purposes: (1) the CTR; (2) the Data Governance Act (DGA); and (3) the proposal for the European Health Data Space regulation (EHDS).[36]

Regarding the CTR, the EDPB does not agree with the assertion that the CTR contains any clauses on consent to data processing. The author of this chapter disagrees with the EDPB's stance on the use of consent to data processing in clinical trials.[37] In its 2021 answers to the questions raised by the Commission regarding the GDPR and health research,[38] the EDPB repeated their stances expressed in their 2019 opinion on the interplay between the GDPR and the CTR, by stating that:

> for data protection purposes, consent is not an appropriate legal basis in research activities where there is a clear imbalance of power between the data

35 EDPB 2021 (n 27), See Q4–6, Q9–11, Q13–17, Q21.

36 European Commission, 'Proposal for a Regulation of the European Parliament and of the Council on the European Health Data Space', *Strasbourg*, 3.5.2022, COM(2022) 197 final, 2022/0140(COD).

37 Pormeister (n 24).

38 EDPB 2021 (n 27), 4–5.

> subject and the controller. It is acknowledged that in clinical trials such an imbalance may exist depending on the circumstances, for instance, when the data subject is not in a good health condition and there is no available therapeutic treatment outside the clinical trial.[39]

First, as previously argued by the author, the EDPB fails to acknowledge the fact that an imbalance of power would render participation in the clinical trial impossible in the first place. This means that if a participant is deemed suitable to partake in a clinical trial, there can be no imbalance of power, and thus consent can be an appropriate legal basis for the processing of personal data in the trial.[40] Second, and more to the point of this chapter, the EDPB has failed to recognise that Art. 28(2) CTR was drafted with the particular aim of allowing for secondary research uses of data obtained for the purposes of a clinical trial by obtaining essentially 'open consent' for the further research uses of the data (See Recital 29 CTR). The author will not repeat her previous work that thoroughly addresses the issue,[41] but it is important to keep in mind that Art. 28(2) CTR presents an example of EU law that at least seems to allow for essentially open consent to be obtained from trial participants for the secondary research uses of their personal data initially obtained for the purposes of a specific clinical trial. The EDPB might argue otherwise, but grammatic and systematic interpretations of the CTR and GDPR allow for this conclusion. Even more so, the EDPB themselves referenced Recital 50 GDPR in their opinion on the interplay of the GDPR and the CTR, noting that the possible secondary use of such data might not even require a new legal basis (hence rendering the discussion of the meaning of consent under Art. 28(2) CTR possibly moot in practice). If secondary research uses of personal data might not even require an independent or new legal basis, then it remains questionable why the EDPB would argue against the concept of open consent to data processing in research. Whether open consent is the most feasible legal basis for data processing in research, is a matter to be determined by the data controller, i.e., the researcher.

Whilst the WP29 was and the EDPB is trying to limit the breadth of GDPR-compliant consent to data processing in research – and thereby the practical means to (re)use data based on the initial consent in research projects other than those foreseen at the time of the collection of the data – other forces within the EU have been working towards the opposite goal.

In 2022, the DGA[42] was adopted. The DGA introduced the concept of 'data altruism', the aim of which is to facilitate means for individuals to give consent for the reuse of their data for, inter alia, purposes of research. Based on Art. 25 DGA,

39 Opinion 3/2019 (n 23), 6.

40 Pormeister (n 24), 135.

41 Ibid.

42 Regulation (EU) 2022/868 of the Parliament and of the Council of 30 May 2022 on European data governance and amending Regulation (EU) 2018/1724 (Data Governance Act), OJ L152/1.

the European Commission will adopt a common 'European data altruism consent form'. As such, the DGA aims to bring about the facilitation of consent as a legal basis for the secondary uses of personal data (including in research). At the same time, the proposal for European Health Data Space (EHDS) regulation has taken the opposite direction: to forego the need for consent, and to provide for an alternative legal basis for the processing of health data for again, inter alia, research purposes.

Whilst the DGA is built on the premise of 'altruistic consent' for the reuse of data, the proposal for a regulation establishing the EHDS was built on the opposite premise: reuse of data without consent.[43] The aim of the EHDS is, inter alia, to make sure that 'researchers, innovators, policy makers and regulators would be able to have access to quality data for their work in a secure way, with a trusted governance and at lower costs than relying on consent'.[44] In essence, the EHDS aims to provide for a legal basis for the reuse of health data alternative to consent. This is a clear exercise of the discretion afforded to EU legislators in Art. 9(2)(j) GDPR, though the proposal itself includes references to Arts. 9(2)(g)–(j) GDPR.[45]

Regardless of the approach taken, both the DGA and EHDS aim to facilitate the secondary use of personal data for research purposes. The efforts of EU legislators to create legal pathways for the secondary use of personal data must be considered when discussing the possible legal bases for establishing and maintaining biobanks. If personal data obtained for whichever purposes can be reused for (other) research purposes without renewed or additional consent, presuming there are additional safeguards in place (e.g., such as those providing for transparency etc.), then it is difficult to comprehend why 'open consent' to data processing in research could not be considered GDPR-compliant (if, for example, such consent were to be regulated in national law based on the discretion afforded to Member States in Art. 9[2][j] GDPR).

Whilst the EDPB engaged in mental gymnastics trying to fit 'broad consent' into the realm of the GDPR, and ended up with the limits being drawn at what could be called 'umbrella consent', EU legislators are striving to make sure (health) data can be reused for, inter alia, scientific research purposes regardless of the initial legal basis or purpose limitations stemming from the original legal basis for data processing.

4.2.5 Critical Concluding Remarks on the EDPB's Approach to GDPR-compliant Consent to Data Processing in Research

As noted in this chapter, the EDPB seems to be of the opinion that GDPR-compliant consent to data processing in research, even in the light of Recital 33 GDPR, could

43 European Commission, 'Proposal for a Regulation of the European Parliament and of the Council on the European Health Data Space', Strasbourg, 3.5.2022, COM(2022) 197 final, 2022/0140(COD).

44 Ibid., 13.

45 Ibid., Recital 37.

not be stretched beyond one consent to data processing being given for 'different research projects that fall within the scope of that broad consent'.[46] The EDPB's exact vision remains unclear, as it also noted that 'Recital 33 GDPR requires that the scope of the research purposes for which the health data will be used is narrowed down (e.g., by areas and types of research questions)'.[47] As previously remarked, the Commission specifically asked the EDPB whether 'cancer research' or 'breast cancer research' as purpose definitions would suffice for this end, and the EDPB failed to give an answer to this question. The EDPB did, however, clearly state that consent to data processing in research cannot be given for unspecified future research projects. Thereby, the EDPB seems to think that exact research projects need to be known, defined and communicated to the individual before or at the time of obtaining consent.

With the EDPB's clear refusal to acknowledge the possibility of open consent to data processing in research under the GDPR, and based on their project-based approach to broad consent, Recital 33 GDPR is effectively stripped of any meaning. Namely, a 'broad consent' as defined by the EDPB (i.e., one covering a multitude of *pre*-defined research projects) could be compliantly drafted under the general rules of consent in Arts. 6(1)(a) and 9(2)(a) GDPR. There would be no need for the existence of Recital 33 GDPR. The general requirement of specificity allows for multiple specific purposes to be listed in one consent form (though, in that case, a separate choice must be given for all different purposes). Thus, if the research projects in which the data is to be processed must be known and communicated prior to obtaining consent, then this is just a regular case of obtaining consent to data processing for more than one specific purpose under the general rules of consent in the GDPR.

Regarding it all in the light of the efforts made by EU legislators with the DGA and the EHDS proposal, the stance of the EDPB on consent to data processing in research seems fruitless, and one might even say counter-productive. If personal data obtained based on specific consent can be reused for further (research) purposes regardless of the limits of the initial consent, it seems rationally pointless and morally questionable to limit the possible breadth of the initial consent.

4.3 The Estonian Example of Open Consent in Biobank Research

4.3.1 Open Consent of the EBB

Since 2002, individuals have been able to join the EBB as 'gene donors' based on an open consent. The EBB consent is qualified by the author as an open consent based on the scarce legal literature available in Estonia concerning EBB consent,[48]

46 EDPB 2021 (n 27), 9, para 31.

47 Ibid.

48 Ants Nõmper, 'Open Consent – A New Form of Informed Consent for Population Genetic Databases' (Dissertation for Obtaining the Degree of Doctor Iuris, University of Tartu 2005).

and derived from the EDPB's definition of 'broad consent' as *not* including 'any kind of – unspecified – future research purposes' – thus meaning that the latter definition could be used for 'open consent' instead. Hence, 'open consent' will be used as referring to consent to data processing for unspecified future research purposes in an area of research, which can be defined as broadly as 'genetic research'.

The open consent of the EBB is established and authorised by the Human Genes Research Act (HGRA), which sets out in § 12(1) that:

> A person's consent to provide a tissue sample, to have a description of the state of health or the genealogy of the person prepared, to entry of the description of the state of health or the genealogy in the Gene Bank in pseudonymised form and to use thereof for genetic research, assessment of personal health risks and prevention of diseases, public health research and statistical purposes shall be prepared in writing and shall be signed by the person who becomes a gene donor.[49]

The consent form is established by a ministerial regulation, as authorised by the HGRA.[50] The EBB consent form has been revised three times (totalling four different redactions) throughout the years but has remained much the same since first being adopted in 2001. The consent was meant to cover both the obtaining and use of biosamples (i.e., the blood sample collected upon joining the EBB), and the processing of personal data for, inter alia, genetic research purposes. The list of elements covered by the consent, as presented to the gene donor at the end of the consent form, has in all versions of the consent form included the use of personal data for purposes of genetic research,[51] public health research and statistical purposes.[52]

As such, the research purposes for which the personal data of EBB donors can be used are essentially unlimited. The consent enables 'any kind of – unspecified – future

49 § 12(1) HGRA (n 3).

50 Ibid., § 12(7).

51 The HGRA uses the phrase 'scientific research' in establishing the legitimate aims for which the EBB may be utilised, whereas the consent form has in all redactions used the phrase 'genetic research' instead. The HGRA uses 'genetic research' in most parts, but in § 16(1), which sets out the purposes for which the EBB can be used, the HGRA has since its first redaction in 2002 used the phrase 'scientific research'. This should not be seen as a purposeful or as a significant deviation, as the EBB was established for purposes of genetic research, and the line between 'scientific research' and 'genetic research' can be simply drawn at whether analysis of genetic data is part of a research project. If genetic data is not included in a project, then the relevant health data should be sought from the national health-related databases instead of the EBB (as the EBB also derives most of the personal data from national databases, though some is obtained from gene donors directly via health questionnaires).

52 The EBB consent form is established by a ministerial regulation and is only available in Estonian. The consent form in effect from 2002–2007, 2007–2010 and 2010–2019 was established by a regulation of the Minister of Social Affairs (regulation no. 125 adopted 17 December 2015) and revised twice. The forth redaction of the consent form in effect from 2019 was adopted by a regulation of the Minister of Health and Labour (regulation no. 39 adopted 11 April 2019). Both the HGRA and the consent form are currently under revision.

research purposes', which has been deemed non-GDPR-compliant by the EDPB in their 2021 answers to the European Commission regarding the GDPR and health research.[53]

The open consent used by the EBB was deemed compliant with the 1995 Directive on data protection by Estonian health law experts at the time the consent was first drafted. A. Nõmper noted in his 2005 doctoral thesis, that '[i]t is therefore also possible under Directive 95/46/EC to obtain open consent, and one need not rely on consent alternatives'.[54] He concluded that '[t]hus, Directive 95/46/EC neither limits specific consent to one research protocol nor prohibits open-ended studies'.[55] By this logic, the open consent legalised by the HGRA and set out in relevant ministerial regulations was deemed compatible with EU data protection law at the time.

Though the HGRA was cosmetically altered[56] in 2019 following the application date of the GDPR, the question of open consent under the GDPR was addressed only in a miniscule part. Though the consent form remained much the same, two things were altered in the ministerial regulation establishing the EBB consent form in 2019 post-GDPR.

Prior to 2019, the consent automatically included the EBB's right to obtain health and certain general data of the gene donor from national databases. Though this was only mentioned in all redactions of the consent form with a single sentence stating that the data controller of the EBB may obtain personal data of a gene donor from 'other databases'. In reality, 'other databases' meant obtaining data from a total of nine(!) national state-run databases and two major hospitals. The gene donors have always had a right to opt out of this and to prohibit the EBB from collecting additional data about them.[57] The fact that one single general sentence in the consent form enabled the EBB to collect data from a multitude of sources, of course, is quite controversial in the light of modern data protection law. To somewhat remedy this situation, the consent form was altered in 2019 to include an option for future gene donors to choose already upon joining the EBB whether to give consent to such data collection or not. However, this new option in the EBB consent form was also very vague and general in its wording, and did not mention any specific sources, or the number of possible databases. Instead, by its wording, it gave the donor the option to allow the EBB to 'supplement, renew and to verify the health data of the gene donor'. This option included a reference to the gene donors' opt out right from this type of data collection but failed to mention any sources from which the data might be obtained (i.e., it did not even mentioned state databases in general).

53 EDPB 2021 (n 27), 9, para 31.
54 Nõmper (n 48), 79.
55 Ibid., 175.
56 These cosmetical changes included, e.g., substituting the 'code' and 'decode' with 'pseudonymise' and 'depseudonymised' to keep in line with the terminology of the GDPR.
57 § 11(6) HGRA (n 3).

Objectively, the described change in the EBB consent form in 2019 did not make anything better – the consent could still not hold up to scrutiny based on the interpretations given to broad consent under the GDPR by the EDPB.

4.3.2 Consent vs. National Law as the Legal Basis for Processing EBB Data

Representatives of state institutions and other informed parties have argued through informal communications that the data processing of the EBB does, in fact, not rely on consent to data processing, but instead relies on the HGRA as the legal basis. According to their arguments, the EBB's consent is to be seen 'only' as consent to human subject research within the meaning of the Oviedo convention,[58] i.e., an additional safeguard from the perspective of data protection (such as the consent to participation in clinical trials is to be seen as an additional safeguard according to the EDPB – though this is very arguable, as the consent to participate is meant not as an 'additional safeguard' for data protection but rather as the primary safeguard for respecting bodily autonomy).

However, that has clearly not been the legislature's intent – as will be shown in what follows, the legislature's intent has been for the EBB consent to serve as both: (1) consent to participation in human subject research; and (2) consent to data processing in genetic research (i.e., open consent to data processing for purposes of genetic research).

As noted in the previous subsection, the scarce legal literature available about the EBB clearly considered the EBB's consent to be consent to data processing within the meaning of the 1995 Directive on data protection.[59] The fact that this was and remained the legislature's intent was evidenced in 2007 when the HGRA underwent a major change with the EBB being transitioned from being a non-profit foundation to being a part of the University of Tartu. In the explanatory note to the law establishing these changes in the HGRA, it is expressly and clearly stated that:

> All of the data processing in the [Estonian] biobank, including the correcting[60] of the data in the biobank, is based on the donor's consent. . . . the gene donors gave their consent to data processing.[61]

58 Convention for the protection of Human Rights and Dignity of the Human Being with regard to the Application of Biology and Medicine: Convention on Human Rights and Biomedicine, Oviedo, 4.IV.1997, ETS No. 164.

59 Nõmper (n 48).

60 The original uses the exact term *'paranduste tegemine'* which translates to 'making corrections', but what was meant here was the obtaining of data from external sources to essentially double-check the health data provided by gene donors via questionnaires. Thus, in essence, it addresses the fact that obtaining data from external sources like national databases and hospitals is based on the donor's consent, which includes consent to data processing.

61 Explanatory note to the 2006 draft law "The law for changing the Human Genes Research Act and the Estonian Academy of Sciences Act 1056 SE" which was adopted in 2007 and came into force on 1 April 2007. The draft law and its explanatory note are availabe in Estonian at <www.riigikogu.ee/tegevus/

Thus, legislators clearly considered the EBB's consent to serve both as consent to participation in human subject research (i.e., primarily for obtaining the blood sample from which the genetic data could be derived) and as consent to data processing (i.e., for the use of the genetic and other personal data in unspecified future genetic research).

It is unclear whether the EDPB's 2021 positions on broad consent under GDPR would entirely preclude open consent being established in national law, as has been the case with the HGRA and the EBB's consent. As acknowledged previously, the EDPB did leave the door slightly open by explaining that:

> [i]t will also be necessary to take into account any provisions in MS law . . . containing further conditions pertaining to processing of health data, since those provisions in MS law could also impact (enable, facilitate or impede) the usability of 'broad consent' in that MS.[62]

4.3.3 Possible Changes in the Legal Basis for the Processing of EBB Data

The HGRA is currently undergoing a reform, part of which is to shift the legal basis of data processing from consent to the HGRA, and to make this clear in both the HGRA and the consent form, which would then remain in place as serving solely as consent to participation in human subject research but no longer consent to data processing. This change has been initiated for a multitude of reasons. One is to prevent possible non-compliance with the GDPR as the Estonian Data Protection Inspectorate has expressed strong criticism of the EBB's consent in informal communications.

Data protection specialists might wonder whether a change in the legal basis for processing is even possible, seen that the EDPB has emphasised that the legal basis for data processing cannot be changed and must be set out prior to the start of the processing, by stating that '[t]he legal basis must be identified at the outset of processing, and information given to data subjects in line with Article 13 and 14 must specify the legal basis'.[63]

However, this would not be a precedent for the Estonian legislator to undertake a change that theoretically should not be possible under data protection law. As previously noted, originally, the EBB was established as a non-profit foundation, which legally acted as the data controller. Due to funding issues, the foundation was dissolved in 2007 and the EBB was incorporated with the University of Tartu, being operated under its Institute of Genomics. This meant that there was a change in the position of data controller. The Data Protection

---

eelnoud/eelnou/339737c4-d255-36ea-9668-b85d87e465e6/Inimgeeniuuringute%20seaduse%20ja%20 Eesti%20Teaduste%20Akadeemia%20seaduse%20muutmise%20seadus> accessed 5 April 2023.

62 EDPB 2021 (n 27), 9, para 30.

63 European Data Protection Board, 'Guidelines. Guidelines 2/2019 on the processing of personal data under Article 6(1)(b) GDPR in the context of the provision of online services to data subjects', Version 2.0, 8 October 2019, 7, para 17.

Inspectorate protested this change, arguing that a change in the data controller would presume obtaining new consent from all gene donors.[64] The legislator recognised that this was not a feasible option and chose to implement the change of the data controller via legislative changes in the HGRA and provided the following justifications and safeguards for *not* requiring a new consent to be obtained from all gene donors:

> For the comprehensive protection of the interests of the gene donors the donors and the public will be notified of the change of the data controller, including being informed of the fact that all gene donors have the right to withdraw their consent to data processing and demand the destruction of their [bio]samples. In addition to the right afforded to gene donors in § 10(1) [of the HGRA] to demand for the decoding information to be destroyed at any time per § 21 [of the HGRA], they have the possibility until 1 July 2008 to demand for their [bio]sample, DNA and health data to be destroyed. Thus, donors are guaranteed, in case they object to their data being processed by [the University of Tartu], the right to demand all of the material pertaining to them to be destroyed and thereby to regain a so-called blank page status. . . .
>
> We concede that the gene donors gave their consent to data processing in circumstances in which the data controller was the [non-profit foundation] EBB and thus, although [the University of Tartu] is at least as trustworthy (and subject to supervision by the state) as the [non-profit foundation] EBB, not all gene donors might agree to the processing of their data in the changed circumstances, i.e., where the data controller is [the University of Tartu]. We emphasise once again that for such cases the gene donors' interests, meaning their expectation that their samples [and data] are being processed by the [non-profit foundation] EBB, are protected by them being notified of the change in the data controller, and by them having the right to withdraw their consent and to demand their samples to be destroyed. . . .
>
> In creating a regulation, which would help fill the gap in the current HGRA in regard to the current data controller ceasing to exist, in addition to protecting the individual's legitimate expectation that the data controller is the [non-profit foundation] EBB, the individual's legitimate expectation of their [bio]sample being part of the gene project has to be protected as well. Due to the fact that the [non-profit foundation] EBB is being liquidated, it is not possible to protect the first legitimate interest. It is, however, possible to ensure that the change in the data controller would not bring about a double breach of the legitimate interests of the individuals. It is possible to ensure that people, who have decided to become donors and have done so in an informed and deliberated manner,

64 Appendix to the explanatory note to the 2006 draft law (n 61).

> can continue being part of the project. Their [bio]samples will not be excluded from the project for the sole reason that there is a change in the data controller.[65]

The same rationale can be applied for changing the legal basis for processing the data of gene donors of the EBB, as this is necessitated by the alleged argument that the current consent form is not GDPR-compliant. If the open consent for data processing used by the EBB so far is no longer in compliance with modern data protection law, then the only way for the EBB to continue existing as a population-based biobank is for its processing to be based on law. The same safeguards can be afforded to gene donors when changing the legal basis for processing as was done when there was a change in the data controller.

Of course, regardless of the legal basis of processing – whether it be open consent or the law – the main concern vis-à-vis gene donors as data subjects should be ensuring transparency.[66]

4.3.4 Regulatory Gaps for Biobanking in Estonia

Though the previously presented solution of relying on the law as a legal basis for data processing instead of consent is a practical solution for the EBB, as it already has its own specific law regulating most aspects of its processing activities (HGRA), this will not be a viable option for other biobanks. Thus, the question of consent to data processing in research remains one of immense practical importance and is in desperate need of clarifications by the EDPB.

The EBB is not the only biobank in Estonia, but the rest remain largely unregulated. Most notably, healthcare service providers – particularly the largest hospitals – collect and preserve biological material and data of patients for (re)use in research. The applicable regulatory framework for biobanks other than the EBB in Estonia is fragmented and can be largely divided into two major parts: (1) human subject research regulations; and (2) data protection law.

Estonia has no national laws on human subject research in general. There is a clause in the Constitution establishing that no-one shall be subjected to medical or scientific research against their free will.[67] Estonia has also ratified the Oviedo convention regulating human rights in biomedicine.[68] Although generally international law like the Oviedo convention should take effect via national regulations, in terms of human subject research the Estonian legislature has failed to implement the Oviedo convention into national law. Based on case law of the Estonian Supreme

65 Explanatory note to the 2006 draft law (n 61).

66 Pormeister (n 6).

67 § 18 of the Constitution of the Republic of Estonia, RT I, 15.05.2015, 2. Available in English at <www.riigiteataja.ee/en/eli/530122020003/consolide> accessed 30 May 2023.

68 Chart of signatures and ratifications of Treaty 164 available at <www.coe.int/en/web/conventions/full-list?module=signatures-by-treaty&treatynum=164> accessed 30 May 2023.

Court, certain rules within the Oviedo convention could be directly applicable.[69] Hence, there is no comprehensive legal regime in Estonia either for research in general or for biobanks specifically.

National data protection law does enable the use of personal data for research purposes without consent; however, these rules are built on a project-specific basis.[70] This means, that they would not suffice for, e.g., long-term storage of data (and biosamples) for the establishment and maintaining of a biobank.

The EDPB's refusal to acknowledge the possibility of open consent to data processing in research, and its insistence on narrowing the concept of GDPR-compliant 'broad consent' to one covering only multiple pre-defined research projects, is effectively creating a scenario whereby healthcare facilities and researchers cannot use consent as a legal basis to data processing in order to establish and maintain biobanks. Without national law to compensate for this gaping hole under the GDPR regime, biobanks in Estonia other than the population-based EBB (that will hopefully be able to continue processing personal data based on the legal act regulating its activities, i.e., the HGRA) would essentially be forced out of existence.

4.4 Concluding Remarks

Without national laws specifically establishing a legal regime for the operation and data processing of biobanks, the only legal basis for data processing under the GDPR that biobanks could rely on would be consent. Generally, consent can only be given for one or more specific purpose(s). However, it is recognised in the recitals of the GDPR that it is not always possible in research to pre-determine exact research projects at the time of the collection of the data. This is particularly pertinent in the case of biobanks, the purpose of which is to collect biosamples and data to facilitate various research projects on a broader scale, as opposed to collecting data for singular or multiple pre-defined research projects. The very point of the existence of a biobank is to serve as a central repository to facilitate essentially unlimited future research projects that cannot be pre-defined at the time of the collection of tissue and data.

Thus, the exception to the requirement of specificity of consent referred to in Recital 33 GDPR is of particular importance to biobanks. Unfortunately, however, none of the authoritative bodies regarding data protection law and the GDPR have given Recital 33 GDPR substantive, systematic and comprehensive meaning. Even when faced with a direct and clear question by the European Commission on whether 'cancer research' or 'breast cancer research' could be stated as processing purposes in a GDPR-compliant consent to data processing, the EDPB failed to provide answers. Instead, the EDPB gave mixed messages. On the one hand, it ruled out the possibility that consent 'for processing health data for "any kind of – unspecified – future research purposes"' (i.e., open consent) could be compliant with the GDPR. On the other hand, when faced with the described direct question from the Commission with

69 20 December 2002 judgement no 3–3–1–58–02 of the Supreme Court of Estonia, 11.

70 § 6 of the Estonian Data Protection Act, RT I, 04.01.2019, 11. Available in English at <www.riigiteataja.ee/en/eli/523012019001/consolide> accessed 31 May 2023.

clear examples, the EDPB referenced the possibility that national laws could affect the question of the legality of broad(er) consent. The EDPB thereby seemed to leave the door open to 'broader consent' in national laws, as compared to the EDPB's own take on consent in light of Recital 33 GDPR. At the same time, the EDPB failed to recognise that its 'one-size-fits-all' approach to consent to data processing under the GDPR is not feasible when it comes to biobanks. Given the prominent and essential role of biobanks in the current era of personalised medicine,[71] it would seem only natural that the governing legal regimes and authoritative bodies in the EU would pay particular attention to this specific area of data processing.

Furthermore, the irony of this discussion lies in the fact that regardless of how specific the initial consent is, there are ways of reusing the same data for (other) research purposes. A theoretical possibility in the form of the 'presumption of compatibility' is even directly built into the GDPR, though this remains for now an unknown and unclear dimension of possibility. Additionally, EU legislators are making efforts to ensure the possibility of secondary use of data in research. Hence, it remains unclear why an individual should not be able to give open consent for their data to be processed in research, e.g., by a biobank – presuming, of course, that appropriate safeguards are in place, including those ensuring that the actual uses of the data are transparent to the individual. This can be attained, e.g., via a dedicated secure website with a user interface providing detailed information on the exact research projects in which the data is being used.

Bibliography

Article 29 Working Party, 'Guidelines on Consent under Regulation 2016/679', adopted 28 November 2017, 17/EN WP 259. As of writing this chapter, the author was unable to find a working weblink for the initial 2017 version of this opinion

Article 29 Working Party, 'Guidelines on Consent under Regulation 2016/679', adopted on 28 November 2017. As last revised and adopted 10 April 2018, 17/EN WP 259 rev.01 <https://ec.europa.eu/newsroom/article29/items/623051/en> accessed 3 April 2023

Baratta R, 'Complexity of EU Law in the Domestic Implementing Process' (19th Quality of Legislation Seminar 'EU Legislative Drafting: Views from Those Applying EU Law in the Member States', 3 July 2014) <https://ec.europa.eu/dgs/legal_service/seminars/20140703_baratta_speech.pdf> accessed 3 April 2023

Casali PG and on behalf of the European Society for Medical Oncology (ESMO) Switzerland, 'Risks of the New EU Data Protection Regulation: An ESMO Position Paper Endorsed by the European Oncology Community' (2014) 25(8) *Annals of Oncology* 1458

Committee on Civil Liberties, Justice and Home Affairs, 'Amendment 191, Proposal for a Regulation, Article 81'. Report on the Proposal for a Regulation of the European Parliament and of the Council on the Protection of Individuals with Regard to the Processing of Personal Data and on the Free Movement of Such Data (General Data Protection Regulation) (COM (2012)0011 – C7-0025/2012-2012/0011(COD)) (22 November 2013) <www.europarl.europa.eu/doceo/document/A-7-2013-0402_EN.html?redirect> accessed 14 March 2023

71 Judita Kinkorová and Ondřej Topolčan, 'Biobanks in the Era of Big Data: Objectives, Challenges, Perspectives, and Innovations for Predictive, Preventive, and Personalised Medicine' (2020) 11(3) EPMA J <www.ncbi.nlm.nih.gov/pmc/articles/PMC7429593/> accessed 24 August 2023.

European Commission, 'Proposal for a Regulation of the European Parliament and of the Council on the European Health Data Space', Strasbourg, 3.5.2022, COM (2022) 197 final, 2022/0140(COD) <https://eur-lex.europa.eu/legal-content/EN/TXT/?uri=CELEX%3A52022PC0197> accessed 4 April 2023

European Data Protection Board, 'EDPB Documents: EDPB Document on Response to the Request from the European Commission for Clarifications on the Consistent Application of the GDPR, Focusing on Health Research', adopted on 2 February 2021

European Data Protection Board, 'Guidelines 05/2020 on Consent under Regulation 2016/679', Version 1.1, adopted 4 May 2020 <https://edpb.europa.eu/sites/default/files/files/file1/edpb_guidelines_202005_consent_en.pdf> accessed 3 April 2023

European Data Protection Board, 'Guidelines: Guidelines 2/2019 on the Processing of Personal Data under Article 6(1)(b) GDPR in the Context of the Provision of Online Services to Data Subjects' (*Version 2.0*, 8 October 2019) <https://edpb.europa.eu/sites/default/files/files/file1/edpb_guidelines-art_6-1-b-adopted_after_public_consultation_en.pdf> accessed 30 May 2023

European Data Protection Board, 'Opinion of the Board Art. 70.1.b. Opinion 3/2019 Concerning the Questions and Answers on the Interplay between the Clinical Trials Regulation (CTR) and the General Data Protection Regulation (GDPR) (Art. 70.1.b))', adopted on 23 January 2019 <https://edpb.europa.eu/our-work-tools/our-documents/opinion-art-70/opinion-32019-concerning-questions-and-answers_en> accessed 3 April 2023

European Data Protection Supervisor, 'Preliminary Opinion on Data Protection and Scientific Research' (6 January 2020) <https://edps.europa.eu/sites/edp/files/publication/20-01-06_opinion_research_en.pdf> accessed 3 April 2023

Explanatory Note to the 2006 Draft Law, 'The Law for Changing the Human Genes Research Act and the Estonian Academy of Sciences Act 1056 SE' Which Was Adopted in 2007 and Came into Force on 1 April 2007. The draft law and its explanatory note are available in Estonian at <www.riigikogu.ee/tegevus/eelnoud/eelnou/339737c4-d255-36ea-9668-b85d87e465e6/Inimgeeniuuringute%20seaduse%20ja%20Eesti%20Teaduste%20Akadeemia%20seaduse%20muutmise%20seadus> accessed 5 April 2023

Kinkorová J and Topolčan O, 'Biobanks in the Era of Big Data: Objectives, Challenges, Perspectives, and Innovations for Predictive, Preventive, and Personalised Medicine' (2020) 11(3) *EPMA J* <www.ncbi.nlm.nih.gov/pmc/articles/PMC7429593/> accessed 24 August 2023

Molnár-Gábor F and others, 'Harmonization after the GDPR? Divergences in the Rules for Genetic and Health Data Sharing in Four Member States and Ways to Overcome Them by EU Measures: Insights from Germany, Greece, Latvia and Sweden' (2022) 84 *Seminars in Cancer Biology* <https://doi.org/10.1016/j.semcancer.2021.12.001> accessed 17 August 2023

Nõmper A, 'Open Consent – A New Form of Informed Consent for Population Genetic Databases' (Dissertation for Obtaining the Degree of Doctor iuris, University of Tartu 2005) <https://dspace.ut.ee/bitstream/handle/10062/818/nomper.pdf?sequence=5&isAllowed=y> accessed 27 December 2022

Peloquin D and others, 'Disruptive and Avoidable: GDPR Challenges to Secondary Research Uses of Data' (2020) 28 *European Journal of Human Genetics* 697, 700

Pormeister, K. 'The Logical Fallacies of the Legal Bases for Data Processing in and beyond Clinical Trials' (2022) 12(2) *IDPL* 132–142 <https://doi.org/10.1093/idpl/ipac003> accessed 3 April 2023

Pormeister K, 'Transparency in Relation to the Data Subject in Genetic Research – An Analysis on the Example of Estonia' (PhD Thesis, Dissertationes Iuridicae Universitatis Tartuensis 76, University of Tartu Press 2019)

Spindler G and Dalby L, 'DS-GVO Art. 9' in Spindler G and Schuster F (eds), *Recht der Elektronischen Medien* (C.H. Beck oHG 2019)

Wolff HA, Brink S and v. Ungern-Sternberg A. (eds), *BeckOK Datenschutzrecht, DS-GVO, BDSG, Grundlagen, Bereichsspezifischer Datenschutz* (C.H. Beck München 2023)

Part III

M2M Communication, AI Systems and Data Protection

5 M2M Communications in 5G Networks

Data Protection and Privacy Aspects

Mykyta Petik

5.1 Introduction

The advent of the fifth-generation (5G) wireless communication standard heralds a new era in the digital landscape, promising unprecedented levels of connectivity, speed, and reliability. With its potential to revolutionize industries ranging from healthcare to autonomous vehicles, 5G technology has captured the imagination of innovators and policymakers alike. Yet, as the information superhighway continues to evolve, this transformation does not come without its attendant challenges. Among these, the security and privacy of machine-to-machine (M2M) communications emerge as pivotal concerns, resonating at the nexus of technological advancement and individual rights.

5G technology represents far more than a mere enhancement over its predecessors in the realm of mobile communications. 5G is not limited to incremental advancements like heightened speed and reduced latency in data transmission. Beyond these improvements, 5G introduces novel features that are set to facilitate transformative changes in the digital landscape.[1] Given the extensive array of applications and the anticipated significance of sectors such as the Internet of Things (IoT), metaverses, artificial intelligence (AI), and cloud and edge computing, the global proliferation and widespread adoption of 5G, and its subsequent evolutions, position it as a potential general-purpose technology (GPT).[2]

One of the most significant changes brought about by 5G is the enhancement of M2M communications. This technology enables machines to interact and communicate autonomously, without direct human intervention, paving the way for more advanced and efficient IoT applications. This shift is expected to have profound implications for various sectors, including manufacturing, healthcare, and transportation, where automation and smart technology play pivotal roles. The low latency and high speed of 5G enhance the ability for real-time data processing in M2M communications. This includes applications in smart cities, autonomous

1 P L Parcu and others, 'The Future of 5G and Beyond: Leadership, Deployment and European Policies' 102622 <http://doi.org/10.1016/j.telpol.2023.102622> accessed 22 December 2023.

2 Ibid.

DOI: 10.4324/9781003502791-8

vehicles, and IoT devices. Real-time processing of potentially personal data necessitates robust data protection measures to ensure compliance with EU standards.

Furthermore, 5G technology significantly bolsters the capabilities of edge computing. By processing data closer to where it is generated, edge computing reduces the need for data to travel to centralized servers, thereby minimizing latency and enhancing data processing speeds. This aspect of 5G is particularly crucial for applications requiring real-time data analysis and processing, such as autonomous vehicles, smart cities, and augmented reality experiences.

Cellular networks, including 5G, due to their widespread coverage, facilitate the implementation of the IoT, offering stable transmissions and reasonable delays. However, these networks were not originally designed to support M2M communications, which are typified by sporadic behavior and the transmission of small-sized data packets.[3]

Key legal challenges and considerations include compliance with the General Data Protection Regulation (GDPR)[4] and ePrivacy Directive (ePD),[5] namely the issue of multi-stakeholder environments and challenge of obtaining consent to processing personal data. The massive data processing capabilities of 5G-enabled technologies like IoT and AI intensify the need for compliance with GDPR. This includes adhering to principles of data minimization, purpose limitation, and ensuring data subject rights. Through the lens of applicable EU legislation, this chapter explores the symbiotic relationship between technological innovation brought by 5G and the safeguarding of individual rights of data subjects, offering an understanding of the complexities that define this digital frontier. In so doing, this chapter seeks to provide an answer to the following research question:

"How does the current EU legal framework address data protection and privacy challenges specific to M2M communications in 5G networks?"

While it is obviously hard to fit the comprehensive answer into one research chapter, the primary focus of this contribution is on analyzing the key legislation relevant to the topic with specific attention to the issue of obtaining consent to processing personal data in M2M communications within 5G networks.

5.2 M2M in 5G Networks

The advent of 5G technology has ushered in a new era of connectivity, promising unprecedented levels of performance and versatility. However, amid the remarkable

3 Catania E and La Corte A, 'IoT Privacy in 5G Networks' [2018] 123.

4 Regulation (EU) 2016/679 of the European Parliament and of the Council of 27 April 2016 on the protection of natural persons with regard to the processing of personal data and on the free movement of such data, and repealing Directive 95/46/EC (General Data Protection Regulation) [2016] OJ L 119/1.

5 Directive 2002/58/EC of the European Parliament and of the Council of 12 July 2002 concerning the processing of personal data and the protection of privacy in the electronic communications sector (Directive on privacy and electronic communications) [2009] OJ L 201.

potential of 5G, the integration of M2M services has emerged as a formidable challenge. While the overarching requirements and principles guiding 5G systems have started to take shape, the intricate technological and regulatory landscape surrounding M2M communications remains veiled in uncertainty.

Harnessing the power of 5G networks to facilitate M2M connectivity unfolds a wealth of advantages. 5G networks offer extensive and comprehensive coverage, spanning both urban and rural areas. This ubiquitous reach ensures that M2M devices can reliably communicate across vast geographic regions, including remote and underserved locations.

There exists a broad consensus within the industry regarding the pivotal role played by several key approaches and technologies in shaping the future of 5G, including the adoption of massive multiple input/multiple output (MIMO) systems, the proliferation of small cell networks, the utilization of high-frequency millimeter-wave (mmWave) communication, and the virtualization of various system components and network functions. These innovations hold immense promise and potential, yet their seamless integration into the framework of 5G to provide efficient support for M2M services remains an unresolved challenge.

5G enables seamless roaming for M2M devices, allowing them to transition effortlessly between different network cells and even across international borders. This uninterrupted connectivity is crucial for applications that require continuous data transmission. The standardized nature of 5G technology ensures that M2M devices and networks are inherently compatible. This eliminates compatibility issues that might arise in heterogeneous network environments, streamlining the deployment of M2M solutions.

5G networks are designed to provide stringent quality of service (QoS) guarantees, ensuring that M2M communications meet predefined performance criteria. Whether it is low latency for real-time applications or high reliability for critical data transfer, 5G can tailor its QoS parameters to suit specific M2M requirements. 5G offers the capability to establish service-level agreements (SLAs), formalizing agreements between service providers and M2M users. These SLAs define the level of service to be delivered, including performance metrics, response times, and service availability, offering transparency and accountability in M2M deployments. 5G ecosystems encompass operational service platforms that streamline the management and orchestration of M2M devices and services. These platforms provide centralized control, monitoring, and configuration capabilities, simplifying the administration of large-scale M2M deployments.[6]

In contrast to interpersonal human communication, M2M communication possesses distinctive characteristics when implemented in 5G networks. M2M communication primarily encompasses massive machine-type communication (mMTC), characterized by the transmission of numerous small data packets and the extensive deployment of devices within a given geographical radio coverage area. This is further reinforced by massive amount of connected devices present in 5G networks.

6 P Bhat and M Dohler, 'Overview of 3GPP Machine-Type Communication Standardization' [2015] 47 <http://doi.org/10.1016/b978-1-78242-102-3.00003-4>.

M2M communication also necessitates interoperability due to the inherent dissimilarity and heterogeneity found in both hardware and software components, as well as within the network infrastructure. This proves a certain challenge, as 5G currently operates largely on legacy equipment and 4G infrastructure due to high cost of upgrading the hardware. The M2M and IoT domains have witnessed exponential growth and present substantial market potential in recent times.[7]

5.3 EU Legal and Policy Framework Applicable to M2M Communications in 5G Networks

Because of GDPR and ePD, the rules on data protection and electronic communications in Member States have been significantly harmonized. The decisions of the Court of Justice of the European Union (CJEU) and the opinions and guidelines of Art. 29 Working Party – an advisory body made up of the representatives of European Data Protection Authorities (DPA), now replaced by European Data Protection Board (EDPB); European Data Protection Supervisor; and BEREC (Body of European Regulators for Electronic Communications) – affect the implementation and application of privacy, security, and data protection legislation, and thus are crucial for developing privacy requirements for M2M communications within 5G networks.

When developing privacy requirements for 5G telecom systems running virtualized multi-component services, exceptional attention must certainly be paid to the legal provisions related to protecting user privacy and personal data. Considering various types and categories of data to be transferred through 5G networks and the technical challenges to distinguish between the types and categories of data, privacy requirements must be developed while keeping in mind the possibility that any piece of data transferred via 5G networks may be considered personal data. The application of EU data protection and privacy rules in mobile communications is a broad topic. Data protection and privacy in the EU is regulated primarily by the GDPR as *lex generalis*. However, when it comes to the issue of security of M2M communications and personal data in 5G networks, there are a number of other relevant legal acts to be assessed, such as the European Electronic Communications Code (EECC). This major piece of legislation, while important for security of data in 5G networks and telecommunications regulation, is not entirely within the scope of this chapter, but is relevant to provide definitions such as that of electronic communications services (ECS).

In 5G networks, various third parties will be involved in processing personal data such as CSPs and third-party application developers. How to coordinate between and balance the competing interests of these actors is one of the most important legal questions to be addressed in the context of data protection and privacy of individuals, especially in light of the data protection by design obligation in Art.

7 M S Bali and others, 'Smart Architectural Framework for Symmetrical Data Offloading in IoT' [2021] 1889 <http://doi.org/10.3390/sym13101889>.

25 GDPR. Different laws – both national and European – may apply, depending on the exact legal qualification of stakeholders; thus, there is a need for legal certainty, which includes stability, consistency, and clarity of the law. Insufficient legal safeguards for activities of new stakeholders in mobile networks also raise legal issues related to loss of control of data, loss of data ownership, and ambiguity of liability of processors and controllers of personal data. These challenges may greatly affect the protection of user rights with regard to the privacy and personal data.

Transferring personal data via cloud-based means and virtualized networks results in a complicated technical environment with multiple stakeholders who pursue different interests and apply different security standards. Software-defined networking (SDN) providers, together with cloud service providers (CSPs), become important stakeholders in the 5G telecom market and will process personal data of end-users, as well as other data – such as M2M communications – which may contain personal data of other individuals.

5.4 Privacy and Data Protection in 5G-enabled M2M Communications: Clarifying the Setting

In the ever-evolving landscape of telecommunications regulations, the framework governing data protection has experienced significant transformations over the past three decades. These alterations, marked by a dynamic pace, have been intrinsically linked to the development of telecommunications services. Consequently, the European Union's legal framework for safeguarding privacy in the realm of digital services has evolved through the interplay of two key legislative instruments: personal data protection regulations, primarily articulated in Regulation 2016/679 (commonly known as GDPR), and a distinct set of provisions dedicated to preserving privacy within the sphere of ECSs, as encapsulated in the ePD.

This section examines the application of these legal instruments to M2M communications, particularly addressing the challenges posed by the concepts of 'personal data' and 'consent' in an automated, machine-driven communication environment. Additionally, we scrutinize the role of the ePD, especially in relation to data confidentiality and the processing of M2M data within 5G networks.

While both GDPR and ePD share the overarching goal of preserving privacy, the context in which these two legislative acts operate differs significantly. GDPR is primarily concerned with the processing of personal data, whereas ePD focuses on aspects such as ensuring the confidentiality of communications, constraining the processing of data related to service usage (metadata) and safeguarding location data. Moreover, these regulations impose obligations on distinct categories of entities. GDPR predominantly governs data controllers and data processors, while ePD's purview extends to providers of publicly accessible ECS. The granular and context-specific nature of ePD regulations positions it as *lex specialis* in relation GDPR. However, it is essential to underscore that viewing ePD solely as a complementary instrument to GDPR is an oversimplification that may lead to misunderstandings. Such a perception tends to create the erroneous impression that ePD primarily pertains to the domain of data protection. In reality, ePD serves a broader purpose, specifically tailored to the realm of ECS and privacy preservation.

5.4.1 ePrivacy Directive

Specific rules on privacy in telecommunications, initially adopted in 1997,[8] were modernized in 2002[9] and 2009,[10] and may be replaced in the near future by the ePrivacy Regulation (ePR).[11] Directive 2002/58/EC (ePrivacy Directive) was adopted in 2002 as a sector-specific piece of legislation with the intention to ensure the protection of privacy, personal data (including location data), and confidentiality of electronic communications. EDPB defines ePD's main goal as "a privacy preserving legal instrument aiming to protect the confidentiality of communications and the integrity of devices".[12] The ePD's scope also includes the regulation of 'cookies' – small files storing data in user's browser. The ePD defines communications as "any information exchanged or conveyed between a finite number of parties by means of a publicly available electronic communications service", and includes information transmitted as a broadcasting service if such transmission contains no data which may lead to identification of the subscriber.[13] The term 'value-added service' means any service processing traffic or location data, excluding when it is necessary for transmission or billing purposes.[14]

The ePD, as it currently stands, is primarily focused on the privacy and confidentiality of electronic communications involving individuals, particularly in relation to public communications networks and services. Its direct applicability to M2M communications is somewhat ambiguous and subject to interpretation, as the directive was originally drafted before the widespread adoption and advancement of M2M technologies. There have been initiatives to update ePD or replace it with a new regulation, which are reviewed further in this chapter.

8 Directive 97/66/EC was adopted in 1997 and referred to ECHR and national constitutions as the basis for the protection of confidentiality: "Whereas confidentiality of communications is guaranteed in accordance with the international instruments relating to human rights (in particular the European Convention for the Protection of Human Rights and Fundamental Freedoms) and the constitutions of the Member States" (Recital 2). The Directive 97/66/EC was aimed at harmonization of national legislation of Member states related to the protection of the right to privacy with respect to the protection of personal data in telecom sector and create conditions for the free movement of such data. See: Directive 97/66/EC of the European Parliament and of the Council [1997] OJ L 24.

9 Directive 2002/58/EC of the European Parliament and of the Council [2002] OJ L 201.

10 Directive 2009/136/EC of the European Parliament and of the Council of [2009] OJ L 337.

11 Proposal for a Regulation of the European Parliament and of the Council concerning the respect for private life and the protection of personal data in electronic communications and repealing Directive 2002/58/EC (Regulation on Privacy and Electronic Communications) [2017] COM/2017/010 final.

12 EDPB 'Guidelines 2/2023 on Technical Scope of Art. 5(3) of ePrivacy Directive' [2023] <https://edpb.europa.eu/our-work-tools/documents/public-consultations/2023/guidelines-22023-technical-scope-art-53-eprivacy_en> accessed 22 December 2023.

13 ePrivacy Directive, Art. 2(d).

14 Ibid., Art. 2(g).

Much of attention was given to the protection of location data in ePD. According to Art. 9(3) of the ePD,

> Processing of location data other than traffic data . . . must be restricted to persons acting under the authority of the provider of the public communications network or publicly available communications service or of the third party providing the value added service, and must be restricted to what is necessary for the purposes of providing the value added service.

This provision applies to any third parties involved in processing personal data through 5G networks, as well, such as CSPs, SDN service providers, etc.[15]

Article 5(1) of the ePD states that Member States are required to ensure the confidentiality of communications and related traffic data transmitted via public communications networks and services through national laws. They must specifically ban unauthorized listening, tapping, storage, or surveillance of communications and traffic data by anyone other than the users themselves, except with user consent or legal authorization, per Art. 15(1). However, this rule does not restrict technical storage essential for the transmission of a communication, as long as it adheres to the principle of confidentiality.[16]

M2M communications often involve the automated exchange of data between devices (terminals).[17] Under Art. 5(3), this would require user consent for storing or accessing information on these devices, unless it is necessary for services explicitly requested by the user. However, obtaining explicit consent in M2M contexts, whereby interaction with users might be minimal or non-existent, poses significant challenges. The provisions of the ePD make it clear that communication taking place in 5G networks in general and the use cases in particular fall within the scope of the Directive, specifically with regard to the electronic communications and location data. It is essential to recognize that ePD was conceived during an era when the Internet was still in its nascent stages. Services such as social networking, voice assistants, and Voice over Internet Protocol (VoIP) communications either did not exist or held far less economic significance than they do today. The original intent behind instituting ePD provisions was to adapt the principles established in data protection regulations to the unique dynamics of the telecommunications sector. This adaptation was primarily aimed at curbing the interception of communications and the excessive processing of related traffic data. Even in contemporary times, Directive 2002/58 remains a foundational source of EU regulatory protection against unwanted electronic communications and lays down obligations related to 'cookie policies' on websites.[18]

15 Ibid., Art. 9(3).

16 ePrivacy Directive, Art. 5(1).

17 F Ding and others, 'Toward a M2M-Based Internet of Vehicles Framework for Wireless Monitoring Applications' [2018] 67700 <http://doi.org/10.1109/ACCESS.2018.2879061>.

18 Rojszczak M, 'OTT Regulation Framework in the Context of CJEU Skype Case and European Electronic Communications Code' [2020] 105440 <http://doi.org/10.1016/j.clsr.2020.105439>.

The core principle of confidentiality emphasizes the paramount importance of maintaining the privacy and non-disclosure of communications between the involved parties. The protection of communication confidentiality stands as a central concern addressed within the framework of the ePD. In a manner akin to how traditional postal services are entrusted with preserving the secrecy of written letters, providers of electronic communication services are obligated to refrain from processing communications unless such processing is deemed technically indispensable.[19]

5.4.2 Proposal for ePrivacy Regulation

There have been calls by the EDPB for amending the ePD and replacing it with a more comprehensive legislative instrument, especially in light of the adoption of the new GDPR in 2016.[20]

The goal of harmonizing EU national laws regarding the confidentiality of communications, as intended by Art. 5(1) of the ePrivacy Directive, was not fully achieved, as was recognized by European Parliamentary Research Service.[21] Prior to the directive's adoption, many Member States had existing regulations on this matter. Even after transposing the directive, variations in legal traditions across the EU led to diverse definitions, conditions, and ways to protect confidentiality. This also resulted in different exceptions being applied, such as in the context of law enforcement monitoring or professional communications.

The ePD does not apply to Internet-based communication services, while EDPB considers such services "functionally equivalent" to traditional telephone

19 Storms S, Valcke P and Kindt E, 'Rage against the Machine: Does Machine-to-Machine Communication Fall within the Scope of the Confidentiality Principle?' [2019] 372 <http://doi.org/10.1093/ijlit/eaz012>.

20 See for example Statement 3/2019 on an ePrivacy regulation adopted on 13 March 2019 by the European Data Protection Board <https://edpb.europa.eu/sites/edpb/files/files/file1/201903_edpb_statement_eprivacyregulation_en.pdf>; and Statement of the EDPB on the revision of the ePrivacy Regulation and its impact on the protection of individuals with regard to the privacy and confidentiality of their communications, adopted on 25 May 2018 <https://edpb.europa.eu/sites/edpb/files/files/file1/edpb_statement_on_eprivacy_en.pdf>.

The EDPB continuously stated that new ePrivacy Regulation must not lower the level of protection offered by ePrivacy Directive, and must complement the GDPR namely with regard to consent rules. The EDPB stated in Statement 3/2019 that "the ePrivacy Regulation is necessary to ensure a level playing field and legal certainty for market operators" and – especially relevantly for 5G networks due to the challenge of obtaining consent before the processing actually takes place – that (Statement on 25 May 2018):

> consent should be obtained systematically in a technically viable and enforceable manner before processing electronic communications data or before using the storage or processing capabilities of a user's terminal equipment. There should be no exceptions to process this data based on the 'legitimate interest' of the data controller, or on the general purpose of the performance of a contract.

21 European Parliamentary Research Service, 'Review of the ePrivacy Directive' [2017] 3.

communications infrastructure.[22] The European Commission published a Proposal for the new ePR replacing ePD in 2017. In February 2021 the Council of the EU confirmed its position on an updated ePrivacy Regulation.[23] The updated Proposal changed the wording on confidentiality in Recital 1 of the Proposal, directly linking it to the right to privacy.[24] The Proposal also uses the definitions established by the EECC, namely the definition of ECS, noting that the new definition of the EECC includes not only services provided via Internet but also 'interpersonal communications services' such as VoIP, messengers, and email services.[25] This definition covers a substantial number of actors and use cases in 5G networks. The Proposal specifically mentions that "transmission of machine-to-machine or Internet of Things services regularly involves the conveyance of signals via an electronic communications network and, hence, constitutes an electronic communications service"[26] potentially covering the massive amount of M2M communications data.

Recital 12 of the given Proposal[27] states that IoT typically involves M2M communications that are considered an ECS.[28] To fully protect privacy and confidentiality rights and to foster a secure and trusted IoT environment in the digital single market, it is important to clarify that this Regulation should encompass the transmission of M2M communications. Consequently, the principle of confidentiality established in this Regulation is also applicable to the transmission of M2M communications. This is the clearest recognition of the applicability of ePrivacy rules to M2M communications yet, and, in turn, to such communications in 5G networks.

Additionally, potential challenges may arise due to the restrictive nature of the provisions of the Proposal related to automated processing of electronic communications data. The Proposal indicates that "any interference of electronic communications data" is prohibited, and interception is qualified as essentially any action performed with the communications data "for purposes other than the exchange of communications".[29] The user consent will be required for scanning and storing the content of the electronic communications, including metadata. While telecom-

22 European Data Protection Board, Statement of the EDPB on the revision of the ePrivacy Regulation and its impact on the protection of individuals with regard to the privacy and confidentiality of their communications, adopted on 25 May 2018 <https://edpb.europa.eu/sites/edpb/files/files/file1/edpb_statement_on_eprivacy_en.pdf>.

23 Council of the EU, 'Confidentiality of Electronic Communications: Council Agrees Its Position on ePrivacy Rules' (2017) <www.consilium.europa.eu/en/press/press-releases/2021/02/10/confidentiality-of-electronic-communications-council-agrees-its-position-on-eprivacy-rules/> accessed 22 December 2023.

24 From Proposal for the ePrivacy Regulation, Recital 1:

> Article 7 of the Charter of Fundamental Rights of the European Union ("the Charter") protects the fundamental right of everyone to the respect for private and family life, home and communications. Respect for the confidentiality of one's communications is an essential dimension of this right, applying both to natural and legal persons.

25 Proposal for the ePrivacy Regulation, Recital 11.

26 Ibid., Recital 15.

27 Ibid.

28 Storms (n 19).

29 Proposal for the ePrivacy Regulation, Recital 15.

munication providers in 5G networks may obtain this consent for the purpose of providing the service of exchange of communications, it might potentially be a challenge for other stakeholders in 5G networks (e.g., CSPs, SDN service providers etc.) to obtain the same consent for their operations with data, since it is unclear whether such operations may qualify as required for purposes of exchanging communications.

However, the timeline of adoption of the ePrivacy Regulation is unclear. It is evident that EU institutions recognize M2M communications as a major point of regulatory interest, yet the way such rules will be applied remains to be seen.

5.4.2.1 Extending the Scope of Article 5(3) ePD and Its Impact on M2M Communications

In November 2023, the EDPB published "Guidelines 2/2023 on Technical Scope of Art. 5(3) of ePD".[30] While the focus of the Guidelines is on the technical scope of ePD in light of the new technological developments, EDPB provides some novel insights into the application of legal provisions of ePD in general, namely on the differences between notions of 'gaining access' to data stored in the terminal equipment and 'stored information'.[31] EDPB's Guidelines suggest to broaden the concept of 'gaining access' and almost seems to be a push for rethinking ePD's provisions. While EDPB has no legal power to amend or interpret legislation, it remains for the CJEU to assess this notion and put EDPB's position to test.

Certain aspects of the ePD can be relevant to M2M communications, such as confidentiality of communications. If M2M communications involve the transmission of personal data over public communication networks, the confidentiality provisions of the ePD could potentially apply. According to EECC, ECS is "a service normally provided for remuneration via electronic communications networks".[32] Provided that the primary function of this transmission service is the conveyance of signals, it should be classified as an ECS, regardless of whether the signal pertains to a M2M communication.[33] Services responsible for the technical transmission of M2M communications are required to maintain the confidentiality of these communications. This applies even if the messages transmitted are generated without direct human involvement. Such communications must remain intact and not be subject to unauthorized interference.[34]

Article 5(3) of the ePD itself states:

> Member States shall ensure that the use of electronic communications networks to store information or to gain access to information stored in the terminal equipment of a subscriber or user is only allowed on condition that

30 Guidelines 2/2023.

31 Ibid., para 39.

32 Directive (EU) 2018/1972 of the European Parliament and of the Council of 11 December 2018 establishing the European Electronic Communications Code [2018] OJ L 321, Article 2(4)

33 Storms (n 19)

34 Ibid.

> the subscriber or user concerned is provided with clear and comprehensive information in accordance with Directive 95/46/EC, inter alia about the purposes of the processing, and is offered the right to refuse such processing by the data controller. This shall not prevent any technical storage or access for the sole purpose of carrying out or facilitating the transmission of a communication over an electronic communications network, or as strictly necessary in order to provide an information society service explicitly requested by the subscriber or user.[35]

The critical analysis of Art. 5(3) of the ePD in relation to M2M communications and data under EU law involves understanding its implications for privacy and data protection in light of new Guidelines published by the EDPB in November 2023. This Article, along with Recital 24, addresses the storing of or access to information in users' terminal equipment, emphasizing user consent or necessity for specific purposes. Recital 24 highlights the importance of protecting terminal equipment as part of users' private spheres. In M2M communications, devices such as smart home appliances, wearables, and connected vehicles all constitute terminal equipment. Protecting these devices from unauthorized data access is crucial, yet complex, given the interconnected nature of M2M ecosystems. The type of information covered by Art. 5(3) ePD is not explicitly defined. In M2M communications, this could range from operational data to personal information, raising questions about the scope of data protection required. Determining what constitutes necessity for service performance in the context of M2M communications can be contentious. For instance, is data transfer between a smart water or gas meter (which might constitute more personal data than is immediately obvious) and the provider's server a necessity, or is it already a violation of applicable provisions of both ePD and GDPR? The answer to this question will not be given by any national DPA or EDPB opinion. The CJEU will most likely have to implement a new test to determine such a delicate border, which is sure to be dynamic and change frequently.

However, observations relevant to M2M in 5G were provided by the EDPB in the Guidelines. According to EDPB, in situations when a device functions solely as an intermediary in a communication process, merely transmitting information without altering its content, this should not be classified as terminal equipment within the specific context of that communication.[36] This perspective implies that if a device's role is limited to acting as a conduit for data transfer – effectively serving as a communication relay – it falls outside the scope of what is defined as terminal equipment under Art. 5(3) of the ePD. Possibly, a substantial amount of 5G infrastructure equipment enabling M2M communications falls under this exception, as well. Expanding on this, the distinction is crucial for understanding the applicability of certain legal provisions, particularly in the realm of data protection and privacy. Devices that do not process or modify the data they relay, but only

35 ePrivacy Directive, Art. 5(3)
36 Guidelines 2/2023, para 59.

facilitate its passage from one point to another, occupy a different legal standing compared to devices that actively process and interact with the transmitted data. This differentiation is significant when considering the legal obligations and privacy implications under EU law, particularly in 5G where multiple devices with varying functions are interconnected.

Moreover, in scenarios where IoT devices connect to a network through a relay device, such as a smartphone or a dedicated hub, and maintain a strictly point-to-point connection with that relay device, the data transmission to the relay might not be subject to Art. 5(3) of the ePD. This is because the communication in such a setup does not occur over a public communication network, which is a key consideration in the application of Art. 5(3) ePD.[37]

However, the situation changes once the relay device receives the information. At this juncture, the information is considered stored on a terminal equipment, bringing it within the ambit of Art. 5(3) ePD. The directive becomes applicable the moment the relay device is tasked with transmitting the received information to a remote server. This distinction is pivotal in understanding the applicability of the ePD in the context of IoT communications.[38]

Following the logic of EDPB's reasoning with regard to IoT, it is possible to carefully presume that since M2M communications in 5G often involve direct data exchanges between devices, bypassing traditional user interfaces, the point-to-point nature of these communications – particularly when they occur within a private network or through a dedicated relay – may initially fall outside the scope of Art. 5(3) ePD. This nuanced interpretation is significant in delineating the legal boundaries of data protection in IoT networks. While the initial transmission from the IoT device to the relay may not trigger the provisions of Art. 5(3) ePD due to the private nature of the connection, the subsequent actions of the relay device – particularly in transmitting data to external servers – activate the requirements of the directive. This underscores the importance of considering the nature and pathway of data transmissions in IoT setups to accurately assess legal obligations under EU privacy laws.

Finally, the EDPB unilaterally extended the application of Art. 5(3) ePD to the notion of 'gaining access',[39] while concerns exist on whether the EDPB even had the legal right to do so. According to EDPB, "Storage and access do not need to be cumulatively present for Art. 5(3) ePD to apply. The notion of 'gaining access' is independent from the notion of 'storing information'. Moreover, the two operations do not need to be carried out by the same entity".[40] If such approach is enforced by the regulators and data protection authorities, in addition to being upheld in the CJEU, it will have a major impact on M2M communications in 5G. Most importantly it will mean the applicability of ePD to M2M communications – with consequences as yet unclear.

37 Ibid., para 58.
38 Ibid., para 60.
39 Ibid., para 32.
40 Guidelines 2/2023, para 29.

5.4.3 GDPR

GDPR is the cornerstone of the EU data protection legal framework. It is not the goal of this chapter to assess the full extent of the impact of GDPR on 5G networks, but rather identify most relevant aspects for the regulation of personal data protection in M2M communications in 5G networks and outline major challenges.

Personal data, according to Art. 4(1) GDPR, is

> any information relating to an identified or identifiable natural person ('data subject'); an identifiable natural person is one who can be identified, directly or indirectly, in particular by reference to an identifier such as a name, an identification number, location data, an online identifier or to one or more factors specific to the physical, physiological, genetic, mental, economic, cultural or social identity of that natural person.[41]

In M2M communications, data transmitted between devices can sometimes be linked to an individual, either directly or indirectly, thus qualifying as personal data under GDPR. For instance, data from smart home devices can reveal information about individuals' habits and preferences, and the massive amount of 5G-connected IoT devices, coupled with high-speed processing of data, will only make such exposure even more impactful in case of a data breach.

Under Art. 4(2) GDPR, processing of personal data encompasses:

> any operation or set of operations which is performed on personal data or on sets of personal data, whether or not by automated means, such as collection, recording, organisation, structuring, storage, adaptation or alteration, retrieval, consultation, use, disclosure by transmission, dissemination or otherwise making available, alignment or combination, restriction, erasure or destruction.[42]

M2M communications often involve several of these actions, particularly when data is collected, transmitted, and analyzed by devices. While Art. 4(2) provides a comprehensive definition of processing, applying this to the specific context of M2M communications in 5G networks involves navigating a series of challenges. It can be argued that in the context of M2M communications, particularly within 5G networks, virtually all actions involving data can be classified as 'processing'. This includes the automatic collection of data from sensors, recording and transmitting this data, storing it for analysis, and even actions like updating software on a device, which may involve processing data about the device. 5G-enabled M2M communications will predominantly involve automated processing, given the minimal human intervention in these operations. This raises questions about the application of GDPR provisions related to automated decision-making and profiling. The

41 GDPR, Art. 4(1)
42 Ibid., Art. 4(2)

expansive definition of processing under Art. 4(2) of the GDPR poses a challenge in determining the full scope of GDPR's applicability to M2M communications. This is because M2M interactions, especially in 5G networks, involve complex and continuous data processing activities.

5.5 Obtaining Consent to Processing Personal Data in M2M Communications

M2M communications typically involve automated data exchanges between devices with minimal or no human intervention. This automated nature makes obtaining explicit, informed consent from individuals (as required by GDPR) problematic. For instance, in an IoT environment, devices continuously communicate data without active human interaction, complicating the process of seeking and recording consent. The European Union's personal data protection legal framework does not offer a single preferred solution that fits all scenarios. The best option for lawful data processing will depend on the specific circumstances of each case. While there is no hierarchical order among the different legal bases for data processing, obtaining the data subject's consent is generally perceived by data controllers as a preferred or default choice for ensuring lawful data processing. However, obtaining and managing data subjects' consent may present challenges and limitations for 5G stakeholders and data controllers, as they must fulfill and demonstrate various requirements for consent validity.

In M2M scenarios, clearly defining what constitutes 'informed consent' is challenging, given the complexity and technical nature of the data processing involved. Users may not fully understand what they are consenting to, especially when it comes to the scope and potential uses of their data. The automated and often user-transparent nature of data exchanges in M2M scenarios makes traditional consent models, whereby users actively opt in, difficult to apply. The dynamic and continuous nature of data processing in M2M communications necessitates a flexible approach to consent that can accommodate changes over time. However, implementing such dynamic consent mechanisms that allow users to easily modify their preferences is technically and practically challenging.

Consent to the processing of one's personal data is not a one-time grant; it needs to be reaffirmed after a certain period of time to confirm the intention of data subject to share their personal data and whenever personal data are employed for purposes beyond the initially granted permission.[43]

Article 6 of the GDPR specifies the legality of processing personal data. It states that processing shall be lawful only if and to the extent that at least one of the following applies: the data subject has given consent, processing is necessary for the performance of a contract, for compliance with a legal obligation, to protect vital interests, for the performance of a task carried out in the public interest or in the

43 Del Re E, 'Which Future Strategy and Policies for Privacy in 5G and Beyond?' [2020] 236 <http://doi.org/10.1109/5gwf49715.2020.9221371>.

exercise of official authority, or for the purposes of legitimate interests pursued by the data controller or a third party. The selection of the six grounds aligns with the overarching principles for lawful restrictions on fundamental rights as delineated in Art. 52(1) of the Charter of Fundamental Rights of the European Union (CFR) and Art. 8(2) of the European Convention on Human Rights (ECHR).[44] Articles 4(11) and 6(1)(a) GDPR define specific requirements to such consent, namely that it should be personal and explicit. In M2M communications within 5G networks, obtaining explicit consent for data processing can be challenging, especially when user interaction is minimal. For IoT devices and applications, ensuring informed and voluntary consent requires clear communication about what data is being collected and how it is being used. The data subjects may not always be aware of the extent and nature of data processing taking place.

Providers of ECS under the EECC may require consent from their subscribers due to the nature of services provided. EECC defines ECS as inter alia "services consisting wholly or mainly in the conveyance of signals such as transmission services used for the provision of machine-to-machine services and for broadcasting",[45] in addition to interpersonal communications services and Internet access services.[46] These providers must obtain consent from their subscribers, whether they are individuals or legal entities, for the processing of electronic communications data and metadata.[47] The only exception to this requirement is when such processing is essential for the transmission of the communication. In this context, 'communication' refers to the exchange or transmission of any information, encompassing both personal and non-personal data, among a specific number of parties through a publicly available ECS.[48] Overall, ensuring proper documentation of the lawful basis for data processing and maintaining accountability for these decisions is both complex and critical, particularly given the complicated data processing ecosystems in 5G M2M communications.

Given these challenges, relying solely on data subjects' consent might not always be a suitable or realistic option to serve the needs of 5G deployment and functioning. Therefore, it is essential to explore alternative lawful grounds for personal data processing, specifically the concept of "legitimate interests" of the data controller or third parties involved.

The EDPB refers to ePD when discussing consent, but specifically notes that the notion of consent in ePD remains the same as the notion of consent in GDPR. Such a connection was established by the CJEU in Case C-673/17 (*Planet49*).[49] It is also noteworthy that directly applying Art. 5(3) ePD would not be possible since

44 C Kuner and others, 'The EU General Data Protection Regulation: A Commentary/Update of Selected Articles' [2021] 325.

45 EECC, Art. 2(4)(c)

46 Ibid., Art. 2(4)(a) and 2(4)(b).

47 Storms (n 19)

48 Ibid.

49 Case C-673/17 *Verbraucherzentrale Bundesverband e. V. v Planet49 GmbH* [2019] ECLI:EU:C:2019:801.

EU Directives do not create obligation for individuals.[50] In M2M environments – considering the amount of equipment and stakeholders, as well as the dynamic nature of 5G architecture – the use of legitimate interest will not always be feasible. It is not possible to retroactively rely on legitimate interest as a ground for processing personal data if the data controller incorrectly or unlawfully obtained the consent of the data subject.[51]

As was pointed out by Eleni Kosta,

> The role of consent in this era is reduced, as the control of the individual over his personal information is overcome by the facilitation of everyday activities in electronic communications and especially the internet, to the extent that the privacy of the individual is not infringed.[52]

It would be extremely hard to obtain an individual's valid consent for the processing by 5G IoT devices before such processing actually takes place because of the almost simultaneous transfer of substantial amounts of personal data. Extensive information about the devices and wearables of the data subject, including sensitive health data such as pulse rate or fitness, will be gathered and processed almost instantly without the possibility of obtaining valid consent the moment such data subject is within the range of 5G-based IoT systems. According to the BEREC publication *A First Assessment Based on Stakeholder Inputs: Report on the Impact of 5G on Regulation and the Role of Regulation in Enabling the 5G Ecosystem*, there is a risk of inability to obtain a valid consent by multiple data processing actors in 5G value chain since such actors will not have a direct relation to end-users.[53]

The dynamic and distributed virtualized architecture of 5G with implemented SDN, NFV, NS and reliance on cloud technologies hinders the exercise of the right to withdraw consent. Another significant challenge is the feasibility of verifying child's consent to data processing. According to Art. 8 of GDPR,

> Where the child is below the age of 16 years, such processing shall be lawful only if and to the extent that consent is given or authorised by the holder of parental responsibility over the child" and "The controller shall make reasonable efforts to verify in such cases that consent is given or authorised by the holder of parental responsibility over the child, taking into consideration available technology.[54]

50 Wiedemann K, 'The ECJ's Decision in "Planet49" (Case C-673/17): A Cookie Monster or Much Ado About Nothing?' 543 <http://doi.org/10.1007/s40319-020-00927-w> accessed 3 January 2023.

51 EDPB, 'Guidelines 05/2020 on Consent Under Regulation 2016/679' [2020] 25 <https://edpb.europa.eu/sites/default/files/files/file1/edpb_guidelines_202005_consent_en.pdf> accessed 22 December 2023.

52 Kosta E, *Consent in European Data Protection Law* (Brill 2013) 399.

53 BEREC 'A First Assessment Based on Stakeholder Inputs – Report on the Impact of 5G on Regulation and the Role of Regulation in Enabling the 5G Ecosystem' (2019) <https://berec.europa.eu/eng/document_register/subject_matter/berec/reports/8910-report-on-the-impact-of-5g-on-regulation-and-the-role-of-regulation-in-enabling-the-5g-ecosystem> accessed 22 December 2023.

54 GDPR, Art. 8.

There exists an obligation of the data controller to undertake 'reasonable efforts' to verify whether the child's parents or caretakers indeed provided their consent to processing the child's personal data.

According to Bert-Jaap Koops, a common misconception – or 'fallacy' – exists around the belief that data protection laws can effectively empower individuals to control their personal data.[55] This fallacy is rooted primarily in the overreliance on the concept of consent as a means of achieving informational self-determination, and the primary issue lies in what can be termed the 'myth of consent'.[56] This concept suggests that the most straightforward method for individuals to exercise control over their data is by providing or denying consent to specific data processing activities. However, this approach oversimplifies the complexities involved in data protection and the realities of how data is managed and used in the digital age. The M2M data in 5G use case, together with advent of ChatGPT, may serve as obvious illustrations of such fallacy. As an alternative, legitimate interest can be used as a ground for processing personal data in certain cases but the data controller must perform a 'balancing test'. According to the Opinion on the notion of legitimate interests of the data controller of Art. 29 Working Party, such test consists of four elements: (a) assessing the controller's legitimate interest, (b) impact on the data subjects, (c) provisional balance, and (d) additional safeguards applied by the controller to prevent any undue impact on the data subjects.[57] Data controllers must carry out and document the assessment to prove minimal impact on privacy before any processing of personal data takes place, and it has to comply with the requirements of the principle of proportionality.[58] Legitimate interests of the data controller must also meet the reasonable expectations of the data subjects.[59] The applicability of the rules outlined by the Art. 29 Working Party's Opinion on the legitimate interests of the data controller to M2M data and communications in 5G networks presents a complex scenario. In M2M communications within 5G networks, data controllers (which could be network operators, service providers, or device manufacturers) must identify their legitimate interests. These could range from network management or service optimization to innovative functionalities. The challenge lies in clearly defining these interests in the context of automated, machine-driven communications, whereby the purposes of data processing might not be immediately apparent or traditionally aligned with user expectations. M2M data can sometimes be non-personal but can become personal when combined with other data or when processed in certain ways. While documenting the assessment process and ensur-

55 Koops B-J, 'The Trouble with European Data Protection Law' 253 <http://doi.org/10.1093/idpl/ipu023>.

56 Ibid.

57 Article 29 Working Party 'Opinion 06/2014 on the Notion of Legitimate Interests of the Data Controller Under Article 7 of Directive 95/46/EC' 33 [2014] 844/14/EN WP 217 <https://ec.europa.eu/justice/article-29/documentation/opinion-recommendation/files/2014/wp217_en.pdf> accessed 22 December 2023.

58 Kuner (n 44)

59 Ibid.

ing compliance with the principle of proportionality in data processing is essential, the dynamic and continuous nature of M2M communications makes ongoing assessment and documentation a complex task.

In some cases, relying on Art. 6(1)(b) GDPR – which allows processing as part of performing a contract – may seem like a more logical alternative. Establishing that data processing is strictly necessary for the performance of a contract in the context of M2M communications can be complex, especially when the link between data processing and service delivery is indirect. For M2M communications that are integral to the delivery of a service (e.g., smart home devices), processing personal data might be justified as necessary for the performance of a contract with the user. At the same time, the link between data processing and service delivery in M2M communications is often indirect. This indirectness might make it difficult to justify that the data processing is strictly necessary for the performance of a contract.

The scale and complexity of 5G networks, along with the potential for vast data collection and processing, amplify these challenges. Ensuring that the data controllers' interests do not override the fundamental rights of individuals requires careful consideration, especially when personal data is not explicitly involved in initial M2M communications but may be implicated as the data is processed further.

5.6 Conclusion

Ensuring data protection and privacy is in line with ePD and GDPR becomes more challenging with 5G. The higher data transmission capabilities and the integration of numerous IoT devices necessitate robust privacy and security measures. The rapid evolution of 5G technology and its applications in M2M communication requires dynamic and adaptable legal frameworks. Current legislation may need updates or clarifications to stay relevant and effective. The applicability of Art. 5(3) ePD to M2M communications in 5G networks is not straightforward. It requires careful consideration of the technology's unique characteristics, including the nature of the networks used, the definition of terminal equipment, and the mechanisms for obtaining user consent. As 5G technology continues to evolve, so too must the legal frameworks governing privacy and data protection, ensuring they remain capable of addressing the novel challenges posed by this advanced technological landscape. In many M2M applications, continuous data processing is essential for functionality. Balancing this requirement with GDPR's stringent consent requirements can lead to conflicts between operational efficiency and compliance with privacy laws.

With the introduction of complex infrastructure and dramatic increase in M2M-processed data, it becomes evident that relying solely on consent as the cornerstone of data protection and individual data control in 5G networks is inadequate. A more nuanced and multifaceted approach is needed, one that takes into account the complexities of data processing, the realities of digital consent, and the power dynamics at play in 5G ecosystem. This approach should include clearer regulations with the emphasis on Art. 5 GDPR[60] principles relating to processing of personal data, namely the principles of lawfulness, fairness, and transparency in personal data processing,[61] and the principle of accountability.[62] A wider and more specific application of Art. 6 GDPR (lawfulness of processing) in 5G networks may be required, as 5G is a complicated technology which is not exclusively a source of challenges, but may also offer solutions. The increased speed of processing data and very low latency means, that mechanisms that enable individuals to have more meaningful control over their personal data may be deployed en masse, despite obvious technical and financial constraints withing M2M communication. 5G networks, with their advanced capabilities, could potentially offer more sophisticated ways to manage consent. This could include real-time consent management tools, more granular control options for users, and enhanced transparency measures. Potentially, creating industry-wide standards for obtaining and managing consent in M2M environments can help address some of the challenges. Utilizing technological solutions such as AI and machine learning to manage dynamic consent could offer more flexibility and adaptability, yet this remains a theoretical possibility rather than a specific plan.

In the context of 5G technology and the processing of personal data, it is imperative that technology providers implement advanced, dynamic, and continuous consent processes and notifications. These measures are essential to safeguard and uphold individuals' rights within M2M-generated data in 5G, including the rights to rectification, erasure, and notification, as outlined in data protection regulations such as the GDPR. Considering the unique challenges of M2M, there may be a need for regulatory adaptations or specific guidelines that address the issue of personal data protection with emphasis on consent.

The interplay between M2M communications and 5G networks in the context of EU data protection revolves around managing the increased volume and complexity of data processing, ensuring robust cybersecurity, maintaining compliance with cross-border data transfer regulations, and addressing the consent and transparency challenges. As both 5G and M2M technologies continue to advance, their alignment with EU data protection standards remains a dynamic and critical area of focus.

Bibliography

Table of Cases

Case C-142/18 Skype Communications Sàrl v Institut belge des services postaux et des télécommunications (IBPT) [2019] ECLI:EU:C:2019:460

Case C-673/17 Verbraucherzentrale Bundesverband e.V. v Planet49 GmbH [2019] ECLI:EU:C:2019:801

60 GDPR, Art. 5.

61 Ibid., Art. 5(1)(a)

62 Ibid., Art. 5(2)

Legislation

Directive 2002/58/EC of the European Parliament and of the Council [2002] OJ L 201
Directive 2002/58/EC of the European Parliament and of the Council of 12 July 2002 Concerning the Processing of Personal Data and the Protection of Privacy in the Electronic Communications Sector (Directive on Privacy and Electronic Communications) [2009] OJ L 201
Directive 2009/136/EC of the European Parliament and of the Council of [2009] OJ L 337
Directive 97/66/EC of the European Parliament and of the Council [1997] OJ L 24
Directive (EU) 2018/1972 of the European Parliament and of the Council of 11 December 2018 Establishing the European Electronic Communications Code [2018] OJ L 321
Proposal for a Regulation of the European Parliament and of the Council Concerning the Respect for Private Life and the Protection of Personal Data in Electronic Communications and Repealing Directive 2002/58/EC (Regulation on Privacy and Electronic Communications) [2017] COM/2017/010 final
Regulation (EU) 2016/679 of the European Parliament and of the Council of 27 April 2016 on the Protection of Natural Persons with Regard to the Processing of Personal Data and on the Free Movement of Such Data, and Repealing Directive 95/46/EC (General Data Protection Regulation) [2016] OJ L 119/1

Bibliography

Article 29 Working Party, 'Opinion 06/2014 on the Notion of Legitimate Interests of the Data Controller under Article 7 of Directive 95/46/EC' 33 [2014] 844/14/EN WP 217 <https://ec.europa.eu/justice/article-29/documentation/opinion-recommendation/files/2014/wp217_en.pdf> accessed 22 December 2023
Bali MS and others, 'Smart Architectural Framework for Symmetrical Data Offloading in IoT' [2021] 1889 <http://dx.doi.org/10.3390/sym13101889>
Bhat P and Dohler M, 'Overview of 3GPP Machine-Type Communication Standardization' [2015] 47 <http://dx.doi.org/10.1016/b978-1-78242-102-3.00003-4>
Catania E and La Corte A, 'IoT Privacy in 5G Networks' [2018] 123
Del Re E, 'Which Future Strategy and Policies for Privacy in 5G and Beyond?' [2020] 236 <http://dx.doi.org/10.1109/5gwf49715.2020.9221371>
EDPB, 'Guidelines 05/2020 on Consent under Regulation 2016/679' [2020] 25 <https://edpb.europa.eu/sites/default/files/files/file1/edpb_guidelines_202005_consent_en.pdf> accessed 22 December 2023
EDPB, 'Guidelines 2/2023 on Technical Scope of Art. 5(3) of ePrivacy Directive' [2023] <https://edpb.europa.eu/our-work-tools/documents/public-consultations/2023/guidelines-22023-technical-scope-art-53-eprivacy_en>
European Parliamentary Research Service, 'Review of the ePrivacy Directive' [2017] 3
Koops B-J, 'The Trouble with European Data Protection Law' 253 <http://dx.doi.org/10.1093/idpl/ipu023>
Kosta E, *Consent in European Data Protection Law* (Brill 2013) 399
Kuner C and others, 'The EU General Data Protection Regulation: A Commentary/Update of Selected Articles' [2021] 325
Parcu PL and others, 'The Future of 5G and Beyond: Leadership, Deployment and European Policies' 102622 <http://dx.doi.org/10.1016/j.telpol.2023.102622>
Storms S, 'Quo vadis, ePrivacy? Confidentiality of Machine-to-Machine Communications' (*CiTiP Blog*, 26 June 2018) <www.law.kuleuven.be/citip/blog/quo-vadis-eprivacy-confidentiality-of-machine-to-machine-communications/>
Wiedemann K, 'The ECJ's Decision in "Planet49" (Case C-673/17): A Cookie Monster or Much Ado about Nothing?' 543 <http://dx.doi.org/10.1007/s40319-020-00927-w> accessed 3 January 2023

6 Training of AI Systems

How to Comply With the GDPR?

Paul Vogel

6.1 Introduction and Problem Outline

In the general discussion about the regulation of artificial intelligence (AI), most of the attention is currently focused on the European Union (EU) draft for an AI regulation (AI Act). However, the training and productive use of AI systems is dependent on an immense database. Such databases in most cases include personal data, especially in practical use. These are comprehensively regulated by the EU's General Data Protection Regulation (GDPR). This chapter is intended to contribute to the investigation of the question of the extent to which data-hungry and non-transparent AI systems are compatible with a regulatory regime that fundamentally demands the most economical and transparent data processing possible.

6.1.1 Discrimination as Undesirable Consequence of the Use of AI

There is a general expectation that intelligent algorithms will be particularly objective and neutral. In contrast to human decision-makers, they are supposed to be able to exclude the conscious or unconscious influence of prejudices, which are said to underlie almost every human decision.[1] However, a different picture often emerges from practical use and empirical studies: Intelligent systems are by no means completely neutral. Like humans, they can exhibit discriminatory tendencies.[2]

With the advent of AI, and in particular of machine learning, the discussion about the prohibition of discrimination has taken on a new dimension. It is no longer only humans who are capable of treating essentially equal things unequally. Discriminatory decisions can also be made by algorithms that adapt their behavior independently in an artificial learning process.

The reason for the risk of discrimination is that an AI system depends on the data used to train it. Errors in the selection and quality of the training datasets are usually directly reflected in the performance of the model; an algorithm cannot

1 T Wischmeyer, 'Regulierung intelligenter Systeme', (2018) 143 *Archiv des öffentlichen Rechts* 1, 26.
2 Ibid., with numerous references.

DOI: 10.4324/9781003502791-9

be more neutral than the data it has learned from.[3] These data are often compiled by a human developer, not by another neutral software or system.[4] Thus, biases and preferences of the programmer flow into every learning algorithm – indirectly through the training data and, of course, usually subconsciously.[5]

6.1.2 Lack of Transparency of AI Systems ("Black Box Character")

What aggravates this situation is that algorithmic discrimination and other violations of the law usually become apparent only at a late stage. Due to the so-called black box character of deep learning systems, trained discriminatory tendencies inherent in the algorithm usually remain hidden. They often only become apparent in the test stage or – even worse – in productive use. And even if such a malfunctioning of the algorithm is known, it often cannot be eliminated within minutes. Rather, in the case of deep learning algorithms, it may take extensive research in the program code to find out where the mismatch is located. And since even the programmer cannot always exhaustively see into the "black box", troubleshooting is anything but trivial.

It needs to be assessed whether and to what extent this state of non-transparency is at all compatible with applicable law. The concerns expressed about opacity seem quite understandable; after all, only a very small part of the population is capable of reading and understanding code.[6] It is therefore a matter of understanding computer programs, knowledge which only a small group of experts possesses, but not the broad section of society.[7]

As a result, in many cases, not even the members of this group of experts are able to fully understand how an algorithm works and – all the more difficult – to make it comprehensible to the technical layperson (especially, the affected person) in case of doubt or dispute. At first glance, therefore, eliminating the black box problem seems very difficult, if not impossible.

6.1.3 Can AI Systems Be Regulated Through Data Protection Law?

It is questionable how the characteristics of AI systems can be legally regulated. The European Commission has already submitted a proposal for an AI regulation (AI Act). Although its entry into force is currently forecast for 2024 at the earliest, this regulation will come with a transition period. Furthermore, the AI Act will also not be a comprehensive set of regulations for AI. The fact that AI systems rely on large amounts of data means that the compatibility of the development and use

3 Ibid., 27.

4 Recently, artificial neural networks have also been developed which in turn configure and train other networks in order to increase the efficiency of the algorithm already in its development phase, cf., M Lenzen, *Künstliche Intelligenz* (C.H. Beck 2019) 67ff.

5 Critically therefore S Ernst, 'Verbraucherschutz durch "faire" Algorithmen – eine Illusion' (2019) *Verbraucher und Recht* 401ff.

6 This is also pointed out by T Wischmeyer, 'Regulierung Intelligenter Systeme' (2018) 143 *Archiv des öffentlichen Rechts* 1, 46.

7 T Wischmeyer, 'Regulierung Intelligenter Systeme', (2018) 143 *Archiv des öffentlichen Rechts* 1, 46.

of AI systems with applicable data protection law must also be examined. This is all the more true as the GDPR shall not be affected by the AI Act.[8] At least at first glance, these characteristics do not appear to be readily compatible with the principles of data protection law.

6.2 Compatibility of AI Systems With the Data Protection Principles of the GDPR

According to Art. 2(1) GDPR, the GDPR applies to any processing of personal data. According to Art. 4(1) GDPR, personal data are "any information relating to an identified or identifiable natural person ('data subject')". It is therefore a question of whether a natural person can be inferred directly or indirectly (i.e., with the help of other indicators) from a piece of information. The GDPR's material scope of application is considered "binary" in this respect: If the reference to a person is to be affirmed, the GDPR is applicable. If, on the other hand, this is not the case, for example because the information in question is completely anonymous, the GDPR is not applicable. A closer look is required for information from which no direct conclusion can be drawn about a data subject, but from which further information or identifiers are required to identify the person behind the information. In such a case, according to Recital 26 of the GDPR, "all the means reasonably likely to be used, such as singling out, either by the controller or by another person to identify the natural person directly or indirectly" must be taken into account to establish the identifiability of the data subject. In this respect, a case-by-case assessment of personal identifiability is also required in the case of the use of AI systems.

6.2.1 The Data Protection Principles

Once the applicability of the GDPR has been confirmed, all requirements of the GDPR are generally applicable to the specific processing. This also and above all includes the data protection principles according to Art. 5 GDPR. All data protection requirements are based on the principles for the processing of personal dataset out in Art. 5 GDPR. For a legally compliant use of AI systems, it is therefore crucial whether the specifics of this technology are compatible with the basic principles enshrined there.

The disregard or insufficient consideration of the principles is directly subject to a fine pursuant to Art. 83(5)(a) GDPR.[9] The abstract and partly vague wording

8 Cf., Art. 2(5a) of the proposal for the AI Act (as amended by the European Parliament on 14 June 2023); regarding the interaction with EU data protection law see also European Data Protection Board & European Data Protection Supervisor, *Joint Opinion 5/2021 on the proposal for a Regulation of the European Parliament and of the Council laying down harmonised rules on artificial intelligence (Artificial Intelligence Act)*, 18 June 2021, 16.

9 See for example the fine of the Information Commissioner's Office against TikTok in April 2023 for the non-compliance with certain data protection principles (such as the principles of lawfulness and transparency), cf., <https://ico.org.uk/about-the-ico/media-centre/news-and-blogs/2023/04/ico-fines-tiktok-127-million-for-misusing-children-s-data/>.

of the data protection principles does not change the character of obligations that must be directly observed, since the following provisions and an already existing body of case law and literature on the old legal situation sufficiently specify the obligations of the controller.[10] Consequently, they are directly binding obligations.[11]

The addressee of all obligations under data protection law is generally the controller, cf., Art. 5(2) GDPR. Pursuant to Art. 4(7) GDPR, this is the body which – alone or jointly with others – determines the purposes and means of the processing of personal data. Whether this body is a natural person or a legal entity is just as irrelevant for the qualification as a controller as the organizational form. The controller must ensure and be able to demonstrate compliance with the data protection requirements. To this end, the controller must implement suitable technical and organizational measures in accordance with Art. 24(1) GDPR to ensure compliance with data protection requirements.[12] In addition, the controller must ensure the technical security of data processing, cf., Art. 32(1) GDPR.

6.2.2 Data Minimization

Intelligent systems are characterized by the special feature of being dependent on large amounts of data. For this reason, conflicts could arise with the data protection principles of data minimization and storage limitation. There are two extreme positions facing each other: On the one hand, AI needs as much data as possible for its training,[13] while on the other hand, data protection law requires the use of as little (personal) data as possible. It must therefore be clarified how the use of intelligent systems can be reconciled with the principles of data minimization and storage limitation.

The principle of data minimization is laid down in Art. 5(1)(c) GDPR and obliges the controller to process personal data "in a manner that is adequate and relevant to the purpose and limited to what is necessary for the purposes of the processing". The wording that the processing must be relevant in relation to the purpose pursued can be translated into the question of whether the processing is suitable for achieving a legitimate objective.[14]

In the age of Big Data and the increasing use of intelligent algorithms, which rely on extensive amounts of data both for their training and for their practical use, the principle of data minimization is particularly challenged.[15] Anonymous data

10 A Roßnagel, 'Commentary on Article 5 GDPR' in S Simitis, G Hornung and I Spiecker gen. Döhmann (eds), *Datenschutzrecht* (Nomos 2019) margin no. 25.

11 J P Albrecht and F Jotzo, *Das neue Datenschutzrecht der EU* (Nomos 2017) part 2 margin no. 1.

12 Bitkom, *Machine Learning und die Transparenzanforderungen der DS-GVO* (2018) 22.

13 Cf., only Datatilsynet – The Norwegian Data Protection Authority, *Artificial intelligence and privacy* (2018) 4.

14 P Schantz, 'Commentary on Article 5 GDPR' in H A Wolff and S Brink (eds), *BeckOK-Datenschutzrecht* (C.H. Beck 2023) margin no. 24.

15 G Hornung, 'Erosion Traditioneller Prinzipien des Datenschutzrechts durch Big Data' in Hoffmann-Riem (ed), *Big Data – Regulative Herausforderungen* (Nomos 2018) 81, 84ff.

do not at all fall within the scope of the GDPR (see Recital 26 GDPR), so the irreversible removal of the personal reference of an item of information would take maximum account of the principle of data minimization.

Consequently, the use of intelligent algorithms requires a reduction of personal data as far as possible. Where possible, anonymous or at least pseudonymized data must be used. Nevertheless, the principle of data minimization in its scope allows the use of extensive amounts of data if this is encompassed by the (legitimate, predefined) purpose of the processing. Beyond that, especially in the case of retention of personal data for the purpose of their later reuse, it may be difficult for intelligent systems to be made to comply with the principle of data minimization.[16]

In particular, it is hard to predict in some cases what data are even necessary and to what extent they can be "limited to what is necessary", if (especially in cases of non-supervised machine learning) it is not possible to predict what results the algorithm will output and to what extent these results will affect the system's learning process; consequently, the purposes of processing may change as learning and development proceeds.[17]

The special feature of AI – that the larger the available data base, the more and better an intelligent system can learn, and the more it can learn, the more valuable this data becomes for future uses – makes it necessary to define the characteristic of the term "necessary" as precisely as possible.[18] However, since the conceivable use scenarios of intelligent algorithms are highly diverse, it is difficult to formulate generally binding guidelines. Because of these difficulties, the German Data Protection Conference (*Datenschutzkonferenz*) felt compelled to emphasize the self-evident fact that the principle of data minimization also applies to AI.[19]

However, the legislator has created the necessary flexibility in Art. 5(1)(c) GDPR through open, undefined legal terms such as "appropriate", "relevant" and "necessary" in order to be able to use AI systems that rely on large amounts of data for their training or productive use in a data protection-compliant manner.[20] This is, of course, subject to the condition that either all possible minimization measures have been taken or that such measures are generally not possible because they would unreasonably limit the usefulness of the system. Accordingly, the principle of data minimization is not an insurmountable obstacle to the use of AI in compliance with data protection law. Nevertheless, the controller is obligated to limit the

16 A Roßnagel, 'Commentary on Article 5 GDPR' in S Simitis, G Hornung and I Spiecker gen. Döhmann (eds), *Datenschutzrecht* (Nomos 2019) margin no. 135.

17 Datatilsynet – The Norwegian Data Protection Authority, *Artificial Intelligence and Privacy* (2018) 18.

18 R Leenes and S de Conca, 'Artificial Intelligence and Privacy – AI Enters the House Through the Cloud' in W Barfield and U Pagallo (eds), *Research Handbook on the Law of Artificial Intelligence* (Edward Elgar 2018) 280, 299.

19 Datenschutzkonferenz, *Hambacher Erklärung zur Künstlichen Intelligenz* (2019) 4.

20 Information Commissioner's Office, *Big Data, Artificial Intelligence, Machine Learning and Data Protection*, version 2.2 (2017) 11.

processing of personal data in the context of training and productive use to the absolute minimum necessary.

6.2.3 Transparency

6.2.3.1 General Remarks on the Transparency Principle

Algorithmic data processing procedures and the outcome of concrete individual decisions are often opaque – not only for the subject of the decision, but also for the user or programmer of the algorithm itself. This is not initially problematic for the use of such procedures by private individuals; private autonomy also includes the fact that individuals do not necessarily have to justify their actions and decisions.[21]

However, if a lack of explanation is likely to infringe the rights of other parties involved or unreasonably restricts their ability to exercise their rights, some sort of justification is required. Data protection law attempts to provide such a correction in cases when personal data of the natural person affected are processed. This follows directly from the fundamental right to data protection (Art. 8 CFR), which could hardly be meaningfully exercised without knowledge as to whether and to what extent one's own personal data are processed.

According to Art. 5(1)(a) GDPR, personal data must be processed in a manner that is comprehensible to the data subject. In the GDPR, the principle of transparency is also – but not only – concretized in the form of a right of access for the data subject (see Art. 15 GDPR).

The wording of Art. 5(1)(a) GDPR ("in a transparent manner in relation to the data subject") may suggest that the principle only requires retrospective transparency, i.e., that the data subject must be enabled to follow the processing operation during or after it has taken place.[22] However, this contradicts the intention of the legislator expressed in the recitals, according to which every natural person should be aware that personal data relating to him or her are being processed and to what extent this is done (Recital 39 GDPR).

This is all the more true in light of the fact that natural persons should have control over their own data (Recital 7 GDPR). In its so-called census ruling, the German Federal Constitutional Court established the principle that an individual must be able to know "who knows what, when and on what occasion about him or her".[23] Accordingly, individuals must be informed in advance (prospectively) about future data processing that will affect them.[24] In addition, according to the GDPR,

21 M Martini, *Blackbox Algorithmus* (Springer 2019) 72.

22 P Schantz, 'Commentary on Article 5 GDPR' in H A Wolff and S Brink (eds), *BeckOK-Datenschutzrecht* (C.H. Beck 2023) margin no. 11.

23 German Constitutional Court (BVerfG), judgment of 15 December 1983, 1 BvR 209, 269, 362, 420, 440, 484/83 – *Volkszählung*.

24 E M Frenzel, 'Commentary on Article 5 GDPR' in B Paal and D A Pauly (eds), *DS-GVO/BDSG* (3rd edn, C.H. Beck 2021) margin no. 21; P Schantz, 'Commentary on Article 5 GDPR' in H A Wolff and S Brink (eds), *BeckOK-Datenschutzrecht* (C.H. Beck 2023) margin no. 11.

all information addressed to the data subject in this regard must be easily accessible and understandable, as well as written in simple and plain language (Recital 39 GDPR, cf., in this respect also Art. 12 GDPR, which specifies the modalities of the provision of information).

Based on these considerations, the GDPR contains provisions in Arts. 13 and 14 that oblige the controller to disclose various information. The requirements of Art. 13 GDPR apply if the personal data was collected directly from the data subject. In contrast, Art. 14 GDPR applies in cases when the data was obtained by other means. These provisions are flanked by a corresponding subjective right of access for the data subject (Art. 15 GDPR).

According to the requirements of Arts. 13–14 GDPR, the controller must in any case provide the data subject with information about his or her identity and contact details, the processing purposes and the legal basis of the data processing (cf., Art. 13[1] and Art. 14[1] GDPR). In addition, according to Arts. 13(2) and 14(2) GDPR, further information must be provided to ensure fair and transparent processing. This includes one piece of information which is particularly relevant in the present context: Art. 13(2)(f), Art. 14(2)(g) GDPR requires stating whether or not automated decision-making (including profiling) is used pursuant to Art. 22(1) and (4) GDPR was applied, "and, at least in those cases, meaningful information about the logic involved, as well as the significance and the envisaged consequences of such processing for the data subject".

Since the use of AI systems could constitute a form of automated decision-making within the meaning of the GDPR, it must first be clarified in the following under which conditions a decision is to be qualified as "automated" in this sense. This is followed by the question of whether and to what extent the described opacity of decision-making when using certain AI systems (especially in the case of so-called *deep learning*) is compatible with the transparency principle of the GDPR.

6.2.3.2 The Ban on Automated Individual Decision-making (Article 22 GDPR)

Article 22 GDPR deals with specific forms of automated processing of personal data. In its paragraph 1, the provision grants the data subject the right not to be subject to a decision based solely on automated processing which produces legal effects concerning him or her, or similarly significantly affects him or her. The provision expressly includes profiling procedures among these measures, although this clarification is merely declaratory in nature due to the legal definition of profiling in Art. 4(4) GDPR, according to which this is a special case of automated processing.[25]

This right is accompanied by exceptions (paragraph 2) and specific restrictions and reservations (paragraphs 3–4). Accordingly, an automated individual decision-making is permissible if, *first*, it is necessary for the entering into, or performance of, a contract between the data subject and a data controller; *second*, if Union or

25 P Schantz, 'Die Datenschutz-Grundverordnung – Beginn einer neuen Zeitrechnung im Datenschutzrecht' (2016) *Neue Juristische Wochenschrift* 1841, 1844.

Member State law authorizes this type of data processing and adequately protects the rights, freedoms and legitimate interests of the data subject; or *third*, if the data subject explicitly consents to the automated decision-making.

With regard to the first and third exemptions, Art. 22(3) GDPR additionally requires that the controller takes appropriate measures to safeguard the rights, freedoms and legitimate interests of the data subject. To this end, the provision lists three corresponding minimum guarantees, namely the right of the data subject to obtain human intervention on the part of the controller, the right to express his or her point of view and the right to contest the decision. A further limitation is contained in Art. 22(4) GDPR, according to which the exceptions of paragraph 2 do not apply if the automated decision is based on special categories of personal data within the meaning of Art. 9(1) GDPR, unless Art. 9(2)(a) or (g) apply and, again, appropriate measures have been taken to protect the rights, freedoms and legitimate interests of the data subject.

6.2.3.2.1 REQUIREMENTS OF ARTICLE 22 GDPR

The first requirement of Art. 22(1) GDPR is the existence of an individual decision based exclusively on automated processing.

The data subject must be *subject to* such an automated decision. This means that he or she must not be involved in the decision-making process at any time or, in any case, must not have had a decisive influence on the outcome of the decision.[26] In this respect, the regulation is based on the predecessor provision at the European level (Art. 15 Data Protection Directive 95/46/EG), according to which there is no decisive influence in this sense if the controller unilaterally determines the conditions of the automated processing and thus the basis of the decision.[27] This may be understood as a lever for a normative limitation of the prohibition: for example, the user of a search engine is not subject to the result, i.e., the decision of the search algorithm, as the decision (i.e., which results are to be shown in what order) is based on the user's decision.[28]

However, the better arguments for the same result, which is ultimately worthy of approval, speak in favor of rejecting the scope of application of the provision only through the characteristic of a legal or factual impairment of the search engine user. After all, the user of a search engine is "subjected" to the result of the search process in such a way that he or she cannot influence the order and completeness of the search results, but this influence lies solely with the operator.[29] The user

26 M Atzert, 'Commentary on Article 22 GDPR' in R Schwartmann, A Jaspers, G Thüsing and D Kugelmann (eds), *DS-GVO/BDSG* (2nd edn, C.F. Müller 2020) margin no. 34.

27 P Gola, C Klug and B Körffer, 'Commentary on Section 6a BDSG' in P Gola and R Schomerus (eds), *BDSG* (12th edn, C.H. Beck 2015) margin no. 3.

28 K V Lewinski, 'Commentary on Article 22 GDPR' in H A Wolff and S Brink (eds), *BeckOK-Datenschutzrecht* (C.H. Beck 2023) margin no. 19.

29 M Atzert, 'Commentary on Article 22 GDPR' in R Schwartmann, A Jaspers, G Thüsing and D Kugelmann (eds), *DS-GVO/BDSG* (2nd edn, C.F. Müller 2020) margin no. 35.

initiates the process and can preset certain parameters to a limited extent; however, the processing and display of the list of results (i.e., the "decision"), which begins after the search form has been submitted, is entirely outside the user's sphere of influence. Intelligent search algorithms, therefore, do not fall outside the scope of Art. 22 GDPR already because their users would not be "subject" to their decisions.

It must also be clarified under which conditions a decision is based *exclusively* on automated processing. In general, it depends on the fact that no natural person has participated in the entire decision-making process.[30] However, the question arises whether in fact any involvement of a natural person is suitable to exclude the prohibition of Art. 22(1) GDPR.

According to all this, the decisive factor is whether a human being has reviewed the decision who, on the one hand, has the authority to correct the result and, on the other hand, has the possibility to do so on the basis of his or her own knowledge.[31] However, the prohibition of Art. 22(1) GDPR cannot be circumvented by a human taking over a merely formal final act of confirmation or execution.[32] This seems agreeable: if a human has the regular task of reviewing decisions made by a computer program in greater or lesser detail, he or she will tend over time to follow the recommendations or judgments of the system effectively "blindly".[33]

Even if such decisions may in many cases coincide with the "gut feeling" of the human decision-maker due to the underlying statistical calculations, this still does not change the fact that the data subject may in a certain way be degraded to a mere object. For this reason, the human making the final decision should at least be in a position to perform an independent assessment and to assert a possibly differing view in the sense of "overriding" the algorithmic (pre-)decision, for even though there is a risk of blind approval in this case as well, the risk that exists with a purely machine-based decision is at any rate somewhat reduced.

If there actually is a decision which is exclusively based on an automated processing of personal data, Art. 22(1) GDPR requires that such decision produces legal effects concerning the data subject or similarly significantly affects him or her.

A decision produces a legal effect in cases in which it alters the legal position of the data subject, establishes or abolishes a right or legal relationship, or interferes with a right.[34] Accordingly, this especially includes legal acts under private

30 Art. 29 Data Protection Working Party, *Guidelines on Automated Individual Decision-Making and Profiling for the Purposes of Regulation 2016/679 (WP 251 rev.01)* (2018) 20.

31 K V. Lewinski, 'Commentary on Article 22 GDPR' in H A Wolff and S Brink (eds), *BeckOK-3* (C.H. Beck 2023) margin no. 23, 24.

32 M Martini, 'Commentary on Article 22 GDPR' in B Paal and D A Pauly (eds), *DS-GVO/BDSG* (3rd edn, C.H. Beck 2021) margin no. 17; G Malgieri and G Comandé, 'Why a Right to Legibility of Automated Decision-Making Exists in the General Data Protection Regulation' (2017) 7 *IDPL* 243, 251; Information Commissioner's Office, *Feedback Request – Profiling and Automated Decision-Making* (2017) 19.

33 A Roßnagel and C Geminn, *Evaluation der Datenschutz-Grundverordnung aus Verbrauchersicht* (2019) 46, cf., <https://www.vzbv.de/sites/default/files/downloads/2019/12/04/19-11-26_gutachten_evaluation_dsgvo.pdf>.

34 M Martini, 'Commentary on Article 22 GDPR' in B Paal and D A Pauly (eds), *DS-GVO/BDSG* (3rd edn, C.H. Beck 2021) margin no. 26.

law, such as the conclusion or termination of a contract. Meanwhile, it is disputed whether the provision only covers *adverse* legal consequences or whether purely beneficial legal consequences are also covered by the term "legal effect".

Further, automated decision-making falls within the scope of Art. 22(1) GDPR if the decision "similarly significantly affects" the data subject. According to the Art. 29 Working Party, the decision must have the potential to significantly affect the circumstances, behavior or choices of the individuals concerned; have a prolonged or permanent impact on the data subject; or at its most extreme, lead to the exclusion or discrimination of individuals.[35] In order to meet the threshold of the criterion "significantly", a decision must, for example, affect someone's financial circumstances (such as their eligibility to obtain credit) or their access to health services.[36] All in all, an automated decision-making will most probably only fall within the scope of Art. 22(1) GDPR if the data subject does not have to accept the decision, as it may restrict his or her free personal or economic development.

For the use of intelligent algorithms, this results in the consequence that only those fully automated processing operations fall within the scope of Art. 22 GDPR which are not merely intended to prepare or support a human decision.[37] In particular, profiling processes that are limited to classifying individuals into groups based on specific characteristics do not fall under the prohibition of Art. 22(1) GDPR – and thus under its consequences with regard to information and disclosure obligations of the controller. Rather, scoring, for example, merely serves to facilitate a person's decision-making, for example, in the question of whether the potential borrower is sufficiently likely to repay his loan installments on time. However, it needs to be noted that the General Attorney at the CJEU, Priit Pikamäe, voted that, at least in many cases, scoring procedures do fall within the scope of Art. 22 GDPR, as in this particular constellation, the score typically determines the final decision (e.g., whether a loan is granted or not).[38]

6.2.3.2.2 CONSEQUENCES OF THE USE OF AI SYSTEMS

As a consequence, many of the AI systems already in use today do not fall within the scope of Art. 22 GDPR. Nevertheless, the relevance of the prohibition of automated individual decision-making should not be underestimated. The ongoing development of intelligent algorithms suggests that decision-making powers will increasingly be transferred to software in the future. The task of the human being will shift in numerous application scenarios from the AI-supported decision-maker

35 Art. 29 Data Protection Working Party, *Guidelines on Automated Individual Decision-Making and Profiling for the Purposes of Regulation 2016/679 (WP 251 rev.01)* (2018) 21.

36 Art. 29 Data Protection Working Party, *Guidelines on Automated Individual Decision-Making and Profiling for the Purposes of Regulation 2016/679 (WP 251 rev.01)* (2018) 22.

37 A Roßnagel and C Geminn, *Evaluation der Datenschutz-Grundverordnung aus Verbrauchersicht* (2019) 46, cf., <https://www.vzbv.de/sites/default/files/downloads/2019/12/04/19-11-26_gutachten_evaluation_dsgvo.pdf>.

38 Opinion of Advocate General Pikamäe of 16 March 2023, Case C-634/21, margin no. 46ff.

to a mere control and auditing role. Consequently, in more and more cases, the automated decision will be based *exclusively* on automated processing. The relevance of Art. 22 GDPR for intelligent algorithms should therefore not be denied hastily.

The provision of Art. 22 GDPR is always one of the first to emerge from data protection law when it comes to AI and intelligent algorithms. The fact that the provision strongly resembles its predecessor provision of Art. 15 Data Protection Directive suggests that the EU legislator did not have the specificities of AI directly in mind. This would at least explain why many of the AI applications in use today are not covered by the scope of Art. 22 GDPR. This is especially true for those algorithms that merely prepare decisions by, for example, assessing a person's creditworthiness by way of scoring or creating a customer profile based on a variety of information, and these measures are only intended to lead to concrete decisions in a later step.

It is true that constellations in which a machine-trained model specifies a probability or a score and on the basis of which a human makes the decision that is ultimately relevant (so-called *human-in-the-loop constellations*) are still likely to dominate at present.[39] However, AI applications are already being used today that make decisions directly, in which no human is endowed with his or her own legal or factual power of determination, but rather the latter primarily monitors the functioning of the system (more or less actively), so-called *human-on-the-loop applications*.[40] Due to the rapidly advancing development of intelligent algorithms, an increase in such constellations is to be expected in the future. The importance of Art. 22 GDPR for the use of intelligent systems will increase proportionally.[41]

6.2.3.3 Information Duties and Right of Access

The principle of transparency according to Art. 5(1)(a) GDPR is concretized in particular by information obligations addressed to the controller (Arts. 13–14 GDPR) and a right to information in favor of the data subject (Art. 15 GDPR). The importance of the obligations to provide information and the right to information regulated in Arts. 13–15 GDPR cannot be overestimated. Only receiving sufficient information from the controller about the (planned or already carried out) data processing will put the data subject be in a position to assess the resulting risks for him or her and to check whether he or she would like to assert further (possibly defensive) rights with regard to the processing of his or her personal data.[42] The corresponding information and disclosure obligations therefore form the core of the fundamental right to data protection.

The information catalog of Arts. 13–14 GDPR could also result in an obligation of the user of AI to inform the data subject (such as the user of a software) about the

39 High-Level Expert Group on Artificial Intelligence, *Ethics Guidelines for Trustworthy AI* (2019) 16.
40 High-Level Expert Group on Artificial Intelligence, *Ethics Guidelines for Trustworthy AI* (2019) 16.
41 P Vogel, *Künstliche Intelligenz und Datenschutz* (Nomos 2022) 141ff.
42 Cf., F Schmidt-Wudy, 'Commentary on Article 13 GDPR' in H A Wolff and S Brink (eds), *BeckOK-Datenschutzrecht* (C.H. Beck 2023) margin no. 2.

use of an intelligent algorithm that processes the data subject's personal data. According to Art. 13(2)(f) or Art. 14(2)(g) GDPR, the obligation to inform includes:

> the existence of automated decision-making, including profiling, referred to in Article 22(1) and (4) and, at least in those cases, meaningful information about the logic involved, as well as the significance and the envisaged consequences of such processing for the data subject.

Article 15(1)(h) GDPR contains a similar right of access for the data subject, which he or she may assert if the controller does not provide the information on their own initiative.

The duty to inform and provide information thus includes, on the one hand, the component *that* a purely automated decision has been or is to be made at all ("if"). However, it also extends to the content and procedural aspects of this decision and its effects ("how").

6.2.3.3.1 EXISTENCE OF AUTOMATED DECISION-MAKING ("IF")

At first glance, the intention of the legislature expressed in Art. 13(2)(f), Art. 14(2)(g) and Art. 15(1)(h) GDPR to oblige the controller to inform the data subject about the existence of automated decision-making seems quite understandable. In many cases, the data subject would not even notice that a decision affecting him or her was not made by a human being, but by a computer program. Such information is significant precisely because of the risks of fully automated processing previously outlined.

However, the implementation of this request by the legislature is certainly debatable. The provisions of Arts. 13–15 GDPR do not make a general reference to Art. 22 GDPR, but only refer to its paragraphs 1 and 4. However, automated individual decision-making pursuant to paragraph 1 is prohibited; information about such a processing (which, in the case of Art. 13 GDPR, has not yet started) is therefore superfluous.[43] Paragraph 4, on the other hand, permits automated individual decisions based on sensitive data within the meaning of Art. 9(1) GDPR under particularly narrow conditions.

It cannot be assumed that the legislator intended to provide only for an obligation to inform or provide information in these exceptional cases, but that the obligation should apply to *every* exceptionally permissible automated individual decision-making.[44] The reference to the provision would then correctly have to include paragraphs 2–4 (instead of paragraphs 1 and 4).

Consequently, the current law, if strictly oriented to the wording, would only allow the controller to provide information about automated decisions that are

43 W Veil, 'Commentary on Article 13 & 14 GDPR' in S Gierschmann, K Schlender, R Stentzel and W Veil (eds), *Kommentar Datenschutz-Grundverordnung* (Bundesanzeiger Verlag 2018) margin no. 118.

44 W Veil, 'Commentary on Article 13 & 14 GDPR' in S Gierschmann, K Schlender, R Stentzel and W Veil (eds), *Kommentar Datenschutz-Grundverordnung* (Bundesanzeiger Verlag 2018) margin no. 118.

exceptionally permissible under Art. 22(4) GDPR, but not those that are necessary, for example, for the performance of a contract under Art. 22(2)(a) GDPR. However, since exceptionally permissible individual decision-making pursuant to Art. 22(2) GDPR requires appropriate safeguards from the controller pursuant to Art. 22(2)(b) and (3) GDPR anyway, which also includes the right to explain one's own position, the risk potential of this flawed norm reference should be manageable for the data subject.

When using AI applications, however, this wording would minimize the number of cases in which the controller must inform its users to those constellations in which an algorithm makes a decision that has a legal effect or similarly significantly affects the data subject without any human intervention. However, this is only the case if the algorithm uses special categories of personal data within the meaning of Art. 9(1) GDPR for this purpose (e.g., health data), and the automated processing is exceptionally permitted under Art. 9(2)(a) or (g) GDPR. Since one of the main purposes of the full harmonization of data protection law was to strengthen the information rights of data subjects,[45] such an understanding of the legislative intent is hardly conceivable.

It can therefore be assumed that the reference to paragraphs 1 and 4 is an editorial mistake and that there should be an obligation to provide information and disclosure in all cases in which a decision is based exclusively on automated processing.[46]

6.2.3.3.2 DETAILS OF AUTOMATED DECISION-MAKING ("HOW")

If applicable, the controller must disclose not only the fact *that* automated decision-making has taken place at all, but also meaningful information about the logic involved and the scope and intended effects of this processing for the data subject ("how"). With regard to the scope of the provision of information and disclosure, the question is discussed as to what meaning should be attached to the insertion "at least in those cases". There are two possible interpretations: On the one hand, it could be understood as a reference back to the normative reference of "automated decision-making including profiling pursuant to Article 22(1) and (4)". In this case, *any* automated decision-making falling within the scope of Art. 22 GDPR would require information, without exception.

It has already been shown that not every AI application falls under the requirements of Art. 22(1) GDPR. However, the parenthetical "at least in those cases" also allows an extension of the information and disclosure obligation to other algorithmic processing operations that do not fall within the scope of Art. 22 GDPR.[47] This is likely to become relevant above all in constellations that are based on a

45 P Schantz, 'Die Datenschutz-Grundverordnung – Beginn einer neuen Zeitrechnung im Datenschutzrecht' (2016) *Neue Juristische Wochenschrift* 1841, 1845.

46 P Vogel, *Künstliche Intelligenz und Datenschutz* (Nomos 2022) 146.

47 A Dix, 'Commentary on Article 13 GDPR' in S Simitis, G Hornung and I Spiecker gen. Döhmann (eds), *Datenschutzrecht* (Nomos 2019) margin no. 18; M Hennemann, 'Commentary on Article 13 GDPR' in B Paal and D A Pauly (eds), *DS-GVO/BDSG* (3rd edn, C.H. Beck 2021) margin no. 32.

comparable risk situation for the personal rights of the data subject. It would then be necessary for the controller to make a balancing decision that takes into account, on the one hand, the risks of (possibly partially) automated processing for the data subject and, on the other hand, the data subject's own interests in keeping specific details of the processing confidential.

Another view, on the other hand, chooses a different connecting factor for the reference to the insertion of the phrase "*in those cases*". Under a narrow semantic interpretation, it refers the word "those" to the profiling explicitly mentioned in Art. 13(2)(f), Art. 14(2)(g) and Art. 15(1)(h) GDPR.[48]

The consequence of this interpretation would be that only when profiling measures are applied, the "how" of the automated individual decision would have to be communicated, i.e., information about the logic involved and the scope and effects of this decision. In all other cases of Art. 22 GDPR which do not fall under the legal definition of profiling (Art. 4[4] GDPR), only an optional provision of information – again based on the comparability of the risk situations – would come into consideration.[49] This interpretation is primarily based on Recital 63 GDPR, according to which a communication of the logic of the automatic processing and its consequences should take place "at least in cases when based on profiling".

However, several considerations speak against the latter reading.

First, the former view is supported by the English language version of the GDPR. There, the insertion in Arts. 13(2)(f), 14(2)(g) and 15(1)(h) GDPR reads "at least in *those* cases" (emphasis added), rather than "at least in *these* cases" (emphasis added).[50] The German version ("*zumindest in diesen Fällen*") and French version ("*au moins en pareils cas*") allow for both interpretations. From a purely semantic point of view, therefore, it is more likely to refer back to automated decision-making, but not to the specifically mentioned example of profiling.

Second, Art. 22(3) GDPR requires the controller to provide appropriate safeguards for each case of automated individual decision-making, which according to the wording of the provision include, among others, "at least" the right to challenge. In order for the data subject to be able to exercise this right at all, he or she must know the essential substantive considerations of the decision, i.e., have been informed about the logic involved. It would therefore make no sense if, according to the intention of the legislature, the controller only had to inform about the "how" of the decision in profiling constellations, but a right of challenge nevertheless exists in all cases of Art. 22 GDPR.

Third, the non-binding character of the recitals is, moreover not suitable for modifying the binding wording of the text of the GDPR. The contrary wording of

48 M Martini, *Blackbox Algorithmus* (Springer 2019) 184ff; in conclusion probably also R Schwartmann and A Schneider, 'Commentary on Article 13 GDPR' in R Schwartmann, A Jaspers, G Thüsing and D Kugelmann (eds), *DS-GVO/BDSG* (2nd edn, C.F. Müller 2020) margin no. 58.

49 M Martini, *Blackbox Algorithmus* (Springer 2019) 184.

50 Ibid.

Recital 63 GDPR is therefore to be regarded as unfortunate, as it does not correspond to the relevant text of the regulation.

After all, the more convincing arguments speak in favor of the first reading, according to which the parenthetical "at least in those cases" in Art. 13–15 GDPR refers to the concept of automated decision-making as a whole and not merely to the subset of profiling.[51]

Thus, it should be noted that the current legal situation only provides for mandatory information or disclosure about the logic and scope of automated decision-making in the narrow scope of Art. 22 GDPR. However, in the case of algorithmic processing operations that involve a comparable risk to the data subject's right to privacy, such information may nevertheless be required. The decision on this lies in the dutifully exercised discretion of the controller, who must keep in mind the threat of a fine under Art. 83(5)(b) GDPR.[52]

6.2.3.4 Result

The lack of transparency resulting from the technical principles of algorithmic decision-making outlined in this chapter raises considerable concerns from the perspective of data protection law. The regulatory regime of data protection law not only seeks to protect the personal data of natural persons by generally prohibiting processing of their personal data and permitting it only by way of exception. Rather, in cases when processing is permitted by way of exception, it requires the controller to provide various guarantees and, conversely, grants the data subject strongly defined rights. Art. 22 GDPR formulates additional requirements for the use of certain AI applications. The importance of this provision will most likely increase significantly.

6.3 A Right to Explanation for Algorithmic Decisions?

In order to resolve the conflict with the principle of transparency, there are voices in legal literature that the GDPR would provide for a "right to explanation" in the case of the use of systems for automated decision-making.[53] At first glance, this sounds quite plausible: if this type of decision-making – as shown – involves a certain risk to the fundamental rights (first and foremost human dignity) of the data subject and it is nevertheless permissible in a specific situation, the data subject should at least

51 P Vogel, *Künstliche Intelligenz und Datenschutz* (Nomos 2022) 149.

52 M Martini, *Blackbox Algorithmus* (Springer 2019) 183ff rightly criticizes the lack of a normative reference point on the question of when algorithmic processing involves a comparable risk, and for this reason an explanation is also owed as to the "how". This ultimately leads to the question of whether and to what extent the GDPR provides for a "right to explanation" for algorithmic decisions. See later in this chapter.

53 See, for example, B Goodman & S Flaxman, *European Union Regulations on Algorithmic Decision-Making and a "Right to Explanation"* (2016) 6ff, cf., <https://arxiv.org/pdf/1606.08813.pdf>.

have the opportunity to learn the basic considerations of the decision.[54] Otherwise, his or her right fundamental right to privacy would be considerably restricted in this respect. Nevertheless, there are certain doubts about the existence and scope of a comprehensive right to explanation for algorithmic decisions, primarily concerning its legal basis.

6.3.1 Legal Basis of a Right to Explanation

The GDPR leaves much room for interpretation regarding the existence and scope of a right to explanation. In any case, a right to explanation is to be located in the third chapter of the GDPR, which provides for the rights of the data subject. Thus, Arts. 13–14 GDPR require the controller to inform the data subject about the existence of automated decision-making within the meaning of Art. 22 GDPR (see earlier in this chapter). In addition, the controller must provide "meaningful information about the logic involved", cf., Art. 13(2)(f) GDPR and – identically – Art. 14(2)(g) GDPR. Also with identical wording, this information obligation of the controller is supplemented by a corresponding right of access of the data subject, cf., Art. 15(1)(h) GDPR.

It has been shown that, according to the opinion expressed here, information from the controller about the "how" of an algorithmic decision-making is only mandatory in the scope of application of Art. 22 GDPR. In addition, however, the information obligations and the corresponding right of access may also be relevant in the case of algorithm-driven processing operations that involve a comparable risk to the data subject's informational self-determination. Although this places the responsibility on the controller to decide on the comparability of the risks according to their due discretion, it also gives the controller a certain degree of flexibility to make the information and disclosure processes dependent on the risk of the processing.

If one speaks of a "right to explanation" in the sense of a subjective right, one is most likely to locate this in the right of access pursuant to Art. 15(1)(h) GDPR, although always in conjunction with the other thematically relevant provisions (Arts. 13[2][f], 14[2][g] and 22[3] GDPR).[55]

6.3.2 Arguments for and Against a Right to Explanation

One of the main advantages commonly expected from a comprehensive right to explanation about the outcome of algorithmic decisions is the improved possibility

54 A Roßnagel & C Geminn, *Evaluation der Datenschutz-Grundverordnung aus Verbrauchersicht* (2019) 36ff, cf., <https://www.vzbv.de/sites/default/files/downloads/2019/12/04/19-11-26_gutachten_evaluation_dsgvo.pdf>.

55 See also M Ebers, 'Explainable AI in the European Union. An Overview of the Current Legal Framework(s)' in L Colonna and S Greenstein (eds), *Nordic Yearbook of Law and Informatics 2020–2021: Law in the Era of Artificial Intelligence* (The Swedish Law and Informatics Research Institute 2022) 103, 111ff.

of detecting errors in the algorithm, for instance in the form of discriminatory tendencies.[56]

In many cases, however, not only the data subject but also the user of an algorithm-based system has an interest in the explanation of a machine decision. A doctor receiving a therapy suggestion for his patient from a software program will regularly not want to implement it blindly, but will first be interested in the reasons for this suggestion.[57] A right to explanation is therefore not merely an end in itself, regardless of the extent to which one attributes to it, but can have a very decisive effect on the technical quality, on the one hand, and the social acceptance of intelligent algorithms, on the other hand.[58]

Furthermore, a right to explanation must not focus solely on protecting the person affected by an algorithmic decision. Current data protection law emphasizes the rights of the data subject, but always tries to reconcile them with the (often conflicting) interests of the data controller, which are themselves regularly protected by fundamental rights.[59]

First of all, it must be taken into account that many novel business models live from the intelligent algorithms on which they are based. They often form the unique selling point of a company that sets it apart from its competitors – which is often why customers use a service in the first place. If the data subject is granted a comprehensive right to explanation, he or she must be enabled to understand the reasons for the decision. Under certain circumstances, this may require the disclosure of details about how the algorithm works. As a rule, however, the data controller has no interest in doing just that. In many cases, the algorithm, the program code and/or the model will qualify as intellectual property, which in turn is subject to special protection, namely copyright protection.[60]

This has also been recognized by the legislature: A right to information pursuant to Art. 15(1)(h) GDPR regarding the existence and logic of automated decision-making "should not adversely affect the rights or freedoms of others, including trade secrets or intellectual property and in particular the copyright protecting the software" (Recital 63 GDPR). Admittedly, according to its wording, this recital only refers to the right to information regarding the "if" and "how" of an automated decision pursuant to Art. 22 GDPR, which precisely does not cover all cases of intelligent algorithms, as the exclusivity of the decision being

56 M Martini, *Blackbox Algorithmus* (Springer 2019) 190.

57 Ibid.

58 See also S Wachter, B Mittelstadt and C Russell, 'Counterfactual Explanations Without Opening the Black Box: Automated Decisions and the GDPR' (2018) 31 *Harvard Journal of Law & Technology* 841, 843.

59 German Constitutional Court (BVerfG), judgment of 6 November 2019, 1 BvR 16/13 – *Recht auf Vergessen I*.

60 S Wachter, B Mittelstadt and L Floridi, 'Why a Right to Explanation of Automated Decision-Making Does Not Exist in the General Data Protection Regulation' (2017) 7 *IDPL* 76, 98; T Wischmeyer, 'Regulierung Intelligenter Systeme', (2018) 143 *Archiv des öffentlichen Rechts* 1, 52; D Kamarinou, C Millard and J Singh, 'Machine Learning with Personal Data' (2016) *Queen Mary School of Law Legal Studies Research Paper No. 247/2016*, 19.

based on automated processing is often lacking (see previously in this chapter). Nevertheless, the recital reflects a general legislative intention to also protect the interests of the controller.

However, the explanation of an algorithmic decision does not necessarily result in an infringement of intellectual property. Numerous pieces of information are conceivable that serve to open up the "black box" for the data subject, at least to some extent, without infringing the rights of the data controller. Examples include the fact and extent of human involvement in the decision-making process, information that provides insight into the quality of the data (such as its sources, how extensively and carefully the training data was collected and labeled), details about the model (including, if applicable, information about the type and weighting of the features and parameters used by the model, insofar as these circumstances do not qualify as trade secrets), and conclusions drawn by the model from the given input data.[61]

Apart from legal obstacles and restrictions of a right to explanation, the factual benefit of such a right to explanation for the data subject must also be critically questioned. It has already been mentioned that disclosure of the source code is not owed due to the copyrights and trade secrets that are generally affected. However, such a disclosure would not bring any added value to the vast majority of those affected – only a small fraction of citizens has sufficient programming knowledge to understand code.[62]

For this reason, the information owed must be subject to a certain degree of abstraction.[63] The data controller must at least be able to describe the general functioning of the algorithmic decision-making process and name the factors involved, at least to the extent that this does not conflict with the protection of trade or business secrets.[64] However, such an abstraction and simplification of the complexity of a machine-learning system, which should not be underestimated, entails the risk that violations of rights or discriminatory tendencies inherent in the algorithm can no longer be detected.[65] A right to explanation would be largely useless under these circumstances.

However, a right to explanation must not be excluded only for the reason that it would not be useful to the data subject. This would impose an infantilization on the

61 N Diakopoulos, 'Accountability in Algorithmic Decision Making' (2016) 59 *Communications of the ACM 57*, 60; see also D Kamarinou, C Millard and J Singh, 'Machine Learning with Personal Data' (2016) *Queen Mary School of Law Legal Studies Research Paper No. 247/2016*, 20.

62 J Burrell, 'How the Machine "Thinks": Understanding Opacity in Machine Learning Algorithms' (2016) 3 *Big Data & Society* 1, 4; B Goodman and S Flaxman, *European Union Regulations on Algorithmic Decision-Making and a "Right to Explanation"* (2016) 6; D Kamarinou, C Millard and J Singh, 'Machine Learning with Personal Data' (2016) *Queen Mary School of Law Legal Studies Research Paper No. 247/2016*, 20.

63 R Schwartmann and A Schneider, 'Commentary on Article 13 GDPR' in R Schwartmann, A Jaspers, G Thüsing and D Kugelmann (eds), *DS-GVO/BDSG* (2nd edn, C.F. Müller 2020) margin no. 60.

64 R Schwartmann & A Schneider, 'Commentary on Article 13 GDPR' in R Schwartmann, A Jaspers, G Thüsing and D Kugelmann (eds), *DS-GVO/BDSG* (2nd edn, C.F. Müller 2020) margin no. 60.

65 T Wischmeyer, 'Regulierung Intelligenter Systeme' (2018) 143 *Archiv des öffentlichen Rechts* 1, 53.

citizen, which would reinforce an objectification of the individual by AI decisions that must be prevented at all costs.[66]

In principle, the purpose of explanations is to enable the data subject to make a free and informed decision on the assertion of his or her rights. Abstracting the specifics of the algorithm and breaking it down into generally understandable statements is therefore not objectionable, but rather the very requirement of an obligation to explain or give reasons. It will often be sufficient to inform the individual about which individual specifics were decisive for a certain result or decision of the algorithm in the individual case.[67] The reduction of complexity may only not be deliberately used to conceal, for example, inherent discrimination or other violations of the law. According to all this, a possibly questionable benefit of a right to explanation is not suitable to substantially limit or even exclude such a right.

6.3.3 Result

As an interim conclusion, it can be noted that the GDPR does include a right to explanation for algorithmic decisions, even if the legislature does not explicitly designate a corresponding right to information of the data subject as such. Rather, pursuant to Art. 15(1)(h) GDPR, the data subject has a right to information about the existence ("if") of automated decision-making within the meaning of Art. 22 GDPR and, within the scope of application of this provision, a right to meaningful information about the logic involved and the scope and intended effects of such processing for him or her ("how").

Due to the parenthetical "at least in those cases", however, the right to information is not exclusively limited to cases of Art. 22 GDPR, but also covers algorithmic processing that entails a comparable risk for the data subject, as such processing is likely to degrade the natural person to a mere object of a machine decision.

It remains unclear where a line is to be drawn with regard to these comparable cases and according to which criteria comparability is determined. The scope of a right to explanation is also not specified in detail by the GDPR. It is only clear that with regard to the content of a right to explanation, the interests and rights of the data controller must be taken into account, as well, namely above all its intellectual property, as well as possibly affected trade secrets.

6.4 Significance of the Risk-based Approach for Technology Regulation Through Data Protection Law

Ambiguities regarding the scope and limits of a right to explanation for decisions of intelligent algorithms result in a high degree of legal uncertainty. Against the backdrop of the threat of sanctions due to the infringement of data subjects' rights

66 P Vogel, *Künstliche Intelligenz und Datenschutz* (Nomos 2022) 184.
67 M Martini, *Blackbox Algorithmus* (Springer 2019) 190.

and the costs of establishing internal company processes to fulfill information and disclosure obligations on the part of the user or programmer of such algorithms, this legal uncertainty can lead to inhibitions regarding their use or further development and thus to an impediment to innovation.[68] Principles therefore need to be defined with the help of which a right to explanation for algorithmic decisions can be shaped. A suitable instrument for this could be the GDPR's *risk-based approach.*

6.4.1 Locating the Risk-based Approach in the GDPR

In itself, the GDPR is based on a *one-size-fits-all* idea: every processing of personal data should be subject to the same requirements, regardless of whether it is carried out by an internationally active large corporation or the classical corner store.[69] On the one hand, this makes sense, as strictly area-specific sets of rules for all conceivable use cases would lead to a complex data protection regime that would be almost impossible for individual data processors to understand. On the other hand, it does not always make sense to impose the same high requirements on every processing operation, regardless of its scope and content.

For this reason, European data protection law follows a risk-based approach, which makes the nature and scope of the obligations of the controller dependent on the risk of the processing for the data subject.[70] This is not an invention of the GDPR; rather, the risk-based approach was already an underlying principle of the Data Protection Directive.[71] A risk assessment is explicitly required in some provisions, such as the obligation to carry out a Data Protection Impact Assessment (DPIA; Art. 35[1] GDPR) or to implement technical and organizational measures, also in the sense of data protection *by design* or *by default*; see Arts. 24(1), 25(1) and (2) GDPR.

Not explicitly mentioned in the wording of the regulation, but as a basic idea behind the provision, the risk-based approach is also the starting point for the lawfulness of processing based on a balancing of interests (Art. 6[1][f] GDPR).[72] When determining the interests of the controller and the data subject to be weighed against each other, the effects of the processing on the data subject's fundamental rights and freedoms – i.e., the risk – must also be explicitly taken into account. Since there is a higher risk to the privacy and informational self-determination

68 A D Selbst and J Powles, 'Meaningful Information and the Right to Explanation' (2017) 7 *IDPL* 233, 236.

69 W Veil, 'DS-GVO: Risikobasierter Ansatz statt rigides Verbotsprinzip – Eine erste Bestandsaufnahme, in Zeitschrift für Datenschutz' (2015) *Zeitschrift für Datenschutz* 347ff.

70 M Martini, 'Commentary on Article 24 GDPR' in B Paal and D A Pauly (eds), *DS-GVO/BDSG* (3rd edn, C.H. Beck 2021) margin no. 2.

71 Art. 29 Data Protection Working Party, *Statement on the Role of a Risk-Based Approach in Data Protection Legal Frameworks (WP 218)* (2014) 2.

72 J P Albrecht, 'Das neue EU-Datenschutzrecht – von der Richtlinie zur Verordnung. Überblick und Hintergründe zum finalen Text für die Datenschutz-Grundverordnung der EU nach der Einigung im Trilog' (2016) *Computer & Recht* 88, 92.

of the data subject when processing sensitive personal data, the GDPR imposes stricter requirements for the processing of special categories of personal data (cf., Art. 9 GDPR).

6.4.2 Relevance of the Risk-based Approach to the Development of New Technologies, Especially AI

Accordingly, the risk-based approach is a guiding principle of European data protection law (and also of information technology [IT] legislation throughout the EU).[73] Consequently, it must also apply to the exercise of data subjects' rights and specifically to a right to explanation of algorithmic decisions – and can possibly give such a right the desired contours. For this purpose, three use cases of intelligent algorithms should be brought to mind.[74]

Case 1 involves the algorithm of a streaming service or an e-commerce platform that identifies users based on their previous behavior on the platform (e.g., last movies watched or products purchased). The algorithm suggests specific titles that it has calculated are most likely to match the user's interests.

Case 2 is based on a system used by an online mail order company for personalized price differentiation. For this purpose, the system determines the purchase history, the terminal device used and the surfing behavior in order to determine the price that should come closest to the maximum amount that the specific user is willing to spend for the desired product. For the present case study, it is to be assumed that the display of a higher price for user A than for user B does not significantly affect the user within the meaning of Article 22(1) GDPR.[75]

Finally, *Case 3* is based on an algorithm that supports a criminal judge in deciding whether or not to suspend a convicted person's prison sentence by calculating his or her recidivism probability and social prognosis on the basis of various parameters.

In all cases, the applicability of the GDPR is assumed. The cases have in common that they do not fall under the scope of application of Art. 22(1) GDPR, as in *Cases 1 and 2*, the automated decision-making does not produce any legal effect or significantly affects the user, and in *Case 3*, the judge's final probation decision is not based *exclusively* on the automated processing, since the judge has the final decision-making authority and is nevertheless obliged to make an independent assessment.

73 P Dunn & G De Gregorio, 'Risk-Based Regulation in European Digital Constitutionalism' *The Digital Constitutionalist*, 21 April 2022.

74 Cf., on the following P Vogel, *Künstliche Intelligenz und Datenschutz* (Nomos 2022) 188ff.

75 However, this is highly disputed in legal literature. See for example G Wagner and H Eidenmüller, 'Down by Algorithms? Siphoning Rents, Exploiting Biases, and Shaping Preferences – Regulating the Dark Side of Personalized Transactions' (2019) 86(2) *University of Chicago Law Review* 581ff.

In all three cases, however, it is questionable whether the data subject affected by the algorithm's decision can demand to be informed by the user about the logic of the system, i.e., whether he or she has a right to explanation under Art. 15(1)(h) GDPR. The Art. 29 Working Party, which advised the European Commission on data protection prior to the entry into force of the GDPR, was decidedly against a dependence of the data subject rights on the risk of the processing.[76] However, the (only briefly substantiated) opinion of the board allows for the interpretation that only the *existence* of data subject rights should not be made dependent on the risk of processing, but that their *scope* allows for corresponding flexibility.

According to these principles, an appropriate differentiation could be made in terms of content with regard to a right to explanation in the aforementioned case constellations. The risk of the processing of personal data by the algorithm in *Case 1*, which evaluates the previous user activities and generates suggestions for further music titles, films or products based on this, poses a low risk to the fundamental rights and freedoms of the user. The user's right to explanation against the user of the algorithm (i.e., the service provider) is limited to very superficial information, such as the personal data used and, if applicable, their influence on the result.

In contrast, the situation in *Case 3* to be assessed significantly differently. For the defendant, whose personal future is largely dependent on the decision of an intelligent algorithm, the automated processing of his personal data poses a particularly high risk. It is true that the judge always makes his or her own assessment in such cases. However, it cannot be ruled out that he or she is significantly influenced – even if unconsciously – by the software's recommendation.[77]

It is not apparent to the defendant on the basis of which parameters and their weighting the algorithm has calculated a concrete probability value. For the further pursuit of his or her rights, for example, it would be highly relevant if it turned out that the program determined an increased probability of recidivism due to trained discriminatory tendencies solely, for example, because of the defendant's ethnicity. If a human judge were to state this fact as a guiding consideration in his or her decision, the sentence would be challengeable in this respect. Accordingly, equally in the case of an algorithmic decision, the defendant must have the opportunity to know the parameters used and their weighting. For these reasons, the scope of the right to explanation and the depth of the obligation to explain should be considerably greater than in *Case 1*.

Case 2, on the other hand, represents a constellation that is somewhere between the aforementioned variants in terms of the required depth of explanation. If a customer has to pay a higher price for a product than other customers, this certainly contradicts his or her interest in doing business at the lowest possible price. Nevertheless, the consequences of the algorithmic decision, according to which the buyer must pay, for example, €50 more than another customer, do not encroach on his

76 Art. 29 Data Protection Working Party, *Statement on the Role of a Risk-Based Approach in Data Protection Legal Frameworks (WP 218)* (2014) 3.

77 See also M Lenzen, *Künstliche Intelligenz* (C.H. Beck 2019) 246.

rights and freedoms to such an extent that the operator of an e-commerce platform would have to explain in detail how the calculation model works.

Nevertheless, the customer has a legitimate interest in knowing which of his or her data has been included in the calculation of the price in order to understand whether possibly incorrect assumptions by the system may have led to an unjustifiably high price. Due to the comparatively low risk, the customer's right to explanation would therefore be fulfilled if he or she were informed, for example, that the system had included in its calculation that he or she had accessed the pages of the online store exclusively with high-priced end devices and had regularly purchased high-value electronic and luxury items in the past.

Admittedly, making the existence of a right to explanation dependent on the risk of processing does not allow for easy solutions and leaves the controller with a certain degree of legal uncertainty.[78] However, more concrete standards would in turn be subject to accusations of inflexibility and lack of technology neutrality: With the rapid development of intelligent algorithms and other technologies, it is hardly possible to comprehensively anticipate cases of high-risk processing operations. Processing operations that are still commonly qualified as particularly risky for an individual's rights and freedoms today may be considered commonplace in 10–20 years. Two decades ago, the tracking of user behavior and the profiling of individuals based on it by international corporations such as Google and Meta for the purpose of targeted advertising would have been considered dangerous, and the processing of surfing behavior for the purpose of improving services would have been considered an unacceptable intrusion into one's privacy. Today, despite some enforcement action going on against profiling models of the global players, targeted advertising is at least tolerated by the majority of Internet users.

Fully automated personalized price differentiation for goods and services is still commonly perceived as unfair today[79] – this attitude may also turn into the opposite over the years. The risk-based approach of the GDPR, therefore, also offers a flexible solution with regard to a right to explanation for algorithmic decisions, which takes into account technological change and the ever-changing social acceptance of new types of technologies and data processing processes, thereby implementing the principle of technology neutrality of data protection law (Recital 15 GDPR) in the best possible way.[80]

78 G Hornung and I Spiecker gen. Döhmann, 'Introduction' in S Simitis, G Hornung and I Spiecker gen. Döhmann (eds), *Datenschutzrecht* (Nomos 2019) margin no. 243 criticize that the GDPR does not contain a clear concept of "risk" that would allow for a proper determination and assessment of the same.

79 F Zuiderveen Borgesius and J Poort, 'Online Price Discrimination and EU Data Privacy Law' (2017) 40 *Journal of Consumer Policy* 347, 355.

80 F Ritter, B Reibach and M Lee, 'Lösungsvorschlag für eine praxisgerechte Risikobeurteilung von Verarbeitungen. Ansatz zur Bestimmung von Eintrittswahrscheinlichkeit und Schadensausmaß bei der Bewertung datenschutzrechtlicher Risiken' (2019) *Zeitschrift für Datenschutz* 532ff set out general criteria for data protection risk assessment in practice.

Also in the field of AI regulation, the EU is pursuing a risk-based approach. In its draft for an AI Act, the European legislator stipulates requirements for the development and marketing of AI systems depending on their risk to the general public or the individual.

Algorithmic transparency is a central building block of trustworthy AI[81] and can, for example, be achieved by way of a subjective right to explanation for the individual, not only with regard to the "if" of the automated decision-making, but also with regard to the "how".

6.5 Conclusion

In summary, it should be noted that the training and use of AI systems raises difficulties also outside the scope of Art. 22 GDPR with regard to compatibility with the data protection principles under Art. 5(1) GDPR. This applies in particular to the transparency principle (Art. 5[1][a] GDPR) and the data minimization principle (Art. 5[1][c] GDPR), which, at least at first glance, conflict with the technical specificities of certain AI systems. However, neither of these principles per se prohibit non-transparent or data-intensive processing of personal data. Rather, like the GDPR as such, they follow a risk-based approach. This is not to be understood in the sense that it makes the *applicability* of data protection provisions dependent on the risk of the processing. This follows a "one-size-fits-all" approach, which – in conjunction with a "binary" material scope of application of the GDPR – subjects any processing of personal data to the obligations of the regulation. However, the substantive *extent* of the obligations imposed by the GDPR very much follows a risk-based approach, as is clear from various places in the text of the regulation. This also applies to the principles of transparency and data minimization. The wording of the latter is already such that even data-intensive processing activities are permissible as long as they are only necessary to fulfill the purpose of the processing. The principle of transparency is embodied in the GDPR in particular in the form of information obligations of the controller and a corresponding right of access of the data subject.

In the context of AI systems, the question is discussed in particular whether the GDPR stipulates a "right to explanation" for algorithm-based decisions. According to the opinion expressed here, this is to be affirmed in principle. However, in line with the risk-based approach, the duty of the data controller to provide an explanation is largely determined by the respective application scenario and the associated risks of the AI application for the respective data subject. All in all, the training and use of AI systems is in any case not generally prevented by the GDPR. The developer or user of an AI system is nevertheless subject to a considerable catalog of obligations including the duty to fulfill data subjects' rights; violations are sanctioned by way of administrative fines or – in the worst case – cease-and-desist orders.

Therefore, provided that it is strictly being viewed at in synopsis with the risk-based approach, the GDPR's "one-size-fits-all" concept does not have to be revised in order for developers and users of AI systems to comply with the GDPR.

81 High-Level Expert Group on Artificial Intelligence, *Ethics Guidelines for Trustworthy AI* (2019) 18.

Even though the AI Act will provide a comprehensive set of regulations for AI systems at the EU level, this will not diminish the importance of the GDPR for the processing of personal data in the context of AI systems. It remains to be seen how the coexistence of the AI Act and the GDPR will play out in practice.

Bibliography

Albrecht J-P, 'Das neue EU-Datenschutzrecht – von der Richtlinie zur Verordnung. Überblick und Hintergründe zum finalen Text für die Datenschutz-Grundverordnung der EU nach der Einigung im Trilog' (*Computer & Recht*, 2016) 88–98

Albrecht J-P and Jotzo F, *Das neue Datenschutzrecht der EU* (Nomos 2017)

Art. 29 Data Protection Working Party, 'Guidelines on Automated Individual Decision-Making and Profiling for the Purposes of Regulation 2016/679, WP 251' (rev.01, 2017, überarbeitet 2018) <https://ec.europa.eu/newsroom/article29/document.cfm?action=display&doc_id=49826> accessed 18 June 2023

Art. 29 Data Protection Working Party, 'Statement on the Role of a Risk-Based Approach in Data Protection Legal Frameworks, WP 218' (2014) <https://ec.europa.eu/justice/article-29/documentation/opinion-recommendation/files/2014/wp218_en.pdf> accessed 18 June 2023

Bitkom, 'Machine Learning und die Transparenzanforderungen der DS-GVO' *Leitfaden* (2018) <www.bitkom.org/sites/default/files/file/import/180926-Machine-Learning-und-DSGVO.pdf> accessed 18 June 2023

Burrell J, 'How the Machine "Thinks": Understanding Opacity in Machine Learning Algorithms' in *Big Data & Society* (SAGE 2016) 1–12

Datatilsynet – The Norwegian Data Protection Authority, 'Artificial Intelligence and Privacy' (2018) <www.datatilsynet.no/globalassets/global/english/ai-and-privacy.pdf> accessed 18 June 2023

Datenschutzkonferenz, 'Hambacher Erklärung zur Künstlichen Intelligenz. Sieben datenschutzrechtliche Anforderungen' *Entschließung der 97. Konferenz der unabhängigen Datenschutzaufsichtsbehörden des Bundes und der Länder* (2019) <www.datenschutz.rlp.de/fileadmin/lfdi/Konferenzdokumente/Datenschutz/DSK/Entschliessungen/097_Hambacher_Erklaerung.pdf> accessed 18 June 2023

Diakopoulos N, 'Accountability in Algorithmic Decision Making' (2016) 59 *Communications of the ACM* 56–62

Dunn P and De Gregorio G, 'Risk-Based Regulation in European Digital Constitutionalism' (*The Digital Constitutionalist*, 21 April 2022) <https://digi-con.org/risk-based-regulation-in-european-digital-constitutionalism/> accessed 20 August 2023

Ebers M, 'Explainable AI in the European Union: An Overview of the Current Legal Framework(s)' in Liane C and Stanley G (eds), *Nordic Yearbook of Law and Informatics 2020–2021: Law in the Era of Artificial Intelligence* (The Swedish Law and Informatics Research Institute 2022) 103–132 <https://irilaw.files.wordpress.com/2022/02/law-in-the-era-of-artificial-intelligence.pdf> accessed 20 August 2023

Ernst S, 'Verbraucherschutz durch "faire" Algorithmen – eine Illusion' *Verbraucher und Recht* (2019) 401–402

Gierschmann S, Schlender K, Stentzel R and Veil W (eds), *Kommentar Datenschutz-Grundverordnung* (Cologne 2018)

Gola P and Schomerus R (eds), *Bundesdatenschutzgesetz* (12th edn, C.H. Beck 2015)

Goodman B and Flaxman S, 'European Union Regulations on Algorithmic Decision-Making and a "Right to Explanation"' (2016) <https://arxiv.org/pdf/1606.08813.pdf> accessed 18 June 2023

High-Level Expert Group on Artificial Intelligence, 'Ethics Guidelines for Trustworthy AI' <https://ec.europa.eu/newsroom/dae/document.cfm?doc_id=60419> accessed 18 June 2023

Hornung G, 'Erosion traditioneller Prinzipien des Datenschutzrechts durch Big Data' in Hoffmann-Riem W (ed), *Big Data – Regulative Herausforderungen* (Nomos 2018) 81–98

Information Commissioner's Office, 'Big Data, Artificial Intelligence, Machine Learning and Data Protection, Version 2.2' (2017a) <https://ico.org.uk/media/for-organisations/documents/2013559/big-data-ai-ml-and-data-protection.pdf> accessed 18 June 2023

Information Commissioner's Office, 'Feedback Request – Profiling and Automated Decision-Making' (2017b) <https://ico.org.uk/media/about-the-ico/consultations/2013894/ico-feedback-request-profiling-and-automated-decision-making.pdf> accessed 18 June 2023

Kamarinou D, Millard C and Singh J, 'Machine Learning with Personal Data, Queen Mary School of Law Legal Studies Research Paper No. 247/2016' (2016) <https://papers.ssrn.com/sol3/papers.cfm?abstract_id=2865811> accessed 18 June 2023

Leenes R and De Conca S, 'Artificial Intelligence and Privacy – AI Enters the House through the Cloud' in Barfield W and Pagallo U (eds), *Research Handbook on the Law of Artificial Intelligence* (Edward Elgar 2018) 280–306

Lenzen M, 'Künstliche Intelligenz' in *Was sie kann und was uns erwartet* (C.H. Beck 2018)

Malgieri G and Comandé G, 'Why a Right to Legibility of Automated Decision-Making Exists in the General Data Protection Regulation' (2017) 7 *IDPL* 243–265

Martini M, *Blackbox Algorithmus. Grundfragen einer Regulierung Künstlicher Intelligenz* (Springer 2019)

Paal BP and Pauly DA (eds), *Datenschutz-Grundverordnung – Bundesdatenschutzgesetz* (3rd edn, C.H. Beck 2021)

Ritter F, Reibach B and Lee M, 'Lösungsvorschlag für eine praxisgerechte Risikobeurteilung von Verarbeitungen. Ansatz zur Bestimmung von Eintrittswahrscheinlichkeit und Schadensausmaß bei der Bewertung datenschutzrechtlicher Risiken' in *Zeitschrift für Datenschutz* (C.H. Beck 2019) 532–535

Roßnagel A and Geminn C, 'Evaluation der Datenschutz-Grundverordnung aus Verbrauchersicht' *Gutachten im Auftrag des Verbraucherzentrale Bundesverbandse. V. (vzbv)* (2019) <www.vzbv.de/sites/default/files/downloads/2019/12/04/19-11-26_gutachten_evaluation_dsgvo.pdf> accessed 18 June 2023

Schantz P, 'Die Datenschutz-Grundverordnung – Beginn einer neuen Zeitrechnung im Datenschutzrecht' in *Neue Juristische Wochenschrift* (C.H. Beck 2016) 1841–1847

Schwartmann R, Jaspers A, Thüsing G and Kugelmann D (eds), *DS-GVO/BDSG. Datenschutz-Grundverordnung, Bundesdatenschutzgesetz, Heidelberger Kommentar* (2nd edn, C.F. Müller 2020)

Selbst AD and Powles J, 'Meaningful Information and the Right to Explanation' in *IDPL* (vol. 7, Oxford University Press 2017) 233–242

Simitis S, Hornung G and Spiecker gen. Döhmann, I (eds), *Datenschutzrecht. DSGVO mit BDSG* (Nomos 2019)

Veil W, 'DS-GVO: Risikobasierter Ansatz statt rigides Verbotsprinzip – Eine erste Bestandsaufnahme' in *Zeitschrift für Datenschutz* (C.H. Beck 2015) 347–353

Vogel P, *Künstliche Intelligenz und Datenschutz. Vereinbarkeit intransparenter Systeme mit geltendem Datenschutzrecht und potentielle Regulierungsansätze* (Nomos 2022)

Wachter S, Mittelstadt B and Floridi L, 'Why a Right to Explanation of Automated Decision-Making Does Not Exist in the General Data Protection Regulation' in *IDPL* (vol. 7, Oxford University Press 2017) 76–99

Wachter S, Mittelstadt B and Russell C, 'Counterfactual Explanations Without Opening the Black Box: Automated Decisions and the GDPR' (2018) 31 *Harvard Journal of Law & Technology* 841–887 <https://papers.ssrn.com/sol3/papers.cfm?abstract_id=3063289> accessed 18 June 2023

Wischmeyer T, 'Regulierung Intelligenter Systeme' (2018) 143 *Archiv des öffentlichen Rechts* 1–66

Wolff HA and Brink S (eds), *Beck'scher Online-Kommentar zum Datenschutzrecht* (44th edn, C.H. Beck 2023)

Zuiderveen Borgesius F and Poort J, 'Online Price Discrimination and EU Data Privacy Law' (2017) 40 *Journal of Consumer Policy* 347–366

7 Training Your Medical/Nursing Robot

From the General Data Protection Regulation to the European Health Data Space

Vera Lúcia Raposo

7.1 Introduction

Medical and nursing robots based on artificial intelligence (AI) systems, like any other AI-based system, require a vast amount of data for their training and testing. Industries developing AI medical/nursing robots have a hard time with the General Data Protection Regulation (GDPR)[1] due to the many constraints it places on data processing and, especially, data repurposing.[2] The development of AI systems requires a huge amount of data, most likely not collected by the AI developers themselves. Under the existing legal framework, the reuse and repurposing of data – particularly sensitive data such as health data – is extremely complex. Aware of this difficulty, the European Union (EU) is in the process of developing the so-called European Health Data Space Regulation (EHDS),[3] which will arguably facilitate the secondary use of personal and non-personal electronic health data.

The chapter will focus on robots that provide medical care and, more broadly, any kind of medical and personal assistance to human patients in order to establish how the development and functioning of these robots can comply with the existing data protection provisions. First, it will characterise the type and tasks of these robots and demonstrate how data are vital for them. Subsequently, it will analyse the challenges raised by the GDPR with regard to obtaining and using the data for purposes related to training AI robots. Finally, it will present, from a critical

1 Regulation (EU) 2016/679 of the European Parliament and of the Council of 27 April 2016 on the protection of natural persons with regard to the processing of personal data and on the free movement of such data, and repealing Directive 95/46/EC (General Data Protection Regulation) [2016] OJ L119/1.

2 In this chapter, the concept of ‘repurposing’ is used to describe the use of data for a different purpose, whereas ‘reuse’ expresses the subsequent use of data in compliance with the original purpose. As we shall see, however, the concept of ‘data repurposing’ is not central in the EHDS. This focuses on the concept of ‘secondary use’, which does not coincide exactly with ‘repurposing’.

3 European Commission Proposal for a Regulation of the European Parliament and of the Council on the European Health Data Space, COM (2022) 197 final <https://eur-lex.europa.eu/legal-content/EN/TXT/?uri=CELE0’X%3A52022PC0197>, accessed 4 August 2023. About this proposal, see Petros Terzis, ‘Compromises and Asymmetries in the European Health Data Space’ (2022) 29 *European Journal of Health Law* 1.

DOI: 10.4324/9781003502791-10

standpoint, the possibilities raised by the EHDS. The chapter will demonstrate that this new regulation may be promising more than it can deliver and anticipate several hurdles to data repurposing.

7.2 Medical and Nursing Robots

Robots are cyber-physical systems composed of hardware and software which are able to interact with the physical world,[4] but there is no consensual definition of what a robot is. Still, some characterising features can be pointed out as common to most robots[5]: sensors (cameras, microphones) that gather information about the physical world (temperature, location), actuators that allow the robot to move around, and system interactions. Not all robots use AI. Robots can – and many of them do – operate without any AI. This study, however, will only deal with AI-based robots.

According to the definition of the High-Level Expert Group on Artificial Intelligence, robotics can be defined as (emphasis in original):

> 'AI in action in the physical world' (also called *embodied AI*). A robot is a physical machine that has to cope with the dynamics, uncertainties and complexity of the physical world. Perception, reasoning, action, learning, as well as interaction capabilities with other systems, are usually integrated into the control architecture of the robotic system. In addition to AI, other disciplines play a role in robot design and operation, such as mechanical engineering and control theory. Examples of robots include robotic manipulators, autonomous vehicles (e.g., cars, drones, flying taxis), humanoid robots, robotic vacuum cleaners, etc.[6]

That is, robots are 'physical agents that [perform] tasks by manipulating the physical world'.[7]

This chapter will focus on AI robotic systems that require health data for their training, thus encompassing medical and nursing robotics. While medical robots can be used to perform all kinds of medical tasks, in addition to or instead of a

4 Eduard Fosch-Villaronga and Tobias Mahler, 'Cybersecurity, Safety and Robots: Strengthening the Link Between Cybersecurity and Safety in the Context of Care Robots' (2021) 41 *Computer Law & Security Review* 2.

5 Bruno Siciliano and Oussama Khatib, 'Introduction' in Bruno Siciliano and Oussama Khatib (eds), *Springer Handbook of Robotics* (Springer 2008) https://doi.org/10.1007/978-3-540-30301-5_1, 1.

6 High-Level Expert Group on Artificial Intelligence, *A Definition of AI: Main Capabilities and Scientific Disciplines* (2019) 5.
This chapter will not discuss what AI is and how it can be defined. For this topic, see High-Level Expert Group on Artificial Intelligence, idem, Section 1.1.

7 European Parliament, *The Impact of the General Data Protection Regulation (GDPR) on Artificial Intelligence*, EPRS | European Parliamentary Research Service (2020), <www.europarl.europa.eu/stoa/en/document/EPRS_STU(2020)641530>.

doctor,[8] nursing robots are focused on caregiving.[9] These can support the elderly in their routine activities, both physical (assisting people with impaired movements to overcome their physical limitations) and mental (providing useful information about medicines, activating the memory of Alzheimer's patients, or even helping those living alone to cope with loneliness). This can be done in a healthcare setting, at an elderly care facility or at the patient's home.

7.3 AI Robots and Data

AI robots – like any other AI system – need data from various sources and in various forms. Huge amounts of data are required to train and test an AI system.[10] The more complex the task to be performed, the more data are required.[11]

However, the complexity of rules, structures and processes across Member States makes it difficult to access and share personal health data. In this regard, there are two main factors to consider: (a) the kind of data; and (b) the kind of technology.

7.3.1 The Kind of Data

Most of the data we need to develop AI robots for medical and nursing care are personal data and, as such, governed by the GDPR. This regulation defines personal data very broadly as 'any information related to an identified or identifiable natural person' (Art. 4[1] of the GDPR).[12]

The concept of personal data defines the material scope of the GDPR: it only applies to data that is considered personal data (though, as stated previously, this is an extremely broad concept), disregarding data that do not refer to human beings (e.g., data on natural phenomena) or data that, though concerning humans, do not refer to particular individuals (e.g., general medical information on human pathologies).

8 Giorgia Guerra, 'Evolving Artificial Intelligence and Robotics in Medicine, Evolving European Law. Comparative Remarks Based on the Surgery Litigation'(2021) 28(6) *Maastricht Journal of European and Comparative Law* 805; Yueh-Hsuan Weng and Chih-Hsing Ho, 'A Comparative Data Protection Analysis of Healthcare Robots (Part 1): Embodiment and Algorithms for HRI' in Siegfried Fina, Mark Lemley, and Roland Vogl (eds), *TTLF Working Papers* (Stanford – Vienna Transatlantic Technology Law Forum 2019) 2, 10.

9 Ibid.

10 For AI systems in general, Sophia Wang, Suzanna Pershing, Aaron Y. Lee, on behalf of the AAO Taskforce on AI and AAO Medical Information Technology Committee, 'Big Data Requirements for Artificial Intelligence' (2020) 31(5) *Current Opinion in Ophthalmology* 318.
Specifically for medical/nursing AI, Thomas Davenport and Ravi Kalakota, 'The Potential for Artificial Intelligence in Healthcare' (2019) 6(2) *Future Healthcare Journal* 94.

11 Thomas Davenport and Rajeev Ronanki, 'Artificial Intelligence for the Real World' (2018) 96(1) *Harvard Business Review* 108.

12 In this regard, Purtova makes the very accurate claim that the GDPR is the law of everything. Nadezhda Purtova, 'The Law of Everything. Broad Concept of Personal Data and Future of EU Data Protection Law' (2018) 10(1) *Law, Innovation and Technology* 40.

In the case of medical and nursing robots, much of the data required is data concerning health – personal data related to the physical or mental health of a natural person, including the provision of healthcare services, which reveal information about his or her health status (Art. 4[15] of the GDPR)[13] – which is an especially sensitive category of data.[14] Sensitive data require additional processing protection, as they represent the core of our private life. Data breaches or unauthorised disclosure of sensitive data constitute a gross violation of fundamental rights. One indicative feature of this special protection is the legal ground for data processing. Any kind of personal data requires a legal ground which enables it to be processed, as set out in Art. 6(1) of the GDPR. However, when it comes to sensitive data, such as health data, an additional legal ground – established in Art. 9(2) of the GDPR – is required.[15]

7.3.2 The Kind of Technology

The GDPR is legislation designed for the Internet, as demonstrated by its multiple references to online lexicon (Internet, social networks, website, links). It is not, however, legislation designed for AI (hence the complete lack of references to specific AI concepts). This is a problem, since AI cannot be created without data, and the restrictions imposed by the GDPR constitute a setback for AI.

The training of AI systems encounters a major obstacle in the GDPR. Article 5 of the GDPR establishes the basic principles of data processing and Art. 5(1)(c) proclaims the principle of data minimisation. According to this principle, the collection and use of personal data must be limited to the bare minimum. This demand clearly clashes with the needs of AI, which requires vast amounts of data.[16] AI cries

13 On the concept of health data in the GDPR, Maria Tzanou, *Health Data Privacy Under the GDPR: Big Data Challenges and Regulatory Responses* (Routledge 2020)

14 Paul Quinn and Gianclaudio Malgieri, 'The Difficulty of Defining Sensitive Data – The Concept of Sensitive Data in the EU Data Protection Framework' (2021) 22(8) *German Law Journal* 1583; Regina Becker, David Chokoshvili, Giovanni Comandé, Edward S. Dove, Alison Hall, Colin Mitchell, Fruzsina Molnár-Gábor, Pilar Nicolàs, Sini Tervo, and Adrian Thorogood, 'Secondary Use of Personal Health Data: When Is It "Further Processing" Under the GDPR, and What Are the Implications for Data Controllers?' (2022) 30(2) *European Journal of Health Law* 129.

Stressing the particular sensitivity of health data, but also the importance of reusing it, Johannes Starkbaum and Ulrike Felt, 'Negotiating the Reuse of Health-Data: Research, Big Data, and the European General Data Protection Regulation' (2019) 6(2) *Big Data & Society* <https://doi.org/10.1177/2053951719862594> accessed 3 July 2023.

15 Ludmila Georgieva and Christopher Kuner, 'Article 9 Processing of Special Categories of Personal Data' in Christopher Kuner and others (eds), *The EU General Data Protection Regulation (GDPR): A Commentary*(Oxford Academic 2020), 365.

16 Centre for Information Policy Leadership (CIPL), 'Artificial Intelligence and Data Protection How the GDPR Regulates AI' (March 2020) 13 <www.informationpolicycentre.com/uploads/5/7/1/0/57104281/cipl-hunton_andrews_kurth_legal_note_-_how_gdpr_regulates_ai__12_march_2020_.pdf> accessed 22 July 2023.

out for Big Data,[17] while the GDPR tries to prevent this,[18] and the very idea of Big Data clashes with the data minimisation principle (Recital 78 and Art. 5[1][c] of the GDPR).[19]

A possible solution could lie in anonymisation procedures, as repeatedly suggested by the European Parliament in its 2020 report on the impact of the GDPR on AI.[20] However, working with anonymised data is not always possible, especially when it comes to personalised AI (as it is the case of many nursing robots), which requires AI developers to know relevant information about those who will use the personalised AI system.[21] Moreover, technological developments have shown that true anonymisation is extremely difficult to achieve because re-identification is possible using a kind of 'reverse engineering'.[22]

The utility of data repurposing for AI development was also acknowledged by Art. 54(1) of the AI Act.[23] According to this provision, AI systems can be developed, within regulatory sandboxes,[24] using personal data that was originally collected for a different purpose, thus not subject to the usual requirements of the GDPR.

7.3.3 The Source of Data for AI Development

Frequently, AI developers do not collect the data they use specifically for training and testing AI, but try to use data collected by other stakeholders and for other purposes. In the case of an AI used for health-related matters, health data are required, which is usually data collected by hospitals to provide healthcare to their patients. For AI developers to use such data, a change of purpose is thus required. Data repurposing refers to the processing of personal data for purposes other than those

17 See Emmanuel Salami, 'AI, Big Data and the Protection of Personal Data in Medical Practice' (2019) 3 *EPLR* 165.

18 Tal Zarsky, 'Incompatible: The GDPR in the Age of Big Data' (2017) 47 4(2) *Seton Hall Law Review* 99.

19 European Parliament (n 7) 47.

20 Ibid.

21 Data minimisation is not the only potential clash between the GDPR and AI, Aleksandr Kesa and Tanel Kerikmäe, 'Artificial Intelligence and the GDPR: Inevitable Nemeses?' (2020) 10(3) *TalTech Journal of European Studies* 68. Additional concerns arise, for instance, from the principle of transparency (Art. 5[1][a] of the GDPR). This principle requires data processing practices that are clear enough for stakeholders to understand how the processing is conducted. Most AI systems, however, are 'black box', which means that what happens between the input (the data provided to 'feed' the system) and the output (the outcome) is frequently unknown. See Warren J. von Eschenbach, 'Transparency and the Black Box Problem: Why We Do Not Trust AI' (2021) 34 *Philosophy & Technology* 1607.

22 Luc Rocher, Julien M. Hendricks and Yves-Alexandre de Montjoye, 'Estimating the Success of Re-Identifications in Incomplete Datasets Using Generative Models' (2019) 10 *Nature Communications* 3069.

23 European Commission, Proposal for a Regulation of the European Parliament and of the Council Laying Down Harmonised Rules On Artificial Intelligence (AI Act) And Amending Certain Union Legislative Acts, COM (2021) 206 final AIA.

24 In the AI context, regulatory sandboxes would allow developers to test AI systems in a controlled environment under regulatory supervision. The goal is to identify potential risks and develop appropriate safeguards, while at the same time allowing innovation to flourish.

for which the personal data were initially collected (Recital 50 of the GDPR). The obvious issue raised here is function creep – that is, a change in the purpose for which the data were originally collected.[25]

However, the GDPR poses severe constraints on the possibility of data repurpose.

7.4 Data Repurposing Under the GDPR

7.4.1 The Compatibility Test

Data repurpose is strongly limited by the principle of purpose limitation:[26] Personal data shall be 'collected for specified, explicit and legitimate purposes and not further processed in a manner that is incompatible with those purposes' (Art. 5[1][b] of the GDPR).[27]

Even though the provision prima facie bans a change of purpose, there is one exception: when the subsequent purpose is compatible with the original one.[28] The legitimacy of data repurposing depends on the compatibility between the new purpose and the original purpose for which the data were collected. According to Recital 50 of the GDPR, the relevant criteria for establishing whether the new purpose is compatible with the previous one are the distance between the new and the original purpose (that is, whether the two purposes are usually pursued together or one comes as a consequence of the other), the alignment of the new purpose with the data subjects' expectations,[29] the nature of the data,

25 For instance, in Singapore, data from the government COVID-19 tracking app were made available to criminal investigations. Mia Sato, 'Singapore's Police Now Have Access to Contact Tracing Data' (January 2021) *MIT Technology Review* <www.technologyreview.com/2021/01/05/1015734/singapore-contact-tracing-police-data-covid/> accessed 24 July 2023. This is a glaring example of health-related data being repurposed for non–health-related purposes, but repurposing can also take place within the field of health. For instance, in the pharmaceutical industry, pharma companies tend to repurpose data from electronic medical records to design clinical trials and develop new drugs. Lucy Hocking, Sarah Parks, Marlene Altenhofer and Salil Gunashekar, *Reuse of Health Data by the European Pharmaceutical Industry* (RAND Corporation 2019).

26 Nikolaus Forgó, Stefanie Hänold and Benjamin Schütze, 'The Principle of Purpose Limitation and Big Data' in Marcelo Corrales, Mark Fenwick and Nikolaus Forgó (eds), New Technology, Big Data and the Law' in *Perspectives in Law, Business and Innovation* (Springer 2017).

27 Despite this principle, the advantages of reusing and repurposing are being increasingly recognised by data protection authorities. For instance, at the beginning of 2023, the French data protection authority CNIL released its guidelines on the reuse of data by data processors for their own purposes. see Commission Nationale de L'informatique et des Libertés (CNIL), *Sous-traitants: la réutilisation de données confiées par un responsable de traitement (12 janvier 2022)* <www.cnil.fr/fr/sous-traitants-la-reutilisation-de-donnees-confiees-par-un-responsable-de-traitement> accessed 14 July 2023.

28 Cécile Terwangne, 'Article 5 Principles Relating to Processing of Personal Data' in Christopher Kuner and others (eds), *The EU General Data Protection Regulation (GDPR): A Commentary*(Oxford Academic 2020) 309, 315–317.

29 Nonetheless, when the legal ground for the primary purpose was not consent, there is no reason to assess the data subject's expectations, because what he or she wants, or does not want, for his or her

their impact on the data subjects' interests and the safeguards adopted by the controller to ensure fair processing and prevent undue impacts.[30] Whether or not further processing is compatible should be assessed on a case-by-case basis, taking into consideration all the relevant circumstances and the key factors previously mentioned. This is the compatibility test, as set out in Art. 6(4) of the GDPR.[31]

It could be asked whether the compatibility assessment also allows the repurposing of sensitive data or, in contrast, whether there is a general ban on repurposing when it comes to sensitive data. The doubt arises because Art. 9 of the GDPR makes no provision for that possibility, arguably leading to the conclusion that the compatibility test is only valid for non-sensitive personal data. However, a different interpretation is that the content of Art. 9 of the GDPR expands on Art. 6 of the GDPR when it comes to sensitive data and, thus, the former is not a repetition of the latter, which is generally applicable to sensitive data. This second interpretation is more plausible in light of the text of both provisions.[32] Moreover, considering that the provision establishing the compatibility test (Art. 5[1][b] of the GDPR) is a general provision that applies to both kinds of data, and that neither this provision nor Recital 50 exclude sensitive data from this test, there is no reason to exclude the possibility of repurposing sensitive data when the compatibility test is satisfied. It is to be expected, though, that the test will lead to a non-compatibility outcome when sensitive data are at stake, as it results from the fact that Recital 50 and Art. 6(4)(c) of the GDPR indicate the nature of the personal data as a criterion to be considered, thus leading to believe that the bar is higher when it comes to sensitive data.[33]

In some cases, the compatibility test will not be required, as other exceptions to the ban on repurposing may operate. For instance, the change of purpose is allowed when a Union or Member State law to which the data controller is subject allows the repurposing (Art. 6[4] and Recital 50 of the GDPR), or when further processing is based on the data subject's consent.

---

data becomes irrelevant in that scenario. This seems to result, *a contrario sensu*, European Health Data Protection Supervisor, 'Preliminary Opinion 8/2020 on the European Health Data Space' (17 November 2020) *Recital* 19, <https://edps.europa.eu/sites/edp/files/publication/20-11-17_preliminary_opinion_european_health_data_space_en.pdf> accessed 12 August 2023.

30 These criteria were suggested by Art. 29 WP in Opinion 03/2013 on purpose limitation (Art. 29 Data Protection Working Party, *Opinion 03/2013 on Purpose Limitation* (2 April 2013) <https://ec.europa.eu/justice/article-29/documentation/opinion-recommendation/files/2013/wp203_en.pdf> accessed 24 July 2023).

31 Waltraut Kotschy, 'Article 6 Lawfulness of Processing' in Christopher Kuner and others (eds), *The EU General Data Protection Regulation (GDPR): A Commentary* (Oxford Academic 2020) 321.

32 For providing additional reasons that justify this interpretation, see Vera Lúcia Raposo, 'Can Personal Data Be Recycled? Data Reuse and Repurposing Under the EHDS' (forthcoming).

33 Tess Blair, 'GDPR: When Is It Permissible to Use Data Beyond Its Original Purpose? The Edata Guide To GDPR' (*Morgan Lewis*, 24 October 2018) <www.morganlewis.com/pubs/2018/10/the-edata-guide-to-gdpr-gdpr-when-is-it-permissible-to-use-data-beyond-its-original-purpose> accessed 27 July 2023.

7.4.2 The Data Subject's Consent

Consent (Arts. 6[1][a] and [2][a] GDPR) has always been the cornerstone of all kinds of data uses. In a 2018 document, the Art. 29 Data Protection Working Party stated: '[w]hen regarded as a whole, the GDPR cannot be interpreted to allow for a controller to navigate around the key principle of specifying purposes for which consent of the data subject is asked'.[34] When consent is used as a legal basis for data processing, the conditions for obtaining valid consent are established in Art. 7 of the GDPR.[35] According to Art. 4(11) of the GDPR, consent must be freely given, specific, informed (for a data subject to be able to assess the possible risks arising from data processing activities to be carried out by AI), unequivocal, and expressed by means of clear affirmative action. This definition is complemented by Recital 32 of the GDPR, which specifies that consent should be granular, i.e., that it should be given for all the purposes of the processing.

Consent is considered crucial for the data subject's self-determination, as repeatedly stated in Opinion 15/2011 of the Art. 29 Working Party[36] and on the guidelines on consent.[37] This understanding, however, is open to criticism.[38] For a start, the alleged freedom to accept or reject data processing is more theoretical than real. Often, consent is informed but not necessarily free. On many occasions, data subjects do not have any real possibility of objecting, as they have no other way to obtain the good or service to which the data processing refers.[39] Moreover, if the information provided is too technical, data subjects might not be able to fully understand the risks involved.[40] The GDPR requires that information be given in plain language (Art. 7[2] of the GDPR), but when it comes to extremely technical matters such as those involved in AI development, it is difficult to provide accurate information in generally accessible language. It is also argued that consent is the trickiest legal ground of all, given its various requirements: it must be informed, it must be opt-in (explicit), it must be possible to withdraw the consent at any given time and it cannot operate when there is an imbalance of powers.[41] These

34 Article 29 Data Protection Working Party, *Guidelines on Consent Under Regulation 2016/67* (Adopted on 28 November 2017, as last Revised and Adopted on 10 April 2018) 28 <https://ec.europa.eu/newsroom/article29/document.cfm?action=display&doc_id=51030> accessed 20 August 2023. These Guidelines were endorsed and updated by the EDPB in European Data Protection Board, *Guidelines 05/2020 on Consent Under Regulation 2016/679* (4 May 2020) <https://edpb.europa.eu/sites/default/files/files/file1/edpb_guidelines_202005_consent_en.pdf> accessed 20 August 2023.

35 Eleni Kosta, 'Article 7 Conditions for Consent' in Christopher Kuner and others (eds), *The EU General Data Protection Regulation (GDPR): A Commentary* (Oxford Academic 2020) 345, 354.

36 Article 29 Working Party, 'Opinion 15/2011 on the Definition of Consent' (13 July 2011) <https://ec.europa.eu/justice/article-29/documentation/opinion-recommendation/files/2011/wp187_en.pdf>.

37 Article 29 Data Protection Working Party (n 34); European Data Protection Board (n 34).

38 European Parliament (n 7) 41.

39 Ibid., 42.

40 Ibid., 41.

41 See European Data Protection Board, *Opinion 3/2019 Concerning the Questions and Answers on the Interplay between the Clinical Trials Regulation (CTR) and the General Data Protection Regulation*

requirements make it extremely difficult for consent to operate as a legal ground for data processing and, consequently, for data repurposing.

7.4.3 The Research Exemption

When it comes to repurposing data for the development of AI systems, another path might be available: scientific research. The concept of scientific research used in the GDPR is very broad,[42] encompassing not only pure scientific knowledge (scientific research *proprio sensu*), but also technological development; that is, its practical employment of knowledge to create new tools.[43] Recital 159 of the GDPR confirms that '[f]or the purposes of this Regulation, the processing of personal data for scientific research purposes should be interpreted in a broad manner including, for example, technological development and demonstration, fundamental research, applied research and privately funded research'. Therefore, the development of AI systems can be considered under the so-called research exemption,[44] which provides a more flexible regime for data processing when the aim is scientific research (Art. 89[1] of the GDPR). Moreover, Art. 5(1)(b) clarifies that secondary uses related to research are to be considered compatible with the original purpose, thus exempting this particular data repurposing from the compatibility test.

However, the obstacle might lie in Art. 6 of the GDPR. This is because the use of data for research purposes is listed in Art. 9(2)(j) of the GDPR, for sensitive data, but not in Art. 6(1) of the GDPR, for general personal data (for instance, demographic details, such as age, gender, and possibly cultural or social preferences, to enhance the robot's ability to provide personalized care). Thus, a more cautious reading of the latter might require finding a legal base in Art. 6 for the repurposing of data on research.[45]

7.5 A Practical Example of Data Repurposing to Train Medical/ Nursing AI Robots

In theory, the GDPR provides legal grounds that allow data repurposing to train medical/nursing AI robots. However, let us conduct a practical exercise to demonstrate the challenges raised by the GDPR.

(GDPR) (Art. 70.1.b)) (Adopted on 23 January 2019) <https://edpb.europa.eu/sites/default/files/files/file1/edpb_opinionctrq_a_final_en.pdf> accessed 4 August 2023.

42 Regarding Scientific Research Under the GDPR, European Data Protection Supervisor, *A Preliminary Opinion on Data Protection and Scientific Research* (6 January 2020) 16–2 <https://edps.europa.eu/sites/edp/files/publication/20-01-06_opinion_research_en.pdf>, accessed 20 August 2023.

43 Interestingly, these two concepts are autonomised in the EHDS, as is clear from Recital 41 and from the various legitimate secondary uses of electronic health data listed in Art. 34(1) of the EHDS.

44 Giulia Schneider and Giovanni Comandè, 'Can the GDPR Make Data Flow for Research Easier? Yes It Can, by Differentiating! A Careful Reading of the GDPR Shows How EU Data Protection Law Leaves Open Some Significant Flexibilities for Data Protection-Sound Research Activities' (2021) 41 *Computer Law & Security Review* 1.

45 Raising this concern, Santa Slokenberga, 'Scientific Research Regime 2.0?, How the Proposed EHDS Regulation May Change the GDPR Research Regime' (2022) *Technology and Regulation* 135–147, 139.

7.5.1 Data Repurpose for an AI Training Set

Imagine a scenario in which AI developers are required to create a training set; that is, the dataset that AI will use for learning. Training sets involve huge amounts of data so it will be impractical to ask for the consent of all the data subjects. However, this same fact also makes it easier to pass the compatibility test (thus excluding the need for consent). When using such a large data pool, the data of a given individual cannot determine the features of the AI model, and therefore, even if that model is used for that same individual (that is, if the AI robot developed based on that model interacts with that person), hardly the latter will suffer negative consequences due to inferences made from his/her data. Since the person is not directly affected by the use of his/her personal data, the compatibility test will most likely not prevent the repurposing of data.[46]

However, this does not mean that the data repurposing will automatically pass the compatibility test. There are two legal risks to consider.

The first is the risk of data misuse, a particularly serious risk for data concerning health or other sensitive conditions.[47] This risk can be mitigated through anonymisation or pseudonymisation and deletion of the data once the model has been constructed. According to Arts. 25 and 32 of the GDPR, AI developers are obliged to implement appropriate measures to ensure an adequate level of security for the relevant risks.

The other potential legal threat concerns inferences about the group.[48] As mentioned previously, in such a large training set, data becomes mere inputs that most likely will not be used to make decisions or predictions about a given individual. However, once an individual's data are included in the training set and considered together with the data provided by individuals sharing his or her same characteristics (i.e., belonging to the same group, such as people who have a rare medical condition), those data can feed inferences about that group of individuals. Even if no person, in particular, is affected by such inferences, the group will be.

As an example, consider the use of a patient's health data about a mental illness that can potentially lead to violent acts to train a model that is then used to take care of elderly patients, some of whom suffering from that mental illness. The inclusion of the patient's data will not affect the patient specifically, but the inclusion of his/her data, along with the data of other similar individuals, may create a risk for the group composed of individuals that suffer from that mental disease and who might be affected by decisions based on such data.[49] For instance, based on the training data, the AI robot might assume that everyone suffering from that mental illness will behave violently and may thus behave more defensively towards these

46 European Parliament (n 7) 46.

47 Ibid.

48 Tore Pedersen and Christian Johansen, 'Behavioural Artificial Intelligence: An Agenda for Systematic Empirical Studies of Artificial Inference' (2020) 35 *AI & Society* 519.

49 European Parliament (n 7) 46.

individuals than towards other people. However, group privacy[50] – even though increasingly advocated by many[51] – is not enshrined in the GDPR.[52] The concept of personal data is meant to protect individuals, not the group to which the individual belongs. Thus, inferences about a group of people – as long as no one is individualised within that group – are not caught by the prohibition on automated decision-making and profiling established in Art. 22 of the GDPR.

In conclusion, it is likely that this data repurposing will pass the compatibility test, but there are still some issues that might change this assessment in the particular case.

7.5.2 Data Repurposing to Personalise an AI System

The scenario is different when data are repurposed to personalise an AI system for a particular individual. Personalised robots are tailor-made products.[53] One size does not fit all, and the product assigned to each individual must fulfil his or her needs, both medical (what medicines that person takes) and non-medical (what time the person usually wakes up). For this purpose to be achieved, the AI robot must combine a 'system of record' (which analyses and stores past interactions and preferences to optimise performance regarding specific users) and a 'system of engagement' (which offers a personalised and natural interaction to enhance the human–robot interaction).[54]

Such a highly custom-made robot requires a huge amount of private information about the individual, which might create some tension with the envisaged aim of privacy – usually referred to as the 'privacy paradox'.[55] This aim raises several legal issues in the light of the GDPR.

50 Alessandro Mantelero, 'From Group Privacy to Collective Privacy: Towards a New Dimension of Privacy and Data Protection in the Big Data Era' in Linnet Taylor, Luciano Floridi and Bart van der Sloot (eds), *Group Privacy: New Challenges of Data Technologies* (Springer 2017) 139.

51 Ibid.

52 European Parliament (n 7) 48.

53 Nikhil Churamani, Paul Anton, Marc Brügger, Erik Fließwasser, Thomas Hummel, Julius Mayer, Waleed Mustafa, Hwei Geok Ng, Thi Linh Chi Nguyen, Quan Nguyen, Marcus Soll, Sebastian Springenberg, Sascha Griffiths, Stefan Heinrich, Nicolás Navarro-Guerrero, Erik Strahl, Johannes Twiefel, Cornelius Weber and Stefan Wermter, *The Impact of Personalisation on Human-Robot Interaction in Learning Scenarios* in Proceedings of the 5th International Conference on Human Agent Interaction (HAI '17). Association for Computing Machinery (New York, 2017) 171 <https://doi.org/10.1145/3125739.3125756> accessed 4 August 2023.

54 Alessandra Rossi, Mariacarla Staffa, Antonio Origlia, Maria di Maro and Silvia Rossi, *BRILLO: A Robotic Architecture for Personalised Long-lasting Interactions in a Bartending Domain* in Companion of the 2021 ACM/IEEE International Conference on Human-Robot Interaction (HRI '21 Companion). Association for Computing Machinery (New York, 2021) 426 <https://doi.org/10.1145/3434074.3447206> accessed 4 August 2023.

55 Christoph Lutz and Aurelia Tamó-Larrieux, 'The Robot Privacy Paradox: Understanding How Privacy Concerns Shape Intentions to Use Social Robots' (2020) 1 *Human-Machine Communication* 87–111. Anna Chatzimichali, Ross Harrison and Dimitrios Chrysostomou, 'Toward Privacy-Sensitive Human – Robot Interaction: Privacy Terms and Human – Data Interaction in the Personal

First, the use/reuse/repurposing of data. Personal AI systems are highly personalised products adapted to fit the user's needs, behaviours and preferences, and to create a deep engagement with the individual.[56] Personalised medical/nursing robots require data about a specific patient (about his or her mental and physical needs, particular tastes, comorbidities, and schedules) to make individualised inferences and act accordingly. For this personalisation to take place, large amounts of data about the person are required, potentially data that were initially collected for therapeutic purposes, which brings us back to the considerations discussed previously regarding the principle of purpose limitation.

The second issue is profiling. The input data (the predictors) concerning the individual are used to evaluate personal aspects relating to that natural person. It refers to the automated processing of data about an individual to make personal inferences about that person, 'in particular to analyse or predict aspects concerning that natural person's performance at work, economic situation, health, personal preferences, interests, reliability, behaviour, location or movements'.[57] Profiling does not necessarily imply the use of AI, nor is AI even mentioned in the GDPR provisions on profiling (or in any other provision, for that matter), but most profiling nowadays is carried out using AI technologies.[58]

For instance, take the case of training an AI robot to look after a patient that is likely to suffer from panic attacks. In order for the robot to be able to cope with such attacks, it must be able to predict them, which, in turn, requires an analysis of the factors that trigger those attacks. A 'psychological profile' of the person is required, including his or her mental history, traumas, concerns, family environment, etc. Based on those data, the AI system will make predictions about the person's behaviour which, in turn, help to profile the individual. Profiling might lead to failing the compatibility test due to the huge threat to individual privacy that it implies.

Nonetheless, profiling is not entirely forbidden by the GDPR. Article 22 of the GDPR allows it under limited circumstances, including when the data subject has provided consent (Art. 22[4] GDPR).[59] As a rule, AI robot personalisation is made at the request of the user and, therefore, the required profiling will most likely have the data subject's consent.

There is a problem, though: some of the individuals who will be using these AI robots might be incapable of providing consent (for instance, for lack of mental

Robot Era' (2021) 12(1) *Paladyn, Journal of Behavioral Robotics* 160) called it the 'personalisation paradox'.

56 European Parliament (n 7) 46.

57 Ibid., 39.

58 On the use of AI for profiling see, for instance, J Kietzmann, J Paschen and E Treen, 'Artificial Intelligence in Advertising: How Marketers Can Leverage Artificial Intelligence Along the Consumer Journey' (2018) 58(3) *Journal of Advertising Research* 263; Thomas Ploug, 'The Right Not to Be Subjected to AI Profiling Based on Publicly Available Data – Privacy and the Exceptionalism of AI Profiling' (2023) 36(14) *Philosophy & Technology* <https://doi.org/10.1007/s13347-023-00616-9>, accessed 4 August 2023.

59 Helena U. Vrabec, *Data Subject Rights under the GDPR* (Oxford Academic 2021) 189–214.

capacity). The GDPR does not address these situations, since this is a matter of national law. In most national legal orders, the solution is that a third party who has the legal right to make decisions on behalf of that person can consent in accordance with the applicable national law.[60]

7.6 The Advent of the European Health Data Space

On 3 May 2022, the European Commission launched the proposal for a Regulation on the EHDS. The EU realised that the limitations on the reuse and repurposing of existing data was a waste of benefits (including economic ones) for EU citizens and EU companies. In the highly regulated healthcare sector, in particular, the waste of data became a concern because it hampers innovation and better medical care. Moreover, the EHDS will be a central building block of Digital Europe and, allegedly, largely facilitate the development of AI medical and nursing robots.

The draft EHDS includes a legal framework for the reuse and repurposing of health data by the industry for innovation and, in particular, AI purposes. The aim is to allow companies operating in this field to have access to a large volume of high-quality health data for research and innovation purposes.

7.6.1 Basic Concepts Under the EHDS

The EHDS deals with all kinds of personal and non-personal electronic health data The challenges of data repurposing clearly have a more drastic effect on the former, as non-personal data lie outside the scope of the GDPR and can therefore be used and repurposed almost without restriction. The more relevant concept, then, is that of personal electronic health data.

The EHDS definition builds on the one established in the GDPR (Art. 2[1][a] of the EHDS), since the EHDS uses the concepts of 'personal data', 'health data' and 'genetic data' as defined in the GDPR. However, the basic concept of 'health data' deriving from the GDPR seems to be extended by the last part of Art. 2(2)(a) of the EHDS to also include 'data referring to determinants of health, or data processed in relation to the provision of healthcare services'. The extension may be more apparent than real, as the definition set out in the GDPR is not as restricted as it might seem, given that the concept of health data in Recital 35 includes 'information . . . collected in the course of . . . the provision of healthcare services'. Thus, the scope of both definitions of health data may end up being the same.[61] The concept of electronic health data is a very broad one and encompasses, for instance, data from

60 Gianclaudio Malgieri and Jędrzej Niklas, 'Vulnerable Data Subjects' (2020) 37 *Computer Law & Security Review* <https://doi.org/10.1016/j.clsr.2020.105415> accessed 4 August 2023.

61 European Data Protection Board and European Data Protection Supervisor, *Joint Opinion 03/2022 on the Proposal for a Regulation on the European Health Data Space*, 13 <https://edpb.europa.eu/system/files/2022-07/edpb_edps_jointopinion_202203_europeanhealthdataspace_en.pdf> accessed 15 July 2023.

electronic health records, clinical trials, other kinds of medical studies, and medical and fitness apps.

The modus operandi of the EHDS involves two main stakeholders: the data holder and the data user. The data holder (Art. 2[2][y] of the EHDS) is the natural or legal person that originally collected the data for their own purposes – presumably in compliance with the GDPR requirements – and is now the holder of the data.[62] This person or entity can be compelled under the EHDS to release the data to the data user if certain conditions are fulfilled. The data user (Art. 2[2][z] of the EHDS), in turn, is the natural or legal person that, based on a data permit, can receive data from the data holder to redirect them for secondary use. The previously mentioned data permit (Art. 2[2][aa] of the EHDS) refers to an authorisation to process data for the so-called secondary uses. It can be issued either by the data holder itself or by the health data access bodies (Art. 36 ff. of the EHDS), which are new bodies to be created in EU Member States to facilitate access to data for secondary uses (but not defined in the EHDS).

A key concept under the EHDS is that of 'secondary use' (Art. 2[2][e] of the EHDS).[63] This does not necessarily refer to subsequent use, but to the uses described in Chapter IV of the EHDS, which are basically those uses that are connected with health but do not refer to the delivery of healthcare (which, under the EHDS, is the 'primary use'). The use of health data to train an AI robot will fall under secondary data use, even if it was the original purpose of the data collection.

The EDHS creates data sharing and release obligations that do not exist in the GDPR.[64] These obligations even apply to data involving intellectual property (IP) rights and/or trade secrets, in which case 'all measures necessary to preserve the confidentiality of IP rights and trade secrets shall be taken' (Art. 33[4] of the EHDS), but there is no real clarification regarding the measures at issue. Still, there is the risk that some data holders, fearing negative outcomes for IP rights, will try to avoid sharing the data with AI developers.

7.6.2 Legitimate Purposes for Secondary Data Uses

Article 34 of the EHDS establishes the permitted purposes for which electronic health data can be accessed and processed for secondary use, including the repurposing of data. The common denominator of the purposes listed in that provision is their connection with the public interest (the public good). Pure profit activities are excluded, as it results from the legitimate purposes set forth in Art. 34 and from

62 For a criticism of the vast scope of this definition, see Terzis (n 3) 10.

63 The very notion of 'secondary use' is new to data protection laws, as it was not included in the GDPR or in the previous Data Protection Directive. See Becker et al. (n 14).

64 Still, this is not a general obligation, as micro-enterprises are exempt from it (Art. 33[2] of the EHDS). However, as any company/entity receiving public funding (from the EU or from the Member State) is under such an obligation (Recital 40 of the EHDS), one might wonder whether micro-enterprises in these conditions are also obliged to share data for secondary uses.

the content of Recitals 37–41.[65] Moreover, the use (including the repurposing) of data can never operate against the individual. As stated in Recital 41 of the EHDS, '[a]ny attempt to use the data for any measures detrimental to the natural person, to increase insurance premiums, to advertise products or treatments, or develop harmful products should be prohibited'. The prohibited uses of electronic health data are developed further in Art. 35 of the EHDS.

Considering the case study described in this chapter – the repurposing of personal health data to train an AI nursing robot – three possible legal grounds can be envisaged: 'innovation activities for products or services contributing to public health or social security, or ensuring high levels of quality and safety of healthcare, of medicinal products or of medical devices' (Art. 34[1][f] of the EHDS); 'training, testing and evaluating of algorithms, including in medical devices, AI systems and digital health applications, contributing to the public health or social security, or ensuring high levels of quality and safety of healthcare, of medicinal products or of medical devices' (Art. 34[1][g] of the EHDS); or 'providing personalised healthcare consisting in assessing, maintaining or restoring the state of health of natural persons, based on the health data of other natural persons' (Art. 34[1][h] of the EHDS).[66]

7.7 Mechanisms for Access to Data Under the EHDS

7.7.1 The Data Permit–based Approach

The EHDS sets up a more flexible, faster and easier mechanism for accessing personal health electronic data and using them in the development of AI medical and nursing robots. However, there is a procedure that must be followed. The core item in this procedure is the data permit and, thus, the data user (the AI developer) becomes a data applicant for this purpose.

There are two different processes for obtaining the data permit. When AI developers wish to have access to data from one single data holder located in one single Member State, they can submit the data access application or request directly to the latter, which will analyse the data access (Art. 49 of the EHDS).[67] If the assessment is positive, the data holder will issue the data permit and release the data to the AI developer in a secure environment, potentially against payment of a fee. The data holder then has three months to inform the relevant health data access body of the data access applications or requests received and the data permits issued. The data

65 See, in particular, the following segments: 'should be made available by data holders to health data access bodies, in order to maximise the impact of the public investment and support research, innovation, patient safety or policy making benefitting the society' (Recital 40); 'Access to data for secondary use should contribute to the general interest of the society' (Recital 41).

66 For a criticism of the overly broad description of these purposes, see Terzis (n 3) 11.

67 A data request does not allow access to the actual data but merely to an 'anonymised statistical format and the data user shall have no access to the electronic health data used to provide this answer' (Art. 47[1] of the EHDS).

holder and the AI developer (data user) will be deemed joint controllers (Art. 26 of the GDPR; Art. 49[3] EHDS).

The procedure becomes far more complex (and consequently lengthy) when several data holders are involved, as established in Arts. 45–46 of the EHDS. When that is the case, the data access request must be submitted to the national health data access body, which will be responsible for appraising the request, mainly by considering the legitimacy of the purpose and the cyber-security measures guaranteed by the AI developer. The decision must be made within a time limit of two months, but this can be extended for two additional months depending on the complexity of the request. If this is the case, the AI developer should be informed about the extension and the justifying reasons (Art. 46[3] of the EHDS). If, after the final deadline, no decision has been made, the data permit will be deemed issued (Art. 46[3] of the EHDS). It is up to the national health data access body (and not the data user; that is, the AI developer) to request the data from the data holder (Art. 46[4] of the EHDS). Article 46(4) of the EDHS states that this contact must be made 'immediately', which is a term open to different interpretations, as the concept might vary according to specific circumstances. The data holder is granted a two-month period (which can be extended in some cases) to release the requested data (presumably, there is no possibility of objecting), but again, the release is not made directly to the data user, but to the national health data access body, which will subsequently pass on those data to the AI developer (Art. 46[4] of the EHDS). The latter can then use the data, but only in conformity with the terms of the data permit (Art. 46[7] of the EHDS).[68]

The data permit is not unlimited in time. It will last for the duration of the secondary purposes invoked for access to the data, but for no longer than five years, even though the time limit can be extended once, but again for no longer than five years (Art. 46[9] of the EHDS).

According to Art. 45(3) of the EHDS, when the request targets several Member States, the data user is not required to contact all the national health data access bodies involved. To facilitate the procedure, it is established that the request may be submitted to a single national data access body of its choice, which will subsequently share the request with the other national health data access bodies involved, using the HealthData@EU platform (Art. 45[3] of the EHDS).

One might think that a data access request submitted to several national data access bodies would receive the same answer from all of them; for instance, by binding the remaining bodies to the decision of the national health data access body where the data request was originally submitted. Otherwise, the process would become far more bureaucratic and lengthier and, moreover, might give rise to potentially opposite decisions from different bodies. Yet this is not the solution deriving from the text of the EHDS. Recital 50 states that '[i]n order to ensure that all health data access bodies issue permits in a similar way, it is necessary to establish a standard common process for the issuance of data permits, with similar requests

68 Terzis (n 3), 6–7.

in different Member States'. Moreover, Art. 54(2) of the EHDS, on mutual recognition, states that '[a] data permit issued by one concerned health data access body may benefit from mutual recognition by the other concerned health data access bodies'. Thus, even though European lawmakers try to encourage common decisions from all the health data access bodies involved,[69] the fact is that, at least in theory, they can decide differently.

7.7.2 Assessment of This Approach

Whether the permit-based approach is suitable in this context is doubtful, as it is very bureaucratic and lengthy, at least lengthier than under the self-assessment model. It may therefore not be as efficient as would be required to really make a difference in innovating digital health. Whether it works also very much depends on how Member States equip their health data access bodies, which can vary greatly across the EU (see, for instance, how data protection authorities are equipped in different Member States). Also, note that if a decision is not released after four months, the authorization to access data will be considered granted (Art. 46[3] EHDS), eventually without taking into consideration all the criteria required for that assessment.

An alternative to this approach may lie in adopting a risk-based approach mechanism, grounded in a self-assessment by the data users (in this case, the AI developers) regarding compliance with the EHDS requirements, with the obligation to keep records of the entire procedure for potential audits.

The risk-based approach would facilitate access to data and make it less rigid and faster, which are the main aims of the EHDS. An obvious concern raised by this alternative design is trust. AI developers and other data users are eager to get their hands on the data, and so one might wonder how objective they will be in that assessment. However, the EU has vast experience with self-assessment procedures. We find them in the EU AI Act, regarding the CE (*Conformité Européenne*, or European Conformity) conformity mark for high-risk AI systems (except for biometric recognition, in the strict cases where this is allowed).[70] The same is true for the Medical Device Regulation,[71] whereby most class I medical devices are only subject to the manufacturer's assessment.[72] Both examples show that trust in self-

69 In addition, a different part of Recital 50 says 'also ensuring coherence between different health data access bodies'.

70 Article 43 of the AI Act. See Vera Lúcia Raposo, 'Ex Machina: Preliminary Critical Assessment of the European Draft Act on Artificial Intelligence' (2022) 30(1) *International Journal of Law and Information Technology* 88, 98–99.

71 Regulation (EU) 2017/745 of the European Parliament and of the Council of 5 April 2017 on medical devices, amending Directive 2001/83/EC, Regulation (EC) No 178/2002 and Regulation (EC) No 1223/2009 and repealing Council Directives 90/385/EEC and 93/42/EEC [2017] OJ L117/1 (MDR).

72 Article 52(7) of the MDR. See Lukas Peter, Ladislav Hajek, Petra Maresova, Martin Augustynek and Marek Penhaker 'Medical Devices: Regulation, Risk Classification, and Open Innovation' (2020) 6(2) *Journal of Open Innovation: Technology, Market, and Complexity* 42.

assessments does not seem to be an issue under EU law, yet this was not the path followed by the European lawmakers in the EHDS.

7.8 The GDPR and the EHDS: Can They Go Together?

The relationship between the GDPR and the EHDS is still unclear, as the former forbids exactly what the latter intends to encourage: the free and easy sharing, use, reuse and repurposing of personal health data.

7.8.1 Legal Grounds for Data Processing

One of the main challenges is the identification of a proper legal ground for data processing from Arts. 6(1) and 9(2) of the GDPR. A fundamental principle of the GDPR is the principle of lawfulness, meaning that any data processing activity must be based on a legal ground in Art. 6(1) of the GDPR, i.e., the real-life scenario must match one of the legal scenarios described in that provision. Moreover, when it comes to sensitive data, such as health data, an additional legal ground must be found in Art. 9(2) of the GDPR.[73]

Access to data for secondary purposes, as established in the EHDS, is still a form of data processing and, as such, is subject to GDPR rules. Any other conclusion would require the EHDS to expressly exclude its data processing activities from the GDPR, which is not the case, nor is there any sign of possible amendments to the GDPR to provide for that same exclusion. Therefore, for AI developers (the data users) to have access to data to train their AI robots, both Arts. 6(1) and 9(2) must be observed, as acknowledged in Recital 37 of the EHDS.

For the EHDS to achieve its aim of facilitating data processing (for the specific purposes defined therein), it is imperative that it brings some flexibility to fulfil the legal grounds established in Arts. 6(1) and 9(2) of the GDPR. Otherwise, its ambitious aims will be frustrated. If Arts. 6(1) and 9(2) were applied as if there were no EHDS, every kind of data processing set out in the latter would be severely restricted by the GDPR requirement for a legal ground.

Therefore, a major contribution of the EHDS will be to allow a more flexible interpretation of Art. 6(1) of the GDPR. We can assume that Art. 6(1)(c) of the GDPR (compliance with a legal obligation to which the controller is subject) will be called on, based on the idea that data holders have the obligation to release the data in the light of the EDHS. In alternative, Art. 6(1)(f) of the GDPR (legitimate interest) can be invoked, given that when the interests claimed by the AI developers (to train medical and nursing AI robots) match the purposes listed in Arts. 34(1)(f)(g)(h) of the EHDS, the legitimacy of those interests is proven.

73 Regarding the lawfulness principle and the obligation to identify a legal ground for data processing, E Gil González and P de Hert, 'Understanding the Legal Provisions that Allow Processing and Profiling of Personal Data – An Analysis of GDPR Provisions and Principles' (2019) 19 *ERA Forum* 597598–597607.

Similarly, Art. 9(2) of the GDPR must also be read in the light of the EHDS: when data users invoke one of the aims referred to in Arts. 34(1)(f)(g)(h) of the EHDS, this shows that they are acting based on a substantial public interest (Art. 9[2][g] of the GDPR) or claiming a public interest in public health (Art. 9[2][i] of the GDPR). Other possibilities mentioned in Art. 9(2) of the GDPR, such as individual treatment (Art. 9[2][h] of the GDPR) or the scientific research exemption (Art. 9[2][j] of the GDPR), are also reinforced by being referred to in Art. 34 of the EHDS.[74] All these legal bases could potentially apply to the training of nursing robots.

7.8.2 Requirements for Data Access: Data Security

A key feature of the GDPR is the technical and organisational procedures to protect data from the earliest stages of data processing. In the GDPR, this is known as data protection by design and by default (Art. 25 of the GDPR). The EHDS also lines up with the GDPR in the demand for data protection measures. For instance, every data transfer must take place in a secure processing environment (Arts. 49[2] and 50 of the EHDS).

To get access to the data for one of the permitted purposes, the AI developer – which is the data applicant here – has to submit a data access application which satisfies the requirements set out in Art. 45 of the EHDS, namely the principles of data minimisation and purpose limitation.

The data must be provided in an anonymised format, but if the purposes of the processing cannot be achieved with anonymised data, then the EHDS allows the data to be pseudonymised. In the latter case, access to pseudonymised data is permitted, but the AI developer must provide the reason why anonymised data are not enough for the envisaged purpose, and the encryption key will be kept only by the national data access body (Recitals 49 and 50 of the EHDS).

Data is pseudonymised when personal identification has been removed and is kept in a separate location.[75] In the health field, these would be the data that refer to the person's medical condition, the biomarkers (pulse and blood pressure, laboratory tests of blood and other tissues, etc.), the medicines being taken, or the procedures performed on that person, but without stating his or her name or other data that could immediately identify the individual. In any case, AI developers are forbidden to attempt to re-identify the data subjects.

74 Nils Lölfing, *The European Health Data Space Proposal of the European Commission* (*Bird&Bird*, 5 May 2022) <www.twobirds.com/en/insights/2022/germany/the-european-health-data-space-proposal-of-the-european-commission> accessed 4 August 2023.

75 Pseudonymous data is still 'explicitly and importantly, personal data, but its processing is seen as presenting less risk to data subjects, and as such is given certain privileges designed to incentivise its use'. See Lilian Edwards, 'Data Protection I: Enter the GDPR' in Lilian Edwards (ed), *Law, Policy and the Internet* (Hart 2018) 88. See also Michèle Finck and Frank Pallas, 'They Who Must Not Be Identified – Distinguishing Personal from Non-Personal Data Under the GDPR' (February 2020) 10(1) *International Data Privacy Law* 11, 21–22.

Article 44(3) of the EHDS forbids data users from identifying pseudonymised data (even though Recital 49 of the EHDS allows for some restrictive exceptions). A failure to comply with this obligation could lead to data users (the AI developers) having their data access permits revoked by data access bodies (Art. 43[3][4] of the EHDS).[76] The provision only envisages this possibility for the case in Art. 46 of the EHDS; that is, when the data permit was issued by a data access body. It does not mention Art. 49 of the EHDS, which refers to cases when the permit was issued by the data holder itself.[77] However, as Art. 49(2) refers to Art. 46 with regard to the issuance of the data permit, it is reasonable to read Art. 43(3)(4) as referring to both situations.

A similar prohibition on re-identification is not imposed with regard to anonymised data. This silence might be due to the fact that anonymised data are traditionally considered unidentifiable. However, we know nowadays that this is not the case, especially when AI techniques are used.[78] The EHDS establishes no penalty for an AI developer that manages to re-identify anonymised data.

7.9 How Optimistic Should We Be?

Data processing in the healthcare sector always poses legal challenges due to the particularly demanding data protection regime imposed by the GDPR, especially for data concerning health and genetics. The introduction of AI into this setting further increases the difficulties, given that training an AI requires an immense amount of data.

When the EHDS was announced, it came with the promise of a more flexible legal arrangement for using, reusing and repurposing data to counterbalance the rigidity of the GDPR legal regime (one might wonder whether the answer would not instead lie in making the GDPR itself more flexible). The hope is that data access and data repurposing will become easier, speedier and more flexible, but prudence recommends that we create no high expectations. We are, after all, in the EU, the land of the brave, where personal data is protected no matter what, whatever the cost, and even notwithstanding the actual benefits of data use. Ultimately, perhaps we should be just moderately optimistic.

Bibliography

Article 29 Data Protection Working Party, 'Opinion 03/2013 on Purpose Limitation' (2 April 2013) <https://ec.europa.eu/justice/article-29/documentation/opinion-recommendation/files/2013/wp203_en.pdf> accessed 24 July 2023

Article 29 Data Protection Working Party, 'Guidelines on Consent under Regulation 2016/67' (Adopted on 28 November 2017, as last Revised and Adopted on 10 April

76 Moreover, Art. 69 EHDS allows Member States to establish additional penalties in their national laws.

77 Also raising this concern, Slokenberga (n 45) 144–145. However, Slokenberga concludes that the cases described in Art. 49 of the EHDS are not covered by the prohibition in Art. 44(3) of the EHDS and recommends that the provision be rewritten.

78 Finck and Pallas (75).

2018) 28 <https://ec.europa.eu/newsroom/article29/document.cfm?action=display&doc_id=51030> accessed 20 August 2023

Becker R, Chokoshvili D, Comandé G, Dove ES, Hall A, Mitchell C, Molnár-Gábor F, Nicolàs P, Tervo S and Thorogood T, 'Secondary Use of Personal Health Data: When Is It "Further Processing" under the GDPR, and What Are the Implications for Data Controllers?' (2022) 30(2) *European Journal of Health Law* 129

Blair, T, 'GDPR: When Is It Permissible to Use Data beyond Its Original Purpose? The Edata Guide to GDPR' (*Morgan Lewis*, 24 October 2018) <www.morganlewis.com/pubs/2018/10/the-edata-guide-to-gdpr-gdpr-when-is-it-permissible-to-use-data-beyond-its-original-purpose> accessed 27 July 2023

Centre for Information Policy Leadership (CIPL), 'Artificial Intelligence and Data Protection How the GDPR Regulates AI' (March 2020) 13 <www.informationpolicycentre.com/uploads/5/7/1/0/57104281/cipl-hunton_andrews_kurth_legal_note_-_how_gdpr_regulates_ai__12_march_2020_.pdf> accessed 22 July 2023

Chatzimichali A, Harrison R and Chrysostomou D, 'Toward Privacy-Sensitive Human – Robot Interaction: Privacy Terms and Human – Data Interaction in the Personal Robot Era' (2021) 12(1) *Paladyn, Journal of Behavioral Robotics* 160

Churamani N, Anton P, Brügger M, Fließwasser E, Hummel T, Mayer J, Mustafa W, Ng HG, Nguyen TLC, Nguyen Q, Soll M, Springenberg S, Griffiths S, Heinrich S, Navarro-Guerrero N, Strahl E, Twiefel J, Weber C and Wermter S, 'The Impact of Personalisation on Human-Robot Interaction in Learning Scenarios' (Proceedings of the 5th International Conference on Human Agent Interaction (HAI '17). Association for Computing Machinery, 2017) 171 <https://doi.org/10.1145/3125739.3125756> accessed 4 August 2023

Commission Nationale de L'informatique et des Libertés (CNIL), 'Sous-traitants: la réutilisation de données confiées par un responsable de traitement' (12 janvier 2022) <www.cnil.fr/fr/sous-traitants-la-reutilisation-de-donnees-confiees-par-un-responsable-de-traitement> accessed 14 July 2023

Davenport T and Ronanki R, 'Artificial Intelligence for the Real World' (2018) 96(1) *Harvard Business Review* 108

Davenport T and Kalakota R, 'The Potential for Artificial Intelligence in Healthcare' (2019) 6(2) *Future Healthcare Journal* 94

Edwards L, 'Data Protection I: Enter the GDPR' in Edwards L (ed), *Law, Policy and the Internet* (Hart 2018) 88

European Commission, 'Proposal for a Regulation of the European Parliament and of the Council Laying down Harmonised Rules on Artificial Intelligence (Artificial Intelligence Act) and Amending Certain Union Legislative Acts, COM' (2021) 206 final AIA

European Commission, 'Proposal for a Regulation of the European Parliament and of the Council on the European Health Data Space, COM' (2022) 197 final. <https://eur-lex.europa.eu/legal-content/EN/TXT/?uri=CELEX%3A52022PC0197> accessed 4 August 2023

European Data Protection Board, 'Guidelines 05/2020 on Consent under Regulation 2016/679' (4 May 2020) <https://edpb.europa.eu/sites/default/files/files/file1/edpb_guidelines_202005_consent_en.pdf> accessed 20 August 2023

European Data Protection Board, 'Opinion 3/2019 Concerning the Questions and Answers on the Interplay between the Clinical Trials Regulation (CTR) and the General Data Protection Regulation (GDPR) (Art. 70.1.b))' (23 January 2019) <https://edpb.europa.eu/sites/default/files/files/file1/edpb_opinionctrq_a_final_en.pdf> accessed 4 August 2023

European Data Protection Board and European Data Protection Supervisor, 'Joint Opinion 03/2022 on the Proposal for a Regulation on the European Health Data Space' 13 <https://edpb.europa.eu/system/files/2022-07/edpb_edps_jointopinion_202203_europeanhealthdataspace_en.pdf> accessed 15 July 2023

European Data Protection Supervisor, 'A Preliminary Opinion on Data Protection and Scientific Research' (6 January 2020) <https://edps.europa.eu/sites/edp/files/publication/20-01-06_opinion_research_en.pdf> accessed 20 August 2023

European Health Data Protection Supervisor, 'Preliminary Opinion 8/2020 on the European Health Data Space' (*Recital*, 17 November 2020) 19 <https://edps.europa.eu/sites/edp/files/publication/20-11-17_preliminary_opinion_european_health_data_space_en.pdf> accessed 12 August 2023

European Parliament, 'The Impact of the General Data Protection Regulation (GDPR) on Artificial Intelligence', *EPRS | European Parliamentary Research Service* (2020a) <www.europarl.europa.eu/stoa/en/document/EPRS_STU(2020)641530>

European Parliament, 'The Impact of the General Data Protection Regulation (GDPR) on Artificial Intelligence', *EPRS | European Parliamentary Research Service* (2020b) <www.europarl.europa.eu/stoa/en/document/EPRS_STU(2020)641530> accessed 13 August 2023

Finck M and Pallas F, 'They Who Must Not be Identified – Distinguishing Personal from Non-Personal Data under the GDPR' (February 2020) 10(1) *International Data Privacy Law* 11, 21–22

Forgó N, Hänold S and Schütze B, 'The Principle of Purpose Limitation and Big Data' in Corrales M, Fenwick M and Forgó N (eds), *New Technology, Big Data and the Law* (Perspectives in Law, Business and Innovation, Springer 2017)

Fosch-Villaronga E and Mahler T, 'Cybersecurity, Safety and Robots: Strengthening the Link between Cybersecurity and Safety in the Context of Care Robots' (2021) 41 *Computer Law & Security Review* 2

Georgieva L and Kuner C, 'Article 9 Processing of Special Categories of Personal Data' in Kuner C and others (eds), *The EU General Data Protection Regulation (GDPR): A Commentary* (Oxford Academic 2020) 365

Gil González E and de Hert P, 'Understanding the Legal Provisions That Allow Processing and Profiling of Personal Data – An Analysis of GDPR Provisions and Principles' (2019) 19 *ERA Forum* 597

Giulia S and Comandè G, 'Can the GDPR Make Data Flow for Research Easier? Yes It Can, by Differentiating! A Careful Reading of the GDPR Shows How EU Data Protection Law Leaves Open Some Significant Flexibilities for Data Protection-Sound Research Activities' (2021) 41 *Computer Law & Security Review* 1

Guerra G, 'Evolving Artificial Intelligence and Robotics in Medicine, Evolving European Law: Comparative Remarks Based on the Surgery Litigation' (2021) 28(6) *Maastricht Journal of European and Comparative Law* 805

High-Level Expert Group on Artificial Intelligence, 'A Definition of AI: Main Capabilities and Scientific Disciplines' (2019)

Hocking L, Parks S, Altenhofer M and Gunashekar S, *Reuse of Health Data by the European Pharmaceutical Industry* (RAND Corporation 2019)

Kesa A and Kerikmäe T, 'Artificial Intelligence and the GDPR: Inevitable Nemeses?' (2020) 10(3) *TalTech Journal of European Studies* 68

Kietzmann J, Paschen J and Treen E, 'Artificial Intelligence in Advertising: How Marketers Can Leverage Artificial Intelligence Along the Consumer Journey' (2018) 58(3) *Journal of Advertising Research* 263

Kosta E, 'Article 7 Conditions for Consent' in Kuner C and others (eds), *The EU General Data Protection Regulation (GDPR): A Commentary* (Oxford Academic 2020) 345

Kotschy W, 'Article 6 Lawfulness of Processing' in Kuner C and others (eds), *The EU General Data Protection Regulation (GDPR): A Commentary* (Oxford Academic 2020) 321

Lölfing N, 'The European Health Data Space Proposal of the European Commission' (*Bird & Bird*, 5 May 2022) <www.twobirds.com/en/insights/2022/germany/the-european-health-data-space-proposal-of-the-european-commission> accessed 4 August 2023

Malgieri G and Niklas J, 'Vulnerable Data Subjects' (2020) 37 *Computer Law & Security Review* <https://doi.org/10.1016/j.clsr.2020.105415> accessed 4 August 2023

Mantelero A, 'From Group Privacy to Collective Privacy: Towards a New Dimension of Privacy and Data Protection in the Big Data Era' in Taylor L, Floridi L and van der Sloot B (eds), *Group Privacy: New Challenges of Data Technologies* (Springer 2017) 139

Pedersen T and Johansen C, 'Behavioural Artificial Intelligence: An Agenda for Systematic Empirical Studies of Artificial Inference' (2020) 35 *AI & Society* 519

Peter L, Hajek L, Maresova P, Augustynek M and Penhaker M, 'Medical Devices: Regulation, Risk Classification, and Open Innovation' (2020) 6(2) *Journal of Open Innovation: Technology, Market, and Complexity* 42

Ploug T, 'The Right Not to be Subjected to AI Profiling Based on Publicly Available Data – Privacy and the Exceptionalism of AI Profiling' (2023) 36(14) *Philosophy & Technology* <https://doi.org/10.1007/s13347-023-00616-9> accessed 4 August 2023

Purtova N, 'The Law of Everything: Broad Concept of Personal Data and Future of EU Data Protection Law' (2018) 10(1) *Law, Innovation and Technology* 40

Quinn P and Malgieri G, 'The Difficulty of Defining Sensitive Data – The Concept of Sensitive Data in the EU Data Protection Framework' (2021) 22(8) *German Law Journal* 1583

Raposo VL, 'Can Personal Data be Recycled? Data Reuse and Repurposing under the EHDS' (forthcoming)

Raposo VL, 'Ex Machina: Preliminary Critical Assessment of the European Draft Act on Artificial Intelligence' (2022) 30(1) *International Journal of Law and Information Technology* 88, 98–99

Rocher L, Hendricks JM and de Montjoye Y-A, 'Estimating the Success of Re-Identifications in Incomplete Datasets Using Generative Models' (2019) 10 *Nature Communications* 3069

Rossi A, Staffa M, Origlia A, di Maro M and Rossi S. 'BRILLO: A Robotic Architecture for Personalised Long-Lasting Interactions in a Bartending Domain' (Companion of the 2021 ACM/IEEE International Conference on Human-Robot Interaction (HRI '21 Companion), Association for Computing Machinery 2021) 426 <https://doi.org/10.1145/3434074.3447206> accessed 4 August 2023

Salami E, 'AI, Big Data and the Protection of Personal Data in Medical Practice' (2019) 3 *EPLR* 165

Sato M, 'Singapore's Police Now Have Access to Contact Tracing Data' (*MIT Technology Review*, January 2021) <www.technologyreview.com/2021/01/05/1015734/singapore-contact-tracing-police-data-covid/> accessed 24 July 2023

Siciliano B and Khatib O, 'Introduction' in Siciliano B and Khatib O (eds), *Springer Handbook of Robotics* (Springer 2008) <https://doi.org/10.1007/978-3-540-30301-5_1> 1

Slokenberga S, 'Scientific Research Regime 2.0?, How the Proposed EHDS Regulation May Change the GDPR Research Regime' (2022) *Technology and Regulation* 135–147, 139

Starkbaum J and Felt U, 'Negotiating the Reuse of Health-Data: Research, Big Data, and the European General Data Protection Regulation' (2019) 6(2) *Big Data & Society* <https://doi.org/10.1177/2053951719862594> accessed 3 July 2023

Terwangne C, 'Article 5 Principles Relating to Processing of Personal Data' in Kuner C and others (eds), *The EU General Data Protection Regulation (GDPR): A Commentary* (Oxford Academic 2020) 309, 315–317

Terzis P, 'Compromises and Asymmetries in the European Health Data Space' (2022) 29 *European Journal of Health Law* 1

Tzanou M, *Health Data Privacy under the GDPR: Big Data Challenges and Regulatory Responses* (Routledge 2020)

Von Eschenbach WJ, 'Transparency and the Black Box Problem: Why We Do Not Trust AI' (2021) 34 *Philosophy & Technology* 1607

Vrabec HU, *Data Subject Rights under the GDPR* (Oxford Academic 2021) 189–214

Wang S, Pershing S, Lee AY and on behalf of the AAO Taskforce on AI and AAO Medical Information Technology Committee, 'Big Data Requirements for Artificial Intelligence' (2020) 31(5) *Current Opinion in Ophthalmology* 318
Weng Y-H and Ho C-H, 'A Comparative Data Protection Analysis of Healthcare Robots (Part 1): Embodiment and Algorithms for HRI' in Fina S, Lemley M and Vogl R (eds), *TTLF Working Papers* (Stanford – Vienna Transatlantic Technology Law Forum 2019) 2
Zarsky T, 'Incompatible: The GDPR in the Age of Big Data' (2017) 47 4(2) *Seton Hall Law Review* 99

Part IV

Blockchain, Robots, Legal Tech and Data Protection

8 Data Protection and Blockchain Technologies

Gerald Spindler

8.1 Introduction and Essential Questions

Blockchain technology, which was developed in 2008 by a still anonymous coder of software (or a group),[1] enabled for the first time the ability to avoid intermediaries as well as to ensure safety regarding the modification and alteration of content. Thus, blockchain technology rapidly became one of the most promising new developments in the digital economy, as it provided for all kinds of digital transactions a new tool that could minimize transaction costs. It also lead to the emergence of digital currencies such as Bitcoin and Ethereum, and tokens which now represent a major part of capital market; at the same time, it led to the development of new governance structures such as the Decentralized Autonomous Organization (DAO) replacing traditional investment structures.[2]

However, the new possibilities also confronted data protection law with new challenges as blockchain technology provides for a total security, not allowing ex post erasures, also establishing decentralized structures. Hence, the following major issues arose from a data protection perspective.

- Is there any processing of personal data?
- Who is the data controller? To whom can actions of supervisory authorities be addressed?

1 Satoshi Nakamoto, 'Bitcoin: A Peer-to-Peer Electronic Cash System' (*Bitcoin*, 1 May 2009) <https://bitcoin.org/bitcoin.pdf> accessed 8 July 2023; see also Marianna Belotti, Nikola Božić, Guy Pujolle and Stefano Secci, 'A Vademecum on Blockchain Technologies: When, Which, and How' (2019) 21 *IEEE Communications Surveys & Tutorials* 3796; UW Chohan, 'A History of Bitcoin' (5 February 2022) 8–9 <https://doi.org/10.2139/ssrn.3047875> accessed 30 June 2023.

2 Wei Cai, Zehua Wang, Jason B Ernst, Zhen Hong, Chen Feng and Victor C M Leung, 'Decentralized Applications: The Blockchain-Empowered Software System' (2018) 6 *IEEE Access* 53019; David Lucking, 'Decentralized Autonomous Organizations' (*Allen & Overy*, 11 July 2016) <www.allenovery.com/en-gb/global/news-and-insights/publications/decentralized-autonomous-organizations> accessed 26 June 2023; Steven A Wright, 'DAOs & ADSs' (2023) *IEEE 15th International Symposium on Autonomous Decentralized System (ISADS)* 1–6; see also Vitalik Buterin, 'Ethereum: A Next-Generation Smart Contract and Decentralized Application Platform' (*Ethereum*, 2014) <https://ethereum.org/669c9e2e2027310b6b3cdce6e1c52962/Ethereum_Whitepaper_-_Buterin_2014.pdf> accessed 26 June 2023; Gerald Spindler, 'Blockchaintypen und ihre gesellschaftsrechtliche Einordnung' (2021) *Recht Digital* 309, 310.

DOI: 10.4324/9781003502791-12

- How should the principle of deletion or data minimization be dealt with?
- How can the right to erasure be implemented?
- How can the transfer of data to countries outside the European Union (EU) be regulated?

The first supervisory authorities, such as the CNIL (Commission Nationale de l'Informatique et des Libertés) in France[3] and the Spanish data protection supervisory authority have taken a position on this, which is to be taken as a basis in the following; however, there are no statements from the European Data Science Academy (EDSA) or the European Data Protection Supervisor (EDPS),[4] or from the Court of Justice of the European Union (CJEU) or German supervisory authorities. First of all, we have to summarize the technological background of blockchain technology and its inherent risks in order to understand and assess the data protection problems, which arise by using blockchain.

8.2 How Blockchain Works

8.2.1 Technical Framework

8.2.1.1 Basics

Digital transactions that want to do without an intermediary but also have to be unique and verifiable must solve the *double-spending* problem[5] which results from the fact that, on the one hand, digital values could in principle be transmitted multiple times without any loss of quality, and on the other hand, the mapping of a transaction in a decentralized network takes time and can therefore be susceptible to double-spending (so-called latencies). Blockchain serves precisely to solve these problems.[6]

In general, blockchain (or distributed ledger technology) is characterized by several elements that work together to enable secure and unambiguously traceable

3 Opinion of Commission Nationale Informatique & Libertés (CNIL), 'Solutions for a Responsible Use of the Blockchain in the Context of Personal Data' (September 2018) <www.cnil.fr/sites/default/files/atoms/files/blockchain.pdf> accessed 30 June 2023.

4 See, however, Opinion of EDPS 'on the proposal for a pilot rule for market infrastructures based on distributed ledger technology' (2021) <https://edps.europa.eu/system/files/2021-06/2021-0219_d0912_opinion_on_pilot_regime_for_market_infrastructures_de.pdf> accessed 6 July 2023 which 8 assumes personal data despite its encryption.

5 See Diogo Duarte, 'An Introduction to Blockchain Technology from a Legal Perspective and Its Tensions with the GDPR' (*Cyberlaw Journal of the Cyberlaw Research Centre of the University of Lisbon School of Law (CIJIC)*, 30 September 2019), 6 <https://doi.org/10.2139/ssrn.3545331> accessed 27 June 2023; Markus Kaulartz, '§ 5 Blockchain-Technologie' in Florian Möslein and Sebastian Omlor (eds), *Fintech-Handbuch* (2nd edn, C.H. Beck 2021) § 5 paras 9ff.

6 For further details, see Christoph Safferling and Christian Rückert, 'Telekommunikationsüberwachung bei Bitcoins-Heimliche Datenauswertung bei virtuellen Währungen gem. § 100a StPO?' (2015) *MMR* 788, 790.

transactions without an intermediary.[7] The *ledger* is a non-relational data storage system that registers transactions, with identical copies of the ledger contained in all *nodes*. All nodes – and thus all computers involved in blockchain – have the same information; recording of the information (transactions) therefore requires a consensus mechanism between the participants, which must be mapped by software (e.g., proof-of-work, but also other).[8] Furthermore, to ensure unambiguity, it must be guaranteed that the contents cannot be changed subsequently.

In the event of conflicting transactions on the network, the transaction that was first recorded in the ledger is assigned validity.[9] The transactions received by the respective nodes are collected in a block (in the case of Bitcoin, a block can be *mined* approximately every ten minutes)[10] and this is virtually proposed for inclusion in the ledger. The task of the *miners*, or more precisely of the *mining node*,[11] is then to use their computing power to determine a so-called *hash value* by trial and error, i.e., a cryptographic image of the previous block and the current block.[12] After successfully determining this hash value and completing the validation or consensus process, the block is then added to the ledger. The incentives for the miners to make their computing power available for this process are of a financial nature; for example, 6.25 Bitcoins plus transaction fees to be determined individually[13] are paid to whoever was the first in the network to determine the correct hash value.[14] The ledger itself is thus the chain of blocks.

---

7 For a description of how this works, see Kaulartz (n 5); Eduard Hofert, *Regulierung der Blockchain* (Mohr Siebeck 2018) 14ff.

8 On the whole see Federal Office for Information Security, 'Towards Secure Blockchains – Concepts, Requirements, Assessments', 23ff <www.bsi.bund.de/SharedDocs/Downloads/EN/BSI/Crypto/Secure_Blockchain.pdf?__blob=publicationFile&v=3> accessed 30 June 2023; Kaulartz (n 5) § 5 paras 13ff; BitFury Group, 'Proof of Stake versus Proof of Work' (*Bitfury*, 2015), 3ff <https://bitfury.com/content/downloads/pos-vs-pow-1.0.2.pdf> accessed 7 July 2023; Tim Swanson, 'Consensus-as-a-Service: A Brief Report on the Emergence of Permissioned, Distributed Ledger Systems' (*Great Wall of Numbers*, 2015), 4 <www.ofnumbers.com/2015/04/06/consensus-as-a-service-a-brief-report-on-the-emergence-of-permissioned-distributed-ledger-systems/> accessed 7 July 2023; Marianna Belotti, Nikola Božić, Guy Pujolle and Stefano Secci, 'A Vademecum on Blockchain Technologies: When, Which, and How' (2019) 21 *IEEE Communications Surveys & Tutorials* 3796, 3802–3803; For further details, see Gerald Spindler, 'Blockchain-Transaktionen und Vertrauensschutz' in Felix Maultzsch and Uwe Blaurock (eds), *Vertrauensschutz im digitalen Zeitalter* (Nomos 2020) 36ff.

9 Kaulartz (n 5) § 5 para 15.

10 Christoph Safferling and Christian Rückert, 'Telekommunikationsüberwachung bei Bitcoins-Heimliche Datenauswertung bei virtuellen Währungen gem. § 100a StPO?' (2015) *MMR* 788, 790.

11 The participants referred to below as *miners* are *mining nodes*.

12 On how hash functions work and their application on blockchain: Harald Pöttinger, 'No Blockchain without Hash Functions' <http://haraldpoettinger.com/blockchain-hashfunktionen/> accessed 7 July 2023.

13 Brian Baker and James Royal, 'What Is Bitcoin Mining and How Does It Work?' (27 March 2023) <www.bankrate.com/investing/what-is-bitcoin-mining/> accessed 30 June 2023.

14 David Scheider, 'Bitcoin Mining – How the Incentive Structure in the Network Determines the Price, in BTC-ECHO' (*BTC Echo*, 25 April 2019) <www.btc-echo.de/bitcoin-mining-wie-die-anreizstruktur-im-netzwerk-den-kurs-bestimmt/> accessed 7 July 2023.

Since each hash value of a subsequent block refers to the hash values of the previous blocks and their information is stored, a unique chain of transactions is generated (a so-called *single version of truth*). This means that in order to change or manipulate earlier transactions, all blocks that exist afterwards would have to be changed and cooperation with other nodes would have to be achieved; together with the high effort required to generate a block, this results in a high level of forgery protection.[15]

Encryption for the respective users is performed using a personal *private key* that is known only to the user and is stored in the user's *wallet* (an electronic memory) and a *public key* that represents the user's address, which is known to everyone. It is not possible to infer the private key from the public key (so-called *asymmetric encryption*).[16] During a transaction, the hash value determined from the transaction data is encrypted by the sender with his private key and thus, in addition to the transaction data as such, is made accessible to the recipient as a digital signature. The recipient can then decrypt the digital signature using the sender's public key, which is known to him, and compare the encrypted version of the hash value thus obtained with the hash value of the transaction data that he has determined himself. In doing so, it can be ensured that a public key only belongs to one person or digital identity, as is realized on the Bitcoin blockchain, for example.[17] After the transaction and the generation of the signature, these are fed into the network together with the public key and checked or validated there by each node.[18] The verification of transactions on a blockchain is carried out by all computers involved in the blockchain; only then is a new block released.

8.2.1.2 Permissioned and Permissionless Blockchain

Ideally, there are two different ways of operating a blockchain: on the one hand, the completely decentralized blockchain as a peer-to-peer network without its own administrator or server, in which case in principle anyone can participate (so-called

---

15 See also Kaulartz (n 5) § 5 para 13; Sigurd Schacht and Carsten Lanquillon, *Blockchain und maschinelles Lernen* (Springer Vieweg 2019) 41; Michèle Finck, 'Blockchain and the General Data Protection Regulation' (July 2019) Study for the European Parliamentary Research Service PE 634.445, 5 <www.europarl.europa.eu/RegData/etudes/STUD/2019/634445/EPRS_STU(2019)634445_EN.pdf> accessed 28 June 2023; Duarte, 'An Introduction to Blockchain Technology From a Legal Perspective and Its Tensions With the GDPR' (n 5) 10–11; Ce Yang, Juan Chen, Bin Zeng and Lei Liao, 'Overview of Blockchain Privacy Protection' *2022 IEEE 8th Intl Conference on Big Data Security on Cloud* (BigDataSecurity) 22 <https://ieeexplore.ieee.org/document/9799487> accessed 6 July 2023.

16 Markus Kaulartz 'Die Blockchain-Technologie' (2016) *CR* 474, 475; Oliver Stiemerling, 'Schutz von Software – Technische Grenzen und neue Möglichkeiten' in Axel Metzger and Jörg Wimmers (eds), *DGRI Jahrbuch 2014* (1st edn, Otto Schmidt 2015) para 286.

17 Duarte, 'An Introduction to Blockchain Technology From a Legal Perspective and Its Tensions With the GDPR' (n 5) 6 <https://doi.org/10.2139/ssrn.3545331> accessed 27 June 2023; Dirk Fox, 'Bitcoin' (2017) *DuD* 507; Markus Kaulartz, 'Die Blockchain-Technologie' (2016) *CR* 474, 475; Ralf Knaier, 'Handelsregister 4.0 dank Blockchain-Technologie?' (2017) *GmbHR* R305, R306; Bastian Liegmann, 'Umsatzsteuerliche Behandlung virtueller Währungen' (2018) *BB* 1175ff.

18 Kaulartz (n 5) § 5 paras 27ff.

permissionless blockchain); on the other hand, the centrally administered blockchain in which not everyone is admitted to blockchain, so-called *permissioned blockchain*.[19] In contrast to the permissionless blockchain, a central authority decides here which rights are granted to the participants in each case; the new blocks proposed in turn by the nodes classified as trustworthy are adopted as soon as they are released by the other nodes classified as trustworthy.[20] There are numerous variations between these poles; thus, software development and maintenance may also be in the hands of a few.[21] Applications for private blockchains are also offered by service providers in the cloud, such as by Microsoft for Ethereum in its own Azure cloud.[22] Furthermore, a distinction is made between the public blockchain, in which everyone can participate, and the private blockchain with a limited group of participants,[23] which does not necessarily go hand in hand with the distinction between permissionless blockchain and permissioned blockchain.[24]

8.2.1.3 The Development of the Necessary Software

The necessary software is developed in completely different ways: In some cases, companies such as Ripple can be found in the financial sector itself offering the information technology (IT) infrastructures, interfaces, etc., but also based on a peer-to-peer network within the framework of a server system including its own consensus protocol (based on the *Byzantine Agreement*).[25] Often, the software is developed as open source software on public platforms, such as Ethereum by the

---

19 Marianna Belotti, Nikola Božić, Guy Pujolle and Stefano Secci, 'A Vademecum on Blockchain Technologies: When, Which, and How' (2019) 21 *IEEE Communications Surveys & Tutorials* 3796, 3799; Duarte, 'An Introduction to Blockchain Technology from a Legal Perspective and Its Tensions with the GDPR' (n 5) 14–15; Federal Office for Information Security, 'Towards Secure Blockchains – Concepts, Requirements, Assessments' <www.bsi.bund.de/SharedDocs/Downloads/EN/BSI/Crypto/Secure_Blockchain.pdf?__blob=publicationFile&v=3> 11ff accessed 30 June 2023; see also BITKOM, 'Fact Paper on Blockchain and Data Protection' (*Bitkom*, 2019), 9ff <www.bitkom.org/sites/default/files/file/import/180502-Faktenpapier-Blockchain-und-Datenschutz.pdf> accessed 30 June 2023; Finck, 'Blockchain and the General Data Protection Regulation' (n 15) 5.

20 Duncan Jones and Jürgen Schreier, 'Security for Permissioned Blockchains' (*Industry of Things*, 2018) <www.industry-of-things.de/sicherheit-fuer-permissioned-blockchains-a-773362/> accessed 7 July 2023; Marianna Belotti, Nikola Božić, Guy Pujolle and Stefano Secci, 'A Vademecum on Blockchain Technologies: When, Which, and How' (2019) 21 *IEEE Communications Surveys & Tutorials* 3796, 3797.

21 S. Michèle Finck, *Blockchain Regulation and Governance in Europe* (Cambridge University Press 2018) 19 citing the Ethereum blockchain.

22 Marley Gray, 'Ethereum Blockchain as a Service Now on Azure' (*Microsoft Azure Blog*, 9 November 2015) <https://azure.microsoft.com/de-de/blog/ethereum-blockchain-as-a-service-now-on-azure/> accessed 7 July 2023.

23 BitFury Group, 'Public versus Private Blockchains' (*Bitfury*, 2015) <https://bitfury.com/content/downloads/public-vs-private-pt1-1.pdf> accessed 7 July 2023; Kaulartz (n 5) § 5 para 40.

24 More closely Federal Office for Information Security, 'Towards Secure Blockchains – Concepts, Requirements, Assessments', 11ff <www.bsi.bund.de/SharedDocs/Downloads/EN/BSI/Crypto/Secure_Blockchain.pdf?__blob=publicationFile&v=3> accessed 30 June 2023.

25 <http://ripple.com> accessed 30 June 2023.

Ethereum Foundation.[26] Again, development is different in the context of loose quasi–joint-venture projects such as Hyperledger, which describes itself as follows: “Hyperledger is an open source collaborative effort created to advance cross-industry blockchain technologies. It is a global collaboration, hosted by The Linux Foundation, including leaders in finance, banking, Internet of Things, supply chains, manufacturing and technology.”[27] Here, the structures can be completely different and are highly dependent on the individual case, but apparently mostly based on a permissioned blockchain.[28]

8.2.2 Risks

Even if blockchain technology therefore seems predestined to overcome old security and counterfeiting problems, a number of risks nevertheless emerge, including the following.[29]

8.2.2.1 Incorrect Data

Interestingly, security risks arise precisely from the high level of forgery protection. Since data cannot be changed later once they have been fed in, incorrect or manipulated data can corrupt an entire blockchain (e.g., in the case of data from sensors in smart products that have been manipulated).[30]

8.2.2.2 So-called 51% Attacks

Furthermore, the first so-called *51% attack* was successfully carried out in January 2019.[31] This “attack” describes a case in which a participant has more than half of the computing power used for mining, so that he can change blockchain to his

26 <http://ethereum.org> accessed 30 June 2023.

27 <www.hyperledger.org/> accessed 30 June 2023.

28 P. C. <www.ibm.com/blockchain/hyperledger> accessed 30 June 2023.

29 For a detailed discussion of the IT security aspects, see Federal Office for Information Security, ‘Towards Secure Blockchains – Concepts, Requirements, Assessments’, 26ff <www.bsi.bund.de/SharedDocs/Downloads/EN/BSI/Crypto/Secure_Blockchain.pdf?__blob=publicationFile&v=3> accessed 30 June 2023.

30 See Federal Office for Information Security, ‘Towards Secure Blockchains – Concepts, Requirements, Assessments’, 58 <www.bsi.bund.de/SharedDocs/Downloads/EN/BSI/Crypto/Secure_Blockchain.pdf?__blob=publicationFile&v=> 3 accessed 30 June 2023.

31 Gate.io, ‘Gate.io Research: Confirmed the 51% Attack and Attackers Accounts’ (*Gate.io*, 08 January 2019) <www.gate.io/article/16735> accessed 30 June 2023; Kraken Bitcoin Exchange, ‘Ethereum Classic (ETC) 51% Attack – Incident Report for Kraken’ (*Kraken Bitcoin Exchange*, 5 February 2019) <https://status.kraken.com/incidents/n31wl183hqmc> accessed 30 June 2023; Nesbitt, ‘Deep Chain Reorganization Detected on Ethereum Classic’ (*The Coinbase Blog*, 7. January 2019) <https://blog.coinbase.com/ethereum-classic-etc-is-currently-bei,ng-51-attacked-33be13ce32de> accessed 30 June 2023; Mike Orcutt, ‘Once Hailed as Unhackable, Blockchains Are Now Getting Hacked’ (*MIT Technology Review*, 19 February 2019) <www.technologyreview.com/s/612974/once-hailed-as-unhackable-blockchains-are-now-getting-hacked/> accessed 30 June 2023.

advantage.[32] However, in doing so, he must manipulate blockchain backward to the point where he wants to encode the deviation, so he must have a majority of computing power, since the other network participants use their own computing power to continue the applicable blockchain.[33] For this reason – and the exorbitantly high resources required – the 51% attack was long considered a purely theoretical case.[34] The probability that an attacker enforces his blockchain is related to the attacker's relative hash rate and the number of transactions.[35]

The hash rate, in turn, is related to the attacker's computing power. If the attacker's hash rate is greater than that of the opponent (the legal network), he can change blockchain. However, even lower values still result in a higher probability of success. Closely related to this is the fact that miners are often combined into so-called *pools* in order to achieve the necessary computing capacity.

In addition, most of these pools are located in one country,[36] in particular apparently in the People's Republic of China. The likelihood of such mining pools coming together to carry out a 51% attack therefore definitely increases.[37]

The only recommended defense is to increase the number of confirmations of a transaction, as this costs the attacker important time.[38] However, from the developer's point of view, it is also pointed out for the Bitcoin system that the system would have to have a lot of Bitcoins from the potential attacker before the time of the attack, so the attack would be even more significantly expensive.[39]

8.2.2.3 Forks

Closely related to the risks of attacks on a blockchain are the risks of responding to them. If the software or client of a blockchain receives an update, for example in response to such an attack, not all nodes and participants may agree with it.

---

32 Federal Office for Information Security, 'Towards Secure Blockchains – Concepts, Requirements, Assessments', 47ff <www.bsi.bund.de/SharedDocs/Downloads/EN/BSI/Crypto/Secure_Blockchain.pdf?__blob=publicationFile&v=3> accessed 30 June 2023; Alexey Malanov, 'Six Myths about Blockchain and Bitcoin: We Put Its Effectiveness to the Test' (*Kaspersky Daily Blog*, 22 August 2017) <www.kaspersky.de/blog/bitcoin-blockchain-issues/14453/> accessed 30 June 2023; Mike Orcutt, 'Once Hailed as Unhackable, Blockchains Are Now Getting Hacked' (*MIT Technology Review*, 19 February 2019) <www.technologyreview.com/s/612974/once-hailed-as-unhackable-blockchains-are-now-getting-hacked/> accessed 30 June 2023.

33 See also Hofert, *Regulierung der Blockchain* (n 7) 21ff.

34 Hans Bechtolf and Niklas Vogt, 'Datenschutz in der Blockchain-Eine Frage der Technik' (2018) *ZD* 66, 70.

35 <www.btc-echo.de/academy/bibliothek/51-attacke/> accessed 30 June 2023.

36 <www.buybitcoinworldwide.com/mining/pools/> accessed 30 June 2023.

37 See also Federal Office for Information Security, 'Towards Secure Blockchains – Concepts, Requirements, Assessments', 47 <www.bsi.bund.de/SharedDocs/Downloads/EN/BSI/Crypto/Secure_Blockchain.pdf?__blob=publicationFile&v=3> accessed 30 June 2023.

38 As recommended by the BTC Academy: <www.btc-echo.de/academy/bibliothek/51-attacke/> accessed 30 June 2023.

39 Gavin Anderson, 'Neutralizing a 51% Attack' (*GavinTech Blog*, 1 May 2012) <https://gavintech.blogspot.com/2012/05/neutralizing-51-attack.html> accessed 30 June 2023.

The new software then creates blocks that are incompatible with the older software – nodes running the older version do not recognize new blocks as valid.[40] So, while some adopt the changes and continue to work with them, another part works without the updates and two strings can be created from the block of the update (one according to the new rules, one according to the old ones); blockchain *forks* and a *fork is* created. A distinction is made between "*soft forks*" and "*hard forks*."[41]

A soft fork is a protocol change that is installed through software updates and narrows the rules of the blockchain; thus, those who use the new version can continue to participate in the old system, and the changes are backwards compatible.[42] A fork occurs with such changes because, conversely, blocks under the old set of rules are not compatible with the stricter rules of the new version, but the majority of miners use the update, creating a new strand. However, the old and new software versions can coexist.

A hard fork, on the other hand, is not backward compatible and requires all miners to update their clients. A hard fork profoundly changes the protocol so that participants who do not implement the change can no longer use the network.[43] The best-known example of a hard fork is the DAO, which, as an investment fund set up on a blockchain (Ethereum), was subjected to an attack by a hacker who took advantage of a vulnerability in the code; in order to eliminate this flaw, the other participants in the blockchain should agree, including by inserting a transaction and thus moving the stolen ethers to another account, to make them available again to the authorized parties.[44] The voting was done with a specific system that uses tokens for voting – *Carbonvote*,[45] which was first used to obtain the participants' approval for the hard fork proposal[46] before any changes were made. With the subsequent implementation of all changes and security updates, the old software was no longer compatible with the new software and the majority of nodes made their

---

40 Bechtolf and Vogt (n 34) 70.

41 Cf., Finck, *Blockchain Regulation and Governance in Europe* (n 21) 203.

42 Raffi Teperdjian, 'The Puzzle of Squaring Blockchain with the General Data Protection Regulation' (2020) 60 *Jurimetrics* 253, 269.

43 David Glance, 'Bitcoin Splits and Bitcoin Cash Is Created. Explaining Why and What Happens Now' (*The Conversation*, 2 August 2017) <http://theconversation.com/bitcoin-splits-and-bitcoin-cash-is-created-explaining-why-and-what-happens-now-81943> accessed 30 June 2023; Tjaden Hess, River Keefer and Emin Gün Sirer, 'Ethereum Is Inherently Secure Against Censorship' (*Hacking, Distributed*, 5 July 2016) <http://hackingdistributed.com/2016/07/05/eth-is-more-resilient-to-censorship/> accessed 30 June 2023.

44 Axel Kannenberg, 'After the DAO Hack: Ethereum Succeeds in the Hard Fork' (*Heise Online*, 20 July 2016) <www.heise.de/newsticker/meldung/Nach-dem-DAO-Hack-Ethereum-glueckt-der-harte-Fork-3273618.html> accessed 30 June 2023; Eike Kühl, 'And Suddenly $50 Million Is Missing' (*Zeit Online*, 20 June 2016) <www.zeit.de/digital/internet/2016-06/the-dao-blockchain-ether-hack> accessed 30 June 2023.

45 <http://carbonvote.com/> accessed 30 June 2023.

46 On the whole, see also Finck, *Blockchain Regulation and Governance in Europe* (n 21) 188; Jeffrey Wilcke, 'To Fork or Not to Fork' (*Ethereum*, 15 July 2016) <https://blog.ethereum.org/2016/07/15/to-fork-or-not-to-fork/> accessed 30 June 2023.

computing power available to the new blockchain. However, some nodes opposed hard forks in principle and continued to use the old software, so this persisting old blockchain was called "Ethereum Classic."[47]

In addition to these so-called *intentional permanent forks*, unintentional short-term forks can also occur when miners have created the same or similar blocks at the same time; these forks disappear again after a short time when the fork with the most transactions (as the longest chain of blocks) then prevails.[48]

8.2.2.4 Software Error

Another error can arise from software errors, such as those that occurred in the form of the so-called *Parity Bug*[49]: The cryptocurrency wallet "Parity," as a so-called *multi-signature wallet*, required consent from multiple parties through their respective private keys for each transaction from a wallet; this functionality apparently depends on a code library that was stored as a multi-signature contract on the Ethereum blockchain. However, due to the programming error, unauthorized parties were able to take over or control the contract, for example by converting this smart contract into a normal wallet and declaring themselves its owner, which apparently happened unintentionally by a user. As a result, a *suicide function* or self-deletion of the contract – together with the code library – was triggered, so that now all multi-signature wallets no longer work and the ethers stored there can no longer be transferred.[50] A proposal to make the wallets available again by inserting a single transaction[51] was not agreed to by the community, with the negative votes totaling 55%.[52] Of particular interest from a legal perspective is the criticism from the community that even within such a structure, it is unclear under what conditions a fork should occur. The example

---

47 See also Kristian G Borkert, 'Die Blockchain hustet . . . Welche Erkältungsmittel hat die Hausapotheke?' in Jürgen Taeger (ed), *Recht 4.0* (OlWIR 2017) 817, 820.

48 See Till Neudecker and Hannes Hartenstein, 'Short Paper: An Empirical Analysis of Blockchain Forks in Bitcoin' in Ian Goldberg and Tyler Moore (eds), *Financial Cryptography and Data Security* (Springer 2019) 1ff.

49 For further coding errors, see Federal Office for Information Security, 'Towards Secure Blockchains – Concepts, Requirements, Assessments' 50 ff with further references <www.bsi.bund.de/SharedDocs/Downloads/EN/BSI/Crypto/Secure_Blockchain.pdf?__blob=publicationFile&v=3> accessed 30 June 2023.

50 See Axel Kannenberg, 'Cryptocurrency Wallet Parity: Bug Freezes Millions Worth of Ether Units' (*Heise Online*, 7 November 2017) <www.heise.de/newsticker/meldung/Kryptogeld-Wallet-Parity-Bug-friert-Ether-Einheiten-im-Wert-von-Millionen-ein-3882902.html> accessed 30 June 2023; see also Matt Suiche, 'The $280M Ethereum's Parity Bug' (*Comae Technologies*, 7 November 2017) <https://blog.comae.io/the-280m-ethereums-bug-f28e5de43513> accessed 30 June 2023.

51 See proposed EIP 999, at <https://github.com/ethereum/EIPs/blob/e30becf4f22200accc14ebec-2c685d93790918a9/EIPS/eip-999.md> accessed 30 June 2023; for discussion, <www.reddit.com/r/ethereum/comments/9083sn/eip999_drama_explained_simply_catch_up_discuss/> accessed 30 June 2023.

52 See also the 'Ethereum Improvement Proposal (EIP 867)', for an orderly approach to such cases, in addition <https://github.com/ethereum/EIPs/issues/866> accessed 30 June 2023; <https://ethereum-magicians.org/t/eip-867-standardized-ethereum-recovery-proposals-erps/139/35> accessed 30 June 2023.

shows – just like with the DAO before – that software errors can certainly lead to malfunctions of blockchain, which can later prove irreparable due to a lack of unity in the community.

8.2.2.5 Other Risks

Other examples include the so-called *chain-splitting bug*, which could have split the blockchain into two incompatible chains simply by inserting a special transaction,[53] the double-spending bug on Bitcoin Core,[54] and numerous distributed denial of service (DDoS) vulnerabilities of various blockchains.[55]

Any cryptography technology on which blockchain is crucially based is – like any other security technology – naturally subject to the risk that the encryption will be "cracked," but the ever-increasing complexity of cryptography technology also makes it likely that many applications will in practice achieve at best a medium standard of security.[56] The introduction of post-quantum cryptography[57] is already being discussed, as quantum computers might be able to decrypt existing cryptography technologies due to their computing capacity.[58] The German Federal Office for Information Security (Bundesamt für Sicherheit in der Informationstechnik, or BSI) therefore sees considerable risks, particularly with regard to so-called long-term security for data encrypted in blockchain, as the cryptography processes have to be replaced after a certain time[59]; the BSI therefore primarily recommends private permissioned blockchains.[60]

---

53 Cory Fields, 'Responsible Disclosure in the Era of Cryptocurrencies' (*Medium*, 10 August 2018) <https://medium.com/mit-media-lab-digital-currency-initiative/http-coryfields-com-cash-48a99b85aad4> accessed 30 June 2023; Hassaan Malik, 'Avoiding Catastrophic Bugs Is Bitcoin's Greatest Challenge in Future, Says Bitcoin Core Developer' (*Blockpublisher*, 21 August 2018) <https://blockpublisher.com/avoiding-catastrophic-software-bugs-is-bitcoins-greatest-challenge-in-future-says-bitcoin-core-developer/> accessed 30 June 2023.

54 Awemany, '600 Microseconds' (*Medium*, 22 September 2018) <https://medium.com/@awemany/600-microseconds-b70f87b0b2a6> accessed 30 June 2023; Julia Magas, 'The Anatomy of Bitcoin Core's Recent Bug' (*Cointelegraph*, 27 September 2018) <https://cointelegraph.com/news/the-anatomy-of-bitcoin-cores-recent-bug> accessed 30 June 2023.

55 Vitalik Buterin, 'Transaction Spam Attack: Next Steps' (*Ethereum*, 22 September 2016) <https://blog.ethereum.org/2016/09/22/transaction-spam-attack-next-steps/> accessed 30 June 2023; Julia Magas, 'The Anatomy of Bitcoin Core's Recent Bug, 2018' (*Cointelegraph*, 27 September 2018) <https://cointelegraph.com/news/the-anatomy-of-bitcoin-cores-recent-bug> accessed 30 June 2023.

56 For the state of the art, see BSI technical guideline, 'Cryptographic Mechanisms: Recommendations and Key Lengths' <www.bsi.bund.de/EN/Themen/Unternehmen-und-Organisationen/Standards-und-Zertifizierung/Technische-Richtlinien/TR-nach-Thema-sortiert/tr02102/tr02102_node.html> accessed 30 June 2023.

57 Cf., 'Quantum Cryptograhpy' <https://de.wikipedia.org/wiki/Quantenkryptographie> accessed 7 August 2020.

58 See TeleTrust, 'Position Paper "Blockchain" (Bundesverband IT-Sicherheit)' (*Teletrust,* 2017) 27<www.teletrust.de/fileadmin/docs/publikationen/broschueren/Blockchain/2017_TeleTrusT-Positionspapier_Blockchain__.pdf> accessed 30 June 2023.

59 Federal Office for Information Security, 'Towards Secure Blockchains' (n 8) 42ff.

60 Ibid 45.

However, it appears that most hacker attacks relate more to the platforms on which virtual currencies traded via blockchain are then exchanged for real currencies; in the third quarter of 2017 alone, approximately 75% of all exchange platforms were victims of cyber attacks.[61] Examples of this are the attacks on the Hong Kong–registered portal Bitfinex, which has already been the victim of DDoS attacks several times[62] and on the former largest Bitcoin trading platform Mt. Gox;[63] but sometimes individual nodes are also attacked[64] or coordinated DDoS attacks are even carried out on larger *mining pools*.[65]

Routing is also said to be vulnerable to attacks, especially in Bitcoin. *Routing* attacks are those in which the perpetrator exploits the Internet infrastructure to intercept or redirect data and thus disrupt the connection of the attacked nodes to the rest of the network. This can be used to isolate individual nodes so that there is a risk of double-spending (as discussed previously in this chapter) and, if a large proportion of computing capacity is isolated, blockchain could be fragmented.[66]

8.2.3 Conclusion

Overall, blockchain is ideally suited for unambiguous transactions or processes, such as property transfers or transactions in the financial sector, as well as for smart contracts. Limitations arise from the low scalability due to the high computing power required;[67] the same applies to the high requirements for storage capacities, so that the lifetime of a blockchain should be limited to a decade (other things being equal).[68] Finally, a thoroughly long time elapses before a transaction is actually validated – apparently up to 60 minutes in the case of the Bitcoin blockchain, for example – which makes real-time financial transactions considerably more difficult, at least in this form of blockchain (proof of work).[69]

---

61 Study at Imperva, 'Global DDoS Threat Landscape Q3 2017' <www.imperva.com/resources/reports/2017-q3-ddos-threat-landscape.pdf> accessed 30 June 2023.

62 Abhishta and others, 'Impact of Successful DDoS Attacks on a Major Crypto-currency Exchange' <https://ris.utwente.nl/ws/portalfiles/portal/92134801/Impact_of_DDoS_Attacks_on_Cryptocurrency_Exchange.pdf> accessed 30 June 2023.

63 Feder and others, 'The Impact of DDoS and other Security Shocks on Bitcoin Currency Exchanges: Evidence from Mt. Gox, 2017' (*Researchgate*, 2017) <www.researchgate.net/publication/322840689_The_impact_of_DDoS_and_other_security_shocks_on_Bitcoin_currency_exchanges_Evidence_from_Mt_Gox/stats> accessed 30 June 2023.

64 See the further examples in Kristian G Borkert, 'Die Blockchain hustet . . . Welche Erkältungsmittel hat die Hausapotheke?' (n 47) 817, 821.

65 Stan Higgins, 'Bitcoin Mining Pools Targeted in Wave of DDOS Attacks' (*CoinDesk*, 12 March 2015) <www.coindesk.com/bitcoin-mining-pools-ddos-attacks> accessed 30 June 2023.

66 Maria Apostolaki, Aviv Zohar and Laurent Vanbever, 'Hijacking Bitcoin: Routing Attacks on Cryptocurrencies' <https://btc-hijack.ethz.ch/files/btc_hijack.pdf> accessed 30 June 2023.

67 See Federal Office for Information Security, 'Towards Secure Blockchains' (n 8) 18.

68 Thus Alexey Malanov, 'Six Myths about Blockchain and Bitcoin: We Put Its Effectiveness to the Test' (*Kaspersky Daily Blog*, 22 August 2017) <www.kaspersky.de/blog/bitcoin-blockchain-issues/14453/> accessed 30 June 2023; also Finck, *Blockchain Regulation and Governance in Europe* (n 21) 31 ff.

69 Peter Roßbach, '§ 4 Blockchain-Technologie' in Florian Möslein and Sebastian Omlor (eds), *Fintech-Handbuch* (1st edn, C.H. Beck 2019) para 55; Kaulartz (n 5) § 5 para 15.

By combining encryption technologies with verification through a decentralized network that cannot be manipulated by a single administrator, the likelihood of forgery is vanishingly small.[70] Finck writes: "It is worth repeating that blockchains do not make trust disappear; they simply replace trust in humans and institutions with trust in technology."[71] In addition to the now numerous blockchain applications in the financial sector,[72] but also local electricity trading in Vienna,[73] the first pilot projects are reported from various countries that want to replace state registers with blockchain,[74] in particular the land register.[75]

However, the specific risks of blockchain must not be ignored, either, especially its dependence on corresponding mining pools that participate in the verification process, as well as the possibility of establishing forks. Software errors can also play a major role in blockchain, not unlike in the "normal" IT world.

8.3 Blockchain Technology and the GDPR

8.3.1 Personal Data

The prerequisite for the application of the EU's General Data Protection Regulation (GDPR) is the processing of personal data, Art. 2(1) GDPR. The reference to persons is thus the linchpin for data protection requirements, whereby Germany, with Art. 4(1) GDPR or Recital 14 GDPR, only includes natural persons in the scope of application, unlike some other Member States, such as Austria, which, according to Section 1(1) sentence 1 Austrian Data Protection Act, grants protection

70 But see also Finck, *Blockchain Regulation and Governance in Europe* (n 21) 30–31, which refers to possible changes and therefore speaks only of "tamper-evident" and not "tamper-proof."

71 Finck, *Blockchain Regulation and Governance in Europe* (n 21) 13.

72 In addition to the many existing cryptocurrencies, the German stock exchange is also testing blockchain solutions for cross-border security transfer and blockchain technology-based settlement of securities transactions <www.deutsche-boerse.com/dbg-de/unternehmen/gruppe-deutsche-boerse/geschaeftsfelder/blockchain-business-areas> accessed 30 June 2023; or the "Spunta" project in the Italian banking sector for blockchain-based interbank clearing <www.fintechfutures.com/2019/02/italian-interbank-dlt-project-spunta-moves-to-pre-production/> accessed 30 June 2023.

73 See: 'Wien Energie Tests Blockchain Technology' <www.wienerstadtwerke.at/eportal3/ep/contentView.do/pageTypeId/71283/programId/72211/contentTypeId/1001/channelId/-49478/contentId/1801181> accessed 30 June 2023.

74 E.g., the commercial register in Malta, see Brigitte Bernhardt, 'Malta Creates First Commercial Register with Blockchain Technology' (*BTC Echo*, 9 May 2019) <www.btc-echo.de/malta-schafft-erstes-handelsregister-mit-blockchain-technologie/> accessed 30 June 2023; similar developments are emerging in France, see Brigitte Bernhardt, 'Hyperledger: France Uses Blockchain Technology from IBM for Commercial Registers' (*BTC Echo*, 18 March 2019) <www.btc-echo.de/hyperledger-frankreich-nutzt-blockchain-technologie-von-ibm-fuer-handelsregister/> accessed 30 June 2023.

75 E.g., in Sweden <www.anlegen-in-immobilien.de/digitalisierung-in-der-immobilienbranche-taugt-die-blockchain-als-grundbuch-ersatz/> accessed 30 June 2023; Honduras, Ghana or Georgia, on this Georg Eder, 'Digital Transformation: Blockchain and Land Titles' (2019), 4ff <www.oecd.org/corruption/integrity-forum/academic-papers/Georg%20Eder-%20Blockchain%20-%20Ghana_verified.pdf> accessed 30 June 2023; in contrast, however, for the German land register Harald Wilsch, 'Die Blockchain-Technologie aus der Sicht des deutschen Grundbuchrechts' (2017) *DNotZ* 761.

to "everyone" and thus also to legal persons beyond the scope of the GDPR.[76] However, a reference to persons is also possible in the case of legal persons, if, for example, the company allows conclusions to be drawn about a natural person[77] or in the case of a one-person company.[78] In the case of transactions between banks (e.g., in the context of currency transfers), a reference to a person and thus the GDPR may therefore not apply.[79]

According to Art. 4(1) GDPR, personal data is any information that relates to an identified or identifiable natural person. The decisive question is therefore always whether the reference to a person can be established in the case of information – the application of the GDPR is only not applicable if the information is completely anonymized; pseudonymization is not sufficient.[80] Without being able to go into this in depth here, the dispute[81] that already arose under the German Data Protection Act is still virulent, namely whether all theoretical possibilities (including those of third parties) of establishing the reference to a person are to be used (so-called *absolute theory*)[82] or whether a reference to a person is only given if it can be established by economically justifiable means that are technically available to the data processor (so-called *relative theory*).[83] As is well known, the CJEU has

---

76 Lutz Schreiber, 'Art. 4' in Kai-Uwe Plath (ed), *DS-GVO/BDSG/TTDSG* (4th edn, Otto Schmidt 2023) Art. 4 para 4; Moritz Karg, 'Art. 4 Nr. 1' in Spiros Simitis, Gerrit Hornung and Spiecker (eds), *Datenschutzrecht* (1st edn, C. H. Beck 2019) Art. 4 Nr. 1 DSGVO para 43, Gerald Spindler, 'Neues zu (internationalen) Bewertungsportalen' (2020) *ZUM* 433, 440.

77 Manuel Klar and Jürgen Kühling, 'Art. 4 DSGVO' in Jürgen Kühling and Benedikt Buchner (eds), *DSGVO BDSG* (3rd edn, C. H. Beck 2020) Art. 4 DSGVO No. 1 para 4; Peter Gola, 'Art. 4 DSGVO' in Peter Gola and Dirk Heckmann (eds), *DSGVO* (3rd edn, C. H. Beck 2022) Art. 4 DSGVO para 28; Stefan Ernst, 'Art. 4 DSGVO' in Boris Paal and Daniel A Pauly (eds), *DSGVO BDSG* (3rd edn, C.H. Beck 2021) Art. 4 DSGVO para 5.

78 Marian Arning and Tobias Rothkegel, 'Art.4 DSGVO' in Juergen Taeger and Detlev Gabel (eds), *DSGVO-BDSG-TTDSG* (4th edn, Deutscher Fachverlag 2022) Art. 4 DSGVO para 17; according to Recital 14 DSGVO, the name, legal form or contact details of the legal person are explicitly excluded from the scope of application, so that for a "strike through" the processing must take place with a recognizable reference to the natural person, see Moritz Karg, 'Art. 4 Nr. 1' in Spiros Simitis, Gerrit Hornung and Spiecker (eds), *Datenschutzrecht* (1st edn, C. H. Beck 2019) Art. 4 Nr. 1 DSGVO paras 43–45.

79 Phillip Quiel, 'Blockchain-Technologie im Fokus von Art. 8 GRC und DS-GVO' (2018) *DuD* 566, 568ff.

80 See only Alexander Roßnagel, 'Pseudonymisierung personenbezogener Daten' (2018) *ZD* 243, 245; Thomas Janicki and David Saive, 'Privacy by Design in Blockchain-Netzwerken' (2019) *ZD* 251, 252; Achim Klabunde, 'Art. 4' in Eugen Ehmann and Martin Selmayr (eds), *DS-GVO* (2nd edn, C. H. Beck 2018) Art. 4 para 32.

81 For a detailed discussion, see Matthias Bergt, 'Die Bestimmbarkeit als Grundproblem des Datenschutzrechts Überblick über den Theorienstreit und Lösungsvorschlag' (2015) *ZD* 365, 366 ff; see also Thilo Weichert, 'Geodaten – datenschutzrechtliche Erfahrungen, Erwartungen und Empfehlungen' (2007) *DUD* 113, 115.

82 Achim Klabunde, 'Art. 4' in Eugen Ehmann and Martin Selmayr (n 80) Art. 4 para 17; for a moderate absolute approach Martin Franzen, 'Art. 4' in M Franzen, I Gallner and H Oetker (eds), *DSGVO* (4th edn, C. H. Beck 2022) Art. 4 DSGVO para 5 according to which the expected effort to be expended by the processed entities must be limited by objective criteria (e.g., costs).

83 Jens Schefzig, 'Big Data = Personal Data?' (2014) *K&R* 772, 773; Benedikt Buchner, 'Art. 4 no. 1' in Kühling and Buchner (n 77) DS-GVO Art. 4 No. 1 paras 25ff; Gola, 'Art. 4' in Gola and

so far excluded only those means that violate legal requirements, but includes the available knowledge of third parties, such as information provided by law enforcement authorities.[84] Moreover, according to Recital 26 p. 3 GDPR, all such means are to be taken into account that are generally likely to be used by the controller or another person for identification purposes. Furthermore, Recital 26, p. 4 GDPR states that all objective factors must be taken into account, including costs, time, and available technology. Thus, in any case, the knowledge of third parties, which is legally accessible to the data processor, will have to be included in order to clarify the question of identifiability[85] – which, by its very nature, moves the scope of application of the GDPR in the direction of a "tightened" relative theory.[86]

Although blockchain in general only assigns a pseudonym to data whose concrete assignment leads to persons outside the blockchain, this does not change the personal reference, since the possibility of identification also exists with pseudonyms.[87] In the case of private (permissioned) blockchains, the reference to persons is obvious,[88] since the central entity holds the relevant data,[89] by concluding a contract with the user; but even in the case of open (permissionless) blockchains, the data can be traced or assigned to persons, since publicly accessible data and analysis tools can be used to trace the information.[90] However, according to Art. 11(2) of the

Heckmann (n 77) DS-GVO Art. 4 para 21; Karg, 'Art. 4 Nr. 1' in Simitis, Hornung and Spiecker gen. Döhmann (n 78) DSGVO Art. 4 no 1 para 60; Gerald Spindler and Lukas Dalby, 'Art. 4' in Gerald Spindler and Fabian Schuster (eds), *Recht der elektronischen Medien* (4th edn, C. H. Beck 2019) DS-GVO Art. 4 para 7; M Arning and T Rothkegel, 'Art. 4' in Taeger, Gabel and Arning (n 78) Art. 4 paras 34ff; Ziebarth, 'Art. 4' in *Sydow/Marsch DS-GVO/BDSG* (3rd edn DSGVO 2022) Art. 4 para 37; *Eßer* in Auernhamer, DSGVO BDSG, 7th edn 2020, Art. 4 DSGVO para 20; *Bucholtz/Stentzel* in Gierschmann and others (eds), *Kommentar DSGVO* (1st edn, Reguvis 2021) Art. 4 No. 1 DSGVO para 11; in this direction also Karg in Simitis, Hornung and Spiecker gen. Döhmann (n 78) Art. 4 DSGVO No. 1 para 62, who, however, advocates a stricter relative theory.

84 Case 582/14 *Breyer v Bundesrepublik Deutschland* [2016] ECLI:EU:C:2016:779 (CR 2016, 791), para 49.

85 Janicki and Saive (n 80) 252; with qualification: Klar and Kühling, 'Art. 4' in Kühling/Buchner (n 77) Art. 4 No. 1 DSGVO para 28.

86 Jürgen Kühling and Manuel Klar, 'Speicherung von IP-Adressen beim Besuch einer Internetseite' (2017) *ZD* 24 (27); Klar and Kühling, 'Art. 4' in Kühling and Buchner (n 77) Art. 4 No. 1 DSGVO para 26; following this Bechtolf and Vogt (n 34) 68.

87 Peter Schantz in Schantz and Wolff (eds), *Das neue Datenschutzrecht* (C. H. Beck 2017) para 303; Klar and Kühling, 'Art. 4' in Kühling and Buchner (n 77) Art. 4 No. 5 DSGVO para 11; Ernst, 'Art. 4 DSGVO' in Paal and Pauly (n 77) Art. 4 DSGVO para 40; Achim Klabunde, 'Art. 4' in Ehmann and Selmayr (n 80) Art. 4 DSGVO para 32; see also Nadine Schawe, 'Blockchain und Smart Contracts in der Kreativwirtschaft – mehr Probleme als Lösungen?' (2019) *MMR* 218, 221; Stefan Tönnissen and Frank Teuteberg, 'DSGVO und die Blockchain' (2020) *DuD* 322, 324 with further references; of other opinion probably Roßnagel, 'Pseudonymisierung personenbezogener Daten' (n 80) 243, 247.

88 Janicki and Saive (n 80) 252; Mario Martini and Quirin Weinzierl, 'Die Blockchain-Technologie und das Recht auf Vergessenwerden' (2017) *NVwZ* 1251, 1253.

89 Björn Steinrötter, 'Datenschutzrechtliche Probleme beim Einsatz der Blockchain' (2021) *ZBB* 373, 379 with further references.

90 Janicki and Saive (n 80) 252; Finck, 'Blockchain and the General Data Protection Regulation' (n 15) 27; Tönnissen and Teuteberg (n 87) 324; Joachim Schrey and Thomas Thalhofer, 'Rechtliche Aspekte der Blockchain' (2017) *NJW* 1431, 1433; Eduard Hofert, 'Blockchain-Profiling' (2017)

GDPR, the obligations and rights under Arts. 15–20 of the GDPR can be reduced if the data subject is difficult to identify, which may be the case especially with pseudonyms.[91] Both the transactions and the keys are therefore to be classified as personal data, especially since the purpose of blockchain is precisely the traceability of transactions.[92]

Various anonymization techniques are being discussed to avoid the application of the GDPR: For example, the data in blockchain is to be completely encrypted so that only the person with the key has access to it. Apart from the fact that the data would then still be personal due to the access of only one person, the benefit of blockchain – the traceability of transactions – would be considerably devalued.[93] The same problem would be encountered if encryption were introduced with a private key that is only used once and then discarded. Traceability would be made more difficult, but not to the extent that one could speak of anonymization.[94] Outsourcing the data outside the blockchain and storing only the transactions themselves does not change the personal reference, either, since the keys are still present and enable the personal reference.[95]

Consequently, in the event that a user processes personal data contrary to its obligations, the scope of application of the GDPR is given – provided that the users are not only legal entities.

It would only be conceivable to apply the exception clause of Art. 23(1)(e) of the GDPR, according to which "other important objectives of general public interest of the Union or a Member State" lead to the non-application of the GDPR.[96]

8.3.2 Justification of Data Processing

Since the GDPR is based on the principle of a general prohibition of the processing of personal data, the processing must always be justified, whereby the GDPR distinguishes between "normal" data, the processing of which can be justified under Art. 6

ZD 161, 163; for Bitcoins: Bechtolf and Vogt (n 34) 69; Paulina Pesch and Rainer Böhme, 'Datenschutz trotz öffentlicher Blockchain?' (2017) 41 *DuD* 93, 95; Michèle Finck, 'Blockchains and Data Protection in the European Union' (2018) 4 *EDPL* 17, 22ff; Paulina Pesch and Christian Sillaber, 'Distributed Ledger, Joint Control? – Blockchains and the GDPR's Transparency Requirements' (2017) *CRi* 166, 168 ff; Christian Rein '§ 14' in Thomas Sassenberg and Tobias Faber (eds), *Rechtshandbuch Industrie 4.0 und Internet of Things* (2nd edn, C.H. Beck 2020) § 14 para 64.

91 Quiel (n 79) 568; Markus Kring and Johannes Marosi, 'Ein Elefant im Porzellanladen – Der EuGH zu Personenbezug und berechtigtem Interesse' (2016) *K&R* 773, 776; Finck, 'Blockchain and the General Data Protection Regulation' (n 15) 18; Steinrötter (n 89) 379.

92 Finck, 'Blockchain and the General Data Protection Regulation' (n 15), 26–29; Teperdjian (n 42) 253, 279; Duarte (n 5) 31; Quiel (n 79) 568; Rein (n 90) 19; Finck, 'Blockchains and Data Protection in the European Union' (n 90) 26; Martini and Weinzierel (n 88) 1253.

93 Cf., Tönnissen and Teuteberg (n 87) 326.

94 For a detailed discussion, see Schauer, 'Blockchain – Zukunftsmusik ohne rechtliche Realisierbarkeit?' (*Recht und Netz*, 6 July 2018) <http://rechtundnetz.com/blockchain-rechtliche-realisierbarkeit/> accessed 10 July 2023.

95 Cf., Quiel (n 79) 568; Finck, 'Blockchains and Data Protection in the European Union' (n 90) 22.

96 Martini and Weinzierl (n 88) 1258.

of the GDPR, and particularly sensitive data under Art. 9 of the GDPR, for which, in addition to specific exceptions, only explicit consent can be considered. The justification criteria of Art. 6(1)(b) of the GDPR – the performance of the contract[97] – and Art. 6(1)(f) – the overriding interests – are often relevant, and in numerous cases also the fulfillment of legal obligations under Art. 6(1)(c) of the GDPR.

Therefore, there are in general no special features specific to the use of blockchain technology with regard to the justification of data processing, since the data on blockchain are always dependent on the actual data processing purpose. In other words, it is in principle irrelevant in which way or with which technology the data is processed, provided that their processing is permissible – unless the technology has special features in terms of data protection law, which are still to be addressed.

However, there are also restrictions, for example with regard to consent pursuant to Art. 6(1)(a), Art. 7 GDPR, which can only be given on the basis of sufficient information about the data processing. Here, it is rightly doubted whether it can be communicated in an obvious and comprehensible way to the average data subject of a data processing what processes blockchain involves and what risks may threaten,[98] especially since even ex ante it cannot necessarily be clear to the data subject who will all be involved in further data processing later on, which may encounter practical problems even in the case of private (permissioned) blockchains.[99] In any case, however, consent can be revoked at any time – regardless of the basis of the law of obligations,[100] with the consequence that data processing must be terminated and the data deleted, unless public law obligations to retain data intervene.

8.3.3 Responsibility and Joint Controllership

One of the central problems of blockchain in terms of data protection law concerns the responsibility for data processing and transmission operations. In terms of a rule

97 Which, however, also poses considerable problems as to whether contractual purposes are limited, for example, by data protection law requirements in the context of content control pursuant to Sections 305ff BGB, see on the whole Malte Engeler, 'Das überschätzte Kopplungsverbot' (2018) *ZD* 55ff with further references; Phillip Hacker, 'Daten als Gegenleistung: Rechtsgeschäfte im Spannungsfeld von DS-GVO und allgemeinem Vertragsrecht' (2019) *ZfPW* 148, 183 ff; Horst Heberlein, 'Art. 6 Rechtmäßigkeit der Verarbeitung' in Eugen Ehmann and Martin Selmayr (eds), *Datenschutz-Grundverordnung* (2nd edn, C.H. Beck 2018), Art. 6 DSGVO para 13; Jürgen Taeger, 'Art. 7 Bedingung für die Einwilligung' in Jürgen Taeger and Detlev Gabel (eds), *DSGVO – BDSG – TTDSG* (4th edn, R&W 2022) Art. 7 DSGVO para 100.

98 Cf., Quiel (n 79) 571.

99 Schrey and Thalhofer (n 90) 1434; also Johannes Hecht, 'Notariat 4.0 und Blockchain-Technologie' (2020) *MittBayNot* 314, 319.

100 In detail on the question of data as consideration Louisa Specht-Riemenschneider, 'Daten als Gegenleistung – Verlangt die Digitalisierung nach einem neuen Vertragstypus?' (2017) *JZ* 763, 764ff; Andreas Sattler, 'Personenbezogene Daten als Leistungsgegenstand' (2017) *JZ* 1036, 1038; Axel Metzger, 'Verträge über digitale Inhalte und digitale Dienstleistungen: Neuer BGB-Vertragstypus oder punktuelle Reform?' (2019) *JZ* 577, 579.

of thumb, the person who decides on the means and purposes of the data processing without being subject to instructions (as distinguished from commissioned data processing) can be considered the controller under Art. 4(7) of the GDPR.[101] This can also happen indirectly, as the CJEU had already assumed in the *Google Spain* decision for a Google subsidiary operating purely in the marketing area.[102]

8.3.3.1 Basics of Joint Controllership

Relevant for the use of blockchain technology (and the decision as to which form of blockchain can be chosen) in this context is the complex and so far still not completely clarified phenomenon of *joint* responsibility ("*joint controllership*") pursuant to Art. 26 GDPR. The CJEU has recently significantly expanded the scope of application by stating that even an indirect, minor influence on the processing operation is sufficient.[103] In the Facebook ruling decided by the CJEU, the coincidence of three factors was declared sufficient for the co-responsibility under data protection law of the operator of a fan page that was operated on Facebook: the opening of the possibility of data processing for a third party (in this case, Facebook), the influence on the data evaluation by determining criteria for evaluation statistics, and the possibility that certain data of the target group can be demanded from the third party.[104] According to this, joint responsibility exists if one's own activity enables the subsequent processing of data by others.[105] In the *Fashion ID* case[106] and the *Jehovah's Witness* case,[107] the CJEU also ruled that it is sufficient for co-responsibility if the processing of personal data is influenced out of self-interest and the purposes

---

101 Case 25/17 *Jehovan todistajat v uskonnollinen yhdyskunta* [2018] ECLI:EU:C:2018:551 (NJW 2019, 285), para 68; Case 131/12 *Google Spain SL, Google Inc. v Agencia Española de Protección de Datos (AEPD), Mario Costeja González* [2014] ECLI:EU:C:2014:317 (NJW 2014, 2257), para 34; Schrey and Thalhofer (n 90) 1433 ff; Martini and Weinzierl (n 88) 1253 ff make a distinction between permission-free and permission-restricted blockchains in terms of liability; crit. Regarding the practical enforceability against responsible parties in blockchains Rainer Böhme and Paulina Pesch, 'Technische Grundlagen und datenschutzrechtliche Fragen der Blockchain-Technologie' (2017) 41 *DuD* 473, 478ff.

102 *Google Spain SL, Google Inc. v Agencia Española de Protección de Datos (AEPD), Mario Costeja González* (n 101) 34; Volker Boehme-Neßler, 'Das Recht auf Vergessenwerden – Ein neues Internet-Grundrecht im Europäischen Recht' (2014) *NVwZ* 825, 827.

103 Case-210/16 *Unabhängiges Landeszentrum für Datenschutz. Schleswig-Holstein v Wirtschaftsakademie Schleswig-Holstein* [2018] ECLI:EU:C:2018:388 (NJW 2018, 2537), paras 37ff; *Jehovan todistajat v uskonnollinen yhdyskunta* (n 101) 68ff.

104 *Unabhängiges Landeszentrum für Datenschutz. Schleswig-Holstein v Wirtschaftsakademie Schleswig-Holstein* (n 103) 37ff.

105 Bernd Wagner, 'Disruption der Verantwortlichkeit' (2018) *ZD* 307, 309; Lukas Lezzi and Jutta Sonja Oberlin, 'Gemeinsam Verantwortliche in der konzerninternen Datenverarbeitung' Verantwortlichkeit' (2018) *ZD* 398, 400; of other opinion Mario Martini, 'Art. 26 Gemeinsam Verantwortliche' in (n 77) Art. 26 DSGVO para 19.

106 Case 40/17 *Fashion ID GmbH & Co. KG v Verbraucherzentrale NRW eV* [2019] ECLI:EU:C:2019:629.

107 *Jehovan todistajat v uskonnollinen yhdyskunta* (n 101) 68.

and means of data processing are thus determined.[108] In the opinion of the CJEU, it is sufficient to enable third parties to further process data – no prior agreement of any kind is required, nor is a coinciding purpose or a joint pursuit of this goal;[109] a marginal connection is sufficient. This means that the circle of responsibility is even wider than in the *Fanpage* decision, in that only indirect influence on the data processing is sufficient, here already the conscious enabling of the subsequent processing, without there being access to the content of the data[110] or active participation in the subsequent processing process by the co-responsible party.

However, the responsibility also ends where the influence of the "joint controller" on the subsequent data processing ceases. Thus, the CJEU stated the following in the *Fashion ID* decision.

> In the light of the foregoing, the answer to the second question must be that the operator of a website, such as Fashion ID, who embeds in that website a social plugin which causes the browser of the visitor to that website to request content from the provider of that plugin and, for that purpose, to transmit personal data relating to the visitor to that provider, may be regarded as the controller within the meaning of Article 2(d) of Directive 95/46. However, this responsibility is limited to the operation or operations of data processing for which he actually decides on the purposes and means, that is, the collection of the data at issue and their disclosure by transmission.[111]
>
> On the other hand, these obligations do not extend to operations of processing of personal data that involve other stages, upstream or downstream of these operations, that the processing of the personal data at issue may entail.[112]

8.3.3.2 Fundamentals for Blockchain

8.3.3.2.1 VALIDATION NODES

The transmission to other participants in blockchain and their data processing is problematic; the verification of a transaction alone requires confirmation by the majority of blockchain participants, as previously explained, so that this alone could constitute data processing by third parties. For the permissionless blockchain, it is therefore pointed out that there is no agreement between the participants, nor is there any influence on the processing of the other blockchain participants,[113]

---

108 *Fashion ID GmbH & Co. KG v Verbraucherzentrale NRW eV* (n 106).

109 *Unabhängiges Landeszentrum für Datenschutz. Schleswig-Holstein v Wirtschaftsakademie Schleswig-Holstein* (n 103) 37ff.

110 *Fashion ID GmbH & Co. KG v Verbraucherzentrale NRW eV* (n 106) with reference to *Jehovan todistajat v uskonnollinen yhdyskunta* (n 101) 68; *Unabhängiges Landeszentrum für Datenschutz. Schleswig-Holstein v Wirtschaftsakademie Schleswig-Holstein* (n 103) 37ff.

111 *Fashion ID GmbH & Co. KG v Verbraucherzentrale NRW eV* (n 106).

112 *Fashion ID GmbH & Co. KG v Verbraucherzentrale NRW eV* (n 106).

113 Thus Janicki and Saive (n 80) 254; Jörn Erbguth and Joachim Galileo Fasching, 'Wer ist Verantwortlicher einer Bitcoin-Transaktion?' (2017) 560, 563; Martini and Weinzierel (n 88) 1254;

Functional processes and results of blockchain are not based on an agreement, but on the individual independent partial actions of all participants.[114] In the same direction goes the argument that there is no common definition of a goal and the means used to achieve it,[115] furthermore that the nodes have no decision-making power over data processing.[116] The mere enabling of further data processing in later nodes is not sufficient.[117]

However, on the one hand, this is not necessarily the case, since the validation nodes or their operators have an important function in the validation process:[118] In contrast to the mining nodes, they carry out transactions and thus disseminate information to all other nodes; the validation nodes record, arrange, and store the personal data, so that in relation to this – against the background of the *Fashion ID* and *Fanpage* decisions – data processing by third parties can very well be affirmed to be enabled.[119] This is because the effectiveness of the entire blockchain depends on the verification process alone, in which all participants are involved. A common purpose within the meaning of Section 705 of the German Civil Code (Bürgerliches Gesetzbuch, or BGB) may not yet be construed from this; however, measured against the criteria shown, which the CJEU has developed, there are nevertheless considerable doubts as to whether *joint controllership* can be assumed.[120] It therefore follows from the principles developed by the CJEU as set out that all those involved in blockchain as validation nodes would be jointly responsible.[121] This result can only be avoided by making clear contractual assignments of tasks.[122]

8.3.3.2.2 MINING NODES

With regard to the mining nodes, on the other hand, it is doubted whether they actually exert an influence on data processing – because they only fulfill a purely technical function.[123] They are involved in such a way that they profit directly

---

similarly Dennis-Kenji Kipker and Hauke Bruns, 'Blockchains für Versorgungsketten im Lebensmittelsektor und der Datenschutz' (2020) *CR* 210, 214.

114 Böhme and Pesch, 'Technische Grundlagen und datenschutzrechtliche Fragen der Blockchain-Technologie' (n 101) 479, who describe this as *a sum of independent behavior* and categorize it as insufficient for joint responsibility.

115 Martini (n 105) 19ff; so also BITKOM (n 19) 29.

116 Böhme and Pesch, 'Technische Grundlagen und datenschutzrechtliche Fragen der Blockchain-Technologie' (n 101) 478ff; Quiel (n 79) 569.

117 Janicki and Saive (n 80) 254 with reference to Flemming Moos and Tobias Rothkegel (2018) *MMR* 596, 599; similarly Rein (n 90) 74; similarly Erbguth and Fasching (n 113) 563; different view for public blockchains Martini and Weinzierl (n 88) 1253 ff; seeing nodes generally as responsible parties Finck, 'Blockchains and Data Protection in the European Union' (n 90) 26.

118 Thus Janicki and Saive (n 80) 253.

119 So also already Martini and Weinzierl (n 88) 1253; so also Bechtolf and Vogt (n 34) 69.

120 This is also considered possible by Quiel (n 79) 569 ff, but without a concrete result.

121 Bechtolf and Vogt (n 34) 69; Kai-Uwe Plath, 'Art. 26' in Kai-Uwe Plath (ed), *DSGVO/BDSG/TTDSG* (4th edn, Otto Schmidt 2023) Art. 26 DSGVO para 27; cf., Finck, 'Blockchain and the General Data Protection Regulation' (n 15) 46–47.

122 CNIL (n 3) p 2.

123 CNIL (n 3) p 2 (so already Martini and Weinzierl (n 88) 1253); openly Rein (n 90) 73.

from participation in the network, but they have no influence on the content of the data to be processed – the mining nodes calculate new blocks, but are not responsible for the personal content of the results, so that joint responsibility cannot be constructed.[124] Also with regard to the previously mentioned *Fanpage* decision, mining nodes should not qualify as data processors, since they technically decide on the addition of further blocks, but only do so in a technically automated manner – unlike in the case of the so-called fan page operators – so that a transfer of the principles of the CJEU case law cannot be considered.[125]

Against the background of the *Fashion ID* decision, however, this result appears doubtful: the mining nodes do not directly influence the data processing and do not have access to the content of the data. According to the CJEU, however, knowingly enabling processing in a phase upstream of this is also sufficient, as this decides – albeit indirectly – on the purposes and means of the processing.[126] In the *Fashion ID* decision, the mere inclusion of the "Like" button was sufficient for joint responsibility, without any kind of access to the data processed by Facebook afterwards. The situation is similar with the mining nodes; although these basically only have a technical task, they deliberately enable subsequent further processing. Also, with regard to the fact that it has been repeatedly emphasized that the concept of the controller is to be interpreted broadly and that this leads to the fact that the existence of a joint responsibility does not necessarily require an equal level,[127] the possibility of the classification of the mining nodes as joint controllers within the meaning of Art. 26 GDPR does not seem so far away. At the very least, they are to be classified as data processors similar to cloud providers, since they provide the infrastructure.[128]

8.3.3.3 Responsibility of the Central Instance

For private (permissioned) blockchains, the picture looks somewhat different: If the central authority specifies the purposes of the data processing, it must at least be qualified as a co-responsible party under Art. 26 GDPR,[129] since it also exercises decision-making powers in this respect. In the case of a permissioned blockchain as in the present case, it is therefore generally assumed that the central instance is responsible.[130] However, much depends on the design of the private blockchain: If

124 Finck, 'Blockchain and the General Data Protection Regulation' (n 15), 46; Martini and Weinzierl (n 88) 1253.

125 Thus Janicki and Saive (n 80) 253ff; Quiel (n 79) 569; see also Johannes Marosi and Luisa Matthé, 'Gemeinsame Verantwortlichkeit eines Fanpage-Betreibers und des dazugehörigen sozialen Netzwerks' (2018) *ZD* 361, 362ff.

126 *Fashion ID GmbH & Co. KG v Verbraucherzentrale NRW eV* (n 106).

127 *Fashion ID GmbH & Co. KG v Verbraucherzentrale NRW eV* (n 106).; in this sense also *Jehovan todistajat v uskonnollinen yhdyskunta* (n 101) 68.

128 Steinrötter (n 89) 381 essentially relies on this.

129 Finck, 'Blockchain and the General Data Protection Regulation' (n 15) 44–45; Janicki and Saive (n 80) 255; Martini and Weinzierel (n 88) 1254; Quiel (n 79) 570.

130 Finck, 'Blockchain and the General Data Protection Regulation' (n 15) 44; Bundesnetzagentur, 'Die Blockchain-Technologie – Grundlagen, Potenziale und Herausforderungen, Status: July 2021'

the central instance is only responsible for the admission of the participants and the allocation of write permissions, but they decide themselves and on their own responsibility about the data processing, a responsibility of central instance for the data processing operations subsequently carried out by the users is ruled out.[131] For even if one were to refer to the *Fashion ID* decision of the CJEU here, in which the installation of a plug-in for Facebook led to the assumption of joint responsibility for the data ascertained and transferred as a result, the CJEU did not hold the website operator who installed the plug-in responsible for the further data processing by Facebook.[132]

However, this result is highly controversial: According to one view, if the central office merely performs the function of a gatekeeper, this does not constitute a sufficient basis for responsibility under data protection law for processing in the network.[133] Others assume that the users or issuers of transactions are responsible if – as in the present case – they have discretion over the content of the transaction.[134] Some advocate joint responsibility of miners, nodes, and initiators.[135] Finck, on the other hand, with reference to the decision of the CJEU in the *Wirtschaftsakademie Schleswig-Holstein* case,[136] assumes that all network participants who use blockchain infrastructure for their own purposes are to be regarded as jointly responsible parties.[137] Still others focus on the individual case and the scope of the central authority's control, so that if there is room for maneuvering, the user or transaction issuer is to be regarded as the responsible party;[138] furthermore, in the case of commercial advantages of the central instance from its network position, this represents a self-interest, and thus, in the wake of the *Fashion ID* decision of the CJEU,[139] the assumption of joint responsibility is to be assumed.[140] However, if the central instance has no economic self-interest, this criterion already fails, or likewise if the central authority lacks a de facto ex post control (for example in the form of a chameleon hash). Nevertheless, if the central

(*Bundesnetzagentur*, July 2021), 22ff <www.bundesnetzagentur.de/DE/Fachthemen/Digitalisierung/Technologien/Blockchain/Links_Dokumente/einfuehrung_bc.pdf?__blob=publicationFile&v=> accessed 10 July 2023; Steinrötter (n 89) 382.

131 Cf., Duarte (n 5) 39; Janicki and Saive (n 80) 254 ff; going further, apparently Anja Dekhuijzen, 'Call for Action on the EDPB to Provide Guidance Concerning GDPR and Blockchain' (2019) *CRi* 33, 35; Rein (n 90) 80: co-responsibility.

132 See above (n 106).

133 Nikolas Guggenberger, 'Part 13.7' in Thomas Hoeren, Ulrich Sieber and Bernd Holznagel (eds), *Multimedia-Recht* (58th edn, C.H. Beck 2022) Part 13.7 para 98.

134 Janicki and Saive (n 80) 255.

135 Quiel (n 79) 570.

136 *Unabhängiges Landeszentrum für Datenschutz. Schleswig-Holstein v Wirtschaftsakademie Schleswig-Holstein* (n 103) 357ff.

137 Finck, 'Blockchain and the General Data Protection Regulation' (n 15) 44–45.

138 Jonas Baumann and Nikolas Hamm, 'Datenschutzrechtliche Verantwortlichkeit in privaten Blockchains (2019) *DSRITB* 221, 230ff following European Parliament Research Service, Blockchain and the General Data Protection Regulation, PE 634.445 – July 2019, 44ff.

139 *Fashion ID GmbH & Co. KG v Verbraucherzentrale NRW eV* (n 106) 582 para 80.

140 Baumann and Hamm (n 138) 230ff.

instance does have the legal possibilities through the contractual arrangement of the write authorizations, joint responsibility would have to be assumed in this respect, whereby this would in turn have to relate to subsequent deletions, etc., which is obviously not provided for.[141]

Furthermore, the distinction between joint responsibility and commissioned data processing is relevant. Here, the decisive factor is whether the subsequent nodes are subject to the instructions of the original "principal"; in this case the central instance – only then is there commissioned data processing pursuant to Art. 27 GDPR.[142] Conversely, the central instance must then conclude corresponding contracts with the nodes and the miners;[143] both are ultimately mutually dependent – the central instance's ability to influence and the requirement to conclude commissioned processing. The fact that the instructions are in the form of an algorithm, which the node processes, does not harm in this respect with regard to commissioned data processing.[144] In particular, the consensus algorithm leads to bound data processing by the nodes during validation.[145] However, since the nodes here are no longer subject to the instructions of the central instance after granting the write authorization to the users, but the users can save the content on blockchain or the blocks of the nodes, the existence of commissioned data processing in relation to the central instance could be doubtful. Nevertheless, since the central instance decides on the admission of the users and the way in which they may use the blocks in the context of granting write authorization, the parallel with cloud computing is again obvious, so that the nodes are also in this case commissioned data processors vis-à-vis the central instance[146] and also vis-à-vis the users, who derive their rights from the contract with the central instance.

8.3.4 Right to Delete

The primary purpose of blockchain technology is to secure clearly traceable, forgery-proof evidence of transactions and entries. However, this is in conflict with the right to erasure of personal data guaranteed by the GDPR in Art. 17(1)(a). The technology is also opposed by the principle of Art. 5(1)(c) GDPR that the storage of personal data must be reduced to a minimum – in other words, that the data must be deleted as soon as possible.[147] The right to erasure according to Art. 17(1)(a) GDPR already exists when the data is no longer needed for the purposes for which it was collected. Furthermore, the right to erasure according to Art. 17(1)(b) GDPR

141 See Baumann and Hamm (n 138) 230ff.
142 Janicki and Saive (n 80) 255; Martini and Weinzierl (n 88) 1254; Quiel (n 79) 569.
143 CNIL (n 3) 3ff; Rein (n 90) 81.
144 Janicki and Saive (n 80) 255; Steinrötter (n 89) 382.
145 Janicki and Saive (n 80) 255.
146 So also Steinrötter (n 89) 383ff.
147 CNIL (n 3) 8 ff; Rein (n 90) 87ff.

arises upon withdrawal of consent by the data subject if there is no other legal basis for the processing.

8.3.4.1 *Primacy of Blockchain?*

According to opinions in the business community, the conflict between the right to deletion and the protection against forgery through protection against subsequent changes in blockchain should be resolved in such a way that the right to deletion has to take a back seat to the overriding interests of blockchain operators in the context of a fundamental rights balancing (right to informational self-determination [Art. 7, 8 CFR]) versus right to entrepreneurial freedom (Art. 16 CFR).[148] However, why there should be an overriding interest in blockchain technology under subordination of other fundamental rights is not quite evident – especially since the GDPR represents a concretization of European constitutional law balancing of the various fundamental rights positions.[149] Thus, the argument with regard to Art. 17 GDPR that deletion is fundamentally unreasonable cannot be accepted either, because the technology is deliberately used here:

> For then the legal system would always have to capitulate when persons deliberately (possibly even purposefully) maneuver themselves into a situation (for example, through the use of a certain technology) that makes it impossible to enforce the law, in order to then plead this very impossibility.[150]

With regard to the mentioned criticism, it has been argued that the GDPR does not require physical deletion of data, but that it is sufficient to make personal data in blockchain unrecognizable.[151] A suitable process for this is seen in particular in the so-called *pruning* procedure, with which information from older blocks can be deleted without impairing the functionality of blockchain.

8.3.4.2 *Deletion by Technical Means*

Deletion of personal data, in the sense of its complete destruction, is hardly feasible on a blockchain from a technical point of view. However, it has not yet been conclusively clarified what is actually meant by "deletion." It is usually considered sufficient if the data can only be retrieved with a disproportionate amount of effort – for

---

148 Thus BITKOM (n 19) 33.
149 Consenting Steinrötter (n 89) 388.
150 Steinrötter (n 89) 388.
151 Deutsche Energie-Agentur, 'Multi-Stakeholder Study-Blockchain in the Integrated Energy Transition' (*Dena,* February 2019) 127 <www.dena.de/fileadmin/user_upload/dena-Studie_Blockchain_Integrierte_Energiewende_DE4.pdf> accessed 10 July 2023.

example, in the context of special software.[152] One solution that has become widespread is that only hash values of personal data are stored in blockchain. The personal data itself should then be stored outside blockchain, with the reference to blockchain then being established via a reference (link).[153] This should make it possible to delete the personal data stored outside blockchain at any time.

Against this background, the following several possible technical solutions can be considered.

8.3.4.2.1 REDACTABLE BLOCKCHAIN

So-called *redactable blockchains* offer the possibility of completely removing affected data by modifying the block in question without changing the block's outer hash value.[154] In redactable blockchains, the inner hash function used in each block of blockchain, from which the outer hash value is later derived together with other components, is replaced by special forms of chameleon hash functions.[155] These are characterized, on the one hand, by their trapdoor function, i.e., that a private key is required to make edits; and on the other hand by the fact that they keep the outer

152 So also Hans-Georg Kamann and Martin Braun, 'Art. 17 Recht auf Löschung („Recht auf Vergessenwerden")' in Eugen Ehmann and Martin Selmayr (eds), *Datenschutz-Grundverordnung* (2nd edn, C.H. Beck 2018), para Art. 17 DSGVO para 34; Tobias Herbst, 'Art. 17 Recht auf Löschung („Recht auf Vergessenwerden")' in Jürgen Kühling and Benedikt Buchner (eds), *DSGVO BDSG* (3rd edn, C.H. Beck 2020) Art. 17 DSGVO para 37; Boris Paal, 'Art. 17 Recht auf Löschung („Recht auf Vergessenwerden")' in (n 77) Art. 17 DSGVO para 30; Spindler/Dalby, 'Art. 17 Recht auf Löschung („Recht auf Vergessenwerden")' in (n 83) Art. 17 DSGVO para 10; Norbert Nolte and Christian Werkmeister, 'Art. 17 Recht auf Löschung („Recht auf Vergessenwerden")' in (n 77) Art. 17 DSGVO para 10 and Kipker/Bruns (n 113) 215, on the other hand, already allow the obliteration of data to be sufficient, so that they are no longer legible controller; Alexander Dix, Art. 17 Recht auf Löschung („Recht auf Vergessenwerden")' in Spiros Simitis and Gerrit Hornung and Indra Spieker gen. Döhmann (eds), *Datenschutzrecht* (1st edn, Nomos 2019) Art. 17 para 5, on the other hand, focuses on physical deletion.

153 CNIL (n 3) 6ff; Bundesnetzagentur (n 130) 22.

154 Giuseppe Ateniese and Bernardo Magri Daniele Venturi and Ewerton Andrade, 'Redactable Blockchain – or – Rewriting History in Bitcoin and Friends' (*Euro S&P 2017*, 11 May 2017), 2ff, 6 <https://eprint.iacr.org/2016/757.pdf> accessed 10 July 2023; Hugo Krawczyk and Tal Rabin, 'Chameleon Signatures' (*NDSS Symposium*, 2000), 3 <www.ndss-symposium.org/wp-content/uploads/2017/09/Chameleon-Signatures-paper-Hugo-Krawczyk.pdf> accessed 10 July 2023; see also Nicolas Hohn-Hein and Günter Barth, 'Immaterialgüterrechte in der Welt von Blockchain und Smart Contract' (2018) *GRUR* 1089, 1090; Felix Krupar and Laurenz Strassemeyer, 'Distributed Ledger Technologien und Datenschutz: Widerspruch oder Evolution?' (2018) *K&R* 746, 751; Martini and Weinzierl (n 88) 1256; David Saive, 'Die drei Kränkungen der Blockchain: Entscheidungshilfe für Blockchain-Implementierungen' (2018) *DSB* 52, 53.

155 Artem Fliunt, M. Zajac and V. Skachek, 'Redactable Blockchain – or – Rewriting History in Bitcoin and Friends' (*Semantic Scholar*, 2018), 5 <https://pdfs.semanticscholar.org/f01c/15b90a5c33719cb452437adc9a5c60a917bb.pdf> accessed 10 July 2023; Dima Grigoriev and Vladimir Shpilrain, 'RSA and Redactable Blockchains' (*Crypotoly ePrint Archive*, 2020), 2ff <https://logic.pdmi.ras.ru/~grigorev/pub/blockchainRSA.pdf> accessed July 10 2023; Krovi Rajasekhar, Sri Harshini Yalavarthy, Sravani Mullapudi and M. Gowtham, 'Redactable Blockchain and It's Implementation in Bitcoin' (2018) *IJET* 401, 403 ff; Tao Ye, Min Luo, Yi Yang, Kim-Kwang Raymond Choo and Debiao He, 'A Survey on Redactable Blockchain: Challenges and Opportunities' (2023) 10(3) *IEEE Transactions on Network Science and Engineering* 1669, 1673.

hash values intact as links between the blocks after edits.[156] In this case, blockchain naturally loses an important advantage attributed to it, in that it becomes deletable again and thus, of course, also manipulatable.

Therefore, similar to the redactable blockchain, a possibility to provide for the deletion[157] or to store the personal data outside blockchain must be provided for in the context of the coding in any case as part of a commissioned processing.[158]

8.3.4.2.2 DATA ENCRYPTION

Another way out is to encrypt the data in blockchain, keeping the decryption code outside blockchain. Destruction of the decryption code then renders the data stored in blockchain unreadable.[159] However, this approach stands or falls with the security of the encryption, and possible future technologies must also be included.[160]

8.3.4.2.3 HASHLINKS

Similarly, the use of so-called hashlinks is proposed, which refer to data in a database outside blockchain that is only available to the data processor – who can then also delete it later.[161] Hashlinks are – simply speaking – nothing more than cryptographically protected hyperlinks. Included in a hashlink are usually a cryptographic hash of the resource, uniform resource locator(s) (URL[s]), and the content type. That is, a hashlink allows a system to determine whether the resource associated with the hyperlink has been modified. Thus, while an external database (like any other database) would in principle be subject to arbitrary change and manipulation, the hashlink on blockchain could at least be used to determine that the underlying data has changed unexpectedly. Arguably, the main problem with the use of hashlinks is that it requires the use of an additional system, which is also very application-specific and (with the development of better cryptographic formats) not easy to update.[162] However, this only postpones the fundamental problem of reconciling forgery protection and subsequent deletion.

The proposal to combine blockchains with *trusted hardware* goes in a similar direction. The data should only be stored and processed within the area protected

---

156 Fliunt (n 155) 3; Rajasekhar, Yalavarthy, Mullapudi and Gowtham (n 155) 403; Ye, Luo, Yang, Choo and He (n 155) 1673.

157 Thus for blockchain, which is subject to approval, Rein (n 90) 88.

158 Finck, 'Blockchains and Data Protection in the European Union' 23; Rein (n 90) 87ff.

159 Kipker and Bruns (n 113) 216; cf., Finck, 'Blockchain and the General Data Protection Regulation' (n 15) 76–77.

160 Spindler and Dalby (n 83) Art. 4 DSGVO no. 1 para 9; similarly Klabunde (n 80) para 15; Moritz Karg, 'Art. 4 Nr. 1 Begriffsbestimmung „Personenbezogenes Datum"' (n 152) Art. 4 no. 1 para 65.

161 Jörn Erbguth, 'Gesetzliche Verantwortung muss der technischen Kontrolle entsprechen' (*Bitcoin Live*, 25 September 2018) <https://bitcoin-live.de/interview-veranstaltungshinweis-gesetzliche-verantwortung-muss-der-technischen-kontrolle-entsprechen/> accessed 10 July 2023.

162 For the whole, see Digitalbazar, 'Javascript Cryptographic Hyperlinks Library' <https://github.com/digitalbazaar/hashlink> accessed 10 July 2023 and <https://datatracker.ietf.org/doc/html/draft-sporny-hashlink-03> accessed 10 July 2023.

by the trusted hardware from any external access.[163] Although deletion is possible in principle and replication and sharing on the trusted hardware is intended to provide a high level of protection for the data against external attacks, this could not yet be achieved with the current state of the art.[164]

8.3.4.2.4 PSEUDONYMIZATION

Whether, on the other hand, effective deletion can also be brought about by pseudonymization appears questionable. The technique used here is to assign pseudonyms to the data stored in blockchain, whereby the concrete personal reference could only be established outside blockchain with the assignment of the plain names to the pseudonyms. By deleting these allocation tables, the files in blockchain could thus also no longer be allocated to individual persons.[165] However, this in turn depends on the question of when it can be assumed that a person is identifiable. If the data volume is large enough and there is the possibility of recourse via an algorithm, the personal reference can also be restored ex post in these cases.[166]

8.3.4.2.5 FORKS

The same applies to the proposal of a "forgotten blockchain," in which all data is virtually netted after a certain time and transferred to a new blockchain.[167] At least until the time when the new blockchain contains the netted data, the right to erasure cannot be carried out in any case. Nor can a "deletion" be carried out by a fork, since the old blockchain still remains in existence.[168]

8.3.4.3 Justifications Vis-à-Vis the Right to Erasure Within the GDPR

It is true that the right to erasure under Art. 17(1) of the GDPR is relatively strong. If consent has been revoked, for example, the data processor can no longer rely on other grounds for justification, in particular not on a balancing of interests pursuant to Art. 6 (1) f) GDPR. Some argue that the wording of Art. 17(1)(b) of the GDPR – "[if] there

---

163 Instructive for Trusted Computing and Trusted Computing Enclaves cf., Lei Zhang, 'Intel SGX and Blockchain: The iExec nd-to-EndTrusted Execution Solution' (*Medium*, 15 Okctober 2018) <https://medium.com/iex-ec/iexec-end-to-end-sgx-solution-fee1e63297b2> accessed 10 July 2023; Samuel Martinet, 'DSGVO und Blockchain: Ist das neue EU-Datenschutzgesetz eine Bedrohung oder ein Anreiz?' (*Cointelegraph*, 6 July 2018) <https://de.cointelegraph.com/news/gdpr-and-blockchain-is-the-new-eu-data-protection-regulation-a-threat-or-an-incentive> accessed 10 July 2023.

164 Researchers have already succeeded in penetrating the area protected by the *trusted hardware and obtaining* personal data: Jacek Varky and Arne Maier, 'Intel SGX and Its Relevance to Blockchain' (*Maibornwolff*, 20 November 2018) <www.maibornwolffde/blog/intel-sgx-relevanz-blockchain> accessed 10 July 2023.

165 Kipker and Bruns (n 113) 216.

166 Cf., Martini and Weinzierl (n 88) 1256.

167 Schauer (n 94).

168 Bechtolf and Vogt (n 34) 70.

is no other legal basis for the processing of the data" – means that the grounds for justification are in a relationship of subsidiarity in the sense that if the primary consent ceases to apply, other grounds for justification will automatically apply, if they are relevant.[169] However, as the European Data Protection Board (EDPB, formerly the Art. 29 Working Party) has pointed out, saying that data processing is based on consent when it is actually based on another legal basis is detrimental to data subjects.[170] This also results from the need to disclose the justification basis prior to the data processing and in relation to a specific purpose.[171] Justification cumulation is therefore ruled out.

The same applies to attempts to continue to assume an overriding interest pursuant to Art. 6(1)(f) of the GDPR despite the existence of the prerequisites pursuant to Art. 17(1) of the GDPR.[172] If the requirements of Art. 17(1)(a)–(c) of the GDPR are met, a balancing pursuant to Art. 6(1)(f) of the GDPR can no longer be relevant, as this only concerns the justification level and cannot undermine the right to erasure. It is also difficult to imagine how the interests of the data processor can still prevail if the data is no longer needed for the purpose for which it was collected.[173]

However, the balancing of interests listed in Art. 17(3) of the GDPR is particularly helpful with regard to legal obligations. Particularly if users or participants perform duties under public law or services of general interest, a legitimate, legally protected interest can often stand in the way of the obligation to delete – however, this can only be assessed in individual cases.

8.3.4.4 Interim Summary

The primary purpose of blockchain is to provide secure and traceable evidence of transactions and entries, which conflicts with the GDPR's requirement to minimize data storage and delete data when it is no longer necessary. Resolving this conflict requires considering the interests of blockchain operators and balancing fundamental rights. It has been stated that it is unreasonable to argue that deletion is fundamentally impossible because it would mean that the law should always capitulate when individuals deliberately use technology to evade its enforcement.

---

169 Winfried Veil, 'Einwilligung oder berechtigtes Interesse? – Datenverarbeitung zwischen Skylla und Charybdis' (2018) *NJW* 3337, 3341; Krusche even goes so far as to assume that the wording suggests that further grounds for justification must be actively sought before the data are deleted after consent has been revoked: Jan Krusche, 'Kumulation von Rechtsgrundlagen zur Datenverarbeitung' (2017) *ZD* 232, 235.

170 Article 29 Data Protection Working Party, WP259 rev.01 (DE), 23, which was adopted by the EDPB in Endorsement 1/2018.

171 Article 29 Data Protection Working Party, WP259 rev.01 (DE), 23; but Veil (n 169) 3342; Krusche (n 169) 235; following this: Kipker/Bruns (n 113) 215; also Martin Keppeler and Wilhelm Berning, 'Technische und rechtliche Probleme bei der Umsetzung der DS-GVO-Löschpflichten' (2017) *ZD* 314, 315 according to which an accumulation of justification grounds before revocation is explicitly possible.

172 But so Kipker and Bruns (n 113) 215.

173 Ultimately, this is also recognized by Kipker and Bruns (n 113) 215.

Technical solutions like the redactable blockchain, however, might affect the meaningful usability of blockchain technology. Other proposed technologies, including the use of hashlinks, simply provide for a postponement of the fundamental problem, because the conflict between forgery protection and subsequent deletion must also be resolved with regard to external databases. Finally, the other technologies mentioned also have individual limitations that do not lead to deletion of personal data within the meaning of Art. 17 GDPR.

Ultimately, the right to deletion according to Art. 17(1) GDPR provides for a very strong right. While technical solutions have not yet led to an appropriate deletion of data, correction can be sought in individual cases via Art. 17(3) GDPR.

8.4 Transmission of Data With International Blockchains

The transfer of data in blockchain also raises difficulties from an international perspective. According to Art. 45 GDPR, an adequate level of protection must generally be maintained in other EU countries; according to Art. 46(2)(c) GDPR, adequate safeguards in the form of standard contractual clauses can also be applied if they have been adopted by the EU Commission in accordance with the review procedure under Art. 93(2) GDPR, and furthermore, after approval by the supervisory authority, contractual clauses under Art. 46(3) GDPR. However, Art. 49(1) GDPR provides for further exceptions for certain cases, in particular, in addition to the explicit consent of the data subject, also the necessity for the performance of a contract with the controller, Art. 49(1)(b) or a contract of the controller with a third party in the interest of the data subject, Art. 49(1)(c) GDPR.

As is well known, the CJEU recently imposed strict criteria here, in particular on the transfer of data to the United States in the Privacy Shield ruling[174] with regard to the decision on an equal level of protection in other EU countries;[175] `only by applying the standard contractual clauses could a transfer in blockchain with participants in other EU countries therefore be justified. Here, too, however, the CJEU applies in principle the basic idea of the comparable level of protection, in that the same legal remedies must be available to the data subject as, for example, in the case of commissioned data processing within the EU, but without the need to establish the adequacy of the level of protection in the third country; rather, what matters here are the appropriate (procedural) safeguards provided by the controller, which in some circumstances must additionally stand alongside the standard data protection clauses.[176]

174 On the lack of adequacy of the U.S. data protection rules with those of the GDPR, cf., Case 311/18 *Facebook Ireland Ltd v Maximillian Schrems* [2020] ECLI:EU:C:2020:559, paras 168ff.

175 *Facebook Ireland Ltd v Maximillian Schrems* (n 174) para 194.

176 *Facebook Ireland Ltd v Maximillian Schrems* (n 174) paras 105, 130ff; see also Datenschutzkonferenz, 'Press release of the Conference of the Independent Data Protection Authorities of the Federation and the States' (*DSK*, 8 July 2020) <https://datenschutzkonferenz-online.de/media/pm/20200616_pm_schrems2.pdf> accessed 10 July 2023.

It would be conceivable to encode these clauses in blockchain – which, however, in turn presupposes that there is a controller who checks and monitors compliance with the adequate data protection standard in other EU countries, which would be possible in principle with the private (permissioned) blockchain, but has not yet been implemented – as far as can be seen. This is because the use of blockchain here also requires the controller to check in each individual case whether additional guarantees such as legal remedies for data subjects or the enforcement of the level of data protection must be provided on a contractual basis, which is likely to encounter considerable problems in the case of a blockchain used globally. On the other hand, it is obvious that these solutions would not work in the case of permissionless blockchains without any central instance/controller.

Even if the use of blockchain is limited to data centers located in the EU; the data transfer – for which Art. 45 et seq. DSGVO intervene – also concerns the mere reading of blockchain. If there is no restriction on the readability of blockchain (even in the case of a public permissioned blockchain), a data transfer to non-EU countries is also possible. It is irrelevant whether this data can be further processed there. The mere transfer of the data to another EU country is sufficient for the data transfer, which can be the case simply by reading out the data. Consequently, a blockchain would have to take the precautions of Art. 45 et seq. DSGVO – or restrict the group of readers to those from the EU.

8.5 Summary

Finally, the use of blockchain technology is restricted from a data protection perspective in multiple ways:

- A processing of personal data is the rule, except it concerns only data of legal entities or the data are anonymized with security by the users.
- A justification of the data processing depends on the respective data processing operations of the users to be determined in the individual case.
- A central instance may be considered as a co-responsible party if it helps to decide for what purposes the users' write permissions are used; otherwise, it is not responsible for subsequent data processing operations on the users.
- Even in the case of a permissionless public blockchain without any central operator, the operators of nodes can be qualified as joint controllers of the data processing.
- A right to erasure can be implemented by technical measures such as the use of hashlinks or a redactable blockchain.
- If blockchain allows that blocks may be read without further territorial restrictions, the requirements of Art. 45 et seq. DSGVO must be complied with.

Regarding the overarching question whether the current rules are fit to address the current challenges that new technologies pose to existing EU data protection laws it clearly and simply can be stated that GDPR and blockchain technology can hardly be reconciled. However, regarding the decentralized blockchain, it is not a specific problem of data protection and the GDPR, but rather more a general problem to which a regulation of blockchain can be addressed as a central instance such as a provider is missing. Hence, it would be advisable to establish similar rules for data protection issues like have been adopted for cryptocurrencies (Markets in Crypto-Assets Regulation, MiCAR),[177] by requiring blockchains to register in a Member State.

Bibliography

Abhishta and others, 'Impact of Successful DDoS Attacks on a Major Crypto-currency Exchange' <https://ris.utwente.nl/ws/portalfiles/portal/92134801/Impact_of_DDoS_Attacks_on_Cryptocurrency_Exchange.pdf> accessed 30 June 2023

Anderson G, 'Neutralizing a 51% Attack' (*GavinTech Blog*, 1 May 2012) <https://gavintech.blogspot.com/2012/05/neutralizing-51-attack.html> accessed 30 June 2023

Apostolaki M, Zohar A and Vanbever L, 'Hijacking Bitcoin: Routing Attacks on Cryptocurrencies' <https://btc-hijack.ethz.ch/files/btc_hijack.pdf> accessed 30 June 2023

Arning M and Rothkegel T, 'Art.4 DSGVO' in Taeger J and Gabel D (eds), *DSGVO-BDSG-TTDSG* (4th edn, Deutscher Fachverlag 2022)

Ateniese G, Venturi BMD and Ewerton Andrade E, 'Redactable Blockchain – or – Rewriting History in Bitcoin and Friends' (*Euro S&P 2017*, 11 May 2017) <https://eprint.iacr.org/2016/757.pdf> accessed 10 July 2023

Baker B, James Royal, 'What Is Bitcoin Mining and How Does It Work?' (27 March 2023) <www.bankrate.com/investing/what-is-bitcoin-mining/> accessed 30 June 2023

Baumann J and Hamm N, 'Datenschutzrechtliche Verantwortlichkeit in Privaten Blockchains' (2019) *DSRITB* 221

Bechtolf H and Vogt N, 'Datenschutz in der Blockchain – Eine Frage der Technik' (2018) *ZD* 66

Belotti M, Božić N, Pujolle G and Secci S, 'A Vademecum on Blockchain Technologies: When, Which, and How' (2019) 21 *IEEE Communications Surveys & Tutorials* 3796

Bergt M, 'Die Bestimmbarkeit als Grundproblem des Datenschutzrechts-Überblick über den Theorienstreit und Lösungsvorschlag' (2015) *ZD* 365

Bernhardt B, 'Hyperledger: France Uses Blockchain Technology from IBM for Commercial Registers' (*BTC Echo*, 18 March 2019) <www.btc-echo.de/hyperledger-frankreich-nutzt-blockchain-technologie-von-ibm-fuer-handelsregister/> accessed 30 June 2023

Bernhardt B, 'Malta Creates First Commercial Register with Blockchain Technology' (*BTC Echo*, 9 May 2019) <www.btc-echo.de/malta-schafft-erstes-handelsregister-mit-blockchain-technologie/> accessed 30 June 2023

Böhme R and Pesch P, 'Technische Grundlagen und datenschutzrechtliche Fragen der Blockchain-Technologie' (2017) 41 *DuD* 473

Borkert KG, 'Die Blockchain hustet . . . Welche Erkältungsmittel hat die Hausapotheke?' in Taeger J (ed), *Recht 4.0* (OlWIR 2017) 817

Bucholtz G and Stentzel R, 'Art. 4 DSGVO' in Gierschmann S and others (eds), *Kommentar DSGVO* (1st edn, Reguvis 2021)

Buterin V, 'Ethereum: A Next-Generation Smart Contract and Decentralized Application Platform' (*Ethereum*, 2014) <https://ethereum.org/669c9e2e2027310b6b3cdce6e1c52962/Ethereum_Whitepaper_-_Buterin_2014.pdf> accessed 26 June 2023

Buterin V, 'Transaction Spam Attack: Next Steps' (*Ethereum*, 22 September 2016) <https://blog.ethereum.org/2016/09/22/transaction-spam-attack-next-steps/> accessed 30 June 2023

Cai W, Zehu Wang Z, Ernst JB, Hong Z, Feng C and Leung VCM, 'Decentralized Applications: The Blockchain-Empowered Software System' (2018) 6 *IEEE Access* 53019

177 Regulation (EU) 2023/1114 of the European Parliament and of the Council of 31 May 2023 on markets in crypto-assets, and amending Regulations (EU) No 1093/2010 and (EU) No 1095/2010 and Directives 2013/36/EU and (EU) 2019/1937, OJ L 150 of 9.6.2023, p. 40 ff.

Lucking D, 'Decentralized Autonomous Organizations' (*Allen & Overy*, 11 July 2016) <www.allenovery.com/en-gb/global/news-and-insights/publications/decentralized-autonomous-organizations> accessed 26 June 2023

Chohan UW, 'A History of Bicoin' (5 February 2022) 8–9 <https://doi.org/10.2139/ssrn.3047875> accessed 30 June 2023

Dekhuijzen A, 'Call for Action on the EDPB to Provide Guidance Concerning GDPR and Blockchain' (2019) *CRi* 33

Dix A, 'Art. 17 Recht auf Löschung ("Recht auf Vergessenwerden")' in Spiros S, Hornung G and Spieker gen. Döhmann I (eds), *Datenschutzrecht* (1st edn, Nomos 2019)

Duarte D, 'An Introduction to Blockchain Technology From a Legal Perspective and Its Tensions with the GDPR' (*Cyberlaw Journal of the Cyberlaw Research Centre of the University of Lisbon School of Law* (CIJIC), 30 September 2019) <https://doi.org/10.2139/ssrn.3545331> accessed 27 June 2023

Engeler M, 'Das überschätzte Kopplungsverbot' (2018) *ZD* 55

Erbguth J, 'Gesetzliche Verantwortung muss der technischen Kontrolle entsprechen' (*Bitcoin Live*, 25 September 2018) <https://bitcoin-live.de/interview-veranstaltungshinweis-gesetzliche-verantwortung-muss-der-technischen-kontrolle-entsprechen/> accessed 10 July 2023

Erbguth J and Fasching JG, 'Wer ist Verantwortlicher einer Bitcoin-Transaktion?' (2017) *ZD* 560

Ernst S, 'Art. 4 DSGVO' in Paal B and Pauly D A (eds), *DSGVO BDSG* (3rd edn, C.H. Beck 2021)

Eßer M, 'Art. 4 DSGVO' in Auernhammer (ed), *DSGVO BDSG* (7th edn, Carl Heymanns 2020)

Feder and others, 'The Impact of DDoS and Other Security Shocks on Bitcoin Currency Exchanges: Evidence from Mt. Gox, 2017' (*Researchgate*, 2017) <www.researchgate.net/publication/322840689_The_impact_of_DDoS_and_other_security_shocks_on_Bitcoin_currency_exchanges_Evidence_from_Mt_Gox/stats> accessed 30 June 2023

Fields C, 'Responsible Disclosure in the Era of Cryptocurrencies' (*Medium*, 10 August 2018) <https://medium.com/mit-media-lab-digital-currency-initiative/http-coryfields-com-cash-48a99b85aad4> accessed 30 June 2023

Finck M, 'Blockchains and Data Protection in the European Union' (2018) 4 *EDPL* 17

Finck M, 'Blockchain and the General Data Protection Regulation' (July 2019) *Study for the European Parliamentary Research Service* PE 634.445, 5 <www.europarl.europa.eu/RegData/etudes/STUD/2019/634445/EPRS_STU(2019)634445_EN.pdf> accessed 28 June 2023

Fliunt A, Zajac M and Skachek V, 'Redactable Blockchain – or – Rewriting History in Bitcoin and Friends' (*Semantic Scholar*, 2018) <https://pdfs.semanticscholar.org/f01c/15b90a5c33719cb452437adc9a5c60a917bb.pdf> accessed 10 July 2023

Fox D, 'Bitcoin' (2017) *DuD* 507

Franzen M, 'Art. 4' in Franzen M, Gallner I and Oetker H (eds), *DSGVO* (4th edn, C. H. Beck 2022)

Glance D, 'Bitcoin Splits and Bitcoin Cash Is Created. Explaining Why and What Happens Now' (*The Conversation*, 2 August 2017) <http://theconversation.com/bitcoin-splits-and-bitcoin-cash-is-created-explaining-why-and-what-happens-now-81943> accessed 30 June 2023

Gola P, 'Art. 4 DSGVO' in Peter G and Dirk H (eds), *DSGVO* (3rd edn, C.H. Beck 2022)

Gray M, 'Ethereum Blockchain as a Service Now on Azure' (*Microsoft Azure Blog*, 9 November 2015) <https://azure.microsoft.com/de-de/blog/ethereum-blockchain-as-a-service-now-on-azure/> accessed 7 July 2023

Guggenberger N, 'Part 13.7' in Hoeren T, Sieber U and Holznagel B (eds), *Multimedia-Recht* (58th edn, C.H. Beck 2022) 98

Hacker P, 'Daten als Gegenleistung: Rechtsgeschäfte im Spannungsfeld von DS-GVO und allgemeinem Vertragsrecht' (2019) *ZfPW* 148

Heberlein H, 'Art. 6 Rechtmäßigkeit der Verarbeitung' in Ehmann E and Selmayr M (eds), *Datenschutz-Grundverordnung* (2nd edn, C.H. Beck 2018)

Hecht J, 'Notariat 4.0 und Blockchain-Technologie' (2020) *MittBayNot* 314

Herbst T, 'Art. 17 Recht auf Löschung ("Recht auf Vergessenwerden")' in Kühling J and Buchner B (eds), *DSGVO BDSG* (3rd edn, C.H. Beck 2020)

Hess T, Keefer R and Sirer EG, 'Ethereum is Inherently Secure Against Censorship' (*Hacking, Distributed*, 5 July 2016) <http://hackingdistributed.com/2016/07/05/eth-is-more-resilient-to-censorship/> accessed 30 June 2023

Higgins S, 'Bitcoin Mining Pools Targeted in Wave of DDOS Attacks' (*CoinDesk*, 12 March 2015) <www.coindesk.com/bitcoin-mining-pools-ddos-attacks> accessed 30 June 2023

Hofert E, 'Blockchain-Profiling' (2017) *ZD* 161

Hofert E, 'Regulierung der Blockchain' (*Mohr Siebeck* 2018) 14

Hohn-Hein N and Barth G, 'Immaterialgüterrechte in der Welt von Blockchain und Smart Contract' (2018) *GRUR* 1089

Janicki T and Saive D, 'Privacy by Design in Blockchain-Netzwerken' (2019) *ZD* 251

Jones D and Schreier J, 'Security for Permissioned Blockchains' (*Industry of Things*, 2018) <www.industry-of-things.de/sicherheit-fuer-permissioned-blockchains-a-773362/> accessed 7 July 2023

Magas J, 'The Anatomy of Bitcoin Core's Recent Bug, 2018' (*Cointelegraph*, 27 September 2018) <https://cointelegraph.com/news/the-anatomy-of-bitcoin-cores-recent-bug> accessed 30 June 2023

Kamann HG and Braun M, 'Art. 17 Recht auf Löschung ("Recht auf Vergessenwerden")' in Ehmann E and Selmayr M (eds), *Datenschutz-Grundverordnung* (2nd edn, C.H. Beck 2018)

Kannenberg A, 'After the DAO Hack: Ethereum Succeeds in the Hard Fork' (*Heise Online*, 20 July 2016) <www.heise.de/newsticker/meldung/Nach-dem-DAO-Hack-Ethereum-glueckt-der-harte-Fork-3273618.html> accessed 30 June 2023

Kannenberg A, 'Cryptocurrency Wallet Parity: Bug Freezes Millions Worth of Ether Units' (*Heise Online*, 7 November 2017) <www.heise.de/newsticker/meldung/Kryptogeld-Wallet-Parity-Bug-friert-Ether-Einheiten-im-Wert-von-Millionen-ein-3882902.html> accessed 30 June 2023

Karg M, 'Art. 4 Nr. 1 DSGVO' in Simitis S, Hornung H and Spiecker I (eds), *Datenschutzrecht* (1st edn, C. H. Beck 2019)

Kaulartz M, 'Die Blockchain-Technologie' (2016) *CR* 474

Kaulartz M, '§ 5 Blockchain-Technologie' in Möslein F and Omlor S (eds), *Fintech-Handbuch* (2nd edn, C.H. Beck 2021)

Keppeler M and Berning W, 'Technische und rechtliche Probleme bei der Umsetzung der DS-GVO-Löschpflichten' (2017) *ZD* 314

Kipker DK and Bruns H, 'Blockchains für Versorgungsketten im Lebensmittelsektor und der Datenschutz' (2020) *CR* 210

Klabunde A, 'Art. 4' in Eugen Ehmann and Martin Selmayr (eds), *DS-GVO* (2nd edn, C. H. Beck 2018)

Klar M and Kühling J, 'Art. 4 DSGVO' in Jürgen Kühling and Benedikt Buchner (eds), *DSGVO BDSG* (3rd edn, C.H. Beck 2020)

Knaier R, 'Handelsregister 4.0 dank Blockchain-Technologie?' (2017) *GmbHR* R305

Krawczyk H and Rabin T, 'Chameleon Signatures' (*NDSS Symposium*, 2000), 3 <www.ndss-symposium.org/wp-content/uploads/2017/09/Chameleon-Signatures-paper-Hugo-Krawczyk.pdf> accessed 10 July 2023

Kring M and Marosi J, 'Ein Elefant im Porzellanladen – Der EuGH zu Personenbezug und berechtigtem Interesse' (2016) *K&R* 773

Krupar F and Strassemeyer L, 'Distributed Ledger Technologien und Datenschutz: Widerspruch Oder Evolution? (2018) *K&R* 746

Krusche J, 'Kumulation von Rechtsgrundlagen zur Datenverarbeitung' (2017) *ZD* 232

Kühl E, 'And Suddenly $50 Million Is Missing' (*Zeit Online*, 20 June 2016) <www.zeit.de/digital/internet/2016-06/the-dao-blockchain-ether-hack> accessed 30 June 2023

Kühling J and Klar M, 'Speicherung von IP-Adressen beim Besuch einer Internetseite' (2017) *ZD* 24

Lezzi L and Oberlin JS, 'Gemeinsam Verantwortliche in der konzerninternen Datenverarbeitung' Verantwortlichkeit' (2018) *ZD* 398

Liegmann B, 'Umsatzsteuerliche Behandlung virtueller Währungen' (2018) *BB* 1175

Malanov A, 'Six Myths about Blockchain and Bitcoin: We Put Its Effectiveness to the Test' (*Kaspersky Daily Blog*, 22 August 2017) <www.kaspersky.de/blog/bitcoin-blockchain-issues/14453/> accessed 30 June 2023

Malik H, 'Avoiding Catastrophic Bugs is Bitcoin's Greatest Challenge in Future, Says Bitcoin Core Developer' (*Blockpublisher*, 21 August 2018) <https://blockpublisher.com/avoiding-catastrophic-software-bugs-is-bitcoins-greatest-challenge-in-future-says-bitcoin-core-developer/> accessed 30 June 2023

Marosi J and Matthé L, 'Gemeinsame Verantwortlichkeit eines Fanpage-Betreibers und des dazugehörigen sozialen Netzwerks' (2018) *ZD* 361

Martinet S, 'DSGVO und Blockchain: Ist das neue EU-Datenschutzgesetz eine Bedrohung oder ein Anreiz?' (*Cointelegraph*, 6 July 2018) <https://de.cointelegraph.com/news/gdpr-and-blockchain-is-the-new-eu-data-protection-regulation-a-threat-or-an-incentive> accessed 10 July 2023

Martini M and Weinzierl Q, 'Die Blockchain-Technologie und das Recht auf Vergessenwerden' (2017) *NVwZ* 1251

Metzger A, 'Verträge über digitale Inhalte und digitale Dienstleistungen: Neuer BGB-Vertragstypus Oder punktuelle Reform?' (2019) *JZ* 577

Moos F and Rothkegel T, 'Gemeinsame Verantwortlichkeit eines Fanpage-Betreibers und des dazugehörigen sozialen Netzwerks' (2018) *MMR* 596

Nakamoto S, 'Bitcoin: A Peer-to-Peer Electronic Cash System' (*Bitcoin*, 1 May 2009) <https://bitcoin.org/bitcoin.pdf> accessed 8 July 2023

Neudecker T and Hartenstein H, 'Short Paper: An Empirical Analysis of Blockchain Forks in Bitcoin' in Goldberg I and Moore T (eds), *Financial Cryptography and Data Security* (Springer 2019) 1

Orcutt M, 'Once Hailed as Unhackable, Blockchains Are Now Getting Hacked' (*MIT Technology Review*, 19 February 2019) <www.technologyreview.com/s/612974/once-hailed-as-unhackable-blockchains-are-now-getting-hacked/> accessed 30 June 2023

Pesch P and Böhme R, 'Datenschutz trotz öffentlicher Blockchain?' (2017) 41 *DuD* 93

Pesch P and Sillaber C, 'Distributed Ledger, Joint Control? – Blockchains and the GDPR's Transparency Requirements' (2017) *CRI* 166

Plath KU, 'Art. 26' in Plath K-U (ed), *DSGVO/BDSG/TTDSG* (4th edn, Otto Schmidt 2023)

Pöttinger H, 'No Blockchain without Hash Functions' <http://haraldpoettinger.com/blockchain-hashfunktionen/> accessed 7 July 2023

Quiel P, 'Blockchain-Technologie im Fokus von Art. 8 GRC und DS-GVO' (2018) *DuD* 566

Rajasekhar K, Yalavarthy SH, Mullapudi S and Gowtham M, 'Redactable Blockchain and It's Implementation in Bitcoin' (2018) *IJET* 401

Rein C, '§ 14' in Sassenberg T and Faber T (eds), *Rechtshandbuch Industrie 4.0 und Internet of Things* (2nd edn, C.H. Beck 2020)

Roßbach P, '§ 4 Blockchain-Technologie' in Möslein F and Omlor S (eds), *Fintech-Handbuch* (1st edn, C.H. Beck 2019)

Roßnagel A, 'Pseudonymisierung personenbezogener Daten' (2018) *ZD* 243

Safferling C and Rückert C, 'Telekommunikationsüberwachung bei Bitcoins-Heimliche Datenauswertung bei virtuellen Währungen gem. § 100a StPO?' (2015) *MMR* 788

Saive D, 'Die drei Kränkungen der Blockchain: Entscheidungshilfe für Blockchain-Implementierungen' (2018) *DSB* 52

Sattler A, 'Personenbezogene Daten als Leistungsgegenstand' (2017) *JZ* 1036

Schacht S and Lanquillon C, *Blockchain und maschinelles Lernen* (Springer Vieweg 2019) 41

Schantz P, 'Anwendungsbereich der Datenschutz-Grundverordnung' in Schantz P and Wolff HA (eds), *Das neue Datenschutzrecht* (C. H. Beck 2017) para 303

Schauer L, 'Blockchain – Zukunftsmusik ohne rechtliche Realisierbarkeit?' (*Recht und Netz*, 6 July 2018) <http://rechtundnetz.com/blockchain-rechtliche-realisierbarkeit/> accessed 10 July 2023

Schawe N, 'Blockchain und Smart Contracts in der Kreativwirtschaft – mehr Probleme als Lösungen?' (2019) *MMR* 218

Schefzig J, 'Big Data = Personal Data?' (2014) *K&R* 772
Scheider D, 'Bitcoin Mining – How the Incentive Structure in the Network Determines the Price, in BTC-ECHO' (*BTC Echo*, 25 April 2019) <www.btc-echo.de/bitcoin-mining-wie-die-anreizstruktur-im-netzwerk-den-kurs-bestimmt/> accessed 7 July 2023
Schreiber L, 'Art. 4' in Plath K-U (ed), *DS-GVO/BDSG/TTDSG* (4th edn, Otto Schmidt 2023)
Schrey J and Thalhofer T, 'Rechtliche Aspekte der Blockchain' (2017) *NJW* 1431
Specht-Riemenschneider L, 'Daten als Gegenleistung – Verlangt die Digitalisierung nach einem neuen Vertragstypus?' (2017) *JZ* 763
Spindler G, 'Blockchain-Transaktionen und Vertrauensschutz' in Maultzsch F and Blaurock U (eds), *Vertrauensschutz im digitalen Zeitalter* (Nomos 2020) 36
Spindler G, 'Blockchaintypen und ihre gesellschaftsrechtliche Einordnung' (2021) *Recht Digital* 309
Spindler G, 'Neues zu (internationalen) Bewertungsportalen' (2020) *ZUM* 433
Spindler G and Dalby L, 'Art. 4 DS-GVO' in Spindler G and Schuster F (eds), *Recht der elektronischen Medien* (4th edn, C.H. Beck 2019) 7
Steinrötter B, 'Datenschutzrechtliche Probleme beim Einsatz der Blockchain' (2021) *ZBB* 373
Stiemerling O, 'Schutz von Software – Technische Grenzen und neue Möglichkeiten' in Metzger A and Wimmers J (eds), *DGRI Jahrbuch 2014* (1st edn, Otto Schmidt 2015) para 286
Suiche M, 'The $280M Ethereum's Parity Bug' (*Comae Technologies*, 7 November 2017) <https://blog.comae.io/the-280m-ethereums-bug-f28e5de43513> accessed 30 June 2023
Swanson T, 'Consensus-as-a-Service: A Brief Report on the Emergence of Permissioned, Distributed Ledger Systems' (*Great Wall of Numbers*, 2015), 4 <www.ofnumbers.com/2015/04/06/consensus-as-a-service-a-brief-report-on-the-emergence-of-permissioned-distributed-ledger-systems/> accessed 7 July 2023
Taeger J, 'Art. 7 Bedingung für die Einwilligung' in Taeger J and Gabel D (eds), *DSGVO – BDSG – TTDSG* (4th edn, R&W 2022)
Teperdjian R, 'The Puzzle of Squaring Blockchain with the General Data Protection Regulation' (2020) 60 *Jurimetrics* 253
Tönnissen S and Teuteberg F, 'DSGVO und die Blockchain' (2020) *DuD* 322
Varky J and Maier A, 'Intel SGX and Its Relevance to Blockchain' (*Maibornwolff*, 20 November 2018) <www.maibornwolffde/blog/intel-sgx-relevanz-blockchain> accessed 10 July 2023
Veil W, 'Einwilligung oder berechtigtes Interesse? – Datenverarbeitung zwischen Skylla und Charybdis' (2018) *NJW* 3337
Wagner B, 'Disruption der Verantwortlichkeit' (2018) *ZD* 307
Weichert T, 'Geodaten – datenschutzrechtliche Erfahrungen, Erwartungen und Empfehlungen' (2007) *DUD* 113
Wilcke J, 'To Fork or Not to Fork' (*Ethereum*, 15 July 2016) <https://blog.ethereum.org/2016/07/15/to-fork-or-not-to-fork/> accessed 30 June 2023
Wilsch H, 'Die Blockchain-Technologie aus der Sicht des deutschen Grundbuchrechts' (2017) *DNotZ* 761
Wright SA, 'DAOs & ADSs' (2023) *IEEE 15th International Symposium on Autonomous Decentralized System* (ISADS) 1
Yang C, Chen J, Zeng B and Liao L, 'Overview of Blockchain Privacy Protection' *2022 IEEE 8th Intl Conference on Big Data Security on Cloud* (BigDataSecurity) 22 <https://ieeexplore.ieee.org/document/9799487> accessed 6 July 2023
Ye T, Luo M, Yang Y, Choo KWR and He D, 'A Survey on Redactable Blockchain: Challenges and Opportunities' (2023) 10(3) *IEEE Transactions on Network Science and Engineering* 1669
Zhang L, 'Intel SGX and Blockchain: The iExec nd-to-EndTrusted Execution Solution' (*Medium*, 15 Okctober 2018) <https://medium.com/iex-ec/iexec-end-to-end-sgx-solution-fee1e63297b2> accessed 10 July 2023
Ziebarth T, 'Art. 4' in Sydow G and Marsch N (eds), *DS-GVO/BDSG* (3rd edn, Nomos 2022)

9 Personal Care Robots Under EU Data Protection Law*

Martin Ebers

9.1 Introduction

Medical progress has led to a demographic transformation. Society is ageing, and the need for caregivers is constantly increasing. Due to lower mortality and increasing survival rates, as well as a sustainable drop in fertility levels, the United Nations (UN) projects that the share of the global population aged 65 years or older will rise from 10% in 2022 to 16% in 2050. Furthermore, the number of persons aged 65 years or older worldwide is projected to be more than twice the number of children under the age of 5 and about the same as the number of children under the age of 12 by 2050.[1] At the same time, the number of people with (especially age-related) disabilities, ranging from hearing loss to Alzheimer's disease and other forms of dementia, increases.[2] Currently affecting more than 55 million people worldwide and with nearly 10 million new cases every year, the World Health Organization (WHO) names dementia as "one of the major causes of disability and dependency among older people globally".[3] The implication of these demographic developments is that an increasing number of elderly persons requiring care will need to be supported by a shrinking younger generation.[4] Considering the

* This work is part of the 'Geriatronics' project, a lighthouse initiative of the Munich Institute of Robotics and Machine Intelligence (MIRMI) at the Technical University of Munich (TUM).

1 United Nations, 'World Population Prospect 2022', ii <www.un.org/development/desa/pd/sites/www.un.org.development.desa.pd/files/wpp2022_summary_of_results.pdf> accessed 21 August 2023; similar number at World Health Organization, 'Aging Fact Sheet' <www.who.int/news-room/fact-sheets/detail/ageing-and-health> accessed 21 August 2023.

2 Cf., F O'Brolcháin, 'Robots and People with Dementia: Unintended Consequences and Moral Hazard' (2017) 26(4) *Nursing Ethics* 963ff.

3 World Health Organization, 'Dementia Fact Sheet' <www.who.int/news-room/fact-sheets/detail/dementia> accessed 21 August 2023.

4 E Fosch Villaronga, H Felzmann, R Pierce, S de Conca, A de Groot, S Robins and A Ponce Del Castillo, 'Nothing Comes Between My Robot and Me: Privacy and Human-Robot Interaction in Robotised Healthcare' in R Leenes, R van Brakel, S Gutwirth and P de Hert (eds), *Data Protection and Privacy: The Internet of Bodies* (1st edn, Hart Publishing 2018); O'Brolcháin, 'Robots and People with Dementia: Unintended Consequences and Moral Hazard' (n 2) 963ff; C Angle, 'Will a Robot Care for My Mom?' (*TedMed*, 2009) <www.tedmed.com/talks/show?id=7193> accessed 21 August 2023.

DOI: 10.4324/9781003502791-13

rising demand of professional care delivery, many older persons can be expected to enter nursing homes and hospitals or substantially increasing the demand for medical care and assistance in daily living, while human resources in health and care decrease.[5]

However, technology offers some solutions. Numerous studies show that *personal care robots* can relieve caregivers or promote therapy and can thus benefit the person being cared for.[6] Psychologically, patients and their relatives can benefit from the use of personal care robots in different ways. For example, studies indicate that interactions with robots such as PARO,[7] a robot baby seal, designed to have a calming effect on patients in hospitals and nursing homes, or AIBO,[8] a robotic dog, can reduce loneliness[9] and improve social connections and communication among elder people by physical interaction or engaging them in play similar to animal-assisted therapy.[10] Moreover, symptoms like loss of memory and inability to recognize children, friends or family members – which is emotionally challenging or even traumatic – can be avoided or relieved by the assistance of personal care robots.[11]

Besides these positive psychological effects, robots have the potential to strengthen the independence of care recipients. Care robots can, for example, be used for removing bed sheets, re-heating and delivering food, walking assistance (especially in post-fall scenarios), helping the user to stand up, monitoring or supporting the care recipients self-management, such as timing, dosages, movement and diet regime, self-assessment or providing timely reminders in order to adhere to medication plans and to mitigate the negative effects of minor cognitive

5 Fosch-Villaronga and others, 'Nothing Comes Between My Robot and Me: Privacy and Human-Robot Interaction in Robotised Healthcare' (n 4) 97ff; O'Brolcháin, 'Robots and People with Dementia: Unintended Consequences and Moral Hazard' (n 2) 963ff; for Europe (and parts of Asia), World Health Organization, 'Health and Care Workforce in Europe: Time to Act' (2022), 7 <www.who.int/europe/publications/i/item/9789289058339> accessed 21 August 2023; for United States, US Department of Health and Human Services, 'Supply and Demand Projections of the Nursing Workforce: 2014–2030' (2017), 4 <https://bhw.hrsa.gov/sites/default/files/bureau-health-workforce/data-research/nchwa-hrsa-nursing-report.pdf> accessed 21 August 2023.

6 Overview on possible robot therapies, E Fosch-Villaronga and J Albo-Canals, 'I'll Take Care of You,' Said the Robot' (2019) 10 (1) *Journal of Behavioral Robotics* 78ff.

7 C D Kidd, W Taggart and S Turkle, 'A Sociable Robot to Encourage Social Interaction Among the Elderly' (*Proceedings 2006 IEEE International Conference on Robotics and Automation*, Orlando, FL, USA, 2006) 3972–3976; G Bardaro, 'Robots for Elderly Care in the Home: A Landscape Analysis and Co-Design Toolkit' (2022) 14(2) *International Journal of Social Robotics* 663.

8 M Fujita, 'On Activating Human Communications with Pet-Type Robot AIBO' (2004) 92(11) *Proceedings of the IEEE* 1804; Bardaro, 'Robots for Elderly Care in the Home' (n 7).

9 H Robinson, B Macdonald, N Kerse and others, 'The Psychosocial Effects of a Companion Robot: A Randomized Controlled Trial' (2013) 14(9) *Journal of the American Medical Directors Association* 661.

10 R Bemelmans, G J Gelderblom, P Jonker and others, 'Socially Assistive Robots in Elderly Care: A Systematic Review into Effects and Effectiveness' (2012) 13(2) *Journal of the American Medical Directors Association* 11.

11 O'Brolcháin, 'Robots and People with Dementia: Unintended Consequences and Moral Hazard' (n 2) 965ff.

impairments (e.g., forgetfulness), as well as minimizing health risks by appropriately responding to medical emergencies.[12] Other possible use-cases are currently being developed and can help the user to remain (even more) independent. As a secondary effect, robots can also reduce social isolation, distance from healthcare services, and the risks of living alone.[13]

One of the main legal challenges and potential obstacles of these uses, however, is the question as to how personal care robots can comply with data protection law. Personal care robots can have huge implications on the users privacy, mainly under three aspects: enabling direct surveillance, creating new access points to traditionally private areas and involving highly sensitive personal information.[14] Moreover, human users can form emotional connections with personal care robots, viewing them as friends or partners. This tendency to anthropomorphize robots (the *anthropomorphization* effect)[15] can lead to misconceptions about data processing and challenge the concept of informed consent. On the other hand, personal care robots (and in particular, the cooperative nature of human–robot interaction) offer a number of opportunities to protect privacy in new ways.

Against this backdrop, the present chapter discusses both the risks and opportunities that arise from the use of personal care robots for privacy and data protection. In doing so, the chapter draws especially from practical experience gained within the "Geriatronics" project – a lighthouse initiative of the Munich Institute of Robotics and Machine Intelligence (MIRMI) at the Technical University of Munich (TUM), Germany.[16]

The remaining parts of this chapter is structured as follows: Section 9.2 first attempts a definition of the term "robot" and a classification of different types of robots, before discussing the use of personal care robots in practice, and in particular, within the Geriatronics project. Section 9.3 thereafter describes the privacy implications of care robots, while Section 9.4 analyzes how to deal with these implications under the General Data Protection Regulation (GDPR) of the European Union (EU).[17] Section 9.5 discusses possible solutions for privacy and data protection. The concluding Section 9.6 summarizes the findings of this work and provides an outlook on how EU data protection law could be improved.

12 Bardaro, 'Robots for Elderly Care in the Home' (n 7) 673; E Broadbent, J Garrett, N Jepsen, V L Ogilvie, H S Ahn, H Robinson, K Peri, N Kerse, P Rouse, A Pillai and others, 'Using Robots at Home to Support Patients with Chronic Obstructive Pulmonary Disease: Pilot Randomized Controlled Trial' (2018) 20(2) *Journal of Medical Internet Research* 1; cf., W Khaksar and others, 'The Robotics in Elderly Healthcare: A Review of 20 Recent Research Projects' (2023) 9 <https://arxiv.org/abs/2302.04478> accessed 18 September 2023.

13 Bardaro, 'Robots for Elderly Care in the Home' (n 7) 673.

14 R Calo, 'Robots and Privacy' in P Lin, G Bekey and K Abney (eds), *Robot Ethics: The Ethical and Social Implications of Robotics* (MIT Press 2012) 187.

15 For a detailed discussion cf., Section 9.3.3.

16 <https://geriatronics.mirmi.tum.de/en/> accessed 4 September 2023.

17 Regulation (EU) 2016/679.

9.2 Personal Care Robots in Practice

9.2.1 What Are Robots?

Typically, the term "robot" refers to cyber-physical systems that combine hardware and software components, network and communication processes, mechanical actuators, controllers, operating systems and sensors to interact with the physical world.[18] In addition to artificial intelligence (AI), other disciplines play a role in robot design and operation, such as mechanical engineering and control theory. Examples of robots include robotic manipulators, autonomous vehicles (e.g., cars, drones, flying taxis), humanoid robots and robotic vacuum cleaners.[19]

Simplified, robots can be described as "[AI] in action in the physical world" or called *embodied AI*.[20]

9.2.2 Classification of Robots

Robots can be categorized in many ways (cf. figure 9.1). For instance, industrial robots can be distinguished from service robots – based on their intended use in industrial automation or their ability to perform tasks for humans.[21] The latter, being sophisticated systems, are increasingly interacting with humans in various settings, including professional, public, private, and healthcare environments. Examples of service robots include feeding robots, exoskeletons, assistants, socially interactive robots, robotic wheelchairs and robotic surgeons. The defining characteristic of these systems is their ability to create an interconnected system where virtual and physical aspects intersect.

Within the category of service robots, another significant distinction lies in the differences between social robots and non-social robots. Social robots are physically embodied, autonomous agents that communicate and interact with humans on an emotional level.[22] They often imitate human behaviours, like talking or exhibiting emotions, and may resemble humans or animals in their appearance, comprising

18 D Quarta, M Pogliani, M Polino, F Maggi, A M Zanchettin and S Zanero, 'An Experimental Security Analysis of an Industrial Robot Controller' (*Proceedings of the 2017 IEEE Symposium on Security and Privacy (SP)*, 2017) 268; E Fosch-Villaronga and T Mahler, 'Cybersecurity, Safety and Robots: Strengthening the Link between Cybersecurity and Safety in the Context of Care Robots' (2021) 41 *Computer Law and Security Review* 1 <www.sciencedirect.com/science/article/pii/S0267364921000017> accessed 4 September 2023.

19 About origin and development of the term robot, K Ishii, 'Comparative Legal Study on Privacy and Personal Data Protection for Robots Equipped with Artificial Intelligence: Looking at Functional and Technological Aspects' (2019) 34 *AI and Society* 509 with further references.

20 High Level Expert Group on AI (2018) 5 <https://ec.europa.eu/futurium/en/system/files/ged/ai_hleg_definition_of_ai_18_december_1.pdf> accessed 4 September 2023.

21 ISO 8373 2012; compare E Fosch-Villaronga and others, 'Privacy Considerations for Socially Assistive Robots. The Privacy Implications of Social Robots. Solutions from Two Conference Workshops' (*Human-Robot Interaction Conference*, Vienna, Austria, 2017) 2.

22 R Campa, 'The Rise of Social Robots: A Review of the Recent Literature' (2016) 26(1) *Journal of Evolution and Technology* 106 <https://jetpress.org/v26.1/campa.htm> accessed 4 September 2023.

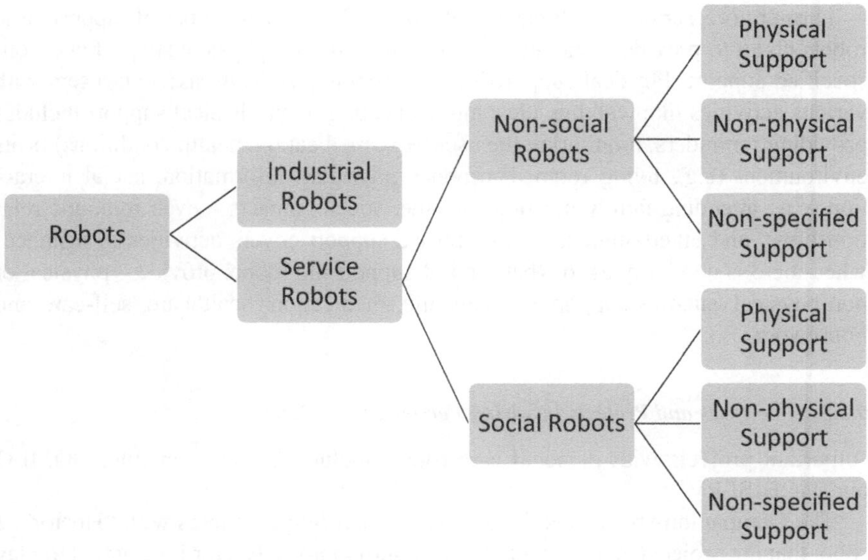

Figure 9.1 Classification of Robots

visible body parts. In contrast to non-social robots, social robots' actions and reactions are based on internal states and perceptions, making them more disruptive as they directly engage with individuals and challenge emotions and feelings. This is because of the tendency of people to anthropomorphize social robots, attributing human-like characteristics to them.[23] The emotional dependence and personalized adaptation of social robots raise specific concerns regarding privacy.[24] In the context of elderly care, robots are expected to be useful in three main areas: assisting the elderly and/or caregivers in their tasks, monitoring health and behaviour, and providing companionship.[25]

Assistance can range from simple tasks performed by specialized robots, such as vacuuming robots and eating aids, to more complex tasks like personal hygiene, requiring advanced robots. Health and behaviour monitoring robots in homes can, comparable with conventional diagnostics, track relevant user behaviour for health and safety purposes, allowing timely alerts to health services when needed. Companionship robots, on the other hand, do not perform assistive tasks but are designed to provide company and social interaction. This type of robot has been commercially available for more than a decade in the form of robotic pets such as the Sony AIBO robot dog, the Pleo dinosaur and the PARO seal.[26]

23 See Section 9.3.3.
24 See Section 9.3.2.
25 A Sharkey and N Sharkey, 'Granny and the Robots: Ethical Issues in Robot Care for the Elderly' (2012) 14 *Ethics and Information Technology* 27.
26 Bardaro, 'Robots for Elderly Care in the Home' (n 7) 663.

Furthermore, service robots can be categorized based on the types of support these robots claim to provide, including physical support, non-physical support and non-specified support. Physical support involves robots physically assisting users with various activities like walking, cleaning, and eating. Non-physical support includes providing reminders, monitoring the user (e.g., medication, health conditions) or its environment (e.g., living room, bedroom), providing information, social interaction (e.g., attending family meetings or other social contacts – even romantic relationships), and entertainment. Non-specified support covers activities in instances when there is no clarity as to what kind of support the robots provide – physical or non-physical, such as support for daily life, medication, healthcare, self-care and housework.

9.2.3 Use-cases and Projects Involving Personal Care Robots

Important projects with personal care robots include CompanionAble, DOMEO and MOBISERV.[27]

The CompanionAble project[28] has linked smart home systems with "Hector", a robot that the project team claims to be fully autonomous. Hector is designed to play the role of a companion for elderly people,[29] helping its users to remain independent, secure, fit and happy by providing friendly reminders; keeping and bringing important objects, such as keys and wallets; offering cognitive stimulation and playing games; and providing seamless video connections to family and friends.[30] Hector is therefore equipped with fall detection mechanisms and can make emergency calls. Hector also enables remote monitoring services and personalized dialogue or interaction possibilities, displaying emotional intelligence through visual, vocal and tactile interfaces, sensor-based movements and natural language recognition.

The DOMEO project[31] was funded by the Ambient Assisted Living Joint Program of the EU.[32] Aimed at improving the wellbeing and autonomy of older people,

27 More projects including reviews can be found in Khaksar and others (n 12) 5.

28 European Commission, 'Integrated Cognitive Assistive and Domotic Companion Robotic Systems for Ability and Security' <https://cordis.europa.eu/project/id/216487> accessed 21 August 2023.

29 A Badii and others, 'CompanionAble: Graceful Integration of Mobile Robot Companion with a Smart Home Environment' (2009) 8(3) *Gerontechnology Journal* 181 <http://doi.org/10.4017/gt.2009.08.03.008.00> accessed 25 September 2023.

30 Ibid.; H-M Gross and others, 'I'll Keep an Eye on You: Home Robot Companion for Elderly People with Cognitive Impairment' (*2011 IEEE International Conference on Systems, Man, and Cybernetics*, Anchorage, Alaska, USA, October 9–12, 2011); H-M Gross and others, 'Further Progress Towards a Home Robot Companion for People with Mild Cognitive Impairment' (*2012 IEEE International Conference on Systems, Man, and Cybernetics (SMC)*, Seoul, Soth Korea, 2012); C Huijnen, A Badii, H den van Heuvel, P Caleb-Solly and D Thiemert, 'Maybe It Becomes a Buddy, But Do Not Call It a Robot – Seamless Cooperation between Companion Robotics and Smart Homes' in D V Keyson, *Ambient Intelligence* (Springer 2011) 324 <https://link.springer.com/chapter/10.1007/978-3-642-25167-2_44> accessed 21 August 2023.

31 AAL Programme, DOMEO – AAL Programme <www.aal-europe.eu/projects/domeo/> accessed 21 August 2023.

32 S Bedaf, G J Gelderblom and L de Witte, 'Overview and Categorization of Robots Supporting Independent Living of Elderly People: What Activities Do They Support and How Far Have They

the project developed mobility assistive and companion robots to support care givers by providing personalized domestic services.[33] During the project, the Kompai robotic platform – which offers remote presence functionalities like monitoring, alarms or memory assistance; sending video streams in case of an emergency; stimulating physical exercise; or observing the user's behaviour[34] – was successfully implemented in the home of users who were suffering from cognitive decline.[35]

The MOBISERV project[36] was also funded by the EU and had several renowned partners representing care organizations, universities, research institutions, and industry from seven countries.[37] The team built a robot companion – which offers structure throughout the day and is able to help its users to remain active by suggesting a variety of activities and reminding them to eat and drink, as well as taking medicine in order to support the independent living of older adults as long as possible, in their home or in various degrees of institutionalization – with a focus on health, nutrition, wellbeing and safety.[38]

9.2.4 The Geriatronics Project

The Geriatronics project[39] of the MIRMI at TUM focuses on the use of personal care robots to assist older people and caregivers.

The term "Geriatronics" refers to a new field encompassing the integration of robotics, mechatronics, information technology, machine intelligence and three-dimensional (3D) technology. The project focuses on optimally supporting the medical care of elderly individuals and promoting self-determination

---

Developed Assistive Technology' (2015) 27(2) *The Official Journal of RESNA* 88 <http://doi.org/10.1080/10400435.2014.978916> accessed 21 August 2023.

33 European Commission, 'Turning a Robot into a Companion for Frail People' <https://ec.europa.eu/programmes/horizon2020/en/print/2485> accessed 21 August 2023.

34 Bedaf and others (n 32).

35 K Zsiga, G Edelmayer, P Rumeau, O Péter, A Tóth and G Fazekas, 'Home Care Robot for Socially Supporting the Elderly: Focus Group Studies in Three European Countries to Screen User Attitudes and Requirements' (2013) 36(4) *International Journal of Rehabilitation Research* 375 <http://doi.org/10.1097/MRR.0b013e3283643d26> accessed 28 September 2023.

36 European Commission, 'An Integrated Intelligent Home Environment for the Provision of Health, Nutrition and Mobility Services to the Elderly' <https://cordis.europa.eu/project/id/248434> accessed 21 August 2023.

37 Ibid.

38 Huijnen and others (n 30); A Iosifidis, A Tefas and I Pitas, 'Multi-View Action Recognition Based on Action Volumes, Fuzzy Distances and Cluster Discriminant Analysis' (2013) 93(6) *Signal Processing* 1445, <http://doi.org/10.1016/j.sigpro.2012.08.015> accessed 28 September 2023; E Marami, A Tefas and I Pitas, 'Nutrition Assistance Based on Skin Color Segmentation and Support Vector Machines' in T Czachórski, S Kozielski and U Stańczyk (eds), *Man-Machine Interactions 2* (Springer 2011) 179; O Zoidi, A Tefas and I Pitas, 'Visual Object Tracking Based on Local Steering Kernels and Color Histograms' (2013) 23(5) *IEEE Transactions on Circuits and Systems for Video Technology* 870, <http://doi.org/10.1109/TCSVT.2012.2226527> accessed 28 September 2023.

39 <www.mirmi.tum.de/en/mirmi/research/health/geriatronics/> accessed 21 August 2023. Project partners are hospitals, nursing and seniors' associations, corporate enterprises and non-profit organizations.

in old age. The collaboration between humans and computers has evolved significantly. With the integration of sensors and sophisticated machine learning (ML) algorithms, robots are transformed into cyber-physical systems capable of learning from their surroundings, past experiences, and interactions with humans.

This goes beyond simply following pre-programmed routines. For instance, in the healthcare sector, care robots utilize sensory data like video and audio to collectively enhance their ML processes.[40] Through this shared knowledge, the robots become adept at distinguishing between real-world events, such as differentiating between a patient fainting and falling accidentally versus intentionally lying down. As a result, care robots can make more informed decisions, leading to improved patient care. Furthermore, voice recognition and emotion decoding capabilities allow the robots to detect patterns indicative of pain, fear or panic in patients. This empowers the robots to respond more effectively to the specific needs and emotions of those under their care. The interconnectedness of robots and the exchange of data and knowledge among them create an environment of continual improvement. This leads to more effective AI functionalities in healthcare settings, promoting better patient outcomes and overall care quality.

The Geriatronics project has three main objectives. The first is the preservation of mobility and social interaction of elderly people. Elderly individuals often encounter challenges in performing everyday tasks due to factors like reduced physical or mental fitness, illnesses, and social isolation. As such, the project intends to address these issues through robotic systems and machine intelligence by facilitating communication between distant family members and acquaintances, and easing the workload of caregivers, allowing them to engage in meaningful conversations with their care recipients.

Second, elderly people should retain their independence for as long as possible. Many seniors, despite their preference for living independently at home, may be compelled to move to nursing homes due to health impairments. However, due to a shortage of skilled personnel, they may not receive sufficient assistance to lead independent lives. Geriatronics assistance systems, employing medical telepresence and personalized diagnostics, offer opportunities for seniors to stay independent.

Finally, the project also offers care for the caregivers themselves. Geriatronics technologies not only assist caregivers in non-care tasks and physically demanding activities but also mitigate the detrimental effects on their health, leading to reduced sick days. While these technologies are not intended to replace nursing staff, they provide valuable support in daily caregiving duties by handling time-consuming or strenuous tasks.

40 L Panait and S Luke, 'Cooperative Multi-Agent Learning: The State of the Art' (2005) 11 *Autonomous Agents and Multi-Agent Systems* 387.

In order to achieve these objectives, three different robots are being tested within the project: GARMI, PARTI and MUCKI.

- GARMI[41] is a humanoid robotic assistant that helps seniors with activities of daily living, such as doing housework. GARMI can also physically assist a patient during rehabilitation exercises and/or even assist the doctor during the first stages of a telemedicine-based doctor visit. GARMI is equipped with measuring devices – for example electrocardiogram (ECG), sphygmomanometer and ultrasound – combined with the use of IoT-sensors. The doctor has access to relevant health parameters to be able to act quickly in cases of emergency and can improve communication with family and friends by adding a new haptic channel to audio-visual communication.
- PARTI[42] is a multimodal teleoperation centre that serves as a control for the household assistant robot GARMI over any kind of Internet connection, built to work autonomously most of the time. Teleoperations are meant to save time due to house visits through enabling doctors to visit their patients virtually to perform basic examinations. This way, they can get a first impression of a person's health condition before driving to people's homes or sending first responders to an apparent emergency. In addition, elderly people who live in villages without medical provision can see a doctor for examinations without travelling great distances.
- MUCKI[43] is a mechatronic avatar for human upper extremities which is used to perform mobilization exercises remotely through bi-directional force feedback between task spaces and assistance of the human digital twin for visualization of muscle activity. The human digital twin[44] comprises an integrative model, which can represent the body under various healthy and diseased physiological states. This technology will be developed to make more personalized medical decisions, including diagnosis, prognosis and treatment planning (e.g., therapy or surgery). This way, new treatments or assistive devices can be tested by simulation prior to the testing on humans, thus making them safer and avoiding unexpected health hazards. MUCKI can also be used for health monitoring and preventive medicine in combination with heterogeneous (wearable) sensor networks and has the potential of being used for teaching and training in the medical field. Telerehabilitation with MUCKI is a highly specialized application based on teleoperation technology developed in the Geriatronics project. The connection between the leader (MUCKI) and follower (GARMI) systems allows responsive and high-precision position-based control of the follower while transmitting force feedback measured at the follower back to the leader; a process known as bi-directional haptic teleoperation. The transparency of the setup is further enhanced using bi-directional video/audio communication channels.

41 <https://geriatronics.mirmi.tum.de/en/garmi/> accessed 28 September 2023.
42 <https://geriatronics.mirmi.tum.de/en/parti/> accessed 28 September 2023.
43 <https://geriatronics.mirmi.tum.de/en/mucki/> accessed 28 September 2023.
44 <https://geriatronics.mirmi.tum.de/en/human-digital-twin/> accessed 28 September 2023.

9.3 Privacy Implications of Personal Care Robots

Personal care robots affect privacy in many ways. They differ from other (smart) devices that also collect data through onboard sensors (e.g., wearables, IoT devices), voice recognition systems (e.g., Cortana, Siri, Alexa) or those that process data in other ways.[45] Unlike these devices, personal care robots have special characteristics, which must be considered. Above all, they perform actions in the physical world and are in constant contact with people, especially caregivers or patients.[46] Moreover, they are used in the care and health sector, which raises additional questions related to the protection of privacy.

Generally speaking, personal care robots have implications on four different aspects of privacy:[47] physical privacy, psychological privacy, social privacy and informational privacy.

9.3.1 Physical Privacy

First, the use of personal care robots presents significant privacy implications concerning physical privacy. Physical privacy describes the extent to which an individual is physically accessible to others, including concepts of personal space and territoriality. Within spatially delimitable places of retreat that are not accessible to everyone, individuals can realize themselves and protect their intimacy. This concerns foremost – but not exclusively – the home of the patient and care recipient.

Personal care robots may inadvertently challenge this notion.[48] By providing assistance within private rooms, these robots gain access to spaces that have traditionally been reserved for human interaction or self-fulfilment only.[49] Consequently, users may experience a breach of their spatial privacy as these machines enter and interact within these intimate environments.

45 M Rueben, C M Grimm, F J Bernieri and W D Smart, 'A Taxonomy of Privacy Constructs for Privacy-Sensitive Robotics' (2017) *ArXiv* 1 <https://arxiv.org/abs/1701.00841> accessed 4 September 2023, presents a taxonomy of privacy as an analytical tool for the Privacy-Sensitive Robotics field.

46 M Rueben, A M Aroyo, C Lutz, J Schmölz, P Van Cleynenbreugel, A Corti and others, 'Themes and Research Directions in Privacy Sensitive Robotics' (*2018 IEEE Workshop on Advanced Robotics and its Social Impacts (ARSO)*, Genova, Italy, 2018) 77 <http://doi.org/10.1109/ARSO.2018.8625758> accessed 28 September 2023.

47 Cf., A Chatzimichali and others, 'Toward Privacy-Sensitive Human – Robot Interaction: Privacy Terms and Human – Data Interaction in the Personal Robot Era' (2020) 12(1) *Journal of Behavioral Robotics* 162 for different types of privacy (other terms); T Heuer, I Schiering and R Gerndt, 'Privacy Framework for Context-Aware Robot Development' (2021) 12(1) *Journal of Behavioral Robotics* 468, 471; Rueben and others, 'Themes and Research Directions in Privacy Sensitive Robotics' (n 46) 78.

48 M E Kaminski, M Rueben, W D Smart and C M Grimm, 'Averting Robot Eyes' 76 (2016) *Maryland Law Review* 983.

49 A Fiske, P Henningsen, A Buyx, 'Your Robot Therapist Will See You Now: Ethical Implications of Embodied Artificial Intelligence in Psychiatry, Psychology, and Psychotherapy' (2019) 21(5) *Journal of Medical Internet Research* <http://doi.org/10.2196/13216> accessed 28 September 2023.

9.3.2 Psychological Privacy

Second, the use of personal care robots presents implications concerning psychological privacy, which describes an individual's ability to control cognitive and affective inputs and outputs, form values and decide when and with whom thoughts are shared or intimate information are disclosed.[50]

As personal care robots become integrated into the lives of users, there is a potential risk of developing psychological dependence on these machines. Relying heavily on robots for emotional support and companionship may lead to a diminished sense of self-reliance and interpersonal connections.[51] Moreover, the presence of personal care robots may inadvertently create chilling effects, causing users to censor their thoughts and emotions in fear of judgment or misuse of their personal data. Such inhibition may result in reduced self-reflection and limit human autonomy as users become accustomed to interacting with non-human entities instead of seeking human interaction for emotional wellbeing.[52] Notably, certain vulnerable user groups – such as children, the elderly or mentally ill people – may be particularly susceptible to these psychological privacy concerns. Children, in their developmental stages, might struggle to differentiate between the companionship provided by robots and genuine human relationships, while the elderly may experience increased isolation if their interactions primarily revolve around robot companions.[53]

Thus, safeguarding psychological privacy becomes imperative to ensure that personal care robots enhance – rather than diminish – users' overall wellbeing and autonomy.

9.3.3 Social Privacy

In addition, the use of personal care robots presents significant privacy implications concerning an individual's ability and efforts to regulate their social contacts, both at the individual and group levels.[54] Social privacy is culturally influenced. Cultural variations, as identified by anthropologists, play a role in shaping the ways people

50 M Burgoon (ed), *Communication Yearbook 6* (Routledge 1982).

51 M Rueben and W D Smart, 'Privacy in Human-Robot Interaction: Survey and Future Work' (2016) *We Robot* 2.

52 Cf. C Lutz and others, 'The Privacy Implications of Social Robots: Scoping Review and Expert Interviews' (2019) 7(3) *Mobile Media and Communication* 412, 426.

53 Cf. S Turkle, W Taggart, C D Kidd and O Dasté, 'Relational Artifacts with Children and Elders: The Complexities of Cybercompanionship' (2006) 18(4) *Connection Science* 347; Lutz and others (n 52).

54 A Westin, *Privacy and Freedom* (1st edn, Atheneum 1967); I Altman, *The Environment and Social Behavior: Privacy, Personal Space, Territory, Crowding* (Brooks/Cole 1975); I Altman, 'Privacy Regulation: Culturally Universal or Culturally Specific?' (1977) 33(3) *Journal of Social Issues* 66, cited after H Leino-Kilpi and others, 'Privacy: A Review of the Literature' (2001) 38 *International Journal of Nursing Studies* 665.

strive to preserve their privacy.[55] *Burgoon* emphasizes the importance of the participants themselves as well as frequency, length and content of social interactions.[56]

To begin with, psychology has shown that users tend to naturally trust computers. They create emotional reactions, change attitudes and affect memories. They are often treated politely or perceived as colleagues.[57] This can have effects on a person's willingness to disclose information.[58] With personal care robots capable of establishing additional social bonds with users, the potential for affection and trust to develop between humans and these machines raises even more concerns about the divulgence of intimate information or secrets.[59] Users often ascribe human-like attributes to their robot companions (*anthropomorphization* effect)[60] and inadvertently reveal sensitive details about their lives more readily, assuming a level of trust akin to human relationships,[61] even when they have clear evidence that this trust is unjustified.[62] Eye contact, facial expressions and a natural voice lead to the illusion of understanding on the user side.[63] Particular influence on users can be achieved through the use of social and physical cues such as language and praise. Physical attractiveness can also influence user behaviour.[64] This trust in the human–robot interaction, sometimes, even trumps trust towards other humans and can be potentially exploited.[65]

55 E Hall, *The Hidden Dimension* (Doubleday and Company 1966); Westin (n 54); Altman, 'Privacy Regulation: Culturally Universal or Culturally Specific?' (n 54).

56 Burgoon (n 50) 221–222.

57 B Reeves, *The Media Equation: How People Treat Computers, Television, and New Media Like Real People and Places* (CSLI 2004); Lutz and others (n 52) 414.

58 Cf., B Kahl, M Füller, T Beer and S Ziegler, 'Acceptance and Communicative Effectiveness of Different HRI Modalities for Mental Stimulation in Dementia Care' in E Di Nuovo, F Broz, F Cavallo and P Dario (eds), *Proceedings of New Frontiers of Service Robotics for the Elderly, IEEE RO-MAN* (2014); Fosch-Villaronga and others, 'Nothing Comes Between My Robot and Me: Privacy and Human-Robot Interaction in Robotised Healthcare' (n 4) 102.

59 K Thomaen, 'Examining the Constitutionality of Robot-enhanced Interrogation' in R Calo, M Froomkin and I Kerr (eds), *Robot Law* (Edward Elgar Publishing 2016) 306.

60 M Scheutz, 'The Inherent Dangers of Unidirectional Emotional Bonds Between Humans and Social Robots' in P Lin, K Abney and G A Bekey (eds), *Robot Ethics: The Ethical and Social Implications of Robotics* (The MIT Press 2012) 205; Ishii (n 19) 515.

61 T J Prescott and J M Robillard, 'Are Friends Electric? The Benefits and Risks of Human-Robot Relationships' (2021) 24(1) *iScience* 101993; E Broadbent, 'Interactions with Robots: The Truths We Reveal About Ourselves' (2017) 68 *Annual Review of Psychology* 627.

62 M Salem, G Lakatos, F Amirabdollahian and K Dautenhahn, 'Would You Trust a (Faulty) Robot?: Effects of Error, Task Type and Personality on Human-Robot Cooperation and Trust' (*Proceedings of the Tenth Annual ACM/IEEE International Conference on Human-Robot Interaction*, 2015) 141–148; P Robinette and others, 'Overtrust of Robots in Emergency Evacuation Scenarios' (*Eleventh Annual ACM/IEEE International Conference on Human Robot Interaction* 2016); P Robinette and others, 'Conceptualizing Overtrust in Robots: Why Do People Trust a Robot That Previously Failed?' in W F Lawless and others (eds), *Autonomy and Artificial Intelligence: A Threat or Savior?* (Springer International Publishing 2017) 129.

63 Kidd, Taggart and Turkle, 'A Sociable Robot to Encourage Social Interaction Among the Elderly' (n 7) 3972–3976.

64 B J Fogg, *Persuasive Technology: Using Computers to Change What We Think and Do* (1st edn, Morgan Kaufmann 2003) 92.

65 Robinette and others, 'Overtrust of Robots in Emergency Evacuation Scenarios' (n 62) 101.

Thus, the growing social integration of personal care robots necessitates careful consideration to ensure the preservation of individuals' social privacy rights and protect against unintended disclosure of private information.

9.3.4 Informational Privacy

Finally, the integration of personal care robots raises significant privacy implications concerning informational privacy. Informational privacy grants an individual's right to control the release of personal information to others, be it individuals or organizations such as hospitals.[66] As highlighted by *Burgoon*, informational privacy extends beyond what is directly under personal control,[67] which should be taken into consideration carefully in the context of personal care robots. These robots collect and process an substantial amount of data, ranging from basic user preferences to sensitive health-related information.

The storage and transmission of such data or cloud connectivity raise concerns about third-party access to user data and introduce security risks, like hacking and other forms of unauthorized access.[68] Additionally, due to the complexity of data processing or a potential lack of user understanding, it is often not apparent at first glance whether or which data is being processed.[69] This is especially true for human-like robots.

Therefore, it is crucial to establish robust data protection measures and transparent data practices to ensure that users' informational privacy remains safeguarded amidst the increasing integration of personal care robots into daily life.

9.4 Challenges Under the GDPR

9.4.1 Quantity and Quality of Processed Personal Data

Different types of robots[70] process different types of data. From a privacy perspective, the majority of the very high amount of data processed by personal care robots is inherently sensitive. The application of the GDPR depends significantly on the type of data concerned. According to Art. 2(1), the GDPR only applies to the processing of personal data, i.e., to any information relating to an identified or identifiable natural person ('data subject') as per Art. 4(1) GDPR. An identifiable natural person is one who can be identified – directly or indirectly, in particular by reference to an identifier such as a name, an identification number, location data, an online identifier or to one or more factors specific to the physical, physiological, genetic, mental, economic, cultural or social identity of that natural person – which is not the case when data is anonymized.

66 Westin (n 54).
67 Burgoon (n 50) 221.
68 Lutz and others (n 52) 422 with further references.
69 Ibid., 413.
70 Cf., Section 9.2.2.

Data processed by personal care robots includes not only personal data in the sense of Art. 4(1) GDPR, but also health-related information, which according to Art. 4(15) GDPR are "special categories of sensitive data" subject to special protection under Art. 9 GDPR.[71] Furthermore, personal care robots handle "biometric data", another category of data under the special regime of Art. 9 GDPR. This occurs when the machines utilize specific technical processes related to the physical, physiological or behavioural traits of an individual, enabling the unique identification of said person, as defined in Art. 4(14) GDPR. Biometric data is typically used by recognition software; for example, for authentication purposes.

Personal care robots do not only process sensitive data, but also data that were previously more difficult to process, because robots of all shapes and sizes, equipped with an array of sophisticated sensors and processors, greatly magnify the human capacity to observe.[72] In addition, they create new access points to traditionally protected spaces. Placed in the most inner sphere of privacy, home robots in particular (e.g., companions) present a novel opportunity for governments, private litigants and hackers to access information about the interior of a living space.[73] Moreover, personal care robots are increasingly becoming human-like and socially interactive in design, making them more engaging and salient to their end-users and the larger community. Many studies demonstrate that people are hardwired to react to heavily anthropomorphic technologies like robots. They sometimes act as if a person were actually present, including having the sensation of being observed and evaluated.[74]

9.4.2 Transparency of Data Processing

Data processing by personal care robots also raises transparency issues. Robots' hidden and complex information processing methods are likely to cause a lack of understanding of the type and scope of information processing.[75] Presently, robots extensively depend on AI and ML to deliver services and execute essential tasks for users. Through the implementation of ML techniques, robots progressively acquire the ability to identify objects, comprehend human emotions and respond effectively to user commands. These autonomous decisions are facilitated

71 While the justification for setting a higher level of protection for special categories of data (such data revealing ethnic origin or sexual orientation) is intuitive, new forms of enhanced analytics challenge the ability to draw a clear distinction between "normal" personal data and "sensitive" data. After all, even an analysis merely relying on "regular" categories can quickly end up revealing sensitive data. Legal literature is therefore calling for a specific intent to process data or an objectified processing context, e.g., in a health context for the special regime of Art. 9 GDPR to apply or focus on the objectified processing context.

72 Calo (n 14) 187ff.

73 Ibid.

74 Cf., Lutz and others (n 52) 426.

75 C Ho, 'Privacy and Transparency in Human-Robot Interaction' in W Barfield, Y Weng and U Pagallo, *Cambridge Handbook on Law, Policy, and Regulations for Human-Robot Interaction* (Cambridge University Press 2024) 589.

by sophisticated algorithmic systems that process vast datasets for model training.[76] The processes are not always visible at first sight, because personal care robots are often designed semi-humanoid (e.g., robot eyes, arms, legs). Sensors (e.g., eyes) are not always identifiable as such. Furthermore, robots are designed to read human emotions and move independently to fulfil their tasks. Therefore patients might not be able to predict the robots' behaviours, including where they go or what they might do next.[77]

Additionally, the process of data processing itself is a *black box* for users. Due to a lack of knowledge or understanding, users will not grasp or be able to retrace the process, especially when and under what circumstances their data (which may be sensitive) will be collected. Also, robots increasingly rely on cloud-based data processing and a multitude of sensors and actuators, making them highly complex and opaque systems, whose data collection is often unknown or misunderstood by users[78] who do not have insight if or which third parties have access to the data collected (e.g., cloud manufacturers).[79]

Finally, it has to be considered that users, even if they acknowledge all or some of the previously discussed factors, tend to be concerned about their privacy and fear a loss of control, but at the same time do not adapt their behaviour accordingly – e.g., by disclosing less or choosing privacy-protecting techniques (the so-called *privacy paradox*).[80] Generally, the hidden nature of data processing by robots catalyzes this psychological effect.

All of this leads to problems for the concept of the basic paradigm of informed consent, since care recipients will have difficulties to truly understand how his or her information will be used.[81]

9.4.3 Inherent Vulnerability of Care Receivers

Obtaining informed consent is especially challenging if the data subject is a care receiver with cognitive impairments, due to the complexity of their capacity, which may be inconsistent and fluctuating. Care receivers, e.g., those suffering from

76 Ibid.

77 Kaminski and others (n 48) 983.

78 M K Lee, K P Tang, J Forlizzi and S Kiesler, 'Understanding Users' Perception of Privacy in Human-Robot Interaction' (*Proceedings of the 6th International Conference on Human-Robot Interaction*, Lausanne, 2011) 181 <http://doi.org/10.1145/1957656.1957721> accessed 28 September 2023.

79 Ho (n 75).

80 S B Barnes, 'A Privacy Paradox: Social Networking in the United States' (2006) 11(9) *First Monday* <https://firstmonday.org/ojs/index.php/fm/article/view/1394> accessed 28 September 2023; T Dienlin and S Trepte, 'Is the Privacy Paradox a Relic of the Past? An In-Depth Analysis of Privacy Attitudes and Privacy Behaviors' (2015) 45(3) *European Journal of Social Psychology* 285; R Gross and A Acquisti, 'Information Revelation and Privacy in Online Social Networks' (*Proceedings of the 2005 ACM Workshop on Privacy in the Electronic Society*, New York, 2005) 71; S Kokolakis, 'Privacy Attitudes and Privacy Behaviour: A Review of Current Research on the Privacy Paradox Phenomenon' (2017) 64 *Computers & Security* 122.

81 Ho (n 75).

dementia, might not be able to consent. The process of obtaining consent therefore may involve additional parties who can provide support to the care receiver. Otherwise, designated proxies could be engaged when the patient's capacity to make decisions is severely impaired. This comes with a lot of uncertainties if the care receiver's state of mind is unclear. Diseases like dementia leave patients with lucid moments and it can be unclear when a proxy or support is needed.

The consent procedure must include both explicit approval for using robotic assistance in healthcare applications and obtaining data protection consent. Such a data protection consent includes the user's willingness to allow the sharing of their information with other relevant parties, thereby ensuring the provision of competent and comprehensive healthcare services. It is imperative to address these dual aspects within the consent process to safeguard both the patient's interests and the privacy of their sensitive data while optimizing the benefits of employing robotic technology in healthcare settings.[82]

9.4.4 Stakeholder Complexity

Identifying controllers and processors, as well as managing their relationships, has been acknowledged as a particularly challenging task in cloud service arrangements.[83] Robotics ecosystems are even more complex because they can involve multiple hardware manufacturers, software developers, cloud service providers, sub-providers and users. It may be a significant challenge to identify and to map all relevant interactions and communications involving, i.e., robot2robot, wearable2robot, robot2cloud, person2robot, sensors2cloud, and sensors2robot. Additionally, the data processing does not have to be necessary to fulfil the primary task of the robot. It can also merely serve to train other systems. Therefore, achieving a comprehensive understanding of the parties responsible for determining the purposes and means of processing personal data becomes even more difficult.

Additionally, the expansive interpretation of controllership in the context of Art. 4(7) GDPR by the European Court of Justice (ECJ),[84] coupled with the potential for joint controllership under Art. 24 GDPR and the increasing decentralization of data collection, storage and processing result in an increase in the number of

82 M Lenca and E Fosch-Villaronga, 'Privacy and Security Issues in Assistive Technologies for Dementia: The Case of Ambient Assisted Living, Wearables, and Service Robotics' in F Jotterand and others (eds), *Intelligent Assistive Technologies for Dementia: Clinical, Ethical, Social, and Regulatory Implications* (Oxford Academic 2019).

83 See D Kamarinou, C Millard and I Oldani, 'Compliance as a Service: A Review of GDPR-Mandated Contractual Relationships Between Providers and Customers of Enterprise Cloud Services' (*Queen Mary School of Law Legal Studies Research Paper No. 287/2018*, 2018); and also W K Hon, C Millard and I Walden, 'Who Is Responsible for Personal Data in Clouds?' in C Millard (ed), *Cloud Computing Law* (Oxford University Press 2013) 193.

84 Cf., CJEU Case C-2010/16 *Wirtschaftsakademie Schleswig-Holstein* ECLI:EU:C:2018:388, paras 26–28. Case C-25/17 *Jehovan todistajat* ECLI:EU:C:2018:551 23. Case 131/12 *Google Spain* ECLI:EU:C:2014:31, paras 28 and 41. Case C-40/17 *Fashion ID* ECLI:EU:C:2019:629.

controllers,[85] creates a (international) web that makes it even more difficult to identify data controllers in the aforementioned context.

9.4.5 Legal Bases for Data Processing

To be lawful, the processing of personal data must meet the requirements under Art. 6(1) GDPR. When biometric or genetic information is involved, the requirements are even higher. According to Art. 9(1) GDPR, the processing of such particularly sensitive data is prohibited except in cases where the conditions of Art. 9(2) GDPR are met.

9.4.5.1 Consent

Research has shown that the evolution of modern technologies (like AI) pushes the concept of informed consent to its limits due to algorithmic opacity.[86] Lack of disclosure, epistemic opacity and explanatory opacity pose a particular challenge for data processing in medicine and care.[87] Still, the processing of personal data is regularly based on consent according to Art. 6(1)(a) GDPR or Art. 9(2)(a) GDPR when certain types of sensitive data, like medical data, are being processed. Their procession is generally prohibited by Art. 9(1) GDPR, but as an exception, Art. 9(2)(a) GDPR stipulates that Art. 9(1) is not applicable where the data subject has given explicit consent to the processing of personal data for one or more specified purposes. While this provision does not contain more specific requirements, the prerequisites for effective consent are regulated in Art. 7 GDPR. Recital 33 GDPR, which can be used for interpretation purposes, clarifies that the expression of consent must be voluntary, for a specific case, in an informed manner and unambiguous.

9.4.5.1.1 LEGAL CAPACITY AND CONSENT

When providing services to care recipients, such as elderly people, the question arises whether care recipients have legal capacity to give consent to data processing. In contrast to national law,[88] the GDPR does not contain provisions on legal capacity. Rather, Art. 8 GDPR only contains a presumption on the capacity of children to give consent, but not for persons with deficiencies such as psychological

85 M Finck, 'Notion of Data Controller in the GDPR' (2021) 11(4) *International Data Privacy Law* 333.

86 As to the question whether individuals are, under EU law, entitled to a right to explanation of automated decision-making, especially when AI systems are used, see M Ebers, 'Explainable AI in the European Union. An Overview of the Current Legal Framework(s)' in L Colonna and S Greenstein (eds), *Nordic Yearbook of Law and Informatics 2020–2021: Law in the Era of Artificial Intelligence* (The Swedish Law and Informatics Research Institute 2022) 103 <https://irilaw.files.wordpress.com/2022/02/law-in-the-era-of-artificial-intelligence.pdf> accessed 28 September 2023.

87 See E Dantas and R Nogaroli, 'The Rise of Robotics and Artificial Intelligence in Healthcare: New Challenges for the Doctrine of Informed Consent' (2021) 4 *Medicine and Law* 1.

88 Cf., Sections 104ff of the German Civil Code.

diseases. Therefore, the issue remains whether it is permissible under the GDPR to apply Member State laws in these cases. In any case, this depends on the legal nature of the consent.[89] Some argue that consent is a sui generis institution under European law which must be interpreted autonomously due to its conclusive regulation in Art. 4(11) and Art. 6–9 GDPR. According to this view, a recourse to Member State laws would be contrary to the aim of the GDPR to establish a uniform level of protection throughout Europe.[90]

Others qualify consent as a (quasi-)juridical act which is subject to Member State laws,[91] as long as its application does not render claims based on EU law impossible in practice or excessively difficult to enforce.[92]

In any case, legal capacity is a mandatory requirement for consent to be effective under the GDPR, regardless of whether recourse to Member State laws is possible or not. The data subject should be "aware" of the processing (Recital 63[1] GDPR). Regarding children, Recital 58(4) GDPR calls for a plain and child-friendly language to give children the opportunity to exert their right to self-determination. Although the GDPR does not contain any regulations for the elderly, the considerations for children can also be applied for those in need of care, because similar problems regarding consent arise for both.

9.4.5.1.2 FREE, REAL CHOICE

Consent has to be informed and should be given freely. In this regard, the prerequisites for informed consent are subject to various uncertainties in care environments, as previously indicated. The Working Party on the Protection of Individuals With Regard to the Processing of Personal Data (Art. 29 Working Party (WP29)) has highlighted in several opinions, that consent can only be valid when the data subject is able to exercise a real choice – meaning that there should be no risk of deception, intimidation, coercion or significant negative consequences (e.g., substantial extra costs, health risks) if the data subject does not consent. Consent will not be considered as freely given in cases when there is any element of compulsion, pressure or inability to exercise free will. Consent must be an unambiguous statement or a clear affirmative action.

9.4.5.1.3 INFORMED CONSENT

To be valid, consent has to be informed. This means that the controller's identity, the existence of a right to withdraw consent, as well as the data processing's

89 P Hacker, *Datenprivatrecht. Neue Technologien im Spannungsfeld von Datenschutzrecht und BGB* (Mohr Siebeck Verlag 2020) 356.

90 T Kienle, 'Datenmündigkeit' (2020) 5 *Privacy in Germany (PinG)* 208, 212.

91 P M Rogosch, *Die Einwilligung im Datenschutzrecht* (Nomos 2013) 40; OLG Karlsruhe, NJW-RR 2018, 1263.

92 Hacker (n 89) 356. This is the so-called principle of effectiveness. For a detailed discussion of this judge-made principle see M Ebers, *Rechte, Rechtsbehelfe und Sanktionen im Unionsprivatrecht* (Mohr Siebeck 2016) 249ff.

purpose, have to be made transparent in clear and plain language.[93] Whether written or oral, such consent must be oriented towards the capacity of the recipient.

9.4.5.1.4 SPECIFIC CONSENT

Further, consent must be given in relation to one or more specific purposes as safeguard against function creep. According to Recital 43 GDPR, consent is presumed not to be freely given if the procedure for obtaining the consent does not allow data subjects to give separate consent for processing operations respectively (e.g., only for some processing operations and not for others) despite it being appropriate in the individual case. Furthermore, Recital 32 GDPR states that consent should be given to each purpose if the processing activities have multiple purposes.

9.4.5.1.5 TRANSPARENCY REQUIREMENTS

Finally, personal care robots must comply with the transparency requirements regulated by Art. 5(1)(a) GDPR, as well as Arts. 12ff. GDPR, because they process personal data.[94] Therefore, data controllers are obliged to inform users of the processing of their personal data in a concise, transparent and intelligible form, and in an easily accessible way. This can be very challenging, considering the involvement of multiple users and the ecosystem's complexity. In order to comply with data protection law data, controllers should inform all users – not only the user setting up the robot – about the identities and roles of those processing personal data who are far from evident for the users.

9.4.5.1.6 FURTHER CHALLENGES

Even if the aforementioned obstacles are overcome, the validity of consent might still be arguable. Care receivers often do not notice some data processing activities since personal care robots are designed to be human-like. Therefore, they cannot consent to specific processes, since they are not informed about every operation. Furthermore, function creep is not traceable. Care receivers are often faced with superior knowledge and they are dependent on care due to illness or old age. Most importantly, psychological or physical impairments might make it (almost) impossible to give consent. The complexity of the systems and of the processes on the one hand, as well as the physical and mental impairments on the other hand, seem to self-contradict in an irresolvable way.

93 For the right to withdraw consent, see Art. 7(3)(3) GDPR. Thereto Albers and Veit 'GDPR Art. 6' in S Brink and A Wolff (eds), *BeckOK DatenschutzR* (44th edn, C.H. Beck 2023) para 36.

94 See also Recital 58 GDPR.

9.4.5.2 Vital Interests of the Data Subject

Art. 9(2)(c) GDPR states that Art. 9(1) GDPR shall not apply in such instances when the data subject is physically or legally incapable of giving consent, and the data processing is necessary to protect the vital interests of the data subject or of another natural person. This, as earlier discussed, is often the case in care environments, e.g., because of mental diseases or guardianship.

However, Art. 9(2)(c) GDPR requires that the data processing is necessary to protect vital interests of the data subject. As an exemption, "vital interest" must be interpreted narrowly and therefore only covers emergency medical care.[95] Yet, personal care robots are predominantly engaged in routine medical procedures or prearranged treatments. The occurrence of processing an individual's personal data to safeguard the vital interests of others is expected to be even less frequent. Therefore, the use of this article as a legal basis should be avoided whenever it is feasible to rely on an alternative for personal data processing.

9.4.5.3 Necessity for Medical Diagnosis, Healthcare or Social Care Treatments

Art. 9(2)(h) GDPR stipulates that Art. 9(1) GDPR does not apply when the data processing is necessary for, among other things,

> medical diagnosis or the provision of health or social care or treatment services on the basis of Union or Member State law or pursuant to contracts with a health professional and subject to conditions and safeguards referred to in paragraph 3.

According to Recital 53(1) GDPR, this exemption takes into account the importance of individual and public health.

In Germany, the legislature has made use of this opening clause. According to Section 22(1)(1b) of the Federal Data Protection Act (Bundesdatenschutzgesetz, or BDSG), the processing of special categories of personal data as referred to in Art. 9(1) GDPR is permitted by public and private bodies if the processing is necessary for the purposes of preventive medicine, medical diagnosis, the provision of health or social care, or treatment or pursuant to a contract with a health professional. In terms of content, this provision is identical to the requirements of the GDPR.[96]

Preventive healthcare includes all health-promoting or therapeutic measures. It aims at the prevention of the development of any impairments.[97] In contrast, nursing and care for the elderly involves the management of such impairments, even though

95 Cf., Schiff 'GDPR Art. 9' in E Ehmann and M Selmayr (eds), *Datenschutzgrundverordnung* (2nd edn, C.H. Beck 2018) para 42.

96 Albers and Veit 'BDSG § 22' (n 93) paras 26, 28.

97 D Heckmann and M Scheurer, 'BDSG § 22' in P Gola and D Heckmann (eds), *Datenschutz-Grundverordnung, Bundesdatenschutzgesetz: DS-GVO/BDSG* (3rd edn, C.H. Beck 2022) para 20.

the use of care robots also has a health-promoting effect. Yet, personal care robots are not so much about these aims but about facilitating everyday life. Since Art. 9(2)(h) GDPR must be interpreted as an exception, many scholars are of the opinion that care activities covered by this provision are limited to professional care.[98]

This also applies to the area of medical diagnostics used to identify diseases or injuries.[99] Care for the elderly and sick is less about determining or classifying findings than about dealing with age-related or disease-related symptoms.

The aforementioned exception can therefore apply only to data processing for care or treatment in the health sector. In principle, all measures that are beneficial to the recovery process of the person concerned are covered by this section. These measures can include effects of care for the elderly and diseased. However, strictly speaking, it is not a matter of alleviating the symptoms themselves, but of making it easier to deal with them in everyday life. It is also not possible to cover all cases, because some age- or disease-related phenomena are not curable.

Additionally, according to Section 22(1)(1b) BDSG and Art. 9(3) GDPR, data processing has to be carried out by qualified personnel.[100] It is evident that this may authorize data processing by healthcare practitioners, but it does not extend to private companies engaged in manufacturing personal care robots or accessing their databases for maintenance or similar purposes. Moreover, it should be noted that typically, health professionals are not engaged in the oversight of robots employed for routine daily tasks – such as retrieving items within a household setting. These tasks are meant to be taken over by robots independently, thus relieving the qualified caregivers.

9.4.6 Evaluation

Due to the previously highlighted privacy problems, the employment of personal care robots presents a difficulty in terms of the GDPR and calls into question several of its fundamental principles. The most significant of them is that personal care robots process a tremendous amount of data, including private biometric or health information that may violate the data minimization principle. Additionally, given that the goal of data processing can change often, some appear to lack a proper legal basis.

Also, data processing is not always (sufficiently) transparent. Transparency is even further strained in robot-care environments because it is difficult to explain to people who are physically or mentally impaired the complexity of stakeholders and the numerous complex data processing operations in those environments when measured against the requirements of the principle of transparency itself.

98 Cf., P Gola, D Heckmann and S Schulz, 'Art. 9' in P Gola and D Heckmann (eds), *Datenschutz-Grundverordnung, Bundesdatenschutzgesetz: DS-GVO/BDSG* (3rd edn, C.H. Beck 2022) paras 39–42; Albers and Veit (n 93) paras 90–94.

99 Heckmann and M Scheurer (n 97) para 22.

100 Ibid., para 17.

Finally, it is important to consider how vulnerable care recipients are on an emotional and physical level. Data processing in healthcare settings is essential, but it needs to be closely monitored and critically assessed.

9.5 Possible Solutions

Design alternatives, data anonymization methods, and the use of dynamic consent could all be used as solutions. First of all, the design and manufacturing processes could already take into account potential privacy implications. Personal care robots could be made to be more transparent by being designed so that they do not have access to certain areas or do not process specific data or signal ongoing data processing. Additionally, by assessing the risk of re-identification, an anonymity risk assessment could offer a framework for determining the degree of pseudo-anonymization. Finally, new approaches to consenting to data processing, like dynamic consent and the idea of conversational privacy, should be taken into account.

9.5.1 Design Options

9.5.1.1 Privacy by Design

Integrating "privacy by design" into the development and deployment of personal care robots can address privacy concerns, enabling their use in compliance with the GDPR. "Privacy by design" is a proactive approach that entails embedding privacy considerations into the design, architecture and operation of systems, technologies and processes.[101] It incorporates not only software and system engineering, but also their operating contexts, including legal, organizational and procedural elements or controls.[102] It is based on several foundational fair information principles that establish privacy as a default setting. "Privacy by design" aims to embed data protection and privacy into early design and the full lifecycle of system operations, in order to make the whole production process more transparent, visible and lawful.[103] The approach has been implemented in the GDPR as one of the data controller's responsibilities. According to Art. 25 GDPR, data controllers are required to implement appropriate technical and organizational measures in compliance with data protection principles, such as data minimization, and to integrate necessary safeguards (e.g., pseudonymization and anonymization) into data processing in

101 A Cavoukian, 'Privacy by Design: The 7 Foundational Principles' (Information and Privacy Commissioner of Ontario, Canada, 2009) 5 <www.ipc.on.ca/wp-content/uploads/Resources/7foundationalprinciples.pdf> accessed 28 September 2023.

102 A Cavoukian and J Jonas 'Privacy by Design in the Age of Big Data' (Information and Privacy Commissioner of Ontario, Canada, 2012).

103 Ho (n 75); European Data Protection Supervisor, 'Opinion 5/2018-Preliminary Opinion on Privacy by Design' (2018) 21ff. As pointed out by the European Data Protection Board (EDPB), "privacy by design" helps to make the data processing more lawful, transparent and fair in order to enforce the individual's rights, unlocking data protection.

order to protect the rights of data subjects. The idea is to prevent privacy violations through technological settings, rather than being reactive and remedial.[104]

The European Data Protection Board (EDPB) published guidelines for data protection by design and by default.[105] These contain interpretation aids for the constituent elements of Art. 25 GDPR and address some of the key principles of the data protection framework. The guidelines further provide guidance on the obligation of "data protection by design" and "by default" according to Art. 25 GDPR. Therefore, they should be used by every organization that processes personal data. Most importantly, data controllers have to implement "appropriate measures and necessary safeguards that provide effective implementation of the data protection principles and, consequentially, data subjects' rights and freedoms by design and by default".[106] Art. 25 GDPR prescribes both design and default elements that should be taken into account. To ensure that organizations comply with the fundamental data principles outlined in Art. 5 and Recital 39 GDPR, the EDPB suggests that the controller should have documentation of the implemented technical and organizational measures.[107]

9.5.1.2 Privacy Design for Personal Care Robots

As discussed earlier, users – especially physically or psychologically impaired persons – may not fully understand the personal care robots' various functions, especially when and under what circumstances their data might be processed. Studies show that users tend to be more tolerant in robots' processing their confidential information and sensitive data when the processing is properly disclosed and necessary for maintaining social robots' functions.[108]

Due to the higher trust towards the robot, the supportive effect can be promoted on the one hand by strengthening the social and emotional bond between robot and care receiver. On the other hand, this increases the dependency of the care receiver even more, raising critical issues. To further deepen trust, some call for implementing into the design not only data protection principles but also fundamental rights principles such as respect for private and family life, confidentiality of communication and freedom of thought, expression and information.[109]

104 Ho (n 75).

105 EDPB, Guidelines 4/2019 on Article 25 Data Protection by Design and by Default Version 2.0 Adopted on 20 October 2020, available at <https://edpb.europa.eu/our-work-tools/our-documents/guidelines/guidelines-42019-article-25-data-protection-design-and_en> accessed 25 September 2023.

106 EDPB, Guidelines 4/2019 (n 105), 4.

107 EDPB, Guidelines 4/2019 (n 105), 7.

108 D S Syrdal, M L Walters, N Otero, K L Koay and K Dautenhahn, 'He Knows When You Are Sleeping. Privacy and the Personal Robot Companion' (Proc. Workshop Human Implications of Human-Robot Interaction, Association for the Advancement of Artificial Intelligence 2007) 28; Ho (n 75).

109 C Michelakaki and S B Vale, 'Unlocking Data Protection by Design and by Default: Lessons from the Enforcement of Article 25 GDPR' (2023) *The Future of Privacy Forum* 22.

9.5.1.3 Limiting Data Processing

Technological solutions include the ability to turn off a robot, limiting its movement in space or time,[110] avoiding anthropomorphic shapes and designing the robot's sensors – especially its "eyes" and "ears" – in a way that makes it clear for the data subject at first glance whether or not data are being processed.[111]

Switching off the robot ends data processing, but problems in standby mode or in automatic start-stop systems are conceivable.

In order to limit the robot's movement in space or time, the bedroom could be off-limits at night or the robot's camera could be mounted too low to see the tops of tables and desks where sensitive documents tend to be. There is a trade-off here, though, since the robot might need to see things up high to do certain tasks in rooms where help is typically needed.[112]

Regarding design of the robot's sensors, a study compared surveillance cameras, a stationary robot and a mobile robot in terms of their efficacy in maintaining privacy. Intriguingly, contrary to expectations, interactions with surveillance cameras exhibited greater privacy-enhancing behaviours as opposed to interactions with the robots.[113] This unexpected outcome might be caused by the anthropomorphic form of the robot, which inadvertently conceals the potential data collection activity.

Another category of technical remedies involves detection or identification. Specific items, groups of items or individuals could be blurred out whenever they are detected. For instance, apprehensions related to the robot capturing confidential documents could be resolved by applying blurring to anything recognized as text. To ensure security, this blurring process should take place at the most foundational level, such as within the camera's firmware, effectively preventing access by the robot's operating system.[114]

9.5.1.4 Privacy Settings in Robots

Engaging with robot privacy settings is challenging. Users often lack clarity regarding the robot's actual operations and therefore cannot decide which settings to make. Anthropomorphic robots that fail to notify or provide feedback to users

110 Rueben and others, 'Themes and Research Directions in Privacy Sensitive Robotics' (n 46) 79.

111 See R Calo, 'The Boundaries of Privacy Harm' (2011) 86 *Indiana Law Journal* 1; C Lutz and A Tamò Larrieux 'RoboCode-Ethicists – Privacy-Friendly Robots, an Ethical Responsibility of Engineers' (2015) 7 *ACM Web Science* 1; A Sanfeliu, M R Llacer, M D Gramunt, A Punsola and Y Yoshimura, 'Influence of the Privacy Issue in the Deployment and Design of Networking Robots in European Urban Areas' (2010) 24(13) *Advanced Robotics* 1.

112 Rueben and others, 'Themes and Research Directions in Privacy Sensitive Robotics' (n 46).

113 Lutz and others (n 52) 424; K Caine, S Šabanović and M Carter, 'The Effect of Monitoring by Cameras and Robots on Privacy Enhancing Behaviors of Older Adults' (*Proceedings of the Seventh Annual ACM/IEEE International Conference on Human – Robot Interaction*, New York, 2012) 343.

114 Rueben and others, 'Themes and Research Directions in Privacy Sensitive Robotics' (n 46) 79.

about how their performance differs from their appearance potentially deceive users in privacy-implicating ways.

One solution to this could be a transparent and easily understandable feedback – one which is given effectively in order to empower care receivers to apply the settings freely. Companies could be guided by feedback of the user or troubleshooting information of the robots themselves. The care receivers have to be informed about that, too, of course, if the data is not anonymized or pseudonymized.

9.5.1.5 Tiers of Authorization and Opt-in Solutions

Implementing privacy safeguards can also involve establishing tiers of authorization and enabling the robot to identify and classify individuals within these tiers. For instance, in a scenario in which the robot coexists with a family, all family members could be granted permission to access information relevant to the family. Conversely, when a visitor arrives at the household, the robot should identify them as an external entity and refrain from revealing certain information. Any new data integrated into the robot's system should be automatically stored at the most stringent clearance level as a default measure.[115]

Another issue arises concerning the classification of information in a manner that enables the robot to discern what data can be shared and with whom. For instance, robots may engage in conversations with humans or even amongst themselves, potentially acquiring additional information for learning purposes, and inadvertently divulge content that another user would have preferred to keep confidential. One potential solution could involve implementing an "opt-in" framework whereby the robot refrains from gathering or sharing specific personal data unless explicit permission is granted by the user "opting in" to permission for the robot to do so. Alternatively, the robot could autonomously identify distinct contexts and adhere to varying privacy regulations associated with each context, including transitions between different contexts.[116]

9.5.2 Data Anonymization

In cases where personal data is processed, the GDPR provides very strict rules that must be observed by data controllers and processors. As discussed previously, this leads to a variety of problems, especially in the case of AI systems and smart robotics, whereby the GDPR takes these new technologies rather insufficiently into account.

Companies and information technology (IT) developers can, however, avoid data protection law if they process non-personal (i.e., anonymous or anonymized) data (cf., Recital 26[5] GDPR). If large, normalized datasets are sufficiently

115 Ibid.

116 H Nissenbaum, 'Privacy as Contextual Integrity' (2004) 79 *Washington Law Review* 119; Rueben and others, 'Themes and Research Directions in Privacy Sensitive Robotics' (n 46) 79.

anonymized, the GDPR draws no normative boundaries for the complex (and often opaque) processing of such datasets, e.g., in AI training.[117]

9.5.2.1 Concept of Anonymous Data in the GDPR

The GDPR differentiates between personal data and non-personal data like anonymous or anonymized data (see Art. 4[1] GDPR and Recital 26[1][5] GDPR). Despite the first impression of a binary approach, the GDPR implements a risk-based set of criteria to determine whether a dataset is to be legally considered personal data. Consequently, this risk must be assessed on a case-by-case basis.[118] This is even more true under ECJ case law and Recital 26 GDPR, whereby the risk of identifiability must be also assessed from the perspective of the data controller (relativist approach) and not (only) from a neutral or generalized standpoint (absolute approach). The ECJ positioned itself not quite clearly towards one or another of those approaches in Case C-582/14 *Breyer v Bundesrepublik Deutschland*. The Court found that "there is no requirement that all the information enabling the identification of the data subject must be in the hands of one person",[119] thus indicating that not only the data controller's perspective is decisive. On the other hand, the Court also stressed in the *Breyer* case that not all possibilities to re-identify a person constitutes "a means likely reasonably to be used to identify the data subject".[120]

Pseudonymized data transmitted to a data recipient is not deemed personal data if the data recipient does not have the ability to re-identify the data subjects, the European General Court recently held in reference to the *Breyer* decision.[121] However, it is currently unclear whether the ECJ will follow this view. In another case, currently pending, the ECJ is expected to decide how to qualify data received by a third party, when such third party does not have the legal means to access "additional identifying information".[122]

Drawing the line between personal and non-personal data is not only difficult from a legal perspective, but also from a technical one. The threshold between personal and anonymous data drawn by data protection law in order to determine the applicability of the dense provisions of the GDPR is not clearly distinguishable. This comes with legal uncertainties for controllers and processors. It is difficult for them to assess whether their efforts are sufficient. Accordingly, they still face

117 M Kolain, C Grafenauer and M Ebers, 'Anonymity Assessment Anonymity Assessment – A Universal Tool for Measuring Anonymity of Data Sets Under the GDPR with a Special Focus on Smart Robotics' (2022) 48(2) *Rutgers University Computer and Technology Law Journal* 6.

118 Cf., M Mourby and others, 'Are 'Pseudonymised' Data Always Personal Data? Implications of the GDPR for Administrative Data Research in the UK' (2018) 34 *Computer Law and Security Review* 222, 228.

119 ECJ, case C-582/14 *Breyer v Bundesrepublik Deutschland* EU:C:2016:779, para 31.

120 ECJ, case C-582/14 *Breyer v Bundesrepublik Deutschland* EU:C:2016:779, paras 45–46.

121 EGC, case T-557/20, *SRB v European Data Protection Supervisor ('EDPS')* EU:T:2023:219.

122 Case C-604/22.

sanctions in case of GDPR breaches[123] since there is no such thing as absolute anonymity from a technical point of view. So far, neither legislation, supervisory authorities nor academics have mastered the task of translating the legal provisions of the GDPR into quantitative and/or qualitative specifications.[124]

9.5.2.2 Anonymization Techniques

Current anonymization methods like k-anonymity,[125] l-diversity[126] and t-closeness[127] instead focus on the likelihood of re-identification and use statistical reasoning to determine the inherent probability of re-identification,[128] but fail to meet the legal criteria previously mentioned. They cannot guarantee sufficiently that an adversary will not find other ways to link certain data points to a natural person. As a result, anonymization techniques that strive to reach a degree of (technical) anonymity tend to be bypassable by even more sophisticated re-identification attacks. These often reveal statistical inferences hardly foreseeable in the setup phase of a data collection. Additionally, the mathematical models and anonymization techniques are by nature also somewhat agnostic towards – or do not perceive – additional knowledge and real-world conditions that can enable a data controller in the process of AI training to trace certain data back to a natural person.[129]

9.5.2.3 Anonymity Risk Assessment

Against this backdrop, the author of this chapter, together with others, has proposed an anonymity risk assessment – an interdisciplinary and risk-based approach to classifying anonymity and measuring the degree of pseudo-anonymization of a given dataset in a legal and technical sense to address these weaknesses. Such an assessment could provide data controllers with a tool to reliably and comprehensively document the conclusion that the data processing in a predefined scope can be considered as processing of anonymous data in a legal sense. Additionally, legal

123 Kolain, Grafenauer and Ebers (n 117) 21. Even though in the overall assessment, pseudonymization might have to be considered under Art. 83(2)(g), see Art. 29 Data Protection Working Party, 'Guidelines on the Application and Setting of Administrative Fines for the Purposes of the Regulation 2016/679' Working Paper 253 17/EN 15.

124 Kolain, Grafenauer and Ebers (n 117) 1.

125 L Sweeney, 'K-Anonymity: A Model for Protecting Privacy' (2002) 10 *International Journal of Uncertainty, Fuzziness and Knowledge-Based Systems* 557–570.

126 A Machanavajjhala, J Gehrke, D Kifer and M Venkitasubramaniam, 'L-Diversity: Privacy Beyond K-Anonymity' (*IEEE 2006 Proceedings of the 22nd International Conference on Data Engineering*, 2006) 24 <https://ieeexplore.ieee.org/stamp/stamp.jsp?tp=&arnumber=1617364> accessed 28 September 2023.

127 N Li, T Li and S Venkatasubramanian, 'T-Closeness: Privacy Beyond K-Anonymity and L-Diversity' (*IEEE 2007 Proceedings of the 23rd International Conference Data Engineering*, 2007) 106 <https://ieeexplore.ieee.org/stamp/stamp.jsp?tp=&arnumber=4221659> accessed 28 September 2023.

128 This technical perspective on anonymity is, however, agnostic to any additional information or real-world context that would allow re-identification through means that exist outside of the given dataset.

129 Kolain, Grafenauer and Ebers (n 117) 21.

entities who develop or handle large normalized datasets would be provided with a methodology to measure the degree of pseudo-anonymization in every relevant system component.[130]

Briefly, we propose a set of two scores to measure the degree of privacy protection within a given system: The "Objective Anonymity Score" includes the metrics k-anonymity, l-diversity, and t-closeness to determine the residual risks of (re-)identifying a natural person under objective statistical measures. The "Subjective Anonymity Score" provides an indicator for the relative anonymity of the processing done by a controller or processor: It considers the cost and time required to successfully re-identify the dataset in question, taking the available manpower and capital of the controller/processor into account. Quantified mathematically, the Anonymity Assessment also considers a qualitative analysis of the available technology at the time of the processing and technological developments as well as the aspect of re-identification through additional information outside the given dataset.[131]

In the field of smart robotics, our method allows developers to plan, build and operate their overall system in a manner that decreases the likelihood of privacy-intrusive re-identification attacks from within. Additionally, it serves as a tool to document and prove legal compliance, e.g., in relation to supervisory authorities in the field of data protection. (Only) those controllers conducting an Anonymity Assessment can claim, on a sufficiently clear factual basis, that they only process anonymized data on specific system components.[132]

Future work can focus on further developing the basic concept of anonymity assessment and needs into an outline for a data protection seal or certificate (Art. 42 GDPR)[133] or in the course of international standardization for specific use-cases.[134]

9.5.3 Dynamic Consent

Consent as one of the legal foundations for collecting and processing data under the GDPR is only valid when it is freely given, specific, informed, and unambiguous (Art. 9[2][a] GDPR).[135] Legal guardians must consent on behalf of minors or impaired people. Individuals are also given the right to change, withdraw or revoke consent at any time.[136]

130 Ibid., 29.

131 Ibid., 23.

132 Ibid., 30.

133 A data protection seal or certificate for anonymization of AI training data could in the long run be certified under Art. 25(3), Art. 42 GDPR. See for this idea in combination with the method of architectural blueprints, C Wirth and M Kolain, 'Privacy by Blockchain Design: A Blockchain-enabled GDPR-compliant Approach for Handling Personal Data' in W Prinz and P Hoschka (eds), *Proceedings of 1st ERCIM Blockchain Workshop 2018, Reports of the European Society for Socially Embedded Technologies* (Deutsches Forschungsinstitut für öffentliche Verwaltung 2018) 1, 2.

134 See DIN SPEC 4997.

135 Cf., Section 9.4.5.1.

136 M M Merlec, Y K Lee, S P Hong, H P In, 'A Smart Contract-Based Dynamic Consent Management System for Personal Data Usage under GDPR' (2021) 21(23) *Sensors* 7994, <https://doi.org/10.3390/s21237994>.

Many researchers still consider informed consent to be the decisive basis for processing personal data by robots in care environments, despite the difficulties highlighted.[137] The special features of human–robot relationships in care (e.g., unpredictable courses of illness, changes of opinion, guardianship, etc.) could be taken into account by shifting the one-time notice and consent focus of privacy laws,[138] even though the principle of purpose limitation generally opposes an "as you go" consent.[139]

9.5.3.1 Basic Concept

"Dynamic consent management" is a novel means of engaging individuals in the use of their personal information.[140] The much-discussed concept[141] was introduced by an Italian research group[142] and aims to address the earlier discussed limitations of paper-based and static consent methods, which afford fewer possibilities and less flexibility for people to systematically define and manage their consent preferences or adjust them to changing life circumstances. The basic concept of dynamic consent is to give control back to the users to dynamically manage their consent on personal data collection and usage.[143] It is designed to address the many issues

137 See Section 9.4.5.1.

138 Fosch-Villaronga, 'Privacy Considerations for Socially Assistive Robots' (n 21) 8; B Custers, F Dechesne, W Pieters, B Schermer and S van der Hof, 'Consent and Privacy' in A Müller and P Schaber (eds), *Handbook of the Ethics of Consent* (Routledge 2018) 247; Mourby (n 118) 5ff. sees informed consent as a promising option under the light of Art. 22(4), but see problems and suggests human interventions.

139 Cf., Chatzimichali (n 47) 170.

140 Merlec and others (n 136).

141 H J Teare, M Morrison, E A Whitley and J Kaye, 'Towards "Engagement 2.00": Insights from a Study of Dynamic Consent with Biobank Participant' (2015) *Digital Health* 1; J Kaye and others, 'Dynamic Consent: A Patient Interface for Twenty-First Century Research Networks' (2015) 23 *European Journal of Human Genetics* 141; K S Steinsbekk and others, 'Broad Consent Versus Dynamic Consent in Biobank Research: Is Passive Participation an Ethical Problem?' (2013) 21 *European Journal of Human Genetics* 897; A S Scott and others, 'Research Applications of Dynamic Consent' in E Kosta, J Pierson and others (eds), *Privacy and Identity Management. Fairness, Accountability, and Transparency in the Age of Big Data* (Springer 2018); I Budin-Ljøsne and others, 'Dynamic Consent: A Potential Solution to Some of the Challenges of Modern Biomedical Research' (2017) 18 *BMC Medical Ethics* 1; M R Asghar, G Russello, 'Flexible and Dynamic Consent-Capturing' (*International Workshop on Open Problems in Network Security*, Lucerne, 2011) 119; M Prictor, M A Lewis, A J Newson and others, 'Dynamic Consent: An Evaluation and Reporting Framework' (2020) 15 *Journal of Empirical Research on Human Research Ethics* 175; M C Mont and others, 'Dynamic Consent, Policy Enforcement and Accountable Information Sharing within and Across Organisations' <www.hpl.hp.com/techreports/2012/HPL-2012-36.pdf> accessed 25 September 2023; S Tokas and O Owe, 'A Formal Framework for Consent Management'(*International Conference on Formal Techniques for Distributed Objects, Components*, Springer 2020) 169.

142 D Mascalzoni, A Hicks, P Pramstaller and M Wjst, 'Informed Consent in the Genomics Era' (2007) 5(9) *Plos Medicine* 1 <http://doi.org/10.1371/journal.pmed.0050192> accessed 28 September 2023.

143 Kaye and others (n 141) 141; Steinsbekk (n 141) 897; Scott and others (n 141).

that are raised by the use of digital technologies in research and clinical care which enable the wide-scale use, linkage, analysis and integration of diverse datasets and the use of AI and Big Data analysis.

Dynamic consent is a personalized, digital interface that enables two-way communication between participants and controllers. It is a practical example of how software can be developed to give research participants greater understanding and control over how their data is used.[144] Dynamic consent involves ongoing engagement with participants, allowing them to see how their samples are used and permitting renegotiation of consent if the samples are to be used for different studies, or if the participant's wishes change.

A flexible and dynamic consent management approach is required to achieve specific, informed, and engaged consent agreements for legal personal data usage with guarantees of transparency, security and privacy. However, there are few solutions that systematically empower individuals to provide tailored consent agreements on distinct personal data, and to take control and decide who will collect, access and/or use their data for specific purposes and periods. In addition, users should be able to delegate consent rights (if necessary or in emergencies when users are unable to provide consent directly), access consent-related information, and withdraw previously given consent at any time.[145]

Determining how to design a proper consent mechanism would have a great influence on whether foundational privacy principles can be implemented for human-robot-interaction (HRI).[146]

9.5.3.2 Design Requirements

To design a dynamic consent management system for the use of personal data under the GDPR, the following design requirements have to be satisfied.[147]

- It has to be clear who the key stakeholders are and what their legitimate roles and responsibilities are.
- It has to be clear how data subjects can be systematically empowered to control their personal data collection and urge consent.
- It has to be clear how individual consent and rights can be explicitly and systematically expressed in a human- and machine-readable format.
- It has to be clear how data subjects should be given access to their personal data collection and usage activity history.
- It has to be clear how data subjects should be notified, and regulators should be informed in case of consent agreement violations.
- It has to be clear what should be done when the consent agreement clauses are violated or the purpose of the given consent is no longer valid.

144 Mascalzoni and others (n 142).
145 Merlec and others (n 136).
146 Ho (n 75).
147 Merlec and others (n 136).

In order to implement these design requirements, Merlec et al.[148] suggest the following.

- A smart-contract-based dynamic consent management system architecture backed by blockchain technology for legal personal data usage based on GDPR.
- User-centric dynamic consent management schemes that leverage smart contracts to enable users to take control of their consent on the personal data collection and usage throughout the data lifecycle. Consent rights can be delegated and audited by users by tracking the log events in blockchain. Users get notified about any consent agreement clause violation and can withdraw the related consent.
- Integration of decentralized InterPlanetary File System (IPFS)[149] nodes with our system – to store data off-chain. The transactions history and access log data are recorded on blockchain to enforce trust and provide tamper-proof data provenance, accountability and traceability.
- Presentation of the security and privacy analysis of the system and evaluate its performance in terms of smart contract algorithm complexity, transaction throughput and latency, computing resource usage and storage network bandwidth utilization.

A prototype of their system was designed and implemented on top of the Quorum blockchain platform[150] to determine its feasibility. The acceptability and reliability of the system were assessed by experimental testing and validation processes. The implemented code and artifacts have been made publicly available.[151]

9.5.4 Conversational Privacy

"Conversational privacy" is another strategy for addressing the flaws in the established "notice and consent" procedure. Here, privacy bots are used, making it easier for users to understand and navigate privacy settings and policies.[152]

148 Ibid.

149 InterPlanetary File System <https://github.com/ipfs-shipyard/ipfs-desktop> accessed 28 September 2023.

150 Quorum: A Permissioned Implementation of Ethereum Supporting Data Privacy <https://github.com/ConsenSys/quorum> accessed 28 September 2023.

151 <https://github.com/mlecjm/sc-dcms> accessed 28 September 2023.

152 Fosch-Villaronga and others, 'Nothing Comes Between My Robot and Me: Privacy and Human-Robot Interaction in Robotised Healthcare' (n 4) 110ff.; compare A B Kocaballi and others, 'The Personalization of Conversational Agents in Health Care: Systematic Review' (2019) 21(11) *Journal of Medical Internet Research* 1; K Kretzschmar and others, 'Can Your Phone Be Your Therapist? Young People's Ethical Perspectives on the Use of Fully Automated Conversational Agents (Chatbots) in Mental Health Support' (2019) 11 *Biomed Inform Insights* 1; R May and K Denecke, 'Security, Privacy, and Healthcare-Related Conversational Agents: A Scoping Review' (2021) 47(6) *Informatics for Health and Social Care* 1.

9.5.4.1 Explaining Complex Privacy Settings

Conversational privacy bots can interact with users, explaining complex privacy settings in clear and simple terms and giving personalized assistance. Through these interactions, users can understand how their data will be used, shared, and protected based on the various settings available, ensuring that users comprehend the implications of their choices and can make informed decisions. Conversational interfaces can present users with hypothetical scenarios to help them understand the consequences of different settings. For instance, conversational privacy bots might explain how enabling facial recognition of personal care robots could enhance convenience but potentially compromise privacy. In this scenario, the bot could explain that facial recognition helps the robot to detect emotions and react in an adequate manner depending on the emotions as well as the privacy implications of facial recognition.

Moreover, by tailoring responses to user inquiries and concerns, conversational interfaces can provide contextual guidance. For example, if a user asks about location tracking, the bot can explain how the feature works, the benefits, and the privacy trade-offs associated with enabling or disabling it. Instead of having to scroll through lengthy menus, conversational privacy bots could assist users with their inquiries and lead them through a step-by-step exploration of the various privacy settings that are significant to them.[153] Users then can interactively modify settings while receiving real-time explanations about the potential impact of each choice. This hands-on approach fosters a better understanding of the implications.

Furthermore, as users engage more with the interface, conversational privacy bots can learn about their preferences and modify their justifications accordingly. This method of progressive learning makes sure that explanations gradually match users' comprehension levels, which is beneficial in care situations.

9.5.4.2 Personalized Recommendations for Privacy Settings

In addition, conversational interfaces can analyze the user's preferences and behaviours to offer personalized recommendations for privacy settings. For instance, if a user expresses a desire for maximum privacy, the bot could suggest opting for stricter data sharing controls or a user could ask the bot if a service provider shares his location with third-party entities, and the bot could provide the user with an opt-out option in response. When users express uncertainty, conversational interfaces can assist in decision-making. By asking probing questions, they can help users to clarify their priorities and guide them towards settings that align with their values. Even more the bot, knowing the users preferences, has the capability to predict the user's choices and thereby decreasing the duration of the interaction. At a certain

153 Cf., H Harkous, K Fawaz, KG Shin and K Aberer, 'PriBots: Conversational Privacy' 2016 *WSF@SOUPS 3* <wwwusenixorg/system/files/conference/soups2016/wfpn16-paper-harkouspdf> accessed 28 September 2023.

point, the user would primarily be confirming or rejecting proposed actions rather than originating them.[154]

Furthermore, conversational privacy bots can gather feedback from users about their understanding of privacy settings and the quality of explanations. This feedback – whether given in the form of text, as a structured message (e.g., with emojis) or through voice – can help improve the interface's effectiveness and user satisfaction over time, thus creating a feedback loop that can optimize the user interface more and more over time.[155]

Finally, even after their initial setup, conversational interfaces can provide continuous support. They could periodically check in with users to ensure that their privacy settings still match their preferences and inform them of any updates or adapt to users' health condition (e.g., dementia getting worse). This facilitates dynamic consent. The ongoing evaluation of the users' privacy settings complements the idea of a dynamic consent that lasts until the preconditions for the given consent have changed.

9.5.4.3 Evaluation

By giving care recipients control over the data processed and allowing them to customize their privacy settings, conversational privacy can complement the idea of dynamic consent. At the same time, conversational privacy can provide a legitimate legal basis for data processing by personal care robots if it can be ensured that patients and care receivers truly understand the privacy information delivered.[156]

9.5.5 Enhancing Transparency in Human–robot Interactions

The relationship between care recipients and the actors involved in providing personal care robot services is characterized by high information asymmetries, which affects the care recipient's autonomy. Users are typically unaware of what data is being collected about them, what information is being inferred from the collected data and how that data is being used.[157] Predictions and actions of robots are opaque, as it often remains unclear why a particular prediction or decision was made and on what basis.

Conventional privacy protection mechanisms aiming for confidentiality mainly offer mechanisms to protect users from unwanted data disclosure (so-called *privacy-enhancing technologies*).[158] However, these privacy-enhancing technologies are

154 Ibid.
155 Ibid.
156 Ibid.
157 Cf., Ibid.; C Zimmermann, 'A Categorization of Transparency-Enhancing Technologies' (2015) *ArXiv* 1, arXiv:1507.04914.
158 PISA Consortium, *Handbook of Privacy and Privacy-Enhancing Technologies* (College Bescherming Persoonsgegevens 2003); Zimmermann (n 157); A Theodoru and others, 'Why Is My Robot Behaving Like That? Designing Transparency for Real Time Inspection of Autonomous

not very well suited to the context of care robot services,[159] since personal care robots process a large amount of personal data to tailor their services to the needs of the care recipient in order to fulfil their task in the best possible way.[160] Also, users often do not primarily seek data minimization, but are willing to disclose data in order to benefit from the use and personalization of services. For these reasons, some scholars argue that a transparency-based approach to privacy protection mechanisms is more suitable.[161]

Transparency-enhancing technologies provide users with information about the collection, analysis and use of data by providers in an effort to reduce the previously mentioned information asymmetries through transparency.[162] This approach is also reflected in European data protection law. Art. 5(1)(a) GDPR states that personal data must be processed lawfully, fairly and in a manner that is transparent to the data subject.

Transparency usually refers to things and concepts that are easy to perceive or detect. The GDPR includes transparency as a proactive requirement for information technologies that process personal data in the sense of making data processing explicit to the user.[163] According to Recital 39 GDPR, the principle of transparency requires that all information and communications relating to the processing of those personal data should be easily accessible and easy to understand, and that clear and plain language should be used. It should be transparent to natural persons that personal data relating to them are collected, used or otherwise processed, and to what extent the personal data are or will be processed. Recital 58 of the GDPR provides that the principle of transparency requires that any information addressed to the public or to the data subject to be concise, easily accessible and easy to un-

---

Robots' <https://robwortham.com/wp-content/uploads/2016/04/TheodorouWorthamAISBImplementingTransparency.pdf> accessed 29 September 2023; J B Lyons, 'Being Transparent about Transparency' (*Trust and Autonomous Systems: Papers from the 2013 AAAI Spring Symposium*) <https://cdn.aaai.org/ocs/5712/5712-24571-1-PB.pdf> accessed 29 September 2023.

159 Cf., for Internet G Müller and others, 'Vertrauensinfrastruktur und Privatheit als ökonomische Fragestellung' in J Buchmann (eds), *Internet Privacy. acatech Studie* (Springer 2012) 143; A Novotny and S Spiekermann, 'Personal Information Markets AND Privacy: A New Model to Solve the Controversy' (*Proc. WI'13*, Leipzig 2013) 1635; D J Solove, 'The End of Privacy? Scientific American' (2018) 299(3) *Scientific American* 100; D J Weitzner and others, 'Transparent Accountable Data Mining: New Strategies for Privacy Protection' (*Technical Report MIT-CSAIL-TR-2006–007*, Massachusetts Institute of Technology Computer Science and Artificial Intelligence Laboratory 2006) <http://dspace.mit.edu/handle/1721.1/30972> accessed 29 September 2023.

160 Zimmermann (n 157) 1.

161 Ibid.; compare A Acquisti and R Gross, 'Imagined Communities: Awareness, Information Sharing, and Privacy on the Facebook' in G Danezis and P Golle (eds), *Privacy Enhancing Technologies* (Springer 2006) 36; Fujitsu Research Institute, 'Personal Data in the Cloud: A Global Survey of Consumer Attitudes' 2010; Gross and Acquisti, 'Information Revelation and Privacy in Online Social Networks' (n 80) 71.

162 Ibid.; M Hansen, 'Marrying Transparency Tools with User-Controlled Identity Management' in S Fischer-Hübner and others (eds), *The Future of Identity in the Information Society. Privacy and Identity. IFIP – The International Federation for Information Processing* (Springer 2007) 199.

163 H Felzmann and others, 'Robots and Transparency: The Multiple Dimensions of Transparency in the Context of Robot Technologies' (2019) 26(2) *IEEE Robotics and Automation Magazine* 71.

derstand, and that clear and plain language and, where appropriate, visualization be used. It also emphasizes the importance of transparency in situations when the multiplicity of actors and the technological complexity make it difficult for the data subject to know and understand whether, by whom and for what purpose personal data relating to him or her are being collected.

Despite these legal requirements, coupled with even more criteria found in the cited recitals – as well as recent intensified research efforts[164] – what transparency means for the field of robotics, remains under-explored.[165] In short, transparency can be described as the "explainability of robotic systems, either from the robot (intelligibility) or user perspective (understandability)".[166]

Felzmann et al. have produced a user-oriented step-by-step guide for implementing transparency in robotic design.[167] Others argue that transparency in the sense of explainability could be detrimental in the context of assistive or personal care robots, since their benefits are partly based on the fact that users do not recognize the robot as such or do not understand the underlying data processing procedures.[168] Otherwise, psychological benefits of the *anthropomorphization* effect may not be realized, and information overload (or a chilling effect) may be a deterrent.

A possible solution to the trade-off between transparency – in terms of data protection compliance – and utility, could be to automate consent based on personalized privacy preferences.[169] Such personal disclosures are based on user profiling, and therefore need to comply with the requirements of the GDPR.[170] What may work in consumer law[171] seems to reach its limits in the context of personal care robots: In particular, Art. 22(4) GDPR stipulates that profiling "shall not be based" on the special categories of data referred to in Art. 9(1) GDPR, unless there is explicit consent. With regard to the requirements for valid consent, the previously discussed observations must be taken into account.[172]

9.6 Outlook

The use of personal care robots raises many ethical and legal concerns about privacy and data protection. Data minimization and transparency are affected by the quantity and quality of personal data processed, the complexity of data transmission,

164 E.g., see <https://sagroups.ieee.org/7001/> accessed 29 September 2023; <https://explainablero-boticsystems.wordpress.com/> accessed 29 September 2023.

165 Felzmann and others (n 163) 11.

166 Ibid.

167 Ibid.

168 K Fischer, 'When Transparent Does Not Mean Explainable' (*Proceedings of Explainable Robotic Systems, Workshop in Conjunction with the HRI Conference*, 2018) <https://explainableroboticsystems.files.wordpress.com/2018/03/1-fischer-being-honest-about-transparency-final.pdf> accessed 28 September 2023 accessed 29 September 2023.

169 Cf., Theodoru and others (n 158).

170 Cf., C Busch, 'Implementing Personalized Law: Personalized Disclosures in Consumer Law and Data Privacy Law' 321 <https://lawreview.uchicago.edu/sites/default/files/04Busch_SYMP_Post-SA%28BE%29.pdf> accessed 28 September 2023; Chatzimichali and other (n 47) 160.

171 Busch (n 170).

172 See Section 9.4.5.1.

stakeholder complexity in care environments and the inherent vulnerability of care recipients, while the traditional concept of consent does not provide satisfactory solutions in this rapidly changing environment.

Design options, data anonymization methods, and the cutting-edge ideas of dynamic consent and conversational privacy are some potential remedies to these problems.

We also propose the creation of a legal framework for personal care robots at the EU level in order to close existing gaps in the protection of patients and care recipients when using personal care robots. The GDPR only provides a very general legal framework that is not tailored to the specificities of robotics. In this respect, a new law could regulate the use of personal data by care robots while providing at the same time the necessary legal basis for data processing. In addition, this regulation could cover a number of other issues that arise in the use of care robots in relation to vulnerable individuals which are currently not covered by the GDPR, particularly such as aspects of physical, psychological and social privacy.[173]

The forthcoming AI Act[174] is unlikely to provide adequate solutions. As noted elsewhere,[175] the AI Act proposal fails to provide effective safeguards for patients and care recipients. In the first place, the proposal does not impose any obligations on manufacturers and professional users towards patients. Second, it does not give individual rights to patients and care recipients. Third, robotics and AI applications used in the care sector are not considered high-risk applications, unless they are medical devices that fall into risk class IIa or higher as defined by the Medical Device Regulation (MDR). It is crucial that legislation in Brussels does not stall and that sector-specific legislation is adopted in areas where particularly vulnerable people interact with robots, such as care robots.

Prior to the creation of any new legislation, however, comprehensive guidelines need to be developed to address the many facets of user privacy, data security and other ethical concerns in the use of care robots. These guidelines would serve as a roadmap for developers, manufacturers and policymakers to engage in responsible practices. Another effective way to ensure compliance and accountability is through certification schemes. Certification can provide a structured evaluation process to assess whether robotic technologies comply with accepted privacy standards. Through certification, producers and developers demonstrate their commitment to ethical privacy practices, thereby fostering consumer confidence and industry accountability.

All of the strategies discussed here require interdisciplinary collaboration, from psychology and design to engineering, communication and law. By combining these disciplines and rethinking conventional approaches, data collection and

173 N Lintvedt, 'Critical Analysis of Consent in Human – Robot Interaction' 30.

174 COM(2021) 206 final.

175 M Ebers, 'AI Robotics in Healthcare between the EU Medical Device Regulation and the Artificial Intelligence Act: Gaps and Inconsistencies in the Protection of Patients and Care Recipients' (2024) *Oslo Law Review*, pending for publication.

human–robot interaction with personal care robots could be effectively and reasonably regulated.

Developing an effective privacy regime for personal care robots requires an integrative and futuristic strategy. Comprehensive guidelines, certification schemes and the possible adoption of new legal frameworks for personal care robots at the EU level, together with new methods to protect user privacy – such as design options, data anonymization, dynamic consent and conversational privacy – pave the way for the ethical and responsible integration of robotic technologies into care environments.

Bibliography

AAL Programme, *DOMEO – AAL Programme* <wwwaal-europeeu/projects/domeo/> accessed 21 August 2023

Acquisti A and Gross R, 'Imagined Communities: Awareness, Information Sharing, and Privacy on the Facebook' in Danezis G and Golle P (eds), *Privacy Enhancing Technologies* (Springer 2006) 36

Albers and Veit 'BDSG § 22' in Brink S and Wolff A (eds), *BeckOK DatenschutzR* (44 edn, C H BECK 2023)

Altman I, *The Environment and Social Behavior: Privacy, Personal Space, Territory, Crowding* (Brooks/Cole 1975)

Altman I, 'Privacy regulation: Culturally universal or culturally specific?' (1977) 33 (3) *Journal of Social Issues* 66

Angle C, 'Will a Robot Care for My Mom?' (*TedMed*, last modified 2009) <www.tedmedcom/talks/show?id=7193> accessed 21 August 2023

Asghar MR and Russello G, 'Flexible and Dynamic Consent-Capturing' (*International Workshop on Open Problems in Network Security, Lucerne*, 2011) 119

Badii A and others, 'CompanionAble: Graceful Integration of Mobile Robot Companion with a Smart Home Environment' (2009) 8(3) *Gerontechnology* 1

Bardaro G, 'Robots for Elderly Care in the Home: A Landscape Analysis and Co-Design Toolkit' (2022) 14(2) *International Journal of Social Robotics* 663

Barnes SB, 'A privacy paradox: Social Networking in the United States' (2006) 11(9) *First Monday* <https://firstmondayorg/ojs/indexphp/fm/article/view/1394> accessed 28 september 2023

Bedaf S, Gelderblom GJ, and de Witte L, 'Overview and Categorization of Robots Supporting Independent Living of Elderly People: What Activities Do They Support and How Far Have They Developed Assistive technology' (2015) 27(2) *The Official Journal of RESNA* 88

Bemelmans R, Gelderblom GJ, Jonker P and others, 'Socially Assistive Robots in Elderly Care: a Systematic Review Into Effects and Effectiveness' (2012) 13(2) *Journal of the American Medical Directors Association* 11

Blake V, 'Regulating Care Robots' (2020) 92 *Temple Law Review* 551

Boukenze B and others, 'Predictive Analytics in Healthcare System Using Data Mining Techniques' (*The Fourth International Conference on Database and Data Mining* 2016), <https://airccjorg/CSCP/vol6/csit65201pdf> accessed 25 September 2023

Broadbent E, 'Interactions with Robots: The Truths We Reveal about Ourselves' (2017) 68 *Annual Review of Psychology* 627

Broadbent E, Garrett J, Jepsen N, Ogilvie V, Ahn HS, Robinson H, Peri K, Kerse N, Rouse P, Pillai A and others, 'Using Robots at Home to Support Patients with Chronic Obstructive Pulmonary Disease: Pilot Randomized Controlled Trial' (2018) 20(2) *Journal of Medical Internet Research* 1

Buchmann (eds), *Internet Privacy acatech Studie* (Springer 2012)

Budin-Ljøsne I and others, 'Dynamic Consent: A Potential Solution to Some of the Challenges of Modern Biomedical Research' (2017) 18 *BMC Medical Ethics* 1

Burgoon M (ed), *Communication Yearbook 6* (Routledge 1982)

Busch C, 'Implementing Personalized Law: Personalized Disclosures in Consumer Law and Data Privacy Law', 321 <https://lawreview.uchicago.edu/sites/default/files/04 Busch_SYMP_Post-SA %28BE%29.pdf> accessed 28 September 2023

Caine K, Šabanović S and Carter M, 'The Effect of Monitoring by Cameras and Robots on Privacy Enhancing Behaviors of Older Adults' (*Proceedings of the Seventh Annual ACM/IEEE International Conference on Human – Robot Interaction*, New York, 2012) 343

Calo R, 'Against Notice Skepticism in Privacy (and Elsewhere)' (2011) 87 *Notre Dame Law Review* 1027

Calo R, 'The Boundaries of Privacy Harm' (2011) 86 *Indiana Law Journal* 1

Calo R, 'Robots and Privacy' in Lin P, Bekey G and Abney K (eds), *Robot Ethics: The Ethical and Social Implications of Robotics* (MIT Press 2012) 187

Campa R, 'The Rise of Social Robots: A Review of the Recent Literature' (2016) 26(1) *Journal of Evolution and Technology* 1

Cavoukian A, 'Privacy by Design: The 7 Foundational Principles' (*Information and Privacy Commissioner of Ontario*, Canada, 2009) 5 <wwwipconca/wp-content/uploads/Resources/7foundationalprinciplespdf> accessed 28 September 2023

Cavoukian A and Jonas J, *Privacy by Design in the Age of Big Data* (Information and Privacy Commissioner of Ontario 2012)

Chatzimichali A and others, 'Toward Privacy-Sensitive Human – Robot Interaction: Privacy Terms and Human – Data Interaction in the Personal Robot era' (2020) 12(1) *Journal of Behavioral Robotics* 162

Custers B, Dechesne F, Pieters W, Schermer B and van der Hof S, 'Consent and Privacy' in Müller A and Schaber P (eds), *Handbook of the Ethics of Consent* (Routledge 2018)

Dantas E and Nogaroli R, 'The Rise of Robotics And Artificial Intelligence In Healthcare: New Challenges For The Doctrine Of Informed Consent' (2021) 4 *Medicine and Law* 1

Dienlin T and Trepte S, 'Is the Privacy Paradox a Relic of the Past? An In-Depth Analysis of Privacy Attitudes and Privacy Behaviors' (2015) 45(3) *European Journal of Social Psychology* 285

Ebers M, 'AI Robotics in Healthcare Between the EU Medical Device Regulation and the Artificial Intelligence Act: Gaps and Inconsistencies in the Protection of Patients and Care Recipients' (2024) *Oslo Law Review*, Pending For Publication

Ebers M, 'Explainable AI in the European Union An Overview of the Current Legal Framework(s)' in Colonna L and Greenstein S (eds), *Nordic Yearbook of Law and Informatics 2020–2021: Law in the Era of Artificial Intelligence* (The Swedish Law and Informatics Research Institute 2022) 103

Ebers M, *Rechte, Rechtsbehelfe und Sanktionen im Unionsprivatrecht* (Mohr Siebeck 2016)

European Commission, 'An Integrated Intelligent Home Environment for the Provision of Health, Nutrition and Mobility Services to the Elderly' <https://cordiseuropaeu/project/id/248434> accessed 21 August 2023

European Commission, 'Integrated Cognitive Assistive and Domotic Companion Robotic Systems for Ability and Security' <https://cordiseuropaeu/project/id/216487> accessed 21 August 2023

European Commission, 'Turning a Robot into a Companion for Frail People' <https://eceuropaeu/programmes/horizon2020/en/print/2485> accessed 21 August 2023

European Data Protection Board (EDPB), *Guidelines 4/2019 on Article 25 Data Protection by Design and by Default Version 20 Adopted on 20 October 2020* <https://edpbeuropaeu/our-work-tools/our-documents/guidelines/guidelines-42019-article-25-data-protection-design-and_en> accessed 25 September 2023

European Data Protection Supervisor (EDPS), 'Opinion 5/2018-Preliminary Opinion on Privacy by Design' (2018) <https://www.edps.europa.eu/sites/default/files/publication/18-05-31_preliminary_opinion_on_privacy_by_design_en_0.pdf>

Federal Trade Commission, 'Internet of Things, Privacy and Security in a Connected World' <wwwftcgov/system/files/documents/reports/federal-trade-commission-staff-report-november-2013-workshop-entitled-internet-things-privacy/150127iotrptpdf> accessed 28 September 2023

Felzmann H and others, 'Robots and Transparency: The Multiple Dimensions of Transparency in the Context of Robot Technologies' (2019) 26(2) *IEEE Robotics and Automation Magazine* 71

Finck M, 'Notion of Data Controller in the GDPR' (2021) 11(4) *International Data Privacy Law* 333

Fischer K, 'When Transparent Does Not Mean Explainable' (*Proceedings of Explainable Robotic Systems, Workshop in conjunction with the HRI Conference*, 2018) <https://explainableroboticsystems.files.wordpress.com/2018/03/1-fischer-being-honest-about-transparency-final.pdf>

Fiske A, Henningsen P and Buyx A, 'Your Robot Therapist Will See You Now: Ethical Implications of Embodied Artificial Intelligence in Psychiatry, Psychology, and Psychotherapy' (2019) 21(5) *Journal of Medical Internet Research* 1

Fogg BJ, *Persuasive Technology: Using Computers to Change What We Think and Do* (1st edn, Morgan Kaufmann 2003)

Fosch-Villaronga E and Albo-Canals J, 'I'll take Care of you,' Said the Robot' (2019) 10(1) *Journal of Behavioral Robotics* 1

Fosch Villaronga E, Felzmann H, Pierce R, De Conca S, De Groot A, Robins S and Ponce Del Castillo A, 'Nothing Comes Between my Robot and me: Privacy and Human-Robot Interaction in Robotised Healthcare' in Leenes R, van Brakel R, Gutwirth Sand de Hert P (eds), *Data Protection and Privacy: The Internet of Bodies* (1st edn, Hart Publishing 2018)

Fosch-Villaronga E and Mahler T, 'Cybersecurity, Safety and Robots: Strengthening the Link Between Cybersecurity and Safety in the Context of Care Robots' (2021) 41 *Computer Law and Security Review* 1

Fosch-Villaronga E and others, 'Privacy Considerations for Socially Assistive Robots the Privacy Implications of Social Robots Solutions from Two Conference Workshops' (*Human-Robot Interaction Conference*, Vienna, Austria, 2017)

Fujita M, 'On Activating Human Communications with Pet-Type Robot AIBO' (2004) 92(11) *Proceedings of the IEEE*

Fujitsu Research Institute, 'Personal Data in the Cloud: A Global Survey of Consumer Attitudes (2010)

Gross H-M and others, 'Further Progress Towards a Home Robot Companion for People with Mild Cognitive Impairment' (*2012 IEEE International Conference on Systems, Man, and Cybernetics (SMC)*, Seoul, Soth Korea, 2012)

Gross H-M and others, 'I'll Keep an Eye on You: Home Robot Companion for Elderly People with Cognitive Impairment' (*2011 IEEE International Conference on Systems, Man, and Cybernetics, Anchorage*, Alaska, USA, October 9–12, 2011)

Gross R and Acquisti A, 'Information Revelation and Privacy in Online Social Networks' (*Proceedings of the 2005 ACM Workshop on Privacy in the Electronic Society*, New York, 2005) 71

Hacker P, *Datenprivatrecht. Neue Technologien im Spannungsfeld von Datenschutzrecht und BGB* (Mohr Siebeck Verlag 2020)

Hall E, *The Hidden Dimension* (Doubleday and Company 1966)

Hansen M, 'Marrying Transparency Tools with User-Controlled Identity Management in Fischer-Hübner S and others (eds), *The Future of Identity in the Information Society. Privacy and Identity. IFIP – The International Federation for Information Processing* (Springer 2007) 199

Harkous H, Fawaz K, Shin KG and Aberer K, 'PriBots: Conversational Privacy' 2016 WSF@SOUPS3<wwwusenixorg/system/files/conference/soups2016/wfpn16-paper-harkouspdf> accessed 28 September 2023

Heckmann D and Scheurer M, 'BDSG § 22' in Gola P and Hecmkann D (eds.), *Datenschutz-Grundverordnung, Bundesdatenschutzgesetz: DS-GVO/BDSG* (3 Aufl 2022, CHBECK 2022)

Heuer T, Schiering I and Gerndt R, 'Privacy Framework for Context-Aware Robot Development' (2021) 12(1) *Journal of Behavioral Robotics* 468

High Level Expert Group on AI (2018) <https://eceuropaeu/futurium/en/system/files/ged/ai_hleg_definition_of_ai_18_december_1pdf> accessed 4 September 2023

Ho C, 'Privacy and Transparency in Human-Robot Interaction' in Barfield W, Weng Y, and Pagallo U, *Cambridge Handbook on the Law, Policy, and Regulation for Human-Robot Interaction* (Cambridge University Press 2024) 589

Hon WK, Millard C and Walden I, 'Who is Responsible for Personal Data in Clouds?' in Millard C (ed), *Cloud Computing Law* (Oxford University Press 2013) 193

Fischer-Hübner S and others (eds), *The Future of Identity in the Information Society Privacy and Identity IFIP – The International Federation for Information Processing* (Springer 2007)

Huijnen C, Badii A, den van Heuvel H, Caleb-Solly P and Thiemert D, 'Maybe It Becomes a Buddy, But Do Not Call It a Robot – Seamless Cooperation between Companion Robotics and Smart Homes' in Keyson DV (ed), *Ambient Intelligence* (Springer 2011)

InterPlanetary File System <https://githubcom/ipfs-shipyard/ipfs-desktop> accessed 28 September 2023

Iosifidis A, Tefas A, and Pitas I, 'Multi-View Action Recognition based on Action Volumes, Fuzzy Distances and Cluster Discriminant Analysis' (2013) 93(6) *Signal Processing* 1445

Ishii K, 'Comparative Legal Study on Privacy and Personal Data Protection for Robots Equipped with Artificial Intelligence: Looking at Functional and Technological Aspects' (2019) 34 *AI and Society* 509

Kahl B, Füller M, Beer T and Ziegler S, 'Acceptance and Communicative Effectiveness of Different HRI Modalities for Mental Stimulation in Dementia Care' in Di Nuovo E, Broz F, Cavallo F and Dario P (eds), *Proceedings of New Frontiers of Service Robotics for the Elderly, IEEE RO-MAN* (IEEE 2014)

Kamarinou D, Millard C and Oldani I, 'Compliance as a Service: A Review of GDPR-mandated Contractual Relationships Between Providers and Customers of Enterprise Cloud Services' (Queen Mary School of Law Legal Studies Research Paper No 287/2018, 2018)

Kaminski M E, Rueben M, Smart WD and Grimm CM, 'Averting Robot Eyes' (2016) 76 *Maryland Law Review* 983

Kaye J and others, 'Dynamic Consent: A Patient Interface for Twenty-First Century Research Networks' (2015) 23 *European Journal of Human Genetics* 141

Khaksar W and others, 'The Robotics in Elderly Healthcare: A Review of 20 Recent Research Projects' (2023) 9 <https://arxivorg/abs/230204478> accessed 18 September 2023

Kidd CD, Taggart W and Turkle S, 'A Sociable Robot to Encourage Social Interaction Among the Elderly' (*Proceedings 2006 IEEE International Conference on Robotics and Automation*, Orlando, FL, USA, 2006)

Kienle T, 'Datenmündigkeit' (2020) 5 *Privacy in Germany (PinG)* 208

Kocaballi AB and others, 'The Personalization of Conversational Agents in Health Care: Systematic Review' (2019) 21(11) *Journal of Medical Internet Research* 1

Kokolakis S, 'Privacy Attitudes and Privacy Behaviour: A Review of Current Research on the Privacy Paradox Phenomenon' (2017) 64 *Computers and Security* 122

Kolain M, Grafenauer C and Ebers M, 'Anonymity Assessment Anonymity Assessment – A Universal Tool for Measuring Anonymity of Data Sets Under the GDPR with a Special Focus on Smart Robotics' (2022) 48(2) *Rutgers University Computer and Technology Law Journal* 1

Koppu S and others, 'Deep Learning Disease Prediction Model for Use with Intelligent Robots' (2020) 87 *Computers and Electrical Engineering* 1

Kretzschmar K and others, 'Can Your Phone Be Your Therapist? Young People's Ethical Perspectives on the Use of Fully Automated Conversational Agents (Chatbots) in Mental Health Support' (2019) 11 *Biomed Inform Insights* 1

Lee MK, Tang KP, Forlizzi J and Kiesler S, 'Understanding Users' Perception of Privacy in Human-Robot Interaction' (*Proceedings of the 6th International Conference on Human-Robot Interaction*, Lausanne, 2011) 181

Leino-Kilpi H and others, 'Privacy: A Review of the Literature' (2001) 38 *International Journal of Nursing Studies* 665

Lenca M and Fosch-Villaronga E, 'Privacy and Security Issues in Assistive Technologies for Dementia: The Case of Ambient Assisted Living, Wearables, and Service Robotics' in Jotterand F and others (eds), *Intelligent Assistive Technologies for Dementia: Clinical, Ethical, Social, and Regulatory Implications* (Oxford Academic 2019)

Li N, Li T and Venkatasubramanian S, 'T-closeness: Privacy Beyond k-Anonymity and l-Diversity' (*IEEE 2007 Proceedings of the 23rd International Conference Data Engineering*, 2007) 106 <https://ieeexplore.ieee.org/stamp/stamp.jsp?tp=&arnumber=4221659>

Lintvedt N, 'A Critical Analysis of Consent in Human – Robot Interaction' (2023) (1) *University of Oslo Faculty of Law Legal Studies Research Paper Series* 1

Lutz C and others, 'The Privacy Implications of Social Robots: Scoping Review and Expert Interviews' (2019) 7(3) *Mobile Media and Communication* 412

Lutz C and Tamò Larrieux A 'RoboCode-Ethicists – Privacy-Friendly Robots, an Ethical Responsibility of Engineers' (2015) 7 *ACM Web Science* 1

Lyons JB, 'Being Transparent about Transparency' (*Trust and Autonomous Systems: Papers from the 2013 AAAI Spring Symposium*) <https://cdnaaaiorg/ocs/5712/5712-24571-1-PBpdf> accessed 29 September 2023

Machanavajjhala A, Gehrke J, Kifer D and Venkitasubramaniam M, 'L-diversity: Privacy Beyond K-anonymity' (*IEEE 2006 Proceedings of the 22nd International Conference on Data Engineering*, 2006) <https://ieeexplore.ieee.org/stamp/stamp.jsp?tp=&arnumber=1617364>

Marami E, Tefas A and Pitas I, 'Nutrition Assistance Based on Skin Color Segmentation and Support Vector Machines' in Czachórski T, Kozielski S and Stańczyk U (eds), *Man-Machine Interactions 2* (Springer 2011)

Mascalzoni D, Hicks A, Pramstaller P and Wjst M, 'Informed Consent in the Genomics Era' (2007) 5(9) *Plos Medicine* 1

May R and Denecke K, 'Security, Privacy, and Healthcare-Related Conversational Agents: A Scoping Review' (2021) 47(6) *Informatics for Health and Social Care* 1

Merlec MM, Lee YK, Hong SP and In HP 'A Smart Contract-Based Dynamic Consent Management System for Personal Data Usage under GDPR' (2021) 21(23) *Sensors* 7994

Michelakaki C and Vale SB, 'Unlocking Data Protection By Design and By Default: Lessons from the Enforcement of Article 25 GDPR' (2023) *The Future of Privacy Forum* 22

Mont MC and others, 'Dynamic Consent, Policy Enforcement and Accountable Information Sharing within and across Organisations' <www.hpl.hp.com/techreports/2012/HPL-2012-36.pdf> accessed 25 September 2023

Mourby M and others, 'Are "Pseudonymised" Data Always Personal Data? Implications of the GDPR for Administrative Data Research in the UK' (2018) 34 *Computer Law and Security Review* 222

Müller G and others, 'Vertrauensinfrastruktur und Privatheit als ökonomische Fragestellung' in Buchmann J (eds), *Internet Privacy. acatech Studie* (Springer 2012) 143

Nissenbaum H, 'Privacy as contextual integrity' (2004) 79 *Washington Law Review* 119

Novotny A and Spiekermann S, 'Personal Information Markets AND Privacy: A New Model to Solve the Controversy' (*Proc WI'13*, Leipzig 2013) 1635

O'Brolchá F, 'Robots and People with Dementia: Unintended consequences and Moral hazard' (2017) 26(4) *Nursing Ethics* 963

Panait L and Luke S, 'Cooperative Multi-Agent Learning: The State of the Art' (2005) 11 *Autonomous Agents and Multi-Agent Systems* 387

PISA Consortium, *Handbook of Privacy and Privacy-Enhancing Technologies* (College bescherming persoonsgegevens 2003)

Prescott TJ and Robillard M, 'Are Friends Electric? The Benefits and Risks of Human-Robot Relationships'(2021) 24(1) *iScience* 101993

Prictor M, Lewis MA, Newson AJ and others, 'Dynamic Consent: An Evaluation and Reporting Framework' (2020) 15 *Journal of Empirical Research on Human Research Ethics* 175

Quarta D, Pogliani M, Polino M, Maggi F, Zanchettin AM, and Zanero S, 'An Experimental Security Analysis of an Industrial Robot Controller' (*Proceedings of the 2017 IEEE Symposium on Security and Privacy (SP)*, 2017)

Quorum: A Permissioned Implementation of Ethereum Supporting Data Privacy <https://githubcom/ConsenSys/quorum> accessed 28 September 2023

Reeves B, *The Media Equation: How People Treat Computers, Television, and new Media Like Real People and Places* (CSLI 2004)

Robinette P and others, 'Conceptualizing Overtrust in Robots: Why Do People Trust a Robot That Previously Failed?' in Lawless WF and others (eds), *Autonomy and Artificial Intelligence: A Threat or Savior?* (Springer International Publishing 2017) 129

Robinette P and others, 'Overtrust of Robots in Emergency Evacuation Scenarios' (*Eleventh Annual ACM/IEEE International Conference on Human Robot Interaction* 2016) <https://ieeexplore.ieee.org/stamp/stamp.jsp?tp=&arnumber=7451740>

Robinson H, Macdonald B, Kerse N and others, 'The Psychosocial Effects of a Companion Robot: A Randomized Controlled Trial' (2013) 14(9) *Journal of the American Medical Directors Association* 661

Rogosch PM, *Die Einwilligung im Datenschutzrecht* (Nomos 2013)

Rueben M, Aroyo A, Lutz C, Schmölz J, Van Cleynenbreugel P, Corti A and others, 'Themes and Research Directions in Privacy Sensitive Robotics' (*IEEE Workshop on Advanced Robotics and its Social Impacts (ARSO), Genova, Italy*, 2018) 77

Rueben M, Grimm CM, Bernieri FJ and Smart WD, 'A Taxonomy of Privacy Constructs for Privacy-Sensitive Robotics' (2017) *ArXiv* 1 <https://arxiv.org/abs/1701.00841> accessed 4 September 2023

Rueben M and Smart WD, 'Privacy in Human-Robot Interaction: Survey and Future Work' (2016) *We Robot* 2

Salem M, Lakatos G, Amirabdollahian F and Dautenhahn K, 'Would You Trust a (Faulty) Robot?: Effects of Error, Task Type and Personality on Human-Robot Cooperation and Trust' (*Proceedings of the Tenth Annual ACM/IEEE International Conference on Human-Robot Interaction*, 2015) 141 <https://ieeexplore.ieee.org/stamp/stamp.jsp?tp=&arnumber=8520654>

Sanfeliu A, Llacer MR, Gramunt MD, Punsola A and Yoshimura Y, 'Influence of the Privacy Issue in the Deployment and Design of Networking Robots in European Urban Areas' (2010) 24(13) *Advanced Robotics* 1

Schaub F, Balebako R, Durity A and Land Cranor LK, 'A Design Space for Effective Privacy Notices' (SOUPS 15: Symposium on Usable Privacy and Security 2015) 1

Schermer B, 'The Limits of Privacy in Automated Profiling and Data Mining' (2011) 27 *Computer Law and Security Review* 46

Scheutz M, 'The inherent Dangers Of unidirectional Emotional Bonds Between Humans and Social Robots' in Lin P, Abney K and Bekey GA (eds), *Robot Ethics: The Ethical and Social Implications of Robotics* (The MIT Press 2012) 205

Schiff 'GDPR Art. 9' in Ehmann E and Selmayr M (eds), *Datenschutzgrundverordnung* (2nd edn, C.H. Beck 2018)

Scott AS and others, 'Research Applications of Dynamic Consent' in Kosta E, Pierson J and others (eds), *Privacy and Identity Management Fairness, Accountability, and Transparency in the Age of Big Data* (Springer 2018)

Sharkey A and Sharkey N, 'Granny and the Robots: Ethical Issues in Robot Care for the Elderly' (2012) 14 *Ethics and Information Technology* 27

Solove DJ, 'The End of Privacy? Scientific American' (2018) 299(3) *Scientific American* 100

Steinsbekk KS and others, 'Broad Consent Versus Dynamic Consent in Biobank Research: Is Passive Participation an Ethical Problem?' (2013) 21 *European Journal of Human Genetics* 897

Sweeney L, 'k-anonymity: A Model for Protecting Privacy' (2002) 10 *International Journal of Uncertainty, Fuzziness and Knowledge-Based Systems* 557

Syrdal DS, Walters ML, Otero N, Koay LK and Dautenhahn K, 'He Knows When you are Sleeping Privacy and the Personal Robot Companion' (*Proc Workshop Human Implications of Human-Robot Interaction, Association for the Advancement of Artificial Intelligence* 2007) 28

Teare HJ, Morrison M, Whitley EA, Kaye J, 'Towards 'Engagement 200: Insights from a Study of Dynamic Consent with Biobank Participant' (2015) *Digital Health* 1

Teare HJA, Morrison M and others, 'Towards "Engagement 20": Insights from a Study of Dynamic Consent with Biobank Participants' (2015) *Digital Health* 1

Theodoru A and others, 'Why Is My Robot Behaving Like That? Designing Transparency for Real Time Inspection of Autonomous Robots' <https://robworthamcom/wp-content/uploads/2016/04/TheodorouWorthamAISBImplementingTransparencypdf> accessed 29 September 2023

Thomaen K, *Examining the Constitutionality of Robot-enhanced Interrogation.* in Calo R, Froomkin M, Kerr I and Robot Law (eds), (Edward Elgar Publishing 2016) 306

Turkle S, Taggart W, Kidd CD and Dasté O, 'Relational Artifacts with Children and Elders: The Complexities of Cybercompanionship' (2006) 18(4) *Connection Science* 347

United Nations, *World Population Prospect 2022* <www.unorg/development/desa/pd/sites/wwwunorgdevelopmentdesapd/files/wpp2022_summary_of_resultspdf> accessed 21 August 2023

US Department of Health and Human Services, 'Supply and Demand Projections of the Nursing Workforce: 2014–2030' (2017) <https://bhwhrsagov/sites/default/files/bureau-health-workforce/data-research/nchwa-hrsa-nursing-reportpdf> accessed 21 August 2023

Weitzner DJ and others, 'Transparent Accountable Data Mining: New Strategies for Privacy Protection' (Technical Report MIT-CSAIL-TR-2006–007, Massachusetts Institute of Technology Computer Science and Artificial Intelligence Laboratory 2006) <http://dspacemitedu/handle/17211/30972> accessed 29 September 2023

Westin A, *Privacy and Freedom* (1st edn, Atheneum 1967)

Wirth C and Kolain M, 'Privacy By Blockchain Design: A BlockChain-enabled GDPR-Compliant Approach for Handling Personal Data' in Prinz W and Hoschka P (eds), *Proceedings of 1st ERCIM Blockchain Workshop 2018, Reports of the European Society for Socially Embedded Technologies* (Deutsches Forschungsinstitut für öffentliche Verwaltung 2018) 1

World Health Organization, 'Aging Fact Sheet' <wwwwhoint/news-room/fact-sheets/detail/ageing-and-health> accessed 21 August 2023

World Health Organization, 'Dementia Fact Sheet' <wwwwhoint/news-room/fact-sheets/detail/dementia> accessed 21 August 2023

World Health Organization, 'Health and Care Workforce in Europe: Time to Act' (2022), 7 <wwwwhoint/europe/publications/i/item/9789289058339> accessed 21 August 2023

Zimmermann C, 'A Categorization of Transparency-Enhancing Technologies' (2015) *ArXiv* 1, arXiv:150704914

Zoidi O, Tefas A and Pitas I, 'Visual Object Tracking Based on Local Steering Kernels and Color Histograms' (2013) 23(5) *IEEE Transactions on Circuits and Systems for Video Technology* 870

Zsiga K, Edelmayer G, Rumeau P, Péter O, Tóth A and Fazekas G, 'Home Care Robot for Socially Supporting the Elderly: Focus Group Studies in Three European Countries to Screen User Attitudes and Requirements' (2013) 36(4) *International Journal of Rehabilitation Research* 375

10 Legal Tech and Data Protection

Enemies or Friends?

Peter Rott

10.1 Introduction

Legal tech generally means the use of technology and software to support legal service providers. Legal tech covers a vast range of services, including software to support legal service providers with practice management, document storage, billing, accounting, electronic discovery and the drafting of contracts or pleadings, tools or a marketplace to connect clients with lawyers, tools for consumers and businesses to complete legal matters by themselves, online legal advice and – perhaps most prominently nowadays – claims management.

Although legal technology is also used by traditional law firms, the notion of 'legal tech' is nowadays closely connected with start-up companies that disrupt the traditional legal market by focusing on legal services that are largely automated.

The connection between legal tech and data protection comes in various forms. For example, legal tech applications can help businesses to comply with data protection legislation. Legal tech claims management companies can help consumers to enforce damage claims against businesses that have breached the law, and indeed we see the first initiatives to that effect in Germany. Finally, legal tech companies themselves heavily rely on data, some of which may be protected (as personal data) by the law, and may therefore be at risk of breaching data protection laws themselves. It is this variety of scenarios that this chapter unfolds, whereby it mainly focuses on issues that – directly or indirectly – affect consumers.

A recurring theme thereby is the question whether legal tech companies are allowed to perform the services they offer, or whether they act in breach of the laws regulating the legal profession. These laws have not been harmonised in any way by EU law, and while Estonia, for example, takes a very liberal approach to legal services that are performed by non-lawyers,[1] other legal systems have traditionally reserved such services to the legal profession. Related problems are shown hereinafter using the example of Germany.

1 See Peter Rott and Karin Sein, 'Obstacles to Legal Tech Services: Examples from Germany and Estonia' (2021) *Journal of European Consumer and Markets Law* 101.

DOI: 10.4324/9781003502791-14

10.2 Legal Tech Companies as Data Controllers

Legal tech companies, as any company, have to comply with data protection legislation.[2] Whereas there is nothing special in that regard when it comes to cookie banners and the like, many legal tech business models require access to or the acquisition of large amounts of data. For example, legal tech companies that are specialised in the enforcement of air passengers' rights will need access to flight schedules, actual flight data, weather data, data regarding industrial actions and many more, and also data from legal databases. When that data is publicly available – or, in the case of legal databases, has been paid for – no data protection issues arise.

There may, however, also be an interest in the personal data of their customers. Obviously, legal tech companies can only use them if one of the grounds of Art. 6(1) General Data Protection Regulation (GDPR) is present. In that regard, the Court of Justice provided for valuable clarification in its *Meta Platforms* judgment of July 2023.[3]

No problem arises when processing is necessary for the performance of a contract to which the data subject is party (Art. 6[1][b] GDPR); a provision that the Court of Justice interpreted narrowly[4] in the sense that the processing must be objectively indispensable for a purpose that is integral to the contractual obligation intended for those users, such that the main subject matter of the contract cannot be achieved if that processing does not occur.

Legal tech companies will, however, also wish to be able to aggregate experience from their many cases, which would allow them, for example, to understand patterns of businesses' behaviours and court practices, to adjust strategies vis-à-vis certain traders, to base their arguments on previous cases or, more generally, to assess the likelihood of success of a certain claim.[5] And even beyond their own business, they may wish to transfer personal data to external service providers that pool data across a whole industry. This is a widespread practice in the insurance industry, with service providers that operate on the basis of several hundreds of thousands of cases per year.[6] Access to such data then provides a crucial advantage over the claimants and their representatives. Collecting data for such purposes is certainly not covered by Art. 6(1)(b) GDPR.

Next, data processing is justified when it is necessary for the purposes of the legitimate interests pursued by the controller or by a third party, except when such

2 Concerning their roles as controllers in various business models, see Ioannis Revolidis and Alan Dahi, 'Datenschutz, Allgemein' in Martin Ebers (ed), *StichwortKommentar Legal Tech* (Nomos 2023), chapter 22 paras 26 ff.

3 Case C-252/21 *Meta Platforms Inc. and others v Bundeskartellamt*, ECLI:EU:C:2023:537.

4 See also Peter Georg Picht, 'CJEU on Facebook: GDPR Processing Justifications and Application Competence' (2023) *Gewerblicher Rechtsschutz und Urheberrecht* 1169, 1171.

5 See also Revolidis and Dahi (n 2) para 43.

6 See Tim Platner, 'Legal Tech und Schadensregulierung – mit Daten und Metadaten aufholen (Teil 2)' (2021) <https://legal-tech.blog/legal-tech-und-schadenregulierung-mit-daten-und-metadaten-aufholen-teil-2>.

interests are overridden by the interests or fundamental rights and freedoms of the data subject which require protection of personal data (Art. 6[1][f] GDPR). This is a rather vague notion, which the Court has also concretised in *Meta Platforms*, and again, it chose a narrow interpretation.[7] The processing of data for the purposes of creating an internal database or contributing to a data pool is surely in the interest of a legal tech service provider, and also in the interest of its other customers,[8] and the Court has recognised in relation to 'product improvement' (in the context of Facebook) that it cannot be ruled out from the outset that the controller's interest in improving the product or service with a view to making it more efficient and thus more attractive can constitute a legitimate interest capable of justifying the processing of personal data and that such processing may be necessary in order to pursue that interest.[9] In contrast, using personal data (from other cases) is in no way in the interests of the individual customer who will normally hope not to need the services of, say, a particular legal tech claims management company for a second time. For the balancing exercise that is enshrined in Art. 6(1)(f) GDPR, the type of information should also be relevant: a missed flight connection is certainly less intrusive than details of a personal injury case, and passing on personal data to an external service provider is probably beyond the expectations of a reasonable customer.

To be safe, legal tech service providers will therefore ask their customers for consent for processing personal data for such purposes[10] under Art. 6(1)(a) GDPR. Article 4(11) GDPR defines 'consent' as meaning 'any freely given, specific, informed and unambiguous indication of the data subject's wishes by which he or she, by a statement or by a clear affirmative action, signifies agreement to the processing of personal data relating to him or her'. First, according to Recital 42 GDPR, consent cannot be regarded as freely given if the data subject has no genuine or free choice or is unable to refuse or withdraw consent without detriment. Thus, the legal tech service provider cannot make consent to such further uses a condition of its services that the customer pays fees for anyway.[11] Moreover, consent must be informed, which means that the purposes must be described in such a way that the customer clearly understands what his or her personal data is used for, and in what way.

10.3 Legal Tech Companies Helping Traders to Comply With Data Protection Law

One business model of legal tech companies consists in the development of software that helps traders to comply with their legal obligations in relation to data

7 Explicitly so: *Meta Platforms* (n 3) para 93.

8 On the relevance of third parties' interests, see Revolidis and Dahi (n 2) para 77.

9 *Meta Platforms* (n 3) para 122.

10 See also Metehan Uzunçakmak and Valentin Zipfel, 'Nationale Wettbewerbsbehörden können in der Missbrauchsaufsicht Verstöße gegen DSGVO des Normadressaten berücksichtigen' (2023) *Newsdienst Compliance* 320026 who conclude that consent appears to be the Court's first choice.

11 For the relevance of fees, see also Picht (n 4) 1170.

protection laws. Relevant tools are sometimes referred to as 'privacy tech'.[12] In 2022, the International Association of Privacy Professionals (IAPP) listed 368 privacy technology vendors.[13]

Among the multitude of services on the market,[14] we will only consider two that are of immediate relevance for the legal tech service provider–customer relationship: cookie banners and data protection declarations.

Cookie banners have been hotly debated in recent years, with questions about the related consent requirements even reaching the Court of Justice, which clarified that the Cookies Directive 2019/136/EC[15] required active consent of the data subject and therefore ruled out an 'opt-out' system.[16] Remaining legal issues, often discussed under the notion of 'dark patterns', centre on allowed or prohibited design of 'accept' and 'reject' buttons, on the amount of information that valid consent requires, and on the number of layers that is acceptable.[17] If the cookie banner does not meet the legal requirements, consent is invalid and the acquisition and use of data is unlawful.

Next, data protection declarations, in which businesses set out their dealings with customers' data – at least in German law – have been qualified as standard terms,[18] and standard terms are invalid if they are unfair. Thus, consent given by acceptance of such unfair standard terms is invalid, and the subsequent acquisition and use of data is unlawful.

Both types of breaches also constitute unfair commercial practices under German law,[19] and they can be pursued by consumer organisations, business organisations

12 See Matthias Struck and Guido Aßhoff, 'Privacy Tech' in Martin Ebers (ed), *StichwortKommentar Legal Tech* (Nomos 2023) chapter 67; Alina Lucia Deparis, 'The Rise of Privacy Techs' (2020) <www.cpomagazine.com/data-privacy/the-rise-of-the-privacytechs/>.

13 See IAPP, *IAPP Privacy Tech Vendor Report 2022* <https://iapp.org/media/pdf/resource_center/2022TechVendorReport.pdf>, 12.

14 For an overview, see Struck and Aßhoff (n 12) para 32 ff.

15 Directive 2009/136/EC of the European Parliament and of the Council of 25 November 2009 amending Directive 2002/22/EC on universal service and users' rights relating to electronic communications networks and services, Directive 2002/58/EC concerning the processing of personal data and the protection of privacy in the electronic communications sector and Regulation (EC) No 2006/2004 on cooperation between national authorities responsible for the enforcement of consumer protection laws [2009] OJ L337/11.

16 Case C-673/17 *Bundesverband der Verbraucherzentralen und Verbraucherverbände – Verbraucherzentrale Bundesverband e.V. v Planet49 GmbH*, ECLI:EU:C:2019:801.

17 See, for example, Carl Christoph Möller, 'Dark Patterns in Consent-Bannern' (2022) *Verbraucher und Recht* 449; Peter Rott, '*Dark patterns* im Verbraucherrecht' in Maria Reiffenstein and Beate Blaschek (eds), *Konsumentenpolitisches Jahrbuch 2023* (Verlag Österreich 2023) 181.

18 See BGH, 16 July 2008 – VIII ZR 348/06 (2008) *Neue Juristische Wochenschrift* 3055 – Payback; KG Berlin, 21 March 2019–23 U 268/13 (2020) *Zeitschrift für Datenschutz* 310 – Google; LG Berlin, 30 April 2013–15 O 92/12 (2013) *Neue Juristische Wochenschrift* 2605 – Apple. See also Peter Rott, 'Data Protection Law as Consumer Law – How Consumer Organisations Can Contribute to the Enforcement of Data Protection Law' (2017) *Journal of European Consumer and Markets Law* 113.

19 For data protection law, see BGH, 28 May 2020 – I ZR 186/17 (2020) *Zeitschrift für Datenschutz* 589; for unfair contract terms see BGH, 31 May 2012 – I ZR 45/11, *Neue Juristische Wochenschrift* 2012, 3577.

and competitors. Notably, they are easily visible on the websites of businesses, and certain business organisations and competitors have specialised in searching traders' websites, sometimes themselves using legal tech, such as web crawlers. Pursuing those breaches has been lucrative business, as courts award a lump sum of €150–250 for the request of an undertaking to end the breach, and this undertaking must be accompanied by the promise of a penalty for further breaches.[20] Moreover, data protection breaches can trigger damages, according to Art. 82 GDPR (on which, see Section 10.4).

One notorious current example from Germany is an alleged breach of data protection laws by using Google Fonts, because Google Fonts are usually not hosted on the website operator's own server but on Google's servers. This implies that whenever a user opens the website, his data – including his Internet protocol (IP) address – are transferred to Google, although Google claims that these data are not analysed and immediately deleted.[21] After a judgment of the Regional Court (Landgericht, or LG) München I that awarded damages of €100 for using Google Fonts,[22] two lawyers started a massive wave of litigation, which will, however, most likely be unsuccessful, as the decision of LG München I is generally regarded to be misguided and the activities of those two lawyers to be fraudulent.[23]

Certainly, however, awareness of data protection law and the obvious willingness of certain actors to enforce it have increased the risk for website operators and have therefore created a market for advice but also for legal tech solutions. Such solutions include cookie and consent tools, data protection declaration generators which can be used to design such declarations, generators for data protection agreements[24] and imprint generators.[25]

We also find tools that are meant to help businesses once a data protection problem has occurred. In such a case, Art. 33 GDPR requires data controllers to notify the personal data breach to the supervisory authority without undue delay and, where feasible, not later than 72 hours after having become aware of it. Insufficient reaction to a data protection problem may trigger a fine, which may be avoided by using legal tech tools.[26]

20 Actually, the business was so lucrative that the German legislator adopted the so-called *Gesetz zur Stärkung des fairen Wettbewerbs* (Act promoting fair competition) (2020) *Bundesgesetzblatt* I, 2568, to protect, in particular, small and medium-sized enterprises (SMEs) from being targeted with warnings and penalties requests.

21 See Daniel Ashkar and Christian Schröder, 'Aktuelle Entwicklungen im Bereich der Data Privacy Litigation' (2023) *Betriebs-Berater* 451.

22 LG München I, 20 January 2022–3 O 17493/20 (2022) *Zeitschrift für Datenschutz* 290.

23 See Ashkar and Schröder (n 21), 451 f.; Jan Spittka, 'Datenschutzklagen als Geschäftsmodell?' (2023) *GRUR-Prax* 31, 33.

24 See, for example, CMS ComplyDPA <https://cms.law/en/deu/innovation/our-products-and-solutions/cms-complydpa>.

25 See Kathrin Strauß, 'Legal Tech & Datenschutz – zwei wie Pech und Schwefel?' (2021) <www.datenschutzexperte.de/blog/datenschutz-im-unternehmen/legal-tech-datenschutz/>.

26 See, for example, the CMS Breach Assistant <https://cms.law/en/int/innovation/legal-tech-tools-and-teams/cms-breach-assistant>.

In the context of data protection declaration generators, or more generally, of contract generators, the mentioned issue of reservation of such services to the legal profession has come up. In Germany, the Legal Services Act (*Rechtsdienstleistungsgesetz*, or RDG),[27] generally speaking, reserves the provision of 'legal services' to the legal profession. A legal service is defined by § 2 para. 1 RDG as 'any activity related to the concrete affairs of others as soon as it requires a legal assessment of the individual case'. The crucial question is whether the automated generation of a legal document, such as a data protection declaration, relates to the 'concrete affairs' of another or whether it merely offers abstract solutions. In the case of the contract generator by SmartLaw, the German Federal Supreme Court (*Bundesgerichtshof*, or BGH) decided that a contract generator was comparable to a manual and did not address an individual case. Thus, such contract generators can be offered by non-lawyers, including legal tech start-ups.[28]

10.4 Legal Tech Companies as Enforcers of Data Protection Law

Most prominently at this moment, legal tech companies act as enforcers of data protection law by collecting damage claims of consumers against companies, with variations on the legal construction applied. In fact, legal tech companies offering this type of services are mushrooming,[29] and they are advertising their services aggressively.[30] In the United States, data protection litigation ranks number one among class actions.[31] Meta (Facebook) reportedly agreed to pay $725 million in settlement of the Cambridge Analytica scandal.[32]

In the Netherlands, the Dutch organisation Stichting The Privacy Collective has brought collective proceedings against the U.S. companies Salesforce and Oracle but was unsuccessful until recently.[33]

27 English translation is available at <www.gesetze-im-internet.de/englisch_rdg/>.

28 See BGH, 9 September 2021–I ZR 113/20 (2021) *Neue Juristische Wochenschrift* 3125. See also LG Frankfurt, 23 February 2023–2–24 S 97/22 (2023) *Beck-Rechtsprechung* 3370, for a 'compensation manager' that can be used for formulating claims against airlines.

29 See also Spittka (n 23) 31.

30 See Tim Wybitul and Kevin Leibold, 'Risiken für Unternehmen durch neue Rechtsprechung zum DS-GVO-Schadensersatz' (2022) *Zeitschrift für Datenschutz* 207.

31 See Kevin Hylton, 'Data Privacy Class Actions on the Rise' (2023) <www.lexisnexis.com/community/insights/legal/b/practical-guidance/posts/data-privacy-class-actions-on-the-rise>. For an overview of data protection class actions, see ClassAction.org, 'Data Breach and Privacy Lawsuits' <www.classaction.org/privacy-and-data-breach>.

32 See Nate Raymond, 'Facebook Parent Meta to Settle Cambridge Analytica Scandal Case for $725 Million', *Reuters* of 23 December 2022 <www.reuters.com/legal/facebook-parent-meta-pay-725-mln-settle-lawsuit-relating-cambridge-analytica-2022-12-23>.

33 See Marcus Jung, 'Haben Salesforce und Oracle gegen die DGSVO verstoßen?' (2020) *Frankfurter Allgemeine* of 2 September 2020 <www.faz.net/pro/d-economy/haben-salesforce-und-oracle-gegen-die-dsgvo-verstossen-16934826.html>. The Rechtbank Amsterdam declared the claim inadmissible, as the Stichting had not proven that the claim was supported by 75,000 consumers, as it had claimed, see Rechtbank Amsterdam, 29 December 2021 – C/13/688682/HA ZA 20–863 <https://uitspraken.rechtspraak.nl/#!/details?id=ECLI:NL:RBAMS:2021:7647> (in Dutch).

In Germany, the pioneers of legal tech enforcement of data protection damage claims have been Europäische Gesellschaft für Datenschutz mbH (EuGD). In a test case in the Regional Court of Munich for one consumer, EuGD won €2,500 in damages for pain and suffering after insufficiently secured personal data had been stolen from the server of the financial services provider Scalable Capital,[34] which triggered EuGD to heavily advertise for more clients that were affected by that data leakage.[35] Of around 33,200 Scalable Capital customers who were affected by the incident, EuGD collected 2,500 clients.[36]

Moreover, according to press reports, EuGD achieved to collect €300 each in compensation for around 2,000 clients from Mastercard following the publication of personal data including the credit card numbers of tens of thousands Mastercard customers in 2019. EuGD itself received another €100 for each customer they represented.[37] Interestingly, in this case, the first instance and appeal courts had already rejected the claim,[38] but the claimant had applied for a second appeal to the BGH, not least to obtain a judgment that would clarify controversial issues of law (on which see hereinafter) – which Mastercard apparently wanted to avoid and therefore settled the dispute. Other current EuGD targets include Facebook, Tesla and Vodafone, all in relation to data leakages.[39]

Another legal tech company that is active in the field of data protection damage claims is Rightmart, which also advertises Facebook data leakage damage claims.[40]

The reasons for this development are manifold. They comprise the extent of breaches of data protection law, including spectacular scandals, the shortage of viable alternative mechanisms, clarifications of data protection law through the case law of the Court of Justice and national courts, and clarifications related to the activities of legal tech companies as enforcers as such.

10.4.1 Clarification of Data Protection Law

Under Art. 82 GDPR, any person who has suffered material or non-material damage as a result of an infringement of this regulation shall have the right to receive compensation from the controller or processor for the damage suffered.

34 LG München I, 9 December 2021–31 O 16606/20 (2022) *Zeitschrift für Bank-und Kapitalmarktrecht* 131. The judgment was followed by LG Köln, 18 May 2022–28 O 328/21 (2022) *Beck-Rechtsprechung* 11236. Reportedly, other courts awarded much smaller amounts, and some rejected damage claims altogether, see Ulrike Barth, 'Nach Datenleck: Scalable Capital muss erneut Schadensersatz zahlen', t:n of 4 March 2023 <https://t3n.de/news/datenleck-scalable-capital-schadensersatz-dsgvo-1538014>. One case is currently pending in the Court of Justice, see Case C-189/22 *SO v Scalable Capital*.

35 See EuGD, 'Urteile zum Scalable Capital Datenleck 2020: 1.200–2.500 EUR Schadensersatz!' <https://eugd.org/schadenersatz/scalable-capital>.

36 See Barth (n 34).

37 See N.N. (tmk), 'Mastercard zahlt Kunden wegen Datenleck 300 Euro', Spiegel online of 4 January 2023 <www.spiegel.de/netzwelt/web/mastercard-zahlt-kunden-300-euro-wegen-datenleck-a-550bf0ba-ceed-49e0-aaa8-507757fcbce6>.

38 See LG Stuttgart, 11 November 2020–14 O 273/20; OLG Stuttgart, 31 March 2021–9 U 34/21, *Beck-Rechtsprechung* 2021, 6282.

39 See EuGD, 'Schadenersatz nach Datenlecks ohne Risiko geltend machen' <https://eugd.org>.

40 See Rightmart, 'Wir lösen Ihr Rechtsproblem' <https://rightmart.de/#wir-loesen-ihr-rechtsproblem>.

10.4.1.1 Data Protection Law in General

As the damage claim under Art. 82 GDPR requires a breach of data protection law in the first place, clarification of individual provisions of the GDPR is helpful. As previously mentioned, the Court of Justice recently – in the case of *Meta Platforms* – gave important guidance on the lawfulness of processing under Art. 6 GDPR, which is absolutely crucial for data protection law. Among others, that decision lay the foundation for follow-on damages claims, to which we now turn.

10.4.1.2 Damages Under Article 82 GDPR

Material damage is a clear-cut legal notion – although causation between a breach of data protection law and material damage may be difficult to prove[41] and the burden of proof is on the claimant, as a general rule of civil procedural law[42] – but they are rare in practice.[43] In the individual case, they may stem, for example, from fraudulent activities after an identity theft, or from the rejection of credit resulting from a negative creditworthiness assessment following a breach of data protection law.

Instead, non-material damage can potentially occur as a mass phenomenon after a breach of data protection law, in particular when that breach has not yet led to material damage but could do so in the future. The preconditions of compensation for non-material damage, however, have been discussed controversially in academic writing and between different courts.

One relevant question is related to a potential requirement of a certain gravity of the breach, which a number of courts applied and therefore rejected damage claims concerning breaches that they thought to be less severe.[44] This barrier has fallen, as the Court of Justice decided in the case of *Österreichische Post* that although the data subject must have suffered damage at all (and the breach, as such, does not suffice), any condition in national law that the damage suffered by the data subject has reached a certain degree of seriousness is in breach of the GDPR.[45]

At the same time, the Court of Justice has made it clear that there must be some damage, whereas the breach as such does not justify a damages claim. Thus, the clarifications by the Court by no means makes bringing data protection non-material damage claims a safe bet now. For example, we can observe that litigation

41 See, for example, OLG Stuttgart, 31 March 2021–9 U 34/21 (2021) *Zeitschrift für Datenschutz* 375.

42 For detailed analysis of relevant case law, see Wybitul and Leibold (n 30) 208 f.; Michael Weber, 'Rechtsprechungslinien zum Anspruch auf immateriellen Schadensersatz nach Art. 82 DSGVO' (2022) *Computer und Recht* 503.

43 See Spittka (n 23) 31; Michael J R Kremer, Jan Conrady and Anja Penners, '"Data Privacy Litigation" – Prozessuale Implikationen des datenschutzrechtlichen Schadensersatzanspruchs nach Art. 82 DS-GVO' (2021) *Zeitschrift für Datenschutz* 128, 130.

44 See the overview by Weber (n 42) 505. In a case decided by AG Goslar, 27 September 2019–28 C 7/19 (2019) *GRUR-RS* 53276, that rejected the claim, the German Federal Constitutional Court, 14 January 2021–1 BvR 2853/19 (2021) *Neue Juristische Wochenschrift* 1005, referred to the uncertainties around the interpretation of Art. 82 GDPR and held that these uncertainties required preliminary reference proceedings in the Court of Justice.

45 Case C-300/21 *UI v Österreichische Post AG*, ECLI:EU:C:2023:370.

related to the Facebook security problem, which allowed third parties to scrape off the personal data of consumers, is dealt with very differently by instance courts. Whereas some courts awarded non-material damage of up to €1,000[46] (and the legal tech claims management company advertises potential damages of up to €5,000), a number courts rejected claims altogether.[47] In August 2023, the Higher Regional Court (*Oberlandesgericht*, or OLG) Hamm was the first appeal court to decide on Facebook scraping claims, and it rejected the claim.[48] In fact, the judgment of OLG Hamm revealed one particular risk of mass litigation for non-material damages: the court required evidence of individual (non-material) harm, and it rejected the general reference to loss of control and the like that the claimant's representative apparently used, with identical wording, in numerous cases. Moreover, the court could not see that there was a great risk linked to the scraping of the claimant's mobile phone number.

10.4.2 Shortage of Alternative Enforcement Mechanisms

Data protection law has traditionally been seen as public law, and it was mainly enforced by data protection authorities that, however, operate with classical public law mechanisms, such as fines of which the victims of breaches do not benefit.

Collective private law enforcement by consumer organisations has been limited to injunctive claims at best for a long time. In Germany, it was explicitly extended to data protection law by the legislature in 2016,[49] but compliance of the new legislation with overarching EU law has been contested.[50] The issue has even reached the Court of Justice, in the cases of *Fashion ID*[51] (concerning the old Data Protection Directive 95/46/EC) and *Meta Platforms Ireland*[52] (concerning the GDPR), but although the Court has confirmed that private law injunctions can operate alongside the public law enforcement system of those two legislative acts,

46 See LG Lübeck, 25 May 2023–15 O 74/22 (2023) *GRUR-RS* 11984 (appeal pending in OLG Schleswig – 5 U 95/23); LG Ravensburg, 13 June 2023–2 O 228/22 (2023) *GRUR-RS* 17418 (appeal pending in OLG Stuttgart – 4 U 107/23).

47 See, for example, LG Augsburg, 2 May 2023–031 O 1709/22 (2023) *GRUR-RS* 13778; LG Augsburg, 9 June 2023–022 O 2669/22 (2023) *GRUR-RS* 13763; LG Baden-Baden, 9 March 2023–3 O 236/22; LG Bochum, 5 June 2023–6 O 86/22 (2023) *GRUR-RS* 14580; LG Deggendorf, 20 June 2023–33 O 461/22 (2023) *GRUR-RS* 14586; LG Köln, 31 May 2023–28 O 138/22 (2023) GRUR-RS 13967; LG Regensburg, 11 May 2023–72 O 731/22 (2023) *GRUR-RS* 17446.

48 OLG Hamm, 15 August 2023–7 U 19/23 (2023) *GRUR-RS* 22505.

49 For an account, see Axel Halfmeier, 'Die neue Datenschutzverbandsklage' (2016) *Neue Juristische Wochenschrift* 1126 ff.

50 On the following, see also the overview by Tobias B. Lühmann, Pascal Schumacher and Lea Stegemann, 'Gegenwart und Zukunft kollektiver Rechtsdurchsetzung im Datenschutzrecht' (2023) *Zeitschrift für Datenschutz* 131, 133.

51 Case C-40/17 *Fashion ID GmbH & Co.KG v Verbraucherzentrale NRW e. V.*, ECLI:EU:C:2019:629.

52 Case C-319/20 *Meta Platforms Ireland Limited v Bundesverband der Verbraucherzentralen und Verbraucherverbände – Verbraucherzentrale Bundesverband e. V.*, ECLI:EU:C:2022:322.

the BGH has referred further questions to the Court of Justice in a second case of *Meta Platforms Ireland*.[53]

This will, of course, change now with the implementation of the Representative Actions Directive (EU) 2020/1828 that allows for redress actions and that expressly includes the GDPR in its scope of application. Predictably though, the qualified entities that Member States will accept will not have the financial and personal resources to enforce consumer protection in the vast array of areas covered by the Directive, given the vast number of breaches of consumer law each year.[54]

Overall, there is a clear gap in the private law enforcement of data protection law that legal tech claims management companies try to fill.

10.4.3 Legal Environment for Mass Claim Management

In turn, it has also been contested whether or not claims management companies could bring claims on behalf of consumers in court, let alone in mass litigation. *Sedes materiae* was again the Legal Services Act. Although the performance of legal services is generally reserved to the legal profession, as mentioned previously, there is an exception for debt collection services.[55] Of course, the Legal Services Act originally had debt collection on behalf of traders and against consumers in mind. Whether or not the new type of debt collection on behalf of consumers against traders is also exempted from the lawyers' privilege was subject to much debate and to litigation, including in the BGH, and it even led to a (modest) reform of the Legal Services Act.[56]

In the meantime, the BGH has clarified most of the controversial points, and the court has made it clear that, in principle, legal tech claims management in such a way that the consumer assigns his claim to the legal tech claims management company, which then enforces it in its own name, is permitted under the Legal Services Act.[57] The BGH has also confirmed the possibility of mass debt collection,[58] which offers enormous efficiency gains, as well as advantages in relation to court fees and lawyers' fees.

Still, there is one particular problem with claims for non-material damages resulting from breach of data protection law: According to § 399 of the German Civil Code, a claim may not be assigned if the performance cannot be made to a person

53 Case C-757/22 *Meta Platforms Ireland Limited v Bundesverband der Verbraucherzentralen und Verbraucherverbände – Verbraucherzentrale Bundesverband e. V.*

54 See, for example, Michael Heese and Ekkehard Schumann, 'Ein Vorabentscheidungsverfahren beim BGH' (2021) *Neue Juristische Wochenschrift* 3023, 3027 f.; Astrid Stadler, 'Zulässigkeit von Inkasso-Bündelungs-und Finanzierungsmodellen nach RDG' (2021) *Recht Digital* 513, 517.

55 § 10 para 1 sent 1 no 1 RDG.

56 Act promoting consumer friendly services in the legal services market (Gesetz zur Förderung verbrauchergerechter Angebote im Rechtsdienstleistungsmarkt) (2021) *Bundesgesetzgblatt* I, 3415.

57 See BGH, 27 November 2019–VIII ZR 285/18 (2020) *Neue Juristische Wochenschrift* 208.

58 See BGH, 13 July 2021–II ZR 84/20 (2021) *Neue Juristische Wochenschrift* 3046; BGH, 13 June 2022 – VIa ZR 418/21 (2022) *Neue Juristische Wochenschrift* 3350, 3352 f.

other than the original obligee without a change of its contents. According to the BGH, this applies to rights that are inalienably connected to a particular person.[59] With regard to non-material damage claims under Art. 82 GDPR, academic authors are divided on that issue,[60] and courts have decided in both directions.[61] As the BGH has recognised the assignability of non-material damage claims in other areas of law,[62] the better arguments seem to speak in favour of assignability.

A similar risk stems from the standard terms of traders that exclude the assignability of customers' claims against these traders. Such attempts have been made not only by airlines[63] but also by landlords in relation of tenants' claims for the reimbursement of excessive rent.[64] Until now, most of them failed as courts have declared such terms unfair and therefore invalid.[65] The German legislature has even introduced an explicit provision in standard terms law that prohibits the exclusion or limitation of the assignability of claims.[66]

EuGD has chosen a different legal construction to avoid this problem, acting as an intermediary between consumers and lawyers while at the same time engaging in third-party financing. Thus, it promises to pay for the court fees and the lawyers' fees in case the claim cannot be enforced. Otherwise, if the case is successful, the defendant will have to pay the court fees and the lawyers' fees, and EuGD keeps 25% of the award in fees. The disadvantage of this model is that the lawyers who cooperate with EuGD have to bring each case individually, and they do not benefit from the degression of court fees that comes with the aggregation of claims.[67]

Overall, the legal environment for legal tech claims management companies in the area of data protection law has clearly become much more favourable recently.[68]

59 See, for example, BGH, 29 April 2014–VI ZR 246/12 (2014) *Neue Juristische Wochenschrift* 2871.

60 In favour of assignability, see for example: Joachim Kohn, 'Der Schadensersatzanspruch nach Art. 82 DS-GVO' (2019) *Zeitschrift für Datenschutz* 498, 499, with further references; Alexander Hellgardt, 'Die Schadensersatzhaftung für Datenschutzverstöße im System des unionalen Haftungsrechts' (2022) *Zeitschrift für Europäisches Privatrecht* 7, 33. Against assignability: Jan Spittka, 'Die Kommerzialisierung von Schadensersatz unter der DS-GVO' (2019) *GRUR-Prax* 475, 477; Susanne Klein, 'Immaterieller Schadensersatz nach der DS-GVO' (2020) *GRUR-Prax* 433. See also the overview by Wybitul and Leibold (n 30) 208.

61 In favour of assignability: LG Essen, 23.9.2021–6 O 190/21. Against assignability: AG Hannover, 9.3.2020–531 C 10952/19 (2019) *Beck-Rechtsprechung* 43221.

62 See, for example, BGH, 12 November 2015–III ZR 204/15 (2016) *Neue Juristische Wochenschrift* 636.

63 See Rott and Sein (n 1) 106 f.

64 See Florian Skupin, 'Die Entwicklung der Lega-Tech-Rechtsprechung im Jahre 2021' (2022) *Recht Digital* 63, 68.

65 Concerning the standard terms of airlines, see Rott and Sein (n 1). In relation to tenancy contracts, the Berlin courts have decided in different directions: In favour of unfairness: LG Berlin (Zivilkammer 65), 30 March 2021–65 S 241/20 (2021) *Beck-Rechtsprechung* 8695. In favour of fairness: AG Berlin-Mitte, 30 June 2021–11 C 246/20 (2021) *Beck-Rechtsprechung* 21855.

66 See new § 308 No 9 lit a) BGB, in effect since 1 October 2021.

67 See also Spittka (n 23) 33.

68 See also Lühmann, Schumacher and Stegemann (n 50) 136.

10.5 Conclusions

Automated solutions as provided by legal tech services providers require a great deal of legal certainty. The GDPR, however, is not exactly a legal instrument that is easy to understand but shines with general principles and vague terminology. Moreover, the legal environment for legal tech services may be unclear, in particular in legal systems that traditionally rely only on the legal profession. Thus, privacy tech and legal tech enforcement of data protection law had a somewhat slow start.

With ongoing clarification of the GDPR, in particular by the Court of Justice, and with adjustments to the legal framework for legal services so as to accommodate the use of legal tech services, legal certainty has increased – and consequently, privacy tech solutions and legal tech claims management services in the area of data protection law are on the rise. The latter, in particular, will play an important role in enforcing data protection law, at least as long as other routes of enforcement are not sufficiently used.

Bibliography

Ashkar, D and Schröder C, 'Aktuelle Entwicklungen im Bereich der Data Privacy Litigation' (2023) *Betriebs-Berater* 451

Barth, U, 'Nach Datenleck: Scalable Capital muss erneut Schadensersatz zahlen', t:n of 4 March 2023 <https://t3n.de/news/datenleck-scalable-capital-schadensersatz-dsgvo-1538014>

ClassAction.org, 'Data Breach and Privacy Lawsuits' <www.classaction.org/privacy-and-data-breach>

Deparis, A L, 'The Rise of Privacy Techs' (2020) <www.cpomagazine.com/data-privacy/the-rise-of-the-privacytechs/>

EuGD, 'Schadenersatz nach Datenlecks ohne Risiko geltend machen' <https://eugd.org>

EuGD, 'Urteile zum Scalable Capital Datenleck 2020: 1.200–2.500 EUR Schadensersatz!' <https://eugd.org/schadenersatz/scalable-capital>

Halfmeier A, 'Die neue Datenschutzverbandsklage' (2016) *Neue Juristische Wochenschrift* 1126

Heese, M and E Schumann, 'Ein Vorabentscheidungsverfahren beim BGH' (2021) *Neue Juristische Wochenschrift* 3023

Hellgardt, A, 'Die Schadensersatzhaftung für Datenschutzverstöße im System des unionalen Haftungsrechts' (2022) *Zeitschrift für Europäisches Privatrecht* 7

Hylton, K, 'Data Privacy Class Actions on the Rise' (2023) <www.lexisnexis.com/community/insights/legal/b/practical-guidance/posts/data-privacy-class-actions-on-the-rise>

IAPP, *IAPP Privacy Tech Vendor Report 2022* <https://iapp.org/media/pdf/resource_center/2022TechVendorReport.pdf>

Jung M, 'Haben Salesforce und Oracle Gegen die DGSVO Verstoßen?' (2020) *Frankfurter Allgemeine Zeitung of 2 September 2020* <www.faz.net/pro/d-economy/haben-salesforce-und-oracle-gegen-die-dsgvo-verstossen-16934826.html>

Klein, S, 'Immaterieller Schadensersatz nach der DS-GVO' (2020) *GRUR-Prax* 433

Kohn, J, 'Der Schadensersatzanspruch nach Art. 82 DS-GVO' (2019) *Zeitschrift für Datenschutz* 498

Kremer, M J R, J Conrady and A Penners, '"Data Privacy Litigation" – Prozessuale Implikationen des datenschutzrechtlichen Schadensersatzanspruchs nach Art. 82 DS-GVO' (2021) *Zeitschrift für Datenschutz* 128

Lühmann, T B, P Schumacher and L Stegemann, 'Gegenwart und Zukunft kollektiver Rechtsdurchsetzung im Datenschutzrecht' (2023) *Zeitschrift für Datenschutz* 131

Möller, C C, 'Dark Patterns in Consent-Bannern' (2022) *Verbraucher und Recht* 449

N N (tmk), 'Mastercard zahlt Kunden wegen Datenleck 300 Euro' Spiegel online of 4 January 2023 <www.spiegel.de/netzwelt/web/mastercard-zahlt-kunden-300-euro-wegen-datenleck-a-550bf0ba-ceed-49e0-aaa8-507757fcbce6>

Picht, P G, 'CJEU on Facebook: GDPR Processing Justifications and Application Competence' (2023) *Gewerblicher Rechtsschutz und Urheberrecht* 1169

Platner, T, 'Legal Tech und Schadensregulierung – mit Daten und Metadaten aufholen (Teil2)'(2021)<https://legal-tech.blog/legal-tech-und-schadenregulierung-mit-daten-und-metadaten-aufholen-teil-2>

Raymond, N, 'Facebook Parent Meta to Settle Cambridge Analytica Scandal Case for $725 Million' *Reuters of 23 December 2022* <www.reuters.com/legal/facebook-parent-meta-pay-725-mln-settle-lawsuit-relating-cambridge-analytica-2022-12-23>

Revolidis I and A Dahi, 'Datenschutz, allgemein' in M Ebers (ed), *StichwortKommentar Legal Tech* (Nomos 2023) 22

Rightmart, 'Wir lösen Ihr Rechtsproblem' <https://rightmart.de/#wir-loesen-ihr-rechtsproblem>

Rott, P, 'Dark Patterns im Verbraucherrecht', in M Reiffenstein and B Blaschek (eds), *Konsumentenpolitisches Jahrbuch 2023* (Verlag Österreich 2023) 181

Rott, P, 'Data Protection Law as Consumer Law – How Consumer Organisations can Contribute to the Enforcement of Data Protection Law' (2017) *Journal of European Consumer and Markets Law* 113

Rott, P and K Sein, 'Obstacles to Legal Tech Services: Examples from Germany and Estonia' (2021) *Journal of European Consumer and Markets Law* 101

Skupin, F, 'Die Entwicklung der Lega-Tech-Rechtsprechung im Jahre 2021' (2022) *Recht Digital* 63

Spittka, J, 'Datenschutzklagen als Geschäftsmodell?' (2023) *GRUR-Prax* 31

Spittka, J, 'Die Kommerzialisierung von Schadensersatz unter der DS-GVO' (2019) *GRUR-Prax* 475

Stadler, A, 'Zulässigkeit von Inkasso-Bündelungs – und Finanzierungsmodellen nach RDG' (2021) *Recht Digital* 513

Strauß, K, 'Legal Tech & Datenschutz – zwei wie Pech und Schwefel?' (2021) <www.datenschutzexperte.de/blog/datenschutz-im-unternehmen/legal-tech-datenschutz/>

Struck, M and G Aßhoff, 'Privacy Tech' in M Ebers (ed), *StichwortKommentar Legal Tech* (Nomos 2023) chapter 67

Uzunçakmak, M and V Zipfel, 'Nationale Wettbewerbsbehörden können in der Missbrauchsaufsicht Verstöße gegen DSGVO des Normadressaten berücksichtigen' (2023) *Newsdienst Compliance* 320026

Weber, M, 'Rechtsprechungslinien zum Anspruch auf immateriellen Schadensersatz nach Art. 82 DSGVO' (2022) *Computer und Recht* 503

Wybitul, T and K Leibold, 'Risiken für Unternehmen durch neue Rechtsprechung zum DS-GVO-Schadensersatz' (2022) *Zeitschrift für Datenschutz* 207

Part V

Behavioural Advertising, Biometrics, Emotions and Data Protection

11 The Mismatch Between GDPR and Behavioural Advertising

What Way Forward?

Federico Galli and Galileo Sartor

11.1 Introduction: The Market of Online Behavioural Advertising

The global online advertising market was valued at $319 billion in 2019 and is projected to reach $1,089 billion by 2027.[1] The United States dominates the online advertising landscape due to its vast market, its worldwide platform leaders in advertising intermediation (such as Google, Facebook, and Amazon), and its large investments in advertising technologies (e.g., Big Data, AI, virtual and augmented reality). The online advertising market in Europe has grown, too, although at a slower pace. According to an estimate by the International Bureau of Advertising (IAB), European online advertising spending has increased in the last 15 years by €4 billion a year, passing from €7.6 billion in 2006 to €64.8 billion in 2019[2] and in the context of increased availability of personal data and rapidly growing advertising technologies, online behavioural advertising (OBA) has become prevalent.[3]

Indeed, in the last 20 years, a complex and dynamic ecosystem has emerged that involves multiple actors in different roles. Advertisers are interested in presenting their offers to potential consumers in order to promote sales. They are willing to pay to have ads displayed, thereby generating the demand for advertising services. Publishers provide space to publish ads together with online content which draw users' attention in the form of news, games, apps, and services. Advertisers are motivated to purchase space on publishers' online interfaces (directly or through intermediaries) to interface with their audience. Between these two categories,

1 Allied Market Search, *Internet Advertising Market Statistics*, 2020 <www.alliedmarketresearch.com/internet-advertising-market>.

2 IAB Europe, *IAB Europe AdEx Benchmark 2019 Study Reveals European Digital Advertising Market Exceeds €64bn in 2019*, 2020 <https://iabeurope.eu/all-news/iab-europe-adex-benchmark-2019-study-reveals-european-digital-advertising-market-exceeds-e64bn-in-2019>.

3 According to the European Commission, online advertising practices include three broad types of advertising: (1) contextual advertising, based on the content of the web pages and keywords used in searches; (2) segmented advertising, based on known characteristics of individuals; and (3) behavioural advertising based on observing behaviour. See European Commission, 'Consumer Market Study on Online Market Segmentation Through Personalised Pricing/Offers in the European Union' (2019) <https://ec.europa.eu/info/publications/consumer-market-study-online-market-segmentation-through-personalised-pricing-offers-european-union_en> access 30 August 2023.

DOI: 10.4324/9781003502791-16

there are many data-driven companies that facilitate the matching of demand and supply in advertising spaces. Advertising intermediaries include multiple actors, such as *advertising networks* (e.g., Google or Facebook),[4] which directly aggregate the supply of advertising space and help marketers elect and buy these spaces; *advertising exchanges*, platforms that sell their aggregated inventory of ad spaces through automated micro-auctions; *supply- and demand-side platforms*, which assist publishers in managing and optimising ad spaces, and advertisers in delivering ads; and *data management platforms*, which collect, aggregate, study, and analyse user data to facilitate the matching between ads and users.[5]

The success of the current OBA market has mainly been driven by the intensive acquisition of users' data and the technologies used to process this data.

Data for targeted advertising can be obtained in multiple ways. They can be volunteered by users via direct actions (such as posting a review on the website or updating their social media profile) or observed by the marketer. In the latter case, marketers acquire data through a host of online tracking technologies, such as cookies, tracking walls, web beacons, device fingerprinting, and Internet of Things (IoT) devices such as smartphones, wearables, smart TVs and various smart home applications.

Personal information can also be derived through deterministic computations or inferences based on observed data. In the latter case, collected data is processed through data analytics and machine learning, then transformed into actionable knowledge.[6] Based on these technologies, individuals can be profiled and grouped into different segments, and their interests, attitudes, and behaviours can be predicted.[7]

Finally, profiles can be built by and exchanged with third-party businesses. Personal data can be sold for further use in advertising to data management platforms and data brokers, or data analytics and market research companies. Data managing companies collect, aggregate, study, and analyse online user data to facilitate the

4 Google is one of the leading advertising networks in Europe. It brings together nearly 2 million advertisers and billions of customers. Through Google Ads services, marketers can place their ads both in the results of search engines like Google Search (the so-called Google Search Network) and on non-search websites, mobile apps, and videos (the Google Display Network). Services are offered under a pay-per-click (PPC) pricing model. Publishers can connect to the network through the Google Ad Sense service, which enables publishers to place third-party ads on their website, earning money based on the number of advertisement ad exposures (impressions) or clicks.

5 Examples of data management platforms include Oracle, Adobe, Salesforce (Krux), and Wunderman (KBM Group/Zipline). Data brokers include U.S. companies with a worldwide presence, such as Acxiom and Experian, and EU companies, such as France's Dawex and qDatum.

6 For example, NLP is commonly used in sentiment analysis to evaluate and classify attitudes and opinions on specific topics, such as consumers' positive or negative reviews and other assessments. See more on this subject, Meena Rambocas, João Gama and others, 'Marketing Research: The Role of Sentiment Analysis' (Universidade do Porto, Faculdade de Economia do Porto 2013).

7 On the uptake of psychological assessments of individuals based on social media data, see: Sandra C Matz and Oded Netzer, 'Using Big Data as a Window into Consumers' Psychology' (2017) 18 *Current Opinion in Behavioral Sciences* 7.

matching between ads and users. They extensively use data processing technologies to build user profiles that include preferences, desires, and needs.

Technology also mediates the delivery of advertising through the so-called programmatic advertising. These include systems, such as real-time bidding (RTB), which allow the automated selling and buying of advertisements. The system handles real-time micro-auctions, in which different marketers bid for the opportunity to target specific individuals based on profiles constructed around them.[8]

11.2 Societal Issues Related to OBA Markets

For a long time, European Union (EU) policymakers have taken a favourable stance towards the growth of online advertising and related industries. Online user tracking and digital advertising have represented, and still represent today, a very important tool for the development of the digital economy and society. As soon as the Internet opened to economic activities, advertising became a significant source of income for businesses; it promoted a series of organisational and technological innovations and permeated the online environment, contributing to shaping access to information and interaction among people. During this period, advertising was considered to strengthen consumer power and market efficiency: every consumer could view offers that best matched their preferences, reducing search costs and maximising the utility of browsing; companies could more effectively reach consumers interested in their products and services; advertising intermediaries, through profiling and content targeting technologies, allowed for efficient allocation of resources.

However, today, a more cautious attitude can be observed. This reflects the emergence of new societal issues. The ability to send targeted ads to individuals provides a growing incentive for massive and indiscriminate collection and sharing of personal data.[9] Most online activities are logged and used to create in-depth profiles of a user preferences and attitudes. As we shall see, users are thus constantly induced to consent to the processing of their personal data. They are forced to engage with a pervasive network of commercial surveillance,[10] the extent of which makes it practically impossible to know how personal data is being used or exchanged.[11]

8 An overview of the real-time bidding ecosystem is described in Jun Wang and others, 'Display Advertising with Real-Time Bidding (RTB) and Behavioural Targeting' (2017) 11 *Foundations and Trends in Information Retrieval* 297.

9 See, in general, S. Zuboff, *The Age of Surveillance Capitalism: The Fight for a Human Future at the New Frontier of Power* (Profile Books, 2019).

10 See Wolfie Christl and Sarah Spiekermann, *Networks of Control, A Report on Corporate Surveillance, Digital Tracking, Big Data & Privacy* (Facultas 2016).

11 See, e.g., Norwegian Consumer Authority, 'Out of Control. How Consumers Are Exploited by the Adtech Industry – and What We Are Doing to Make It Stop', 14 January 2020 <https://storage02.forbrukerradet.no/media/2020/01/2020-01-14-out-of-control-final-version.pdf> last access 30 August 2023 studying the data exchange practices of ten commonly used smart-phone app, noting the exchange with an average of 135 third parties involved in advertising and/or consumer behavioural profiling.

Current targeted advertising practices can also affect users beyond strict data privacy and affect autonomy in decision-making.[12] The strategic or uncontrolled use of profiles and personal information can erode users' ability to make adequately informed choices based on their preferences. People may be led to purchase unnecessary goods, spend too much time on viewing content, engage in risky financial transactions, or indulge in their weaknesses. The opportunity for undue influence is emphasised by psychographic techniques and emotion recognition technologies,[13] which allow for the exploitation of personality traits inferred from online behaviour to reveal opportunities for manipulation.

Problems regarding OBA are not limited to the commercial domain. Not only are users constantly bombarded with advertising messages, but the information they receive – including political propaganda – is also similarly influenced by the aim of capturing the user's attention.[14] Capturing attention can occur by providing users with useful and relevant information, but it can also be achieved by exposing them to messages – including fake news – that satisfy or excite them, confirm their biases, trigger negative feelings (e.g., anger or excitement), and provide additive symbolic rewards and punishments. Furthermore, users tend to receive content and messages that have attracted or satisfied similar individuals in the past, leading them to remain trapped in their own ideas (so-called filter bubbles).[15] In the long term, this can lead to polarisation and extremism, thus deteriorating public discourse.

11.3 The GDPR and Online Behavioural Advertising

As personal data moves the entire OBA ecosystem, the first framework called into play to regulate advertising markets in the EU is data protection laws.

In fact, the General Data Protection Regulation (GDPR)[16] applies to OBA when personal data processing operations are involved. While advertisers may argue that they are not processing personal data, given the fact that they do not tie personal

12 Regarding manipulation in OBA, see Ryan Calo, 'Digital Market Manipulation' (2013) 82 *The George Washington Law Review* 995, where he updates the concept of "market manipulation" elaborated by Hanson and Kysar to describe how companies exploit consumers' cognitive limitations to the reality of digital marketplaces by using the tool of persuasion through the personalisation of every aspect of the consumer experience. In the same line of research, see also: Daniel Susser, Beate Roessler and Helen Nissenbaum, 'Technology, Autonomy, and Manipulation' (2019) 8(2) *Internet Policy Review*.

13 See Mateja Durovic and Tommaso Corno, Chapter 13 of this book.

14 Claudio Celis Bueno, *The Attention Economy: Labour, Time and Power in Cognitive Capitalism* (Rowman & Littlefield 2016).

15 On this topic, two seminal contributions are Cass R Sunstein, *Infotopia: How Many Minds Produce Knowledge* (Oxford University Press 2006) and Eli Pariser, *The Filter Bubble: What the Internet Is Hiding from You* (Penguin UK 2011).

16 Regulation (EU) 2016/679 of the European Parliament and of the Council of 27 April 2016 on the protection of natural persons with regard to the processing of personal data and on the free movement of such data, and repealing Directive 95/46/EC [2016] OJ L119/1.

information to the user's profile,[17] scholarly work[18] and established case law of the European Court of Justice (ECJ)[19] already explained that this is generally the case based on the potential of OBA to single out persons, regardless of their names being identified. Also, regardless of the distinction between personal and non-personal data, one must remember that another prominent piece of EU data protection law also applies to the processing in the context of targeted advertising, namely the e-Privacy Directive.[20] The latter protects user privacy in electronic communication and contains important rules on data collection on users' devices (such as with cookies).

In theory, EU data protection law sets a highly restrictive framework for OBA. First of all, the GDPR always requires a legal basis for data processing operations involved in OBA. Among such bases are the data subject's consent, the necessity for the performance of a contract, legal obligation, vital interest, tasks to be performed in the public interest, and legitimate private interest. While, in theory, companies are free to decide the basis for the processing, as we shall see in the next section, the data subject's consent should be regarded as the most adequate legal basis. Moreover, according to Art. 5(3) of the e-Privacy Directive, the data subject's consent is required when data are collected directly on the user's device.

Second, it requires that data processing involved in targeted advertising respects data processing principles contained in Art. 5(1). Among these principles, purpose limitation and data minimisation are particularly relevant, as they constitute the foundation of the proportionality criterion underlying the protection of the European fundamental rights to data protection.[21] They respectively legitimise a privacy intrusion insofar as the collected data are strictly limited and necessary to pursue lawful, specific, and pre-established purposes.

Third, the Regulation provides data subjects targeted with OBA with a wide array of individual rights, among which are the rights to withdraw consent for data processing anytime and – if the legal basis used is the legitimate interest – to object to the processing of data for marketing purposes.

17 For example, Katharine Kemp, '"A Rose by Any Other Unique Identifier": Regulating Consumer Data Tracking and Anonymisation Claims" (2022) 21 *Competition Policy International TechReg Chronicle* (August 2022) shows that many advertisers give consumers the impression in privacy policies that collected data cannot have an impact on the individual (e.g., it will not be added to the individual consumer's profile) so it should be considered outside the scope of data protection regulation.

18 See, e.g., Frederik J Zuiderveen Borgesius, 'Singling Out People Without Knowing Their Names – Behavioural Targeting, Pseudonymous Data, and the New Data Protection Regulation' (2016) 32 *Computer Law & Security Review* 256.

19 Court of Justice of the European Union, Case 582/14 Breyer [2016], ECLI:EU:C:2016:779

20 Directive 2002/58/EC of the European Parliament and of the Council of 12 July 2002 concerning the processing of personal data and the protection of privacy in the electronic communications sectors [2002] OJ L201/37.

21 On the principle of proportionality in EU data protection law, see, among others, Lorenzo Dalla Corte, 'On Proportionality in the Data Protection Jurisprudence of the CJEU' (2022) 12(4) *International Data Privacy Law* 259.

Fourth, the GDPR prohibits automated decision-making that includes profiling and that may have a legal or similar effect on data subjects. As we will discuss in the next section, according to Art. 29 of the Working Party (WP), this may also include certain OBA practices based on several factors that may suggest a particularly significant effect on the data subjects.

Fifth, data controllers are required to adopt a privacy-by-design approach to data processing and adequate security measures to mitigate the risks connected to data processing. When the risks are particularly high, they must implement a Data Protection Impact Assessment (DPIA), which is a core tool of the accountability principle; namely, to proactively estimate risk connected to data processing and adopt technical and organisational measures to prevent such risks from materialising into privacy harms.

Finally, the GDPR provides an enforcement framework highly relevant to the OBA ecosystem. It entrusts national data protection authorities with supervisory power on the application of substantive rules, possibly through transnational cooperation with other digital protection acts (DPAs) and the consistency mechanisms provided by the European Data Protection Board.

11.4 The Regulatory Mismatch

Despite the robust legal framework existing to protect privacy in the online advertising sector, data protection experts are still desperately waiting to see tangible improvements in people's privacy. A 2020 EU Agency for Fundamental Rights survey[22] shows that, after two years of the GDPR being in force, most EU citizens are still concerned about their personal data being misused. For example, around 30% worry about advertisers, businesses, and foreign governments' access to information without them knowing. Other empirical findings show that citizens are generally aware of their rights, but few of them consider them adequate to limit data collection and exchange in advertising networks.[23]

In the next section, we shall discuss some potential reasons for this, identifying five mismatches between the GDPR and OBA.

11.4.1 Data Protection Principles

Where extensive data collection is the norm, data protection principles often clash with online advertising practices.

22 European Union Agency for Fundamental Rights (FRA), 'Our Rights Matter: Data Protection and Privacy, Fundamental Rights Survey' (2020) <https://fra.europa.eu/en/publication/2020/fundamental-rights-report-2020> accessed 30 August 2023.

23 See, e.g., Among all, see, e.g., Edith G Smit, Guda Van Noort and Hilde A M Voorveld, 'Understanding Online Behavioural Advertising: User Knowledge, Privacy Concerns and Online Coping Behaviour in Europe' (2014) 32 *Computers in Human Behavior* 15, as well as Joanna Strycharz, Jef Ausloos and Natali Helberger, 'Data Protection or Data Frustration? Individual Perceptions and Attitudes Towards the GDPR' (2020) 6 *European Data Protection Law Review* 407.

For example, while the GDPR expects organisations to provide a detailed account of the personal data flows,[24] including who the data controllers are and with whom data are shared, OBA data practices often do not show such a degree of transparency. Reports provide systemic non-compliance with certain information items in privacy policies, the use of vague language and generic terms, and the lack of granularity of categories of collected and pursued purposes.[25] To a certain extent, this degree of opacity is intrinsic to the ad tech ecosystem, and the blame cannot be placed solely on the individual website.[26] For example, publishers should tell in advance the user the identity of the trader on behalf of whom the website will display the ad. However, in RTB–auction-based systems, it is often impossible to predict who will win an auction, as this depends on multiple factors, not least how the algorithms make the RTB work.

Next, the GDPR places a strong emphasis on the principle of data minimisation, which mandates that personal data should be adequate, relevant, and limited to what is necessary for the purposes for which it is processed.[27] However, the OBA ecosystem relies on a comprehensive and continuous collection of user data. While this extensive data gathering serves the purpose of creating detailed user profiles for targeted advertising, it frequently exceeds what is strictly necessary for ad delivery.[28]

Third, the principle of purpose limitation demands that personal data are collected for "specified, explicit and legitimate purposes" and not further processed in a manner that is incompatible with those purposes.[29] In our context, while initial data collection may be for the purpose of serving relevant ads, the complexity of the OBA ecosystem often leads to the use of personal data for unforeseen or secondary purposes.[30] Data collected may find its way into other analytics, or even

24 This can be derived from the general principle of lawfulness, fairness, and transparency contained in Art. 5(1)(a), as well as from the information items that must be disclosed to data subjects before the processing takes place, according to Arts. 13 and 14 of the GDPR.

25 Giuseppe Contissa and others, 'Claudette Meets GDPR: Automating the Evaluation of Privacy Policies Using Artificial Intelligence' (2018) <https://www.beuc.eu/sites/default/files/publications/beuc-x-2018-066_claudette_meets_gdpr_report.pdf>. More recently, Alexander J Wulf and Ognyan Seizov, '"Please Understand We Cannot Provide Further Information": Evaluating Content and Transparency of GDPR-Mandated AI Disclosures' (2022) *AI & Society* 1.

26 According to Michael Veale and Frederik Zuiderveen Borgesius, 'Adtech and Real-Time Bidding Under European Data Protection Law' (2022) 23 *German Law Journal* 226, the actor-based complexity of RTB makes it one of the most solid barriers for ensuring GDPR-compliance.

27 Art. 5(1)(c) of the GDPR.

28 Ioanna D Constantiou and Jannis Kallinikos, 'New Games, New Rules: Big Data and the Changing Context of Strategy' (2015) 30 *Journal of Information Technology* 44. According to the authors, while traditional business strategies would respond to the need to collect data intentionally and purposefully to inform specific theoretical models and provide predefined input to the decision-making process, Big Data can be made business-relevant after its collection, but its relevance may not straightforwardly be derived from original data records.

29 Art. 5(1)(b) of the GDPR.

30 See Michèle Finck and Asia Biega, 'Reviving Purpose Limitation and Data Minimisation in Personalisation, Profiling and Decision-Making Systems', *Max Planck Institute for Innovation & Competition Research Paper* (11 January 2021) <https://doi.org/10.48550/arXiv.2101.06203>.

be sold to third parties for unrelated purposes. Moreover, it is hardly ever the case that purposes are specifically determined in privacy policies. OBA often relies on vague and broad disclosure mechanisms that do not adequately inform users about the precise purposes of data collection.

11.4.2 Data Controllership

Under the GDPR, establishing the roles of data controller and data processor is crucial in determining responsibilities and ensuring compliance. The data controller is the entity determining purposes and means of the processing and therefore is the one considered ultimately accountable if processing does not comply with the GDPR. Controllers can act alone or jointly with others. If multiple controllers exist, they must transparently determine their responsibilities (in particular, with regard to data subjects' rights and information) and comply with them.[31] On the other hand, the data processor acts on behalf of the controller, carrying out the actual processing activities and being responsible for implementing data security measures.

In OBA, determining the data controller among all the stakeholders can be convoluted. While some entities may act as data controllers for specific processing activities, the overall division of roles remains ambiguous. The consequence of this is that each actor in OBA attempts to allocate significant responsibility elsewhere, possibly misclassifying themselves, for example, either as data processors or not processing data at all. Also, OBA often involves collective decision-making regarding data processing activities. Advertisers, publishers, and advertising networks jointly collaborate to target users with personalised ads based on their online behaviour. These collaborative efforts can blur the lines between data controllers and processors.

This complex situation creates significant problems both for data subjects and DPAs. Data subjects are not generally aware of the specific entities involved in data processing, making it challenging to know which party to contact regarding data-related requests. Similarly, such opacity has long left DPAs struggling to know who to enforce against first, engaging in disagreements with entities about their status within data protection before coming to substantive conclusions about enforcement. Courts have increasingly used joint controllership to deal with the many actors who can influence how data is processed online, including in the value chain in online advertising,[32] but this has to be decided case by case and stifle a systematic allocation of responsibilities.

A clear example of this shortcoming and how new daring interpretations are needed to bypass it is provided by the recent litigation brought forward by the Belgian DPA against IAB Europe, the latter being a membership organisation coordinating various efforts concerning the RTB.[33] On 2 February 2022, the Belgian

31 Article 26 of the GDPR.

32 Court of Justice of the European Union, C-40/17 Fashion ID GmbH & Co.KG v Verbraucherzentrale [2019], ECLI:EU:C:2019:629 where the Court concluded that a website embedding a social network plug-in is a joint controller together with the social media platform, as it profits from visibility and optimisation of its products and services (paras. 78–79).

33 A summary of the proceeding can be found at <www.dataprotectionauthority.be/citizen/iab-europe-held-responsible-for-a-mechanism-that-infringes-the-gdpr> accessed 30 August 2023.

DPA issued a decision the Transparency and Consent Framework (TCF), a standard designed by IAB to facilitate the compliance of RTB with consent-based protection set by the GDPR,[34] declaring it in breach of Arts. 5–6 of the regulation. It is striking is that while previous DPAs' investigations in the OBA ecosystem have addressed dubious processing practices by organisations holding personal data, the Belgian DPA's decision has taken action against IAB Europe itself, characterising the association as a joint controller together with all actors participating in the RTB ecosystem. What is odd is that IAB Europe itself process no personal data in the RTB ecosystem and does not profit from it but is just the entity designing and managing the standard (i.e., TCF), which, however, is inextricably part of the processing undertaken by all actors in RTB interested in legally operating in Europe.

11.4.3 Legal Bases and Consent

11.4.3.1 The Quest for a Legal Basis

As anticipated in the previous section, data subjects' consent is today considered the only possible legal basis for a legitimate OBA practice. We got to this juncture after a long debate, the main point of contention being whether controllers can use the contractual necessity and the legitimate interest as a legal basis for collecting data to engage in OBA practices.

As early as 2010, Art. 29 WP in Opinion 2/2010 on online behavioural advertising[35] did not even consider using contract and legitimate interest as a legal basis for OBA, as it assumed that consent was necessary. The opinion was influenced by the discussion around the e-Privacy Directive, which at the time was amended to replace implicit with explicit consent. The Group used the *lex specialis* argument to hold that affirmative consent was also needed under the then-in-force general Data Protection Directive.[36] The problem is, however, far from obvious: the cookie consent mandate outlined in the e-Privacy Directive cannot serve as the sole legal basis for processing personal data for OBA purposes. An autonomous legal basis must be found in the general data protection law.[37]

The discussion has resurfaced after the entry into force of the GDPR, especially considering the newly added Recital 47, which states that "the processing

34 Autorité de Protection des Données, Decision on the merits 21/2022 of 2 February 2022 (Case number DOS-2019–01377). For an extended comment on this decision, we refer to Michael Veale, Midas Nouwens and Cristiana Santos, 'Impossible Asks: Can the Transparency and Consent Framework Ever Authorise Real-Time Bidding After the Belgian DPA Decision?' (2022) *Technology and Regulation* 12.

35 Article 29 Working Party, Opinion 2/2010 on online behavioural advertising, Adopted on 22 June 2010.

36 Directive 95/46/EC of the European Parliament and of the Council of 24 October 1995 on the protection of individuals with regard to the processing of personal data and on the free movement of such data [1995], OJ L281/31.

37 Frederik J Zuiderveen Borgesius, 'Personal Data Processing for Behavioural Targeting: Which Legal Basis?' (2015) 5 *International Data Privacy Law* 163.

of personal data for direct marketing purposes may be regarded as carried out for a legitimate interest". This provision cast doubts on whether the EU legislature intended to include the OBA under this legitimate interest exemption.

At this point, the topic was taken up by the European Data Protection Board (EDPB), with somewhat conflicting opinions. In the 2017 Guidelines on Art. 22,[38] the Board has emphasised that in certain cases, OBA may qualify as automated decision-making having a similarly significant effect on the data subject (see *infra*), which should be prohibited unless explicit consent is obtained. In the 2019 Guidelines on contractual necessity in online service,[39] the Board seems to have come to a resolution arguing that the necessity to perform a contract cannot provide a general valid reason for the controller/provider to collect data for OBA, even if the service is backed up only by advertising revenues. Regarding legitimate interest, there is a slightly different stance. The 2014 Opinion on legitimate interest[40] suggests that simple one-to-one marketing initiatives may be covered by a legitimate interest, subject to adequate safeguards and measures, and after meeting the balancing test. In more complex cases, including those involving extensive profiling, data sharing, or behavioural advertisement, consent should be the basis. The same rationale was reaffirmed in the 2021 Guidelines on targeting in social media:[41] if targeting is based on declared data, then legitimate interest is a sufficient legal basis; if it is based on observed or inferred data, consent is needed.

A decisive milestone has been set by the recent ruling by the ECJ in the case *Meta Platforms Inc and Others v Bundeskartellamt*.[42] This case originates in a 2019 decision of the German Federal Cartel Office,[43] which condemned Facebook for conditioning the use of its social network on the user's consent to a wide range

38 Article 29 Working Party, Guidelines on Automated individual decision-making and Profiling for the purposes of Regulation 2016/679, Adopted on 3 October 2017 as last Revised and Adopted on 6 February 2018.

39 European Data Protection Board, Guidelines 2/2019 on the processing of personal data under Art. 6(1)(b) GDPR in the context of the provision of online services to data subjects, Version 2.0, 8 October 2019.

40 Article 29 Working Party, Opinion 06/2014 on the notion of legitimate interests of the data controller under Art. 7 of Directive 95/46/EC, Adopted on 9 April 2014.

41 European Data Protection Board, Guidelines 8/2020 on the targeting of social media users, Version 2.0, Adopted on 13 April 2021.

42 Court of Justice of the European Union, C-252/21 Meta Platforms Inc and Others v Bundeskartellamt [2023], ECLI:EU:C:2023:537

43 Bundeskartellamt, B6–22/16. According to the Authority, it was acceptable to make the use of Facebook conditional on consent to the collection of data generated through Facebook itself, i.e., to exclude from Facebook those users who refused to consent to be tracked when using Facebook. However, the combination of data generated by services different from Facebook would require separate user consent, which should be "voluntary", such that refusal to consent to this processing operation would not affect the use of the social network. Ultimately, the decision declared that this conduct, since it was inconsistent with the GDPR, constituted an abuse of Facebook's dominant position on the market for online social networks. An English summary of the decision can be found at <www.bundeskartellamt.de/SharedDocs/Meldung/EN/Pressemitteilungen/2019/07_02_2019_Facebook.html> accessed 30 August 2023.

of processing operations over their data, including the combination, under the same user profile, of data collected by Facebook, by Facebook-owned services, and by third parties. Facebook brought an action against that decision before the Düsseldorf Higher Regional Court, and the Court referred the matter to the ECJ for a preliminary ruling, having doubts, first, as to whether national competition authorities can review whether the processing of personal data complies with the GDPR and, second, the interpretation and application of certain GDPR provisions. Among the latter point, two significant questions relate to OBA, namely (1) whether a social network can collect user data from services and websites other than the social network based on the justification of necessity to perform the social media contract; and (2) whether data processing for purposes such as "content personalisation", "personalised advertising", "measurement and analytics to enable advertising to improve the service", among others, may be justified under the legitimate interest legal basis.

By its judgement delivered on 4 July 2023, the Court ruled that, generally, data processing for advertising purposes is lawful if and to the extent that the data subject has given consent for one or more specific purposes. In the absence of such consent, or where that consent was not valid, the contractual performance and the legitimate interest can be provided as justification as long as they are strictly necessary. Regarding contractual necessity, the Court stresses the fact that the processing for advertising must be "objectively indispensable" for a purpose that is integral to the contractual obligation intended for those users, such that the main subject matter of the contract cannot be achieved if that processing does not occur.[44] For the legitimate interest, the Court applies the three-tier test proposed by Art. 29 WP and states that processing for advertising purposes can be based on legitimate interest if: (1) the controller has informed data subjects of such legitimate interest; (2) the processing is carried out only insofar as is strictly necessary for the purposes; and (3) it is apparent from a balancing of the opposing interests, having regard to all the relevant circumstances, that the interests or fundamental freedoms and rights of those users do not override that legitimate interest of the controller or of a third party.[45] On the latter issues, the Court also finds that, in the absence of consent on their part, the interests and fundamental rights of those users are presumed to override the interest of the operator of an online social network in personalised advertising through which it finances its activity.[46]

Therefore, the ECJ seems to have ended the discussion: individual consent is the only legal basis providing a general justification for OBA data processing.

11.4.3.2 Consent and Its Limits

We severely doubt that admitting that only consent can provide a legal basis for OBA is necessarily the best option to ensure higher data subject protection. Consent is

44 C-252/21 *Meta Platforms Inc and Others v Bundeskartellamt* [2023], para. 98.
45 Ibid para. 126.
46 Ibid para. 117.

typically the most challenging legal basis to establish because the GDPR requires it to be: (1) free, namely that it represents a genuine and real choice of the data subjects; (2) specific, i.e., the data subject must be able to consent to each different purpose of the processing, if present; (3) informed, namely the data subject must be aware of a bare minimum of characteristics related to the processing; and (4) unambiguous, i.e., that consent must be provided through affirmative action and cannot be assumed by implicit behaviours.[47] Several criticisms have already pointed to the impracticability of such rigorous consent in the OBA ecosystem, given a mix of socio-technical complexity, consumer cognitive limitations, and dubious business practices.

Under present socio-technical conditions, individuals are frequently asked for consent for complex data processing operations involved in OBA. These operations often use advanced technologies and intricate organisational arrangements, making it challenging for most users to assess the risks and privacy costs associated with OBA. Moreover, personal data can be aggregated and analysed in unpredictable ways, giving rise to information that was not expected when consent was given, leading to unexpected uses and "context creep" for data subjects.[48] After all, the GDPR's consent framework often treats consent as a one-time event rather than an ongoing process, but OBA relies on continuous data gathering to update user profiles and deliver personalised advertisements.

The impracticability of valid consent in OBA has clearly emerged in the already-mentioned OpenRTB investigation undertaken by the Belgian DPA. The DPA has noted that, in this regard, consent faces several challenges. First, the processing objectives imposed by IAB Europe on TCF participants are excessively ambiguous and, at times, even misleading, making it difficult to establish specific consent ("measure content performance"; "apply market research to generate audience insights"). Second, the involvement of numerous parties makes it excessively time-consuming for data subjects to comprehend to whom they are granting consent, and to be adequately informed. Third, the consent requests scrutinised by the Belgian DPA fail to furnish adequate summaries regarding the categories of collected data, and they lack the necessary level of detail regarding the various processing activities conducted by each vendor. Finally, users are unable to effectively retract their consent because, upon doing so, ad tech vendors are essentially unable to process the personal data of a data subject, rendering it impossible to determine the source of the withdrawal request.

On top of technical complexity, the impracticability of consent is based on empirical findings on consumer cognitive limitations. In fact, for consent to be effective, data subjects not only need complete and legally compliant information but

47 Art. 4(11) of the GDPR.

48 See, e.g., the study by Blase Ur and others, 'Smart, Useful, Scary, Creepy: Perceptions of Online Behavioral Advertising' *Proceedings of the Eighth Symposium on Usable Privacy and Security* (2012) <https://doi.org/10.1145/2335356.2335362>, which shows that users have deep concerns about data collection, and most participants believed that advertisers collect personally identifiable information. They also misunderstand the role of advertising networks, basing their opinions on an advertising network on that company's non-advertising activities.

also the motivation and ability to understand it. Both recipient- and disclosure-related factors must be considered.

The first category encompasses the data subject's motivation and biases. Motivation refers to the individual's level of interest and willingness to engage with the information provided. In many cases, consumers may lack the motivation to thoroughly review and understand lengthy privacy policies or consent forms, especially when the process is perceived as tedious or time-consuming or when access to a service is made dependent on a consent decision.[49] Additionally, biases – whether cognitive or emotional – can influence how consumers interpret and respond to consent requests. Pre-existing beliefs, trust in the data collector, or emotional responses can all shape an individual's decision-making process.[50]

Disclosure-related factors refer to the quality and comprehensibility of the information presented to the data subject. While *informativeness* is a critical aspect for informed consent, indicating whether the provided information is clear, concise, and adequately explains the data processing activities involved, privacy policies are filled with vague terms, legal jargon, or non-informative details.[51] This lack of informativeness can result in confusion or misunderstanding, rendering consent ineffective. *Completeness* is another vital element, signifying whether the disclosure covers all relevant aspects of data processing, potential risks, and the intended purposes. However, privacy policies are hardly complete: data controllers frequently retain valuable pieces of information, such as how they convert personal data into profiles, and the risks of relevant processing operations.

On top of this, dubiously legal practices are carried out systematically by ads-displaying websites. Users are often presented with pre-checked boxes or bundled consent options that encompass various purposes, making it difficult for them to opt out and exercise meaningful choices. In addition, service providers often fall short of enabling users to exercise this right effectively. Users may not have straightforward means to opt out of data collection and profiling. Even when opt-out options are available, they may not be clearly communicated or may require users to navigate a complex web of settings and preferences.

Given these factors, insisting on regulating OBA through GDPR-consent-based protection while neglecting all the emerging evidence about its failures seems like an unproductive approach. Either consent-based regulation is pushed through, however, with the result that most part of the OBA market is declared outside the law,[52]

49 On motivation to read privacy policy, see Edith G Smit and others (n. 23).

50 For an overview of how different cognitive biases affect privacy decisions and how these are leveraged by website designers, see Ari Ezra Waldman, 'Cognitive Biases, Dark Patterns, and the "Privacy Paradox"' (2020) 31 *Current Opinion in Psychology* 105.

51 On language and informativeness in privacy policies, see Tatiana Ermakova and others, 'Privacy Policies and Users' Trust: Does Readability Matter?' in *AMCIS 2014 Proceedings, Human Computer Interaction* (2014) <https://aisel.aisnet.org/amcis2014/HumanComputerInteraction/GeneralPresentations/14> accessed 30 August 2023.

52 After the landmark ruling of the ECJ, the Norwegian DPA has declared that Meta's data collection practices for the purpose of targeted advertising are unlawful and has consequently imposed a

or one should come to the realisation that, as things stand, consent may not provide adequate safeguards and alternative forms of protection should be considered.

One could even push the argument forward and ask, with a view to providing greater protection to data subjects, while embracing the spirit of the GDPR,[53] if it would not be better to rather allow OBA based on legitimate interest. Indeed, while consent requires data subjects to analyse the risks of data processing, legitimate interest shifts the burden on the data controllers, who must balance their own interests with the rights, freedoms, and interests of data subjects. A strict interpretation and guidance of this balancing test, plus greater control on accountability by supervisory agencies, would arguably provide higher protection than consent as it is now.

11.4.4 Legitimate Profiling

OBA normally entails profiling under Art. 4(4) of the GDPR, as it always implies an assessment of an individual's characteristics, although the GDPR is quite ambiguous on the legal regime applicable to profiling. The first ambiguity pertains to whether profiling is to be regarded as a kind of data processing or as a purposed process entailing different processing (e.g., data collection, data analysis, data use, etc.). Article 29 WP[54] seems to take the first stance and requires that profiling abide by all general provisions, including data protection principles and legal bases.[55] A second concern relates to the degree to which profiling is covered by Art. 22. It is not clear whether profiling is covered regardless of an automated decision taking place. In the negative, the prohibition of Art. 22 would not apply to OBA unless a decision is taken; thus, it would not apply to the assessments performed through data analytics. On the positive, data analysis would be prohibited if the resulting assessment may have an impact on the data subjects' rights and freedom or similarly significantly affect the data subject.

In any case, it is noteworthy that Art. 29 WP itself holds that, in certain cases, OBA may amount to a decision having a significant effect on data subjects.[56] This may happen, depending on the particular features of the case, including the intrusiveness of the profiling process, including the tracking of individuals on different

---

temporary ban on Facebook and Instagram's OBA. See <www.datatilsynet.no/contentassets/36ad4a92100943439df9a8a3a7015c19/urgent-and-provisional-measures–meta_redacted.pdf>.

53 See, Tuulia Karjalainen, 'All Talk, No Action? The Effect of the GDPR Accountability Principle on the EU Data Protection Paradigm' (2022) 8 *European Data Protection Law Review* 19, where the author suggests that legitimate interest legal basis and the accountability principle enshrined in the GDPR reform should be seen as alternative to data subjects' and public preventive control.

54 Article 29 Working Party, Guidelines on Automated individual decision-making and Profiling for the purposes of Regulation 2016/679, Adopted on 3 October 2017, as last revised and adopted on 6 February 2018.

55 Guidelines on Automated Individual Decision-making, p. 9. In particular, according to Art. 29 WP, profiling should be transparent, and the data subject shall have the right to know how profilin works; it must be fair, thus not leading to unfair discrimination; controllers must make sure they comply with data minimisation and purpose limitation principles; a legal basis is always required, though no precedence should be given to one over the other.

56 Guidelines on Automated individual decision-making, p. 22.

websites, devices, and services; the expectations and wishes of the persons concerned; the manner in which the advertisement is made available; or the exploitation of the vulnerability knowledge of the data subjects involved. The assessment must be made case by case; however, the criteria listed by the WP seem to cover much of the risks connected to OBA types of processing.

First, tracking across multiple platforms is deeply invasive, as it collects data not only about what users do on a specific website but also their online behaviour across the entire Internet ecosystem. Second, empirical studies suggest that the average user does not fully grasp the extent of data tracking and the depth of profiling practices and has instead high expectations regarding online privacy.[57] Third, excessive ad repetition can lead to user annoyance and frustration, while certain forms of advertising may subtly influence users beyond their reasonable perception. Finally, multiple sources have raise a voice against the OBA practices that exploit users' vulnerabilities, such as by targeting them with health-related advertisements based on their search history or by categorising them based on sensible attributes, such as political opinions or sexual orientation.[58]

From these factors, one might derive that, to a large extent, OBA practices would be prohibited under Art. 22, par. 1. In that case, however, the exceptions in par. 2 would still apply, among which explicit consent. The discussion thus goes back to consent again. Given the higher demand of explicit consent, what was said previously about ordinary consent under Art. 6(1)(a) holds true even more.

11.4.5 Risk Assessment and Privacy by Design

The GDPR promotes a risk-based approach. The data controller is responsible to carry out a risk assessment considering the nature, scope, context and scope of the envisaged processing.[59] Such risk assessment should, then, lead the data controller to implement appropriate technical and organisational measures to be able to demonstrate that processing is performed in accordance with the Regulation. On top of that, in cases whereby the processing is likely to result in a "high risk" to data subjects' rights and freedoms, the GDPR mandates a DPIA, namely a structured process used to assess and manage the potential risks and impacts.[60]

57 See, among others, Moritz Büchi and others, 'Making Sense of Algorithmic Profiling: User Perceptions on Facebook' (2023) 26 *Information, Communication & Society* 809, where the authors show the lack of awareness and differently surprising reactions in Facebook behavioural advertising.

58 José González Cabañas, Ángel Cuevas and Rubén Cuevas, 'Unveiling and Quantifying Facebook Exploitation of Sensitive Personal Data for Advertising Purposes' (2018) *27th USENIX Security Symposium (USENIX Security 18)* <https://www.usenix.org/system/files/conference/usenixsecurity18/sec18-cabanas.pdf>, where the Authors have shown that Facebook labels 73% EU users with potential sensitive interests and that this information may maliciously be used by third parties to unveil Facebook users' identity accessed 30 August 2023.

59 Art. 24 of the GDPR.

60 According to Art. 35 of the GDPR, the DPIA entails the following activities: the identification of the data processing activities, an assessment of the necessity and proportionality requirements, an

According to Art. 35(3) and the guidelines on DPIA released by the Art. 29 WP,[61] data controllers engaged in OBA practices should carry out a DPIA, as the implied processing operations are likely to result in high risk for data subjects. For example, OBA extensively relies on profiling and predicting user behaviour based on various aspects concerning the data subject's online activities, such as their interests, behaviour, and preferences. Moreover, OBA often combines data from various sources and across different platforms to build comprehensive user profiles. Moreover, OBA frequently employs innovative technologies and techniques to track and target users.

The extent to which OBA actors perform a DPIA is not clear. The IAB produced guidelines on how a DPIA should be carried out by data controllers in OBA,[62] but there is no actual figure on whether these guidelines are followed. In any case, the DPIA in the GDPR presents a systemic flaw, which makes it particularly ineffective in ensuring accountability in OBA: there is no actual mechanism to involve data subjects in risk assessment. First, the controller is under no obligation to consult the data subject or their representative during the DPIA.[63] Moreover, after the DPIA has been carried out, the data controller has an obligation to provide the related documentation only to the DPA and only when an investigation is underway, though no obligation exists to disclose it to data subjects whether and how a DPIA has been carried out. This shortcoming can lead to a DPIA process being primarily reliant on the organisation's perspective. As a result, certain risks associated with OBA, which may only be evident to data subjects who experience them first-hand, could be overlooked or underestimated. At the same time, without meaningful engagement in the DPIA process, data subjects may remain in the dark about how their data is being used and the potential consequences.

Within the risk assessment approaches, the GDPR also promotes the concept of privacy by design,[64] encouraging organisations to consider data protection from the outset of any data processing activity. With its reliance on third-party tracking and data sharing, online advertising often falls short of this principle. The complexity of the ad tech ecosystem makes it challenging to implement robust privacy safeguards, leaving user data vulnerable. The same holds for privacy by default, as OBA infrastructure's defaults lean towards collecting extensive data rather than not, which may exceed what is necessary for ad targeting.

---

evaluation of risks to data subjects, and the implementation of risk mitigation measures. The DPIA must be documented, and assessments and measures must be reviewed and updated regularly.

61 Article 29 Working Party, Guidelines on Data Protection Impact Assessment (DPIA) and determining whether processing is "likely to result in a high risk" for the purposes of Regulation 2016/679, wp248rev.01.

62 IAB Europe Legal Committee, GDPR Data Protection Impact Assessments (DPIA) for Digital Advertising under GDPR (2020) <https://iabeurope.eu/knowledge-hub/guide-gdpr-data-protection-impact-assessments-dpia-for-digital-advertising-under-gdpr>.

63 As clearly stated by Art. 35(9) of the GDPR, this option is completely left to the discretion of the data controller.

64 Art. 25(1) and (2) of the GDPR.

One of the most apparent frustrations of these principles relates to the widespread deployment of dark patterns.[65] In OBA, this refers to manipulative and deceptive design techniques employed by advertisers and websites to trick or coerce users into taking actions they may not intend to. These patterns exploit user psychology and lack transparency, often leading individuals to unknowingly consent to data collection or engage with ads. They can include misleading prompts, confusing opt-in processes, and concealed data tracking, ultimately eroding user privacy and trust in online advertising practices.

Standard settings in OBA ecosystems also tend to frustrate the integrity and security of personal data.[66] The volume of data involved in automated exchanges of data such as data management platforms (DMP) and RTB is massive, with thousands of entities processing billions of data points regularly. However, reports suggest that there is often inconsistent application of adequate security measures to protect this data during transmission and storage. There have been multiple claims that OBA is responsible for frequent data leaks and distribution of malicious ads, as well as unauthorised access to user data during OBA processes.

Some OBA companies may argue that they implement security measures, such as pseudonymisation, processing data without being able to identify an individual. However, relying solely on pseudonymisation does not necessarily meet the GDPR's rigorous security requirements. Moreover, although benefiting from relaxed repurposing requirements, pseudonymised data are still personal data under the GDPR, and unless advertisers anonymise data – which is hardly the case given the need to signal users out to effectively target them with personalised advertising[67] – they still must have a legal basis and comply with data protection principles.

11.5 Taking Stock and the Way Forward: A Crossroads?

In the current situation, it seems that the GDPR and the broader EU data protection regime are unsuitable to address privacy challenges connected to OBA markets.

The assumption that informational self-determination on the data subjects' side and the freedom to exploit personal data to conduct business on the traders' side would provide a win-win situation for all parties involved has not met the reality test.

If that objective were accomplished, all of the following would be true: (1) companies would process personal data insofar as such data are strictly necessary for providing advertising; (2) beyond strict necessity, companies would process personal data based on a free, informed, unambiguous, freely given consent expressed by the data subject; which in turn means that (3) companies disclose what information

65 Christoph Bösch and others, 'Tales from the Dark Side: Privacy Dark Strategies and Privacy Dark Patterns' (2016) 2016(4) *Proceedings on Privacy Enhancing Technologies* 237.

66 Information Commissioner's Office, 'Update Report into Adtech and Real Time Bidding' (20 June 2019) <https://ico.org.uk/media/about-the-ico/documents/2615156/adtech-real-time-bidding-report-201906.pdf> accessed 31 August 2023, p. 23.

67 Sophie C Boerman, Sanne Kruikemeier and Frederik J Zuiderveen Borgesius, 'Online Behavioral Advertising: A Literature Review and Research Agenda' (2017) 46 *Journal of Advertising* 363.

is created on users' profiles and would are the risks connected to it, without making underlying service conditional on the obtaining of consent; (4) companies would refrain from carrying out profiling practices when, based on genuine risk assessment, there is evidence that they might affect data subject's behaviours; and (5) certain technological settings, such as RTB, would be ruled out to move towards more privacy-preserving options.

However, reality does not fit this ideal picture. Data subjects are largely swayed into consenting to data processing by the design or the market forces underlying current OBA ecosystems. If they can choose, they generally consent their privacy away without understanding much of the underlying processing operations. On the other hand, data controllers systematically reject accountability, and if they accept it, they do little to translate data protection principles into practices. They maintain full secrecy on profiling practices and derived information items for competitive advantage while resting on technological settings provided by leading market players or coordinating entities.

The mismatch is not only a matter of effectiveness but is also visible considering the larger societal move in the relationships between data-driven advertising companies and individuals.[68] Personally identifiable information has become less significant than the probabilistic insights that enable anticipating and influencing people's behaviour. Individual data only hold relevance when they can be analysed with data from others, possibly gathered in different contexts. Individual consent has lost its power, probably due to its excessive and unnecessary use, de facto disabling its legal effects. Moreover, it misses societal interests behind privacy that go beyond their ability to make free decisions about their own informational selves.[69] On the other hand, we have come to the realisation that business interest cannot provide a lawful basis for OBA practices, either via legitimate interests or via contractual obligations, as it cannot override clearly emerging risks for individuals' rights and freedoms. Profiling techniques, which are growing increasingly intricate, have become the standard method of processing, yet technical and legal prerequisites for enhancing transparency have not been established. The principle of privacy by design seems to be entirely thwarted, to the point that its promoter Ann Cavoukian talked about "surveillance by design" to suggest how the market leans toward privacy-invasive technological solutions rather than privacy-preserving ones.[70]

68 See, Jens-Erik Mai, 'Big Data Privacy: The Datafication of Personal Information' (2016) 32(3) *The Information Society* 192. The author advances the idea of a datafication model of privacy, whereby regulation would be concerned with the ability to classify and sort people based on the available data and the kind of information protected should be produced by data processing and analysis. In a similar vein, see the reconstruction in Alessandro Mantelero, 'The Future of Consumer Data Protection in the EU Rethinking the "Notice and Consent" Paradigm in the New Era of Predictive Analytics' (2014) 30(6) *Computer Law & Security Review* 643.

69 For a critique on the individual dimension of consent and the need to move to a collective approach to data protection, see Alessandro Mantelero, 'Personal Data for Decisional Purposes in the Age of Analytics: From an Individual to a Collective Dimension of Data Protection' (2016) 32(2) *Computer Law & Security Review* 238.

70 Ann Cavoukian, 'Op-Ed: Beware of "Surveillance by Design"' (*The Post*, 2011) <https://financialpost.com/technology/op-ed-beware-of-surveillance-by-design> accessed 30 August 2023.

We believe that this deadlock can largely be attributed to an inconsistency inherent in the current data protection framework: the coexistence of the ideas that data is an inalienable asset protected by a fundamental right with fundamental societal stakes attached to it, but at the same time that consent to data processing can provide a counter-performance to a direct or indirect economic benefit.[71] This contradiction may be visible in Art. 7(4) and in the persistent political[72] and doctrinal debate[73] on whether the GDPR actually prohibits bundling consent to the provision of online services. Therefore, the way to overcome this situation is to take two different directions, between which we believe a choice will have to be made, or at least a balance will have to be struck. One must either: (1) accept that privacy is exclusively in the individual sphere, with the possibility of the data subject surrendering his or her data in exchange for direct or indirect benefits, while doing everything to allow the expression of a genuine and free choice, or (2) go beyond the idea of individual informational self-determination and find other regulatory regimes that support the idea that there is more to privacy-compliant online advertising than the individual protection of personal data.

The first avenue entails re-establishing the data protection information and consent paradigm, making sure by a legislative mandate that the socio-technical apparatus behind OBA makes its best effort to ensure that consent is informed and free. The second path implies an acknowledgement that the OBA ecosystem can no longer be regulated exclusively by limiting data collection and that different regulatory objectives should be targeted to preserve privacy and other social interests.

71 More extensively on this point, see Federico Galli, Francesca Lagioia and Giovanni Sartor, 'Consent to Targeted Advertising' (2022) 33 *European Business Law Review* 485.

72 Art. 7(4) of the GDPR states that when assessing whether consent is freely given, an account shall be taken of whether, inter alia, the performance of a contract, including the provision of a service, is conditional on consent to the processing of personal data that is not necessary for the performance of that contract. While the EDPB argues that the wording of Art. 7 para. 4, in conjunction with Recital 43, means that the legal grounds of consent and contract performance are included in Art. 6(1)(a) and (b) "cannot be merged and blurred", others challenge an interpretation of the provision as an outright rejection of the current dominant online business model. For example, Klement posits that Art. 7 para. 4 cannot be interpreted as prohibiting "bundling" per se. He argues that the controller's obligation to "take utmost account" of the effect of the conditionality upon the data subject's ability to consent "freely" means that a certain level of conditionality must, in principle, be permitted under specific circumstances. See Klement, J H, in S Simitis, G Hornung and I Spieker gen. Döhmann (eds), *Datenschutzrecht, Nomos, Baden-Baden*, 2019, Artikel 7, pt. 1.

73 The possibility of prohibiting the "bundling" of consents was indeed considered by the EU legislature. The Parliament proposed to include that the controller should not be permitted to make the execution of a contract or the provision of a service "conditional on the consent on the processing or use of data that is not necessary for the execution of that contract or the provision of the service". This option was, however, clearly rejected in the final version of the GDPR; see the European Parliament legislative resolution of 12 March 2014 on a proposal for a regulation of the European Parliament and of the Council on the protection of individuals with regard to the processing of personal data and on the free movement of such data (General Data Protection Regulation) (COM(2012)0011 – C7–0025/2012–2012/0011(COD)), Art. 7 para. 4.

We do not think that the two avenues are necessarily mutually exclusive. However, choosing to opt for one avenue over another bears political significance on the relationships between individuals and society.

11.6 Reinstating Privacy in OBA: Designing a Data Protection–friendly Framework

One way to fix the current situation is by providing individuals with knowledge and tools to effectively control their data flow in online advertising. In our view, the GDPR's goal of ensuring privacy by design and by default through self-regulation and accountability obligations in the GDPR, while being the right way forward, has so far failed to be implemented as it left its implementation to self-regulation and accountability. Co-regulatory initiatives are desperately needed to bring privacy to the forefront in the design of OBA.

A discussion has been going on for some time involving privacy advocates, ad tech companies and networks, and browser vendors (the so-called gatekeepers) regarding the need for a new model for online advertising that takes into account the issues described previously. In the remainder of this section, we will highlight three proposals and show that if the discussion is only left to market players, much is to be lost at the expense of privacy.

11.6.1 Privacy-friendly Interfaces

If control of personal data is to be reinstated, effective ways for data subjects to provide meaningful consent to behavioural advertising are needed.

One currently discussed hot topic is to what extent privacy interfaces influence the way data subjects consent to the underlying processing operations. The discussion has revolved around the topic of dark patterns and deceptive design in privacy policy and cookie banners. Such tactics can include burying privacy settings deep within convoluted menus, using confusing language, or employing misleading visuals to induce users into providing more data or consenting to invasive tracking.

The discussion has prompted the user experience (UX) industry to a new wave of "ethical design"[74] practices, emphasising transparency, user-centricity, and the establishment of trust. Ethical design principles prioritise creating user interfaces that are clear, intuitive, and respectful of user preferences. Such interfaces empower users to make informed decisions about their data and privacy. Advocates

74 See, e.g., Elvis Hsiao, 'Ethical Design: Obligations of a UX Designer That Are Never Talked about Enough' (*BoorCamp UX Design*, December 2022) <https://bootcamp.uxdesign.cc/ethical-design-obligations-of-a-ux-designer-thats-never-talked-about-enough-452692529a2b> accessed 30 August 2023; Nick Lawrence, 'UI/UX Design: 5 Major Ethics' (*UX Planet*, January 2022) <https://uxplanet.org/ui-ux-design-5-major-ethics-116a7fc14df7> accessed 30 August 2023). Studies and courses are also emerging to teach ethical design to UX students, see Giovanna Nunes Vilaza and Per Bækgaard, 'Teaching User Experience Design Ethics to Engineering Students: Lessons Learned' (2022) 4 *Frontiers in Computer Science* 793879.

for bright design argue that it can lead to stronger and more sustainable relationships between businesses and users. When users feel in control and well-informed, they are more likely to engage with online content willingly, thereby fostering a healthier digital ecosystem.

Recently, regulators have started to take part in the debate.[75] Given the multiple complaints on cookie banners filed with several EU DPAs by Max Schrems' privacy advocacy organisation NOYB (meaning "none of your business"),[76] the EDPB decided to establish a task force to coordinate actions.

The last report[77] mapped recurrent trends and provided an assessment under the e-Privacy Directive and the GDPR. For some practices, it seems that consensus has not been reached; for example, when websites refrain from displaying a reject button on the cookie banner's first layer. For other practices, such as in the case of pre-ticked boxes on the second layer of the cookie banner (after the user clicks on the "Settings" button of the first layer) or deceptive "link design" on the cookie banner's first layer, the view of the Board is that it will not allow a valid consent. Regarding the configuration of some cookie banners in terms of colours and contrasts of the buttons, where the "accept all" button is more clearly highlighted over other available options, the Board agreed that a general banner standard concerning colour and/or contrast cannot be imposed on data controllers.

Critical discussion on privacy interfaces has also reached EU lawmakers and triggered two important provisions contained in the Digital Services Act (DSA) and the Digital Markets Act (DMA).[78] Article 25(1) of the DSA broadly formulates a prohibition on designing and organising the interface to deceive recipients, setting a standard whose content will have to be clarified ex post on a case-by-case basis. Moreover, Art. 25(3) empowers the European Commission to issue guidance about specifically manipulative practices. Among the letters, two may affect the obtaining

75 Before the GDPR, the discussion on how cookie banners should be designed to ensure an informed consent was mostly taken on by some national DPA. For example, the Italian DPA issued guidelines in 2014 on how simplified information could be given in cookie consent requests. The guidelines were updated in 2021, based on subsequent debate at EU level and respective the stricter stance of the GDPR on information and consent.

76 Among its initiatives, the privacy advocacy group has developed a mass scanning system to automatically detect unlawful cookie banners and, if the controller does not react, automatically file a complaint the SA. In particular, in March 2021, NOYB scanned the web for illegal cookie banners and filed more than 700 complaints across Europe. From the initially scanned websites, at least 56% introduced more compliant cookie banners, including Coca-Cola, Raiffeisen, and Mastercard. As of the time of writing, 60 cookie cases have been closed. More information can be found at the related NOYB web page <https://noyb.eu/en/data-protection-authorities-support-noybs-call-fair-yesno-cookie-banners> accessed 30 August 2023.

77 European Data Protection Board, Report of the work undertaken by the Cookie Banner Taskforce, Adopted on 17 January 2023.

78 Respectively, Regulation (EU) 2022/2065 of the European Parliament and of the Council of 19 October 2022 on a Single Market For Digital Services and amending Directive 2000/31/EC, [2022], OJ L277/1 and Regulation (EU) 2022/1925 of the European Parliament and of the Council of 14 September 2022 on contestable and fair markets in the digital sector and amending Directives (EU) 2019/1937 and (EU) 2020/1828, OJ L265/1.

of consent by users in OBA: (1) giving more prominence to certain choices when asking the recipient of the service for a decision; and (2) making repeated requests to the user where that choice has already been made, especially by presenting pop-ups.

The DMA does not contain any specific rule on interface design and dark patterns, as it is more oriented to ensure competition in data-intensive markets. It contains a series of obligations/prohibitions for gatekeepers relevant to advertising, such as tracking end-users outside of the gatekeepers' core platform service for the purpose of targeted advertising, without effective consent having been granted, or preventing users from un-installing any pre-installed software or app if they wish so. However, Art. 13 establishes that the gatekeeper's behaviours should comply with obligations regardless of their contractual, commercial, or technical nature or consist of the use of behavioural techniques or interface design. This means that a constraint is put on how the interface may impair the autonomy of business and end-users on the platform, including in data collection and exchange.[79]

We do think that such provisions are overall an improvement in the regulatory debate; however, they fail to get to the point. If the objective is to reinstate privacy choice, a data protection–friendly environment should at least provide for the availability and easy accessibility of a "do not collect data" button. A privacy-friendly environment may also entail making this option a pre-selected choice, with the possibility of users choosing lower levels of protection. It should also be possible to register this choice so that users who refuse to be tracked are relieved of the need to repeat their selection each time they access a website.

11.6.2 Default Setting and Consent Management Entities

As we wrote previously, we think that one of the reasons that has turned consent into being practically meaningless is that users are exposed to too many consent decisions. Thus, we reckon that to make consent more effective, we need to start thinking about reducing consent decisions. To do that, two avenues could be pursued: (1) mandating and regulating default settings; and (2) enabling the uptake and coordinating consent management entities.

Differently from privacy interfaces, default settings do not refer to how websites should design their interface and cookie banners, but rather go to the root of the problem and regulate the user's accessibility to adjust their privacy preferences in the browser. The concept aims to empower users by allowing them to set default privacy preferences in web browsers. These preferences would be automatically conveyed to website publishers, reducing the burden on users to repeatedly configure privacy settings on each website they visit. They could encompass options like prohibiting data collection, preventing third-party tracking, and disallowing data sales, giving users more control over their personal data.

79 Art. 5(1) of the DMA may also be read as a provision referring to privacy dark patterns, since it requires that when consent for the purposes of those practices enlisted in Art. 5(1) has been refused or withdrawn by the end-user, the gatekeeper shall not repeat its request for consent for the same purpose more than once within a period of one year.

This debate has led certain browsers to implement "user-accessible privacy options". For example, Firefox has implemented the Enhanced Tracking Protection[80] systems, which among other features, allow a user who enables this option to automatically select "Reject All" in cookie banners.[81] Similarly, Apple's Intelligent Tracking Prevention mechanism includes a machine learning system that works by learning which domains are used to track a user.[82]

At the same time, the possibility of users' accessible options standardisation, such as the 2009 "Do-Not-Track" (DNT) initiatives,[83] has re-emerged. Global Privacy Control (GPC) and Advanced Data Protection Control (ADPC) represent new standardised privacy signals that allow users to pre-select via their browser privacy choices; whereas the GPC is designed to send a single signal to websites to stop them from being able to sell the user's data, the ADPC is seeking to provide users with more granular control on the data privacy, reflecting the more complex legislative framework we have in the EU.[84] What seems the current situation is that promoters of these standards just present them as technical implementations of legal provisions, namely the "user-enabled privacy controls" provision defined by the California Consumer Privacy Act (CCPA) and the "by defaults" measure included in Art. 25 of the GDPR. As with the DNT, at the moment they both require the specific website/service to respect the user option.[85]

We argue that besides presenting these options as an implementation of privacy by designs, legislative backing is needed to make them effective and enforceable. Lawmakers could, for example, enact specific data protection legislation that includes provisions for privacy signal compliance. These laws should clearly define what constitutes tracking, and the consequences for non-compliance. Supervisory authorities would be responsible for monitoring websites, conducting investigations, and imposing fines or penalties on non-compliant organisations. For this system to function effectively, cooperation from web browsers is essential. Browsers should actively support and facilitate the transmission of user privacy preferences, ensuring that users' choices are respected and enforced across the digital landscape.

80 Firefox, Enhanced Tracking Protection in Firefox for desktop <https://support.mozilla.org/en-US/kb/enhanced-tracking-protection-firefox-desktop>.

81 Cookie banner handling works with a list of domains. Only domains on that list will get automated handling regarding their cookie banners <https://community.mozilla.org/en/campaigns/firefox-cookie-banner-handling/> accessed 31 August 2023.

82 Apple, 'Safari Privacy Overview' (*Safari White Paper*, Apple 2019) <www.apple.com/safari/docs/Safari_White_Paper_Nov_2019.pdf>.

83 The DNT default was conceived as an hypertext transfer protocol (HTTP) header field which could be set by the user through the browser in order to signal his or her choice to reject consent to each website's owners. All browsers implemented the DNT signal in 2011–2012 and it was widely adopted by users. However, subsequent reports showed that few website owners and publishers respect the signal. The incoherent reaction to DNT can be seen in Google's integration of it into Chrome, while at the same time declining to honour the signal on its web pages.

84 Global Privacy Control (GPC) <https://globalprivacycontrol.org/> and Advanced Data Protection Control: <www.dataprotectioncontrol.org/> accessed 30 August 2023. While GPC is a W3C standard and seems to have already reached a certain degree of consensus, ADPC is a technical specification proposed by a group of researchers from the University of Vienna and NOYB.

85 In the Project's GitHub, one can read (<https://privacycg.github.io/gpc-spec/> accessed 30 August 2023):

To facilitate consent-based protection, another option is to promote and supervise the fiduciary role of "data and consent management platforms".

In the current situation, DMP and consent management platforms (CMP) are entities partaking in the OBA ecosystems, making their own share out of the entire advertising operations by serving for the ultimate purpose.[86] DMP allows the gathering and analysis of user's data to create profile to be sold onto the markets. On the other hand, CMP serve the purpose of collecting, store, and share the "consent signal"[87] of a data subject. While these actors should ensure that data collection and exchange respect the GDPR, this is often not the case.

Lawmakers should promote the creation and oversight of corresponding entities that run similar operations but in the ultimate purpose of favouring data subject's interests. For example, DMP platforms could emerged to collect users' data and to manage them in their interest. On the one hand, they could be designed so that they prioritise user privacy and control. This could involve implementing robust data anonymisation techniques, enabling users to easily opt in or out of data collection, and providing clear and user-friendly interfaces for managing their data preferences. On the other hand, based on users' options, they could collectively negotiate vis-à-vis advertisers about data use conditions, monetary or other advantages to be obtained in exchange for the use of their data. This may also include the development of data protection software agents able to implement the data protection policies chosen by users when they access websites.

In this way, one crucial aspect characterising OBA networks – namely, the unbalance in knowledge and bargaining power between data subjects and controllers – could be overcome. Individuals would be alleviated from being unburdened of the need to directly engage with the management of their personal data; they would entrust their data and related management to third-party fiduciaries which could exercise some kind of collective control to ensure that data are processed consistently with agreements. Collective actions would, indeed, play a significant role in rebalancing this power dynamic. Users could join forces to negotiate with data controllers, demanding fair compensation or services in exchange for their valuable data. This collective bargaining would strengthen the position of data subjects, ensuring that their interests are better represented in the data ecosystem.

At the same time, while regulating on compliance with privacy signals and promoting trusted DMP, we argue that a regulation should also ensure that users' accessible and collective bargaining options are known and understood by most users. The issue of transparency and clarity in these users' privacy-empowering mechanisms is critical, since without the ability to quickly understand the options, they would certainly rely on the default selected by the browser or giving away

86 For a description and a legal qualification under GDPR, see Cristiana Santos and others, 'Consent Management Platforms under the GDPR: Processors and/or Controllers?' in Nils Gruschka, Luís Filipe Antunes, Kai Rannenberg and Prokopios Drogkaris (eds), *Privacy Technologies and Policy. 9th Annual Privacy Forum, APF 2021 Oslo, Norway, June 17–18, 2021 Proceedings* (Springer 2021).

87 The Consent Signal is a text-based digital representation of the user's consent in a standardised format, stored in the user's browser, and provided to third-party vendors by the CMP.

their data to non-trusted intermediaries. Indeed, one frequently cited criticism of privacy-empowering mechanisms is the fact that they divide users into two groups: those who enabled the option and those who did not, assisting in fingerprinting (identifying) a web browser – and thus its user.

11.6.3 Controlled Browsers' Gatekeeping

Lately, a great focus has been on replacing third-party cookies with other solutions that could be viewed, at least partially, as privacy preserving. In the present day, almost all the major browsers have started to block third-party cookies and to look for new methods for data collection for the purpose of online targeted advertisement.

Multiple proposals have been presented to the Private Advertising Technology Community Group and the Web Incubator Group by the likes of Google, Apple, and Microsoft, which rely on the idea of entrusting the browser with the tasks of collecting data and delivering ads in ways that protect privacy and ensure consent.[88] One of the most talked-about projects in the ad tech world has been Google's "Federated Learning of Cohorts" (FLoC),[89] which was recently replaced by an equivalent called "Topics".[90] The stated purpose of FLoC/Topics is to give advertisers a way of targeting ads without exposing the personal details of individual users. It does this serving a publicly available application programming interface (API) that may be queried by ad services to fetch a limited number of "topics" that have been associated with the websites visited by the user. These topics would be reset periodically and prevent the divulging of any other information on the user. The topics are inferred by the browser or explicitly mapped by the website. In the first case, the browser will leverage a machine learning classifier model to map site hostnames to topics. The list of topics is predefined by Google, with the proposal pushing for it "to be sourced from an external party that incorporates feedback and ideas from across the industry" and is based on the categories identified by the IAB in the so-called audience taxonomy.[91] Other similar solutions have been proposed by Microsoft (PARAKEET), by IAB Europe (Unified ID 2.0), and by Apple under its "Apple advertising and privacy" policy.

88 For an overview of these proposal and the overall trends, and the consequences from a privacy point of view, we refer to the work by Sergio Guida, 'Third-Party Cookies and Alternatives: What Consequences in Terms of Consent?' (2021) *European Journal of Privacy Law & Technologies* 135.

89 Google, Building a privacy-first future for web advertising, <https://blog.google/products/ads-commerce/2021-01-privacy-sandbox/> accessed 30 August 2023. Different analyses of the FLoC can be found in reports and scientific technical literature, e.g., Florian Turati, "Analysing and Exploiting Google's FLoC Advertising Proposal" (MA thesis, ETH Zurich, Department of Computer Science 2022).

90 The Topic variation was proposed by Google after a series of negative comments, from both competitors and other players. As FLoC, the service is implemented directly in the Chrome browser, and Google is planning on activating it gradually as a test phase. See more on Topic at Google's web page, Get to know the new Topics API for Privacy Sandbox <https://blog.google/products/chrome/get-know-new-topics-api-privacy-sandbox/> accessed 30 August 2023.

91 IAB Audience Taxonomy <https://iabtechlab.com/standards/audience-taxonomy/> accessed 30 August 2023.

These solutions have been presented under the heading of "privacy sandboxes",[92] thus suggesting that users' privacy is taken care of. Indeed, browsers would exercise their gatekeeping functions by retaining all personal data connected to users' browsing history, thereby preventing the actual bits of information that identify/profile the user to flow from browsers to other nodes of the network. Advertising companies will still be able to rely only on first-party cookies, but this represents an infinitely smaller amount of information about the users. At the same time, the kind of information that would be exchanged with advertisers is rather the "group" or the "topic" in which users have been placed by the algorithmic systems run by the browsers, based on undisclosed browsing behaviours. This means, for example, that advertisers would receive aggregated data about users' interests and preferences rather than specific individual information. For instance, instead of knowing that John Doe visited a specific online store, advertisers might learn that a group of users who share similar interests in electronics or fashion have visited the same store, thus being able to target them with relevant products and services.

While many of these proposals do, in fact, provide enhanced data protection mechanisms, we would like to draw attention to their significance in terms of privacy regulation.

First, the shift towards anonymised, grouped data aims to strike a balance between user privacy and the advertising industry's desire for targeting and personalised content delivery. At the same time, it also raises questions about the underlying vision of "privacy" purported by ad tech gatekeepers. For instance, processing personal data only on browsers without them leaving Google's servers is certainly a privacy-preserving option. At the same time, it is not necessarily the case that information on whether users are included in certain cohorts or can be described by certain topics is necessarily the best option for users. Problems may relate to the transparency of these algorithms and how they categorise users, potentially leading to concerns about the fairness and accuracy of such profiling.

Second, it should be noted that these technical solutions are being proposed as open standards, to be adopted by all the actors involved. The major difference with the other standards, however, is that while they generically "invite" ad tech companies to comply or describe vague standards that *should* be implemented (such as the DNT), the new browser-based advertising standards are designed in a way as to limit access to the whole advertising network unless the standard is adopted. This "regulatory approach"[93] leverages the centrality and power of advertising intermediaries, which in the last ten years have built a vast ecosystem in which end-users and other players are forced to play by the rules of the house, and supposedly shift the responsibility/burden of respecting the privacy norms from the provider of a service to the user, through the entire technological infrastructure which should be "compliant by design".

92 A sandbox can be described as an isolated environment, where there is a strict separation from the outside. In this context, the environment is the browser, and the separation is with the other actors, websites, ad tech companies, etc.

93 Laurence Diver, 'Digisprudence: The Design of Legitimate Code' (2021) 13(2) *Law, Innovation and Technology* 325.

While this may be an effective way to regulate privacy, there are drawbacks that relate to dimension of power. Take Google, for example: the company is the leading provider of ad tech services across virtually every step of the value chain between marketers and publishers, as well as operating the Chrome browser and the Android mobile system; thus, their decisions affect the space at large.[94] Google is in the position of being able to add a feature in Chrome, then use the large user base of the browser to force competitors to implement the same, effectively creating a standard. However, in a sensitive domain such as that of advertising, the decision should not be made by a single player with a dominant position, but instead be reached by consensus, with the input of regulators, who could go beyond the surface and determine what privacy we should protect, and if the defence implementations put forward are genuine and not a smokescreen for anti-competitive conduct.

All in all, we need to figure out the role that regulators (should) play in building a privacy-preserving system that benefits users.

Some regulators have indeed been investigating the new "privacy sandbox" advanced by OBA gatekeepers. For example, in October 2021, the French Commission Nationale de l'Informatique et des Libertés (CNIL) issued a complete picture of alternatives to third-party cookies for targeted advertising to ensure that the different proposals advanced comply with the rules on cookies and data protection.[95] On the competition side, the UK's Competition and Markets Authority (CMA) has warned that the Google FLoC/Topics proposal may run against fair competition in that "it could undermine the ability of publishers to generate revenue".[96] The investigation has since been closed, with an agreement on commitments by Google not to design or implement the privacy sandbox in a way that favours its own activities, and not to use certain data – including Chrome browser data – in its advertising businesses.[97]

94 The warnings of many authors that Google's proposal is likely to further advantage it over other publishers and advertising platforms has attracted the attention of competition regulators, the online advertising industry, and critics of their platform power. See Mark Nottingham, 'Playing Fair in the Privacy Sandbox: Competition, Privacy and Interoperability Standards' (2021) *SSRN Scholarly Paper ID 3891335* <https://papers.ssrn.com/abstract=3891335> accessed 30 August 2023. See also, in this regard, Damien Geradin, Dimitrios Katsifis and Theano Karanikioti, 'Google as a de Facto Privacy Regulator: Analysing the Privacy Sandbox from an Antitrust Perspective' (2021) 17 *European Competition Journal* 617; Ariel Ezrachi and Viktoria H S E Robertson, 'Competition, Market Power and Third-Party Tracking' (2019) 42(1) *World Competition*.

95 Commission Nationale de l'Informatique et des Libertés, 'Alternatives to Third-Party Cookies: What Consequences Regarding Consent?' (23 November 2021) <www.cnil.fr/en/alternatives-third-party-cookies-what-consequences-regarding-consent> accessed 30 August 2023.

96 CMA to investigate Google's 'Privacy Sandbox' Browser Changes, *Press Release* <www.gov.uk/government/news/cma-to-investigate-google-s-privacy-sandbox-browser-changes> accessed 31 August 2023.

97 Available at https://competitionandmarkets.blog.gov.uk/2023/04/28/googles-privacy-sandbox-commitments-implementation-and-what-comes-next/ accessed 30 August 2023. In the field of competition, some help may also come from the DMA when it will be fully in force. Although no specific provisions exist now to restrict a shift to more browser-based advertising, Art. 19 leaves the possibility for the EU Commission to investigate practices that are not included in the list of prohibited practices but hinder fair competition within core platform services or are unfair in a way that is not effectively addressed by regulation.

Finally, collaborative standardisation processes should be promoted so that ways of designing the OBA ecosystem, different from those unilaterally imposed gatekeepers, could be promoted. An example of such a process is the Dovekey proposal,[98] which was an attempt at reaching a consensus between Google and smaller ad tech companies. Policymakers could more directly engage in this type of more open consensus-reaching standardisation proposals, as this may heavily impact the Internet ecosystem of the future.

11.7 Beyond Data Protection: Regulating Data Use in OBA

The second approach assumes that, in the current situation, the GDPR alone cannot ensure the privacy of users targeted with OBA and that other regulatory tools could and should limit data exchanges and processing in OBA to preserve privacy and other social interests.

Underlying this approach is not only the acknowledgement that the GDPR may not be fit to address privacy issues in OBA but also that paradigms other than informational data protection may better represent privacy issues in the current online economy. Instead of looking at privacy only as having control over or limiting access to one's own information, societal issues in OBA suggest that equal emphasis should be put on the dimension of individual and collective decision-making, namely how data are used to interfere with individual and groups' choices, opportunities, and decisions.[99]

In the following subsections, we shall consider some regulatory steps that could be undertaken in the field of OBA that go beyond information data protection and tackle the use of data. We acknowledge that some of these steps have, albeit mildly, been taken forward by recently approved digital market regulations, especially the DSA. Indeed, for some aspects, the DSA could be looked at as a regulation on data use. We argue, however, that these options should be pursued with a more systematic approach via a proportionality assessment.

11.7.1 Substantive Prohibitions

Shifting the focus from collection to data use allows us to reflect on which data uses should be prohibited because of their unbearable detrimental effects on individuals and society. Prohibiting OBA may entail different degrees of restrictions.

One option could be to ban OBA altogether, namely to sanction whoever uses personal data to carry out online advertising. As extreme as it may seem, this option is supported by many voices in policy circles and in the advertising ecosystem.

98 See GitHub page <https://github.com/google/ads-privacy/blob/master/proposals/dovekey/README.md> accessed 30 August 2023. In the Dovekey proposal, the user data and the automated assessment of interests would be done in a server structure hosted by an independent entity. This would reduce the reliance on Google, which is the owner of the main browser.

99 Herman T Tavani, 'Informational Privacy: Concepts, Theories, and Controversies' in *The Handbook of Information and Computer Ethics 131* (Wiley Online Library 2008).

For example, during the legislative works for the DSA, a group of Members of the European Parliament (MEPs) supported the idea of introducing a general ban on advertising based on the collection of personal data.[100] While opposing voices warn that such a move would endanger part of the current online economy,[101] at least those ad-funded free services, many research initiatives show that such an outcome may not necessarily be true.[102] Less intrusive, more sustainable and more democratic online advertising forms are possible. For example, contextual advertising still relies on targeting individual users but, instead of their personal data, is based on the context of the content users are engaging with. From the advertisers' side, it works by allowing them to purchase ad space on types of web pages or websites based on the content on the page. This can be based on a website so that, for example, ads for riding courses are placed next to articles about horses or keywords input by the users so that, for instance, ads for flights to England are placed next to articles about English football. As a matter of fact, contextual advertising already drives one of the biggest online advertising markets: search advertising. Search advertising benefits from an incredibly strong signal about what the user is interested in, i.e., the searched-for term.

We warn against considering contextual advertising as the everlasting compromise. Targeting methods in contextual advertising are evolving significantly beyond the ability to target based on content and keywords on a page. The more sophisticated contextual platforms can now target based on text, image, audio, location, and semantics of content on individual pages.[103] While this information does not pertain to the user but to the text, some misuse can nonetheless be foreseen, such as tailoring the advertising message and layout to the tone of the webpage. Still, this undoubtedly represents a minor risk with respect to privacy-invasive advertising.

100 European Parliament, Resolution of 20 October 2020 with recommendations to the Commission on a Digital Services Act: adapting commercial and civil law rules for commercial entities operating online (2020/2019[INL]), para 17. The request has been reiterated after the ECJ ruling on advertising by asking for a moratorium on tracking users online. See, Théophane Hartmann, 'Ten MEPs Ask EU Commission for a Moratorium on Tracking of Users, Euractiv' (20 July 2023) <www.euractiv.com/section/data-privacy/news/ten-meps-ask-eu-commission-for-a-moratorium-on-tracking-of-users/> accessed 30 August 2023.

101 See, for instance, IAB Europe's Concerns <https://iabeurope.eu/wp-content/uploads/2021/04/IAB-Europe_What-Would-an-Internet-Without-Targeted-Ads-Look-Like_April-2021.pdf> accessed 30 August 2023.

102 See, among others, the arguments put forward in BEUC Press Release, 'Why It's Time to Ban Surveillance Ads', November 2021 <www.beuc.eu/blog/why-its-time-to-ban-surveillance-ads/> and the Norwegian Consumer Council Report, 'Time to Ban Surveillance-based Advertising. The Case Against Commercial Surveillance Online' June 2021 <https://storage02.forbrukerradet.no/media/2021/06/20210622-final-report-time-to-ban-surveillance-based-advertising.pdf>.

103 Reports from the industry show that three broad kinds of contextual information are emerging as an asset: categories (what are the topics on the page?), sentiment (is the tone negative or positive?), and emotions (what emotions are being conveyed?). See, e.g., the report by Duncan McCann, Will Stronge and Phil Jones, 'The Future of Online Advertising – Exploring the Impacts of Surveillance-Based Advertising, Current Trends in Adtech and the Challenges and Opportunities of a Total Ban on the Use of Personal Data' (2021), p. 36.

Rather than banning OBA altogether, one more moderate approach would be to prevent OBA from bringing about certain unwanted effects. For example, there is a wide consensus that behavioural advertising should not be designed to deceive and manipulate users to make choices they would not otherwise make. In this field, regulation could learn from the prohibitions on unfair commercial practices contained in the Unfair Commercial Practices Directive (UCPD).[104] Indeed, there has been a huge discussion in recent years about the possibility of applying the UCPD to online advertising. The UCPD is a prominent example of how market legislation can blacklist certain practices that bring about unfair outcomes to consumers and markets, thus providing an easy-to-use legal ground to sanction practices. Discussion of the application, and possible reform, of UCPD to digital markets is still open.[105]

Lighter restrictions may entail the prohibition of using certain data categories in the advertising process as a proxy for unwanted outcomes. For example, such an option would prohibit the use of certain categories of data to profile users or to target advertising altogether. For example, advertisers may be forced not to use health-related information or biometric data to serve advertising. Similarly, profiling of users based on their political or religious orientations could be prohibited, as this would avoid the manipulation of individuals based on their political bias or religious beliefs.

It seems that this option has been pursued in the DSA. Art. 26(3) prohibits providers of online platforms from displaying ads to users based on profiling using special categories of personal data. However, from reading the provision, it is not clear whether the special categories of data cannot be used when they represent the input of profiling or also the output thereof. This makes a big difference, as many special categories of data are not directly collected by advertisers but might be inferred based on common personal data categories.

Another less restrictive approach would be to ban OBA practices when vulnerable groups are involved. There are hints of these options, too, in the DSA, where Art. 28(2) requires online platforms not to present ads on their interface based on profiling when they have a reasonable certainty that users are minors. While enhanced protection of minors is to be welcomed, critical literature suggests a broader look at vulnerability.[106] This perspective would entail considering vulnerability as a multifaceted concept that extends beyond traditional categories

104 Directive 2005/29/EC of the European Parliament and of the Council of 11 May 2005 concerning unfair business-to-consumer commercial practices in the internal market and amending Council Directive 84/450/EEC, Directives 97/7/EC, 98/27/EC and 2002/65/EC of the European Parliament and of the Council and Regulation (EC) No 2006/2004 of the European Parliament and of the Council [2005], OJ L 149/22.

105 See, ex multis, Natali Helberger and others, 'EU Consumer Protection 2.0. Structural Asymmetries in Digital Consumer Markets', A joint report from research conducted under the EUCP2.0 project, Commissioned by BEUC, March 2021 <https://www.beuc.eu/brochure/eu-consumer-protection-20-structural-asymmetries-digital-consumer-markets-0> Also refer to the thoughts contained in Federico Galli, 'Online Behavioural Advertising and Unfair Manipulation Between GDPR and UCPD' in Martin Ebers and Cantero Marta Gamito (eds), *Algorithmic Governance and Governance of Algorithms. Legal and Ethical Challenges* (Springer 2021); Federico Galli, *Algorithmic Marketing and EU Law on Unfair Commercial Practices* (Law, Governance and Technology Series, Springer 2022).

106 Natali Helberger and others (n. 23).

and demographics, such as age or socioeconomic status. It would involve recognising that vulnerability can be highly contextual and situational, influenced by factors like personal circumstances, mental health, cultural background, and life events. By adopting a more nuanced understanding of vulnerability in the context of online advertising, regulatory frameworks like the DSA could be better equipped to safeguard not only minors but all individuals who may find themselves in vulnerable situations due to a variety of interconnected factors.

These two options may, however, carry the risk of cherry-picking particular informational practices or stigmatising certain categories of people. The admissibility of certain categories of data in advertising practices may be deeply dependent on context. Problems may be very specific, as different normative considerations and different solutions come into play; for example, when speaking about data leading to discrimination in hiring, and contributing to depression in teens. So, responses need to be tailor-made, and this challenges the idea of a general regulation on data use in advertising, as a case-by-case and sector-by-sector approach would be.

11.7.2 Disclosing Ads Selection Criteria and Risks

Regulating data use may not necessarily require the imposition of bans but instead lead to mandatory information disclosures, regarding not data collection but its use. A parallel can be drawn with tobacco regulation, whereby warning labels on cigarette packages inform consumers about the health risks associated with smoking. Similarly, data use disclosures could provide users with clear, concise information about how their data is being used by advertisers, enabling them to make meaningful and informed decisions about the ad they engage with.

On data use transparency regulation, the EU seems better equipped. In the past five years, the EU has discussed moving the regulatory focus in targeted advertising from protecting personal data to ensuring transparency in how these data are managed and processed for advertising purposes. The focus is no longer only on the possibility of data subject to knowing what data is processed but on the possibility of knowing how the use of data leads to the display of a certain advertisement. We are here beyond the traditional data protection principle of transparency of the data processing, which precisely concerns the data and the purposes of the processing: the key information asset is how data processing systems are set to influence decision-making based on personal data, thus enabling data subjects to make an informed decision and understand the extent to which the digital representation of themself affects commercial offers.

Although well-established consumer directives already included some relevant provisions,[107] the core of this regulatory movement is again the DSA. Art. 26(1)

107 We refer to Art. 5 of the P2B Regulation (Regulation (EU) 2019/1150 of the European Parliament and of the Council of 20 June 2019 on promoting fairness and transparency for business users of online intermediation services OJ L186/57) and Art. 3(4)(b) and 6(a) of the Omnibus Directive (Directive (EU) 2019/2161 of the European Parliament and of the Council of 27 November 2019 amending Council Directive 93/13/EEC and Directives 98/6/EC, 2005/29/EC and 2011/83/EU of

requires that all online platforms displaying advertising must ensure that the recipients of the service can clearly and unambiguously identify a set of information, including: (1) that the content displayed is an advertisement; (2) the entity on whose behalf the advertisement is presented; (3) the entity who paid for the advertisement, if different from point *b*; and (4) meaningful information directly and easily accessible from the advertisement about the main parameters used to determine the recipient to whom the advertisement is presented and – where applicable – about how to change those parameters. The information is to be provided in real time and for each individual message, at the moment when the user is presented with the ad.

This last point – the obligation to provide *meaningful information about the main parameters used to determine the recipient* – seems to us to be of great importance.

In practice, relevant advertisements will have to be accompanied by the profile characteristics used as the basis to direct the advertisement to the recipient. For example, advertisements for gyms will have to show that the recipient is targeted due to a range of criteria which might include their interest in sports, their age, and the fact they live near the advertised gym. While the criteria may be fairly clear-cut in that example, advertisements for less popular or more controversial subjects will also be obliged to show how the recipient is targeted. This might be because the recipient has liked specific groups on social media or because of the search history of their search engine. In short, the recipient will need to be informed about the particulars relevant to the advertisements shown and about their digital label.

From a legal/systematic perspective, the new provision is equally remarkable: it means that users are to be provided with a sort of "justification" of why they see a certain ad. This goes well beyond "meaningful information about the logic involved" in the advertising system[108] and concerns the right to an explanation – the actual presence of which within the GDPR is much debated.

Having said this, the actual effectiveness of this provision will depend on how it will be translated into practice. The specificity of the description of the selection parameters employed may affect the practical value of the information provided in the user's decision-making process. For instance, there might be uncertainty regarding whether parameters like "consumer behaviour" or "user browsing history" (which, by the way, have already been used by major OBA intermediaries for some time now) can offer sufficient specificity to inform users about how commercial messages are tailored. At the same time, parameters too specific may pose additional problems for the protection of trade secrets, and the DSA explicitly states that information on parameters must not entail the disclosure of the inner workings of their selection algorithms.

Also, any effort to implement the provision will have to overcome the fundamental epistemic challenge tied to many automated systems used in OBA today.[109] These can

---

the European Parliament and of the Council as regards the better enforcement and modernisation of Union consumer protection rules, OJ L 328/7).

108 This could be drawn from Arts. 13(2)(f) and 14(2)(g) GDPR, as long as OBA automated systems are considered types of automated decision-making systems under Art. 22 (cfr., Section 11.4.4).

109 Cf., Adrien Bibal and others, "Legal Requirements on Explainability in Machine Learning" (2021) 29 *Artificial Intelligence and Law* 149.

be best portrayed as "black boxes" not only because, in certain cases, they are run by private companies not disclosing their functioning but also because they incorporate complex machine learning functionalities that cannot be easily explained even by those who run the systems. For example, some selection parameters may be automatically learned and implicit in the machine-learned model (e.g., psychological or social weaknesses) or be learned through proxies (such as with many sensitive personal data).

Finally, there is reasonable doubt as to whether this information will be used by consumers. We should indeed be cautioned against overemphasising transparency and individualised explanations as a general remedy to potentially unfair practices in OBA.[110] A parallel may be drawn between consent and individualised explanations, as both rely on the data subject's informed initiative. As it has been observed in Section 11.4.3.2, in online environments, consent provides little if no protection at all, given the disparity in knowledge and power between controllers and data subjects, and also the limited time and energy available to the latter, and their inability to pool their interests and resources and coordinate their activities. The same may also apply to the advertising explanations, which may remain underused by users.

One may wonder whether the addressee of this transparency movement should be the general public rather than the individual user. This would mean that selection parameters are disclosed in a publicly available section of the platforms rather than on the individual web page of the user. This option is foreseen in the DSA, but only with respect to Very Large Online Platforms (VLOP) and Very Large Online Search Engines (VLOSE).[111] Art. 39 imposes additional transparency requirements on VLOP and VLOSE, namely to make publicly available, through a searchable tool that allows multi-criteria queries and through APIs, a repository containing information about advertising displayed, the person on whose behalf it is displayed, and the selection criteria, especially when an ad was intended to be displayed only to specific segments of users. The information is to be made available until one year after the end of the related ad campaign. Significantly, access to the repository is not subject to the requirements foreseen in Art. 40 for vetted researchers to access data for systemic risk monitoring. At the same time, only vetted researchers can be heard by the Commission and the Board in order to issue guidelines on how to structure this repository and which functionalities are to be made available.

11.7.3 Regulatory Attitudes

As a last point, we would like to address how regulation on data use in OBA may approach the object of regulation, regardless of its content (namely, whether mandate

110 See, for instance, the doubts about the need and usefulness of new information disclosures promoted by the DSA in Arno R Lodder and J Morais Carvalho, "Online Platforms: Towards an Information Tsunami with New Requirements on Moderation, Ranking, and Traceability" (2022) 33(4) *European Business Law Review*.

111 On 25 April 2023, the Commission has published the VLOP/VLOSE designated list, including the following platforms which are relevant for OBA networks: Google, Meta, Amazon etc. The list is available at the following Press Release webpage <https://digital-strategy.ec.europa.eu/en/policies/dsa-vlops> accessed 30 August 2023.

disclosures or substantive prohibitions are leveraged). We build on the regulation theory provided by Amnon Reichman, who speaks of three distinct "regulatory attitudes":[112] namely, the top-down command-and-control attitude, performance-based regulation, and the managerial approach.

The top-down command-and-control approach involves government or regulatory authorities setting specific rules, standards, and regulations that organisations or individuals must follow. It is characterised by a strict, prescriptive framework that dictates activities, often with little flexibility or discretion. An example of this approach in marketing space is provided by the previously mentioned UCPD, which establishes top-down prohibited selling practices and entrusts consumer agencies as well as individual consumers to enforce those prohibitions.

In the context of regulation on data use in OBA, a top-down command-and-control approach would entail EU legislators or regulatory agencies issuing detailed regulations governing data use in OBA, either specifying the types of data that can be used or mandating specific information items and setting strict penalties for non-compliance. This approach would bring uniformity in data use regulation, strong enforcement power on supervisory agencies, and clear expectations for advertisers and data subjects.

At the same time, relying only on command-and-control top-down regulation in a technology-intensive environment such as OBA is practically impossible; this seems obvious to anyone who thinks about it seriously. This attitude has the potential to stifle unpredictable and beneficial innovations, and it has limited flexibility and a potential lag in adapting to rapidly evolving technology. Also, regulators may lack the specific competence to establish what should be done and what should not to accomplish the regulatory objective. For example, generally mandating that profiling should not be carried out based on sensitive data does not tell how this should be realised in practice (by marking and phasing special categories of data used?; using security measures, such as anonymisation or pseudonymisation? etc.) and cannot fully represent the diversity of profiling systems that may be at play in OBA networks. Similarly, as said previously, mandating top-down what information is to be disclosed on the way data are used may require some technical clarifications that cannot be predicted in advance.

The second approach is performance-based regulation. In this regulatory approach, the focus is on setting performance goals and outcomes that organisations or individuals must achieve rather than specifying detailed processes or methods to achieve them. It allows greater flexibility in how compliance is achieved, as long as the desired outcomes are met.

An example of this alternative approach is provided by the DSA regulation on VLOP and VLOSE, and, to a certain extent, by the GDPR itself. Art. 34 requires

112 Amnon Reichman and Giovanni Sartor, 'Algorithms and Regulation' in Hans-W Micklitz, Oreste Pollicino, Oreste, Amnon Reichman, Andrea Simoncini, Giovanni Sartor and Giovanni De Gregorio (eds), *Constitutional Challenges in the Algorithmic Society* (Cambridge University Press 2021) 131.

VLOP and VLOSE to conduct a systemic risk assessment and to adopt mitigation measures in relation to the algorithmic systems run by the platforms, including those used in advertising services. The systemic risks are defined based on the desired outcomes of the regulation, namely, to uphold fundamental rights (such as privacy, data protection, freedom of expression, etc.), as well as general interest in a high level of consumer protection and the protection of minors. Control over this kind of performance-based regulation relies on abundant documentation that needs to be drafted by the VLOP/VLOSE and is ensured by an interaction with the EU Commission and the Member State's digital services coordinator where the platform is established.

The GDPR is also an example of this performance-based regulation, at least to a certain extent. The accountability principle requires data controllers, regardless of their size, to comply with the data protection principles and to provide proof of that. This means that data controllers must carry out a risk assessment on data protection rights and adopt technical and organisational measures to mitigate such risks. The DPIA is a key tool for that, as it offers the needed proof to show compliance.

In the field of OBA, performance-based regulation in this context would define desired outcomes related to user data protection and privacy without prescribing specific methods. For example, it would require advertisers not to manipulate and deceive data subjects into clicking on ads or to discriminate against protected groups in the delivery of advertising. In addition, it could set performance targets for the transparency of data usage practices and mandate the effectiveness of opt-out mechanisms.

This co-regulatory approach is undoubtedly beneficial: it would encourage innovation and adaptability, enable creative compliance solutions, and focus on end results. At the same time, there could be a potential for ambiguity in meeting performance goals, challenges in defining and measuring outcomes, and potential variability in compliance approaches. Much of the effectiveness of this approach will also depend on the level of control over compliance and accountability programmes. One cannot overlook the fact that conflicts of interest may arise, especially when advertisers and intermediaries have to implement mitigation measures that may result in less effective advertising.

Finally, the last approach that could be taken involves regulators ensuring that the regulatees have the governance structure and management procedures to self-regulate. This approach recognises the importance of empowering these entities to take responsibility for their own compliance with data use regulations while still maintaining oversight and providing guidance.

In the context of regulating data use in OBA, the managerial approach involves regulatory authorities verifying that the regulated entities have established robust governance structures and effective management procedures to facilitate self-regulation. It would ensure that OBA stakeholders have established governance frameworks that clearly delineate responsibilities for data use and transparency disclosure. This might involve, for instance, the creation of internal compliance committees or teams tasked with overseeing data-related activities; and transparent, representative, and accountable procedures for adopting codes of conduct or technical standards. Also, regulatory authorities may promote training and education programmes for OBA industry personnel to enhance their understanding of data uses and best practices. Overall, this approach would acknowledge that industry participants are in the best position to understand the nuances of their data usage and they can adapt more swiftly to changes in technology and consumer preferences. Regulatory oversight in this approach is focused on ensuring that the industry's self-regulatory mechanisms are effective and aligned with broader data protection goals.

The GDPR could provide a model in certain respects. The GDPR requires data processing entities to implement organisational measures to ensure privacy interests are taken seriously by data controllers. In certain cases, this entails the mandatory designation of a technically and legally competent professional (i.e., the Data Protection Office, or DPO) that must monitor and ensure that data protection requirements are complied with by the controller. The DPO serves as a linchpin in ensuring that organisations have the governance structure and management procedures necessary for self-regulation. A similar entity is also foreseen by Art. 41 of the DSA but is limited to VLOP/VLOSE. A regulation on data use that takes on a government-and-management approach may consider extending this measure to all OBA stakeholders.

A caution of this approach pertains to its effectiveness in bringing about the desired policy goals. In some cases, a managerial approach may lack the legal teeth needed for effective enforcement.[113] While it encourages self-regulation, it may not provide strong mechanisms to penalise non-compliance adequately. Moreover, potential variance in compliance is based on different organisations. Without strict, uniform rules, some entities may prioritise compliance more than others, potentially leading to uneven protection of users. Finally, some problems may arise from the professional competence of self-regulatory or standardisation bodies to discern permitted uses from unlawful ones, especially when some of the risks connected to data uses go beyond mere security matters and encompass broader issues such as manipulation and psychological integrity of users.[114]

11.8 Conclusion

In the present chapter, we analysed the regulatory mismatch between existing European Union (EU) data protection law and online behavioural advertising (OBA) practices and address the way forward of data privacy regulation in this field.

After exploring the OBA market and societal interest at stake, we have unveiled the critical relationship between the General Data Protection Regulation (GDPR) and OBA data processing, identifying five shortcomings.

First, many data protection principles are disregarded in the OBA, the most obvious being data minimisation, given the excessive and unnecessary amount of data processed. Second, it is difficult to apply the distinction between data controllers and data processors set forth by the GDPR, with the consequence that allocating

113 This is shown, for example, by the various issues characterising the DPO in the day-by-day management of privacy compliance, Francesco Ciclosi and Fabio Massacci, 'The Data Protection Officer, an Ubiquitous Role Nobody Really Knows' (2022) *arXiv preprint arXiv:2212.07712*.

114 In this vein, Hans W Micklitz, 'The Role of Standards in Future EU Digital Policy Legislation. A Consumer Perspective' Report Commissioned by BEUC and ANEC, July 2023.

responsibility in the network is challenging. Third, we looked at the course towards the view that consent is the only possible legal basis for the lawful processing of personal data. However, we emphasised the impossibility of obtaining valid consent in the OBA, given the socio-technical complexity, the cognitive limitations of users, and the antiprivacy practices of websites. Fourth, we found that while according to authoritative interpretation, the GDPR would prohibit processing consisting of profiling and automated decisions in the OBA, this prohibition is rejected and not enforced. Finally, there is little accountability on the part of data controllers, both for risk management practices (with little awareness of the OBA's privacy impact assessment) and for privacy by design and security, especially in the real-time bidding (RTB).

We have argued that these shortcomings may be attributed to the fact that the GDPR and EU data protection law do not coherently take a stance on the possibility of using consent to online advertising in exchange for direct or indirect benefits.

We therefore proposed two options to overcome this deadlock. One would be to push consent regulation forward and put the necessary efforts to enable users to express genuine consent to processing. This approach entails that regulations may take part in the design of a new techno-legal framework for OBA to reinstate (more) privacy. We have suggested moves that need cooperation between regulatory bodies and private companies engaged in OBA. These include user-friendly interfaces, rethinking default settings, introducing consent management entities, and considering controlling browsers' gatekeeping.

On the other hand, we proposed to overcome the current situation by shifting the focus of regulatory action to data use rather than data collection. This approach would entail that more emphasis is put on the way personal data are transformed and used to influence decision-making process of people and groups. Within this regulatory move, different options could be pursued: one pertains to prohibiting OBA, to various degrees. Otherwise, a new type of transparency movement could be promoted to benefit collective groups, rather than individuals, which would uncover how data are used in profiling and automated decision-making. Different regulatory attitudes may be adopted: top-down command-and-control regulation, performance-based regulation, and a managerial approach.

We would like to stress that, within these second avenues, different options should be pursued more coherently considering a proportionality assessment of risks stemming from OBA. This means that the higher the countervailing interests are at stake, the stricter the regulatory move should be. For example, in the case of political advertising, broadly scoped bans on OBA could be set in top-down command-and-control regulation. This approach could contribute to preventing highly risky societal development, such as undue influence over elections, politics, and, more generally, public opinion. At the same time, less strict regulatory actions could be devised in the case of commercial OBA. The transparency-oriented and performance-based attitude of the DSA may seem promising. However, we will see how it will translate into practice.

On the other hand, the choice between redesigning a data protection-friendly OBA market and shifting regulation to data use may not be mutually exclusive.

The two avenues could be equally pursued – or at least, a balance should be struck between the two. However, choosing one avenue over another may bear great significance. This decision extends far beyond mere regulatory mechanics; it holds profound implications for how individuals perceive their privacy rights, the distribution of power between the public and private sectors, and the overall fabric of society within the evolving landscape of OBA environments.

The first option is based on the vision that users can be empowered through more privacy-preserving OBA networks by means of a technological reorientation. This still puts a great emphasis on individual choice and control, and their ability to actually act upon technology to improve their privacy choice. On the other hand, the current proposals of overcoming third-party cookie-based advertising seem to shift the burden of privacy protection to gatekeepers and companies that are themselves interested in fostering a self-regulating environment. At the same time, this option is predicated on the idea that governments can command technological advancement for the benefits of users, which may require a delicate balance between innovation and regulation of all affected, potentially diverging (see privacy vs. competition) interests.

The second avenue is premised on the idea that the individual alone is not able and should not decide if and to what extent to allow data exchange for the purposes of OBA when societal interests are at stake. This may instil a paternalistic flavour into personal data management, as governments would basically discriminate between lawful and unlawful personal data uses. At the same time, it can prevent a largely free and uncontrolled market from using personal data to influence people's decisions and opinions, thus ensuring that public values are taken into account when regulating OBA practices.

Bibliography

Article 29 Working Party, Guidelines on Automated individual decision-making and Profiling for the purposes of Regulation 2016/679, Adopted on 3 October 2017 as last Revised and Adopted on 6 February 2018

Article 29 Working Party, Opinion 06/2014 on the notion of legitimate interests of the data controller under Art. 7 of Directive 95/46/EC, Adopted on 9 April 2014

Article 29 Working Party, Opinion 2/2010 on online behavioural advertising, Adopted on 22 June 2010

Article 29 WP, Guidelines on Data Protection Impact Assessment (DPIA) and determining whether processing is "likely to result in a high risk" for the purposes of Regulation 2016/679, wp248rev.01

Autorité de Protection des Données, Decision on the merits 21/2022 of 2 February 2022 (Case number DOS-2019–01377)

Bibal A and others, 'Legal Requirements on Explainability in Machine Learning' (2021) 29 *Artificial Intelligence and Law* 149

Boerman SC, Kruikemeier S and Zuiderveen Borgesius FJ, 'Online Behavioral Advertising: A Literature Review and Research Agenda' (2017) 46 *Journal of Advertising* 363

Bösch C and others, 'Tales from the Dark Side: Privacy Dark Strategies and Privacy Dark Patterns.' (2016) *Proceedings on Privacy Enhancing Technologies* 237

Büchi M and others, 'Making Sense of Algorithmic Profiling: User Perceptions on Facebook' (2023) 26 *Information, Communication & Society* 809

Bueno CC, *The Attention Economy: Labour, Time and Power in Cognitive Capitalism* (Rowman & Littlefield 2016)

Cabañas JG, Cuevas Á and Cuevas R, 'Unveiling and Quantifying Facebook Exploitation of Sensitive Personal Data for Advertising Purposes', *27th USENIX Security Symposium (USENIX Security 18)* (2018) <https://www.usenix.org/system/files/conference/usenixsecurity18/sec18-cabanas.pdf> accessed 30 August 2023

Calo MR, 'Digital Market Manipulation' (2013) 82 *The George Washington Law Review* 995

Chen G and others, 'Understanding Programmatic Creative: The Role of AI' (2019) 48 *Journal of Advertising* 347

Chen J, *Regulating Online Behavioural Advertising Through Data Protection Law* (Edward Elgar Publishing 2021)

Christl W and Spiekermann S, *Networks of Control, A Report on Corporate Surveillance, Digital Tracking, Big Data & Privacy* (Facultas 2016)

Ciclosi F and Massacci F, 'The Data Protection Officer, an Ubiquitous Role Nobody Really Knows' (2022) *arXiv preprint arXiv* 2212.07712

Commission Nationale de l'Informatique et des Libertés, 'Alternatives to Third-Party Cookies: What Consequences Regarding Consent?' (23 November 2021) <www.cnil.fr/en/alternatives-third-party-cookies-what-consequences-regarding-consent> accessed 30 August 2023

Constantiou ID and Kallinikos J, 'New Games, New Rules: Big Data and the Changing Context of Strategy' (2015) 30 *Journal of Information Technology* 44

Contissa G and others, 'Claudette Meets GDPR: Automating the Evaluation of Privacy Policies Using Artificial Intelligence' (2018) <https://www.beuc.eu/sites/default/files/publications/beuc-x-2018-066_claudette_meets_gdpr_report.pdf> accessed 30 August 2023

Dalla Corte L, 'On Proportionality in the Data Protection Jurisprudence of the CJEU' (2022) 12 *International Data Privacy Law* 259

Diver L, 'Digisprudence: The Design of Legitimate Code' (2021) 13 *Law, Innovation and Technology* 325

Ermakova T and others, 'Privacy Policies and Users' Trust: Does Readability Matter?' *AMCIS 2014 Proceedings, Human Computer Interaction* (2014) <https://aisel.aisnet.org/amcis2014/HumanComputerInteraction/GeneralPresentations/14> accessed 30 August 2023

European Commission, 'Consumer Market Study on Online Market Segmentation Through Personalised Pricing/Offers in the European Union' (2019) <https://ec.europa.eu/info/publications/consumer-market-study-online-market-segmentation-through-personalised-pricing-offers-european-union_en>

European Data Protection Board, Guidelines 2/2019 on the processing of personal data under Art. 6(1)(b) GDPR in the context of the provision of online services to data subjects, Version 2.0, 8 October 2019

European Data Protection Board, Guidelines 8/2020 on the targeting of social media users, Version 2.0, Adopted on 13 April 2021

European Data Protection Board, Report of the work undertaken by the Cookie Banner Taskforce, Adopted on 17 January 2023

European Union Agency for Fundamental Rights (FRA), 'Our Rights Matter: Data Protection and Privacy, Fundamental Rights Survey' (2020) <https://fra.europa.eu/en/publication/2020/fundamental-rights-report-2020> accessed 30 August 2023

Ezrachi A and Robertson VH, 'Competition, Market Power and Third-Party Tracking' (2019) 42 *World Competition*

Finck M and Biega A, 'Reviving Purpose Limitation and Data Minimisation in Personalisation, Profiling and Decision-Making Systems' *Max Planck Institute for Innovation & Competition Research Paper* (11 January 2021) <https://doi.org/10.48550/arXiv.2101.06203> accessed 30 August 2023

Galli F, *Algorithmic Marketing and EU Law on Unfair Commercial Practices* (Alma Mater Università di Bologna, Springer 2022)

Galli F, Lagioia F and Sartor G, 'Consent to Targeted Advertising' (2022) 33 *European Business Law Review* 485

Galli F, 'Online Behavioural Advertising and Unfair Manipulation Between GDPR and UCPD' in Martin E and Cantero Marta G (eds), *Algorithmic Governance and Governance of algorithms – legal and Ethical Challenges* (Springer 2021)

Geradin D, 'What Is a Digital Gatekeeper? Which Platforms Should Be Captured by the EC Proposal for a Digital Market Act?' (2021) *{SSRN} Scholarly Paper 3788152* <https://papers.ssrn.com/abstract=3788152> accessed 26 May 2023

Geradin D, Katsifis D and Karanikioti T, 'Google as a de Facto Privacy Regulator: Analysing the Privacy Sandbox from an Antitrust Perspective' (2021) 17 *European Competition Journal* 617 <https://doi.org/10.1080/17441056.2021.1930450> accessed 31 August 2023

Guida S, 'Third-Party Cookies and Alternatives: What Consequences in Terms of Consent?' (2021) *European Journal of Privacy Law & Technologies* 135

Helberger N and others, 'EU Consumer Protection 2.0. Structural Asymmetries in Digital Consumer Markets', A joint report from research conducted under the EUCP2.0 project, Commissioned by BEUC, March 2021 <https://www.beuc.eu/brochure/eu-consumer-protection-20-structural-asymmetries-digital-consumer-markets-0> accessed 31 August 2023

Karjalainen T, 'All Talk, No Action? The Effect of the GDPR Accountability Principle on the EU Data Protection Paradigm' (2022) 8 *European Data Protection Law Review* 19

Kemp K, "A Rose by Any Other Unique Identifier': Regulating Consumer Data Tracking and Anonymisation Claims' (2022) 21 *Competition Policy International TechReg Chronicle*

Kretschmer M, Pennekamp J and Wehrle K, 'Cookie Banners and Privacy Policies: Measuring the Impact of the GDPR on the Web' (2021) 15 *ACM Transactions on the Web* 20:1 <https://dl.acm.org/doi/10.1145/3466722> accessed 31 August 2023

Lodder AR and Carvalho JM, 'Online Platforms: Towards an Information Tsunami with New Requirements on Moderation, Ranking, and Traceability' (2022) 33 *European Business Law Review*

Mai J-E, 'Big Data Privacy: The Datafication of Personal Information' (2016) 32 *The Information Society* 192

Mantelero A, 'The Future of Consumer Data Protection in the EU Re-Thinking the "Notice and Consent" Paradigm in the New Era of Predictive Analytics' (2014) 30 *Computer Law & Security Review* 643

Mantelero A, 'Personal Data for Decisional Purposes in the Age of Analytics: From an Individual to a Collective Dimension of Data Protection' (2016) 32 *Computer Law & Security Review* 238

Matz SC and Netzer O, 'Using Big Data as a Window into Consumers' Psychology' (2017) 18 *Current Opinion in Behavioral Sciences* 7

McCann D, Stronge W and Jones P, 'The Future of Online Advertising – Exploring the Impacts of Surveillance-Based Advertising, Current Trends in Adtech and the Challenges and Opportunities Oft a Total Ban on the Use of Personal Data. (october 2021)' (2021) 7 *Retrieved February* 2021

Micklitz HW, "The Role of Standards in Future EU Digital Policy Legislation. A Consumer Perspective", Report Commissioned by BEUC and ANEC, July 2023

Norwegian Consumer Council, 'Out of Control. How Consumers Are Exploited by the Adtech Industry – and What We Are Doing to Make It Stop', 14 January 2020 <https://storage02.forbrukerradet.no/media/2020/01/2020-01-14-out-of-control-final-version.pdf> last access 30 August 2023

Norwegian Consumer Council, 'Time to Ban Surveillance-based Advertising. The Case Against Commercial Surveillance Online' June 2021 <https://storage02.forbrukerradet.no/media/2021/06/20210622-final-report-time-to-ban-surveillance-based-advertising.pdf> last access 31 August 2023

Nottingham M, 'Playing Fair in the Privacy Sandbox: Competition, Privacy and Interoperability Standards' (2021) *{SSRN} Scholarly Paper ID 3891335* <https://papers.ssrn.com/abstract=3891335> accessed 28 February 2022

Pariser E, *The Filter Bubble: What the Internet Is Hiding from you* (Penguin UK 2011)

Rambocas M, Gama J, and others, 'Marketing Research: The Role of Sentiment Analysis' (Universidade do Porto, Faculdade de Economia do Porto 2013)

Reichman A and Sartor G, 'Algorithms and Regulation', *Constitutional Challenges in the algorithmic Society* (Cambridge University Press 2021)

Santos C and others, 'Consent Management Platforms under the GDPR: Processors and/or Controllers?' in Gruschka N, Antunes LF, Rannenberg K and Drogkaris P (eds), *Privacy Technologies and Policy. 9th Annual Privacy Forum, APF 2021 Oslo, Norway, June 17–18, 2021 Proceedings* (Springer 2021)

Simitis S, Hornung G and Spiecker genannt Döhmann I, *Datenschutzrecht: DSGVO Mit BDSG* (Nomos 2019)

Smit EG, Van Noort G and Voorveld HA, 'Understanding Online Behavioural Advertising: User Knowledge, Privacy Concerns and Online Coping Behaviour in Europe' (2014) 32 *Computers in Human Behavior* 15

Strycharz J, Ausloos J and Helberger N, 'Data Protection or Data Frustration? Individual Perceptions and Attitudes Towards the GDPR' (2020) 6 *European Data Protection Law Review* 407

Sunstein CR, *Infotopia: How Many Minds Produce Knowledge* (Oxford University Press 2006)

Susser D, Roessler B and Nissenbaum H, 'Technology, Autonomy, and Manipulation' (2019) 8 *Internet Policy Review*

Tavani HT, 'Informational Privacy: Concepts, Theories, and Controversies' (2008) *The Handbook of Information and Computer Ethics* 131

Turati F, 'Analysing and Exploiting Google's FLoC Advertising Proposal' (Master's thesis, ETH Zurich, Department of Computer Science 2022)

Ur B and others, 'Smart, Useful, Scary, Creepy: Perceptions of Online Behavioral Advertising' *Proceedings of the Eighth Symposium on Usable Privacy and Security* (2012) <https://doi.org/10.1145/2335356.2335362> accessed 30 August 2023

Veale M and Borgesius FZ, 'Adtech and Real-Time Bidding Under European Data Protection Law' (2022) 23 *German Law Journal* 226

Veale M, Nouwens M and Santos C, 'Impossible Asks: Can the Transparency and Consent Framework Ever Authorise Real-Time Bidding After the Belgian DPA Decision?' (2022) *Technology and Regulation* 12

Vilaza GN and Bækgaard P, 'Teaching User Experience Design Ethics to Engineering Students: Lessons Learned' (2022) 4 *Frontiers in Computer Science* 793879

Waldman AE, 'Cognitive Biases, Dark Patterns, and the "Privacy Paradox"' (2020) 31 *Current Opinion in Psychology* 105

Wang J and others, 'Display Advertising with Real-Time Bidding (RTB) and Behavioural Targeting' (2017) 11 *Foundations and Trends in Information Retrieval* 297

Wulf AJ and Seizov O, '"Please Understand We Cannot Provide Further Information": Evaluating Content and Transparency of GDPR-Mandated AI Disclosures' (2022) *AI & Society* 1

Zuiderveen Borgesius FJ, *Improving Privacy Protection in the Area of Behavioural Targeting* (Wolters Kluwer Law & Business 2015)

Zuiderveen Borgesius FJ, 'Personal Data Processing for Behavioural Targeting: Which Legal Basis?' (2015) 5 *International Data Privacy Law* 163

Zuiderveen Borgesius FJ, 'Singling Out People Without Knowing Their Names – Behavioural Targeting, Pseudonymous Data, and the New Data Protection Regulation' (2016) 32 *Computer Law & Security Review* 256

12 Beyond Procedural Fetishism

The Inadequacy of GDPR in Regulating Facial Recognition Technologies and Public Space Surveillance

Monika Zalnieriute

12.1 Introduction

In preparation for the upcoming 2024 Olympics, France has unveiled its plans to use real-time closed-circuit television (CCTV) cameras for AI surveillance of 'anomalies' in the crowds – i.e., unattended baggage, crowd rushes and fights.[1] While this law specifically rules out the use of facial recognition technology (FRT), a month before this, the French Senate voted to adopt a different law permitting FRT to be used in public spaces for three years.[2] In Greece, a police program is being implemented which would allow authorities to use hand-held devices to gather biometric information – with this data being crossed checked across the private, policing and immigration sectors.[3] Similarly, private companies in Spain and Hungary have piloted technology allowing customers to make payments using FRT or palm biometrics.[4] In France, FRT and biometrics have been used to track employees during the course of their work.[5]

From public spaces to banking, policing and welfare, FRT is assisting governments and business alike to monitor crowds and employees, collect taxes, police cities and identify customers. FRT involves processing of a person's facial image, typically for verification, identification, categorization or counting. Concerns

1 'Paris 2024 Olympics: Concern Over French Plan for AI Surveillance' *BBC News* (19 July 2023) <www.bbc.com/news/world-europe-66122743> accessed 25 August 2023.

2 Masha Borak, 'French Senate Votes in Favor of Public Facial Recognition Pilot | Biometric Update' (15 June 2023) <www.biometricupdate.com/202306/french-senate-votes-in-favor-of-public-facial-recognition-pilot> accessed 25 August 2023.

3 'Greece: New Biometrics Policing Program Undermines Rights' (*Human Rights Watch*, 18 January 2022) <www.hrw.org/news/2022/01/18/greece-new-biometrics-policing-program-undermines-rights> accessed 25 August 2023.

4 Tom Phillips, 'Merchants in Spain and Hungary Pilot Cardless Payments Service That Combines Face and Palm Biometrics' (*NFCW*, 15 September 2020) <www.nfcw.com/2020/09/15/367868/merchants-in-spain-and-hungary-pilot-cardless-payments-service-that-combines-face-and-palm-biometrics/> accessed 25 August 2023.

5 'La Formation Restreinte de la CNIL Prononce Une Sanction de 50 Millions D'euros à L'encontre de la Société GOOGLE LLC' (*CNIL*, 20 January 2019) <www.cnil.fr/fr/la-formation-restreinte-de-la-cnil-prononce-une-sanction-de-50-millions-deuros-lencontre-de-la> accessed 17 March 2020.

DOI: 10.4324/9781003502791-17

around an increased use of live automated FRT in airports, train stations and city streets across the globe have led many NGOs, local municipalities and legislators in Europe, the Americas and Asia-Pacific to call for regulation or even outright bans on FRT use. However, regulatory solutions still lag behind. Indeed, one of the leading data protection laws in the world – the General Data Protection Regulation (GDPR) of the European Union (EU) – provides only a non-specific and generalist approach towards managing FRT use. However, an increasing use of FRT in public spaces changes the balance of power between governments and their populations: it enables the state to locate and identify individuals in seconds from a distance, and without the person's knowledge or consent, and without the significant human resources needed in traditional policing or migration.

This chapter focuses on how FRT use in public spaces expands state and corporate power, undermining the rights to privacy, freedom of expression, due process and equal treatment. This approach has its foundations in early surveillance scholarship, which focuses on how surveillance infrastructure alters legal, policing and military practices in a way that changes the individual's relation to society.[6] Significant parts of this scholarship thus focus on privacy and surveillance,[7] suggesting both normative and descriptive definitions for these concepts.[8] The general argument is that public surveillance cannot negate individual expectations of privacy merely by existing in public – these spaces instead could (and should) have adequate privacy protections.[9] The first wave of scholarship analyzed the ability

6 Rachel Hall, 'Surveillance and Public Space' *Oxford Research Encyclopedia, Communication* (Oxford University Press 2017) 1; Kelly Gates and Shoshana Magnet, 'Communication Research and the Study of Surveillance' (2007) 10 *Communication Review* 277; John Gilliom, *Overseers of the Poor: Surveillance, Resistance, and the Limits of Privacy* (University of Chicago Press 2001); Mark Andrejevic, *ISpy: Surveillance and Power in the Interactive Era* (University of Kansas Press 2007); William Bogard, *The Simulation of Surveillance: Hypercontrol in Telematics Societies* (Cambridge University Press 1996); David Lyon, *Surveillance Studies: An Overview* (Polity Press 2007); John McGrath, *Loving Big Brother: Performance, Privacy, and Surveillance Space* (Routledge 2004).

7 Gary T. Marx, 'Coming to Terms: The Kaleidoscope of Privacy and Surveillance' in Beatte Roessler and Dorota Mokrosinska (eds), *Social Dimensions of Privacy: Interdisciplinary Perspectives* (Cambridge University Press 2015); Koops et al note that privacy concerns are not limited only to informational concerns Bert-Jaap Koops and others, 'A Typology of Privacy' (2016) 38 *University of Pennsylvania Journal of International Law* 483.

8 On the definition of surveillance, see Lyon (n 6) 3: 'the focused, systematic and routine attention to personal details for purposes of influence, management, protection or direction'; Kevin D Haggerty and Richard V Ericson (eds), *The New Politics of Surveillance and Visibility* (University of Toronto Press 2006) 3: 'the collection and analysis of information about populations in order to govern their activities'; On the definition of privacy, see Koops and others (n 7) 492; Marx (n 7) 35; Adam D Moore, *Privacy Rights: Moral and Legal Foundations* (Pennsylvania University Press 2010); Bryce Clayton Newell, 'Transparent Lives and the Surveillance State: Policing, New Visibility, and Information Police' (Doctoral thesis, University of Washington 2015) 28; Daniel J Solove, Marc Rotenberg and Paul M Schwartz, *Information Privacy Laws* (Aspen Publishers 2006) 40–51.

9 Tjerk Timan, Bryce Clayton Newell and Bert-Jaap Koops (eds), *Privacy in Public Space: Conceptual and Regulatory Challenges* (Edward Elgar 2017); Bryce Clayton Newell, Tjerk Timan and Bert-Jaap Koops, *Surveillance, Privacy and Public Space* (Routledge 2019); Nicole A Moreham, 'Privacy in Public Places' (2006) 65 *The Cambridge Law Journal* 606; Joel Reidenberg, 'Privacy in Public'

of CCTV cameras in public spaces to encourage self-discipline and affect public attitudes regardless of their 'real' utility,[10] which was followed by the conception of virtual platforms (i.e., the Internet) as 'public spaces' capable of surveilling individual behaviours and interactions.[11] Most recently, research has shifted attention to ideologically loaded public spaces such as protest-sites and universities.[12]

Building on this work, looking in particular at FRT-enabled surveillance and pointing to the absence of oversight and accountability mechanisms, I demonstrate how FRT has significantly strengthened state and corporate power. I suggest that existing regulatory mechanisms, such as the GDPR, do not adequately account for the significant risks of FRT to undermine due process, political protests, equal protection and privacy. The GDPR and the FRT jurisprudence is engaging in what I call procedural fetishism – which is the tendency to focus on procedural safeguards, assuming that these adequately protect against power expansion, rather than dealing directly with the substantive macro-issues on FRT use. To counter such procedural fetishism in FRT governance, I argue that laws and jurisprudence on FRT must avoid procedural fetishism and go beyond procedural safeguards to engage with substantive questions on how to limit the power that FRT expands. The new laws governing FRT use must redistribute power not only by breaking and taxing tech companies, fortifying regulatory enforcement and increasing public scrutiny by adopting prohibitive laws, but also by democratizing big tech companies by making them public utilities and giving people a say on how these companies should be governed. Crucially, we must also decolonize FRT governance discourse through recognizing the colonial practices of extraction and exploitation, and listening to the voices of Indigenous peoples and communities of the so-called Global South. With these mutually reinforcing efforts, a new FRT regulation will debunk the corporate and state agenda of procedural fetishism to ensure that political protests, privacy and due process can flourish in the modern state.

12.2 Facial Recognition Technology: What Is It, and How Does It Work?

FRT augments traditional surveillance methods by detecting and comparing a person's eyes, nose, mouth, to skin textures and shadows to identify individuals.[13]

(2014) 69 *University of Miami Law Review* 141; Helen Fay Nissenbaum, 'Towards and Approach to Privacy in Public: Challenges of Information Technology' (1997) 7 *Ethics & Behaviour* 207; Beatte Roessler, 'Privacy and/in the Public Sphere" (2016) 1 *Yearbook for Eastern and Western Philosophy* 243.

10 Hall (n 6) 12; Bogard (n 6).

11 Hall (n 6) 9.

12 Sara Solarova and others, 'Reconsidering the Regulation of Facial Recognition in Public Spaces' (2023) 3 *AI and Ethics* 625, 1–11; Bryce Clayton Newell, 'Privacy and Surveillance in the Streets: An Introduction' in Bryce Clayton Newell, Tjerk Timan and Bert-Jaap Koops (eds), *Surveillance, Privacy and Public Space* (Routledge 2019) 4. Hall (n 6) 4; Torin Monahan, 'The Right to Hide? Anti-Surveillance Camouflage and the Aestheticization of Resistance' (2015) 12 *Communication and Critical/Cultural Studies* 159.

13 Andrew Guthrie Ferguson, 'Facial Recognition and the Fourth Amendment' (2021) 105 *Minnesota Law Review* 1105; Jagdish Chandra Joshi and Karunesh K Gupta, 'Face Recognition Technology: A

Identifying individuals by their facial features has existed since the 19th century in the form of police sketches, facial mapping (using CCTV) and morphological analysis.[14] FRT is merely an extension of this process[15] – one which significantly expands its capabilities by introducing an algorithmic element. At its core, FRT is a digital matching software which functions by breaking down the digital images of faces into identifiable parts.[16] In this sense, the data functions in a similar way to a digital fingerprint – as various characteristics are identified on the face (i.e., eyebrow or lip position), and these are translated into individual 'data-points' capable of recognition by the software.[17] By then presenting these 'clusters' of characteristics, the software can compare stored information with subsequently captured facial images, returning either a correct match ('one-to-one' matching for verification purposes) or several potential matches ('one-to-many' matching for identification purposes).[18] FRT thus deals with data templates and not directly with images (even though it needs images for the purposes of comparison).[19] The algorithm follows a general path of acquisition and pre-processing, feature extraction, classification and verification/identification.[20]

Review' (2016) 1 *The IUP Journal of Telecommunication* 53; Relly Victoria Virgil Petrescu, 'Face Recognition as a Biometric Application' (2019) 3 *Journal of Mechatronics and Robotics* 237; Mary Grace Galterio, Simi Angelic Shavit and Thaier Hayajneh, 'A Review of Facial Biometrics Security for Smart Devices' (2018) 7, 37 Computers; Ian Berle, *Face Recognition Technology: Compulsory Visibility and Its Impact on Privacy and the Confidentiality of Personal Identifiable Images* (Springer 2020).

14 Marcus Smith, Monique Mann and Gregor Urbas, *Biometrics, Crime and Security* (Routledge 2018) 124.

15 Ibid.

16 Ferguson (n 13) 1105.

17 Ibid., 1111.

18 Smith, Mann and Urbas (n 14) 126.

19 Vera Lúcia Raposo, '(Do Not) Remember My Face: Uses of Facial Recognition Technology in Light of the General Data Protection Regulation' (2023) 32 *Information & Communications Technology Law* 45, 47.

20 Berle (n 13) 13; Galterio, Shavit and Hayajneh (n 13) 1; Benedikt Driessen and Markus Dürmuth, 'Achieving Anonymity against Major Face Recognition Algorithms' in Bart de Decker and others (eds), *Communications and Multimedia Security*, vol. 8099 (Springer 2013) 3:

> First, one needs to find the approximate position of the face in the image; this is called face detection and a separate line of research. Most work on face recognition considers this job to be completed before; commonly used face image databases such as the FERET [a dataset developed by the US Department of Defense used to assist security, intelligence, and law enforcement personnel between 1993 and 1997] database annotate the images with the eye coordinates. Second, images are normalized, which usually includes an affine transformation [that is, the vectors between points of the space] to align the eyes, histogram equalization, and sometimes masking of the background. Third, in feature extraction algorithm-dependent features the probe image [is] extracted. Representing an image by a set of features can be seen as a step-in data reduction that aims at extracting a compact but discriminating description of the image. Ideally, the output of this step is at the same time robust against changes in posture, lighting, face expression, etc. Finally, the pre-processed probe image is matched against gallery images. . . . the output of a face recognition algorithm is a list of identifiers, where the algorithm estimates that the first identifier (e.g., name) is the most likely one, matching the subject on the probe image.

Given the extent of data obtained, FRT covers a range of different software types: 'feature-based' FRT works by identifying the features of a face, person's eyes, nose, mouth and distance between these components, whereas 'appearance-based' FRT focuses on face as a whole during the matching process.[21] More advanced FRT that has emerged in recent years looks to the typical facial traits in addition to any combination of skin textures, shadows and three-dimensional (3D) modeling ('eigenface' features).[22] FRT as a 'touchless' biometric will also grow in prominence a post-pandemic world, and is touted as an irreplaceable aid in tackling future emergencies.[23] All of these FRT types, however, fall within the larger category of biometric identification (from the Greek: *bios* [life] and *metron* [measurement]), as they pinpoint unique biological markers that can identify someone referring to their intrinsic physical or behavioural characteristics.[24] Compared with traditional mechanisms of biometric identification (i.e., fingerprints), FRT significantly expands the processing power of these techniques and allows for a more automated identification process.

Unsurprisingly, due to the relative ease of use and extreme processing power, FRT has become extremely prevalent within public spaces. Here, high-resolution panoramic cameras are used to scan the faces of people in designated public areas, with the data then being transmitted through an online network to a centralized platform. FRT software then compares a collected image of an individual's face – taken from a CCTV surveillance camera, for example – against existing database of facial images of identified individuals (a so-called watch list), looking for a match between a face on the database and the more recently collected image.[25] Some FRT tools go further and purport to classify people by gender or race or make predictions about their emotions and intent; or – most recently – perform 'smart' or 'automated' surveillance by real-time analytics of live video screening. FRT surveillance is particularly disturbing because it does not necessarily aim to identify any particular individual, but instead seeks to monitor the observed space more generally and collect or compare data. The purpose of this monitoring is often two-fold – involving either a 'purposeful' verification of identify, or a more 'purposeless' surveillance and identification for future use. The former approach often occurs where such general face surveillance also attempts to locate particular

21 Ferguson (n 13) 6; Joshi and Gupta (n 13) 53–54; Petrescu (n 13) 240; Galterio, Shavit and Hayajneh (n 13) 3.

22 Galterio, Shavit and Hayajneh (n 13) 3; Petrescu (n 13) 240–241; Berle (n 13) 11.

23 Jeffrey Neuburger, 'Will the Role of Facial Recognition Grow in a Post-COVID-19 World?' (*New Media and Technology Law Blog*, 31 March 2020) https://newmedialaw.proskauer.com/2020/03/31/will-the-role-of-facial-recognition-grow-in-a-post-covid-19-world/.

24 Regulation 2016/679 of the European Parliament and of the Council of 27 April 2016 on the Protection of Natural Persons with Regard to the Processing of Personal Data and on the Free Movement of Such Data, and Repealing Directive 95/46/EC [2016] OJ L119/1 (GDPR) Art. 4/14; Raposo (n 19) 47.

25 Lucas D Introna and Helen Fay Nissenbaum, 'Facial Recognition Technology: A Survey of Policy and Implementation Issues' (The Center for Catastrophe Preparedness & Response 2009) 11.

individuals due to criminal or other suspicion.[26] This is typically known as face identification among law enforcement circles, and involves the comparison of static images collected after a crime has been committed, and comparing it with available databases.[27] Databases of drivers' license photos, mugshots and other images are used for making matches.

The 'purposeless' or generic face surveillance can be actualized in three ways; first, by scanning stored video footage;[28] second, by real-time monitoring;[29] and third, by data mining third-party stored images.[30] Primarily, FRT can be used to scan video surveillance from public places (i.e., public transport, street cameras) – 'data mining' for any faces that appear and then assigning a digital FRT 'template' for current identification.[31] Another mechanism for monitoring public spaces using FRT is through real-time monitoring, which involves matching individuals to previously stored facial templates (which are linked to their pre-filled personal information) in real time.[32] Finally, third-party images from social media sites such as Facebook and Google are also a target for FRT, as parties could acquire those images and match them to existing surveillance to not only improve identification but gather further intelligence about the targeted individuals (i.e., location, interests, relationships).[33]

12.3 From Marketing Tactics to Peaceful Protests: How the Various Uses of FRT Expand Power

FRT is used in many different ways today, by both private companies and public authorities. This chapter mainly focuses on FRT use in public and semi-public spaces, and not in private contexts, such as identifying oneself for smartphone security. However, FRT is deployed in public spaces by both public and private actors.

26 Ferguson (n 13) 12; 'How Facial Recognition Became a Routine Policing Tool in America' <www.nbcnews.com/news/us-news/how-facial-recognition-became-routine-policing-tool-american1004251> accessed 24 June 2020.

27 Ferguson (n 13) 13.

28 See, e.g., Chris Burt, 'Motorola Could Offer Facial Recognition with Police Body Cameras with WatchGuard Acquisition' (*Biometric Update*, 23 July 2019) <www.biometricupdate.com/201907/motorola-could-offer-facial-recognition-with-police-body-cameras-with-watchguard-acquisition> accessed 24 June 2020; Sidney Fussell, 'Did Body Cameras Backfire?' (*The Atlantic*, 1 November 2019) <www.theatlantic.com/technology/archive/2019/11/border-patrol-weighs-body-cameras-face-recognition/600469/> accessed 24 June 2020.

29 See, e.g., 'China's New "super Camera" Can Instantly Pinpoint Specific Targets among Tens of Thousands of People – China Power – ABC News (Australian Broadcasting Corporation)' (8 October 2019) <www.abc.net.au/news/2019-09-26/chinas-new-500-megapixel-super-camera/11539176> accessed 8 October 2019.

30 Petrescu (n 13) 242; Ferguson (n 13) 10–12.

31 Ferguson (n 13) 1116.

32 Ibid., 1117.

33 Ibid., 1118–1119.

One of the earliest public displays of automated FRT was at the 1970 World's Fair in Osaka, Japan, when the Nippon Electric Company (NEC) exhibited a program which would match a user's face with one of seven categories, each representing a famous person.[34] While the program was, as computer scientist Takoe Kanade wrote in his doctoral thesis, "not very reliable", "attraction itself was very successful". The NEC's attraction captured a dataset of photographs from people 'young and old, males and females, with glasses and hats', and at different orientations, 688 of which Takeo Kanade could use in his doctoral thesis on pattern recognition, picture processing and facial recognition.[35] Kanade's thesis enabled rapid identification of human outlines and facial features using computerized subroutines, correctly identifying 75% of people in a photographic set.[36]

However, it took until the 1990s to commercialize FRT, given the substantial difficulties associated with both artificial intelligence (AI) algorithms and the 'noise' associated with real-world data collection.[37] In 1993, the US Department of Defense began a more systematic attempt to develop a Facial Recognition Technology (FERET) program, which was successful enough to justify 'real-time' uses.[38] Simultaneously, private groups such as the Visionics Corporation, Miros Inc., and Viisage Technology emerged as frontrunners in the development of real-time systems to prove the viability of FRT for security and law enforcement purposes.[39] Since then, development of FRT has globalized and increased in pace – Neurotechnology in Lithuania, Veritas in Spain, Idemia in France and many others have worked on FRT, which has become a popular tool for both private companies and public authorities.

12.3.1 Expanding Private Power Through FRT

FRT use has risen sharply within private and commercial settings in recent years.[40] From retail stores to the gambling industry, FRT has become an effective means to increase customer experience, or conversely, actively engage in crime prevention.[41] These vastly differing applications of FRT in the private sector are particularly

34 Kelly Gates, *Our Biometric Future: Facial Recognition Technology and the Culture of Surveillance* (NYU Press 2011) 25; Takeo Kanade, *Computer Recognising Human Faces* (Birkhauser 1977) 33–34.

35 Kanade (n 34) 34.

36 Ibid., 9.

37 Gates (n 34) 47.

38 Ibid., 49; P Jonathon Phillips, Patrick J Rauss and Sandor Z Der, 'FERET (Face Recognition Technology) Recognition Algorithm Development and Test Results' (*Army Research Laboratory* 1996) 7, 54 <https://pdfs.semanticscholar.org/31de/9b3dd6106ce6eec9a35991b2b9083395fd0b.pdf?_ga=2.230812767.1905244237.1592970696-144232886.1592801485> accessed 24 June 2020.

39 Gates (n 34) 49–50.

40 Max Zahn, 'Controversy Illuminates Rise of Facial Recognition in Private Sector' (*ABC News*, 8 January 2023) <https://abcnews.go.com/Business/controversy-illuminates-rise-facial-recognition-private-sector/story?id=96116545> accessed 22 August 2023.

41 Berle (n 13) 20–23.

disturbing because there is a significant lack of transparency and no ability for people to actively consent to its use – meaning corporate power is expanded at the expense of the individual.

Within the commercial sector, FRT is commonly used for non-identification purposes such as classification (i.e., assigning an individual to a demographic based on facial features) or characterization (i.e., inferring customer reactions or feelings).[42] This allows companies to gain data and analyze the demographic entering and purchasing at a store, while also allowing targeted advertisements to be displayed to these customers. For example, the French software company Quividi developed a Smartscreen network in 2015, which has been installed in 41 shopping centres across Australia and New Zealand. These screens contain hidden cameras which determine age, gender and mood to offer a personalized advertisement to passing customers.[43] Not only does the fact that the cameras are hidden mean that individuals remain unaware of the processing of their biometric data, but the benefits are solely reserved for those deploying this technology (i.e., private retail and tech companies) and not the unwitting bypassers. This significantly expands the advertising power of these private companies by allowing them to subtly influence potential customers.

While Quividi insists that the software uses facial detection and not recognition, other companies have not shied away from deploying FRT in these spaces. Not only do companies such as Amazon continue to offer gender recognition as a feature of FRT (with further technologies also being able to detect sexual orientation from the biometric templates produced by FRT),[44] but the technology has recently been used to exclude certain individuals from private premises. In January 2023, Kelly Conlon (an American lawyer) was prevented from entering the Radio City Music Hall in New York – due to FRT identifying her as being on an 'attorney exclusion list' banning employees from entering when their firm is engaged in litigation with the company.[45] These commercial FRT uses often lack adequate consent and significantly infringe on individual's rights to privacy, all while not being bound by state or local regulations due to the activities being conducted on private property.[46] FRT therefore gives private companies the power to achieve their goals (in this case the 'protection' of company information) by any means necessary.

42 Raposo (n 19) 48–49.

43 Eden Gillespie, 'Are You Being Scanned? How Facial Recognition Technology Follows You, Even as You Shop' (*The Guardian*, 24 February 2019) <www.theguardian.com/technology/2019/feb/24/are-you-being-scanned-how-facial-recognition-technology-follows-you-even-as-you-shop> accessed 22 August 2023.

44 Raposo (n 19); James Vincent, 'Automatic Gender Recognition Tech Is Dangerous, Say Campaigners: It's Time to Ban It' (*The Verge*, 14 April 2021) <www.theverge.com/2021/4/14/22381370/automatic-gender-recognition-sexual-orientation-facial-ai-analysis-ban-campaign> accessed 22 August 2023.

45 Zahn (n 40).

46 Dave Gershgorn, 'Retail Stores Are Packed with Unchecked Facial Recognition' (*The Verge*, 14 July 2021) <www.theverge.com/2021/7/14/22576236/retail-stores-facial-recognition-civil-rights-organizations-ban> accessed 22 August 2023.

Moreover, by virtue of their private nature, the ability of individuals to decry these uses is limited significantly.

Additionally, many companies have also sought to use FRT as a means of crime prevention – especially within gambling, banking and larger commercial locations. Not only are companies such as Walmart, Apple, Macy's and 7-Eleven either using the technology in stores currently or proposing to do so in the future,[47] but larger locations such as New York's Madison Square Garden arena are adding it to their security protocols.[48] Additionally, gambling locations have also employed the technology to identify those on self-exclusion registers or those known to cheat, and banks have been planning to install FRT at automated teller machines (ATMs) in the pursuit of secure transactions.[49] These uses are enabled by private tech companies providing the software. For example, FaceFirst is one the most popular FRT software provider in the United States, claiming to work with one-quarter of North America's largest retailers.[50] The cooperation between these private organizations and tech companies means that the actions of private institutions are becoming more similar to law enforcement bodies, as FRT allows retailers to take a more active role in securitization and gathering evidence than previously. Therefore, the use of FRT by companies stands in a blind spot – as their private nature makes it difficult to enforce traditional regulations, even though the FRT data obtained is implemented for traditionally public means (i.e., crime prevention). FRT use thus significantly expands the power of private companies, bestowing them with a quasi-law enforcement role.

12.3.2 Expanding State Power Through FRT

FRT has also been used by public authorities in many different ways. Generic surveillance – mostly through real-time monitoring of public spaces and events – has been particularly controversial. Recently, for example, the UK government used almost a million CCTV cameras during the King's Coronation to deploy live FRT and identify any individuals on their watchlist (i.e., alleged criminals) "in order to keep the public safe".[51] This event constituted the largest use of mass FRT surveillance in public spaces in UK history.[52] Using FRT in these circumstances al-

47 Ibid.; Fight for the Future, 'Ban Facial Recognition in Stores' (*Ban Facial Recognition in Stores*) <www.banfacialrecognition.com/stores> accessed 22 August 2023.

48 Zahn (n 40).

49 Berle (n 13); 'Seven Bank Plans Japan's First Facial Recognition ATM Service' (*Nikkei Asia*) <https://asia.nikkei.com/Business/Finance/Seven-Bank-plans-Japan-s-first-facial-recognition-ATM-service> accessed 22 August 2023.

50 Lauren Debter, 'Retailers Quietly Deploying Controversial Technology to Combat Crime Spree' (*Forbes*) <www.forbes.com/sites/laurendebter/2022/01/31/retailers-quietly-deploying-controversial-technology-to-combat-crime-spree/> accessed 22 August 2023.

51 Mary-Ann Russon, 'How Will AI Facial Recognition Be Used at the King's Coronation?' (*Evening Standard*, 4 May 2023) <www.standard.co.uk/tech/facial-recognition-technology-coronation-met-police-privacy-artificial-intelligence-b1078801.html> accessed 23 August 2023.

52 Ibid.

lows governments to expand their power by both enabling police to arrest and detain individuals with a history of activism before any actual suspicion arises. Moreover, the UK government sought to justify this with regard to the rhetoric of public safety – a common technique for justifying and normalizing power expansion through technology.

Additionally, the FRT software used by the government is often riddled with biases and only serves to reinforce existing racial discrimination. For instance, the FRT used at the coronation was retrospectively identified as having a significant racial bias when deployed at certain thresholds.[53] FRT has also been used to increase the surveillance capabilities of police in specific (mostly non-white) areas. Research by Amnesty International has shown that non-white neighbourhoods in New York (i.e., Bronx, Brooklyn and Queens) are disproportionately exposed to invasive FRT and thus are more often the targets of stop-and-frisk procedures.[54] Authorities in Israel have also used FRT systems to scan the faces of Palestinians and apply automatic restrictions on their movement.[55] FRT thus enables government authorities to strengthen and reinforce racist policing and assert more control over certain populations, undermining due process and equal protection.

Even more concerningly, governments often controversially deploy FRT to tackle global protest movements – functioning both as a means by which to retrospectively track protestors and as a prophylactic against future criminal behaviour. As of 2021, half of the U.S. federal agencies which employ law enforcement officers (about 20) were reported to be using FRT.[56] AI systems have thus been extensively integrated into government activities – with FRT being used as a means to shape police investigations and shift substantial surveillance power into the hands of government institutions.[57]

This was particularly evident in 2020, during the protests following the killing of George Floyd in Minneapolis, Minnesota, where several people involved were arrested and charged after being identified through the use of FRT.[58] Similarly,

53 Lindsay Clark, 'Facial Recog System Used by Met Police Shows Racial Bias' <www.theregister.com/2023/05/25/facial_recognition_system_used_by/> accessed 23 August 2023.

54 'USA: Facial Recognition Technology Reinforcing Racist Stop-and-Frisk Policing in New York – New Research' (*Amnesty International*, 15 February 2022) <www.amnesty.org/en/latest/news/2022/02/usa-facial-recognition-technology-reinforcing-racist-stop-and-frisk-policing-in-new-york-new-research/> accessed 23 August 2023.

55 'Israeli Authorities Using Facial Recognition to Entrench Apartheid' (*Amnesty International*, 2 May 2023) <www.amnesty.org/en/latest/news/2023/05/israel-opt-israeli-authorities-are-using-facial-recognition-technology-to-entrench-apartheid/> accessed 23 August 2023.

56 Nicol Turner Lee and Caitlin Chin, 'Police Surveillance and Facial Recognition: Why Data Privacy Is Imperative for Communities of Color' (*Brookings* 2022) <www.brookings.edu/articles/police-surveillance-and-facial-recognition-why-data-privacy-is-an-imperative-for-communities-of-color/> accessed 22 August 2023.

57 Ferguson (n 13) 1106–1107.

58 Tate Ryan-Mosley and Richards, 'The Secret Police: Cops Built a Shadowy Surveillance Machine in Minnesota after George Floyd's Murder' (*MIT Technology Review*, 3 March 2020) <www.technologyreview.com/2022/03/03/1046676/police-surveillance-minnesota-george-floyd/> accessed 16 April 2023.

Derrick Ingram was tracked to his apartment using FRT and charged with third-degree assault on a police officer, after he shared a photo of himself protesting at the Black Lives Matter (BLM) protest.[59] These events attracted public outcry and resulted in International Business Machines (IBM) and Amazon agreeing not to sell their FRT software to U.S. authorities until more regulations are put in place. However, other companies (i.e., Microsoft, Clearview AI) are still selling their FRT products to law enforcement.[60] In any event, the self-imposed private moratoriums cannot account for the significant increase in state power these technologies facilitate, which results from such profit-driven private-public collaboration between tech companies and public authorities. FRT is thus not only used by governments to prevent protests before and during events, but also to track politically active individuals. These technologies thus expand the surveillance and investigative capabilities of the police so that any individual can be tracked and detained at any point in time and for any charges.

And it's not just U.S. authorities, FRT has also been used to curb peaceful protests in other countries. For instance, FRT has been used in Russia to prevent dissent against President Vladimir Putin and the current government. Recently, FRT was used to retrospectively arrest and convict Nikolay Sergeyevich Glukhin following his peaceful protests on the Moscow metro in 2019.[61] Moreover, FRT has also been used preventatively to detain individuals flagged by the system as politically active. For example, Andrey Chernyshov was detained by police officers in mid-2022 while on the Russian metro after being flagged by FRT for his involvement in previous anti-war protests.[62] As the war with Ukraine has progressed, research has also found that FRT has been used in Russia to prevent protests from occurring – with more than 141 people being preventively detained throughout 2022 (mostly on public holidays or days of national significance).[63] All of these detentions occurred while travelling on the metro, which as recently as 2021 had a new FRT pay system (Face Pay) installed for the purposes of ensuring easier travel.[64] As such, the

59 'Podcast – Facial Recognition and Policing Protesters' (*Amnesty International Canada*) <https://amnesty.ca/podcast-facial-recognition-and-policing-protesters/> accessed 22 August 2023; Adrienne Green, 'What Happened After Derrick Ingram's Standoff with the NYPD' (*Intelligencer*, 25 May 2021) <https://nymag.com/intelligencer/2021/05/derrick-ingram-nypd-standoff.html> accessed 22 August 2023.

60 Matthew Guariglia, 'IBM, Amazon Agree to Step Back From Face Recognition. Where Is Microsoft?' (*Electronic Frontier Foundation*, 10 June 2020) <www.eff.org/deeplinks/2020/06/ibm-amazon-end-and-pause-fr-programs-where-microsoft> accessed 23 August 2023.

61 *Glukhin v Russia, App No 11519/20, Third Section Judgment* (*Eur Ct Hum Rts*, 4 July 2023) <https://hudoc.echr.coe.int/?i=001-225655>; Monika Zalnieriute, 'Glukhin vs Russia' (2023) 117(4) *American Journal of International Law*, pp. 695–701.

62 'How Facial Recognition Is Helping Putin Curb Dissent' *Reuters* (28 March 2023) <www.reuters.com/investigates/special-report/ukraine-crisis-russia-detentions/> accessed 23 August 2023.

63 Ibid.

64 Pjotr Sauer, 'Privacy Fears as Moscow Metro Rolls Out Facial Recognition Pay System | Russia | The Guardian' (*The Guardian*, 15 October 2021) <https://amp.theguardian.com/world/2021/oct/15/privacy-fears-moscow-metro-rolls-out-facial-recognition-pay-system> accessed 23 August 2023.

use of FRT in a seemingly innocuous area eventually led to its integration to police enforcement mechanisms, significantly expanding state power.

Furthermore, wider integration of FRT into government-run services is becoming increasingly normal. As of 2022, 70% of governments across the world use FRT on a large-scale basis – including in airports (60%), public transport (30%) and schools (20%).[65] Countries such as Australia, France and Japan have all introduced FRT to allow individuals to check in to flights without the need for a boarding pass or even a physical passport.[66] Ecuador has even gone as far as to create electronic passports which are authenticated via biometric measures such as FRT.[67] Moreover, FRT has also been deployed by governments in other public spheres such as schools – with the city government of Delhi, India choosing to integrate FRT into a dozen schools during 2021,[68] and Australia also trialling FRT in various schools across New South Wales and Victoria states.[69] The technology has even been integrated into the voting processes in Egypt, India and Bangladesh,[70] with voter turnout being decreased at polls with FRT compared to polls without.[71] Thus, by deploying FRT in these spaces, governments both normalize its use and assert more coercive control over democratic processes.

FRT thus not only allows governments to quickly identify individuals and stifle protests or political dissent, but its wide acceptance as an effective and helpful tool also means it can be implemented in more 'mundane' government activities in the name of 'efficiency'. However, such varied use of FRT has sparked controversy

65 Paul Bischoff, 'Facial Recognition Technology (FRT): 100 Countries Analyzed' (*Comparitech*, 8 June 2021) <www.comparitech.com/blog/vpn-privacy/facial-recognition-statistics/> accessed 24 August 2023.

66 Michael Gebicki, 'Facial Recognition Technology Set to Transform Air Travel' (*The Sydney Morning Herald*, 31 October 2022) <www.smh.com.au/traveller/travel-news/facial-recognition-technology-set-to-transform-air-travel-20221031-h27i5y.html> accessed 24 August 2023; | Alessandro Mascellino, 'Multi-Touchpoint Face Biometrics Systems Unveiled at Airports in Japan and France | Biometric Update' (14 April 2021) <www.biometricupdate.com/202104/multi-touchpoint-face-biometrics-systems-unveiled-at-airports-in-japan-and-france> accessed 24 August 2023.

67 'New ABIS for Biometric Passport Issuance in Ecuador' (*Innovatrics*) <www.innovatrics.com/references/new-abis-for-biometric-passport-issuance-in-ecuador/> accessed 24 August 2023.

68 REUTERS, 'Facial Recognition Tech in Delhi Schools Sparks Privacy Concerns' (*Daily Sabah*, 2 March 2021) <www.dailysabah.com/world/asia-pacific/facial-recognition-tech-in-delhi-schools-sparks-privacy-concerns> accessed 24 August 2023.

69 Sarah Basford Canales, 'Australian Schools Have Been Trialling Facial Recognition Technology, Despite Serious Concerns About Children's Data' (*Gizmodo Australia*, 10 March 2020) <https://gizmodo.com.au/2020/03/australian-schools-trial-facial-recognition-technology-looplearn/> accessed 24 August 2023.

70 'Bangladesh Voter Registration Project Using Biometrics to Detect and Prevent Duplicate Registrations' (*GovTech*, 27 July 2010) <www.govtech.com/security/Bangladesh-Voter-Registration-Project-using-Biometrics.html> accessed 24 August 2023; 'Mobile Biometric Solution MorphoTablet Secures the Voting Process in Egyptian Parliamentary Elections | Biometric Update' (18 December 2015) <www.biometricupdate.com/201512/mobile-biometric-solution-morphotablet-secures-the-voting-process-in-egyptian-parliamentary-elections> accessed 24 August 2023.

71 Feyaad Allie, 'Facial Recognition Technology and Voter Turnout' (2023) 85 *The Journal of Politics* 328.

and concern among civil liberties groups and privacy advocates, who argue that the technology can be used to stifle dissent and violate the rights of individuals merely expressing their opinions or participating in society.[72] Despite these concerns, governments typically defend the use of FRT by framing it either as a simple tool of efficiency or as a necessary measure to maintain 'public safety' and order during a time of civil unrest. FRT is thus part of the broader trend whereby city spaces are increasingly technologized and securitized to enhance monitoring by – and mobilization of – police forces and other authorities.[73]

12.3.3 Public and Private Power Comes Together

In both commercial spaces and law enforcement processes, private companies have been collaborating with public actors to develop the infrastructure for increased surveillance. In the past, this has included police purchasing private FRT or image databases from private companies – often in secret. For example, one of the biggest and oldest technology companies, IBM,[74] has a history of providing governments with technological infrastructure. In recent years, the company has shifted focus from personal computers to AI and FRT,[75] which culminated in the company collaborating with the repressive Philippine government to provide FRT software. In 2019, a report by *The Intercept* revealed that police forces in the Philippines had been provided FRT video software by IMB during 2012, and that this software enabled President Rodrigo Duterte's war on drugs and extrajudicial killings.[76] This technology thus allowed the excessive crime suppression tactics of the Davao police, which were widely known to many human rights organizations.[77] Despite the fact that IBM claimed the deal with the Philippines was for "legitimate public safety activities",[78] it also asserted that the software ceased to be provided in 2012. Nonetheless, IBM continued providing more generic FRT software to the same police forces, with its 'Face Capture' technology being mentioned in a public disclosure in a 2013/2014 presentation.[79] This practice is not new, with IBM supplying previous authoritarian regimes (i.e., Germany's Nazi Party) with technology to

72 Vikram Dodd, 'Police Accused Over Use of Facial Recognition at King Charles's Coronation' (*The Guardian*, 3 May 2023) <www.theguardian.com/uk-news/2023/may/03/metropolitan-police-live-facial-recognition-in-crowds-at-king-charles-coronation> accessed 31 August 2023.

73 Jathan Sadowski and Frank Pasquale, 'The Spectrum of Control: A Social Theory of the Smart City' (2015) 20 *First Monday* 12.

74 Encyclopedia Britannica, 'IBM | Founding, History, & Products' (*Encyclopedia Britannica*) <www.britannica.com/topic/International-Business-Machines-Corporation> accessed 14 October 2020.

75 Eric Reed, 'History of IBM: Timeline and Facts' (*TheStreet*, 24 February 2020) <www.thestreet.com/personal-finance/history-of-ibm> accessed 14 October 2020.

76 George Joseph, 'Inside the Video Surveillance Program IBM Built for Philippine Strongman Rodrigo Duterte' (*The Intercept*, 20 March 2019) <https://theintercept.com/2019/03/20/rodrigo-duterte-ibm-surveillance/> accessed 17 June 2020.

77 Ibid.

78 Ibid.

79 Ibid.

identify and target specific groups of people – specifically, the unique punch-card technology which ran the census and identified Jewish individuals.[80]

More recently, private companies have been continuing this trend of providing governments with the means to target specific populations. For example, Clearview AI – a platform which pairs FRT algorithms with a database of 30 billion photos (primarily from social media) – not only markets itself to law enforcement, but has been under fire for providing services both to U.S. and Australian police forces.[81] These collaborations are often secretive and involve a significant merging between the private and public actors – and increase power for both, often with little awareness from the public.

12.4 No FRT Regulation and the Hope of the GDPR

Despite the increasing deployment of FRT in many cities squares, schools, shopping malls and streets across the globe, its use is not uniformly regulated. Law enforcement agencies, as well as private companies, are experimenting with FRT with discretion and on an ad hoc basis, with neither appropriate legal frameworks to govern its use nor sufficient oversight or public awareness.[82] In the EU, there is no legislation that would directly regulate the use of FRT. The major legislative effort which proposes to regulate use of AI, including FRT, in the future is the European Commission's proposed AI Act.[83] This Act, introduced as a draft proposal in April 2021, would be the first piece of legislation to horizontally regulate AI usage by classifying different AI types into risk-based categories (i.e., unacceptable, high, limited and minimal risk) based on their sector and application.[84] For example, under the AI Act, AI tools assisting in the administration of justice as defined as being 'high risk'.[85] The AI Act sets out extensive legal requirements for such

80 Edwin Black, *IBM and the Holocaust: The Strategic Alliance Between Nazi Germany and America's Most Powerful Corporation-Expanded Edition* (Crown Publishers 2001).

81 Jordan Valinsky Business CNN, 'Clearview AI Has Billions of Our Photos. Its Entire Client List Was Just Stolen' (*CNN*) <www.cnn.com/2020/02/26/tech/clearview-ai-hack/index.html> accessed 6 March 2020; Angela Chen, 'What Happens When Life Insurance Companies Track Fitness Data?' (*The Verge*, 26 September 2018) <www.theverge.com/2018/9/26/17905390/john-hancock-life-insurance-fitness-tracker-wearables-science-health> accessed 31 December 2019.

82 Monika Zalnieriute, 'Burning Bridges: The Automated Facial Recognition Technology and Public Space Surveillance in the Modern State' (2021) 22 *Columbia Science and Technology Review* 314, 284.

83 Proposal for a Regulation of the European Parliament and of the Council Laying Down Harmonised Rules on Artificial Intelligence (AI Act) and Amending Certain Union Legislative Acts 2021.

84 Joshua P Meltzer and Aaron Tielemans, 'The European Union AI Act: Next Steps and Issues for Building International Cooperation in AI' 1 <https://policycommons.net/artifacts/4136169/the-european-union-ai-act/4944759/> accessed 27 August 2023.

85 Proposal for a Regulation of the European Parliament and of the Council Laying Down Harmonised Rules on Artificial Intelligence (AI Act) and Amending Certain Union Legislative Acts (n 78) reads:

> Certain AI systems intended for the administration of justice and democratic processes should be classified as high-risk, considering their potentially significant impact on democracy, rule of law, individual freedoms as well as the right to an effective remedy and to a fair trial. In

'high-risk' systems, including data governance principles, accuracy and security requirements, transparency, and documentation and record-keeping.[86] Nonetheless, the current proposal is still in the process of being adopted – a process which was estimated at the time of writing this chapter to continue until at least the end of 2023.[87] Interestingly, the precursor for the proposal – a draft EU White Paper on AI released in February 2020, appeared to call for a discussion about a temporary five-year ban on FRT use. However, the final proposal removed mention of such a moratorium.[88]

However, pending these legislative developments, so far, the use of FRT in EU has only been regulated indirectly through the more generic data protection and privacy laws, such as the GDPR[89] and the Law Enforcement Directive 2016/680.[90] Additionally, the European Data Protection Board (EDPB),[91] national data protection authorities and the Consultative Committee of the Convention 108+[92] have recently discussed how GDPR and Law Enforcement Directive, as well as the Council of Europe Data Protection Convention 108,[93] regulate the use of FRT.

The GDPR was introduced by the EU in 2018 and is a comprehensive data protection law regulating how companies and governments deal with the

particular, to address the risks of potential biases, errors and opacity, it is appropriate to qualify as high-risk AI systems intended to assist judicial authorities in researching and interpreting facts and the law and in applying the law to a concrete set of facts. Such qualification should not extend, however, to AI systems intended for purely ancillary administrative activities that do not affect the actual administration of justice in individual cases, such as anonymisation or pseudonymisation of judicial decisions, documents or data, communication between personnel, administrative tasks or allocation of resources.

86 Ibid., Chapter 2 of Title III.

87 'EU AI Act: First Regulation on Artificial Intelligence | News | European Parliament' (8 June 2023) <www.europarl.europa.eu/news/en/headlines/society/20230601STO93804/eu-ai-act-first-regulation-on-artificial-intelligence> accessed 28 August 2023.

88 For more on the timeline, see Amrita Khalid, 'The EU's Agenda to Regulate AI Does Little to Rein in Facial Recognition' (*Quartz*, 20 February 2020) <https://qz.com/1805847/facial-recognition-ban-left-out-of-the-eus-agenda-to-regulate-ai/> accessed 10 June 2020.

89 GDPR (n 24).

90 Directive 2016/680 of the European Parliament and of the Council of 27 April 2016 on the Protection of Natural Persons with Regard to the Processing of Personal Data by Competent Authorities for the Purposes of the Prevention, Investigation, Detection or Prosecution of Criminal Offences or the Execution of Criminal Penalties, and on the Free Movement of Such Data, and Repealing Council Framework Decision 2008/977/JHA [2016] OJ L119/89 2016. (Law Enforcement Directive)

91 European Data Protection Board, 'Guidelines 05/2022 on the Use of Facial Recognition Technology in the Area of Law Enforcement' (2022) <https://edpb.europa.eu/system/files/2022-05/edpb-guidelines_202205_frtlawenfo rcement_en_1.pdf>.

92 Consultative Committee of the Convention for the Protection of Individuals with Regard to Automatic Processing of Personal Data Convention 108, 'Guidelines on Facial Recognition T-PD(2020)03rev4' (*Council of Europe, Directorate General of Human Rights and Rule of Law* 2021) <https://r m.coe.int/guidelines-on-facial-recognition/1680a134f3>.

93 Council of Europe, 'Convention for the Protection of Individuals with Regard to the Automatic Processing of Individual Data' (1981) *ETS* 108 <www.coe.int/en/web/data-protection/convention108-and-protocol>.

processing of personal data related to natural persons.[94] As such, the GDPR provides a 'one-size-fits-all' approach to data protection – given its provisions are not adjusted to different sectors, technologies or applications. The main purpose of the GDPR is to give a comprehensive (but generic) outline of the rights of each data subject and the obligations on data-holders and third parties. Importantly, however, the GDPR does not generally apply to the activities of law enforcement authorities (which are instead regulated by the Law Enforcement Directive 2016/680)[95] – only covering the surveillance for law enforcement purposes conducted by private companies.[96] However, public authorities engaging in FRT surveillance for other purposes than law enforcement are covered under the GDPR.

The data collected through FRT is protected under the GDPR, as it falls within the category of 'biometric data' defined under Art. 4/14 as a variant of personal data.[97] This means that in synthesizing the facial templates, FRT creates a form of 'personal data resulting from specific technical processing relating to the physical, physiological or behavioural characteristics of a natural person'.[98] Additionally, FRT data is also likely to fall under a special category of sensitive personal data (i.e., 'sensitive data' in Art. 9 GDPR), as it relates to the processing of an extremely visible feature (i.e., a face) which can reveal a person's racial origin or uniquely identify them.[99] Thus, the data obtained through FRT must comply with the rights and obligations outlined throughout the GDPR.

To begin with, before private companies or public authorities can process data using FRT, Art. 5(1)(a) of the GDPR requires that a proper legal basis exists for the use of FRT. These grounds are further outlined in Art. 6, and include: the data subject consenting, to comply with legal obligations, to protect vital interests of data subject, to carry out a task for the public interest or to achieve the legitimate interests of the controller or third-party (all of which, save consent, require an element of necessity).[100] Additionally, since FRT is a new technology which processes personal data, Arts. 32 and 35 of the GDPR place extra obligations on data processers. For example, Art. 32 requires that procedural safeguards appropriate to the level of risk posed by data processing (i.e., encryption, confidentiality, evaluation of methods) are implemented.[101] Article 35 further requires that new technologies are accompanied by a data protection risk assessment which outlines the potential risks of the technology and the measures introduced to address them.[102]

94 GDPR (n 24) Art. 1.
95 (Law Enforcement Directive) (n 93).
96 GDPR (n 24) Art. 2; Raposo (n 19) 46.
97 GDPR (n 24) 4/14; Raposo (n 19) 47.
98 GDPR (n 24) Art. 4.
99 Ibid., Art. 9.
100 Ibid., Art. 6.
101 Ibid., Art. 32.
102 Ibid., Art. 35.

12.5 The Inadequacy of GDPR Approach in Regulating FRT: No One-Size-Fits-All

However, even though the GDPR restricts FRT use to certain situations and encourages specific safeguards to be put in place, it does not do enough to prevent the abuse of state and corporate power which FRT enables. Not only are the one-size-fits-all regulations inadequate for constraining the unique features of this technology, but the legislation also implicitly sanctions FRT use in spaces where it should be fundamentally challenged. As such, the current approach is inadequate in two senses: first, due to its focus on procedural safeguards, the GDPR is unable to adequately constrain FRT use; and second, the GDPR fails to address the substantive issues arising from FRT use. I address these arguments in turn.

12.5.1 The GDPR's Approach – Procedural Fetishism

In spite of the significant challenges that FRT poses to due process, individual privacy and freedom of expression, discussed in earlier sections, the GDPR does little to address the fundamental power disbalance enabled by FRT. Instead, its focus is largely on how companies and governments can effectively integrate FRT into their processes and mitigate these aforementioned risks. This approach is laden with what I call procedural fetishism – an overemphasis and focus on procedural safeguards which redirects public attention from more substantive questions about the concentration and limits of power to procedural micro-issues.[103] In the area of surveillance, procedural fetishism is characterized by a failure to discuss the substantive legality of how new technologies affect the lives of individuals and the public, focusing instead on introducing procedural safeguards to mitigate any risks (which assumes their proportionality, functionality and effectiveness).[104] Indeed, rather than setting out situations when FRT use should be prohibited, the GDPR merely legitimizes the use of FRT in any circumstances, assuming enough safeguards have been put in place. Such an approach missed the very first step – asking whether, in particular circumstances, FRT should be used at all. Such procedural fetishism also implicitly approves the use of FRT by both the government authorities and companies alike, legitimizing it in the eyes of the public.[105]

The main way the GDPR purports to protect personal sensitive data obtained by FRT is by imposing stricter requirements for both the legal grounds for processing (Art. 9) and the securitization of that data (Arts. 24–25 and 32). Article 9 of the GDPR restricts the processing of personal data to ten specified circumstances – such

103 Monika Zalnieriute, 'Against Procedural Fetishism: A Call for a New Digital Constitution' (2023) 30(2) *Indiana Journal of Global Legal Studies* 227–264.

104 Monika Zalnieriute, 'Procedural Fetishism and Mass Surveillance under the ECHR: Big Brother Watch v. UK' (*Verfassungsblog: On Matters Constitutional*, 2 June 2021) 4 <https://verfassungsblog.de/big-b-v-uk/> accessed 03 May 2024.

105 Monika Zalnieriute, '"Transparency-Washing" in the Digital Age: A Corporate Agenda of Procedural Fetishism' (2021) 8 *Critical Analysis of Law* 39.

as when consent is obtained, and when it is necessary for legitimate activities to protect vital interests of the data subject, or for reasons of substantial public interest.[106] Out of the ten exceptions, six require that the data processing is accompanied by "specific measures to safeguard the fundamental rights and interests of the data subjects".[107] As such, the GDPR's focus on mandating procedural safeguards not only relies on the data controller's assessment of the appropriate protections, but it also validates the use of FRT in these areas – thus overestimating the ability of any safeguards to adequately protect the rights of the individual and failing to ask the fundamental question as to whether the processing of such personal data should be permitted to begin with.

Moreover, the GDPR obliges the data controller to take into account the nature and risks of the technology to implement appropriate technical measures (Arts. 24–25 and 32) and, in the case of new technologies, undertake a Data Protection Impact Assessment (DPIA; Arts. 35–36). Law enforcement authorities across the globe, however, start using FRT without fail to undertaking these DPIAs – as in the famous case *Bridges*, decided by England's Court of Appeal in 2020.[108] In *Bridges*, the South Wales Police had failed to carry out a proper DPIA for its FRT use and had not complied with the public sector equality duty.[109] However, even if the police authorities undertake DPIAs, this GDPR approach arguably functions to facilitate the processing of data via new technologies, such as FRT, rather than subject them to a substantive assessment of the merits behind its use. Moreover, the automated nature of FRT (as evidenced in this case) also poses significant difficulties for data controllers adhering to the GDPR – as the ability of FRT to 'adapt' and 'automate' its processes means that such data protection assessments may become obsolete as newer (and less predictable) risks arise.

The procedural fetishism found in the GDPR is not limited to data protection laws; it is also prevalent in the nascent FRT jurisprudence. Many recent court decisions from across the world demonstrate that FRT jurisprudence does not go beyond the discussion of procedural safeguards, instead focusing on whether the safeguards introduced by the government or company are sufficient to justify any incursions on fundamental human rights. For example, while the first court decision on FRT in the world – the *Bridges* case – ruled that South Wales law enforcement's use of automated FRT was unlawful because it was not 'in accordance with law' for the purposes of Art. 8 of the European Convention on Human Rights (ECHR),[110] the court only ruled so because the police failed to put adequate procedural safeguards in place.[111]

106 GDPR Art 9.
107 Ibid.
108 *R (on the application of Edward Bridges) v The Chief Constable of South Wales Police* [2020] Court of Appeal (Civil Division) C1/2019/2670; EWCA Civ 1058.
109 Ibid., 210.
110 *R (on the application of Bridges) v Chief Constable of South Wales Police [2020] EWCA Civ 1058.*
111 Zalnieriute, 'Burning Bridges' (n 74) 284–307.

Moreover, the European Court of Human Rights (ECtHR) has also recently taken a similar approach to the legality of the FRT use by law enforcement, grounded in procedural fetishism. In 2023 in *Glukin v Russia*, the Court found that Russia's use of FRT to track down a peaceful protestor breached Arts. 8 and 10 of the Convention – but largely because the government failed to put in sufficient procedural safeguards to warrant an incursion on the rights to privacy and freedom of expression.[112] Even more so, in 2022, France's Conseil d'État (Council of State) held that the use of FRT to identify suspects during criminal proceedings was 'absolutely necessary' for the purposes of national French legislation, implementing Art. 10 of the EU *Law Enforcement Directive* – given the extent of data which could assist the police and the proportionality to the aim pursued.[113]

These judgments, while mostly finding that the use of FRT or surveillance has resulted in a breach of fundamental human rights (not the French one!), fail to actively engage with the risks surrounding the use of FRT and its ability to significantly expand state and corporate power and undermine both the rights of the individuals and the civic life of the public. Skipping the substantive questions such as whether mass-FRT surveillance could be ever proportional, the courts become complicit in the normalization of FRT use by governments and companies – instead relying entirely on the assumption that adequate safeguards can exist, and that the infringements on human rights caused by FRT only stem from an absence of adequate protections.[114] This approach, grounded in procedural fetishism, is similar to the one taken through the GDPR, as they both promote FRT use in any way – as long as certain 'safeguards' are in place.

12.5.2 Substantive Questions We Ignore: Power Shifts and FRT

However, procedural safeguards are unlikely to protect against the abuse of power and violations of fundamental rights and civil liberties that FRT use enables – because talking about procedural safeguards alone does not address the questions about how FRT use enables mass surveillance, which, in turn, can have a chilling effect on the rights to freedom of expression and association, privacy, and due process, resulting in discriminatory treatment, among other concerns. It can be easily misused by law enforcement to target certain groups of people, such as political

112 *Glukhin v Russia* (n 61).

113 *Conseil d'Etat, Décision n° 442364, 26 April 2022* <www.conseiletat.fr/fr/arianeweb/CE/decision/2022-04-26/442364> accessed 17 July 2023; Directive 2016/680 of the European Parliament and of the Council of 27 April 2016 on the Protection of Natural Persons with Regard to the Processing of Personal Data by Competent Authorities for the Purposes of the Prevention, Investigation, Detection or Prosecution of Criminal Offences or the Execution of Criminal Penalties, and on the Free Movement of Such Data, and Repealing Council Framework Decision 2008/977/JHA [2016] OJ L119/89 [2016] OJ L119/89.

114 Monika Zalnieriute, 'Glukhin vs Russia' (2023) 117(4) *American Journal of International Law* 695–701

activists or marginalized communities, and such targeting often leads to further discrimination and injustice. Therefore, FRT augments the state and corporate power against customers and citizens – and the ability or capacity of procedural safeguards to rectify such an imbalance is limited, if not illusory.

12.5.2.1 FRT Use and Public Space Surveillance

For example, the growing prevalence of public space surveillance through FRT has a chilling effect on public discourse by threatening the right to protest anonymously, a notion fundamental to protest movements. Protest movements must be able to access tangible physical public locations – often places such as streets, roads and parks. Given the practicality of gathering large numbers of citizens, these public spaces have become foundational to social and political movements and symbolic of democratic freedom, being understood as a "foundational space for democracy".[115] In occupying these spaces, groups become visible and disruptive forces capable of airing dissent and demanding change.[116] Public spaces, particularly for the purpose of protest, thus allow individuals to "touch upon the balance of power, rule of law and democratic governance"[117] and challenge power structure by questioning how governments maintain the integrity of these public spaces.[118]

FRT use in public spaces – whether to retribute against protestors or engage in generic surveillance activities – interferes with the ability of citizens and communities to engage in public protest anonymously. Historically, protestors have always often been capable of retaining anonymity, but the increased deployment of FRT in public spaces is constantly challenging this right, which is fundamental to social movements and protests. The general understanding of protests – as a means of facilitating democratic participation – is that individuals forfeit their individual voice for the benefit of social disruption and are, in turn, granted the right of anonymity. Thus, a sense of safety arises out the fact that demonstrating requires an individual to join a collective and express an idea larger than themselves. Without this promise of anonymity, protestors are unlikely to feel safe when gathering in public and manifesting their disagreement with current norms – as surveillance tools create fear that their data will be weaponized against them to punish their dissent. As such, the goals

115 Richard Sennett, *The Spaces of Democracy* (Ann Arbor: University of Michigan, College of Architecture and Urban Planning 1998).

116 Daniel Trottier and Christian Fuchs, 'Theorising Social Media, Politics and the State: An Introduction' in Daniel Trottier and Christian Fuchs (eds), *Social Media, Politics and the State* (Routledge 2015) 33; Alberto Melucci and Leonardo Avritzer, 'Complexity, Cultural Pluralism and Democracy: Collective Action in the Public Space' (2000) 39 *Social Science Information* 507.

117 Jens Kremer, 'The End of Freedom in Public Places? Privacy Problems Arising from Surveillance of the European Public Space' (Doctoral dissertation, University of Helsinki 2017) 73.

118 'Protestbewegung – Warum Einen Öffentlichen Platz Besetzen? (Why Occupy a Public Space?)' (*Deutschlandfunk*,2014)<www.deutschlandfunk.de/protestbewegung-warum-einen-oeffentlichen-platz-besetzen.1184.de.html?dram:article_id=299327> accessed 17 June 2020.

of protesting can only truly be achieved if protestors remain anonymous, a right that is increasingly challenged and eroded by FRT-enabled surveillance.

As surveillance technologies such as FRT become the norm for monitoring and controlling collective action across many countries, scholars have become increasingly focused on the chilling effect this may have on dissent.[119] In particular, using FRT to track and detain individual protestors (i.e., Derrick Ingram during BLM, Nikolay Sergeyevich Glukhin in Russia) shifts the power balance between individuals and the state. The individual no longer is a 'free autonomous citizen', and thus public space surveillance negatively affects the rule of law and democratic participation.[120] Such tools, particularly FRT, disempower protestors with regard to their biological information[121] – which both threatens them[122] and simultaneously breaks down their collective image. Surveillance can thus be conceptualized as a disciplinary process, since these tools can actualize punishment and retribution against individual protestors who would normally be part of a collective. The prevalence of surveillance technologies is also indicative of what Deleuze called the 'controlled' society.[123]

Indeed, the use of FRT in public spaces – whether to retribute against protestors or engage in generic surveillance activities – can be seen largely as an attempt to maintain the status quo of neoliberal governmentality. The modern surveillance state has become the Foucauldian prison – where individuals are located, identified and classified as threats to society.[124] The widespread use of FRT is thus reflective of a power shift which Foucault claims began following the Second World War; where the population as a statistical body became the dominant object of power over the individual.[125] A good tangible example of this power shift is the

119 Lucas Melgaco and Jeffrey Monoghan, 'Introduction: Taking to the Streets in the Information Age' in Lucas Melgaco and Jeffrey Monoghan (eds), *Protests in the Information Age* (Routledge 2018); Luis Fernandez, *Policing Dissent: Social Control and the Anti-Globalization Movement* (Rutgers University Press 2008); P Gillham, 'Securitizing America: Strategic Incapacitation and the Policing of Protest since the 11 September 2001 Terrorist Attacks' (2011) 5 *Sociology Compass* 636; P Gillham, B Edwards and J Noakes, 'Strategic Incapacitation and the Policing of Occupy Wall Street Protests in New York City, 2011' (2013) 23 *Policing and Society* 81; Jeffrey Monoghan and K Walby, 'Making up "Terror Identities": Security Intelligence, Canada's Integrated Threat Assessment Centre, and Social Movement Suppression' (2012) 22 *Policing and Society* 133; Jeffrey Monoghan and K Walby, '"They Attacked the City": Security Intelligence, the Sociology of Protest Policing, and the Anarchist Threat at the 2010 Toronto G20 Summit' (2012) 60 *Current Sociology* 653.

120 Irena Nesterova, 'Mass Data Gathering and Surveillance: The Fight against Facial Recognition Technology in the Globalized World' 6 <www.shs-conferences.org/articles/shsconf/pdf/2020/02/shsconf_glob2020_03006.pdf> accessed 2 June 2020.

121 J Pugliese, *Biometrics: Bodies, Technologies, Biopolitics* (Routledge 2012).

122 T Monahan, 'Dreams of Control at a Distance: Gender, Surveillance, and Social Control' (2009) 9 *Cultural Studies ↔ Critical Methodologies* 286.

123 Gilles Deleuze, 'Postscript on the Societies of Control' (1992) 59 *October* 3; Zygmunt Bauman and David Lyon, *Liquid Surveillance: A Conversation* (Polity Press 2013); Melgaco and Monoghan (n 115).

124 Michel Foucault, *Discipline and Punish: The Birth of the Prison* (Pantheon Books 1977) 196–197.

125 Michel Foucault, *Security, Territory, Population: Lectures at the Collège de France 1977–1978* (Palgrave Macmillan UK 2009) 25; Claudio Celis Bueno, 'The Face Revisited: Using Deleuze and

emergence of smart (or connected) cities – where information and communication technologies are applied to infrastructure or civil processes to create city-wide networks.[126] Songdo (South Korea),[127] Masdar City (the United Arab Emirates),[128] Barcelona (Spain),[129] London (UK),[130] and Copenhagen (Denmark) have all implemented such smart cities.[131] Can procedural safeguards alone protect us from this shift in power, which fundamentally alters and redefines not only privacy expectations, but also civic and political life of the public? Or do we need law of a different kind – for example, laws that prohibit FRT use in public settings or laws that demand breaking tech companies and making them public utilities? These possibilities are discussed in the final section of this chapter.

12.5.2.2 FRT Use and Discriminatory Treatment

FRT deployment has also resulted in discriminatory treatment, and it is very questionable how procedural safeguards alone could rectify this. Academic researchers have long argued that FRT is not a 'neutral' process[132] but instead reinforces historical inequalities through its biases and inaccuracies.[133] For example, FRT has been shown to perform poorly when identifying women, children and individuals with darker skin tones.[134] This was illustrated at the King's Coronation in the UK and many

---

Guattari to Explore the Politics of Algorithmic Face Recognition' (2020) 37 *Theory, Culture & Society* 73, 88.

126 Sadowski and Pasquale (n 73) 2–3.

127 'Songdo IBD' <http://songdo.com/> accessed 30 June 2020.

128 'Masdar City, a Zero-Waste, Zero-Carbon City in the Desert | Living Circular' <www.livingcircular.veolia.com/en/city/masdar-city-zero-waste-zero-carbon-city-desert> accessed 30 June 2020.

129 Ross Tieman, 'Barcelona: Smart City Revolution in Progress' (26 October 2017) <www.ft.com/content/6d2fe2a8-722c-11e7-93ff-99f383b09ff9> accessed 30 June 2020.

130 'Smarter London Together' (*London City Hall*, 7 June 2018) <www.london.gov.uk//what-we-do/business-and-economy/supporting-londons-sectors/smart-london/smarter-london-together> accessed 30 June 2020.

131 Copenhagen Capacity, 'Smart City in Greater Copenhagen' <www.copcap.com/set-up-a-business/key-sectors/smart-city> accessed 30 June 2020.

132 Clare Garvie, Alvaro Bedoya and Jonathan Frankle, 'The Perpetual Line-Up' (*Centre on Privacy and Technology* 2016) <www.perpetuallineup.org/> accessed 11 November 2019; B F Klare and others, 'Face Recognition Performance: Role of Demographic Information' (2012) 6 *Information Forensics and Security, IEEE Transactions On* 7 1789; Joy Buolamwini and Timnit Gebru, 'Gender Shades: Intersectional Accuracy Disparities in Commercial Gender Classification' *Proceedings of Machine Learning Research* (2018) <http://proceedings.mlr.press/v81/buolamwini18a/buolamwini18a.pdf> accessed 17 June 2020.

133 Matthew Schwartz, 'Color-Blind Biometrics? Facial Recognition and Arrest Rates of African-Americans in Maryland and the United States' (Thesis in partial fulfilment of a Master of Public Policy, Georgetown University 2019) 15.

134 Salem Hamed Abdurrahim, Salina Abdul Samad and Aqilah Baseri Huddin, 'Review on the Effects of Age, Gender, and Race Demographics on Automatic Face Recognition' <https://link-springer-com.wwwproxy1.library.unsw.edu.au/content/pdf/10.1007/s00371-017-1428-z.pdf> accessed 2 June 2020; 'Amazon's Face Recognition Falsely Matched 28 Members of Congress with Mugshots' (*American Civil Liberties Union*) <www.aclu.org/blog/privacy-technology/surveillance-technologies/amazons-face-recognition-falsely-matched-28> accessed 2 June 2020.

other events. Given that marginalized groups already face systemic issues of inequality, FRT surveillance serves to increase and reinforce already existing discrimination. Discrimination and bias are thus often introduced into the FRT software at three stages in the technical process – either whilst learning, simplifying or after applying the technology. First, the machine learning process may introduce bias depending on the training dataset and system design. Second, an element of technical bias may be inherent to the simplification of reality (i.e., faces) into code; and third, emergent bias could arise from user interactions which specific populations after the technology's implementation.[135] These biases are particularly prevalent in the law enforcement context, as the training data comes from photo databases relating to past criminal activity.[136] This becomes even more dangerous in jurisdictions, such as the United States, where people of colour are more likely to be *pulled over*,[137] *searched*,[138] *arrested*,[139] *incarcerated*,[140] and *wrongfully convicted*[141] than white women. As a result, minorities and people of colour become overrepresented in FRT training systems,[142] and police use of FRT can result in a high number of false positives due to functioning in this already discriminatory environment. The FRT not only infringes on protesting rights, but can also disproportionately diminishes the freedom of assembly for those who are already marginalized. Many claim that algorithms cannot be understood as neutral, but rather as a social mechanism which "reifies existing power and class structures".[143]

135 Rebecca Crootof, '"Cyborg Justice" and the Risk of Technological – Legal Lock-In' (2019) 119 *Columbia Law Review* 1, 8; Batya Friedman and Helen Fay Nissenbaum, 'Bias in Computer Systems' (1996) 14 *ACM Transactions on Information Systems* 330, 333–336.

136 Henriette Ruhrmann, 'Facing the Future: Protecting Human Rights in Policy Strategies for Facial Recognition Technology in Law Enforcement' (May 2019) 46 <https://citrispolicylab.org/wp-content/uploads/2019/09/Facing-the-Future_Ruhrmann_CITRIS-Policy-Lab.pdf> accessed 1 June 2020; Garvie, Bedoya and Frankle (n 132).

137 'New Data Reveals Milwaukee Police Stops Are About Race and Ethnicity' (*American Civil Liberties Union*) <www.aclu.org/blog/criminal-law-reform/reforming-police/new-data-reveals-milwaukee-police-stops-are-about-race-and> accessed 2 June 2020; Frank R Baumgartner, Derek A Epp and Kelsey Shoub, *Suspect Citizens What 20 Million Traffic Stops Tell Us About Policing and Race* (Cambridge University Press 2018).

138 'New Data Reveals Milwaukee Police Stops Are About Race and Ethnicity' (n 144); Camelia Simoiu, Sam Corbett-Davies and Sharad Goel, 'The Problem of Infra-Marginality in Outcome Tests for Discrimination' (2017) 11 *The Annals of Applied Statistics* 1193; Lynn Lanton, 'Police Behavior during Traffic and Street Stops, 2011' <www.bjs.gov/content/pub/pdf/pbtss11.pdf> accessed 2 June 2020.

139 'NAACP | Criminal Justice Fact Sheet' (*NAACP*) <www.naacp.org/criminal-justice-fact-sheet/> accessed 2 June 2020; Megan Stevenson and Sandra Mayson, 'The Scale of Misdemeanor Justice' (2018) 98 *Boston University Law Review* 371.

140 'The Color of Justice: Racial and Ethnic Disparity in State Prisons' (*The Sentencing Project*) <www.sentencingproject.org/publications/color-of-justice-racial-and-ethnic-disparity-in-state-prisons/> accessed 2 June 2020.

141 Samuel Gross, Maurice Possley and Klara Stephens, 'Race and Wrongful Convictions in the United States' (*National Registry of Exonerations* 2017) <www.law.umich.edu/special/exoneration/Documents/Race_and_Wrongful_Convictions.pdf> accessed 2 June 2020.

142 Ruhrmann (n 136) 63; Garvie, Bedoya and Frankle (n 132).

143 Bueno (n 125) 76; Jonathan Beller, *The Message Is Murder: Substrates of Computational Capital* (Pluto Press 2018); Trevor Paglen, 'Invisible Images (Your Pictures Are Looking at You)' (The New Inquiry, 8 December 2016) <https://thenewinquiry.com/invisible-images-your-pictures-are-looking-at-you/>

To truly understand the problems of bias and discrimination that are inherent to the application of FRT, it is necessary to delve into its history and production. Even though biometrics are often heralded as being futuristic technologies, they are in fact one of the oldest forms of identification, and FRT is merely the latest extension in such techniques which measure the human form.[144] While biometric identification dates back to around 2558 BCE in Ancient Egypt – when individual body measurements were used to identify and verify the identity of workers[145] – the technology became particularly prevalent in the colonial context of the 19th century.[146] This was largely because this time of slavery and mass assimilation posed significant issues of identity and mobility to missionaries, such that biometric identification (i.e., fingerprinting, photography, anthropomorphic science) allowed European authorities to 'fix' and control the populations they deemed unruly.[147] The British (namely, William Herschel) established the practice of using fingerprints when Britain was 'administrating' India to "tell the difference" between their Indian subjects.[148] The Belgians measured facial characteristics and conducted blood tests to categorize Rwandans into groups and construct specific races amongst them, with policy being that specific groups were preferred for specific roles in the colony.[149] This categorization later gave rise to much of the scholarship on eugenics – since the pioneer of this practice asserted that criminality was inherently linked to physicality and one's fingerprints.[150] Therefore, facial biometrics were a fundamental aspect of various colonial regimes throughout history.

In modern contexts, FRT's reliance on the racialized colonial order is best exemplified by its resources extraction process, which often occurs in formerly colonial spaces. As a result, many FRT and AI systems use methods and resources which are rooted in colonization. For example, the Mahalanobis distance function (which determines statistical similarity and informs machine learning today) was developed using a subset of population data from the Bengal Province in India during the 1920s to classify unknown individuals into castes based on head size.[151] Given the prevalence of this function in FRT today, it serves to both reinforce colonial standards of the caste system in the modern context and influence other classification systems inherent in FRT.[152] Conversely (yet unsurprisingly), the application of FRT preferentially favours Caucasian skin tones, with projects such as the Dark Database demonstrating

---

accessed 16 June 2023; Safiya Umoja Noble, Algorithms of Oppression: How Search Engines Reinforce Racism (New York University Press 2018); Virginia Eubanks, *Automating Inequality: How High-Tech Tools Profile, Police, and Punish the Poor* (St Martin's Press 2018).

144 Sara M Smyth, *Biometrics, Surveillance and the Law* (Routledge 2019) 13, 21.

145 Ibid., 21–22.

146 Ibid., 13.

147 Ibid.

148 Ibid., 29.

149 Ibid., 30.

150 Ibid., 30–31.

151 Simon Michael Taylor, Kalervo N Gulson and Duncan McDuie-Ra, 'Artificial Intelligence from Colonial India: Race, Statistics, and Facial Recognition in the Global South' (2021) *Science, Technology, & Human Values* 01622439211060839, 3.

152 Ibid., 4.

the FRT often does not detect nor enroll darker skin tones into the system – meaning that the system inherently privileges Caucasian skin (whilst 'forgetting' people of colour).[153] It is not surprising, then, that several critics have suggested that FRT bears resemblance to the outdated practices of phrenology and physiognomy[154] – as these popularized (but delegitimized) scientific methods also seek to maintain power relationships within society, in a similar fashion to FRT today.

12.6 What Should We Do? Beyond Procedural Fetishism

Since the current applications of FRT in both commercial and government sectors are riddled with risks to democratic participation and rights to peaceful assembly, and encourage discriminatory policing practices, legislatures should seek to impose further regulatory mechanisms and entirely ban FRT use in certain circumstances. While current laws such as the GDPR do attempt to regulate AI use in some fashion, their focus on procedural safeguards as a way to limit the risks associated with FRT is insufficient to restrain both companies and governments from exploiting these technologies. As the risks posed by the use of FRT strike at the heart of rule of law, both legislatures and judiciaries must instead engage with substantive questions about how to limit corporate and state power in the face of these new technologies. While recent scholarship has suggested several avenues to protecting individuals from abuse (i.e., regulation,[155] standards of algorithmic accountability[156] and auditing processes),[157] I argue that dealing with the fundamental questions surrounding FRT use – and avoiding procedural fetishism – is necessary to ensure that the 'chilling effect' of FRT is eliminated.

153 Dennis Delgado, 'The Dark Database: Facial Recognition and Its" Failure" to Enroll' (2021) 17 *Media-N* 69.

154 Bueno (n 125) 75; Beller (n 143); Gates (n 34); Paglen (n 143); 'Sci-Fi Crime Drama with a Strong Black Lead' (*The New Inquiry*, 27 June 2015) <https://thenewinquiry.com/sci-fi-crime-drama-with-a-strong-black-lead/> accessed 16 June 2020; 'Noble (n 143). Physiognomy's New Clothes – Blaise Aguera y Arcas – Medium' <https://medium.com/@blaisea/physiognomys-new-clothes-f2d4b59fdd6a> accessed 16 June 2020.

155 Marion Oswald, 'Algorithm-Assisted Decision-Making in the Public Sector: Framing the Issues Using Administrative Law Rules Governing Discretionary Power' (2018) 376 *Philosophical Transactions of the Royal Society* A <https://royalsocietypublishing.org/doi/abs/10.1098/rsta.2017.0359> accessed 10 September 2018; Andrew Tutt, 'An FDA for Algorithms' (2017) 69 *Administrative Law Review* 83.

156 Corinne Cath and others, 'Artificial Intelligence and the "Good Society": The US, EU, and UK Approach' (2018) 24 *Science and Engineering Ethics* 505.

157 Brent Mittelstadt, 'Auditing for Transparency in Content Personalization Systems' (2016) 10 *International Journal of Communication* 4991; Pauline T Kim, 'Auditing Algorithms for Discrimination' (2017) 166 *University of Pennsylvania Law Review Online* 189.

12.6.1 Holding FRT Companies Accountable for Power Abuse

One way we can start addressing substantive issues surrounding the FRT use is by holding the private companies creating and deploying FRT technologies to account. As discussed in Section 12.3.3, these private actors play a significant role in increasing surveillance of public and private spaces, and their products are often readily integrated into policing or other areas in the name of 'efficiency'. For example, in both commercial spaces (i.e., Quividi) and law enforcement processes (i.e., Clearview AI), telecommunications service providers and tech giants have been cooperating with private and public actors to develop the infrastructure for increased surveillance. In the past, this has included police purchasing private FRT or image databases – often in secret.

Thus, we need to make the companies providing the FRT infrastructure accountable. Creating public and consumer pressure may be effective in some senses (i.e., backlash from the BLM protests stopping IBM and Amazon from providing FRT, as explained in Section 12.3.3).[158] However, such pressure relies heavily on self-imposed moratoriums which depend entirely on the companies themselves. Yet we need measures that are not just aspirational but legal in nature and that deal with the substantive questions of power surrounding FRT use. Such more substantive change, however, could be achieved through adapting existing legal instruments (i.e., human rights law) to private actors, and by targeting the structure and functioning of FRT companies. This could include the introduction of significant taxes or implementation of anti-competition laws for big tech, democratizing FRT companies to align their practices with public utility, and decolonizing technological infrastructure to deal with the substantive issue of these technologies continuing to ensure these spaces do not continue to marginalize specific groups. I discuss these in turn.

12.6.1.1 Private Accountability Through Human Rights Law

One way to hold private companies accountable could be through human rights law and an international legally binding treaty on business and human rights. Such treaty has been discussed since 1970s, and currently is being debated again at the United Nations (UN).[159] However, currently, private companies fall within the hu-

158 Guariglia (n 60).

159 *See Binding Treaty*, Bus. & Hum. Rts. Res. Ctr., business-humanrights.org/en/binding-treaty (providing the latest developments and progress on the UN Treaty on Business and Human Rights); *see also Open-Ended Intergovernmental Working Group on Transnational Corporations and Other Business Enterprises with Respect to Human Rights*, U.N. Hum. Rts. Council <www.ohchr.org/EN/HRBodies/HRC/WGTransCorp/Pages/IGWGOnTNC.aspx>; Human Rights Council, Elaboration of an International Legally Binding Instrument on Transnational Corporations and other Business Enterprises with Respect to Human Rights, 26th Sess., U.N. Doc. A/HRC/26/L.22/Rev.1 (25 June 2014) (resolution adopted by 20 votes in favour, 13 abstentions and 14 against); Human Rights Council, Human Rights and Transnational Corporations and Other Business Enterprises, 26th Sess., U.N. Doc. A/HRC/26/L.1 (23 June 2014).

man rights gap – human rights laws that could protect against human rights infringements from FRT often apply only to government bodies,[160] and this is the same within international human rights law. Moreover, the current approach encouraging 'corporate and social responsibility' (CSR) and imposing solely ethical – as opposed to legal – obligations on private tech companies is also insufficient to deal with the significant problems FRT causes.[161] This inadequacy is evidenced by what I call 'transparency-washing' by tech companies – i.e., when a company performatively promotes transparency and respect for human rights while acting in ways that undermine both.[162]

Additionally, the human rights gap is greater in certain jurisdictions, such as Australia, where no federal level human rights framework exists. In such jurisdictions, binding human rights obligations must be adopted for police, governments and tech companies. It is not enough to merely rely on the 'goodwill' of these institutions, especially when they consistently fail to respect and undermine the rights to privacy, freedom of expression, due process and equal protection. Existing human rights laws that apply to private companies, such as data protection laws, should not only bind companies with certain safeguards, but should limit their power fundamentally, so that human rights are not infringed by the use of FRT. Hard legal obligations are especially important, given the increasing role that companies play in providing both public and private surveillance technologies.

12.6.1.2 Accountability Through Structural Changes and Leadership Shifts

Apart from human rights law, new laws address the substantive problems with FRT by targeting the structure and function of the tech companies producing these technologies. Regulatory action, in this sense, would serve to protect individuals by ensuring that certain companies cease to be 'gatekeepers' of both private and public FRT uses. Recently, it has been suggested that antitrust and competition law may be a means by which to 'break down' big tech companies such that they are no longer dominating and propelling the expansion of power via FRT.[163] This approach is already appearing in the political realm, with the EU Commission enacting two pieces of legislation in late 2022 which aim

160 Monika Zalnieriute, 'From Human Rights Aspirations to Enforceable Obligations by Non-State Actors in the Digital Age: The Case of Internet Governance and ICANN' (2019) *Yale Journal of Law & Technology* 278.

161 Ibid.

162 Zalnieriute, 'Transparency-Washing' (n 105).

163 Manuel Wörsdörfer, 'Big Tech and Antitrust: An Ordoliberal Analysis' (2022) 35 *Philosophy & Technology* 65; Zephyr Teachout, *Break 'Em Up: Recovering Our Freedom from Big Ag, Big Tech, and Big Money* (St Martin's Publishing Group 2020); Nicolas Petit, *Big Tech and the Digital Economy: The Moligopoly Scenario* (Oxford University Press 2020) <https://cadmus.eui.eu/handle/1814/68567> accessed 25 September 2022; Dina Srinivasan, 'The Antitrust Case against Facebook: A Monopolist's Journey Towards Pervasive Surveillance in Spite of Consumers' Preference for Privacy' (2019) 16 *Berkeley Business Law Journal* 39.

to ensure that platform giants operate fairly – the Digital Markets Act (DMA) and the Digital Services Act (DSA).[164] As suggested by Kieron O'Hara, these companies could also be targeted by preventing anticompetitive mergers and stifling competition by obliging tech companies to divest any companies they acquire – a good example being Facebook's acquisitions of Instagram and WhatsApp.[165] Tech companies could also be segregated into specific sectors (i.e., 'ring-fenced'), or forced to split businesses into separate corporations to break apart their power dynamics.[166]

These regulatory approaches can be supported by introducing increased tax for such companies – which has already been implemented at the national level by the Organization for Economic Co-operation and Development's landmark international tax deal which became effective in 2023 and implements a minimum corporate tax rate of 15% across 136 countries (representing 90% of the global gross domestic product).[167] In using existing tools of antitrust and competition law, alongside developing newer legislation dealing specifically with tech 'giants', the wealth and power conferred by FRT software can be redistributed amongst other private and public actors. This may prevent some of the substantive issues of FRT (i.e., FRT use being solidified into public spaces, the integration of FRT in commercial contexts, etc.), as larger tech companies will no longer be monopolizing the market and pushing for integration into the public sector. The ability of private companies to take on a quasi-enforcement role will also be curtailed by such legislative changes.

However, alongside these traditional tools, it is important to implement more radical solutions. This could include reconceptualizing FRT digital service companies as public utilities, such as closely regulated private companies or even government-run organizations.[168] The aim of this reform would be to place big FRT companies under public control at the state, national or regional level[169] – thus reversing the expansion of the private into the public that is currently occurring

164 Council Regulation (EC) 2022/1925 of 14 September 2022 on Contestable and Fair Markets in the Digital Sector and Amending Directives (EU) 2019/1937 and (EU) 2020/1828 (Digital Markets Act) [2022] L265/1; Council Regulation (EC) 2022/2065 of 19 October 2022 on a Single Market for Digital Services and amending Directive 2000/31/EC (Digital Services Act) [2022] L227/1.

165 Kieron O'Hara, 'Policy Question: How Can Competition against the Tech Giants Be Fostered?', *Four Internets* (Oxford University Press 2021) <https://oxford.universitypressscholarship.com/10.1093/oso/9780197523681.001.0001/oso-9780197523681-chapter-10> accessed 7 October 2021.

166 Teachout (n 163).

167 Organisation for Economic Co-operation and Development, 'International Community Strikes a Ground-Breaking Tax Deal for the Digital Age' (2021) <www.oecd.org/tax/international-community-strikes-a-ground-breaking-tax-deal-for-the-digital-age.htm> accessed 25 September 2022.

168 Dan Schiller, 'Reconstructing Public Utility Networks: A Program for Action' (2020) 14 *International Journal of Communication* 12; Vincent Mosco, *Becoming Digital: Toward a Post-Internet Society* (Emerald Group Publishing 2017); James Muldoon, *Platform Socialism: How to Reclaim Our Digital Future from Big Tech* (Pluto Press 2022).

169 Thomas M Hanna and Michael Brennan, 'There's No Solution to Big Tech Without Public Ownership of Tech Companies' (*Jacobin*, 2020) <https://jacobin.com/2020/12/big-tech-public-ownership-surveillance-capitalism-platform-corporations> accessed 25 September 2022.

with FRT. Such as approach also succeeds in addressing substantive problems with FRT use, as it focuses on structural issues such as exploitation, surveillance and manipulation.[170]

12.6.2 Banning the Use of FRT in Public Spaces

Another way to avoid the procedural fetishism prevalent in current approach to FRT regulation would be to completely ban certain FRT uses because even with all conceivable limits being put in place, the use of FRT can problematic – especially in certain contexts, such as its use in public spaces. In such context, not only does the FRT challenge the centrality of public spaces and anonymity for protest movements, but it is also discriminatory in nature. Indeed, many scholars, politicians, activists and regulators have argued that a ban on FRT use is the only practical way to ensure the technology is not abused by the law enforcement. For example, U.S. scholar Ferguson argues for a blanket ban on facial surveillance techniques, a ban or probable-cause standard for facial tracing and facial identification, and limitations to facial verification alongside increase accountability for issues with error, bias and transparency.[171]

Yet, it is not only scholars who are proposing bans on FRT. For example, informal resistance groups are on the rise over the past few years. These include groups such as Fight for the Future – which runs a project called Ban Facial Recognition and operates an interactive map of where the U.S. government deploys FRT around the country.[172] Amnesty International also runs a project called Ban the Scan, which similarly maps the New York Police Department (NYPD) surveillance machinery and can tell you the exposure to FRT of certain routes through New York.[173] And its not just activists, either – public institutions advising legislatures in some countries, such as the UK and Australia, are also clear on FRT use; for example, the UK Equality and Human Rights Commission and the Australian Human Rights Commission encouraged their governments to place a moratorium on FRT use in police practices and law enforcement generally, before legislation can be formally introduced.[174]

170 James Muldoon, 'Don't Break Up Facebook – Make It a Public Utility' (2020) <https://jacobin.com/2020/12/facebook-big-tech-antitrust-social-network-data> accessed 25 September 2022.

171 Ferguson (n 13) 63–73.

172 'Ban Facial Recognition' <www.banfacialrecognition.com/> accessed 16 April 2023.

173 'Inside the NYPD's Surveillance Machine' <https://banthescan.amnesty.org/decode/> accessed 28 August 2023.

174 See For example, the UK Equality and Human Rights Commission had, in March 2020, called on suspension, see Equality and Human Rights Commission, 'Facial Recognition Technology and Predictive Policing Algorithms Out-Pacing the Law' (12 March 2020) <www.equalityhumanrights.com/en/our-work/news/facial-recognition-technology-and-predictive-policing-algorithms-out-pacing-law> accessed 16 September 2020. And for Australia, see Edward Santow and others, 'Human Rights and Technology Final Report' (*Australian Human Rights Commission* 2021) <https://tech.humanrights.gov.au/downloads?_ga=2.200457510.901905353.1624842000-1160604841.1624842000> accessed 28 June 2021.

Moreover, FRT use by law enforcement has already been banned in some jurisdictions. Belgium and Luxembourg are the only two countries known to have banned FRT use in public spaces and by law enforcement.[175] However, 17 municipalities in the United States have implemented local bans on the use of FRT by the government – including San Francisco and nearby Berkeley (banning local agencies, e.g., transport, police),[176] a general ban by Massachusetts municipalities,[177] and FRT use in police body-cameras being banned in California, New Hampshire and Oregon.[178] Additionally, the Automated Facial Recognition Technology (Moratorium and Review) Bill[179] proposes to ban FRT in the UK.

Similarly, the EU AI Act[180] lists a set of AI practices that would be prohibited under the legislation, and the use of real-time biometric identification systems in public spaces by law enforcement will generally be prohibited under Art. 5(1)(d).[181] However, its prohibition could be undermined by law enforcement agencies interpreting the provided exceptions broadly. In particular, the exceptions provided cover situations when FRT use may be beneficial for finding "potential victims of crime" or for preventing a "specific, substantial and imminent threat . . . or terrorist attack".[182] This approach bans certain uses of FRT, recognizing the disproportionality of the FRT-enabled mass surveillance in public spaces. This is perhaps better than the vague terms used in the GDPR, such as "legal obligations" or "legitimate interests".[183] However, the EU AI Act, as well as UK Bill, are yet to be adopted.

12.6.3 Decolonizing FRT Discourse and Laws

Crucially, given the significant discriminatory impact of the FRT on marginalized communities and the racism and colonial roots of the development of the FRT technology, we must decolonize FRT governance discourse through recognition of

175 Bischoff (n 65).

176 Kate Conger, Richard Fausset and Serge Kovaleski, 'San Francisco Bans Facial Recognition Technology' (*The New York Times* 2019) <www.nytimes.com/2019/05/14/us/facial-recognition-ban-san-francisco.html>.

177 Christopher Jackson and others, 'Regulation of Facial Recognition Systems at the Municipal Level' <https://escholarship.org/uc/item/7qp0w9rn>.

178 Max Read, 'Why We Should Ban Facial Recognition Technology' (*Intelligencer*, 30 January 2020) <https://nymag.com/intelligencer/2020/01/why-we-should-ban-facial-recognition-technology.html> accessed 1 June 2020.

179 Lord Clement-Jones, 'Automated Facial Recognition Technology (Moratorium and Review) Bill [HL]' (2020 2019) <https://services.parliament.uk/bills/2019-20/automatedfacialrecognitiontechnologymoratoriumandreview.html/>.

180 Proposal for a Regulation of the European Parliament and of the Council Laying Down Harmonised Rules on Artificial Intelligence (AI Act) and Amending Certain Union Legislative Acts (n 78).

181 Ibid., 5(1)(d).

182 Ibid.

183 GDPR Art 6(1).

colonial practices of extraction and exploitation, and pay attention to the voices of Indigenous peoples and communities of the so-called Global South.[184] As I explain in my recent work on procedural fetishism,[185] this must include decolonial ways to theorize, analyze and critique tech companies,[186] because people in the so-called Global South relate very differently to major tech companies than do those who live in the so-called Global North.[187] A good example of decolonial discourse is a Non-Aligned Technologies Movement (NATM) – a worldwide alliance of civil society organizations, which aims to create "technosocial spaces beyond the profit-motivated model of Silicon Valley and the control-motivated model of the Chinese Communist Party".[188] However, decolonization efforts must go beyond civil society or mere declarations from policy-makers. For example, the EU's focus on regulating AI as a consumer "product-in-use" requiring individual protection in its AI Act undermines EU claims to regulate "ethical" AI, for it completely ignores the exploitative practices and global implications of AI production and use. The new laws must recognize and explicitly acknowledge the power disparities, exploitation and coloniality of AI production as a collective rights deprivation.[189]

12.7 Conclusion

If law enforcement agencies and private companies can resort to FRT for mere convenience and experimenting, our rights to privacy, public protest, dues process and equal protection are undermined, along with significant impact on the rule of law and democratic process. Indeed, public space surveillance has potential to curtail and stifle political discourse in our democracies. For instance, the High Court of Australia – Australia's highest court – has emphasized the importance of the right to protest to Australian democracy: besides casting their vote in elections, Australians have no other ways to express their political views.[190] It is similar in many other contemporary democracies today.

Before tech companies and public authorities develop FRT further and use it in increasingly more invasive ways, it is imperative that this public and private surveillance infrastructure is limited. We need prohibitive laws limiting the use of FRT

184 See Zalnieriute, 'Against Procedural Fetishism: A Call for a New Digital Constitution' (n 103).

185 Ibid.

186 See Zahra Takhshid, 'Regulating Social Media in the Global South' (2022) 24 *Vanderbilt Journal of Entertainment and Technology* 1, 1–56; Abeba Birhane, 'Algorithmic Injustice: A Relational Ethics Approach' (2021) 2 *Patterns* 1, 1–33; Jason Edward Lewis et al., 'Indigenous Protocol and Artificial Intelligence Position Paper' (22 December 2021, 9:19 PM) <https://spectrum.library.concordia.ca/id/eprint/986506/>; Stefania Milan and Emiliano Treré, 'Big Data from the South(s): Beyond Data Universalism' (2019) 20 *Sage Journal of Television & New Media* 319, 326.

187 Rafael Grohmann & Willian Fernandes Araujo, Ai for Everyone?: Critical Perspectives 247–266 (2021).

188 Non Aligned Technologies Movement <https://nonalignedtech.net/index.php?title=MainPage> accessed 30 May 2023.

189 Catriona Gray, 'Data Dispossession' *Sociological Review* (5 May 2021) <https://thesociological-review.org/magazine/may-2021/digital-social-life/data-dispossession/>.

190 *Brown v Tasmania* [2017] HCA 43.

in both public and private spaces, and we need hard legal obligations for both those who develop and those who deploy them. This means tangible regulation on FRT use. Unfortunately, existing regulatory mechanisms – such as the GDPR – do not account for the significant risks of FRT to undermine privacy, due process, political protests and equal protection. The approach of the GDPR and FRT jurisprudence is permissive, grounded in what I call procedural fetishism – a tendency to focus on procedural safeguards, assuming that these can adequately protect against power expansion and abuse. Such proceduralist laws and jurisprudence cannot limit the power expansion enabled through FRT.

To counter such procedural fetishism in FRT governance, we need new laws and jurisprudence on FRT to go beyond their traditional emphasis on procedural safeguards to engage with substantive questions about how to limit the state power that FRT expands. We need tangible substantive laws that will limit the power of both public and private actors: breaking and taxing FRT companies, fortifying regulatory enforcement and decolonization of the FRT governance discourse, among other things. The legal reforms could start with an explicit ban on police and private use of FRT in public spaces. This is not drastic. In fact, a ban is a modest first step in the long journey ahead to push back against escalating FRT surveillance worldwide.

Acknowledgements

The author is grateful to Jessica Whetters for excellent research assistance.

Bibliography

Allie F, 'Facial Recognition Technology and Voter Turnout' (2023) 85 *The Journal of Politics* 328

'Amazon's Face Recognition Falsely Matched 28 Members of Congress with Mugshots' (*American Civil Liberties Union*) <www.aclu.org/blog/privacy-technology/surveillance-technologies/amazons-face-recognition-falsely-matched-28> accessed 2 June 2020

Andrejevic M, *ISpy: Surveillance and Power in the Interactive Era* (University of Kansas Press 2007)

'Ban Facial Recognition' <www.banfacialrecognition.com/> accessed 16 April 2023

'Bangladesh Voter Registration Project Using Biometrics to Detect and Prevent Duplicate Registrations' (*GovTech*, 27 July 2010) <www.govtech.com/security/Bangladesh-Voter-Registration-Project-using-Biometrics.html> accessed 24 August 2023

Bauman Z and Lyon D, *Liquid Surveillance: A Conversation* (Polity Press 2013)

Baumgartner FR, Epp DA and Shoub K, *Suspect Citizens What 20 Million Traffic Stops Tell Us About Policing and Race* (Cambridge University Press 2018)

Beller J, *The Message Is Murder: Substrates of Computational Capital* (Pluto Press 2018)

Berle I, *Face Recognition Technology: Compulsory Visibility and Its Impact on Privacy and the Confidentiality of Personal Identifiable Images* (Springer 2020)

Bischoff P, 'Facial Recognition Technology (FRT): 100 Countries Analyzed' (*Comparitech*, 8 June 2021) <www.comparitech.com/blog/vpn-privacy/facial-recognition-statistics/> accessed 24 August 2023

Black E, *IBM and the Holocaust: The Strategic Alliance Between Nazi Germany and America's Most Powerful Corporation-Expanded Edition* (Crown Publishers 2001)

Bogard W, *The Simulation of Surveillance: Hypercontrol in Telematics Societies* (Cambridge University Press 1996)

Borak M, 'French Senate Votes in Favor of Public Facial Recognition Pilot | Biometric Update' (15 June 2023) <www.biometricupdate.com/202306/french-senate-votes-in-favor-of-public-facial-recognition-pilot> accessed 25 August 2023

Bueno CC, 'The Face Revisited: Using Deleuze and Guattari to Explore the Politics of Algorithmic Face Recognition' (2020) 37 *Theory, Culture & Society* 73

Buolamwini J and Gebru T, 'Gender Shades: Intersectional Accuracy Disparities in Commercial Gender Classification' *Proceedings of Machine Learning research* (2018) <http://proceedings.mlr.press/v81/buolamwini18a/buolamwini18a.pdf> accessed 17 June 2020

Burt C, 'Motorola Could Offer Facial Recognition with Police Body Cameras with WatchGuard Acquisition' (*Biometric Update*, 23 July 2019) <www.biometricupdate.com/201907/motorola-could-offer-facial-recognition-with-police-body-cameras-with-watchguard-acquisition> accessed 24 June 2020

Business JV, 'Clearview AI Has Billions of Our Photos. Its Entire Client List Was Just Stolen' (*CNN*) <www.cnn.com/2020/02/26/tech/clearview-ai-hack/index.html> accessed 6 March 2020

Canales SB, 'Australian Schools Have Been Trialling Facial Recognition Technology, Despite Serious Concerns About Children's Data' (*Gizmodo Australia*, 10 March 2020) <https://gizmodo.com.au/2020/03/australian-schools-trial-facial-recognition-technology-looplearn/> accessed 24 August 2023

Capacity C, 'Smart City in Greater Copenhagen' <www.copcap.com/set-up-a-business/key-sectors/smart-city> accessed 30 June 2020

Cath C and others, 'Artificial Intelligence and the Good Society: The US, EU, and UK Approach' (2018) 24 *Science and Engineering Ethics* 505

Chen A, 'What Happens When Life Insurance Companies Track Fitness Data?' (*The Verge*, 26 September 2018) <www.theverge.com/2018/9/26/17905390/john-hancock-life-insurance-fitness-tracker-wearables-science-health> accessed 31 December 2019

'China's New "super Camera" Can Instantly Pinpoint Specific Targets among Tens of Thousands of People – China Power – ABC News (Australian Broadcasting Corporation)' (8 October 2019) <www.abc.net.au/news/2019-09-26/chinas-new-500-megapixel-super-camera/11539176> accessed 8 October 2019

Clark L, 'Facial Recog System Used by Met Police Shows Racial Bias' <www.theregister.com/2023/05/25/facial_recognition_system_used_by/> accessed 23 August 2023

Clayton Newell B, Timan T and Koops B-J, *Surveillance, Privacy and Public Space* (Routledge 2019)

'The Color of Justice: Racial and Ethnic Disparity in State Prisons' (*The Sentencing Project*) <www.sentencingproject.org/publications/color-of-justice-racial-and-ethnic-disparity-in-state-prisons/> accessed 2 June 2020

Conger K, Fausset R and Kovaleski S, 'San Francisco Bans Facial Recognition Technology' [2019] The New York Times. <www.nytimes.com/2019/05/14/us/facial-recognition-ban-san-francisco.html>

Consultative Committee of the Convention for the Protection of Individuals with Regard to Automatic Processing of Personal Data Convention 108, 'Guidelines on Facial Recognition T-PD(2020)03rev4' (Council of Europe, Directorate General of Human Rights and Rule of Law 2021) <https://r m.coe.int/guidelines-on-facial-recognition/1680a134f3>

Council Regulation (EC) 2022/1925 of 14 September 2022 on Contestable and Fair Markets in the Digital Sector and Amending Directives (EU) 2019/1937 and (EU) 2020/1828 (Digital Markets Act) [2022] L265/1

Council Regulation (EC) 2022/2065 of 19 October 2022 on a Single Market for Digital Services and amending Directive 2000/31/EC (Digital Services Act) [2022] L227/1

Council of Europe, 'Convention for the Protection of Individuals with Regard to the Automatic Processing of Individual Data' (1981) *ETS* 108 <www.coe.int/en/web/data-protection/convention108-and-protocol>

Crootof R, '"Cyborg Justice" and the Risk of Technological – Legal Lock-In' (2019) 119 *Columbia Law Review* 1

Debter L, 'Retailers Quietly Deploying Controversial Technology to Combat Crime Spree' (*Forbes*) <www.forbes.com/sites/laurendebter/2022/01/31/retailers-quietly-deploying-controversial-technology-to-combat-crime-spree/> accessed 22 August 2023

Deleuze G, 'Postscript on the Societies of Control' (1992) 59 *October* 3

Delgado D, 'The Dark Database: Facial Recognition and Its" Failure" to Enroll' (2021) 17 *Media-N* 69

Directive 2016/680 of the European Parliament and of the Council of 27 April 2016 on the Protection of Natural Persons with Regard to the Processing of Personal Data by Competent Authorities for the Purposes of the Prevention, Investigation, Detection or Prosecution of Criminal Offences or the Execution of Criminal Penalties, and on the Free Movement of Such Data, and Repealing Council Framework Decision 2008/977/JHA [2016] OJ L119/89 2016

Dodd V, 'Police Accused over Use of Facial Recognition at King Charles's Coronation' *The Guardian* (3 May 2023) <www.theguardian.com/uk-news/2023/may/03/metropolitan-police-live-facial-recognition-in-crowds-at-king-charles-coronation> accessed 31 August 2023

Driessen B and Dürmuth M, 'Achieving Anonymity against Major Face Recognition Algorithms' in de Decker B and others (eds), *Communications and Multimedia Security*, Vol 8099 (Springer 2013)

Edkins J, *Face Politics* (Routledge 2015)

Encyclopedia Britannica, 'IBM | Founding, History, & Products' (*Encyclopedia Britannica*) <www.britannica.com/topic/International-Business-Machines-Corporation> accessed 14 October 2020

Equality and Human Rights Commission, 'Facial Recognition Technology and Predictive Policing Algorithms Out-Pacing the Law' (12 March 2020) <www.equalityhumanrights.com/en/our-work/news/facial-recognition-technology-and-predictive-policing-algorithms-out-pacing-law> accessed 16 September 2020

'EU AI Act: First Regulation on Artificial Intelligence | News | European Parliament' (8 June 2023) <www.europarl.europa.eu/news/en/headlines/society/20230601STO93804/eu-ai-act-first-regulation-on-artificial-intelligence> accessed 28 August 2023

Eubanks V, *Automating Inequality: How High-Tech Tools Profile, Police, and Punish the Poor* (St Martin's Press 2018)

European Data Protection Board, 'Guidelines 05/2022 on the Use of Facial Recognition Technology in the Area of Law Enforcement' (2022) <https://edpb.europa.eu/system/files/2022-05/edpb-guidelines_202205_frtlawenfo rcement_en_1.pdf>

Ferguson AG, 'Facial Recognition and the Fourth Amendment' (2021) 105 *Minnesota Law Review* 1105

Fernandez L, *Policing Dissent: Social Control and the Anti-Globalization Movement* (Rutgers University Press 2008)

Foucault M, *Discipline and Punish: The Birth of the Prison* (Pantheon Books 1977)

Foucault M, *Security, Territory, Population: Lectures at the Collège de France 1977–1978* (Palgrave Macmillan UK 2009)

Friedman B and Nissenbaum HF, 'Bias in Computer Systems' (1996) 14 *ACM Transactions on Information Systems* 330

Fussell S, 'Did Body Cameras Backfire?' (*The Atlantic*, 1 November 2019) <www.theatlantic.com/technology/archive/2019/11/border-patrol-weighs-body-cameras-face-recognition/600469/> accessed 24 June 2020

Future F for the, 'Ban Facial Recognition in Stores' (*Ban Facial Recognition in Stores*) <www.banfacialrecognition.com/stores> accessed 22 August 2023

Galterio MG, Shavit SA and Hayajneh T, 'A Review of Facial Biometrics Security for Smart Devices' (2018) 7 *Computers* 37

Garvie C, Bedoya A and Frankle J, 'The Perpetual Line-Up' (*Centre on Privacy and Technology* 2016) <www.perpetuallineup.org/> accessed 11 November 2019

Gates K, *Our Biometric Future: Facial Recognition Technology and the Culture of Surveillance* (NYU Press 2011)

Gates K and Magnet S, 'Communication Research and the Study of Surveillance' (2007) 10 *Communication Review* 277

Gebicki M, 'Facial Recognition Technology Set to Transform Air Travel' (*The Sydney Morning Herald*, 31 October 2022) <www.smh.com.au/traveller/travel-news/facial-recognition-technology-set-to-transform-air-travel-20221031-h27i5y.html> accessed 24 August 2023

Gershgorn D, 'Retail Stores Are Packed with Unchecked Facial Recognition' (*The Verge*, 14 July 2021) <www.theverge.com/2021/7/14/22576236/retail-stores-facial-recognition-civil-rights-organizations-ban> accessed 22 August 2023

Gillespie E, 'Are You Being Scanned? How Facial Recognition Technology Follows You, Even as You Shop' (*The Guardian*, 24 February 2019) <www.theguardian.com/technology/2019/feb/24/are-you-being-scanned-how-facial-recognition-technology-follows-you-even-as-you-shop> accessed 22 August 2023

Gillham P, 'Securitizing America: Strategic Incapacitation and the Policing of Protest since the 11 September 2001 Terrorist Attacks' (2011) 5 *Sociology Compass* 636

Gillham P, Edwards B and Noakes J, 'Strategic Incapacitation and the Policing of Occupy Wall Street Protests in New York City, 2011' (2013) 23 *Policing and Society* 81

Gilliom J, *Overseers of the Poor: Surveillance, Resistance, and the Limits of Privacy* (University of Chicago Press 2001)

Glukhin v Russia, App No 11519/20, Third Section Judgment, (Eur Ct Hum Rts, 4 July 2023) at https://hudoc.echr.coe.int/?i=001-225655 R (on the application of Bridges) v Chief Constable of South Wales Police [2020] EWCA Civ 1058 R (on the application of Edward Bridges) v The Chief Constable of South Wales Police [2020] Court of Appeal (Civil Division) C1/2019/2670; EWCA Civ 1058

'Greece: New Biometrics Policing Program Undermines Rights' (*Human Rights Watch*, 18 January 2022) <www.hrw.org/news/2022/01/18/greece-new-biometrics-policing-program-undermines-rights> accessed 25 August 2023

Green A, 'What Happened After Derrick Ingram's Standoff With the NYPD' (*Intelligencer*, 25 May 2021) <https://nymag.com/intelligencer/2021/05/derrick-ingram-nypd-standoff.html> accessed 22 August 2023

Gross S, Possley M and Stephens K, 'Race and Wrongful Convictions in the United States' (*National Registry of Exonerations*, 2017) <www.law.umich.edu/special/exoneration/Documents/Race_and_Wrongful_Convictions.pdf> accessed 2 June 2020

Guariglia M, 'IBM, Amazon Agree to Step Back From Face Recognition. Where Is Microsoft?' (*Electronic Frontier Foundation*, 10 June 2020) <www.eff.org/deeplinks/2020/06/ibm-amazon-end-and-pause-fr-programs-where-microsoft> accessed 23 August 2023

Haggerty KD and Ericson RV (eds), *The New Politics of Surveillance and Visibility* (University of Toronto Press 2006)

Hall R, 'Surveillance and Public Space' in *Oxford Research Encyclopedia, Communication* (Oxford University Press 2017)

Hamed Abdurrahim S, Abdul Samad S and Baseri Huddin A, 'Review on the Effects of Age, Gender, and Race Demographics on Automatic Face Recognition' <https://link-springer-com.wwwproxy1.library.unsw.edu.au/content/pdf/10.1007/s00371-017-1428-z.pdf> accessed 2 June 2020

Hanna TM and Brennan M, 'There's No Solution to Big Tech Without Public Ownership of Tech Companies' (*Jacobin*, 2020) <https://jacobin.com/2020/12/big-tech-public-ownership-surveillance-capitalism-platform-corporations> accessed 25 September 2022

House TW, 'United States and European Commission Announce Trans-Atlantic Data Privacy Framework' (25 March 2022) <www.whitehouse.gov/briefing-room/statements-releases/2022/03/25/fact-sheet-united-states-and-european-commission-announce-trans-atlantic-data-privacy-framework/> accessed 25 September 2022

'How Facial Recognition Became a Routine Policing Tool in America' <www.nbcnews.com/news/us-news/how-facial-recognition-became-routine-policing-tool-american1004251> accessed 24 June 2020

'How Facial Recognition Is Helping Putin Curb Dissent' *Reuters* (28 March 2023) <www.reuters.com/investigates/special-report/ukraine-crisis-russia-detentions/> accessed 23 August 2023

'Inside the NYPD's Surveillance Machine' <https://banthescan.amnesty.org/decode/> accessed 28 August 2023

Introna L and Nissenbaum HF, *Facial Recognition Technology: A Survey of Policy and Implementation Issues* (The Center for Catastrophe Preparedness & Response 2009)

'Israeli Authorities Using Facial Recognition to Entrench Apartheid' (*Amnesty International*, 2 May 2023) <www.amnesty.org/en/latest/news/2023/05/israel-opt-israeli-authorities-are-using-facial-recognition-technology-to-entrench-apartheid/> accessed 23 August 2023

Jackson C and others, 'Regulation of Facial Recognition Systems at the Municipal Level' <https://escholarship.org/uc/item/7qp0w9rn>

Jee C, 'A New Face Recognition Privacy Bill Would Give Us More Control Over Our Data – MIT Technology Review' (*MIT Technology Review*, 8 October 2019) <www.technologyreview.com/f/613129/a-new-face-recognition-privacy-bill-would-give-us-more-control-over-our-data/> accessed 8 October 2019

Joseph G, 'Inside the Video Surveillance Program IBM Built for Philippine Strongman Rodrigo Duterte' (*The Intercept*, 20 March 2019) <https://theintercept.com/2019/03/20/rodrigo-duterte-ibm-surveillance/> accessed 17 June 2020

Joshi JC and Gupta KK, 'Face Recognition Technology: A Review' (2016) 1 *The IUP Journal of Telecommunication* 53

Kanade T, *Computer Recognising Human Faces* (Birkhauser 1977)

Khalid A, 'The EU's Agenda to Regulate AI Does Little to Rein in Facial Recognition' (*Quartz*, 20 February 2020) <https://qz.com/1805847/facial-recognition-ban-left-out-of-the-eus-agenda-to-regulate-ai/> accessed 10 June 2020

Kim PT, 'Auditing Algorithms for Discrimination' (2017) 166 *University of Pennsylvania Law Review Online* 189

Klare BF and others, 'Face Recognition Performance: Role of Demographic Information' (2012) 6 *Information Forensics and Security, IEEE Transactions On* 7 1789

Koops B-J and others, 'A Typology of Privacy' (2016) 38 *University of Pennsylvania Journal of International Law* 483

Kremer J, *The End of Freedom in Public Places? Privacy Problems Arising from Surveillance of the European Public Space* (Doctoral dissertation, University of Helsinki 2017)

Kukielski K, 'The First Amendment and Facial Recognition Technology' (2022) 55 *Loyola of Los Angeles Law Review* 231

'La Formation Restreinte de la CNIL Prononce Une Sanction de 50 Millions D'euros à L'encontre de la Société GOOGLE LLC' (*CNIL*, 20 January 2019) <www.cnil.fr/fr/la-formation-restreinte-de-la-cnil-prononce-une-sanction-de-50-millions-deuros-lencontre-de-la> accessed 17 March 2020

Lanton L, 'Police Behavior During Traffic and Street Stops, 2011' <www.bjs.gov/content/pub/pdf/pbtss11.pdf> accessed 2 June 2020

Lee NT and Chin C, 'Police Surveillance and Facial Recognition: Why Data Privacy Is Imperative for Communities of Color' (*Brookings* 2022) <www.brookings.edu/articles/police-surveillance-and-facial-recognition-why-data-privacy-is-an-imperative-for-communities-of-color/> accessed 22 August 2023

Lord Clement-Jones, 'Automated Facial Recognition Technology (Moratorium and Review) Bill [HL]' (2020 2019) <https://services.parliament.uk/bills/2019-20/automatedfacialrecognitiontechnologymoratoriumandreview.html/>

Lyon D, *Surveillance Studies: An Overview* (Polity Press 2007)

Marx GT, 'Coming to Terms: The Kaleidoscope of Privacy and Surveillance' in Beatte R and Dorota M (eds), *Social Dimensions of Privacy: Interdisciplinary Perspectives* (Cambridge University Press 2015)

Mascellino | Alessandro, 'Multi-Touchpoint Face Biometrics Systems Unveiled at Airports in Japan and France | Biometric Update' (14 April 2021) <www.biometricupdate.com/202104/multi-touchpoint-face-biometrics-systems-unveiled-at-airports-in-japan-and-france> accessed 24 August 2023

'Masdar City, a Zero-Waste, Zero-Carbon City in the Desert | Living Circular' <www.livingcircular.veolia.com/en/city/masdar-city-zero-waste-zero-carbon-city-desert> accessed 30 June 2020

McGrath J, *Loving Big Brother: Performance, Privacy, and Surveillance Space* (Routledge 2004)

Melgaco L and Monoghan J, 'Introduction: Taking to the Streets in the Information Age' in Lucas M and Jeffrey M (eds), *Protests in the Information Age* (Routledge 2018)

Meltzer JP and Tielemans A, 'The European Union AI Act: Next Steps and Issues for Building International Cooperation in AI' <https://policycommons.net/artifacts/4136169/the-european-union-ai-act/4944759/> accessed 27 August 2023

Melucci A and Avritzer L, 'Complexity, Cultural Pluralism and Democracy: Collective Action in the Public Space' (2000) 39 *Social Science Information* 507

Mittelstadt B, 'Auditing for Transparency in Content Personalization Systems' (2016) 10 *International Journal of Communication* 4991

'Mobile Biometric Solution MorphoTablet Secures the Voting Process in Egyptian Parliamentary Elections | Biometric Update' (18 December 2015) <www.biometricupdate.com/201512/mobile-biometric-solution-morphotablet-secures-the-voting-process-in-egyptian-parliamentary-elections> accessed 24 August 2023

Monahan T, 'Dreams of Control at a Distance: Gender, Surveillance, and Social Control' (2009) 9 *Cultural Studies ↔ Critical Methodologies* 286

Monahan T, 'The Right to Hide? Anti-Surveillance Camouflage and the Aestheticization of Resistance' (2015) 12 *Communication and Critical/Cultural Studies* 159

Monoghan J and Walby K, 'Making up "Terror Identities": Security Intelligence, Canada's Integrated Threat Assessment Centre, and Social Movement Suppression' (2012) 22 *Policing and Society* 133

Monoghan J and Walby K, '"They Attacked the City": Security Intelligence, the Sociology of Protest Policing, and the Anarchist Threat at the 2010 Toronto G20 Summit' (2012) 60 *Current Sociology* 653

Moore AD, *Privacy Rights: Moral and Legal Foundations* (Pennsylvania University Press 2010)

Moreham NA, 'Privacy in Public Places' (2006) 65 *The Cambridge Law Journal* 606

Mosco V, *Becoming Digital: Toward a Post-Internet Society* (Emerald Group Publishing 2017)

Muldoon J, 'Don't Break Up Facebook – Make It a Public Utility' (2020) <https://jacobin.com/2020/12/facebook-big-tech-antitrust-social-network-data> accessed 25 September 2022

Muldoon J, *Platform Socialism: How to Reclaim Our Digital Future from Big Tech* (Pluto Press 2022)

'NAACP | Criminal Justice Fact Sheet' (*NAACP*) <www.naacp.org/criminal-justice-fact-sheet/> accessed 2 June 2020

Nesterova I, 'Mass Data Gathering and Surveillance: The Fight against Facial Recognition Technology in the Globalized World' <www.shs-conferences.org/articles/shsconf/pdf/2020/02/shsconf_glob2020_03006.pdf> accessed 2 June 2020

Neuburger J, 'Will the Role of Facial Recognition Grow in a Post-COVID-19 World?' (*New Media and Technology law Blog*, 31 March 2020) https://newmedialaw.proskauer.com/2020/03/31/will-the-role-of-facial-recognition-grow-in-a-post-covid-19-world/

'New ABIS for Biometric Passport Issuance in Ecuador' (*Innovatrics*) <www.innovatrics.com/references/new-abis-for-biometric-passport-issuance-in-ecuador/> accessed 24 August 2023

'New Data Reveals Milwaukee Police Stops Are About Race and Ethnicity' (*American Civil Liberties Union*) <www.aclu.org/blog/criminal-law-reform/reforming-police/new-data-reveals-milwaukee-police-stops-are-about-race-and> accessed 2 June 2020

Newell BC, 'Privacy and Surveillance in the Streets: An Introduction' in Bryce Clayton N, Tjerk T and Bert-Jaap K (eds), *Surveillance, Privacy and Public Space* (Routledge 2019)

Newell BC, 'Transparent Lives and the Surveillance State: Policing, New Visibility, and Information Police' (Doctoral Thesis, University of Washington 2015)

Nissenbaum HF, 'Towards and Approach to Privacy in Public: Challenges of Information Technology' (1997) 7 *Ethics & Behaviour* 207

O'Hara K, 'Policy Question: How Can Competition against the Tech Giants Be Fostered?', *Four Internets* (Oxford University Press 2021) <https://oxford.universitypressscholarship.com/10.1093/oso/9780197523681.001.0001/oso-9780197523681-chapter-10> accessed 7 October 2021

Organisation for Economic Co-operation and Development, 'International Community Strikes a Ground-Breaking Tax Deal for the Digital Age' (2021) <www.oecd.org/tax/international-community-strikes-a-ground-breaking-tax-deal-for-the-digital-age.htm> accessed 25 September 2022

Oswald M, 'Algorithm-Assisted Decision-Making in the Public Sector: Framing the Issues Using Administrative Law Rules Governing Discretionary Power' (2018) 376 *Philosophical Transactions of the Royal Society A* <https://royalsocietypublishing.org/doi/abs/10.1098/rsta.2017.0359> accessed 10 September 2018

Paglen T, 'Invisible Images (Your Pictures Are Looking at You)' (*The New Inquiry*, 8 December 2016) <https://thenewinquiry.com/invisible-images-your-pictures-are-looking-at-you/> accessed 16 June 2020

'Paris 2024 Olympics: Concern Over French Plan for AI Surveillance' *BBC News* (19 July 2023) <www.bbc.com/news/world-europe-66122743> accessed 25 August 2023

Petit N, *Big Tech and the Digital Economy: The Moligopoly Scenario* (Oxford University Press 2020) <https://cadmus.eui.eu/handle/1814/68567> accessed 25 September 2022

Petrescu RVV, 'Face Recognition as a Biometric Application' (2019) 3 *Journal of Mechatronics and Robotics* 237

Phillips PJ, Rauss PJ and Der SZ, 'FERET (Face Recognition Technology) Recognition Algorithm Development and Test Results' (Army Research Laboratory 1996) <https://pdfs.semanticscholar.org/31de/9b3dd6106ce6eec9a35991b2b9083395fd0b.pdf?_ga=2.230812767.1905244237.1592970696-144232886.1592801485> accessed 24 June 2020

Phillips T, 'Merchants in Spain and Hungary Pilot Cardless Payments Service That Combines Face and Palm Biometrics' (*NFCW*, 15 September 2020) <www.nfcw.com/2020/09/15/367868/merchants-in-spain-and-hungary-pilot-cardless-payments-service-that-combines-face-and-palm-biometrics/> accessed 25 August 2023

'Physiognomy's New Clothes – Blaise Aguera y Arcas – Medium' <https://medium.com/@blaisea/physiognomys-new-clothes-f2d4b59fdd6a> accessed 16 June 2020

'Podcast – Facial Recognition and Policing Protesters' (*Amnesty International Canada*) <https://amnesty.ca/podcast-facial-recognition-and-policing-protesters/> accessed 22 August 2023

Proposal for a Regulation of the European Parliament and of the Council Laying Down Harmonised Rules on Artificial Intelligence (Artificial Intelligence Act) and Amending Certain Union Legislative Acts 2021

'Protestbewegung – Warum Einen Öffentlichen Platz Besetzen? (Why Occupy a Public Space?)' (*Deutschlandfunk*, 2014) <www.deutschlandfunk.de/protestbewegung-warum-einen-oeffentlichen-platz-besetzen.1184.de.html?dram:article_id=299327> accessed 17 June 2020

Pugliese J, *Biometrics: Bodies, Technologies, Biopolitics* (Routledge 2012)

Raposo VL, '(Do Not) Remember My Face: Uses of Facial Recognition Technology in Light of the General Data Protection Regulation' (2023) 32 *Information & Communications Technology Law* 45

Read M, 'Why We Should Ban Facial Recognition Technology' (*Intelligencer*, 30 January 2020) <https://nymag.com/intelligencer/2020/01/why-we-should-ban-facial-recognition-technology.html> accessed 1 June 2020

Reed E, 'History of IBM: Timeline and Facts' (*TheStreet*, 24 February 2020) <www.thestreet.com/personal-finance/history-of-ibm> accessed 14 October 2020

Regulation 2016/679 of the European Parliament and of the Council of 27 April 2016 on the Protection of Natural Persons with Regard to the Processing of Personal Data and on the Free Movement of Such Data, and Repealing Directive 95/46/EC [2016] OJ L119/1 GDPR

Reidenberg J, 'Privacy in Public' (2014) 69 *University of Miami Law Review* 141

Reuters, 'Facial Recognition Tech in Delhi Schools Sparks Privacy Concerns' (*Daily Sabah*, 2 March 2021) <www.dailysabah.com/world/asia-pacific/facial-recognition-tech-in-delhi-schools-sparks-privacy-concerns> accessed 24 August 2023

Roessler B, 'Privacy and/in the Public Sphere' (2016) 1 *Yearbook for Eastern and Western Philosophy* 243

Ruhrmann H, 'Facing the Future: Protecting Human Rights in Policy Strategies for Facial Recognition Technology in Law Enforcement' (May 2019) <https://citrispolicylab.org/wp-content/uploads/2019/09/Facing-the-Future_Ruhrmann_CITRIS-Policy-Lab.pdf> accessed 1 June 2020

Russon M-A, 'How Will AI Facial Recognition Be Used at the King's Coronation?' (*Evening Standard*, 4 May 2023) <www.standard.co.uk/tech/facial-recognition-technology-coronation-met-police-privacy-artificial-intelligence-b1078801.html> accessed 23 August 2023

Ryan-Mosley T and Richards, 'The Secret Police: Cops Built a Shadowy Surveillance Machine in Minnesota after George Floyd's Murder' (*MIT Technology Review*, 3 March 2020) <www.technologyreview.com/2022/03/03/1046676/police-surveillance-minnesota-george-floyd/> accessed 16 April 2023

Sadowski J and Pasquale F, 'The Spectrum of Control: A Social Theory of the Smart City' (2015) 20 *First Monday*

Sakin N, 'Will There Be Federal Facial Recognition Regulation in the US?' <https://iapp.org/news/a/u-s-facial-recognition-roundup/> accessed 28 August 2023

Santow E and others, 'Human Rights and Technology Final Report' (*Australian Human Rights Commission* 2021) <https://tech.humanrights.gov.au/downloads?_ga=2.200457510.901905353.1624842000-1160604841.1624842000> accessed 28 June 2021

Sauer P, 'Privacy Fears as Moscow Metro Rolls out Facial Recognition Pay System | Russia | The Guardian' (*The Guardian*, 15 October 2021) <https://amp.theguardian.com/world/2021/oct/15/privacy-fears-moscow-metro-rolls-out-facial-recognition-pay-system> accessed 23 August 2023

Schiller D, 'Reconstructing Public Utility Networks: A Program for Action' (2020) 14 *International Journal of Communication* 12

Schwartz M, 'Color-Blind Biometrics? Facial Recognition and Arrest Rates of African-Americans in Maryland and the United States' (Thesis in Partial Fulfilment of a Master of Public Policy, Georgetown University 2019)

'Sci-Fi Crime Drama with a Strong Black Lead' (*The New Inquiry*, 27 June 2015) <https://thenewinquiry.com/sci-fi-crime-drama-with-a-strong-black-lead/> accessed 16 June 2020

Sen. Blunt R [R-M, 'S.847–116th Congress (2019–2020): Commercial Facial Recognition Privacy Act of 2019' (14 March 2019) <www.congress.gov/bill/116th-congress/senate-bill/847> accessed 28 August 2023

Sennett R, *The Spaces of Democracy* (University of Michigan, College of Architecture and Urban Planning 1998)

'Seven Bank Plans Japan's First Facial Recognition ATM Service' (*Nikkei Asia*) <https://asia.nikkei.com/Business/Finance/Seven-Bank-plans-Japan-s-first-facial-recognition-ATM-service> accessed 22 August 2023

Simoiu C, Corbett-Davies S and Goel S, 'The Problem of Infra-Marginality in Outcome Tests for Discrimination' (2017) 11 *The Annals of Applied Statistics* 1193

'Smarter London Together' (*London City Hall*, 7 June 2018) <www.london.gov.uk//what-we-do/business-and-economy/supporting-londons-sectors/smart-london/smarter-london-together> accessed 30 June 2020

Smith M, Mann M and Urbas G, *Biometrics, Crime and Security* (Routledge 2018)
Smyth SM, *Biometrics, Surveillance and the Law* (Routledge 2019)
Solarova S and others, 'Reconsidering the Regulation of Facial Recognition in Public Spaces' (2023) 3 *AI and Ethics* 625
Solove DJ, Rotenberg M and Schwartz PM, *Information Privacy Laws* (Aspen Publishers 2006)
'Songdo IBD' <http://songdo.com/> accessed 30 June 2020
Srinivasan D, 'The Antitrust Case against Facebook: A Monopolist's Journey towards Pervasive Surveillance in Spite of Consumers' Preference for Privacy' (2019) 16 *Berkeley Business Law Journal* 39
Stevenson M and Mayson S, 'The Scale of Misdemeanor Justice' (2018) 98 *Boston University Law Review* 371
Taylor SM, Gulson KN and McDuie-Ra D, 'Artificial Intelligence from Colonial India: Race, Statistics, and Facial Recognition in the Global South' (2021) *Science, Technology, & Human Values* https://doi.org/10.1177/01622439211060839
Teachout Z, *Break 'Em Up: Recovering Our Freedom from Big Ag, Big Tech, and Big Money* (St Martin's Publishing Group 2020)
Tieman R, 'Barcelona: Smart City Revolution in Progress' (26 October 2017) <www.ft.com/content/6d2fe2a8-722c-11e7-93ff-99f383b09ff9> accessed 30 June 2020
Timan T, Newell BC and Koops B-J (eds), *Privacy in Public Space: Conceptual and Regulatory Challenges* (Edward Elgar 2017)
Trottier D and Fuchs C, 'Theorising Social Media, Politics and the State: An Introduction' in Daniel T and Christian F (eds), *Social Media, Politics and the State* (Routledge 2015)
Tutt A, 'An FDA for Algorithms' (2017) 69 *Administrative Law Review* 83
Umoja Noble S, *Algorithms of Oppression: How Search Engines Reinforce Racism* (New York University Press 2018)
'USA: Facial Recognition Technology Reinforcing Racist Stop-and-Frisk Policing in New York – New Research' (*Amnesty International*, 15 February 2022) <www.amnesty.org/en/latest/news/2022/02/usa-facial-recognition-technology-reinforcing-racist-stop-and-frisk-policing-in-new-york-new-research/> accessed 23 August 2023
Vincent J, 'Automatic Gender Recognition Tech Is Dangerous, Say Campaigners: It's Time to Ban It' (*The Verge*, 14 April 2021) <www.theverge.com/2021/4/14/22381370/automatic-gender-recognition-sexual-orientation-facial-ai-analysis-ban-campaign> accessed 22 August 2023
Wörsdörfer M, 'Big Tech and Antitrust: An Ordoliberal Analysis' (2022) 35 *Philosophy & Technology* 65
Zahn M, 'Controversy Illuminates Rise of Facial Recognition in Private Sector' (*ABC News*, 8 January 2023) <https://abcnews.go.com/Business/controversy-illuminates-rise-facial-recognition-private-sector/story?id=96116545> accessed 22 August 2023
Zalnieriute M, 'Against Procedural Fetishism: A Call for a New Digital Constitution' (2023) 30(2) *Indiana Journal of Global Legal Studies* 227
Zalnieriute M, 'Burning Bridges: The Automated Facial Recognition Technology and Public Space Surveillance in the Modern State' (2021) 22 *Columbia Science and Technology Review* 314
Zalnieriute M, 'From Human Rights Aspirations to Enforceable Obligations by Non-State Actors in the Digital Age: The Case of Internet Governance and ICANN' (2019) *Yale Journal of Law & Technology* 278
Zalnieriute M, 'Glukhin vs Russia' (2023) 117(4) *American Journal of International Law* 695
Brown v Tasmania [2017] HCA 43 Conseil d'Etat, Décision n° 442364, 26 April 2022 <www.conseiletat.fr/fr/arianeweb/CE/decision/2022-04-26/442364> accessed 17 July 2023
Zalnieriute M, '"Transparency-Washing" in The Digital Age: A Corporate Agenda of Procedural Fetishism' (2021) 8 *Critical Analysis of Law* 39
Zalnieriute M, 'Procedural Fetishism and Mass Surveillance under the ECHR: Big Brother Watch v. UK' (*Verfassungsblog: On Matters Constitutional*, 2 June 2021) <https://verfassungsblog.de/big-b-v-uk/> accessed 3 May 2024

13 The Privacy of Emotions

From the GDPR to the AI Act, an Overview of Emotional AI Regulation and the Protection of Privacy and Personal Data

Mateja Durovic and Tommaso Corno

13.1 Introduction

Artificial intelligence (AI) systems represent one of the fastest-moving aspects of technological innovation with which – both consciously and not – users interact daily on a global scale. These systems represent an enormous opportunity for the development of global economies, processing large amount of data to drive productivity, sustainability and push both the private and public sector towards desirable outcomes thanks to the insights provided by them.

In the European Union (EU), the drive towards the adoption and promotion of excellence in the field of AI has been first stated through Ursula von der Leyen's Commission's Political Guidelines,[1] calling for coordination within the EU on addressing the implications of AI systems and prioritising investments in the field. Such commitment has then been acted upon first through a White Paper on "Artificial Intelligence – A European Approach to Excellence and Trust",[2] and second through a proposal for a "Regulation Laying Down Harmonised Rules on Artificial Intelligence (Artificial Intelligence Act) and Amending Certain Union Legislative Acts" (the AI Act, or Proposed Regulation).[3]

The Commission's work and proposals, however, do not limit themselves at making a case for a wider adoption of AI in order to bring the EU at the forefront of its implementation in government, security and commerce (to name a few ambits of application). In fact, the White Paper on AI is based on two distinct yet equally necessary objectives: excellence and trust. In relation to the latter, a need to contrast the threats that the implementation of AI can pose – such as discrimination, opaque decision-making, the intrusion of privacy and the use of AI for criminal purposes – has been identified, and the development of an appropriate legislative

1 Ursula von der Leyen, 'A Union that Strives for More: My Agenda for Europe. Political Guidelines for the Next European Commission 2019–2024' (*European Commission* 2019) 13.

2 Commission, 'On Artificial Intelligence – A European Approach to Excellence and Trust' (White Paper) COM(2020) 65 final (AI White Paper).

3 Commission, 'Proposal for a Regulation of the European Parliament and of the Council Laying Down Harmonised Rules on Artificial Intelligence (Artificial Intelligence Act) and Amending Certain Union Legislative Acts' COM(2021) 206 final.

DOI: 10.4324/9781003502791-18

framework for this has since commenced, culminating in the aforementioned regulation proposal.

This chapter focuses on a relatively small area of AI, emotion recognition, and its implications in relation to data protection and privacy in the context of current and future regulatory frameworks. As described by Andrew McStay, one of the biggest social opportunities behind these technologies is that they can represent a giant leap towards achieving an increasingly naturalised relationship between humans and machines.[4] While, as this chapter will discuss, this does not come without risks that must be addressed, this can explain the growing attention that companies and institutions have been giving to emotion recognition technologies and the debate that arises therefrom. The use of such technologies, in fact, poses particular questions on its legitimacy in relation to the quality and nature of the data collected, and considerations are to be made both in relation to the current EU legal framework of the General Data Protection Regulation (GDPR) and in light of the Proposed Regulation on Artificial Intelligence.

The issues arising from the use of AI for emotion recognition may also be seen as intrinsic to the purpose of this technology, and thus a general consideration of the ethical implications and concerns that these raise is useful in understanding the degree of compatibility between emotion recognition and data protection.

This chapter therefore begins with an introduction to emotion recognition AI and the academic debate behind its legitimacy. It then proceeds to evaluate the way AI (in its broader sense) fits within the GDPR framework and how this would change if the AI Act (in its current form before the European Commission) were to become law. This first part will set out the general principles against which the issues relating to emotion recognition are considered; that is, looking at the ethical implications of processing data relating to users' emotions and evaluating this technology's compatibility with the GDPR, the principles of data protection and an eventual AI Act. The outcome of this necessarily leads to further considerations being made in relation to the void left by the Proposed Regulation when tackling the issues specific to emotional AI, and evaluating the possible avenues to guarantee the protection of personal data and privacy through self-regulation.

Given the current state of the law, the current prospective outcomes of the AI Act and the ethical considerations at stake, these issues are all but trivial. The development of these technologies will have a strong influence over society, extending well beyond the realm of consumer relationships, making a comprehensive review of emotional AI's critical aspects and of the pathways to its safe and responsible development fundamental to the development of a (currently lacking) substantial body of literature on the matter.

4 Andrew McStay, 'The Right to Privacy in the Age of Emotional AI' (*OHCR* 2018) 2 <www.ohchr.org/sites/default/files/Documents/Issues/DigitalAge/ReportPrivacyinDigitalAge/AndrewMcStayProfessor_of_Digital_Life,_BangorUniversityWalesUK.pdf> accessed 20 June 2023.

13.2 The Interaction Between AI and the GDPR, and the Proposed AI Act

Technological innovation has consistently represented a great opportunity for Europe and the world, yet its implications in terms of safeguarding people's privacy and personal data have – in an equally consistent manner – represented a concern for European lawmakers. The beginning of a global endeavour in terms of data protection dates back to 1981, when the Data Protection Convention (Convention 108)[5] was adopted with the aim of preserving the rights protected by Art. 8 European Convention on Human Rights (ECHR). This was following the determination – reached in the 1970s – that the growing use of information technology brought to light the shortcomings of the ECHR itself in terms of protection against the misuse of personal data.[6]

In 1995, European harmonisation on the matter of data protection began as means to ensure consistency in the application of the objectives set out by Convention 108 and the development of the internal market. With this in mind, the Data Protection Directive[7] entered into force on 13 December. The next step in the process of development of the European legislative framework on the matter of privacy and data protection was the passing of the GDPR,[8] which gave form to the legal landscape that we know today regarding this topic.

This brief explanation of the development of data protection legislation across Europe is useful to understand what has prompted legislative change in contrasting the misuse of users' information throughout the years. When the Data Protection Directive entered into force, the Internet still counted a small user base, and consequently no reference to it was made in the instrument's text. Between 1995 and 2016, the Internet became a global hub for the exchange and processing of personal data. Enormous companies operating in tech emerged, gathering unprecedented amounts of personal information from very large user bases. At the same time, the use of cookies drastically changed the way advertising is delivered, targeting specific users based on preferences and interests. In a world that was more interconnected than ever, European legislation had to tackle new issues in the way data was collected and processed in order to protect users' fundamental rights. The Internet, its growth and the new challenges connected to it made a piece of legislation that directly addressed this "new world" of data processing, giving birth to the GDPR.

5 Convention for the Protection of Individuals with regard to Automatic Processing of Personal Data (Data Protection Convention) (28 January 1981) ETS 108.

6 Council of Europe, 'Explanatory note to the Convention for the Protection of Individuals with Regard to Automatic Processing of Personal Data' (1981) ETS 108, para 4.

7 Directive 95/46/EC of the European Parliament and of the Council of 24 October 1995 on the protection of individuals with regard to the processing of personal data and on the free movement of such data [1995] OJ L 281/31.

8 Regulation (EU) 2016/679 of the European Parliament and of the Council of 27 April 2016 on the protection of natural persons with regard to the processing of personal data and on the free movement of such data, and repealing Directive 95/46/EC (General Data Protection Regulation) [2016] OJ L 119.

In a similar way, the GDPR does not make any mention of AI in its text. While the two are fundamentally compatible, and several provisions are particularly relevant to the various applications of AI, the fast-paced development of the latter also poses a series of challenges to some applications of the GDPR.[9] In its White Paper on AI, the Commission held that while EU legislation remains applicable as a matter of principle regardless of whether AI is involved, an assessment of the adequacy of such enforcement in addressing risks is required.[10] Similarly to the need for the development of a new legal framework that took into account the Internet's role in users' lives and the new threats posed by it, the rapidity with which AI is developing can lead to breaches of fundamental rights and threats to the security and wellbeing of citizens, raising questions about the appropriateness of the GDPR alone to deal with this.[11] Issues relating to transparency, oversight on decision-making, profiling and purpose limitation may emerge from the development of these technologies, and the boundaries of the current GDPR framework are tested by the systems through which AI stores, uses and learns from personal data.[12] In brief, it seems like AI is moving too fast for the GDPR alone to be sufficient in safeguarding citizens' rights.

As the EU tries to catch up with the rapid development of AI in terms of its regulation, the Proposed Regulation on Artificial Intelligence puts forward four objectives: (1) ensuring that AI systems available in Europe are complying with existing EU laws and comply with the EU's values and fundamental rights; (2) ensuring that the legal framework in which AI sits is sufficiently certain; (3) enhancing governance and effective enforcement of the law applicable to AI systems; and (4) preventing market fragmentation in the area of AI.

In doing so, the Proposed Regulation sets out a series of mandatory requirements and harmonised technical standards that are applied following a risk-based approach. From the prohibition of certain "unacceptable" AI practices to the imposing of different levels of transparency requirements for different systems, the Proposed Regulation generates greater oversight on the single market for AI technology, thus regulating both its commercialisation and its use through measures that are examined further in this chapter in the context of emotion recognition.

How does this the interplay between the GDPR and the AI Act then unfold when the provisions of the AI Act are triggered? This question is not one that finds an easy answer, in particular because of the general reticence exercised by European lawmakers in explicitly and directly enforcing data protection provisions through the Proposed Regulation.[13] This approach has been made explicit in the Act itself,

9 European Parliament, 'The impact of the General Data Protection Regulation (GDPR) on artificial intelligence' (EPRS 2020) II-III.

10 COM(2020) 65 final (n 2) 10.

11 Council of Europe, 'Algorithms and Human Rights: Study on the Human Rights Dimensions of Automated Data Processing Techniques and Possible Regulatory Implications' DGI(2017)12, 29.

12 European Parliament (n 9) II.

13 Cristiano Codagnone, Giovanni Liva and Teresa Rodriguez De Las Heras Ballell, 'Identification and Assessment of Existing and Draft EU Legislation in the Digital Field' (European Parliament

which explicitly states it should not be seen as the legal ground for the processing of personal data,[14] but can hardly be defined as satisfactory. Stating that the AI Act operates without prejudice to European legislation (including the GDPR) answers very few questions about how the two can operate together, and when and how the triggering of the Proposed Regulation's provisions will reflect in the involvement of the GDPR. Questions remain in relation to the classification of AI systems as triggering the high-risk presumption found in Art. 35 GDPR, the absence of an explicit need for compliance with the GDPR in certain provisions of the AI Act, the lack of clarity on the applicability of Art. 22 GDPR to AI systems and the lack of explicit remedy provisions in the AI Act, among others.[15] While these are pressing questions that are worthy of consideration when looking at how Europe's data protection landscape will evolve once the AI Act enters into force, they are beyond the scope of this chapter and are best left to specialist literature. This is because the data protection and privacy implications of emotional AI extend far beyond the law itself. As will be discussed later in this chapter, the nature of the data collected by these systems is such that it often falls outside the meaning of "personal" data, making the role of the GDPR – whatever this may be – substantially irrelevant while still preserving some critical elements from the perspective of privacy and fundamental rights. It is perhaps exactly from this that the issues discussed in this chapter arise. While ultimately of a legal nature, these stem from wider principles which are instrumental to the evaluation of the risks that emotional AI may pose. For this reason, it is first essential to understand how these systems work and why they are so deeply contested from a scientific and ethical perspective.

13.3 Emotion Recognition AI: A Highly Contested Technology

13.3.1 What Is Emotion Recognition AI? Theory and Criticisms

In June 2022, Microsoft announced that emotion recognition AI would be removed from their software.[16] Similarly, in May, nearly 30 activist groups formally asked in a letter to Zoom CEO Eric Yuan for the company to stop investing in the technology, and most importantly to keep it out of its platform.[17] Why is this the case?

Emotion recognition AI relies on a series of processes to infer emotions in users, be this from their facial expressions, their tone of voice or any other action

---

2022) 62 <www.europarl.europa.eu/thinktank/en/document/IPOL_STU(2022)703345> accessed 17 June 2023.

14 COM(2021) 206 final, Recital 41.

15 Codagnone, Liva and Rodriguez De Las Heras Ballell (n 13) 63.

16 Elliott Lewis, 'Microsoft Is Removing Emotion Recognition Features from Its Facial Recognition Tech' (*NBC News*, 27 June 2022) <www.nbcnews.com/tech/tech-news/microsoft-removing-emotion-recognition-features-facial-recognition-tec-rcna35087> accessed 12 July 2022.

17 Mike Gleason, 'Privacy Groups Urge Zoom to Abandon Emotion AI Research' *TechTarget* (12 May 2022) <www.techtarget.com/searchunifiedcommunications/news/252518128/Privacy-groups-urge-Zoom-to-abandon-emotion-AI-research> accessed 12 July 2022.

performed that may be used to identify their emotional state, such as choice of words. This technology, therefore, uses machine learning to expand on a series of "standardised" actions or expressions that people use when they find themselves in any given emotional state.

There are several forms of emotion recognition technologies, which process different types of biometric data through a range of algorithms in order to determine the emotional state of the individual interacting with the technology. Generally speaking, emotion recognition takes place in the form of facial expression recognition (FER), speech emotion recognition (SER), text or other forms of audio/video data collection. Some emotion recognition systems even use physiological signals (such as galvanic skin response, heart rate and breathing patterns) to determine the emotional state of the data subject, and while these may have a higher accuracy than systems relying on the aforementioned parameters, they do not represent the form of emotion recognition AI to which people may find themselves frequently exposed.[18] It is therefore more useful, in considering the implications of these technologies, to focus on those that do not require the collection of physiological data, of which data subjects would be well aware and which do not attempt at a "humanisation" of computers in order to infer an emotional state.

Even within the same form of emotion recognition, several models and processes have developed in the attempt to achieve greater accuracy and a broader range of detectable emotions. It is perhaps starting from this final point that critics of emotion recognition technology have attacked these systems. A 2020 study published on the *Journal of Artificial Intelligence and Systems* found that while some systems had an accuracy of better than 98% in detecting target emotions, to that point only seven basic emotions had been identified through the use of AI.[19] Such recognition is consistent with Paul Ekman's basic emotion theory, which classifies emotion in six broad categories and sets forth the idea that emotions are instinctive, that different people react similarly when exposed to similar stimuli, that basic emotions are expressed similarly by different people and that there is a consistency in the physiological reaction to basic emotions by different people.[20] In short, basic emotion theory considers a very limited amount of emotions as dominant in humans, suggesting that our reactions to these are genetically hardwired in us.

This claim, unsurprisingly, is a matter of great debate in the scientific community. While other models to explain human emotion have developed, basic emotion theory – most likely thanks to its simplicity and ability to label emotions in broad categories – remains the dominant source of inspiration and theoretical framework for most emotion recognition AI systems. While basic emotion theories have as an objective categorising emotional states based on data inputs from data subjects'

18 Maria Egger, Matthias Ley and Sten Hanke, 'Emotion Recognition from Physiological Signal Analysis: A Review' (2019) 343 *Electronic Notes in Theoretical Computer Science* 35.

19 Anvita Saxena, Ashish Khanna and Deepak Gupta, 'Emotion Recognition and Detection Methods: A Comprehensive Survey' (2020) 2 *Journal of Artificial Intelligence and Systems* 53.

20 Paul Ekman, 'An Argument for Basic Emotions' (1992) 6 *Cognition and Emotion* 169; Ibid., 62.

behaviours or reactions, theories have been advanced against the existence of any form of basic emotion, leaving space for an understanding of emotion as unique to each person.[21]

Moving beyond the theoretical framework that underpins emotion recognition AI systems, even greater doubts can be raised when looking at the application of basic emotion theory to these technologies. The use that these systems make of data inputs appears to be more arbitrary than scientifically based, even if basic emotion theory were to be accepted. It has been pointed out that "simply measuring the face does not tell you whether your interpretation of it in that instance is correct or incorrect", underlining thus the importance of context when determining emotional states and consequent reactions to these.[22]

In light of this debate, it is first clear that the understanding of emotions from a scientific perspective is all but a completed endeavour. Clashing theories are still in place, while emotion recognition AI systems appear to have adopted a single one of those, out of convenience rather than scientific backing. Furthermore, the application of basic emotion theory to this field is also questioned as a result of its lack of contextualisation and appreciation for the multiple modes through which emotional reactions can be expressed.

13.3.2 The Debate Behind the Use of Emotion Recognition AI

Even assuming that the data collected and the output are accurate, the applications of emotion recognition technology are countless – and for this precise reason, they can both be used in pursuit of valuable outcomes or misused in order to manipulate people. For example, FER may be employed for security purposes such as the prevention of fraud or other types of crime,[23] while tech companies have also developed software for the detection of the emotional state of people contacted by call centres.[24] Both cases are examples of how these technologies can be a double-edged sword. Using real-time FER can help identify emotional states associated with crimes such as fraud or terrorism, yet the employment of these can be controversial. Would it be fair for people to be stopped and searched on the grounds of a particular detected emotion, for example? Similarly, call centres may use the data collected in real time to change their approach towards consumers, leaving space for an abuse of emotional intelligence to manipulate them into performing determinate actions.

21 Mark A Cohen, 'Against Basic Emotions, and Toward a Comprehensive Theory' (2005) 26 *The Journal of Mind and Behavior* 229.

22 Madhumita Murgia, 'Emotion Recognition: Can AI Detect Human Feelings from a Face?' (*Financial Times*, London, 12 May 2021) <www.ft.com/content/c0b03d1d-f72f-48a8-b342-b4a926109452> accessed 7 June 2023.

23 Kostantina Vemou and Anna Horvath, 'TechDispatch #1/2021 – Facial Emotion Recognition' (*European Data Protection Supervisor*, 26 May 2021) <https://edps.europa.eu/data-protection/our-work/publications/techdispatch/techdispatch-12021-facial-emotion-recognition_en> accessed 22 July 2022.

24 Cogito, 'Real Time Coaching' (*Cogito*, n.a.) <www.cogitocorp.com/products/real-time-coaching> accessed 22 July 2022.

An example of this is the development of Zoom IQ for sales, a function introduced by telecommunications company Zoom that analyses transcripts from meetings held on its platform to aid sales teams in determining their next steps in negotiation. The system utilises a range of parameters, such as the attribution of positive or negative correlations to words, talking speed, talk/listen ratios, patience and engaging questions to determine sentiment among customers and adapt salespeople's approach to negotiation.[25] Zoom is only the last of a series of tech companies venturing in this field, with Uniphore and Sybil already producing software that measures reactions and engagement among customers,[26] and this move has proven itself quite unpopular among rights groups, which have argued that employing such techniques is a violation of privacy and human rights.[27]

The main issue that applies to these scenarios is whether it is acceptable for companies or public bodies to use data such as emotion, which represents one of the most intimate aspects of one's person, in order to incentivise certain outcomes over others or to interfere with their lives under the pretext of safety and security. This raises serious ethical questions about the development and employment of such technologies, which both human rights groups and academics have harshly contested.[28] The use of emotion recognition by public authorities has also been singled out by the UN High Commissioner for Human Rights, Michelle Bachelet, for the risks associated with the undermining of human rights such as that to privacy, liberty and a fair trial in the 2021 report on "The Right to Privacy in the Digital Age".[29]

Another point often raised in relation to emotion recognition AI is the potential for reactivity that it carries among users. This can be described as one's changing of their behaviour in response to their knowledge of being observed, which has been brought up as a potential consequence of the implementation of emotion

25 Zoom, 'Understanding Zoom IQ for Sales Metrics' (*Zoom Support*, 22 June 2022) <https://support.zoom.us/hc/en-us/articles/5233822805389-Understanding-Zoom-IQ-for-Sales-metrics> accessed 22 July 2022.

26 Kate Kaye, 'Companies Are Using AI to Monitor Your Mood During Sales Calls. Zoom Might Be Next' *Protocol* (13 April 2022) <www.protocol.com/enterprise/emotion-ai-sales-virtual-zoom> accessed 22 July 2022.

27 Rohitha Naraharisetty, 'Activists Call on Zoom to Halt 'Emotion Detection' AI Tool' (*The Swaddle*, 19 May 2022) <https://theswaddle.com/activists-call-on-zoom-to-halt-emotion-detection-ai-tool/> accessed 17 July 2022.

28 Alexa Hagerty and Alexandra Albert, 'AI is Increasingly Being Used to Identify Emotions – Here's What's at Stake' (*The Conversation*, 15 April 2021) <www.theconversation.com/ai-is-increasingly-being-used-to-identify-emotions-heres-whats-at-stake-158809> accessed 19 February 2023; Ben Willis, 'Emotion Recognition Tech Fundamentally Flawed, Says Human Rights Charity' (*Global Government Forum*, 12 February 2021) <www.globalgovernmentforum.com/emotion-recognition-tech-fundamentally-flawed-human-rights-charity/> accessed 19 February 2023; Kate Crawford, 'Artificial Intelligence is Misreading Human Emotion' *The Atlantic* (27 April 2021) <www.theatlantic.com/technology/archive/2021/04/artificial-intelligence-misreading-human-emotion/618696/> accessed 19 February 2023.

29 United Nations High Commissioner for Human Rights, 'The Right to Privacy in the Digital Age' (13 September 2021) A/HRC/48/31.

recognition as means of evaluating engagement in classrooms or worker motivation. The issues relating to this phenomenon have been set out as follows by Sandra Wachter:

> Applying emotion-recognition software to employees also poses a threat to diversity because it forces people to act in a way that adheres to an algorithmic and artificial "mainstream" standard, and so infringes on peoples' autonomy to express themselves freely.[30]

Finally, the issues surrounding emotion recognition AI are not limited to ethical considerations, but relate to the scientific side of such technologies, as well. As emotion recognition relies on biometric data such as facial expressions or tone of voice, in order to determine one's emotional state, such technology requires some parameters which, albeit adapting through machine learning, are used as an indication for certain emotional states rather than others. The risk that causes much criticism is that of a standardisation of emotion recognition: most of these technologies, in fact, are based on "basic emotion" theory, which takes a biological approach to analysing how we react to emotive stimuli and supports the idea that all mankind is fundamentally designed to react in similar ways to the same emotional states.[31]

However, this approach appears to be all but certain. There seems, in fact, to be growing support for the idea that several factors – which can include, for instance, culture and background – influence emotional responses. The science behind emotion recognition, despite it being backed by multi-billion–dollar investments, has thus been harshly criticised by groups opposing the use of such technology, who have referred to it as a "pseudoscience", raising concerns over the impact that this may have on cultural and ethnic minorities.

As it stands, it seems clear that emotion recognition AI is not flawless, and it carries risks with it that, if the technology is misapplied or used for unethical purposes, can go to the very root of people's rights and liberties. The significance that emotions have as part of one's person, the potential for misuse of emotion recognition, the behavioural and social consequences of the widespread use of these technologies and the uncertainty surrounding the science upon which these are based all represent solid grounds for the undertaking of extensive ethical considerations on the matter, and it comes as no surprise that there is such harsh criticism surrounding their development and use. The following section will examine with more depth the implications of the issues raised in relation to emotion recognition, looking at their place within the framework of the GDPR and the potential threats for data protection that they pose.

30 Sandra Wachter, 'Every Smile You Fake – An AI Emotion-Recognition System Can Assess How 'Happy' China's Workers Are in the Office' (*Berkman Klein Center*, 15 June 2021) <https://cyber.harvard.edu/story/2021-06/every-smile-you-fake-ai-emotion-recognition-system-can-assess-how-happy-chinas> accessed 29 January 2023.

31 Hagerty and Albert (n 28).

13.4 Areas of Concern With Emotion Recognition AI

It appears clear that emotional AI is all but uncontroversial from a number of standpoints, ranging from the technological to the ethical. This, in turn, necessarily entails legal considerations to be made on the status of these systems, how they are currently regulated and the impact of future legislation on the matter. In particular, in evaluating emotional AI one must identify its most critical aspects: those that allow these systems to potentially fall outside the scope of or bypass regulatory frameworks.

On this matter, one fundamental note must be made before beginning any analysis of how emotional AI fits within the framework of current and upcoming legislation. Both the GDPR and the AI Act define personal data as those that can be used to identify (or single out) an individual.[32] Notably, the AI Act does state that facial images amount to personal data but, similarly to the GDPR, fails in setting out the reach of such definition and the impact that anonymisation techniques may have in making the final data fall outside (or within) the scope of the legislation. While it has been suggested that these may still lead to the data in question to be considered personal, this remains a matter of opinion rather than law, and techniques such as the use of soft biometrics may easily lead to the data collected falling outside the meaning of "personal".[33] Pursuant to Recital 26 GDPR, the test when data is anonymised is whether the means reasonably likely to be used can lead to the singling out of a natural person. It goes without saying that, given this definition, it is very simple for developers and users of emotion recognition AI to fall outside the scope of current data protection regulations.

The following analysis, therefore, is to be taken as relating, first, to those emotional AI systems that do operate in such a way as to fall within the scope of the GDPR and, second, to highlight the inconsistencies that the processing of emotional data creates in relation to the principles of data protection. While this may appear to be a redundant exercise at first, Section 13.4.2 will look at the significance of these inconsistencies, drawing upon the relevance of emotional data as a deeply personal form of information that, while not recognised under current or prospective regulatory frameworks, is worthy of protection in compliance with the same fundamental principles enshrined in the GDPR.

13.4.1 In Relation to Data Protection and the GDPR

The initiation and development of European regulation in the ambit of privacy and data protection has largely been driven by a necessity to protect fundamental rights from the rapid development of new technologies, which in turn pose challenges in relation to the way data protection practices and legislation are understood, governed and applied. Similarly to the way in which the Internet and social media

32 Art. 4(1); GDPR COM(2021) 206 final, Art. 3(33).

33 Andrew McStay, 'Emotional AI, Soft Biometrics and the Surveillance of Emotional Life: An Unusual Consensus on Privacy' (2020) 7 *Big Data and Society* 1.

challenged the Data Protection Directive with new systems and technologies, AI – and in particular, emotion recognition systems – pose novel risks in relation to the way in which the GDPR may effectively protect fundamental rights. This does not mean that emotion recognition is per se incompatible with the GDPR, and neither that the current legislative framework does not apply to these technologies, but rather that the way they operate may – in some cases – muddle the waters of how these rules can protect fundamental rights when the systems use can display bias, opacity and excessive intrusion into one's personal sphere.

The question that emerges from this is that of identifying the challenges that emotion recognition poses and evaluate both how protection from its shortcomings can be achieved through the GDPR and the remaining risks that these new technologies pose to fundamental rights and rights protected under the current regulations on data protection.

13.4.1.1 Accuracy of Data

Among the principles of the processing of personal dataset out in Art. 5 GDPR is that of accuracy of the data collected, held and processed, which is further reinforced by data subjects' right to rectification under Art. 16 GDPR.

As mentioned in Section 13.3.3, the scientific principles behind emotion recognition AI systems – and consequently, their actual ability to detect emotions in users – are contested to the point that they have also been described as "complete pseudoscience". The doubts relating to the scientific backing of these systems also reflects in empirical findings. One study, led by Dublin's City University,[34] found that emotion recognition systems tend to be less accurate at detecting emotional states compared to humans, raising further doubts as to how such systems may in fact be considered sufficiently accurate for the purposes of the GDPR, and posing a risk to data subjects that interact with this AI.

The explanation of what constitutes "accurate" data is fundamentally unclear, although EU case law can help in clarifying this. In Case C434/16 *Novak*, in fact, the Court held that the evaluation of accuracy must be made in light of the purposes for the collection of such data. Similarly, it is believed that the meaning of accuracy also refers to the input that is given to machines and the way these work.[35] Therefore, if a certain AI is made to interpret emotional data following "basic emotion" theory, it is not clear whether any inaccuracy (in real terms) that is the product of following such theory is to be considered as such. Furthermore, the fact that emotion recognition AI operates as means of interpretation (basically acting as a

34 Damien Dupré and others, 'A Performance Comparison of Eight Commercially Available Automatic Classifiers for Facial Affect Recognition' (2020) 15 *PLoS ONE* <https://journals.plos.org/plosone/article/file?id=10.1371/journal.pone.0231968&type=printable> accessed 17 January 2023.

35 European Union Agency for Fundamental Rights, 'Data Quality and Artificial Intelligence – Mitigating Bias and Error to Protect Fundamental Rights' (*FRA*, 2019) <https://fra.europa.eu/en/publication/2019/data-quality-and-artificial-intelligence-mitigating-bias-and-error-protect> accessed 17 June 2023.

substitute for a human observer), it seems unclear whether in exact outputs from such systems are actually to be considered "inaccurate" for the purpose of data protection regulation, thus potentially opening the door for breaches of fundamental rights when such inaccuracies produce outcomes that would otherwise be avoided.

An example of this is when the inaccuracies of emotion recognition AI produce discriminatory outcomes, the implications of which are described in the following subsections.

13.4.1.2 Discrimination

Among the risks directly associated with the use of emotion recognition AI and its lack of accuracy is the discriminatory data output that several of these technologies have demonstrated. This is particularly true in relation to FER, which has been found – as recognised also by the Commission in their White Paper on Artificial Intelligence – in some cases to display racial and gender bias.[36]

Studies have shown that some emotion recognition systems tend to be both more imprecise and attribute emotions with more negative connotation to people of colour.[37] Error rates in Black data subjects for speech recognition systems can occur up to twice than in white subjects, according to Stanford's Fair Speech initiative. Similarly, emotion recognition does not – contrary to claims on its usefulness – represent an effective aid to people with disabilities, with the technology demonstrating the potential to misinterpret the expressions of autistic people and people with other conditions that can lead to atypical facial expressions such as Parkinson's or Bell's palsy.[38]

Within the framework of the GDPR, discrimination is tackled prevalently through two provisions. The first, Art. 9(1), prohibits the processing of personal data belonging to protected categories – this includes is data revealing ethnic or racial origin, and biometric data for the identification of unique natural persons – with exceptions provided in Art. 9(2) which permit the processing of protected data when, for example, data subjects consent to such processing, the processing is necessary for employment or social security purposes, the processing is necessary to protect "vital interests" of the subject or the data in question is manifestly made public by the subject.

The second provision acting as to prevent discrimination in data processing is Art. 22 GDPR, which relates to algorithmic decision-making. Article 22(1) prohibits such decision-making, yet Art. 22(2) sets out three exceptions to the rule, these being (1) when this is necessary to enter into or perform a contract between the

36 Joy Buolamwini and Timnit Gebru, 'Proceedings of the 1st Conference on Fairness, Accountability and Transparency' (2018) 81 *PMLR* 77.

37 Luren Rhue, 'Racial Influence on Automated Perceptions of Emotion' (2018) <https://papers.ssrn.com/sol3/papers.cfm?abstract_id=3281765> accessed 12 June 2022; Allison Koenecke and others, 'Racial Disparities in Automated Speech Recognition' (2020) 117 *PNAS* 7684.

38 Gerald Quinn, 'Rights of Persons with Disabilities: Report of the Special Rapporteur on the Rights of Persons with Disabilities' (28 December 2021) A/HRC/49/52.

data subject and data controller; (2) when this is authorised by Union or Member State law, and suitable measures are in place to safeguard the data subject's rights, freedoms and legitimate interests; or (3) when the data subject explicitly consents to this. The provision then directly relates to non-discrimination in its fourth paragraph, where it is stated that, if the exceptions in paragraph 2 apply, special categories of data mentioned in Art. 9 cannot be used in algorithmic decision-making, unless the exceptions in Art. 9(2) apply and appropriate safeguard measures are in place.

Therefore, the GDPR establishes two levels of protection from discrimination for data subjects: The first level is an outright ban on the processing of data that may lead to discrimination, subject to proportionate exceptions. The second level applies to cases in which, exceptionally to the norm, algorithmic decision-making is permitted. This second level reiterates the prohibition on the processing of special category data, adding an additional layer of protection to the exceptions in Art. 9 by further requiring suitable safeguarding measures to be in place.

While it may seem that the GDPR establishes an efficient and proportionate system for the safeguarding of personal data that may lead to discrimination and the violation of data subjects' fundamental rights, the way emotion recognition and biometric data technologies operate poses new challenges on this matter. The issues outlined here, in fact, do not derive from the type of data that these systems process, but are the product of technical flaws that have been encountered in several of these technologies. In fact, facial emotion recognition does not necessarily process data relating, for instance, to one's ethnicity, and could potentially even avoid falling within the scope of "biometric" data as defined by the GDPR. The data it is concerned with and processes are the parameters used to determine the data subject's emotional state, and the data output is the determination of an emotion. Therefore, the data processed by many of these systems can avoid falling within the scope of Art. 9, and yet can still present a heavy bias due to the way in which, for example, negative emotions are more often portrayed in people of colour.

The fact that these systems could thus avoid the prohibition set out in Art. 9 means that greater risks for discrimination emerge in the contexts of algorithmic decision-making permitted by Art. 22, as the additional safeguards for the data subject's rights, freedoms and legitimate interests are not required. Therefore, emotion recognition AI systems that do not use data that is "uniquely identifying" of the data subjects would be relieved of the restrictions that protect them from non-discrimination.

Even when taking into consideration systems that may fall under Art. 9 as, perhaps, they process and store facial images of the data subjects, the exceptions contained within Arts. 9(2) and 22(2) would expose data subjects to practices that, unbeknownst to them, may disfavour them as a result of the technological and scientific flaws that they may present. Since these technologies do not directly relate to ethnicity or gender, but rather use biometric data (intended in a broader sense than that defined in the GDPR), the ways in which biases can be engrained and develop within emotion recognition AI may be opaque to users, thus posing an ulterior risk regardless of whether these are considered within or outside of the scope of Arts. 9 and 22(4).

The risk of discrimination posed by emotion recognition AI, which has been demonstrated to exist particularly in relation to gender and racial biases, is therefore dual. First of all, the rapid development of technology in this ambit may mean that these technologies, despite the fundamental rights violations risks that they carry, might be able to circumvent the prohibition set out in Art. 9. Second, even if they are to be caught by Art. 9, a lack of knowledge relating to the bias risks that accompany these technologies entails that data subjects may be induced into accepting their use, exposing themselves to a potential for racial and gender-based discrimination.

13.4.1.3 Human Decision-making – Art. 22 GDPR Exceptions and Safeguards

Article 22 GDPR is not only designed to prevent algorithmic decisions that derive from potential discriminatory data processing practices, such as profiling, but is designed to protect data subjects from any such decision that may unjustly interfere with their fundamental rights and interests.

If emotion recognition truly has "no proven basis in science" and can be considered "absolute pseudoscience" at worst,[39] then all of its applications in the context of algorithmic decision-making, where these fall within the exceptions in Art. 22, represent potential issues for the protection of people's data and fundamental rights. Technologies used to detect emotional states in order to shortlist candidates for employment positions, for example, may present threats that extend beyond discrimination of any kind, and relate solely to the potential for inaccuracy that these may present.

In 2021, HireVue had to discontinue its facial analysis screening over concerns regarding the appropriate use of its AI system in employment decisions.[40] The software, which should help reduce recruiters' biases, is often used as an automated pre-recruitment process, which filters applicants based on their responses. If the use of AI itself in these contexts without human supervision is per se arguably problematic, it is even more so when emotion recognition is involved.

As previously explained, the science of basic emotion theory is highly disputed, and as a consequence its application does not guarantee accurate and trustworthy results. Even if Art. 22(4) were to apply, it seems unclear what safeguarding measures could be put in place to prevent such inaccuracies, since as previously explored, the question of accuracy is one that heavily relates to the theory of emotion used by the AI and is thus in itself a concept open to interpretation.

39 Lewis (n 16).

40 Roy Maurer, 'HireVue Discontinues Facial Analysis Screening' (*SHRM*, 3 February 2021) <www.shrm.org/resourcesandtools/hr-topics/talent-acquisition/pages/hirevue-discontinues-facial-analysis-screening.aspx> accessed 17 January 2023.

13.4.2 Is Emotional Data Special? The Broader Relationship Between Emotion Recognition and Data Protection

Sections 13.4.1.1–13.4.1.3 have approached the data protection implications of emotion recognition AI by looking at how these technologies touch upon some established principles of data protection that are at the core of the legislative framework of the GDPR. While such an approach is useful in considering the challenges posed to the current system, it fails to exhaustively answer the question as to whether and how emotion recognition threatens data protection and privacy in a broader – and perhaps more philosophical and normative – sense.

In plainer terms, beyond understanding the relationship between emotion recognition and the GDPR, one must also ask if there is "something special" to emotion recognition that makes it inherently threatening in terms of privacy and data protection, and thus warranting a greater level of protection for data subjects. The issues related to this topic transcend its positioning under current or future legislative frameworks, and require ethical considerations – largely based on human rights – in assessing the legitimacy of these systems in relation to data protection. The evaluation of emotion recognition systems must transcend the legal meaning and the accuracy of these systems, as these are insufficient for an assessment of their legitimacy.

Clearly, this does not mean that the law and the accuracy of the systems do not have a role in evaluating the systems; rather, it means that a fundamental consideration based on ethics must also be made and supported by these contextual factors. The definition of personal data under current legislation does not protect the data subject's biometric information (in the case of emotion recognition)[41] when the data collected does not allow for the identification of the subject. The wide range of practices that this caveat would allow without the controls and limitations of a legal framework for privacy and data protection warrant themselves consideration of what emotion recognition entails, and whether it is inherently – and beyond the realm of the GDPR's underlying principles – at odds with the reach that Member States, companies and users ought to have within one's personal life and, ultimately, individuality.

As mentioned in the introduction, emotion recognition is a tool that has the potential to naturalise the interaction between humans and technology. However, McStay follows up to that by noting that emotion – when quantified – achieves economic value.[42] It is perhaps this step that transforms what – setting technical and scientific considerations aside – is a revolutionary tool in the way we define our relationship with technology into an arguably unethical and dubiously legitimate instrument for "mass surveillance".[43] It is necessary to look at the foundation for a

41 McStay (n 4) 5.

42 Ibid., 2.

43 ARTICLE 19, 'Emotional Entanglement: China's Emotion Recognition Market and Its Implications for Human Rights' (*ARTICLE 19*, 2021) 36–37 <www.article19.org/wp-content/uploads/2021/01/ER-Tech-China-Report.pdf> accessed 20 February 2023.

right to privacy – and what this entails – to understand the implications of collecting and using emotional data and how these reflect in the fields of human rights and, more broadly, ethics.

Many ethical critiques of the implementation of emotion recognition in public spaces relates to the dignity of the individuals whose emotions are – allegedly – identified and collected. When looking at the reasons behind the right to privacy, there are convincing arguments that place the protection of dignity as the key objective that this aims to achieve.[44] The EU GDPR itself enshrines the importance of safeguarding dignity as an aim of privacy rules.[45] In the case of emotion recognition, it may very well be the case that these technologies are not only capable of attacking individual dignity, but that such an incompatibility with the preservation of dignity falls within their nature. Let us, for example, consider the case of FER systems deployed in public spaces for advertisement purposes. The data collected can be prevented from falling within the legal meaning of "personal data" if it does not allow for the identification of a particular individual. However, this does not mean that the use of the technology does not represent a practice that is infringing upon individuals' privacy and dignity. Privacy is a concept that extends beyond legal meaning, and is a matter of choice rather than of secrecy.[46] While allowed by data protection laws, this practice makes inferences that closely relate to the individual subject to the technology, which may be undesired. It is difficult to see how this, especially when occurring in continuous iterations over a wide pool of data subjects, does not represent an invasion of both individual and collective – as argued by Floridi – privacy.

The use of emotion recognition technologies, in fact, presents numerous critical aspects in relation to the protection of privacy. These include, for example, the lack of knowledge on data subjects' part, the use of data that can be described as sensitive and the constant and arbitrary judgments that these technologies make.[47] While these can be considered invasive of every subject's privacy, the impact they can have on vulnerable subjects and the potential for profiling that these processes possess represents particular risks to the preservation of human dignity and to human rights more generally. As a result, one of the possible undesirable outcomes of the deployment of emotion recognition AI in public spaces is that, by processing what is not legally considered personal data and infringing on individuals' privacy, a risk emerges for the revealing of real or inferred personal information.[48]

44 Luciano Floridi, 'On Human Dignity as a Foundation for the Right to Privacy' (2016) 29 *Philosophy and Technology* 307.

45 Art. 88 GDPR.

46 Saif M Mohammad, 'Ethics Sheet for Automatic Emotion Recognition and Sentiment Analysis' (2022) 48 *Computational Linguistics* 239, 263.

47 ARTICLE 19 (n 43) 36–37.

48 Mark Latonero, 'Governing Artificial Intelligence: Upholding Human Rights and Dignity' (*Data and Society*, 2018) 13 <www.datasociety.net/wp-content/uploads/2018/10/DataSociety_Governing_Artificial_Intelligence_Upholding_Human_Rights.pdf> accessed 20 February 2023.

Interactions, and at times interferences, with the day-to-day vicissitudes of data subjects through these technologies can – depending on the systems used for machine learning and for inferring conclusions – lead to a categorisation of people who are simply expressing particular facial features, tones of voice or other forms of biometric data collected by the AI systems. These use the visible, audible or otherwise detectable aspects of a person's features or behaviour to determine one's subjective and undetectable (at least in a direct manner) mental and emotional state. As argued by Luke Stark and Jesse Hoey, emotion is reflected in a variety of phenomena, not all of which are visible.[49] The practical risk of revealing personal information and profiling, therefore, comes in addition to another more fundamental and ethically crucial one, which is the question of emotion recognition violating people's mental and emotional privacy.[50] In turn, this risk must be evaluated on the basis of another consideration, which is of what the public and private spheres consist. It is perhaps this final distinction that explains the critical aspects of emotion recognition in public spaces: the ethical implications and legitimacy of these systems highly depend on how we understand emotional expression and the weight of subjective human experience that arises from such understanding.[51] Similarly to our physical aspect (which we can still, to an extent, conceal in public spaces), our emotional state is an element of individuals' private sphere that is inevitably attached to the person, even when this person is in a public space. Emotion recognition technologies purportedly use what basic emotion theory could describe as unequivocal indicators of an emotional state to determine the nature of the subjective element of human experience and emotion.

The private and public spheres, when discussing emotion, are inevitably intersecting,[52] and when discussing emotion recognition it can further be argued that the public display of expressions, body language or other physically detectable behaviour is not wholly private when it takes place in a public space. However, it is for this same reason that the processing of data for emotion recognition purposes is particularly problematic, as data subjects have no choice about what is processed and whether it is processed. These practices take information that is capable of being collected in order to draw conclusions about something that is wholly subjective and can be defined as private within the private sphere itself. By this, it is meant that emotions are complex and can be difficult to identify and express, even for those who are experiencing them. By indirectly collecting emotional information, which is inferred by observing other publicly visible indicators, users of emotion recognition AI are reaching within individuals' private sphere while, on the surface, operating solely with what is publicly available. By recalling the concept

49 Luke Stark and Jesse Hoey, 'The Ethics of Emotion in Artificial Intelligence Systems' (*Proceedings of the 2021 ACM Conference on Fairness, Accountability and Transparency*, March 2021) 783.

50 McStay (n 4).

51 Stark and Hoey (n 49) 786.

52 Luke Stark, 'The Emotional Context of Information Privacy' (2016) 32 *The Information Society* 14.

of mental and emotional privacy, it is difficult to uphold the ethical legitimacy of these technologies when used without consent and in public spaces.

The analysis provided here clearly points towards the uniqueness of emotional data. Its subjective nature, its inevitability and its unseverability from the individual entail that data subjects can hardly escape being subjected to a violation of users' part of their emotional privacy. This warrants consideration of emotional data as that which is both different from all other data, and particularly sensitive. From an ethical perspective, the apparently inevitable growth in the use of these technologies for a range of purposes means that great attention must be placed on how it is regulated, and that this will have to be done on an ad hoc basis. Regardless of how emotion recognition systems interact with existing legal frameworks, it is evident that there is more to this type of data than its mere "personal" dimension: the role of privacy, the ethical weight of subjectivity and, more broadly, the understanding of emotions as a personal and social phenomenon make this a type of data which must be protected in particular ways – and, perhaps, more extensively.

13.4.3 The Position Following the Artificial Intelligence Act

Emotion recognition is a perfect example of how the rapid development of AI can represent a challenge to legal frameworks for data protection, namely the GDPR, and to the ethics of the relationship between people and technology. As with the GDPR's adoption in 2016 as a response to the new challenges posed by the Internet and its evolving data processing practices, the Proposal for a Regulation Laying Down Harmonised Rules on Artificial Intelligence (the AI Act) aims at preserving the rights of people throughout the European Union in light of the growth, evolution and future prospects for the widespread adoption of AI systems in Europe.

Both technologies that are presently available and those that are yet to come in the field of emotion recognition pose unique challenges to the current system, through which individuals' privacy and data are protected in the safeguarding of their fundamental rights and safety. For this reason, the AI Act as put forward by the European Commission sets out a series of measures that – both directly and indirectly – regulate the way emotion recognition AI can be marketed within the Union and used on EU subjects.

13.4.3.1 Transparency Requirements (Title IV)

Title IV of the Proposed Regulation sets out transparency requirements for AI systems that pose a particular threat as regards the manipulation of users. These obligations would apply to three categories of systems, namely those interacting with humans, those that are used to detect emotions or associate users with social categories through biometric data, and those that generate or manipulate digital content.

Earlier in this chapter, it was set out that emotion recognition technologies have a high potential for misuse and manipulation. An overall lack of transparency with users relating to the fact that their facial expressions, tone of voice or other biometric information may be used for a range of purposes can be problematic, to say the least, both from an ethical point of view and in light of users' perspectives of how processors and controllers collect and use personal data, in particular in contexts of everyday use such as social media.[53]

The AI Act aims to resolve such lack of transparency by imposing obligations on users of technologies defined in Art. 3 as emotion recognition or biometric categorisation systems.[54] These entail that all those using such systems must inform the people exposed to these technologies about their operation. Transparency, here, is understood as communication to exposed subjects relating to the processes involving emotion recognition. There is one exception to the transparency requirements set out in Art. 52, which is that of AI systems used for biometric categorisation to detect, prevent and investigate criminal offences, in which case subjects exposed to these forms of AI do not need to be informed.

It must be noted here that the imposing of transparency requirements represents a form of regulation of specific AI systems, regardless of whether they are considered high-risk systems. The exclusion of these systems from automatically falling within high-risk AI is indicative of the Commission's opinion that emotion recognition generally represents a form of AI with limited – or at least not always high – associated risks.[55] It is also true, however, that several applications of these technologies will in fact cause them to fall under the category of high-risk AI, as explained in what follows, and that this entails another level of transparency requirements which are not based on communication, but rather on interpretability.[56] Such systems would be required to further comply with a much larger set of regulations described in Section 13.5, which in all effect would further control the use of emotion recognition AI and prevent its misuse and the violation of users' rights.

Despite this, the starting point for emotion recognition under the AI Act would be that of particular – but not necessarily high – associated risks, and therefore limited regulations of these systems. This entails that, provided that a system is in fact defined for the purposes of the Proposed Regulation as an emotion recognition system (which in itself is a point worthy of debate; see in what follows), it is solely required to comply with the transparency requirements set out in Art. 52, and its escalation into the high-risk AI category would be subject to meeting the descriptions contained in Annexes II and III as described in what follows.

53 Gabriel Grill and Nazanin Andalibi, 'Attitudes and Folk Theories of Data Subjects on Transparency and Accuracy in Emotion Recognition' *(Proceedings of ACM in Human Computer Interaction (PACM)*, 2022).

54 COM(2021) 206 final, Art. 52.

55 Tambiama Madiega, 'Artificial Intelligence Act' (*European Parliamentary Research Service*, January 2022) <www.europarl.europa.eu/RegData/etudes/BRIE/2021/698792/EPRS_BRI(2021)698792_EN.pdf> accessed 7 July 2022.

56 Anastasiya Kiseleva, 'Making AI's Transparency Transparent: Notes on the EU Proposal for the AI Act' (*European Law Blog*, 29 July 2021) <www.europeanlawblog.eu/2021/07/29/making-ais-transparency-transparent-notes-on-the-eu-proposal-for-the-ai-act/> accessed 20 June 2023.

13.4.3.2 Emotion Recognition as a High-risk AI System

As previously mentioned, the requirement of disclosure is simply a starting point that applies to all emotion recognition AI systems. This does not exclude that additional and more onerous requirements may be placed both on developers and users of these systems on the basis of other provisions contained within the proposed AI Act. Title III of the Act deals with AI systems that are considered "high risk", and it may be that case that some emotion recognition systems do in fact fall within such category. The first three chapters of Title III are the most relevant in relation to the implications of this in the context of data protection and emotion recognition systems, as they deal with determining what is considered "high risk" (in addition to Annex III), with the requirements for all such systems and with the obligations that are imposed upon the providers and users of high-risk AI.

13.4.3.2.1 IS EMOTION RECOGNITION AI A HIGH-RISK SYSTEM?

The first of these three chapters is, perhaps, the most relevant in the discussion of the implications on data protection of emotion recognition technologies. As previously explained in this chapter, emotion recognition AI will only be considered "high risk" if it satisfies the conditions set out in Art. 6 of the Proposed Regulation, subject to amendments pursuant to Art. 7. The resulting requirements and regulatory framework for these technologies, therefore, depends on the satisfaction of Art. 6, in absence of which the requirement of notice will remain the sole restriction to the use of emotion recognition technology. Similarly, emotion recognition AI that does not fall within the scope of Art. 6 would not be subject to the requirements concerning its providers and developers, and while the technology would still have to be compliant with GDPR requirements and those set out in other harmonised bodies of law, the AI-specific aspect that is set out in the second chapter of Title III would not apply to such technologies.

There are two elements to Art. 6 that set out what AI systems are considered high risk. In the first case, AI systems are those that are a safety component of a product – or a product in itself – that is covered by Union legislation listed in Annex II, in the case that the product involving such AI system is required to undergo third-party conformity assessment prior to its placement on the market. This specifically applies to goods that are caught by harmonised Union legislation relating to civil aviation, two- or three-wheel vehicles or quadricycles, agricultural and forestry vehicles, marine equipment, rail systems, motor vehicles and their trailers, and aircraft. In order for an AI system to be considered high risk under this paragraph, both the applicable legislation and third-party assessment requirements must be met.

In absence of this, Art. 6 of the proposed AI Act sets out an additional list of systems that are considered high risk, which may be subject to amendments by the Commission under Art. 7, but only if the systems are intended to be used in one of the areas listed in points 1–8 of Annex III. Currently, Annex III of the Act covers biometric identification, management and operation of critical infrastructure, educational and vocational training, employment and workforce management, access to services, law enforcement, migration and the administration of justice. All AI operating within the descriptions provided for high-risk AI within these categories will be considered to pose a higher level of threat to data subjects, and will therefore have to comply with the requirements set out in Title III. In the realm of emotion recognition systems, this provision would entail that software for the assessment of candidates or to monitor the emotional state of workers, which is one of the uses for which the "dynamic emotion recognition" system developed by the Chinese tech company Taigusys has been employed,[57] would fall within the category of high-risk AI. Similarly, emotion recognition software used by law enforcement for security purposes – such as to police large events – would be considered high risk for the purposes of Art. 6 (provided that they are not caught by the ban set out in Art. 5).

However, there are also emotion recognition systems that do not fall within the scope of Art. 6, and therefore are not bound by the requirements and obligations set out in what follows. An example of this would be the aforementioned systems employed by call centres to detect target customers' emotions and adapt their approach to maximise chances of sale, which would remain solely subject to the transparency requirements in Art. 52. Arguably, these may be sufficient to warn consumers about how their data is being used and to warn them about the associated risks. However, if we consider more vulnerable groups, such as the elderly, the risk associated with the use of subliminal techniques is certainly higher, and transparency may not be sufficient to comprehend the implications of the use of such technologies. Cases such as this fall between the cracks of the AI Act, as the potential for manipulation (especially of more vulnerable groups), is evident, while the absence of an evident risk of physical or psychological harm entails that Art. 5 will hardly apply to these systems. In the first place, the way in which high-risk AI is categorised in the Proposed Regulation entails the exclusion of several systems of emotion recognition, which would consequently only be subject to a duty of transparency. In light of the issues mentioned previously, the sufficiency of this is debatable, especially when considering the nature of the data being collected and used, which is extremely personal and – as regards the processing of the data itself – of which the accuracy is all but certain.

It seems clear that already in the definition of what makes a system high risk, some significant issues emerge – including the way emotional AI can or cannot fall within the scope of the provision. Setting aside the question of whether emotional AI should be generally banned (which is perhaps the most generally accepted amongst critics of the AI Act's approach to these technologies), the current provisions in Arts. 6–7 are arguably excessively rigid, restricting the Commission to the amendment of Annex III only insofar as the purpose of the system sits within

57 Elise Leise, 'Chinese Firm Taigusys Launches Emotion-Recognition System' (*AI Magazine*, 17 June 2021) <www.aimagazine.com/data-and-analytics/chinese-firm-taigusys-launches-emotion-recognition-system> accessed 20 February 2023.

a predetermined and inflexible range of purposes. Given the incontestable fact – shown by the historical development of legislation concerning data and technology briefly presented in Section 13.2 – that modern legal frameworks must be designed to adapt to evolving technologies and have often failed to do so sufficiently,[58] the implementation of the recommendation that the AI ought to allow the Commission to add high-risk systems in areas outside points 1–8 (and allow the European Artificial Intelligence Board to propose such changes) is not only desirable, but necessary.[59] Given an initial scenario whereby, most likely, emotional AI will solely be subject to the transparency requirements set out in Title IV, the possibility of adding these systems – alongside any other systems (some of which may be developed following the passing of the AI Act) that prove to pose a threat to the safety and privacy of data subjects – to the list in Annex III is fundamental in the achievement of a legislative framework capable of adapting to a rapidly developing technological landscape. In absence of this, the issues identified in this section will not only persist, but their solution – should the risks associated with emotional AI substantially materialise – would require more time-consuming and complex legislative procedures.

13.4.3.2.2 OBLIGATIONS OF PROVIDERS AND USERS, AND THE EFFECT ON HIGH-RISK EMOTION RECOGNITION SYSTEMS

Having discussed what AI systems fall within the category of high risk, and how this applies to those that undertake emotion recognition, it is useful to discuss the implications when these systems do, in fact, fall within the scope of Title III. Setting aside notification and conformity assessments, what is particularly relevant to this are the requirements that high-risk systems must satisfy and the obligations that are imposed on their providers and users, as it is these provisions that will affect the way emotion recognition AI is developed and employed on EU-based data subjects.

The requirements that all high-risk AI systems must meet in order to be conforming with the Act are set out in Chapter 2 of Title 3, and include, among other provisions, a duty of compliance (which takes into account the purpose of the systems themselves),[60] the establishment of risk-management systems, transparency obligations and data governance provisions. In terms of risk-management, Art. 9 sets out that all high-risk systems must be subject to a four step process that: (1) identifies and analyses foreseeable risks; (2) estimates and evaluates risks arising from the normal use of the systems and their reasonable misuse; (3) evaluates other possible arising risks based on data analysis; and (4) leads to the adoption of

58 Rebecca Crootof, 'Jurisprudential Space Junk: Treaties and New Technologies' in Chiara Giorgietti and Natalie Klein (eds), *Resolving Conflicts in the Law* (Brill 2019).

59 Sam Clarke and others, 'Submission of Feedback to the European Commission's Proposal for a Regulation Laying Down Harmonised Rules on Artificial Intelligence' (*European Parliament* 2021) F2665626, 2.

60 COM(2021) 206 final, Art. 8.

risk-management measures. Of these steps, two deal with the tackling of risks prior to actual use of the high-risk systems in the first place through their identification on a broader level, and subsequently by looking at the purpose of the systems themselves and the potential for abuse. However, responsibilities continue throughout the lifetime of the systems, with the analysis of data being the fulcrum of the iterative process that leads to the evaluation of previously unidentified risks.

While there is no definition of "risk" provided in the Proposed Regulation, it is possible to infer this from the language of the Act itself, in particular from the criteria set out in Art. 7 for the amendment of Annex III. It seems, in fact, that "risk" is a flexible concept that varies by taking into consideration the purposes that a particular system is designed to serve,[61] the extent of the potential impact on vulnerable individuals and the reversibility of the materialisation of such risk. This does not mean, however, that there is no single basis for the understanding of what can constitute a "risk" for the purposes of the AI Act. The provisions contained therein, in fact, indicate that "risk" entails both the potential for causing harm to the health and safety of people exposed to the AI systems in question (both physically and psychologically, as per Art. 5), and the potential for an adverse impact on the fundamental rights of the same. This leads to a discussion of the challenges in the identification and tackling of risks in emotion recognition AI, and of the legal implications of this would be in light of the AI Act becoming law.

While the previous section has brought to light some evident risks associated with emotion recognition AI, some of these may not be as straightforwardly identified and assessed. Most risks, such as discrimination, are consequential or related to the operation of these systems: the way they operate leads to outcomes that are considered a risk, as they are an obstacle to the respect of the fundamental rights of those exposed to the technology. This allows for the process set out in Art. 9 to operate with greater ease: having seen the potential for a risky outcome, the system can be adapted to limit such risks.

However, it has been previously mentioned that the whole underlying theory to emotion recognition technologies is a highly contested one, and that this can (and does) lead to inaccurate results in many cases. Taking this in the context of high-risk AI systems – which per Annex III are used in particularly impactful areas such as employment, migration or the administration of justice – it is arguable that emotion recognition does pose a particular threat, as the shortcomings of these technologies are complex in identification precisely because they might be accurate in light of the theory employed, yet this may not reflect in accuracy regarding the actual emotions of the data subjects. For example, if basic emotion theory is employed, these systems may very well be able to detect what, under such theory, is considered to be surprise or disgust. However, the fact that basic emotion theory is under heavy fire regarding its ability to take into account the variety of emotions we perceive daily means that the true accuracy of these systems is clearly lower than the theoretical one. For the purposes of the AI Act, though, it seems more plausible that

61 Ibid., Art. 8–9.

accuracy can and will be considered from a theoretical point of view: the system itself works, but the underlying framework could represent a systemic threat and will not be considered under Art. 9, thus arguably failing in tackling all risks – in this case systemic risks, which are insufficiently addressed by the Act, according to the Ada Lovelace Institute in its recommendations to the EU – associated with the use of emotion recognition systems that fall within the scope of Title III.[62]

In light of this issue, the safeguards set up in Art. 15 of the proposed AI Act regarding accuracy and robustness of AI systems further come under attack. It is the very understanding of what emotion consists of that will determine the accuracy of these systems: if an evaluation is based on the same theoretical principles – such as basic emotion theory – as the system itself, it will certainly score higher than if a standardised approach is taken for all emotion recognition systems, perhaps employing a more complete theoretical framework. The key question to be asked here is: how can we tell whether an emotion recognition system truly is *accurate*? Can the successful following of a series of instructions producing outputs that are aligned with one particular theory of emotion be sufficient for this to be the case? The wording of the Act could suggest that the requirement is a greater one by referencing the purpose for which the system is put in place.[63] However, this does not resolve the issue of conflicting theories, leaving as a viable solution that of empirically determining whether a system's output coincides with an individual users' perceptions, which from a practical perspective presents greater challenges and may, at the same time, raise doubts in relation to potential discrepancies in the labelling of similar feelings between individuals. It thus remains to be seen what approach will be taken by providers of emotion recognition systems, and whether this will become an object of dispute both academically and in the courts.

On a brighter note, Art. 15 may help address the issue of discrimination that was raised in the previous section and which represents a challenge for the protection of personal data in the contexts of emotion recognition. The Article in question provides, in fact, that the systems "shall be resilient as regards errors, faults or inconsistencies that may occur within the system . . ., in particular due to their interaction with natural persons".[64] While the accuracy of the systems themselves is an object of dispute because of their underlying theoretical framework, the racial bias that some emotion recognition systems present transcends this. Such errors are not due to a dubious scientific backing, but rather to the difficulty that these systems have in achieving correct outcomes *given* the emotion theory employed. Furthermore, in the case of systems that learn continuously, these inaccuracies give rise to the risk of feedback loops, whereby inaccuracies are exacerbated as time passes due to improper learning patterns that accept discriminatory outcomes. The resilience requirement in Art. 15(3) is designed to prevent this from happening, by imposing

62 Ada Lovelace Institute, 'People, Risk and the Unique Requirements of AI' (*Ada Lovelace Institute*, 2022) <www.adalovelaceinstitute.org/policy-briefing/eu-ai-act/> accessed 31 August 2023.

63 COM(2021) 206 final, Art. 15(1).

64 Ibid., Art. 15(3).

an obligation to ensure that the operation of the AI systems is adaptable in light of these errors, thus providing that, for instance, any form of inaccuracy linked to the discriminatory operation of emotion recognition is promptly resolved.

A fundamental aspect to the functioning of this and to the prevention of discriminatory or inaccurate outcomes in high-risk contexts is the provision on human oversight set out in Art. 14 of the proposed AI Act. It has been previously noted how one of the greatest concerns relating to the use of emotion recognition systems is the movement towards the automation of decisions, based on emotional reactions or alleged deception picked up by AI, that have a profound impact on people's lives.[65] This is not an uncommon practice, to different extents, among significantly large businesses like Unilever or IBM, and similarly the provision of emotion recognition software (or at least some form of inferring system based on facial, speech or text recognition) by companies such as HireVue has attracted great attention recently. In light of the discriminatory outcomes of some emotion recognition AI systems (which represent an indisputable issue) and of the challenging of basic emotion theory (which is an object of contention), the imposition of human oversight can help significantly reduce the impact of both by ensuring that users or providers are aware of the impact of such systems on decision-making, and of the risks associated with their use. In particular, knowledge on the functioning, capacities and limitations of the systems would allow – taking once again the example of recruiters – for identification and correction of racially discriminating outputs and avoid over-reliance on a system's conclusions when screening candidates.

In reality, however, this may be more complex to put in practice. The purpose of emotion recognition AI is that of providing an insight into the data subject's psyche, detecting subtle cues that indicate a particular state of mind or feeling. It is hard to see how human oversight could consistently minimise imprecisions in this process, as it seems implausible that all individuals who are assigned oversight would be able to identify such cues (or their absence) independently and accurately, concluding whether the program's output is consistent and truthful. A solution to this could be the disclosure of all relevant input data to the overseer, who would then be aided in identifying potential biases due to external factors (such as accent or timbre in speech recognition, or skin tone in FER). Despite this, human oversight in the context of emotion recognition is a highly observational task which is not free of challenges, thus leaving open the question of whether having a person overseeing the operation of these systems can effectively mitigate their potential systemic inaccuracies.

Finally, it is worth noting when looking at the requirements for high-risk AI systems the relationship of transparency that the proposed AI Act imposes between providers and users. Under the Proposed Regulation, in fact, the design and development of AI systems must be such that users are enabled to interpret their outputs

65 Grace Brennan, 'Emotion Analytics Used in AI Recruitment Tools Are Not Only Unethical But Incorrect' (*The Sociable*, 27 February 2020) <www.sociable.co/technology/emotion-analytics-ai-recruitment-tools-incorrect/> accessed 31 August 2023.

and use them appropriately.[66] The same issues explored previously with regards the determination of accuracy, limitations and risks apply to this provision. While it is positive that users are informed of the potential weaknesses of emotion recognition AI systems, as it fosters a balanced employment of them, the nature of what consists a weakness or inaccuracy is central to such disclosure, which will in turn influence the way these technologies are applied.

Following the requirements for the marketing of high-risk AI systems, the proposed AI Act also sets out a series of obligations with which providers and users of these must comply. Most of these relate to the application of the provisions of Chapter 2, ensuring that the AI systems placed on the market are compliant with their requirements through a quality management system. Perhaps more interestingly on the topic of data protection, Art. 29 sets out the obligations that fall upon users of high-risk systems, thus introducing a level of responsibility for those who make use of these technologies in addition to their designers and manufacturers. These obligations contribute to addressing the issues specific to emotion recognition AI that have been identified in this chapter in relation to the protection of personal data.

First, Art. 29(3) is significant for ensuring that purpose limitation takes place by making users responsible for only using relevant input data in view of the intended purpose of the system in question. As discussed in this chapter, purpose limitation represents one area of concern with emotion recognition AI, as a result of the extensive collection of data is used to determine a particular outcome. It is enough to think of the amount of parameters that are, for example, used in FER to understand how wide-ranging the data collected for each data subject can be, and even more so in the case of multimodal systems. The provision on purpose limitation comes alongside another two provisions within Art. 29 that refer to the way data is used and stored, namely 29(5)–29(6), that require users to both keep logs generated by AI systems for appropriate periods of time and to use the information provided pursuant to Art. 13 (on transparency and provision and information to users) to carry out a Data Protection Impact Assessment. In light of this final point, the transparency obligation imposed on providers is of particular relevance, as it allows for the ensuring of an appropriate assessment of the threats that a given emotion recognition AI system may pose to the protection of personal data, ensuring that two levels of risk mitigation take place.

Second, an additional level of protection is granted by placing an obligation on users to suspend their use of a high-risk AI system and notify providers when a risk to health, safety or the protection of fundamental rights arises,[67] thus further tackling the challenge posed by systems that present discriminatory outputs. This, however, would be highly reliant on users' ability to recognise such outputs and to the tracing back of the risk to the operation of the systems. Once again, the meaning of inaccuracy and risk come in play: while protection from discrimination, for example,

66 COM(2021) 206 final, Art. 13(1).
67 Ibid., Art. 29(4), 65(1).

could be guaranteed to a greater extent through this measure, it once again seems complex to identify a risk based on the way the theoretical framework upon which the AI system is based, thus leaving open the question of whether, given the particular challenges posed by emotion recognition, effective protection of personal data and fundamental rights can be guaranteed under the proposed AI Act.

13.4.3.2.3 THE USE OF EMOTIONAL AI IN HIGH-RISK SITUATIONS: IS THE AI ACT SUFFICIENT?

Setting aside the debate about whether all emotion recognition AI systems should be classified as high risk (or more) and whether these systems are unethical from a data protection perspective regardless of their application, it is perhaps useful to evaluate whether the framework for high-risk systems proposed by the AI Act would be sufficient to safeguard the principles of data protection enshrined in the GDPR when dealing with this particular type of technology.

Generally speaking, it seems that this area of the AI Act does address the issues that AI systems – and emotion recognition in particular – raise in relation to these general principles, in particular in relation to accuracy, discrimination, human oversight and purpose limitation. This, however, does not come without some questions persisting on the way that the Proposed Regulation would be able to address challenges in the delicate context of emotion recognition AI, especially in relation to the role of human inference as opposed to that of machines in determining how reliable and accurate these systems are.

First of all, there is a contrast between the approach of the Court in *Novak*, where a purpose-centred understanding of accuracy was taken, and the idea that the latter relates to the relationship between data inputs and outputs in light of the machine's processes. This is to say that there is a substantial difference for the purposes of the AI Act between accuracy understood as the machine producing an accurate output when looking solely at what it was designed to accomplish, or understood instead as consistently identifying and processing data inputs producing a predictable outcome given those inputs and the system's learning history.

In light of this, the inaccuracies produced by some emotion recognition AI systems that have caused debate and a general scepticism towards their compatibility with data protection can be categorised as either objective or subjective. Such a distinction allows separation of those inaccuracies which can be quantified, and relate to a system's failure to correctly identify and process certain data inputs (in the case of FER, for example, a frown or smile), and those that do not fall within the relationship between the input and its processing but rather to an inaccurate outcome as a result of an interpretation all issue that is inherent to the system's theoretical framework. For example, it is objectively and mathematically possible to identify discrimination in emotion recognition systems, as a failure to identify certain inputs on people belonging to a specific group will lead to an unexpected output given the inputs that take place in the physical world as opposed to those registered by the system. Conversely, determining whether a machine accurately labels a data subject as "happy" or "anxious" can be a more complex and nuanced operation, as it involves elements of subjectivity and interpretation. Perhaps, this is exactly the issue with trying to ensure data protection when dealing with emotion recognition systems: determining their overall accuracy involves converting a subjective perception into an objective "label" that is then to be contrasted with a system's output.

It seems that Title III of the proposed AI Act surely does include useful measures for the mitigation of objective inaccuracies and the consequent protection of fundamental rights, such as non-discrimination, that these systems can put at risk. Nevertheless, it seems evident from Section 13.4 that a relative uncertainty surrounds instead subjective inaccuracies, and that both the standard for measuring these (purpose-based or founded on the relationship between input and output) and the way in which analysis is conducted will be fundamental to effectively mitigating the risks borne by emotion recognition AI, especially when dealing with fundamental sectors such as employment, justice or security. Human oversight and the approach to the obligations set out in Arts. 14 and 29 will be of paramount importance to this endeavour, and the inclusion of such provisions definitely marks an important step in ensuring that emotion recognition AI in high-risk context will not be used as a tool for automated decision-making.

13.4.3.3 Remaining Concerns Following the Artificial Intelligence Act

While the Proposed Regulation does have an extensive impact on the extent and way in which emotion recognition AI may be employed, there remains a degree of lack of satisfaction among some as to how the limiting of these technologies has been undertaken. For instance, a group of digital rights organisations – composed of ARTICLE19, EDRi, Bits of Freedom, Access Now and IT-Pol – has called for the amendment of the AI Act to first, change the definition of emotion recognition to include data that does not allow a unique person's identification within the term "biometrics-based data", and second, impose a general prohibition on emotion recognition systems (which should not, however, include mere assistance systems).[68]

The rationale for such request, which is also supported by the claims made by Michelle Bachelet,[69] the European Data Protection Board and the Special Committee on Artificial Intelligence in a Digital Age (AIDA) of the European Parliament,[70] is that the use of these technologies represents an intrusion in one's private life that cannot be justified or proportionate to the aims such technologies serve. Indeed, the AI Act does not address the question of whether it is ethical at all for AI to collect data which, in the first place, represents one of the deepest levels of one's identity and is perhaps too invasive to be considered proportionate to its purposes and,

68 AccessNow and others, 'Prohibit Emotion Recognition in the Artificial Intelligence Act' (*AccessNow*, 2022) <www.accessnow.org/cms/assets/uploads/2022/05/Prohibit-emotion-recognition-in-the-Artificial-Intelligence-Act.pdf> accessed 12 September 2023.

69 Ibid.

70 Codagnone, Liva and Rodriguez De Las Heras Ballell (n 13).

second, is of dubious accuracy and could lead to interferences with and infringements of people's natural liberty and fundamental rights.

This final point is laid out in the preamble to the Proposed Regulation itself,[71] which recognises the risks relating to the use of emotion recognition when the accuracy of the outcome and of the training data cannot be guaranteed. While the Commission aims to overcome such threats by defining emotion recognition a high-risk AI when used by law enforcement and in matters relating to migration, this is not necessarily sufficient to overcome the unethical and manipulative use that may be made of such AI systems. As emotion recognition is directly defined in Annex III as a high-risk AI in these two cases, the triggering of the measures for high-risk AI in other applications of these technologies would be highly dependent on the enforcement and governance surrounding the AI Act. However, there is space to argue that emotion recognition systems are fundamentally invasive of users' privacy, regardless of the way they are employed, and that there is a near-constant need for greater oversight on their use. In light of this, the employment of emotion recognition AI for purposes outside of the scope of legislation set out in Annex II or not mentioned in Annex III may be problematic, as it would allow for a series of emotion recognition systems to be used for potentially manipulative purposes such as call-centre emotional analysis without being subject to the controls set out in Title III.

It thus seems that if and when the AI Act becomes EU law, the debate over the marketing and employment of emotion recognition AI will be all but over. While the employment of these technologies will undergo strict controls in relation to areas such as employment and workers management, law enforcement, vocational training, access to public benefits and several others, such controls may not apply in other areas where similar concerns regarding accuracy of data, discrimination and transparency may be involved. Similarly, the definition of what emotion recognition systems consist of at the moment limits such denomination to technologies that allow the identification of a unique person, thus apparently omitting all those that collect data that do not uniquely identify data subjects yet may still have a profound impact on their experiences or pose a threat both to their personal liberty and to their fundamental rights. It remains to be seen whether further steps will be taken to limit recourse to these technologies both in light of the GDPR and of an eventual adoption of the AI Act, yet it seems clear that the concerns raised by academics and organisations have not been fully and exhaustively addressed by the Proposed Regulation, and that the future of data protection and privacy in relation to emotion recognition will still heavily rely on the GDPR and, in some cases, find little help in legislation designed to address AI-related concerns.

13.5 The Way Forward: A Possibility for Industry Self-regulation?

Emotional AI, and AI more generally, is unique in the methods and pace of evolution, making it difficult to generate a comprehensive yet not overly restrictive

71 COM(2021) 206 final, para 38.

legislative framework for these technologies to be developed and operate in. Until now, the way emotional AI has made its way into our daily interactions with technology has largely been determined and subject to providers' and users' common sense and responsibility, perhaps driven by moral responsibility and certainly by the fear of loss of consumer confidence. There is no set of industry rules that specifically relate to emotion recognition technologies, no common pledge by companies that have invested in its development setting the boundaries for its use, yet some form of self-regulation – one that is driven by market forces – has already been taking place. There is no doubt that this cannot be sufficient to ensure that the critical issues set out here are appropriately dealt with.

However, the relatively small body of academic literature and recommendations made by leading academics on the topic of emotional AI regulation does seem to stress the importance of self-regulation. This is the case in McStay's recommendations to the Office of the United Nations High Commissioner for Human Rights (OHCHR) and the Special Rapporteur on the right to privacy, which place at their heart the need for the application of moral pressure to entities other than law-makers.[72] While it is also true that this should not substitute or detract any effort in raising awareness with data protection organisations,[73] the relevance that is given here to the role of non-lawmaking bodies is significant in understanding the direction that the regulation of the use and development of these technologies can be expected to take. The argument for self-regulation is also important in light of the evident lacunae that the AI Act (introduced after McStay's recommendations) features in relation to this particular form of AI technologies. The ambitious endeavour of the European Union to regulate the world of AI appears – at least as it stands – to have insufficiently addressed the reality and implications of emotion recognition. It may be the case that the law-making body is the one to have failed in addressing the issues that this technology can bring about. For this reason, McStay's argument remains actual and should lead towards a questioning of whether regulators should do more to fill the gaps left by the AI Act, or whether self-regulation through public pressure may be enough to achieve this.

If the literature on the regulation of emotional AI is scarce, it may well be said that on the topic of its self-regulation, it is close to none. Evaluating the possibility of self-regulation for emotional AI, therefore, must draw on considerations made regarding AI as a whole. After all, it cannot be forgotten that emotion recognition represents one fragment of a much wider family of systems, of which the processes – ranging from machine learning to the algorithms used to reach conclusions – are highly similar. The opportunities and risks that the self-regulation of AI can present, therefore, may be examined in the context of emotion recognition, considering the implications that the particularities of these systems can bring about.

This said, both sectoral and academic literature on the topic of AI self-regulation tend to be sceptical of the sufficiency of this in absence of outside regulatory forces. An institutionalist approach, or at least one that places the role of regulatory bodies

72 McStay (n 4) 8.
73 Ibid.

at the top of the framework that ought to define the way in which the world of AI operates, seems to be preferable both from an ethical and a practical point of view. This is the position held by Thomas Ferretti, arguing for a justified prevalence of government in regulating AI as opposed to the sector's self-regulation. Ferretti's justification lies in three points – legitimacy, stability and efficiency – all three of which can be guaranteed to a greater extent through hard-letter law or institutions.[74]

First, the argument for legitimacy rests on the claim that the principles by which AI should be governed must be made legitimately.[75] In the case of technology that interacts with society at large, the idea of systems that adapt to the limits imposed by each individual when operating in public spaces appears unrealistic. There is thus a need for general restrictions to be imposed, and legitimacy in this sense may be better achieved through the democratic process than by entrusting companies to identify and apply moral and ethical frameworks that align with what society at large perceives to be an acceptable use of data.

Second, and perhaps centrally to the topic of this chapter, Ferretti's institutionalist approach argues that the priority of centralised and institutional regulation derives from the stability in compliance and AI safety that this brings.[76] What must be considered here is that AI brings with itself a novel way of using personal data that can lead to inferences being made in relation to the data subject, potentially leading to the disclosure of an excessive amount of data compared to what was originally envisaged and accepted by them.[77] In the case of emotional AI, as discussed in the previous sections, this issue is further exacerbated by the questions surrounding the systems' accuracy and the nature of their output data. If companies that employ or develop these systems accept the use of possibly inaccurate and discriminatory technology resting on dubious scientific grounds, how can these companies – either independently and directly or through a common endeavour – be better placed than an institutional actor in regulating emotional AI? From a safety perspective, it seems evident that the standards for the control of these technologies in a way that tackles the issues explored in this chapter can only be set and enforced efficiently if a party that can effectively balance all considerations – technological advancement and economic development on one side, and data protection and privacy on the other – takes on this role. This view has also been shared by companies deeply involved in the development and use of AI like Google, which in its recommendations for the regulation of AI underlines that for this precise reason – the need for "balanced, fact-based guidance" – the self-regulation of AI cannot be a sufficient safeguard against the risks that may emerge.[78] The stability and safety point raised by Ferretti holds particularly for emotional AI, which is both rapidly developing

74 Thomas Ferretti, 'An Institutionalist Approach to AI Ethics: Justifying the Priority of Government Regulation Over Self-Regulation' (2022) 9 *Moral Philosophy and Politics* 239, 240–241.

75 Ibid., 247.

76 Ibid., 248.

77 Ibid., 249.

78 Google AI, 'Recommendations for Regulating AI' (*Google* 2020) 1 <https://ai.google/static/documents/recommendations-for-regulating-ai.pdf> accessed 20 February 2023.

and in great need of an impartial and scientific approach towards its regulation, challenging the assumptions upon which emotion-inferring algorithms are based. Self-regulation, in absence of such an endeavour, will hardly lead to companies rethinking emotion theory as accepted by them in the development of the systems they sell or employ, and will thus hardly lead to meaningful considerations in terms of safety, which institutional regulation, instead, will be incentivised to undertake.

Finally, institutional regulation is described by Ferretti as more efficient in tackling the distributive inequalities that AI systems may generate, for example, through access to these technologies.[79] Such an argument may be seen as touching the complexities of emotion recognition AI only slightly, but some considerations may still be made. In particular, when looking at who makes use (and who profits) from the collection of emotional data, this will in many cases be companies and corporations that seek to utilise the data to drive sales and profits. In other words, the use of emotion recognition AI systems yields a clear winner, while on the other hand, consumers may – at times – enjoy an improved targeting of advertisement, while however risking a highly disproportionate level of manipulation and invasion of their privacy. Having made this consideration, the argument for institutional actors being more efficient in the context of regulating emotion recognition is simple. Returning to the example of companies employing these systems for advertisement, it is self-evident that the ultimate aim of this is to profit from the use of technology. This necessarily entails that, to some extent, the disparity in the benefit granted by their use will be persistent, and that there is an incentive for companies to use less efficient means to comply with their moral obligations towards consumers (assuming that such obligations are recognised by them). In substance, self-regulation would lead companies to seek solutions that still allow them to maintain this power imbalance with their consumers and drive profit. On the other hand, government-led regulation has the ability to take a wider range of factors into consideration, aiming (hopefully) at the achievement of a more just distribution of resources and acting with an interest in being efficient in this.

The institutionalist approach to the regulation of AI, through the argument proposed by Ferretti, is closely applicable to the peculiarities of emotion recognition systems. The additional risks posed by these technologies, in particular due to the nature of the data involved, are clear indicators of the fact that if institutional regulation is generally favourable where AI is involved, this is even more so the case in relation to emotional AI. While the invasion of people's interior privacy is a cause of concern and the byproduct of the use of these technologies, their development is almost inextricably linked to such outcomes. The reason for their development, sale and employment is that of using information extrapolated from their mental state in order to achieve an objective – be this the sale of a product or the monitoring of individuals for security purposes. While market and public pressure may represent a reason to take a step back, companies that choose to employ these technologies have an incentive to do so to the limit of what the law prescribes. It is thus the law,

79 Ferretti (n 74) 254.

that made by Member States and international institutions, which sets the limit, and which is thus best placed to do so in a comprehensive, legitimate, stable and efficient manner.

13.6 Conclusion

Emotion recognition AI, like many other types of AI technologies that can be found on the market or are yet to be developed, has traits – and consequently risks – that are unique to its case. It is not a coincidence that, in drafting the proposed AI Act, the European Commission decided to make specific reference to emotional AI in Title IV and recognise the "special" category of technology that these systems represent. The aim of this chapter has been that of unpacking the nature of this category, bringing its critical aspect to light and reaching the (widely accepted) conclusion that there is good reason for concern in relation to emotion recognition technologies.

Starting from a general perspective on the risks that emotional AI entails, related to discrimination, data accuracy and consent, to name a few, the possibility for these technologies to fall outside the scope of current privacy and data protection frameworks is, in and of itself, a cause for concern. These risks are also enough to suggest that – looking at the future – the European Commission has significantly misidentified or underestimated the privacy and data protection issues that come with emotion recognition systems, and that the development of the AI Act to this point has been unsatisfactory from this perspective. This extends well beyond the failure to prohibit these systems altogether, although that would be the recommended course of action with very few and very specific exceptions. The possibility for the materialisation of serious risks as a result of some systems falling both outside of the prohibited practices and high-risk systems provisions of the Act are exemplary of the unsatisfying outcome that the AI Act (as it stands) will produce.

The impact and scope of AI regulation is to be understood also beyond the European reality, focusing on the global impact that current and future Union regulatory frameworks can have on technological development and commerce. The "Brussels effect" will exist for all developers and users who will want to continue engaging with the European Union and its citizens, and will thus lead towards global adaptation on the matter of AI. The current failure of the AI Act in regulating emotion recognition systems will have (or rather will not have, in a positive sense) an impact on the protection of privacy and personal data across the globe. Developers and users will, fundamentally, remain subject to the risks that these systems entail, without proper safeguards and incentives for users to act in a manner that is fully consistent and not endangering of their fundamental rights.

Where does this leave the AI market, when looking at the future? If regulatory frameworks develop consistently with what appears to be the case in the European Union, it seems that the protection of data subjects exposed to emotional AI will almost uniquely be dependent on the responsibility of providers and users. Public scrutiny – which to this point has achieved some success in holding larger corporations accountable for their use of these technologies – will be key in ensuring this and promoting the development of sector guidelines for those involved in interacting with emotional AI. However, this represents a condition that can hardly be maintained efficiently in the long term and is subject to abuse by those who manage to slip through the net of the public lens. Institutional regulation is key to achieving an efficient, just and structured control of these systems. While it may very well be the case that the European Parliament will amend the text of the AI Act to cover emotional AI in a more comprehensive way, such a claim is speculative. In absence of such action, the evolution of these systems and their applications will have to be closely monitored, to understand which of the identified risks actually materialise and counteract these. As with the evolution of the EU from the GDPR to the AI Act, the development of an efficient framework for emotional AI may be a matter of time. The legitimate question, given the precedent, is: will Europe act in time?

Bibliography

AccessNow and others, 'Prohibit Emotion Recognition in the Artificial Intelligence Act' (*AccessNow* 2022) <www.accessnow.org/cms/assets/uploads/2022/05/Prohibit-emotion-recognition-in-the-Artificial-Intelligence-Act.pdf> accessed 12 September 2023

Ada Lovelace Institute, 'People, Risk and the Unique requirements of AI' (*Ada Lovelace Institute*, 2022) <www.adalovelaceinstitute.org/policy-briefing/eu-ai-act/> accessed 31 August 2023

ARTICLE 19, 'Emotional Entanglement: China's Emotion Recognition Market and Its Implications for Human Rights' (*ARTICLE 19*, 2021) <www.article19.org/wp-content/uploads/2021/01/ER-Tech-China-Report.pdf> accessed 20 February 2023

Brennan G, 'Emotion Analytics Used in AI Recruitment Tools Are Not Only Unethical But Incorrect' (*The Sociable*, 27 February 2020) <www.sociable.co/technology/emotion-analytics-ai-recruitment-tools-incorrect/> accessed 31 August 2023

Buolamwini J and Gebru T, 'Proceedings of the 1st Conference on Fairness, Accountability and Transparency' (2018) 81 *PMLR* 77

Clarke S and others, 'Submission of Feedback to the European Commission's Proposal for a Regulation Laying Down Harmonised Rules on Artificial Intelligence' (European Parliament 2021) F2665626

Codagnone C, Liva G and Rodriguez De Las Heras Ballell T, 'Identification and Assessment of Existing and Draft EU Legislation in the Digital Field' (European Parliament 2022) <www.europarl.europa.eu/thinktank/en/document/IPOL_STU(2022)703345> accessed 17 June 2023

Cogito, 'Real Time Coaching' (*Cogito* n.a.) <www.cogitocorp.com/products/real-time-coaching> accessed 22 July 2022

Cohen M A, 'Against Basic Emotions, and Toward a Comprehensive Theory' (2005) 26 *The Journal of Mind and Behavior* 229

Commission, 'On Artificial Intelligence – A European Approach to Excellence and Trust' (White Paper) COM (2020) 65 final (AI White Paper)

Commission, 'Proposal for a Regulation of the European Parliament and of the Council Laying Down Harmonised Rules on Artificial Intelligence (Artificial Intelligence Act) and Amending Certain Union Legislative Acts' COM (2021) 206 final

Council of Europe, 'Algorithms and Human Rights: Study on the Human Rights Dimensions of Automated Data Processing Techniques and Possible Regulatory Implications' DGI(2017)12

Council of Europe, 'Explanatory Note to the Convention for the Protection of Individuals with Regard to Automatic Processing of Personal Data' (1981) *ETS* 108
Crawford K, 'Artificial Intelligence is Misreading Human Emotion' *The Atlantic* (27 April 2021) <www.theatlantic.com/technology/archive/2021/04/artificial-intelligence-misreading-human-emotion/618696/> accessed 19 february 2023
Crootof R, 'Jurisprudential Space Junk: Treaties and New Technologies' in Giorgietti C and Klein N (eds.), *Resolving Conflicts in the Law* (Brill 2019)
Dupré D and others, 'A Performance Comparison of Eight Commercially Available Automatic Classifiers for Facial Affect Recognition' (2020) 15 *PLoS ONE* <https://journals.plos.org/plosone/article/file?id=10.1371/journal.pone.0231968&type=printable> accessed 17 January 2023
Ekman P, 'An Argument for Basic Emotions' (1992) 6 *Cognition and Emotion* 169
Egger M, Ley M and Hanke S, 'Emotion Recognition from Physiological Signal Analysis: A Review' (2019) 343 *Electronic Notes in Theoretical Computer Science* 35
European Parliament, 'The Impact of the General Data Protection Regulation (GDPR) on Artificial Intelligence' (EPRS 2020)
European Union Agency for Fundamental Rights, 'Data Quality and Artificial Intelligence – Mitigating Bias and Error to Protect Fundamental Rights' (FRA, 2019) <https://fra.europa.eu/en/publication/2019/data-quality-and-artificial-intelligence-mitigating-bias-and-error-protect> accessed 17 June 2023
Ferretti T, 'An Institutionalist Approach to AI Ethics: Justifying the Priority of Government Regulation Over Self-Regulation' (2022) 9 *Moral Philosophy and Politics* 239
Floridi L, 'On Human Dignity as a Foundation for the Right to Privacy' (2016) 29 *Philosophy and Technology* 307
Gleason M, 'Privacy Groups urge Zoom to abandon Emotion AI Research' (2022)*TechTarget* <www.techtarget.com/searchunifiedcommunications/news/252518128/Privacy-groups-urge-Zoom-to-abandon-emotion-AI-research> accessed 12 July 2022
Google AI, 'Recommendations for Regulating AI' (Google 2020) <https://ai.google/static/documents/recommendations-for-regulating-ai.pdf> accessed 20 February 2023
Grill G and Andalibi N, 'Attitudes and Folk Theories of Data Subjects on Transparency and Accuracy in Emotion Recognition' *(Proceedings of ACM in Human Computer Interaction (PACM)*, 2022)
Hagerty A and Albert A, 'AI Is Increasingly Being Used to Identify Emotions – Here's What's at Stake' (*The Conversation*, 15 April 2021) <www.theconversation.com/ai-is-increasingly-being-used-to-identify-emotions-heres-whats-at-stake-158809> accessed 19 February 2023
Kaye K, 'Companies Are Using AI to Monitor Your Mood During Sales Calls. Zoom Might Be Next' *Protocol* (13 April 2022) <www.protocol.com/enterprise/emotion-ai-sales-virtual-zoom> accessed 22 July 2022
Kiseleva A, 'Making AI's Transparency Transparent: Notes on the EU Proposal for the AI Act' (*European Law Blog*, 29 July 2021) <www.europeanlawblog.eu/2021/07/29/making-ais-transparency-transparent-notes-on-the-eu-proposal-for-the-ai-act/> accessed 20 June 2023
Koenecke A and others, 'Racial Disparities in Automated Speech Recognition' (2020) 117 *PNAS* 7684
Latonero M, 'Governing Artificial Intelligence: Upholding Human Rights and Dignity' (*Data and Society*, 2018) <www.datasociety.net/wp-content/uploads/2018/10/DataSociety_Governing_Artificial_Intelligence_Upholding_Human_Rights.pdf> accessed 20 February 2023
Leise E, 'Chinese Firm Taigusys Launches Emotion-Recognition System' (*AI Magazine*, 17 June 2021) <www.aimagazine.com/data-and-analytics/chinese-firm-taigusys-launches-emotion-recognition-system> accessed 20 February 2023

Lewis E, 'Microsoft Is Removing Emotion Recognition Features from Its Facial Recognition Tech' (*NBC News*, 27 June 2022) <www.nbcnews.com/tech/tech-news/microsoft-removing-emotion-recognition-features-facial-recognition-tec-rcna35087> accessed 12 July 2022

Madiega T, 'Artificial Intelligence Act' (European Parliamentary Research Service, January 2022) <www.europarl.europa.eu/RegData/etudes/BRIE/2021/698792/EPRS_BRI(2021)698792_EN.pdf> accessed 7 July 2022

Maurer R, 'HireVue Discontinues Facial Analysis Screening' (*SHRM*, 3 February 2021) <www.shrm.org/resourcesandtools/hr-topics/talent-acquisition/pages/hirevue-discontinues-facial-analysis-screening.aspx> accessed 17 January 2023

McStay A, 'Emotional AI, Soft Biometrics and the Surveillance of Emotional Life: An Unusual Consensus on Privacy' (2020) 7 *Big Data and Society* 1

McStay A, 'The Right to Privacy in the Age of Emotional AI' (OHCR 2018) <www.ohchr.org/sites/default/files/Documents/Issues/DigitalAge/ReportPrivacyinDigitalAge/AndrewMcStayProfessor_of_Digital_Life,_BangorUniversityWalesUK.pdf> accessed 20 June 2023

Mohammad SM, 'Ethics Sheet for Automatic Emotion Recognition and Sentiment Analysis' (2022) 48 *Computational Linguistics* 239

Murgia M, 'Emotion Recognition: Can AI Detect Human Feelings from a Face?' (*Financial Times*, London, 12 May 2021) <www.ft.com/content/c0b03d1d-f72f-48a8-b342-b4a926109452> accessed 7 June 2023

Naraharisetty R, 'Activists Call on Zoom to Halt 'Emotion Detection' AI Tool' (*The Swaddle*, 19 May 2022) <https://theswaddle.com/activists-call-on-zoom-to-halt-emotion-detection-ai-tool/> accessed 17 July 2022

Quinn G, 'Rights of Persons with Disabilities: Report of the Special Rapporteur on the Rights of Persons with Disabilities' (28 December 2021) A/HRC/49/52

Rhue L, 'Racial Influence on Automated Perceptions of Emotion' (2018) <https://papers.ssrn.com/sol3/papers.cfm?abstract_id=3281765> accessed 12 June 2022

Saxena A, Khanna A and Gupta D, 'Emotion Recognition and Detection Methods: A Comprehensive Survey' (2020) 2 *Journal of Artificial Intelligence and Systems* 53

Stark L, 'The Emotional Context of Information Privacy' (2016) 32 *The Information Society* 14

Stark L and Hoey J, 'The Ethics of Emotion in Artificial Intelligence Systems' (*Proceedings of the 2021 ACM Conference on Fairness, Accountability and Transparency*, March 2021)

United Nations High Commissioner for Human Rights, 'The Right to Privacy in the Digital Age' (13 September 2021) A/HRC/48/31

Vemou K and Horvath A, 'TechDispatch #1/2021 – Facial Emotion Recognition' (*European Data Protection Supervisor*, 26 May 2021) <https://edps.europa.eu/data-protection/our-work/publications/techdispatch/techdispatch-12021-facial-emotion-recognition_en> accessed 22 July 2022

Von Der Leyen U, 'A Union That Strives for More: My Agenda for Europe. Political Guidelines for the Next European Commission 2019–2024' (European Commission 2019)

Wachter S, 'Every Smile You Fake – An AI Emotion-Recognition System Can Assess How "Happy" China's Workers Are in the Office' (*Berkman Klein Center*, 15 June 2021) <https://cyber.harvard.edu/story/2021-06/every-smile-you-fake-ai-emotion-recognition-system-can-assess-how-happy-chinas> accessed 29 January 2023

Willis B, 'Emotion Recognition Tech Fundamentally Flawed, Says Human Rights Charity' (*Global Government Forum*, 12/02/2021) <www.globalgovernmentforum.com/emotion-recognition-tech-fundamentally-flawed-human-rights-charity/> accessed 19 February 2023

Zoom, 'Understanding Zoom IQ for Sales Metrics (*Zoom Support*, 22 June 2022) <https://support.zoom.us/hc/en-us/articles/5233822805389-Understanding-Zoom-IQ-for-Sales-metrics> accessed 22 July 2022

Table of Legislation

Convention for the Protection of Individuals with regard to Automatic Processing of Personal Data (Data Protection Convention) (28 January 1981) ETS 108

Directive 95/46/EC of the European Parliament and of the Council of 24 October 1995 on the protection of individuals with regard to the processing of personal data and on the free movement of such data [1995] OJ L 281/31

Regulation (EU) 2016/679 of the European Parliament and of the Council of 27 April 2016 on the protection of natural persons with regard to the processing of personal data and on the free movement of such data, and repealing Directive 95/46/EC (General Data Protection Regulation) [2016] OJ L 119

Index

For Product Safety Concerns and Information please contact our
EU representative GPSR@taylorandfrancis.com Taylor & Francis
Verlag GmbH, Kaufingerstraße 24, 80331 München, Germany